Biographical Dictionary of
Modern European Radicals
and Socialists
Volume 1: 1780–1815

Biographical Dictionary of Modern European Radicals and Socialists
Volume 1: 1780–1815

EDITED BY

DAVID NICHOLLS

Senior Lecturer in History, Manchester Polytechnic

AND

PETER MARSH

Principal Lecturer in History, Manchester Polytechnic

THE HARVESTER PRESS · SUSSEX
ST. MARTIN'S PRESS · NEW YORK

First published in Great Britain in 1988 by
THE HARVESTER PRESS LIMITED
16 Ship Street, Brighton, Sussex

First published in the United States of America by
St. Martin's Press, Inc., 175 Fifth Avenue, New York, NY 10010

British Library Cataloguing in Publication Data

Biographical dictionary of modern European
  radicals and socialists.
  Vol. 1 : 1780–1815
  1. Radicalism—Europe—Biography
  I. Nicholls, David II. Marsh, Peter
  322.4'4'0922   HN380.R3

  ISBN 0–7108–1045–8

Library of Congress Cataloging-in-Publication Data

Biographical dictionary of modern European radicals and socialists
  edited by David Nicholls and Peter Marsh.
    p. cm.
    Bibliography: p.
    Includes index.
    Contents: v. 1 1780–1815.
    ISBN 0–312–01968–8 : $30.00
    1. Radicals--Europe--Biography--Dictionaries. 2. Socialists--
  -Europe--Biography--Dictionaries.   I. Nicholls, David, 1948–
  II. Marsh, Peter E.
  HN380.Z9R32 1988
  322.4'4'0922--dc19
  [B]   87–36961
                                                        CIP

Typeset in 9 on 10 point Times Roman by Photo·graphics, Honiton,
Devon

Printed in Great Britain by Mackays of Chatham

Contents

Introduction

In seeking to compile a biographical dictionary of European radicals active in the period from 1780 onwards, the term 'radical' has been interpreted in its widest sense, in order to do justice to the heterogeneity of the forces of social and political change that were beginning to develop from the late eighteenth century onwards. The term 'radical' was originally used in England in its literal Latin sense of pertaining to a root, but from the Civil War period it began to take on its more familiar political meaning, referring to change which was of a thorough and fundamental nature. As a noun, applied to reformers who held advanced and progressive views, it came into general use during the early nineteenth century, and as such has been incorporated into the historical vocabulary.

Some historians have, however, questioned the conceptual utility of the term 'radical'. Indeed, it has been applied to reformers of so many different political persuasions and from such widely divergent class backgrounds as to make a nonsense of any intention to use it as anything more than a broad descriptive category. It has therefore proved almost impossible to identify a radical tradition in *one* country let alone a unitary tradition that could be sought across the diverse political histories of the states of continental Europe.

It may seem somewhat perverse therefore to embark on a multi-volume project that aims to provide biographies of the major European radicals since 1780. However, the very impreciseness of the term 'radical' gives it a certain heuristic value that justifies its retention as an analytical category. Historical writing on the political and ideological development of modern Europe has quite justifiably concentrated on the central ideas, values and representatives of the two most powerful bodies of thought which shaped that development, namely liberalism and socialism. However, the search for the forerunners and 'bearers' of the liberal and socialist traditions has inevitably imposed a teleological structure on the past which has sometimes hidden or ignored alternative currents of thought of considerable diversity. A history of Europe's ideological development which privileges liberal or socialist categories because these emerged as dominant and systematised inevitably oversimplifies the complexity of that development.

This point could not be better illustrated than by reference to the period covered by the first volume of this dictionary. In the years from 1780 to 1815 the forces of change developing in European society were complex and diverse, varying markedly from country to country and region to region. With the benefit of hindsight it is possible to trace the beginnings of the great movements of liberalism, nationalism and socialism; yet the period was characterised above all by an ideological eclecticism. Ideas and movements for change multiplied and the intellectual landscape of one individual might embrace *inter alia* mesmerism, proto-socialism and a religiously-derived cosmology. As Engels said of the utopian socialists, their programmes comprised 'a mish-mash allowing of the most manifold shades of opinion'.[1] To extract the 'socialist' features and neglect the other ingredients in this 'mish-mash' does no service to historical understanding.

Moreover, the very eclecticism of radical thought often played a crucial role in 'masking' class relations, particularly in the early period of industrial capitalism before a fully-articulated 'scientific' socialism had emerged, and when both the nascent bourgeoisie and working class could find common cause in wresting power from an aristocratic polity.[2] The advanced reformers before 1848 — the 'radicals' — often operated at the nexus of class relations, and it is important therefore to understand their ideas and policies. After 1848 the mantle of root-and-branch reformer was increasingly taken up by socialists and the later volumes of this *Biographical Dictionary* will reflect that fact.

In compiling this volume we have employed much the same definition of the term 'radical' as did Joseph Baylen and Norbert Gossman in their companion volumes on Britain.[3] In other words the term has been used to apply to those individuals who wished to change existing economic, social and political structures by political action and/or theoretical criticism which could not be incorporated in the prevailing ideological consensus of their time and place. Because of the geographical scope of the dictionary, which includes countries at vastly different levels of political, social and economic development, that ideological consensus varied quite considerably. For this reason a radical in eastern Europe in the 1790s would appear remarkably moderate in the context of revolutionary France. Nonetheless, such an individual might well be imprisoned or executed for advocating reforms that had long since been accepted elsewhere. And, by the same token, political reformers excluded from these pages because they were moderate by comparison with other of their compatriots, would have appeared the most extreme radicals had they advocated their policies elsewhere. In sum, the individuals chosen for inclusion have been judged according to the political and social context of their own societies and not by any universalist conception of radicalism. In this task of selection we have been greatly assisted by the expertise of our many specialist contributors.

At the start of the period covered by this volume there was a superficial similarity between the political structures across continental Europe. The characteristic state-form was that of the absolute monarchy, backed up by the support of the landed nobility and the Church, and seemingly secure and stable. However, this apparent stability masked an intellectual ferment and political questioning of the established forms of authority with individuals increasingly prepared to articulate the need for change and reform. As Rudé has pointed out:

The great question was: should the way to reform be sought by enlarging the authority of an 'enlightened' monarch at the expense of the estates; should aristocratic or other 'intermediate bodies' be strengthened as a check on the power of the Crown; or should the power of both be balanced, or eclipsed, by vesting greater responsibility in the hands of the people themselves?[4]

Rudé's formulation captures the *political* controversies of the period but it is important to note that these political upheavals were accompanied by economic change, the growth of new social classes and groupings, and the emergence of a rationalising and critical ideology which questioned existing spiritual and moral values also. The years 1780 to 1815, therefore, were marked by the growth of considerable social, political and ideological pluralism in Europe, and it is important that an examination of radical figures does full justice to the varying forms in which critics of the existing order chose to express themselves.

Three crucial influences helped to shape the development of radical thought and activity during this period: the Enlightenment, the French Revolution, and the unevenness of economic and social development across Europe. The first two bequeathed the critical values which were at the heart of radical thought. In particular, the attack on hereditary, absolute monarchy, the emphasis on natural law and natural rights, the advocacy of social and religious freedoms, equality of opportunity in politics, all helped to encourage a common intellectual currency in which European radicals could exchange their ideas across national and, to a lesser extent, social boundaries. The combined stimuli of the Enlightenment and the French Revolution interacted with the third influence, the pace of economic and social change, to shape the contours of radicalism across Europe. Unevenness of economic and social development influenced the political arrangements and forms of authority to which radicals addressed their criticisms and to some extent determined the uneven spread of radical ideas across the multifarious states and societies of Europe. As Hobsbawm has noted, there was a marked difference between the states of eastern Europe and those to the west of 'a line running roughly along the river Elbe, the western frontier of what is today Czechoslovakia, and then south to Trieste'.[5] In the east agrarian serfdom still prevailed and economic and social development was slow. In the west mercantile capitalism was developing and was creating the very social groups who would question and seek to change existing economic, social and political relations.

There were thus significant economic and social differences between the states and regions of Europe which substantially affected their receptivity to the radical currents which developed during the late eighteenth and early nineteenth centuries as a consequence of the Enlightenment and the French Revolution. These economic and social differences were reflected in the differing forms of political authority with which radicals had to contend. Leaving aside the parliamentary system of Britain, continental Europe displayed quite wide-ranging forms of operation of the system of hereditary, absolute monarchy — for example in France, Spain, Prussia and the Austrian Empire. Furthermore, republican forms of government existed in Switzerland and some parts of Italy whilst at the other extreme, eastern Europe and Russia were characterised by rigid autocracy and despotic rule. Generally speaking, it was in western and parts of southern Europe that the 'checks' on absolute monarchy had developed to their greatest extent, although even here these checks were mainly in the form of aristocratic élites seeking limitations on the individual power of the monarch rather than any concession to 'democratic' or popular institutions. Nevertheless, there was enough disturbance to the traditional order to give encouragement to the proponents of radical ideas and to the classes who, by the turn of the century, were seeking to challenge that order more fundamentally.

The tensions which existed between monarchy and aristocracy in various states of Europe by the end of the eighteenth century weakened their capacity to face the more radical ideas and actions of classes excluded completely from political participation and held back economically and socially by the hierarchy of rank and privilege. Economic development was gradually beginning to change the societies of Europe, especially those in the west, and the growth of the professional, mercantile, and industrial bourgeoisie was to provide the appropriate seedbed for the propagation of radical values. The national context in which this section of society operated, however, determined the extent to which their sense of inequality and denial of opportunity would take radical political forms. Equally, the possibilities for cooperation with monarchical and aristocratic interests and a shared fear of the 'common people' would tend to blunt their radical appetites often before truly democratic and egalitarian reforms had been consolidated. To this extent 'middle-class radicalism' varied considerably in the range of objectives it encompassed and the forms of change it proposed and was very much subject to the pressures which other groups and classes could exert upon it within individual states. Generally speaking, the demands were for limited representative government, equality of opportunity, national self-determination, civil and religious freedoms, and the protection of personal property by the state. Only in those states where economic development was most extensive was this programme broadened to include the demands of subordinate groups such as the artisans and even then the attachment to 'economic democracy' of many European radicals during the period from 1780 to 1815 was a very tenuous one.

Thus, European radicalism's development was conditioned by the economic, social and political divisions of the continent and by the ability of radical spokesmen to overcome these divisions through the articulation of alternatives which seemed relevant in a variety of different contexts. In this respect, the key factor in stimulating the growth of radicalism and its spread throughout Europe was the French Revolution of 1789. The revolution not only heightened the sense of identity of the nascent European bourgeoisie and its perception of its grievances, it also put a question-mark against monarchical rule and aristocratic privilege. Moreover, it developed the concepts, ideas and political tactics which could be adopted by individuals and groups seeking change throughout Europe. The title 'Jacobin', for example, was rapidly appropriated by reformers elsewhere in Europe who embraced the principles of the revolution. The French revolutionary armies and the Napoleonic campaigns also carried French political ideas and democratic forms of organisation into parts of

Europe where the indigenous radical presence might otherwise have remained marginal and uninfluential.

Inevitably, therefore, the French radical tradition and its representatives must loom large in a volume covering the period 1780 to 1815. So too must the ideas and currents of thought which it stimulated, not only the accepted revolutionary traditions of liberalism and Jacobinism but also the sub-currents of early socialism, communism and feminism. However, in compiling this volume of the *Biographical Dictionary*, an attempt has been made to give adequate representation to the radical movements outside France, whilst acknowledging that without the stimulus of the revolution and French revolutionary foreign policy, such movements might have been relatively weak.

Of the 187 radicals included in this volume, therefore, the overwhelming majority (86) were active in France.[6] The German states, particularly those occupied by France in the Revolutionary Wars, provide the second largest cohort (43), and the establishment of sister-republics elsewhere (such as the Cispadane, Cisalpine, Batavian, Helvetic) brought to the centre of power radical activists in Italy (14), Holland (7), and Switzerland (6). Elsewhere, French revolutionary ideas were relatively weak, though they nevertheless formed the basis for a number of 'Jacobin conspiracies' within the polyglot Austrian Empire, and the dictionary contains biographies of eight Austrians, five Hungarians, and one Czech. Habsburg control of the Austrian Netherlands also encouraged rebellion in Belgium, where nationalist and democratic movements preceded (like those in Holland) the outbreak of the revolution, though they subsequently became intermeshed with and overtaken by events in France. These intersecting and overlapping developments can be traced in the lives of the three Belgians recorded here. Nationalism was also a major stimulus to Polish radicalism where the indignities of partition and foreign occupation led a number of aristocrats and intellectuals to turn to Jacobin ideas — and the dictionary includes biographies of six of the more important Polish reformers. France was, therefore, the epicentre of radicalism during this period, sending out a series of shockwaves across continental Europe. Only those countries far removed from France remained relatively untouched — Greece and Norway each have only one representative in this dictionary, while the five Russians included were radical in their background and autocratic society by virtue of an attachment to the Enlightenment and not to revolutionary ideas. The one exception is Spain, which remained largely insulated from French influence behind the Pyrenees, a fact reflected in the inclusion here of only one Spanish activist.

In terms of the sociological coverage of the dictionary, information provided by contributors on the occupations of the radicals and their parents, while not complete, is sufficient to enable us to make a number of general observations concerning class background.[7] In the first place, very few of the radicals were born into the lowest class. Of the 157 for which we have some information on parental occupations, only four came from peasant families and three are described as being born into poor circumstances. In addition one was the son of a porter, one the son of a barber, two were the children of caretakers, one the child of a poor wine-grower, and one of a poor farmer. By contrast twenty-six were born into noble families, and the nobility no doubt also provided some of the individuals listed as civil servants and government officials, army officers and churchmen. Of these three groups, twenty-five of the radicals were the children of civil servants and government officials, five of army officers, and eight of churchmen (both Catholic and Protestant). A further ten are described as coming from prominent, wealthy, or bourgeois backgrounds, and twenty-two were the children of fathers engaged in business, financial, commercial or industrial activities (textile manufacturers, wood merchants, bankers etc.). Twenty-three were children from artisan or petit bourgeois backgrounds although these varied considerably ranging through cook, butcher, barber, silversmith, goldsmith, master brewer, master joiner, sea captain, engineer, and innkeeper. A further twenty-five were born into what might loosely be described as the professional middle class, embracing lawyers, doctors, lecturers and teachers.

This professional middle class is in some ways the most significant radical cohort. Fifteen of the fathers were involved in some area of legal work.[8] Moreover, this weighting towards the influence of a legal training is carried over dramatically when one examines the occupations of the radicals themselves where approximately a quarter were involved in the legal profession or had studied law at university. The role of the professions and of intellectuals in eighteenth-century radical politics, and especially the corrosive effect which the legally-trained could bring to bear upon the Establishment, is convincingly demonstrated by the biographical details in this dictionary. In addition to the law, careers in the church, the universities, the army, the civil service, and in medicine were all productive of radical minds. Over half of the radicals were members of one or more of these professions at some time in their lives. Many gave vent to their discontents through writing in some form or other — so that nearly a third used their pens as journalist, poets, publicists, and playwrights in order to challenge the dominant consensus of their time.

In terms of gender only six of the radicals included here were women. This is in part a reflection of male dominance of eighteenth-century politics and society, but also partly an indication of the limitations of our historiography. Hence, while the overwhelming impression created by this dictionary is of a radical politics dominated by men and articulated by a professional middle class, non-participation by women and the poorer sections of the community should not simply be 'read off' from this. We know that male artisans and women played crucial roles in the French Revolution though their identities and biographies are frequently unknown to us, or are only now being uncovered. It is research on the lives of just such individuals that we would particularly welcome for inclusion in future volumes.

The French Revolution and its impact is therefore the most significant feature of the period 1780–1815. In France alone the revolution down to 1795 went through a series of progressively more radical phases—constitutional monarchy, democratic republic, proto-socialist—associated with the programmes of particular factions (Feuillants, Girondins, Jacobins, Babouvists and so on). While generally we have had to draw a line between reformers by including as 'radical' those prepared to rid themselves of the monarchy and move in the direction of democratic and more popular forms of political and social organisation, we have been wary of undue rigidity. After all, the political factions themselves were not rigid or homogeneous parties. Moreover, alignment with a moderate political faction did not preclude the advancement of progressive social policies, or colonial reforms, or perhaps the dissemination of ideas by a gift for trenchant journalism. Again, the consideration of each individual according to the definition of 'radical' outlined above has allowed us to cut across what are often loose and artificial political categories.

Selection for inclusion has, therefore, ultimately rested with ourselves as editors. We have, however, endeavoured to mitigate this responsibility by drawing on the combined wisdom of our contributors and the advice of many specialists in the history of this period. This has helped us but it is no fail-safe device. Historians notoriously differ in their interpretations, not least of all as to what constitutes 'progressive' change. In the case of German Jacobinism, for example, there are widely divergent opinions on the significance of those who drew upon or were inspired by the French Revolution, as the different views of writers such as Blanning and Grab make clear.[9] This should serve to demonstrate the difficulties of historicist or teleological standpoints. It is for this reason that we have determined from the outset to make this project on European radicalism and socialism an open-ended one. It is hoped to produce seven volumes covering the period from 1780 to 1980 in a chronological sequence.[10] However, we intend also to produce a supplementary volume of radicals and socialists who were originally excluded either through ignorance on our part or lack of contributors. While endeavouring to include the major figures we would nevertheless not wish to delay the progress of the series either because of the tardiness of contributors or the inability to find an immediate contributor. Indeed, it is our hope that the appearance of this first volume will stimulate suggestions for later volumes and, where omissions are identified, for inclusion in the supplementary volume. In sum we would prefer by the end of the project to have erred on the side of commission rather than omission. We would therefore welcome correspondence from individuals prepared to contribute to the project. Suggestions for contributions and inclusions in later volumes should be sent to the editors at the following address: Department of English and History, Ormond Building, Lower Ormond Street, Manchester M15 6BX.

The real worth of this biographical dictionary therefore rests with the knowledge and scholarship of our many contributors, drawn from around the world. Tapping this pool of international talent and expertise has inevitably taken time, and this volume has been seven years in gestation. We sincerely hope that subsequent volumes can be produced at much shorter intervals. Many of the biographies that are included are available in English for the first time, and we hope that this will facilitate comparison and contrasts between the reforming traditions of the various European states and assist an understanding of both the basis for, and the obstacles to, their current search for greater cooperation and unity.

The biographical entries have been produced as far as possible to conform to the following format—brief ascription of 'radicalism', account of life, summary of radical contributions, assessment of radicalism, further bibliographical information. The bibliographies are not intended to be exhaustive as this would have rendered the project unwieldy. Contributors were asked to indicate the sources that they considered the most useful and informative and to take into account as far as possible the needs of an English readership. We have also employed the 'quod vide' convention to indicate cross-references. A number of parallel projects will be found particularly useful by readers of this volume, notably A. Kuscinski, *Dictionnaire des conventionnels* (Paris, 1917), S. Scott and B. Rothaus (eds.), *Historical dictionary of the French Revolution* (2 vols., Westport, CT, 1985), and H. Reinalter (ed.), *Jakobiner in mitteleuropa* (Innsbruck, 1977).

The production of this first volume has incurred a number of specific debts. In particular we are grateful to Manchester Polytechnic for providing financial assistance at various stages. In the early days we were allowed to use the facilities of the Institute of Advanced Studies and owe our thanks to its Dean, John Langrish. The Faculty of Humanities, Law and Social Science provided us with a research grant and typing facilities. The research grant allowed us to employ for one term a research assistant, Tim Kirk, who assisted in translating a number of contributions and in writing several of the German and Austrian entries for which we had not been able to find contributors. Where there have been technical problems in translation—for example in the transliteration of Russian names—we have followed the conventions recommended by our contributors. Finally, our greatest personal debts are to Carol and Christine who have provided the necessary encouragement and diversion to sustain us through the production of this first volume and we therefore dedicate it to them.

D.N. and P.M.
August 1987

Notes

1. F. Engels, *Socialism: utopian and scientific* (Westport, 1977), p.44.
2. This has been argued for British radicalism at greater length elsewhere. See, D. Nicholls, 'The English middle class and the ideological significance of radicalism, 1760–1886', *Journal of British Studies*, 24 (Oct. 1985), pp. 415–33.
3. J.O. Baylen and N.J. Gossman (eds.), *Biographical Dictionary of modern British radicals. Vol. 1: 1770–1830* (Sussex, 1979), p.5.

4. G. Rudé, *Revolutionary Europe 1783–1815* (London, 1964), p.34.
5. E.J. Hobsbawm, *The Age of Revolution 1789–1848* (London, 1962), p.26.
6. It should be noted that the information in this paragraph on the geographical distribution of radicalism relates to area of *activity* and not specifically to place of birth. This gives a better sense of the location of the centres of radicalism, and makes some allowance for its cosmopolitan nature. Hence, for example, in the numerical breakdown Marat has been recorded as French not German, Arndt as German not Swedish, Buonarotti as French rather than Italian, and so on.
7. It is stressed that these are only tentative observations. Information on the parental background of thirty of the radicals was either not given or was insufficiently precise. Moreover, class and occupational titles disguise vast disparities in wealth and status — for example, the inpoverishment of many who still nevertheless could lay claim to noble titles and privileges. Finally, many radicals were engaged in several occupations during their lifetimes.
8. This total does not include judges who have been counted with the government officials.
9. See the review article, which discusses the work of H. Scheel, Walter Grab and others, by T.C.W. Blanning in *Historical Journal*, 23, 4 (1980), pp. 985–1002. The debate has essentially rested on the extent to which a genuine 'German' Jacobinism developed, with a momentum of its own, independent of the 'revolution from above' initiated by French occupation.
10. The scheduled division is as follows: 1780–1815, 1816–48, 1849–70, 1871–90, 1891–1914, 1915–39, 1940–80. Of course, individuals do not conveniently confine their activities to one particular period. The aim will be to include them in the volume which best embraces their major period of activity, although inevitably this choice will sometimes be quite arbitrary.

List of contributors

1. Beik, Paul H. (Swarthmore College, Pennsylvania) for Maillard.
2. Benda, Kálmán (Budapest, Hungary) for Hahnóczy, Martinovics, Szentmarjay
3. Bienvenu, Richard (University of Missouri-Columbia) for Prieur de la Côte d'Or.
4. Boros-Kazai, Andras (Vermillion, South Dakota, USA) for Batsányi, Berzeviczy.
5. Chaudhuri Nupur (Kansas State University) for Chabot, Chaumette, Gouges, Manuel, Tallien.
6. Cleland, Joel S. (Lander College, Greenwood, South Carolina) for Billaud-Varenne, Carnot, Couthon, Gregoire, Merlin de Douai, Vincent.
7. Coppa, Frank J. (St. John's University, New York) for Pagano.
8. Davies, Stephen (Manchester Polytechnic) for Castella, Grenus, La Harpe, Ochs, Zschokke.
9. Doyle, William (University of Bristol) for Le Peletier de Saint-Fargeau, Raynal, Sieyès.
10. Edelstein, Melvin (The William Paterson Cellege of New Jersey) for Barère.
11. Edmonds, Bill (Macquarie University, New South Wales) for Chalier, L'Ange, Monnet.
12. Friuglietti, James (Eastern Montana College) for Monge, Romme.
13. Garrioch, David (Monash University, Victoria) for Bailly, Chénier, Hérault de Séchelles, Santerre.
14. Geggus, David P. (University of Florida) for Sonthonax.
15. Gilli, Marita (Université de Franche Comté) for Cloots, Dorsch, Forster, Fröhlich, Hofmann, Kant, Kerner, List, Wedekind.
16. Gough, Hugh (University College, Dublin) for Bazin, Bonneville, Brissot de Warville, Carra, Condorcet, Lebois, Loustalot, Marat, Maréchal, Robespierre.
17. Grab, Walter (Tel Aviv, Israel) for Albrecht, H.C., Albrecht, J.F.E., Bohl, Brunner, Butenschön, Grossmann, Heiligenstedt, Meyer, Rebmann, Riem, Schmieder, Schnieder, Schutz, Trenck, Unzer, Vollmer, Wachter, Würzer, Ziegenhagen.
18. Gray, Marion W. (Kansas State University) for Hippel.
19. Hanson, Paul R. (Butler University, Indianapolis) for Lindet, Pache, Philippeaux, Prieur de la Marne.
20. Harrison, Joseph (University of Manchester) for Marchena.
21. Jones, W. Gareth (University College of North Wales) for Novikov, Radishchev.
22. Kądziela, Lukasz (University of Warsaw) for Horodyski, Jasiński, Kołłataj, Kosciuszko, Maruszewski, Orchowski.
23. Kirby, David (School of Slavonic and East European Studies, University of London) for Lofthuus.

24. Kirk, Tim (University of Warwick) for Ascher, Böhmer, Clauer, Dirnbock, Knigge, Lehne, Metternich, Muller, Prandstetter, Taufferer, Wenninger.
25. Körner, Alfred (Bohn, W. Germany) for Hebenstreit von Streitenfeld, Riedel.
26. Lovett, Clara M. (Columbian College, The George Washington University, Washington D.C.) for Abbamonti, Galdi, Gorani, Ranza.
27. Lyons, Martyn A. (The University of New South Wales) for Amar, Baby, Bayle, Hébert, Jagot, La Revellière-Lépeaux, Lavicomterie, Lebas, Ruhl, Vadier, Voulland.
28. McPhee, Peter (Victoria University of Wellington, New Zealand) for Théroigne de Méricourt.
29. Macrakis, A. Lily (Regis College, Weston, Massachusetts) for Rigas Pheraios.
30. Malino, Frances (University of Massachusetts-Boston) for Hourwitz.
31. Mansfield, Paul (Macquarie University, New South Wales) for Collot d'Herbois.
32. Mejdřicka, Květa (Prague, Czechoslovakia) for Opiz.
33. Miller, Marion S. (University of Illinois, Chicago) for Gioannetti, Gioia, Poggi, Russo.
34. Moore, Bob (Bristol Polytechnic) for Daendels, Fijnje, Gogel, Paulus, Vreede.
35. Moran, Daniel J. (Standford University) for Arndt, Huber, Oelsner, Posselt, Reinhard, Usteri.
36. Mühlpfordt, Günter (Halle, DDR) for Bahrdt.
37. Murray, William J. (La Trobe University, Victoria) for Audouin, Danton, Desmoulins, Fabre d'Eglantine, Fréron, Kéralio, Pétion de Villeneuve, Robert, Saint-Just.
38. Neugebauer-Wölk, Monika (Historische Kommission zu Berlin) for Cotta.
39. Nicholls, David (Manchester Polytechnic) for Bourbotte, Cambon, Chasles, Drouet, Jeanbon Saint-André, Lebon.
40. Noether, Emiliana P. (University of Connecticut) for Ceracchi, Compagnoni, L'Aurora, Pimentel, Salvador.
41. O'Meara, Patrick J. (University of Dublin) for Fonvizin, Kretchetov, Pnin.
42. Polasky, Janet (University of New Hampshire) for Verlooy, Vonck, Walckiers.
43. Popkin, Jeremy (University of Kentucky) for Archenholtz,Goerres, Valckenaer, Van der Capellen tot den Poll.
44. Rose, R. Barrie (University of Tasmania) for Babeuf, Buonarotti, Fauchet, Germain, Lacombe, Leclerc, Léon, Roux, Varlet.
45. Rosenstrauch-Königsber, Edith (Vienna, Austria) for Blumauer, Hackel.
46. Slavin, Morris (Youngstown State University, Ohio) for Momoro.

47. Stone, Bailey (University of Houston, Texas) for Thuriot de la Rosière.
48. Sutherland, Donald M.G. (University of Maryland) for Carrier, Fouche.

ABBAMONTI, Giuseppe (1759–1819)
Italian Jacobin

Abbamonti was born of a prominent family in the small town of Caggiano (province of Salerno), and educated at the faculty of law in Naples. He joined the conspiracy of 1793–94 in his native kingdom of Naples and had to flee into exile, first to Oneglia, on the Ligurian coast, where he was a schoolteacher for a time, then to Milan. In the Lombard capital he became very active in local politics and a founder of the radical *Giornale dei patrioti italiani* (1797). In Milan he also wrote *Saggio sulle leggi fondamentali dell'Italia libera* and *Progetto di constituzione per la Lombardia*. He argued that the republican and democratic governments made possible by the impact of the French Revolution in Europe would need broad popular support in order to remain in power. To this end, they needed to ameliorate social and economic conditions that produced vagrancy, mendicity, and homelessness.

Having returned to his native region, he became a member of the Directory of the Repubblica Partenopea. For his role in that revolutionary government, he was sentenced to death in 1799, but pardoned in 1801. His political fortunes rose again during the Napoleonic régime, when he became a councillor of state. Under Joseph Bonaparte and Joachim Murat he represented the democratic (or 'patriot') faction within the government, alongside his colleague and fellow Salernitan Matteo Galdi (q.v.), in contrast to the moderately liberal faction of Francesco Ricciardi and Giuseppe Zurlo. Despite this, his career as a magistrate continued under the Bourbon restoration, until his death in Naples in 1819.

Abbamonti was among the most radical members of the Jacobin movement in Italy. Best known for his extreme views on education, he advocated free elementary education for all children, with those who were to receive secondary education being selected by their own classmates when they reached the age of ten. Furthermore, pupils would be involved in all aspects of instruction, curriculum planning and school discipline. These views place him alongside other radical theorists of the late eighteenth and nineteenth centuries who laid the foundations of modern progressive education.

There is no biography of Abbamonti but further information can be found in the following secondary sources: D. Carpanetto, *L'Italia del '700* (Turin, 1980); F. Venturi, *Italy and the Enlightenment* (London, 1972); S.J. Woolf, *A History of Italy* (London, 1979); C. Zaghi, *La Rivoluzione francese e l'Italia* (Naples, 1966); C. Zaghi, *Potere, chiesa e società* (Naples, 1985).

CLARA M. LOVETT

ALBRECHT, Heinrich Christoph (1763–1800)
German Jacobin and publicist

Albrecht was born in Hamburg and attended the Johanneum Gymnasium there before studying theology, philosophy and English language in Göttingen. His translations of Shakespeare's epic poems *Venus and Adonis* and *The Rape of Lucrece* were published in Halle in 1783. After returning to his home town, Hamburg, he founded a school in the suburb of Eppendorf, and taught there for a time. Albrecht frequented the houses of liberal Hamburg merchants such as Georg Heinrich Sieveking and Johann Friedrich Ernst Westphalen, whose sister-in-law he later married. He was also a welcome guest at the house of J.H.A. Reimarus, a friend of the recently deceased Gotthold Ephraim Lessing, whose tradition Albrecht attempted to develop in the journal, *Neue Hamburgische Dramaturgie*, of which sixteen issues appeared in 1791, and where the performances of F.L. Schröder's theatre troupe were reviewed. He defended the ideas of human rights and popular sovereignty in several Enlightenment journals and, in 1791, published a *Hamburgische Monatsschrift*, which appeared for some six months. Like his friend F.W. von Schütz (q.v.), Albrecht was a member of the Christian-Jewish Freemasons' lodge

'Einigkeit und Toleranz' [Unity and Toler-
ance], where he made a speech on October
4, 1792 on 'The Improvement of the
Jewish Nation'. He also took part in H.G.
Sieveking's short-lived 'Readers' Society',
whose statutes were modelled on those of
the Mainz Jacobin Club.

In his *Geheime Geschichte eines Rosen-*
kreuzers (Secret Story of a Rosicrucian)
Albrecht sought to expose the obscurantist
tendencies of that organisation; in his
Materialien zu einer kritischen Geschichte
der Freimaurerei (Material for a Critical
History of Freemasonry) (1792) he reiter-
ated Lessing's ideas on the origins and
aims of the secret associations. In two
anonymous pieces, *Rettung der Ehre*
Adolphs, Freiherrn von Knigge (The Saving
of the Honour of Adolph, Freiherr von
Knigge) and *Erläuterungen über die Rechte*
der Menschen (Elucidation of the Rights
of Man) Albrecht defended Knigge (q.v.),
one of the pioneer protagonists of bourgeois emancipation, against the attacks of
his conservative opponents J.G. Zimmer-
mann and Jean André de Luc.

Albrecht's major work, *Versuch über*
den Patriotismus (Essay on Patriotism)
(Hamburg, 1792) argued for freedom of the
press; the national unification of Germany;
and the abolition of estates in a republic
based on popular sovereignty. The work
is one full of sympathy for the lower classes
and replete with Jacobin ideology. In
his *Untersuchunggen über die englische*
Staatsverfassung (Examinations of the
English Constitution) (1794) Albrecht
vehemently criticised the anti-democratic
policy of William Pitt, the suspension of
Habeas Corpus and the persecution of
dissidents; his description of the misery of
the English working class anticipates in
part Friedrich Engels' *Condition of the*
English Working Class (1844). After his
marriage in 1794 to Margarethe Elisabeth
von Axen and his move to Kielseng near
Flensburg, he wrote the play, *Die Revol-*
ution in England (The Revolution in
England) (Schleswig, 1796), which not only
brought out the parallels between the
execution of Charles I (1649) and that of
Louis XVI (1793), but also put speeches

into the mouths of representatives of the
lower classes, which recalled the fierce
attacks on the German princes by Thomas
Münzer, the peasant leader of 1525.
Albrecht also published two poems in G.C.
Meyer's (q.v.) Jacobin periodical *Der neue*
Mensch.

Albrecht's last years were spent on the
Kielseng estate where he operated a grain
mill and owned a nearby brickworks. He
died in 1800. Albrecht was therefore a
prominent German radical, a leading publicist of Jacobin ideas, and an advocate and
defender of republican and democratic
ideals on behalf of the lower classes.

Details of Albrecht's life are to be
found in Berend Kordes, *Lexikon der jetzt*
lebenden schleswig-holsteinischen, lauen-
burgischen und eutinischen Schriftsteller
(Schleswig, 1797) p. 14f.; J.G. Meusel,
Das gelehrte Deutschland oder Lexikon
der jetzt lebenden Deutschen Schriftsteller
(Lemgo, 1795–1834) Vol. 1, pp. 60–62. See
also W. Grab, *Demokratische Strömungen*
(Hamburg, 1966), pp. 67–74; W. Grab,
Leben und Werke norddeutscher Jakobiner
(Stuttgart, 1973), pp. 35–47; Walter Koch,
'Christoph   Albrecht   and   Christine
Westphalen', *Jahrbuch des Instituts für*
deutsche Geschichte, Vol. 11, (1982), pp.
381–85.

W. GRAB

ALBRECHT, Johann Friedrich Ernst
(1752–1814)
German Jacobin, radical playwright,
novelist and pamphleteer

Albrecht was born in Stade, the son of a
doctor. He studied medicine in Erfurt,
took his doctorate there on January 16,
1772 and shortly afterwards married the
fifteen-year old daughter of his teacher,
Johann Paul Baumer. He lectured in Erfurt
until 1776, when he accepted a position as
private physician to Baron Karl Rheinhold
Manteuffel in Reval, the capital of the
Russian province of Estonia. On trips to
St Petersburg and other Russian towns he
formed an unfavourable impression of
social conditions in the tsar's empire. On
his return his wife Sophie embarked on a

stage career and quickly became famous. In 1783 she joined the theatre group of G.F.W. Grossmann (q.v.) and the following year played the role of Luise Millerin in the première of Schiller's *Kabale und Liebe*. Schiller was delighted with her work and later included some of her poems in his *Thalia*. Albrecht accompanied his wife on tour to Leipzig, where Schiller was their guest for several months, to Dresden, where Sophie became a member of the Saxon Court Theatre, and to Prague, where she appeared in the festivities at the coronation of Leopold II as king of Bohemia. Albrecht worked for some time as a book-seller in Prague.

Between 1776 and 1810 Albrecht published more than sixty novels, stories, plays, and biographical and historical works, which were usually full of contemporary references and often appeared under pseudonyms and with false and fictitious places of publication. His *romans à clef* praised France as the home of freedom, human rights and popular sovereignty, contained ironic and scathing criticism of the social and political conditions under the *ancien régime* and derided the obscurantism and patronage of the Russian and Prussian courts (on Friedrich Wilhelm II: *Saul II genannt der Dicke, König von Kanonenland*; on Potemkin: *Pansalvin, Fürst der Finsternis*; on Catherine II: *Miranda, Queen of the North, Lover of Pansalvin*; on Tsar Paul I: *Staub I, König der Unterwelt*; on General Suvorov: *Kakodämon der Schreckliche, Pansalvins und Mirandas Donnerkeil, Revisor des Codex der Menschenrechte*).

In 1795 Albrecht and his wife moved to Altona, where they made contact with the Jacobin circle around Würzer (q.v.) and Schütz (q.v.), and the Verlagsgesellschaft von Altona. Albrecht also made the acquaintance of Rebmann (q.v.), who had sought refuge with Würzer early in 1796. Albrecht and Rebmann probably worked together on the radical pamphlet *Der politische Tierkreis oder die Zeichen unserer Zeit*, published under the pseudonym Huergelmer, which also appeared under the title *Das neueste graue Ungeheuer*.

From March to September 1796 Albrecht published the Jacobin journal *Der Totenrichter* at the Verlagsgesellschaft von Altona. The journal pilloried the gaping social contrast between the luxury of the Hamburg merchants and the misery of the poor majority of the population. It was here that Rebmann, who fled to Paris in June 1796, published his *Briefe auf einer Reise durch Holland und Frankreich*.

On September 1, 1796 Albrecht opened the Altona National Theatre which, in the course of the following years, became the focal point of north German Jacobinism. Albrecht's plays (*Masaniello von Neapel, Die Befreiung, Klaus Störzenbecher*, and others) dealt with the defence of popular rights against the infringements of the ruling class. In 1798 Sophie divorced Albrecht and married one Herr von Hahn, with whom she lived on an estate on the Elbchausee. After Hahn's death in 1806 she went back to Albrecht. After the occupation of Hamburg by Danish troops in 1801, the National Theatre went bankrupt. Albrecht tried to keep things going by touring Holstein but the economic crisis which followed the continental blockade of 1806 made it impossible to continue. He took up medicine again and wrote several popular works on medical topics, mostly about hygiene, gynaecological problems and venereal diseases; some of these works remained in print until the beginning of the twentieth century. In 1813 Albrecht was head physician at the military hospital in Hamburg. When General Davout fortified the city and expelled thousands to Altona, Albrecht took care of the sick refugees, contracted typhus and died after a short illness. Sophie Albrecht died in poverty in Altona in 1840.

Albrecht's importance as a radical lay chiefly in his activities as a playwright, pamphleteer, novelist, and proprietor of the Altona National Theatre, helping to popularise Jacobin ideas and bring them to the attention of the German public.

Biographical entries on Albrecht are to be found in J.G. Meusel, *Das gelehrte Deutschland oder Lexikon der jetzt lebenden Deutschen Schriftsteller* (Lemgo,

1795–1834), Vol. 1, pp. 44–47; D.L. Lübker and H. Schröder, *Lexikon der schleswigholsteinischen, lauenburgischen und eutinischen Schriftsteller von 1796 bis 1828* (Altona and Schleswig, 1829–1831), pp. 9–14; Hans Schröder, *Lexikon der hamburgischen Schriftsteller bis zur Gegenwart* (Hamburg, 1851–1883), Vol. 1, pp. 40–42; and *Neue Deutsche Biographie* (Berlin, 1953), Vol. 1, p. 181. Further information can be found in: P.Th. Hoffmann, *Die Entwicklung des Altonaer Nationaltheater* (Altona, 1926); M. Thiel, *J.F.E. Albrecht (1752–1814): Arzt, medizinischer Volksschriftsteller, politischer Belletrist* (Diss. med., Berlin 1870), and W. Grab, *Demokratische Strömungen in Hamburg und Schleswig-Holstein zur Zeit der ersten französischen Republik* (Hamburg, 1966).

W. GRAB

AMAR, Jean Pierre André (1755–1816)
French revolutionary regicide and terrorist

Amar was born in Grenoble, where his father was Director of the Mint. By the age of 24, he was an *avocat au Parlement* and moved in aristocratic circles, becoming a Freemason, and purchasing the office of *Trésorier de France* in Dauphiné in 1784. Amar, however, had some difficulty in paying for this office, and in the 1780s, was gradually forced to sell the family's property. In 1788 he had an illegitimate son, for whom he was apparently reluctant to accept financial responsibility. Only in 1795 was the mother awarded damages, and Amar ordered to contribute to his son's upbringing until he attained the age of majority.

His political career began in 1790 with election to the *district* of Grenoble. In 1792 he was elected to the National Convention as representative of the Isère, receiving 276 votes out of 494. He voted for the death of Louis XVI and defended the legitimacy of his trial, against Lanjuinais. In March 1793, Amar urged the establishment of the Revolutionary Tribunal which he was later to influence directly. He was

sent *en mission* to the Ain, and his home department of the Isère, where he arrested several hundred suspects. On his return, he denounced General Kellermann, and on 14 June he was elected a member of the Committee of General Security.

On this police committee, his main responsibilities were for conducting interrogations, and for the south-eastern region of France. He presented the report to the Convention, which recommended the outlawing of the Brissotins, and he personally arrested Rabaut St Etienne, Protestant pastor and Girondin sympathiser. He was also responsible for the dossier against Chabot (q.v.), Basire and Fabre d'Eglantine (q.v.) implicated in the financial scandal concerning the India Company. In this Amar fell foul of Robespierre (q.v.) who reproached him with not fully drawing out the political dimension of the affair, which was to become the *conspiration de l'étranger*. On 15 Germinal Year II, Amar's contribution to the Terror was recognised, when he was elected president of the National Convention.

Amar had never been a Robespierrist, and he thus survived the Thermidorian reaction until after the rising of Germinal Year III, when he was arrested and imprisoned in the Chateau d'Ham. In Brumaire Year IV, he benefited from the general amnesty, but was arrested again as an accomplice of Babeuf (q.v.) in the Conspiracy of the Equals. He was acquitted of this charge by the High Court at Vendôme, and was exiled from Paris in Floréal Year IV. He retired to the South-east, but at Chambéry, was threatened with assassination by the widow of a guillotined suspect. He played no further political role, and withdrew so completely from public life that his death was announced prematurely in 1803. He played no role in the Cent Jours, and did not, like many other Jacobins, rally to the Empire. By the Bourbon Restoration, he had been converted by Swedenborgian mysticism. He died of apoplexy in Paris, at the age of 61.

Amar was a *déclassé* aristocrat, who became a convinced Jacobin. He never lost a certain elegance of manner, more reminiscent of the lifestyle of an Old Regime *parlementaire*, than of a Republican terrorist. Sénart described him in the Committee of General Security as vindictive and cruel, ambitious, proud and too fond of female company. He never played a leading role, but was a useful, if irritating associate, a dedicated enemy of Girondism, of monarchy, and of his own class.

There is no full biography of Amar but details of his life can be found in A. Kuscinski, *Dictionnaire des conventionnels* (Paris, 1917); and R.J. Caldwell, 'André Amar and the fall of the Mountain', *Proceedings of the Consortium on Revolutionary Europe, 1750–1850* (1975).

MARTYN LYONS

ARCHENHOLTZ, Johann Wilhelm von (1741–1812)
German journalist and periodical publisher

The son of a Hanoverian noble family, Archenholtz served as a cadet in the Prussian Army during the Seven Years' War and was promoted to officer's rank at the age of nineteen. Wounded in 1760, he left the army after the war and spent more than a decade travelling and living by his wits. After an accident lamed him in 1780, he began to pursue a career as a writer. His travel book, *England und Italien*, first published in 1785, became an international bestseller. His praise of English civil and political liberty reflected the ideology of the Wilkite movement that he had witnessed in London; in the context of German political institutions, his views had clear radical implications. In 1787 Archenholtz settled in Hamburg, the liveliest centre of German journalism, and set about systematically exploiting his countrymen's interest in English affairs by publishing several journals and volumes of translations; he also wrote a highly successful history of the Seven Years' War.

Archenholtz's first impressions of the French Revolution were heavily influenced by his friend Campe's publications, which glorified the French movement, and in mid-1791 he decided to relocate to Paris, planning to publish a journal about the revolution for a German audience. He associated with other German radicals living in Paris, such as Karl Reinhard (q.v.) and Konrad Oelsner (q.v.). Archenholtz quickly realised that the real centre of political power in France had passed from the assembly to the clubs, particularly the Jacobins, but he was dismayed by the violence of their internecine quarrels and alarmed by the rapid disintegration of the constitutional system put into place in September 1791. As he became more critical of the course the revolution was taking, he felt less and less secure in Paris and finally returned to Hamburg in June 1792, where he founded a new periodical, the *Minerva*, which he continued to edit until 1809. At first, his Parisian radical friends, such as Oelsner, supplied him with correspondence, and the magazine quickly became one of the best German sources of information about events in France. Even when he separated himself from the Paris radicals in 1794, Archenholtz did not openly denounce the revolution but strove to provide an objective picture of events. He continued to defend the achievements of the revolution's first years, although he admitted that the French had failed to create workable new institutions. He opposed the Austro-Prussian invasion in 1792, predicting that it would end in military defeat, but he did not welcome the subsequent French occupation of German territory and condemned the annexation of the Rhineland to France.

During the Napoleonic period, Archenholtz accommodated himself to political realities sufficiently to keep his publication alive, but his sympathies became more anti-French. The defeat of Prussia in 1806 depressed him severely; he was unable to share the confidence of some of his collaborators in the possibility of a Prussian revival. He quit the *Minerva* in 1809 and died in February 1812.

Archenholtz's devotion to individual freedom and the ideal of constitutional government was sincere but hardly original. His major contribution to the development of German radicalism was in his creation of successful journalistic vehicles for conveying news and ideas from England and France.

Aside from Archenholtz's own works, there is only one significant study: Friedrich Ruof, *Johann Wilhem von Archenholtz, eine deutscher Schriftsteller zur Zeit der französischen Revolution und Napoleons* (Berlin, 1915).

J. POPKIN

ARNDT, Ernst Moritz (1769–1860)
Poet and essayist, opponent of Napoleon, and herald of German nationalism

Arndt was born in Schoritz, on the Swedish island of Ruge, on December 26, 1769. His father was a liberated serf. Arndt was educated at home by his mother until the age of 12, after which he attended school in Stralsund, thanks to an unknown benefactor. In 1789 he suffered a severe personal crisis, and spent the next ten years in a restless search for a vocation. He studied theology and history at the University of Greifswald in 1791–92, and in 1793 at Jena, where he came under the influence of J.G. Fichte. After qualifying for the Lutheran ministry he returned home, and worked for two years as a tutor and an assistant clergyman in the household of a local pastor. In 1798, however, Arndt renounced the ministry, and set off on an eighteen-month journey of self-discovery, which took him south to Vienna and Italy, and west to Paris, where he spent the summer of 1799 familiarising himself with the revolution and its aftermath.

Arndt returned from his travels with a stronger sense of his own identity, as a writer (a craft he now took up for the first time) and, more ambiguously, as a German. He had travelled as a Swedish subject because he believed that Germans were looked down upon, a feeling that was given a political edge during his return voyage up the Rhine, where the sight of the ruined castles along its banks inspired him with a deep resentment toward France.

This journey marks the beginning of his political career. In 1800 he settled in Greifswald as an assistant professor of history. Although his first attempt to report his experiences, *Reisen durch einen Theil Deutschlands, Ungarns, Italiens und Frankreich in den Jahren 1798 und 1799* (Altona, 1802), was largely apolitical, it was closely followed by an impassioned indictment of French aggression, *Germanien und Europa* (Altona, 1803), in which Arndt laments the inability of Germany to defend itself, or to play the great role in Europe that history and geography had assigned it. Much more impressive was another work of the same year, *Versuch einer Geschichte der Leibeigenschaft in Pommern und Rüge*, published in Berlin. In it Arndt offered a close analysis of serfdom as an economic and political institution, in effect arguing that the weakness of the political community in central Europe flowed from the debasement of its humblest members. This book was very well-received, and contributed to the abolition of serfdom in Sweden a few years later, and secured Arndt an appointment to the chair in history of Greifswald in 1806.

It was, however, as an opponent of France that Arndt first gained the attention of the public. Shortly after receiving his chair Arndt published what proved to be the first of four volumes entitled *Geist der Zeit* (Altona, 1806), which insisted that the new French Imperium was by its nature despotic and anti-German. His call for national resistance went unheeded, however, and with the collapse of Prussia the following year Arndt became a political fugitive. He lived in Stockholm until 1809, where he worked as a publicist and translator in the state chancellery. After the deposition of King Gustavus IV (March 29, 1809) by a faction friendly to France, Arndt returned secretly to Berlin. But the appearance of a second volume of *Geist der Zeit* (Stockholm, 1809) once again made his position precarious. His call for a universal rising to expel the French and create a united Germany was unacceptable to official circles in Prussia. In 1810 he returned briefly to Greifswald, where he was not allowed to resume his teaching post. He spent the next year living in seclusion, mainly in Berlin, where he became acquainted with the leading figures of the Prussian reform movement. In 1812 he joined the stream of German patriots into Russia, and became secretary to the 'German Committee' headed by the former Prussian Minister, Baron Karl von Stein.

During the next two years Arndt became one of the most prominent voices demanding the overthrow of the French. Part of his popularity flowed from his gifts as a poet, which were modest by the standards of the official culture, but proved ideally suited to the crafting of marching songs and ballads [published as *Lieder für Deutsche* (Leipzig, 1813)]. To Arndt the struggle against Napoleon was in fact the popular rebellion he had been advocating since 1805. In a series of fire-breathing pamphlets and essays [see especially 'Katechismus für den deutschen Kriegs- und Wehrmann', 'Was bedeutet Landsturm und Landwehr?' and the third volume of *Geist der Zeit* (Berlin, 1814)] he called upon the people of Germany to throw off their shackles, whether imposed by the foreigner or by the past. Arndt believed that he was witnessing not simply a 'Befreiungskrieg' (War of Liberation), but a true 'Freiheitskrieg' (War of Independence), and that the military exertions of the nation in arms would inevitably give rise to profound political change. In his view the outcome of a European war fought by mass armies and popular militia would not be a return to the status quo in Germany, but the establishment of a constitutional nation-state capable of guaranteeing both the civil rights and the international position of its citizens.

That this was not the aim of the allied governments was, however, obvious, and with the coming of peace Arndt's 'Jacobinical' ideas were no longer tolerable. From 1815–17 he edited an irregular periodical called *Der Wächter*, which attacked the reactionary policies pursued in Berlin. When the University of Bonn was founded in 1818 Arndt was given the chair in modern history, as a reward for his services during the war. But the appearance of the fourth volume of *Geist der Zeit* in Berlin that same year once again made his position insupportable. Arndt's repeated calls for freedom of the press, free trade, and representative government had already made him suspect in any case, but they were especially unacceptable coming from an employee of the state. In the summer of 1819 he was arrested and his papers confiscated. His trial for sedition before the Central Investigatory Commission in Mainz ended in acquittal, but he was not allowed to resume his professorship – though he retained the benefit of his stipend.

For the next twenty years he lived as a private scholar and writer, until, in 1840, he was reinstated in his professorship by the new, nominally liberal-minded Prussian king, Frederick William IV. In 1841 he became rector of the university. With the onset of revolution in 1848 Arndt, then 78 years old, again took his place on the political stage, entering the National Assembly in Frankfurt as a supporter of the centrist liberal Heinrich von Gagern. When Frederick William refused the crown of a united Germany, however, Arndt retired completely from public life. He died on January 29, 1860 in Bonn.

Posterity's image of Arndt has been defined almost entirely by the xenophobically patriotic ballads and pamphlets of the War of Liberation. His abiding sympathy for the underprivileged masses, particularly the enormous, inarticulate peasantry of northern Europe, is largely forgotten. It is in fact hard to think of any German of his generation who had more confidence in the political potential of ordinary people than he did. This is of course a result of his own origins; he was and remained an authentically popular figure, who did not hesitate to address himself to the broadest possible audience. That he was also an anti-revolutionary figure is unquestionable, if by that one means that he was an opponent of the French Revolution. But the very depth of his opposition radicalised him, leading him to seize upon revolutionary means – popular militia, representative assemblies, a free press – to strengthen and improve his own society. The post-war Prussian establishment was not wrong to fear him, and it is in no way surprising to discover that, during the 1820s, works by other writers might be suppressed outright simply on the grounds that their style resembled his.

The most important source of information on Arndt's life is his autobiography, *Erinnerungen aus dem äusseren Leben* (Leipzig, 1840). The best edition of his works is Heinrich Meisner and Robert Geerds (eds), *Ernst Moritz Arndt: Ausgewählte Werke*, (16 vols. in 4, Leipzig, 1908). There is a substantial secondary literature on Arndt in German, almost all of which is dominated by the national issue. A representative example is Rudolf Thiele, *Ernst Moritz Arndt: Sein Leben und Arbeiten für Deutschlands Freiheit, Ehre, Einheit und Grosse* (Gütersloh, 1894). There is a similar work in English, Alfred George Pundt, *Arndt and the National Awakening in Germany* (London, 1935). Much more sophisticated is Karl Heinz Schäfer, *Ernst Moritz Arndt als politischer Publizist* (Bonn, 1974), which has a large bibliography. For a Marxist interpretation see Herbert Scurla, *Ernst Moritz Arndt, der Vorkämpfer für Einheit und Democratie* (East Berlin, 1952).

DANIEL J. MORAN

ASCHER, Saul ('Theodiscus') (1767–1822)

German radical thinker and supporter of Enlightenment ideas

Ascher was born in Landsberg an der Warthe on February 6, 1767. Little is known of his early life. A Jewish writer, he lived in Berlin where he ran a bookshop until 1810, when he gained a doctorate at Halle, gave up his business and retired to write full time. In 1789 he married Rahel Spanier and they had one daughter. Ascher occupied himself in the earlier part of his career with the question of Jewish emancipation, and criticised Joseph II's *Toleranzedikt* in his *Bemerkungen über die bürgerliche Verbesserung der Juden* (1788). This was followed by a book dealing with the religious politics of the Jewish question: *Leviatan oder Religion in Rücksicht des Judentums*. Ascher was a supporter of Enlightenment ideas and unsympathetic to the German Romantic movement. Among the early Romantics he attacked in print were both Fichte, for his anti-semitism, in the tract *Eisenmenger II*, and Heinrich von Kleist.

In his *Die Revolution in geschichtsphilosophischer Perspektive* (1802) Ascher developed an historical philosophy of revolution. He rejected the 'categorical imperative' postulated by Immanuel Kant (q.v.), with its emphasis on autonomous individual decision-making, and posited instead an interpretation of revolution as the culminating crisis in an historic constellation of forces. He dated the beginnings of social conflict from the emergence of private property and traced the origins of oppression and inequality to the end of a prehistoric Golden Age for which he used the term 'Geselligkeit' ('sociability') as opposed to modern 'Gesellschaft' society, a distinction which anticipates that between 'Gemeinschaft' (community) and 'Gesellschaft' in nineteenth-century German social thought. Modern society must transcend its origins and re-establish the principle of 'sociability', and revolutions are the point at which this restoration of the Golden Age can be achieved. For Ascher the French Revolution was an opportunity for the liberation of mankind from authority and prejudice, and it would be followed by a chain-reaction of other revolutions.

During the French occupation Ascher was a staunch supporter of Napoleon, (*Napoleon oder der Fortschritt der Regierung*). His mockery of nascent German nationalism made him unpopular; he continued to attack the Romantics for their nationalistic glorification of an idealised German past and their implicit exclusion of Jews from German society. *Die Germanomanie*, which warned against nationalist excesses enjoyed the distinction of being burnt by members of a *Burschenschaft*, one of the student associations common in German universities, and usually characterised by extreme national chauvinism and reactionary ideas.

In his later works, and in particular in his *Ansicht von dem künftigen Schicksal des Christentums* (1820), he dealt with the theme of the coming of a future universal religion. He was also interested in the political development of Europe and he thought that a united Europe would emerge from the alliance of European sovereigns. This theory found expression in his essay *Europas politischer und ethischer Zustand seit dem Kongreß zu Aachen*. Ascher died in Berlin on December 8, 1822.

Ascher's writing concentrated on three areas. The emancipation and assimilation of the Jews in European society was a lifelong pre-occupation and an understandable one for a Jewish thinker who had himself enjoyed a non-denominational education and become integrated into German society. The philosophical ideas of the Enlightenment and the philosophical history of the revolution, led him to collaborate with Kotzebue as a publisher, and earned him the derision of Heinrich Heine, who described his work as humourless and insubstantial. He was also an anti-nationalist or internationalist; he supported Napoleon, who, he believed, would bring about Jewish emancipation and European union.

Ascher's work has not been reprinted since the following editions from the late eighteenth and early nineteenth centuries: *Bemerkungen über die bürgerliche Verfassung der Juden* (Frankfurt am Oder, 1788); *Leviatan oder Religion in Rücksicht des Judentums* (Berlin, 1792); *Eisenmenger II. Nebst einem vorausgesetzten Sendschreiben an den Herrn Professor Fichte in Jena* (Berlin, 1794); *Napoleon oder der Fortschritt der Regierung* (Berlin[?], 1808); *Die Germanomanie* (Berlin[?], 1815); *Ansicht von dem künftigen Schicksal des Christentums* (Berlin[?], 1820); *Europas politischer und ethischer Zustand seit dem Kongreß zu Aachen* (Berlin[?], 1820). His article

'Die Revolution in geschichtsphilosophischer Perspektive', which was first published in 1802, is reprinted in Jörn Garber, *Revolutionärer Vernunft. Texte zur jakobinischen und liberalen Revolutionsrezeption in Deutschland 1789–1810* (Kronberg Taunus, 1974), which also includes a discussion of Ascher's philosophical, social and political ideas. Walter Grab has also written briefly on Ascher: 'Saul Ascher. Ein jüdischdeutscher Spätaufklärer zwischen Revolution und Restauration', *Jahrbuch des Instituts für deutsche Geschichte*, vol. 6 (Tel Aviv, 1977), pp. 131–79.

TIM KIRK

AUDOUIN, Pierre Jean (1764–1808)
French radical journalist, member of the National Convention

Audouin was born in Paris and on the eve of the revolution was a lawyer of modest circumstances. He immediately adopted the most extreme ideas which he propagated, in fairly subdued tones, in his daily newspaper, the *Journal universal* (November 23, 1789–Germinal 30 Year III). He abandoned the more moderate tone of his newspaper as the insurrection of 10 August approached, and was one of the organisers of that event.

Audouin was elected to the National Convention in September 1792. He played an active role in the Convention, where he was for a while one of the secretaries, and where he voted for the death of the king 'within twenty-four hours', but his main influence continued to be exerted through his newspaper which was heavily subsidised. It ceased to appear after the fall of Robespierre (q.v.), and in the reaction that followed Audouin was able to combine attacks on 'the aristocracy of the rich', of 'the millionaire faction', with denunciations of 'the Robespierre remains' ('la queue de Robespierre'). In this way he survived the Thermidorian reaction and went on to be elected to the Council of Five Hundred in the Directory. There he attacked royalists, spoke in favour of the sale of émigré wealth and in general inveighed against 'refractory priests, royalist cut-throats, rebels and Vendémiaire conspirators'. However, he called for an amnesty in Messidor, Year V. He suggested that the coup d'état of 18 Fructidor be made a national festival. He reappeared briefly during the rule of Napoleon, in 1802, but lost his position as Commissioner of Commercial Relations in the Orient the following year. He then went to Bayonne as *controleur principal des droits réunis*, and died there in 1808.

Audouin's radicalism was mainly exhibited in his journalism and through his involvement in the insurrection of 10 August. He continued to espouse radical anti-clerical and anti-royalist views during the period of the Directory but moderated his politics sufficiently to serve the Directory and Napoleon in minor official capacities.

There is no biography of Audouin, but see the entry in A. Kuscinski, *Dictionnaire des Conventionnels* (Paris, 1917).

BILL MURRAY

**BABEUF, François Noel ('Gracchus')
(1760–1797)**
*French popular leader and
revolutionary communist, leader of the
Conspiracy of Equals*

Babeuf was born at St Quentin on November 23, 1760 and was baptised François Noel, adopting the name Gracchus in 1793. He was the son of a *garde*, or excise-man, employed by the royal tax farmers. Born into poverty, Babeuf began his working life as a labourer on the Picardy canal, but by 1783 had married and established himself at Roye as a *feudiste*, or specialist in feudal estate administration. Without formal education, he prescribed for himself a rigorous course of study, and became a corresponding member of the Royal Academy of Arras. His first involvement in politics occurred in May 1787, with the beginnings of the national agitation against the privileged orders. During the elections to the Estates-General in 1789 he publicly attacked the relics of the feudal system and advocated a single tax and a national system of

education; demands which also formed part of his first major work, the *Cadastre perpétuel*, a reforming tract published in 1789.

From 1790 to the end of 1792 Babeuf made a reputation for himself as a local agitator, 'the Marat of the Somme'. He led campaigns in Picardy against the indirect taxes, against feudal dues and other seigneurial rights, and for the dividing up of town commons, and the lands of the Church and of the seigneurs among the poor peasants, demonstrating talents as a popular journalist and pamphleteer, as a legal advocate, and as a crowd leader.

After August 10, 1792 Babeuf was elected first to the Somme Department, and then to the District of Montdidier, where his revolutionary zeal as an administrator made him many enemies. At the beginning of 1793 he was charged with forgery by his enemies, and forced to take refuge in Paris, where he made contacts with the sans-culotte leaders and served in the important post of secretary of the Paris food administration. He was also named to the national Commission des Subsistances.

In November 1793 Babeuf was arrested on the forgery charge and spent eight months in gaol. Released shortly after Thermidor he re-entered Paris politics, founding his *Journal de la Liberté de la Presse* (subsequently the *Tribun du Peuple*) to press for an end to the Revolutionary Government and a return to democracy. This stance brought him into conflict with the Thermidorian reaction, and his journal adopted an increasingly popular and Jacobin tone until he was arrested again in February 1795. After spending ten months in prison, much of it at Arras, Babeuf was released again in October and re-founded his *Tribun du Peuple*, using it to campaign for the overthrow of the Directory and the realisation of a régime of common property and complete equality.

Driven underground by repression, Babeuf became chief propagandist of the Conspiracy of the Equals, dedicated to the same objectives. Among the other leaders were Buonarroti (q.v.), Félix Le Peletier, Darthé, Antonelle and Silvain Maréchal (q.v.). Babeuf was arrested when the Conspiracy was betrayed in May 1796. After a year's imprisonment and a highly publicised trial before the High Court of Vendôme he was sentenced to death, not for communist conspiracy, but for advocating the restoration of the supplanted Jacobin Constitution of 1793. He was executed at Vendôme on May 27, 1797, after failing an attempt at suicide.

Babeuf has been described as the first modern revolutionary communist. The sources of his communism have been attributed variously to the influence of Enlightenment Utopianism, and particularly that of Rousseau, Mably and Morelly, to his contacts with the vigorous communal traditions of the peasants of Picardy, and to his experience of the wartime directed economy of the Jacobin government. All three factors seem to have played a part.

Four main stages may be detected in the evolution of Babeuf's ideas. Firstly, in the 1780s he displayed clear sympathy with the common Utopian notions of the age, but his interest was literary rather than practical. Secondly, the onset of the Revolution encouraged him to formulate a reform programme in the *Cadastre perpétuel* (1789). This discussed but discarded the idea of a thorough-going equal redistribution of landed property, proposing instead a system of redistributive taxation and government-financed social welfare. Thirdly, by mid-1790 Babeuf had returned to the possibilities of directly redistributing land, and 'the Agrarian Law', as this was termed by contemporaries, became central to his thinking and remained so until 1795. In its defence he cited the classical exponents of the Agrarian Law: Lycurgus, Camillus, Gracchus, and Cassius. No clear public programme was ever put forward, though at different times Babeuf proposed dividing out the lands of the Church, the seigneurial domain lands and the lands of Vendéan rebels. The Agrarian Law remained rather a private ideal, suitable for discussion and propagation among like-minded militants as a long term goal, while the demands of everyday political life made more moderate practical reforms

appropriate. Finally, from the summer of 1795, Babeuf adopted the attainment of pure communism as an immediate, practical objective. In discussions with Charles Germain (q.v.), a fellow-prisoner at Arras, he definitively rejected the Agrarian Law and proposed instead the complete abolition of private property and of money, to be replaced by an administered economy in which the products of the soil and the workshop would be collected in public warehouses, and distributed in absolutely equal shares to all citizens. Details of the new system were published in the *Tribun du Peuple* at the end of 1795 and in the propaganda of the Conspiracy. Others emerged in the proceedings of the trial and in Buonarroti's 1828 history of the Conspiracy.

Babeuf's communism was concerned almost exclusively with distribution and hardly at all with production. There was to be some central allocation of apprenticeships to occupations according to foreshadowed needs, and an active policy of encouraging the dissemination of scientific and technological advances. Apart from that the land was apparently to be left to peasant households, and the workshops to the artisans.

Thus while the Babouvist movement may have represented to some extent a reaction against the encroachment of developing capitalism on traditional modes of production, Babeuf's communism was itself based on such modes and did not take into account the impact and the possibilities of the Industrial Revolution.

Marx depicted Babeuf as the 'spokesman of the proletariat' in the French Revolution, and some subsequent historians have followed suit. In fact he did develop, in his writings, an interpretation of French society as based on the exploitation of the vast majority of propertyless *prolétaires*, (proletarians), by a minority of 'aristocrats' or *propriétaires* (property-owners). At first deriving the institution of property from conquest and fraud, Babeuf moved ultimately to a theory of economic exploitation: the property-owners, he explained, were able to squeeze the propertyless by high prices through their monopoly of the ownership and sale of necessities, and by low wages through their monopoly of the sources of employment. At the same time, and particularly after 1794, Babeuf and his followers stressed the importance of recruiting the support of workers, sans-culottes and the poor generally, and directed their propaganda accordingly. Babeuf did not however identify or attempt to appeal to anything resembling a modern industrial proletariat, and the attempt to depict him in this guise is an anachronism.

The conspirators of 1796 planned to move towards communism by several stages. First, there would be a popular insurrection, accompanied by an immediate redress of the worst inequalities: the seizure and distribution of food and clothing supplies and of surplus accommodation according to need. At the same time a 'Jacobin' political dictatorship would be restored on the pattern of 1793–4, which would impose progressive taxes in kind, to support the agents of the régime and the needy. A 'national community' would be founded, endowed with all public lands, in which the full communist order would be immediately realised, and which would progressively attract the totality of citizens, thanks to the protection and active encouragement of the revolutionary government. Efforts would be made as soon as practicable to return to the democratic constitution of 1793. This is essentially the version of the conspirators' aims as presented by Buonarroti and absorbed into the radical tradition of the nineteenth century. But while it is true that Babeuf did advocate a revolutionary dictatorship in 1796, his attitudes to democracy and dictatorship were more complex. Throughout the first years of the revolution he had been a strong defender of the widest possible democracy, with representative government supplemented by the devices of direct democracy: petitions, binding mandates, popular scrutiny and recall, and of efforts to involve marginal elements, such as women and the poor in political activity. In 1794 he had condemned the Jacobin dictatorship in strong terms. By 1796 he had nevertheless come to believe that thanks to the repressive skill and propaganda of the Directory the majority of the people had become corrupt or misled: a short purifying period of *ad hoc* dictatorship was therefore necessary before a return to democracy. But in no sense was Babeuf the advocate of a permanent, institutional dictatorship of the kind advocated by Buonarroti.

Thanks to the circumstances of his trial and execution, Babeuf's immediate reputation was as a 'martyr of liberty', together with Robespierre (q.v.) and the Prairial victims, part of a common revolutionary democratic tradition, and his communism was not at first taken seriously. After Buonarroti's account was published in 1828, Babouvist ideas penetrated the French secret societies of the 1830s and 1840s, where they contributed to the contemporary resurgence of socialist and communist speculation, but generally as a departure point for more modern formulations. Later in the nineteenth century a greater recognition was given to the pioneering originality of Babeuf's ideas, and in 1877 Jules Guesde stressed the direct affiliation of his newly founded Parti des Travailleurs with the Conspiracy of the Equals, while in 1902 Jean Jaurès paid a similar tribute on behalf of the young French Socialist Party. In 1919, in one of the first proclamations of the Communist International, Trotsky hailed Babeuf as the first of a long line of revolutionary heroes and martyrs whose struggle had prepared the way for the world proletarian revolution, and modern Soviet and Marxist historians have given him massive attention.

In addition to Babeuf's own writings cited in the text, the following secondary sources should be consulted: M. Dommanget, *Pages choisies de Babeuf* (Paris, 1935); J.A. Scott (ed. and trans.), *The defense of Gracchus Babeuf before the High Court of Vendôme* (Boston, 1967); R.B. Rose, *Gracchus Babeuf: the first revolutionary communist* (Stanford and London, 1978); R.B. Rose, 'Babeuf and the class-struggle', *Australian Journal of Politics and History*,

22 (1976); K.D. Tonnesson, 'The Babouvists: from utopian to practical socialism',
Past and Present, 22 (1962); F.M. Buonarroti, *Conspiration pour l'égalité dite de
Babeuf* (2 vols., Paris, 1957); Colloque
International de Stockholm, *Babeuf et les
problèmes du babouvisme* (Paris, 1963);
V. Daline, *Gracchus Babeuf à la veille
et pendant la grande révolution française*
(Moscow, 1976); and R. Legrand, *Babeuf
et ses compagnons de route* (Paris, 1981).
    R.B. ROSE

BABY, Jean François (?–1796)
French revolutionary terrorist

Little is known of Baby's early life. He
was a bankrupt businessman from Tarascon
(Ariège), who still owned enough property
to describe himself as a *propriétaire* or a
rentier. During the French revolutionary
terror, he emerged as one of the leading
Jacobin militants of the south-western
region, and an active agent of the Conventionnel Vadier (q.v.).

He was *procureur* of his commune of
Tarascon, and denounced the local administrations of municipality and department
for their moderate policies. He became
procureur-général of the district, and a
suppléant to the National Convention in
the Year II, (i.e. reserve deputy for the
Ariège department). He met Vadier on
one of his many visits to Paris, and returned
to the south-west to become part of Vadier's political clientèle, providing information on local suspects and counter-
revolutionaries.

In Toulouse, he was appointed *commissaire civil* of the *armée révolutionnaire* of
the Haute-Garonne, and he persuaded it
to send an expedition to the Ariège. Here
he arrested Darmaing, Vadier's principal
opponent in the department. In Frimaire
Year II, Clauzel, deputy for the Ariège,
denounced the violent activities of Baby
and his colleagues, and the Convention
passed an order for his arrest. It seems
likely, however, that the intervention of
Vadier secured immunity for Baby on this
occasion. Baby encouraged the formation

of local committees of revolutionary *surveillance*, and earned the well-known local
nickname of the 'Hyena of the Gévaudan',
a reference to a legendary wild beast of
the Languedoc.

At the end of this mission, denounced
by the clergy of St Girons, Baby withdrew
to Paris. In the Year III he was arrested
and imprisoned in Toulouse until the
amnesty of Brumaire Year IV. On 24
Floréal Year IV he was arrested as an
accomplice in the Babouvist conspiracy,
for Babeuf (q.v.) had named him as a
possible member of a renewed National
Convention. Implicated in the affair of the
camp de Grenelle, Baby could not escape
the denunciations against him. He was
reported to have promised the deputy
Lakanal that he was ready to assassinate
the Directory, and members of both legislative councils. These seditious words were
enough to secure his conviction, and he
was executed in 1796.

Baby was an example of a local extremist
and dechristianiser, who made a brief
impact in his region during the terror,
before escaping to the relative anonymity
of Paris. There, however, his radical activities showed both the persistence and the
failure of extreme forms of Jacobinism
during the period of the Directory.

There are no biographies of Baby.
    MARTYN LYONS

BAHRDT, Karl Friedrich (1740–1792)
*German democrat, writer and
philosopher*

Karl Friedrich Bahrdt was born at Bischof-
swerda, Saxony, on 25 August. He was
the son of the rector of Leipzig University,
Professor Johann Friedrich Bahrdt
(1713–1775), and studied there himself,
taking a master's degree in 1761. From
1762 he lectured, and was professor at
Leipzig (1766–1768), Erfurt (1768–1771),
and Gießen, in Hesse (1771–1775). He
then became head of boarding school
colleges of the new 'Philanthropium' type,
first in Grisons, Switzerland (1775–1776),
and then in the Palatinate (1777–1779). He
travelled to Holland and England during

this time, and praised England and British liberty as his model and ideal. As a result of his sharp, radical criticism of absolutism and authority he was removed from office and banned by the Imperial Court Council in Vienna for heresy (1778–1779). He was forbidden to preach, or to write or teach on theological subjects, and was threatened with banishment from the Holy Roman Empire if he did not recant.

Instead of recanting Bahrdt published his *Glaubensbekenntnis* (1779) and fled to Halle in Prussia, where he found asylum under Frederick II, whose minister, Zedlitz, allowed the outlawed radical to lecture at the university but, in accordance with Frederick's wishes, only on classical philology, ethics, and rhetoric. He received no salary, and was not permitted to teach theology. In Halle Bahrdt delivered public lectures, which attracted students, citizens, soldiers, and whole families, including women. In this respect his work was an important milestone in the pre-history of the extension of university education, and of women's emancipation. Although there were sometimes almost 1,000 people present in the audience, Bahrdt did not receive an official appointment.

In August 1786 Frederick II was succeeded by his less able nephew Frederick William II, who was unlike his uncle in many respects, hating the Enlightenment, and favouring orthodoxy, mysticism, and spiritualism. He was under the influence of his court favourites, led by Woellner, who became his first minister in 1788. At first Bahrdt tried to win over the new government with his books: *System der moralischen Religion*, later re-issued under the title *Moral für alle Stände*, and *Über Pressefreiheit*. The latter was often used and cited during the years 1787–1797, even by the courts of justice, in the struggle against increasing censorship and religious liberty and the rights of freedom of thought, of speech and of the press.

Bahrdt's endeavours proved to be in vain. The reactionary Woellner issued his notorious anti-Enlightenment *Religionsedikt* in July 1788, the month of his appointment as minister, and Bahrdt changed his position to one of resolute radical opposition. In his satirical comedy *Das Religionsedikt*, he compromised Woellner, Frederick William, and their camarilla.

The death of Frederick the Great had proved to be a turning point, and since that time Bahrdt had organised the enlightened opposition against orthodoxy, obscurantism, anti-rationalist absolutism and especially against the new masters of Prussia, in a secret society called the 'Union of 22', later abbreviated to the 'German Union' or simply 'Union'. First he founded a local lodge, whose members consisted of students and citizens. When it was prohibited in 1787 he rebuilt it on a larger scale as a secret national and international corresponding society. Bahrdt's illegal lodge served as a pretext for his removal from the university in the autumn of 1787 and, forced to leave his university lectern, he retired to a vineyard near Halle, where he lectured to the people and lived as a freelance writer. In order to disguise assemblies and meetings of visitors and couriers, and not least for the benefit of his family, he became an innkeeper as well. As a result of the popularity of Bahrdt's aims, the effectiveness of his slogans, and the success of his 'chain' method of enrolment, where each member had to recruit new ones, the 'Union' expanded rapidly in 1787 and 1788 until it covered all the states of Europe, except Spain, Portugal, and the Turkish Balkans. Never before had an organisation grown so rapidly in such a short time. There were about 700 members, mainly intellectuals and adherents of the radical Enlightenment. Bahrdt, an anglophile who had become a master of the Grand Lodge of England in 1788, asserted that the 'Union' was of English origin. The 'Union' constituted a German system of para-freemasonry, alongside English, Scottish, French, Swedish and other types of genuine, para- and pseudo-freemasonry. Its name, 'German Union', expressed something of the desire for political unification among the nationally-fragmented Germans. Most members were Germans, but Bahrdt was an Enlightenment cosmopolitan and insisted that the organisation should not be confined to one nation. It was also an international organisation, with members in sixteen European countries. Fifty-two leading central European radicals were correspondents, friends, disciples, and adherents of Bahrdt. Twenty-four of them became members, correspondents, or candidates for membership of the 'Union'. Ten belonged to its staff of co-organisers. The centres of the 'Union' were in Halle, Leipzig, Vienna, Marburg and Heidelberg. Bahrdt composed five plans or programmes for the 'Union', and wrote a 'programme book', entitled *Über Aufklärung und deren Beförderungsmittel*. His ultimate aim was the unification of Europe through the Union. Unlike the freemasons and the Illuminati, Bahrdt excluded all princes and ministers (as a gesture of anti-absolutism) but admitted women and Jews (in the spirit of humanity and emancipation).

As a consequence of these activities, and for writing his satire against the *Religionsedikt*, Bahrdt was arrested in April 1789, on the king's orders and at Woellner's request. His house was searched, but one room, containing the most incriminating papers, was overlooked. Bahrdt was accused of *lèse-majesté*. In order to break his resistance Woellner threatened him, in May, with execution by beheading. Since he remained unmoved by this, the minister hoped to shock him into co-operation by announcing, in July, a sentence of life-imprisonment. But neither the threat of the death penalty, nor that of life imprisonment could shake him, and he remained unmoved by other forms of pressure: the appalling conditions in his cell, which ruined his health and the temporary prohibition of his writing or receiving visitors, even members of his family. Bahrdt admitted nothing and was sentenced on suspicion. His hope that the students, citizens and soldiers of the city would free him by storming his Halle Bastille proved to be in vain. After the victory of the revolution in France, Woellner changed his tactics towards Bahrdt, fearing that he might become a martyr of a German revolution. In response to public criticism of his

persecution of Bahrdt, he advised the king to reduce his sentence. Meanwhile, the 'Union' was being persecuted in Austria, Prussia, Saxony and elsewhere. Spying, denunciations, exposés, treachery, fear and indiscretions eventually led to its dissolution. Regional groups continued to exist until 1796.

In prison Bahrdt, a prolific writer, wrote thirteen volumes and many letters. His *Handbuch der Moral für den Bürgerstand*, asserts that only burghers and peasants make up the nation, from which the nobility are excluded. His autobiographical writings in prison include: *Geschichte und Tagebuch meines Gefängnisses*, a history and diary of his imprisonment, which includes the story, with documents, of the English origins which he claimed for the 'Union'; and his *Geschichte seines Lebens, seiner Meinungen und Schicksale*, an autobiography in four volumes. Even in prison Bahrdt continued to criticise the ruling class, often in anonymous or pseudonymous novels.

Following his release Bahrdt returned to his vineyard and wrote his most radical and revolutionary books, against absolutism and the rule of nobility, and in particular against the corrupt post-frederician government of Prussia. *Rindvigius* was a biographical novel directed against the Woellner party at court and the king; *Rechte und Obliegenheiten der Regenten und Untertanen* expounded a theory of state and society, with radical demands for social reform, and proposals for a state based on the 'people's welfare'. It asserted the duty of a people in distress to revolt and depose incompetent rulers. The work was published illegally in the autumn of 1791, although printing had been forbidden twice, by the censors in both Berlin and Halle. *Prüfung der Schrift des Hofrats Rönneberg über symbolische Bücher in Beziehung aufs Staatsrecht* was a tract directed against attempts, officially approved and assisted by Woellner, to justify the *Religionsedikt* in terms of civil law. *Der klägliche König* was an anonymous satirical parody in the form of a drama, directed against the Woellner camarilla. His last work, *Anekdoten und Charakterzüge. Aus der wahren Geschichte*, written shortly before his death, and published posthumously, was an attempt to dissuade the European princes and governments from intervention against revolutionary France. He warned them to leave France alone, or their own peoples might revolt against them.

But Bahrdt's health had suffered, especially during his imprisonment in Halle. In the first days of the first coalition war waged by Prussia and Austria against revolutionary France, he died at Nietleben after a haemorrhage in April 1792, at the age of 51.

Bahrdt is notable for the whole range of his radical thinking, going beyond orthodox Enlightenment views to embrace the causes of social reform and welfare. He was a prolific writer and agitator and a keen supporter of the French Revolution. Bahrdt must also be recognised as an early advocate of European union and a firm opponent of state nationalism through his organisation 'the Union' as an international corresponding society cutting across national boundaries.

Some of Bahrdt's works have not been reprinted since they were first published: *Glaubensbekenntnis* (1779); *System der moralischen Religion* [(2 Vols., Berlin, 1786; the fourth edition was entitled *Moral für alle Stände* (1797)]; *Über Aufklärung und deren Beförderungsmittel* (Leipzig, 1788); *Rindvigius* (Libau, Latvia, 1791); *Rechte und Obliegenheiten der Regenten und Untertanen* (Riga, 1792); *Prüfung der Schrift des Hofrats Rönneberg über symbolische Bücher in Beziehung aufs Staatsrecht* (Halle, 1791); *Der klägliche König* (Danzig, 1792); and *Anekdoten und Charakterzüge. Aus der wahren Geschichte* (Hamburg, 1793).

Other works have recently been reissued as new editions, many of them accompanied by critical introductions. *Das Religionsedikt*, which first appeared in Vienna in 1788 has recently been republished, with an epilogue by L. Lütkehaus, in Heidelberg, 1985. *Handbuch der Moral für den Bürgerstand* (Halle, 1789),

appeared in a new edition with an introduction by G. Koneffke (Vaduz, 1979); a new edition of *Geschichte und Tagebuch meines Gefängnisses* (Halle, Berlin, Frankfurt am Main, Vienna, 1790), is in preparation. Bahrdt's *Geschichte seines Lebens, seiner Meinungen und Schicksale* (Halle, Berlin, Frankfurt am Main, Vienna, 1790) is available in an unabridged new edition with a commentary and epilogue by G. Mühlpfordt, (Stuttgart 1983, 1986).

G. MÜHLPFORDT

BAILLY, Jean Sylvain (1736–1793)
French revolutionary, president of the National Assembly and mayor of Paris

Bailly was born in Paris, son of the keeper of the king's paintings in the Louvre, and received a good education. Under the instruction of Lacaille he took up astronomy and his observations of comets, of the planets, and of the moon earned him a place in the Academy of Science in 1763. His most important work was on the moons of Jupiter. He also had literary pretensions and entered a number of competitions, winning a prize from the Berlin Academy in 1768 for an *Eloge de Leibnitz*, a work which revealed Bailly's sympathy towards the *philosophes*. He benefited from the patronage of d'Alembert and Buffon, and subsequently became a friend of Benjamin Franklin and a member of the Neuf Soeurs freemasons' lodge. There he joined many other prominent men of the day, including Voltaire. His fame as an astronomer and author won him admission to the fashionable salons of Paris and to the Court. In the following years he wrote most of his major works on the history of astronomy, as well as trying to establish the existence of the lost continent of Atlantis. He was highly thought of in government circles, and was included in a commission appointed to investigate Mesmerism. In 1784 he was elected to the French Academy, and in 1785 was appointed to a commission investigating conditions in the Hôtel Dieu, the main hospital in Paris. The report, written by Bailly, was highly critical and proposed a far-reaching reorganisation of the whole Paris hospital system.

Bailly married in 1787, at the age of 51. His first real entry into political life came in 1789, with the calling of the Estates General. He was named president of his electoral district, and was elected to the Estates General, winning the largest number of votes of any of the deputies for Paris. Elected president of the Assembly of the Third Estate, he continued in this role when the Third Estate broke away and declared itself the National Assembly. He was first to take the Tennis Court Oath. On 15 July, after the taking of the Bastille, the Assembly named him mayor of Paris, and in this capacity he received Louis XVI at the hôtel de ville on July 17, 1789. He was re-elected mayor in 1790, defeating Danton (q.v.), and held the position until late 1791, despite attacks on his administration by the radical press. The municipality's use of troops against the crowd on the Champ de Mars on July 17, 1791 earned Bailly the condemnation of the increasingly powerful Left, and on November 18, 1791 he resigned. He left Paris and lived in the provinces for nearly two years, but on a visit to Melun was recognised and arrested. Taken to Paris, he was tried for his role in the Champ de Mars massacre and was executed on November 12, 1793.

Bailly took a radical stand in 1789, but as revolutionary politics moved to the left he increasingly found himself among the moderates, and eventually retired from politics. A man of the Enlightenment, he welcomed the revolution and hoped for a constitutional monarchy, displaying considerable courage in dealing both with the Court and with the people of Paris. When Louis XVI visited Paris in July 1789, Bailly made it clear publicly that the king came not as an absolute monarch, but at the invitation of the people of the city. This earned him the hatred of royalists, just as his continued support for a constitutional monarchy and his part in the Champ de Mars massacre later won him the condemnation of the Left. He is therefore chiefly to be remembered as a radical for his role in the early stages of the revolution and his contribution to the early development of Parisian municipal organisation.

Bailly's major writings are: *Essai sur les satellites de Jupiter* (Paris, 1766); *Histoire de l'astronomie ancienne* (Paris, 1775); *Lettres sur l'Atlantide de Platon* (Paris, 1775); *Histoire de l'astronomie moderne* (3 vols., Paris, 1779–82); *Discours et mémoires* (Paris, 1790); *Mémoires d'un témoin de la Révolution* (3 vols., Paris, 1804; repr. 2 vols., Geneva, 1975). His work in the administration of Paris is documented in S. Lacroix (ed.), *Actes de la Commune de Paris pendant la Révolution* (Paris, 1894–98; 2nd series, 1900-14; repr. New York, 1973). There are a number of modern biographies: G.A. Brucker, *Jean-Sylvain Bailly, revolutionary mayor of Paris* (Urbana, Ill., 1950; repr. Westport, Conn., 1984); George A. Kelly, *Victims, authority, and terror: the parallel deaths of d'Orléans, Custine, Bailly, and Malesherbes* (Chapel Hill, N.C., 1982); and Edwin B. Smith, *Jean-Sylvain Bailly: astronomer, mystic, revolutionary, 1736–1793* (Philadelphia, 1954). A reproduction of the portrait of Bailly by David may be found in M. Reinhard, *Nouvelle Histoire de Paris. La Révolution, 1789–99* (Paris, 1971), p. 16.

D. GARRIOCH

BARÈRE DE VIEUZAC, Bertrand (1755–1841)

*French revolutionary terrorist known as the 'Anacreon of the Guillotine';
spokesman for the Committee of Public Safety*

Barère was born in Tarbes in the Pyrénées on September 10, 1755. The son of a well-off lawyer and noble mother, he enjoyed material comfort and good local social connections. Although a commoner, he profited from the Old Regime. His family owned a fief at Vieuzac, the title of which he used. At the mainly noble Collège of Sorèze, he grew comfortable in aristocratic society. Due to a dispensation, he was admitted early to the law school at the University of Toulouse. His father, who bought him the office of councillor at the seneschal's court in Bigorre, obtained permission for his son to fill the post six years early. Barère remained in Toulouse, where he was a successful lawyer before the Parlement. He married a poor noble's daughter. He also pursued the craft of writer, winning admission to the literary academies of Montauban and Toulouse. He joined the Masonic Lodge.

Under the impact of the Enlightenment, Barère became a 'reforming traditionalist'. His *Eulogies*, written from 1782–88, reveal a royalist and a Catholic, but a 'liberal'. He accepted royal absolutism, but the king should rely on enlightened ministers. The Parlements were the protectors of liberty. He argued for religious toleration and free thought and expression. Opposed to the guilds, he favoured a free-market economy. He advocated reform of criminal justice and the abolition of torture. He wanted careers to be based on merit not birth. A humanitarian, he was shocked by mass poverty and begging.

During a vist to Paris in 1788, in which he witnessed the political struggles, Barère was converted into an opponent of the Parlements. Championing the cause of the commoners, he was elected a deputy of the Third Estate of Bigorre. Never a leader in the Estates-General, nonetheless he became a moderate revolutionary. He voted for the National Assembly, took the Tennis Court Oath, and refused to join the other orders on June 23. Praising the nobles for the night of August 4, he surrendered his feudal rights and renounced his compensation for his venal office. He joined the Breton Club and became a journalist for *Le Point du Jour*. Although he mixed with high society, including the Duke of Orléans, he quit the conservative *Société de 1789*. While he accepted July 14 and the October Days, he distrusted direct popular action. He was no democrat, supporting property qualifications for voting and holding office. He supported the Constituent's religious reforms, growing bitter at the non-juring priests. While he did not play an important role in institutional reforms, he obtained the *département* of the Hautes-Pyrénées

with Tarbes as its capital.

In 1791, he opposed all efforts to strengthen royal power. He also opposed a republic and was silent about the Massacre of the Champ de Mars. He joined the Feuillants after their split with the Jacobins, serving as their president, but soon rejoined the Jacobins. He opposed the conservative changes in the constitution. He supported Robespierre (q.v.) when he proposed to grant political rights to free Negroes and mulattos as well as equal rights for Jews and Protestants. He supported free public education and public relief for the poor. While moving to the left, Barère tried to follow a middle course. He feared both counter-revolution by the right and radical popular revolution. If he distrusted the king and aristocracy, he was not yet a democrat and republican.

Elected by his *département* as a judge of the court of appeals in Paris, Barère stayed in the capital until January 1792. After a brief visit to Tarbes, he returned to Paris just before the revolution of August 10, 1792, which he accepted. Danton (q.v.), the Minister of Justice, hired him as a legal assistant.

Barère was elected by the Hautes-Pyrénées as a deputy to the Convention, where he sat with the Plain. Trying to prevent a rupture between Paris and the provinces, he sought to preserve unity between the Mountain and the Girondins. Opposing Roland's proposal for a departmental guard, he also attacked the Paris Commune. He rejected Louvet's charge that Robespierre aspired to be a dictator, but the latter was insulted by his unflattering remarks. He was not enthusiastic about revolutionary expansionism. He played a statesmanlike role in the trial of Louis XVI, during which he voted with the Mountain. As president of the Convention, he personally interrogated the king. His oratory was instrumental in convincing moderates to reject Vergniaud's motion that the Convention's verdict should be ratified by the primary assemblies. After voting for the death penalty, he spoke effectively against Buzot's proposal for a reprieve. Barère had become a regicide.

Barère's shifting political behaviour between January and June 1793 can be explained by his mistaken conviction that he could mediate between the factions to restore the Convention's unity. Appalled by the Girondins' ineptitude, he was equally frightened by the Mountain's alliance with Parisian radicalism. The defection of General Dumouriez, whom he had once praised, left him vulnerable. Along with Danton, he played a leading role in the creation of the Committee of Public Safety to which he was the first to be elected. There he shared responsibility for foreign policy with Danton, whose policy of a negotiated peace he supported. He tried to forestall the insurrectional movement against the Girondins. Opposing Gaudet's motion to reorganise the Paris Commune, he proposed instead the creation of a Commission of Twelve to investigate it. On June 2 he asked the twenty-two Girondins whose arrest was demanded to resign voluntarily. When they refused, Barère suggested that the deputies march from the hall to demonstrate that the Convention was free. Failing to save the Girondins, he accepted June 2 because he saw that conciliation was impossible.

When the Committee of Public Safety was reorganised on July 10, he and Lindet were the only two members of the Dantonist committee to be re-elected. Accepting the idea that only coercion and total military victory could save the revolution, Barère became a terrorist. Designated by the committee as its spokesman to the Convention, his eloquence was invaluable in consolidating the committee's power. As its *rapporteur*, he proposed the *levée-en-masse*, the arrest of the Girondins, and the trial of Marie Antoinette. On September 5, he praised the Commune's proposal for the Terror, while recommending the creation of a Revolutionary Army. He defended the Law of Suspects and helped formulate the Law of 14 Frimaire. Supporting Robespierre's efforts to crush the committee's enemies, he stood by him in resisting the Dantonist challenge, stifling the Girondins' defence, and opposing radical dechristianisers. He participated in the elimination of the ultras and citras, even helping to silence Danton.

Barère busied himself with police measures and the war effort, while becoming an expert on commercial policy. An Anglophobe, he proposed the Navigation Act. He defended the Law of the Maximum as necessary, while proposing flexibility in its application. He delivered speeches on French military victories, extolling republican heroism to bolster morale. Barère became a *de facto* minister of cultural propaganda, mobilising artists and scientists for the war effort. He gave the report on the use of the French language, which proposed eliminating dialects. On May 11 he reported the proposal to eliminate begging by creating a national system of public relief. By hard work and his affable personality, he did much to hold the committee together. When it split into factions, he tried to avoid a break. He remained loyal to Robespierre almost to the end. He accepted the Police Bureau and swallowed his scruples about the law of 22 Prairial. Barère tried to work out a reconciliation in the joint meeting of the two executive committees on July 22. It was only on 8 Thermidor, after Robespierre attacked his enemies without giving names, that Barère turned against him. On 9 Thermidor, he proposed a decree to disarm the Commune and read the report outlawing the Robespierrists.

Barère was stunned by the Thermidorian reaction. He hoped that 9 Thermidor would restore harmony in the Committee of Public Safety. He intended that the terror should continue and fought to preserve the Revolutionary Government. He failed. By the draw of the lot, he had to leave the committee on September 1. As a deputy, he proposed to consolidate the revolution on the basis of democracy and the division of émigré property into small plots, but his motion failed. He defended himself against charges of dictatorship by blaming the Robespierrists and arguing that the decisions of the Revolutionary Government were collective. On March 5, 1795 he was arrested pending trial. Due to the insurrection of 12 Germinal, the

Convention decreed his deportation to Guyana with Collot d'Herbois (q.v.) and Billaud-Varenne (q.v.). Although they were deported, by some mystery he remained behind. He was ordered to stand trial in Saintes, but it never occurred. Escaping from prison, he hid in Bordeaux. His efforts to win an amnesty from the Directors were to no avail.

When Bonaparte came to power, Barère flattered him to get his freedom. He obtained an amnesty from Fouché (q.v.), the Minister of Police. Barère hoped Bonaparte would give him a government post, but instead he commissioned him to refute Lord Grenville's attack on his 'imperialistic' foreign policy. In October 1800, fearing he would be incriminated by the actions of his Jacobin friend Demerville, he revealed a plot on Napoleon's life to the police. Demerville was executed and other Jacobins were deported. In 1803, Bonaparte commissioned him to write regular weekly reports on public opinion. During the next four years, he was a paid secret agent for Bonaparte. He published a panegyric of the emperor and an unsuccessful anti-English newspaper. A double agent, he also received money from a Spanish agent for Godoy and confided in Russian diplomatic agents. Napoleon dismissed him abruptly in 1807. He lived a marginal existence thereafter. When the Bourbons returned to power, he tried to win Louis XVIII's favour by publicly praising the Charter. During the Hundred Days, he served Napoleon. With Fouché's help, he was elected deputy from the Hautes-Pyrénées. He tried to convince Napoleon to accept a real parliamentary régime. During the Restoration, he hid in Paris to escape arrest. In 1816, to avoid deportation, he escaped to Belgium.

He lived in Mons for six years and Brussels for eight, working on his memoirs and other writings. He had friends among the French exiles such as Vadier (q.v.), David, Baudot, and Buonarotti (q.v.). Thanks to the July Revolution, he was able to return to France in 1830. He stayed in Paris for two years, writing critical sketches of Parisian life. Returning to Tarbes in 1833, he was elected to the departmental council of the Hautes-Pyrénées, where he served for six years. Although he criticised the policies of the July Monarchy, financial distress forced him to seek a pension from the government. He received a literary pension from Thiers and another from Louis Philippe. Barère died in Tarbes in 1841 at the age of eighty-five, still believing in the revolution.

Barère's contribution to radicalism cannot be measured in terms of ideas or writings, but must be sought in his services to the Committee of Public Safety. His influence was limited by his reputation as a devious and unprincipled turncoat. But political partisanship has obscured his important contributions to the revolution. An amiable and ambitious Gascon, capable of seeing both sides of an issue, he was not inclined to radicalism. He evolved with the political circumstances. In the Convention, when his efforts at mediation failed, he became a terrorist. Never a leader or a fanatical party man, he could be in turn something of a Girondin, a Dantonist, and a Robespierrist without ever being truly one of them. But Barère was highly esteemed by the deputies for trying to preserve the Convention's unity. On April 6, 1793, he was chosen first for the Committee of Public Safety, receiving more votes than any other member ever received. He was one of only two members of the Dantonist committee re-elected on July 10. His was the eloquence that the deputies wanted to hear. As the designated spokesman of the Committee of Public Safety, Barère was at the height of his fame in the Year II. He was nicknamed the 'Anacreon of the Guillotine'. Due to his hard work and efforts to preserve the unity and authority of the committee, he was one of its most valuable members. After 9 Thermidor, his efforts to perpetuate the Revolutionary Government and the terror ended in failure. Vilified as a terrorist by the Thermidorians and condemned by the radicals for betraying Robespierre, his political career came to an end. Fearing for his life, and impoverished, he became a pitiable man. He tried to restore his reputation by his memoirs, but failed because he distorted the truth. While anathema to nineteenth-century historians of all tendencies, recent American historians have restored his reputation. R.R. Palmer found consistency in his efforts to preserve revolutionary unity, while Leo Gershoy explained his shifts by his personality traits. Both stress his invaluable service to the Revolutionary Government.

For Barère's unreliable memoirs see his *Mémoires de Bertrand Barère* (4 vols., Paris, 1842–44; English trans., 1896). For his views during the Constituent Assembly, see *Le Point du Jour* (26 vols., Paris, 1789–91). Sympathetic coverage of Barère as a member of the Committee of Public Safety can be found in R.R. Palmer, *Twelve Who Ruled* (Princeton, 1941). The best biography is Leo Gershoy, *Bertrand Barère: A Reluctant Terrorist* (Princeton, 1962). See also Auguste Kuscinski, *Dictionnaire des Conventionnels* (Paris, 1917).

MELVIN EDELSTEIN

BATSÁNYI (a. k. a. Bacsányi), János (1763–1845)

Republican poet, essayist and translator, member of the Hungarian Academy of Sciences

Batsányi was born into an impoverished gentry family in Tapolca, Hungary. He studied law at the University of Pest and made his first literary contacts while in the employ of the aristocratic Orczy family. In 1787 he became a clerk with the treasury office in Kassa (today: Kosice, Czechoslovakia); while in that city, he co-founded the first Hungarian literary magazine, the *Magyar Museum*. His progressive anti-royalist sentiments resulted in the loss of employment; he was briefly the secretary of Miklós Forgács, Lord Lieutenant of Nyitra County.

On November 11, 1794, Batsányi was arrested on charges of complicity in the Hungarian Jacobin conspiracy led by I. Martinovics (q.v.). Although the charges could not be proven, he was imprisoned for a year. After his release, he moved to Vienna, became a bank employee, started a series of literary publications, and married the celebrated Austrian poetess Gabriella Baumberg.

When France invaded Habsburg territories in 1809, Batsányi co-authored a Napoleonic proclamation addressed to the Hungarians. He subsequently moved to Paris and received an annuity from Napoleon. After 1815, Habsburg authorities imprisoned him in Dijon, Brünn and Spielberg. Released upon intercession from his wife, Batsányi was exiled to Linz. For the remainder of his life—almost half a century—he was relegated to being an observer of developments in central Europe. While he became half-forgotten in his native land, his prestige abroad increased; he maintained correspondence with intellectuals from various lands, wrote and published political pamphlets in German, and a history of Hungarian literature in French. He died in Linz on May 12, 1845.

Considered among the most distinguished lyric poets of Hungary's literary revival, Batsányi was primarily a political poet, who addressed Hungarians and mankind in general. ('Come, let us go forth as Men and Citizens, on the Road of Justice, to fulfil our sacred duty. There is no virtue without Humanity, and no Humanity without Homeland.') He supported the Europeanist literary programme of his progressive contemporaries but was also influenced by the nationalism of Ossian—whom he translated. His poems on the miseries of the national past and the grievances of the people recall the rebellious Hungarian poetry of earlier centuries and foreshadow the patriotic literature of the Reform Era, especially Ferenc Kölcsey's 'Anthem'. Torn between doubt and hope, he brooded over the fate of his homeland, placing it in the context of Europe:

Will the world awaken from its deadly slumber?

Will it ever break the chains that it
encumber?
Or to the century's utter shame eternal,
Will it be toppled down, Freedom's
new-raised altar?

(*Epistle to Barcsay*, 1792)

By prophesying and expecting the radical
transformation of social and political institutions to take place in consequence of the
French events, Batsányi also represented
a new poetic attitude. His 1789 poem *On
the Changes in France* voiced revolutionary
conviction and revealed that he was more
progressive than his Hungarian contemporaries:

Ye countries and nations tried by vicissi-
tude,
Groaning in the throes of unseemly
servitude;
Unable as yet to break out in defiance
From your ignominious, imprisoning
irons;
You whose blood Nature asks, you
anointed hangmen,
You, too, butchers of your faithful
feudal bondmen,
Come and foresee your fate, which as
yet but tarries—
But keep your watchful gaze steadily
on Paris!

In another poem, *The Seer*, Batsányi
envisaged social justice based on rationalism:

Let us endow schools of morality
For studious nations, where philosophy
Shall teach no harm or falsehood to slip
past us,
Justice and liberty our only masters.

Batsányi was one of the earliest representatives of political literature in Hungary and is generally viewed as a forerunner of the committed revolutionary
poets of the mid-nineteenth century. He
personified the plebeian Hungarian intelligentsia of his time, who simultaneously
supported the resistance movement of
nationalist gentry and also advocated the
ideas of Enlightenment and social progress.
The following sources provide further

information on the life of Batsányi, his
literary work, and the Hungarian Jacobin
movement with which he was involved:
Lajos Horánszky, *Batsányi János és kora*
(János Batsányi and his age) (Budapest,
1907); Ferenc Szinnyei, *Batsányi János*
(Budapest, 1904); Kálmán Benda, *A
magyar jakobinusok* (The Hungarian Jacobins) (Budapest, 1957); Kálmán Benda
(ed.), *A magyar jacobinusok iratai* (The
writings of the Hungarian Jacobins)
(Budapest, 1957); Beatrix Boreczky, *A
magyar jacobinusok* (Budapest, 1977);
Denis Silagi, *Jakobiner in der Habsburger
Monarchie* (Wien and München, 1962);
Sándor Eckhardt, *A francia forradalom
eszméi Magyarországon* (The ideals of the
French Revolution in Hungary) (Budapest,
1924); and Ernst Wangermann, *From
Joseph II to the Jacobin trials* (Oxford,
1959).

ANDRAS BOROS-KAZAI

BAYLE, Moise (1755–?1811)
*Regicide and French revolutionary
terrorist*

Bayle was born in Chêne, near Geneva,
into a Protestant family, which had fled
France after the Revocation of the Edict
of Nantes in 1685. He became a book-
keeper at Marseilles, where he was elected
first *officier municipal*, then *procureur-
général-syndic* of the department of Bou-
ches-du-Rhône in March 1792.

Although Bayle never joined the Jacobin
Club, he was a regicide who voted for the
death of the king within 24 hours. On
March 9, 1793 he was sent on a recruitment
mission to the Rhône valley, but arrived
in Marseilles when the federalist revolt
against Parisian Jacobinism was at its
height. Rather than be trapped by the
federalists of his home town, Bayle took
refuge in Montélimar, where he and his
colleague Boisset attempted to raise Provence against the Marseillais rebels. He
attacked the federalists in the Convention
on June 1, 1793. On August 13, 1793 he
was elected a member of the Committee
of General Security, for which he became
Treasurer on 4 Frimaire Year II. On Ier

Brumaire Year II, he was elected president of the National Convention. Bayle did not forget his fellow-southerners. He opposed the violence of Fréron (q.v.), sent to suppress the revolt in Marseilles; and if Marseilles, unlike the rebel city of Lyon, did not lose its name by official decree, this was partly due to the intervention of Bayle.

Bayle's membership of the Committee of General Security did not cease until 15 Fructidor Year II, but after the rising of Germinal Year III, an order was issued for his arrest on a charge of fomenting disorder in the south. Bayle escaped, but later gave himself up. At the beginning of the Year IV, he owed thousands of *livres* in debts, and was living in abject poverty with his five children and pregnant wife. At the end of Vendémiaire Year IV, he was released, and he secured temporary employment in the Directory's police ministry, in the bureau for émigrés. The Consulate exiled him to Switzerland until 1803. He was then appointed as a financial administrator in the *arrondissement* of Malmédy, and was last heard of there in 1811.

Bayle was never a Robespierrist: Sénart wrote that Bayle suppressed evidence against Tallien (q.v.), in order to protect him from Robespierre's (q.v.) wrath. Nor was he a bloodthirsty terrorist, for even his enemies agreed on Bayle's mildness and moderation. He was nevertheless a regicide, and an active member of the terrorist police committee, where he was responsible for correspondence and accounts. His career illustrates the adherence of Protestants to the revolutionary cause, and the importance of southern Jacobinism in launching him to prominence.

Further information on Bayle is available in the following: Michel Eude, 'Les députés méridionaux membres des comités de gouvernement en 1793–1794', *Actes du 96e congrès national des sociétés savantes (Toulouse, 1971), section d'histoire moderne et contemporaine* (Paris, 1976).

MARTYN LYONS

BAZIN, Jacques Rigomer (1771–1818)
French Jacobin and Saint-Simonian

Born in Le Mans in March 1771 into a wealthy bourgeois family, Bazin was a *clerc de procureur* there before the revolution. In the spring of 1792 he enrolled as a volunteer in the army, but was invalided out before the end of the year with an injury that appears to have left him with a permanent limp. During the summer of 1793 he emerged as the leader of a radical group within the *société populaire*, called the *Bazinistes*, which was critical of the moderate policies of the elected administrative authorities and gathered support from the artisans and labouring poor. In December 1793, after the administrative authorities had been replaced by representatives on mission, he was made *agent national* for the District of Le Mans and worked closely with one of them, Philippeaux (q.v.), who was representative for Le Mans and had himself been an activist in the *société populaire* prior to his election to the National Convention. When Philippeaux was arrested as a Dantoniste in March 1794, however, Bazin quickly followed, and along with ten other members of the *société populaire* was sent to Paris to stand trial before the revolutionary tribunal, accused of conspiring to discredit the authority of the National Convention. He was acquitted on 2 May and celebrated his release in a pamphlet, *Les membres de la société populaire du Mans traduits et acquittés au tribunal révolutionnaire à leurs concitoyens*. When he returned to Le Mans in August 1794, however, he was promptly imprisoned again for resuming his political activity, until September 1795.

Once released, he worked briefly as professor of history in the newly created *école centrale* of the Sarthe, established a printing business, and emerged as leader of a neo-Jacobin group, the *exclusifs*, which was made up of several former members of the *société populaire*. He visited Paris frequently, establishing contacts with several activists close to Babeuf (q.v.), including Antonelle and Maréchal (q.v.), and on September 28, 1796 launched in Le Mans a newspaper, the *Chronique de la Sarthe*, which was the mouthpiece of the *exclusifs*, publishing regular denunciations of local administrative bodies, large landowners, speculators, royalists and priests. In September 1797, after the Fructidor coup, he founded a constitutional circle in the city, helping to set up others throughout the Sarthe too, and organising groups of Jacobins to tour royalist areas in the west of the department in a caravan on propaganda missions. He was elected to the Municipality of Le Mans in March 1798, but by this time the Directory was determined to stem the growth of Jacobinism. It therefore annulled his election and closed down the *Chronique* which, it alleged, was 'rédigé dans des principes contraires à la constitution de l'an III'. Bazin attempted to circumvent the ban by reviving the paper under other titles, but these were closed down too and, like many other provincial Jacobin leaders, he moved to Paris in the summer of 1798. There he contributed articles to the surviving Jacobin press and with R.-F. Bescher edited the *Démocrate ou le Défenseur des Principes* in the summer of 1799, reporting the debates of the neo-Jacobin Manège Club, of which he was a member.

With Bonaparte's accession to power, democratic political activity was driven underground. Bazin resumed teaching for several years, working in Versailles, and wrote a play, *Jacqueline d'Olzebourg*, which was performed in 1803. In May 1804 he was briefly arrested, as a known opponent of the régime, but soon released. By now he had formed a friendship with Saint-Simon, sharing an apartment with him for several years, and in 1807 published a pamphlet-series of *Lettres philosophiques* which, besides containing many elements of Saint-Simon's thought, were intended to revive the spirits of the surviving republican groups in the capital. Among their subscribers were many former Jacobins and Babouvists, and it appears that they were partly designed to pass on coded messages to readers who were members of the *Philadelphe* secret society, the aim of which was the elimination of Bonaparte and the

establishment of a democratic republic. He ceased publication in late 1807, giving as his reason 'un plan d'une plus grande étendue' and, when the Malet conspiracy was uncovered in the summer of 1808, was arrested and detained, without trial, for nine months. On April 15, 1809 he was released, on condition that he live in Rouen under police surveillance, but he stayed secretly in Paris instead, with the help of Saint-Simon, was re-arrested and spent the next five years in prison, first at the Bicêtre, then at the Château d'Ham.

Released in 1814 by the allied armies, he published a revised edition of the *Lettres philosophiques* and a periodical, *Le Lynx*, in which he included an unfavourable review of Saint-Simon's *De la Réorganisation de la société Européenne*, and showed that much of his earlier radicalism had given way to patriotism. He openly supported Napoleon during the Hundred Days, following the Napoleonic armies in their retreat south of the Loire in the hope of publishing a newspaper for them, and was consequently imprisoned at the beginning of the Second Restoration. On his release, he returned to Le Mans to publish a number of moderate republican brochures, critical of the Restoration. For one of these, *Le Catéchisme Politique* published in November 1816, he was found guilty of endangering the security of the state and sentenced to five months imprisonment. He was released on appeal in February 1817. In 1818, however, when his play *Jacqueline D'Olzebourg* was performed in Le Mans, he was publicly insulted by an army officer and killed in the ensuing duel.

Bazin's political views underwent gradual change during the course of his career. During the revolution he was a radical Jacobin with views close to those of the Parisian Enragés such as Roux (q.v.) or Varlet (q.v.). Throughout the Directory he supported the ideals of the constitution of 1793, was passionately anti-clerical, and advocated sweeping measures of reform to alleviate poverty. Yet, although he was in close contact with several of Babeuf's colleagues, and openly condemned Babeuf's execution, he was never a Babouviste, because of his attachment to democratic politics and to the principle of private property. During the Empire his social views were influenced by those of Saint-Simon, while his links with the *Philadelphes* reveal a move from constitutional Jacobinism to conspiratorial politics. Five years in prison, from 1809–1814, changed this, however, for his subsequent writings were both more intensely patriotic and committed to a liberal rather than radical republic. A man of evolving views, Bazin nevertheless provided a thread of continuity between the Jacobinism of the revolution and the liberalism of the Restoration, as well as an example of the interchange between provincial and Parisian politics typical of many other radicals.

Bazin's major publications were newspapers or periodicals, notably the *Chronique de la Sarthe* (1796–8), *Le Démocrate* (1799), and *Le Lynx* (1815–1817). The remainder of his work is made up of his play, *Jacqueline d'Olzebourg, mélodrame en trois actes* (Paris, 1803), the *Lettres philosophiques* (Paris, 1807 and 1814), and a number of pamphlets written in his later years, during the early Restoration: *Cathéchisme politique à l'usage des constitutionnels* (Le Mans, 1816); *La Charte expliquée aux habitants des campagnes* (Le Mans, 1816); *Doutes éclaircis par un constitutionnel* (Le Mans, 1816); *Etrennes d'Aristide à maître Pierre* (Le Mans, 1816); *Lettre à un révolutionnaire d'aujourd'hui par un révolutionnaire d'autrefois* (Le Mans, 1816); *Lettre constitutionnel* (Le Mans, 1816); *Mon Procès* (Le Mans, 1816); *Des Réactions* (Le Mans, 1816); *Séride* (Le Mans, 1816); *Le Trône et l'autel, ou réponse à M. de Châteaubriand, par un ci-devant révolutionnaire* (Le Mans, 1816); *Premier coup d'oeil sur la session de mil huit cent dix-sept* (Le Mans, 1817); *De la monarchie sans charte* (Le Mans, n.d.). The details of Bazin's revolutionary career are covered in M. Reinhard, *Le départment de la Sarthe sous le régime du Directoire* (Saint-Brieuc, 1936); for his activity under the Empire, see J. Dautry, 'Saint-Simon et les anciens babouvistes de 1804 à 1809', *Annales*

historiques de la Révolution française, (1960); for an appreciation of his later years, D.-C. Barbier, *A la mémoire de Rigomer Bazin* (Le Mans, 1818). Details of his trial in 1794 are in Archives Nationales, W356, No. 744.

HUGH GOUGH

BERZEVICZY, Gergely (1763–1822)
Hungarian political economist and writer

Born to a prominent family of Protestant noblemen in Nagylomnic in the Szepesseg (Spis) region, Berzeviczy matriculated at Kesmark (Kezmarok) and received his law degree in 1783. Between 1784 and 1787 he studied at Göttingen, and travelled throughout Germany, France, Belgium and England. Upon his return to Hungary, he obtained a post with the Council of Imperial Viceroy. Although he developed close contact with the movements of enlightened noblemen and pro-Jacobin intellectuals, he escaped the suspicion of the Habsburg secret police. In the aftermath of the arrests in 1795, he deemed it prudent to resign his position and returned to his property in Kakaslomnic. However, Berzeviczy's was not a passive retirement: he continued to write his socio-economic studies and remained committed to the idea of emancipating Hungary's serfs.

In an anonymous pamphlet, *Der Majestatprozess in Ungarn* (1800), he condemned the trial and execution of the Hungarian Jacobins and tried to clear the stigma attached to their names. Early in the nineteenth century, he corresponded with German scientists, and became one of the major representatives of Hungarian scientific life abroad. In 1802 he was elected to membership in the Göttingen scientific society. In 1807 he travelled to Warsaw and Danzig in order to study Hungarian foreign-trade possibilities in the region. His study concerning this trip (*Die Erweiterung des nordischen Handels*, Vienna 1814) was proposed to the Congress of Vienna for consideration. He died at Kakaslomnic (today Vel'ka Lomnica, Czechoslovakia) on February 23, 1822.

In 1797 Berzeviczy published *De commercio et industria Hungariae*, the first Hungarian economic writing that, in addition to advocating complete freedom of foreign trade, criticised the mercantilist policies of Vienna, and pointed out its oppressive anti-Hungarian character. He applied Adam Smith's ideas concerning free competition and the elimination of medieval restrictions to the expressly rural environment of central Europe, and called for its 'rationalisation'. In his view, agriculture was nothing more than a special kind of productive endeavour, a capitalistic enterprise, which was to be freed of all restrictions. This called for an end to the patriarchal attitude of the latifundia: the landholder was expected to operate without the compulsory labour and other services provided by his serfs, but he was also to be made free of worries about the welfare of his tenant-employees.

Berzeviczy's main work is the theoretical manuscript *Oeconomia Publico Politica*, probably completed in 1818, and first published (in Hungarian) in 1902. He was among the first to state that the feudal conditions of Hungary stood in the way of progress, and warned the nobility about the potentially catastrophic situation of serfs brought on by the growing predominance of commodity-production. Considering himself somewhat of an outsider, he levelled harsh charges of oppressing the serfs against his fellow landlords; claiming that even within the limits of regulations introduced by the enlightened rulers, 'the barbarian lords' had many opportunities to exploit their serfs. Berzeviczy's charges appeared not only in his Latin-language pamphlets written around the beginning of the century, but also in his articles written later for the journals of Vienna; to the point that, even though the Hungarian noblemen were reluctant to make statements in foreign publications, they were forced to answer these articles, and attempt to put a gloss on their serfs' predicament.

Berzeviczy was made into an opponent of the prevailing social order primarily by his familiarity with the ideas of the Enlightenment and by his humanitarian concern for the oppressed. In addition, his faith in the feudal agrarian system was shaken by purely economic calculations. In this he was influenced in equal measure by the Josephine ideas of *Aufklärung* and the findings of the parliamentary committees commissioned by the 1791 Diet. He organised and analysed the data at his disposal with merciless logic, calculated the services and productivity of the serfs with modern statistical methods, and determined that they were practically unable to earn a decent human living under the prevailing conditions of servitude. (The reports of these committees were generally conservative, but they raised several points which could have contributed to the solution of the problems. In vain, Berzeviczy proposed the discussion of the reports and their use: they were never discussed until the Diet of 1825–27.) Berzeviczy even excused the execution of Louis XVI on rational grounds, asserting that the ruler did not perform his functions in the requisite manner.

His great erudition and his travels made him immune to Romantic parochialism and somewhat impatient with domestic points of view; he was not caught up in the struggle for the use of the Hungarian language in public life, a central issue of his times, and generally ignored narrowly Hungarian considerations. Thus, he had the critical and reformist spirit of Istvan Szechenyi, without the great love of his race that the other man had exhibited.

As early as 1790 Berzeviczy worked out a bold constitutional plan for Hungary, advocating separation from Austria, and proposed that an English prince be placed on the Hungarian throne, so that he could promote industry and trade. As Napoleon's armies approached in 1809, Berzeviczy took up this plan once again. He called for the creation of a constitutional monarchy, characterised by the following main points: the nobility were to retain their distinct legal status but were to participate in the bearing of public burdens; serfs were to be emancipated from the rule of landlords and allowed to cultivate their own land as free peasants; special taxes for landholders and churches were to be eliminated; the properties of the Roman Catholic church were to become nationalised, and clergymen were to receive a state salary; peasants were to be represented on the lower table of the National Diet, and the various branches of the government were to be separated. Berzeviczy also proposed that these goals could only be realised by an authoritarian head of state, because the peoples of Hungary were too fragmented to recognise their own common interest.

Berzeviczy's major works are: *De commercio et industria Hungariae*, (Locse, 1797); *De conditione et indole rusticorum in Hungaria* (Locse, 1806); *Ansichten des asiatisch-europaischen Welthandels* (Pest, 1808); and *De Dominio Austriae in Hungariae* (pamphlet, 1790).

Additional information on Berzeviczy can be found in the biographies by Eva H. Balazs, *Berzeviczy Gergely a reformpolitikus 1763–1795* (Budapest, 1967), and Jeno Gaal, *Berzeviczy Gergely elete es muvei* (Budapest, 1902). See also, Kálmán Benda, *A magyar jakobinusok* (Budapest, 1957); Kálmán Benda (ed.), *A magyar jakobinusok iratai*, vols. 1–3 (Budapest, 1952–57); and Denis Silagi, *Jakobiner in der Habsburger Monarchie* (Vienna, Munich, 1962).

ANDRAS BOROS-KAZAI

BILLAUD-VARENNE, Jacques Nicolas (1762–1819)

French Jacobin, member of the Committee of Public Safety, terrorist

A native of La Rochelle and the son of an attorney to the présidial court, Billaud-Varenne was trained in law, but was unsuccessful in that profession or the others that he tried—teaching and writing. He produced a number of political tracts attacking the Catholic Church and the government. These suggest that Billaud was already a radical before 1789. Strongly influenced by Rousseau, his tracts anticipated much of the Hébertist programme imposed by the revolutionary crowds on the Convention in 1793 and 1794.

Billaud became an active revolutionary from the beginning, joining the Friends of the Revolution in 1790 and later the Jacobin Club. He also worked as a secretary to Danton (q.v.). By the summer of 1792, Billaud was calling for exile of the king and the arrest of Lafayette. In September he was chosen by electors in Paris as a delegate to the National Convention where he became one of the most radical members of the Jacobin faction known as the Mountain.

It was Billaud who proposed that the Convention declare September 22, 1792 the first day of the Republic. In 1793 he published a tract entitled *Elements of Republicanism* calling for a more equitable distribution of property and universal right to employment. On July 26, 1793 he joined with the equally radical Collot d'Herbois (q.v.) to push through a law which imposed the death penalty on persons convicted of hoarding. When revolutionary crowds invaded the Convention on 5 September, he supported their demand for a militia of armed sans-culottes empowered to requisition grain from peasants who refused to relinquish their surplus. His popularity with the sans-culottes compelled the Convention to make Billaud (along with Collot d'Herbois) a member of the Committee of Public Safety.

Billaud was an energetic member of the Committee, taking charge of its correspondence with authorities in the departments. He worked constantly for greater central control over local authorities and did much to prepare the Law of 14 Frimaire (December 4, 1793) which made all locally-elected officials agents of the Convention. This law further consolidated the Jacobin dictatorship.

Billaud stood with his colleagues on the Committee when it arrested Hébert (q.v.) and his followers during the crisis of Ventôse (March 1794). But his own ideas were far closer to those of the Hébertists than the Robespierrists. He quarrelled increasingly with Robespierre (q.v.) and Saint-Just (q.v.) in the Committee and came to fear that Robespierre would destroy him. Billaud thus joined with other anti-Robespierrists on 9 Thermidor (July

27, 1794) to have his colleague arrested and subsequently guillotined. The removal of Robespierre, however, undermined the position of all Jacobins with the result that Billaud was removed from the Committee several weeks later. In 1795 he was arrested, tried as a terrorist, and sent to Guiana where he remained until 1815. Afterwards he drifted to Haiti where he died in 1819.

Billaud-Varenne was one of the most radical members of the Committee of Public Safety. Unlike Robespierre and others, he did not see the Law of Ventôse (March 13, 1794) as a temporary concession to appease the sans-culottes. The act called for the property of enemies of the revolution to be seized and distributed to indigent patriots. Billaud thought the law just. Basing his arguments on Rousseau's *Social Contract*, he contended that unequal distribution of property resulted in a contract of the wealthy few against the poor. He urged that only confiscation and redistribution could lay the basis for a true republic and this only if other measures were taken to prevent future concentration of wealth. Among such measures would be guaranteed employment as well as wage and price legislation.

It would be incorrect to view Billaud as a socialist or proto-socialist. His ideas were more correctly those of sans-culottic radicalism. There is no abhorrence of private property *per se* and no call for social ownership of the means of production. Instead there is a vision of a republic of small property-holders free from the economic and political tyranny of the rich. Such was the vision that inspired the radicalism of the artisan and the small property-holder of the nineteenth century.

Billaud-Varenne's ideas can be studied in his *Les élémens du républicanisme* (Paris, 1793), and *Principes régénérateurs du système social* (Paris, 1795). The standard biography is Jacques Guilane, *Billaud-Varenne: l'ascète de la Révolution* (Paris, 1969).

JOEL S. CLELAND

BLUMAUER, Aloys (1755–1798)
Austrian Enlightenment radical, poet, Illuminatus and Jacobin

Blumauer was born on December 22, 1755 in Steyr, Upper Austria, son of a manufacturer of small iron goods. After eleven years at the Jesuit school in Steyr he left in 1772, with excellent reports, to become a Jesuit novice in Vienna. In 1773 the Jesuit order was dissolved and he returned to secular life and together with friends from his novitiate made the acquaintance of Sonnenfels and Gottfried van Swieten, who determined his later career. Through Sonnenfels he was introduced to the court theatre (*Burgtheater*), where his rather weak and insignificant play *Erwine von Sternheim* was successfully performed in 1780.

From 1781 to 1794 Blumauer edited the *Wiener[ischen] Musenalmanach* (partly in collaboration with his friend Joseph Franz Ratschky), where he also published his own poetry. Blumauer's work was very satirical, critical and anticlerical, and illustrated his clear commitment to the ideas of the Enlightenment (*Glaubensbekenntnis eines nach Wahrheit Ringenden, Gebet eines Freymaurers, An die Weisheit*). From 1782 to 1784 he edited the *Wiener Realzeitung*, where he published his important essay *Über Osterreichs Aufklärung und Literatur*, in which he clearly analysed the position of Austrian literature in his day, and stated its tasks, possibilities and weaknesses.

Following the Josephinian censorship reform, he became a book censor under Gottfried van Swieten in 1782, and in the same year he was accepted into the masonic lodge *Zur wahren Eintracht*, an élite lodge, which served as a substitute for an academy of arts and sciences, and which was led by the famous mineralogist Ignaz von Born, on whom the Sarastro of Mozart's *Magic Flute* was based. Blumauer worked closely with von Born as editor of the *Journal für Freymaurer*.

Blumauer was also accepted into the secret order of the Illuminati, the effective counter pole to the mystic Rosicrucians, who were widespread in Austria. The Illuminati order was founded by Weishaupt in Bavaria as a school of wisdom, politicised by von Knigge (q.v.), and in Austria stood for the radical Enlightenment.

The work which made Blumauer famous was *Virgils Æneis travestiert*, on which he worked for at least seven years, without completing it (nine books instead of twelve). In undermining the status of the legendary founder of Rome, and having him found the Vatican instead of the empire, the work used anachronisms and other similar devices to attack the aspirations to secular power of the contemporary Vatican, and essentially served the aims of the Josephinian reforms. The work had great influence, even in the non-German speaking Habsburg dominions, and particularly in those with newly-emerging literatures. There were several imitations and translations, including Ukrainian (Ruthenian) and White Russian. The Hungarian translation of 1794 was prohibited by the censor. Volume 3 (Books 7–9) appeared in 1788, but the publication of the subsequent volume (Books 10–12) of the *Æneis* was prevented by the arrest of Blumauer's landlord Johann Hackel (q.v.), who was charged with complicity in the 'Jacobin conspiracy'. Blumauer himself was allowed to remain free, but was put under secret surveillance, and finally cautioned.

Since the accession of Francis II in 1792 it had only been possible to have political discussions in private. Hackel's house had been a salon during this time, in which enlightened spirits met and discussed political matters, and particularly the events in France. After von Born's death the house became—through Blumauer—a centre for the intellectuals of the radical Enlightenment, almost exclusively former freemasons, and often also former Illuminati. Blumauer dined almost daily at the table of his landlady Katharina Hackel, and his friends and visitors were often also present. These dinners offered the opportunity for discussing all the major questions of the day, and in particular the revolution in France. One of the main points of dis-

cussion was attitudes to the French constitution, and later the assessment of the Jacobin terror. There were strong disagreements, as the interrogation records of the Jacobin trials testify.

Soon after the accession of Francis II Blumauer resigned from his post as censor, which he felt no longer accorded with his outlook. Censorship had gradually departed from the educational principles envisaged by Gottfried van Swieten, and become a 'policing institution' (cf. Sashegyi, *Zensur und Geistesfreiheit*, p. 237). After the accession of Francis II government policy was determined solely by fear of the printed word.

After signing a partnership contract with bookseller Rudolph Gräffer in 1786, Blumauer became sole proprietor of the bookshop in 1793. He died in Vienna in March 1798, leaving considerable debts. On April 24, 1798 his *Æneis* was banned by imperial decree—his poetry had already been proscribed earlier as an offence to morality and religion. His works continued to appear abroad, but were only published again in Vienna during the French occupation in 1809. Bookseller Anton Pichler, who published them on behalf of the French authorities, was penalised for this after the departure of the French.

Blumauer was one of the most brilliant, and at the same time one of the most popular representatives of Josephinian Enlightenment literature, whose greatest literary work, the *Æneis* was extremely influential throughout the Habsburg dominions and beyond. He was a resolute supporter of the radical Enlightenment and, after the death of Joseph II, active in circles and groups whose members became increasingly interested in the French Revolution, and recognised and discussed its significance. They were eventually denounced to the authorities and charged with participation in the 'Jacobin conspiracy'. Blumauer himself played a decisive role in this group, but kept very much in the background.

There have been several editions of selected works of Blumauer, from an eight-volume collection first published in Leipzig from 1801 to 1806 to a four-volume collection published in Vienna in 1884. The latter claims to contain Blumauer's manuscript *Nachlaß* (personal papers etc.) but the documents are not Blumauer's. Further information on Blumauer can be found in the following: Bärbel Becker-Cantarino, *Aloys Blumauer and the Literature of the Austrian Enlightenment* (European University Papers, Series 1, Vol. 90, Berne, Frankfurt am Main, 1973); Paul P. Bernard, *Jesuits and Jacobins. Enlightenment and Enlightened Despotism in Austria* (Urbana, Chicago, London, 1971)—only to be used with strong reservations; Leslie Bodi, 'Enlightened Despotism and Literature of Enlightenment', in *German Life and Letters*, Vol. 22 (Oxford, 1969); Paul von Hoffmann-Wellenhof, *Aloys Blumauer. Literarhistorische Skizze aus dem Zeitalter der Aufklärung* (Vienna, 1885); Alfred Körner, *Die Wiener Jakobiner* (Stuttgart, 1972); Edith Rosenstrauch-Königsberg, *Freimaurerei im josephinischen Wien. Aloys Blumauers Weg vom Jesuiten zum Jakobiner* (Vienna, 1975), and 'Aloys Blumauer—Jesuit, Freimaurer, Jakobiner', in *Jahrbuch des Instituts für deutsche Geschichte der Universität Tel Aviv* (1973), pp. 145–171; Oskar Sashegyi, *Zensur und Geistesfreiheit unter Joseph II. Beitrag zur Kulturgeschichte der habsburgischen Länder* (Budapest, 1958); Denis Silagi, *Jakobiner in der Habsburger-Monarchie. Ein Beitrag zur Geschichte des aufgeklärten Absolutismus in Österreich* (Vienna, Munich, 1962); Ernst Wangermann, *From Joseph II to the Jacobin Trials. Government Policy and Public Opinion in the Habsburg Dominions in the Period of the French Revolution* (Oxford, 1959), and *The Austrian Achievement 1700–1800* (London, 1973).

EDITH ROSENSTRAUCH-
KÖNIGSBERG

BOHL, August Jakob (1762–1808)
German Jacobin writer

Bohl, who grew up in poor circumstances, attended the Catholic seminary in Bruchsal from 1785 to 1787 and became a chaplain in Philippsburg, where his 'passion for innovation' attracted the attention of the church authorities. In 1791 he was transferred first to Gernsheim, and then to Hambach, in the diocese of Speyer. It was here that he wrote the anonymous satire *Das Zölibat ist aufgehoben*, which derided the church's monasticism and obscurantism, and the anonymous tragedy *Die Mönche in Niederland und Kaiser Joseph II*, which criticised the clerical rebellion in Belgium against the emperor's reforms. In both plays Bohl pleaded for complete social and political equality of all citizens, including Protestants and Jews, criticised and derided Catholic hypocrisy and the inhuman behaviour of many aristocrats towards their subjects, and demanded the abolition of the celibacy of Catholic priests. Both plays were published by the Speyer bookseller Philipp Wilhelm Hauth. When the papers of the revolutionary priest Joseph Brunner (q.v.) were seized by the authorities in Tiefenbach in 1793, letters from Bohl were found from which his authorship of both plays could be established. On February 20, 1794 the investigation before the ecclesiastical court in Bruchsal began. Bohl fled to his parents in Rastatt to avoid arrest. After his return in August 1794 he was put on trial and charged with 'adherence to the French madness'; *Das Zölibat* was designated a scandalous play, because it 'had praised the French Revolution to heaven'. Bohl was sentenced to four weeks' detention and had to retake his theological course. He died in 1808.

Little else is known of Bohl, who remained in the service of the church until his death. His investigation and trial seems to have had the effect desired by the church authorities: the rebellious priest refrained from publishing attacks against the pillars of the feudal hierarchy.

There is no biography of Bohl, but information on his work as a radical playwright can be found in Gerhard Steiner, *Jakobinerschauspiel und Jakobinertheater* (Stuttgart, 1973).

W. GRAB

BÖHMER, Georg Wilhelm (1761–1839)
German journalist, supporter of the French Revolution and of French annexation of the left bank of the Rhine

Böhmer was born in Göttingen, the son of Georg Ludwig Böhmer, on February 7, 1761. He studied theology at Göttingen University from 1779, and taught canon law and ecclesiastical history there from 1785. In 1787 he founded the journal *Magazin für das Kirchenrecht, die Kirchen- und Gelehrtengeschichte.* In 1788 he became Professor of Protestant Theology at the *Gymnasium* in Worms. Here he continued to write, although the liberal tendencies of his work made him unpopular with the authorities. He followed the course of political events in France very closely, and welcomed the revolution. On the occupation of Mainz by French troops on October 4, 1792 Böhmer immediately entered the service of the French, subsequently became the secretary of General Custine, and delivered the German version of the general's address to the Mainz Club on October 25, 1792.

Böhmer became a member of the Mainz Club on October 25, 1792 and occupied a number of other important positions. He was an election commissar and, although not one of its leading personalities, he was a deputy (for Oberolm) in the short-lived Rhineland National Convention. He was also editor of the Rhineland *National-Zeitung* from October 1791 to April 1793.

When the French left Mainz in July 1793 following the fall of the city to the Prussians after a long siege, Böhmer was taken hostage as security for those Germans taken to France, and was imprisoned in the fortress at Ehrenbreitstein, near Koblenz on the Rhine and, later, at Petersburg near Erfurt. He was released in 1795, and emigrated to France, where he served in a number of offices both under the Directory and under Napoleon. Along with Nimis and Blau, he edited the Paris-based German-language newspaper, *Pariser Zuschauer*, thousands of copies of which were distributed in the Rhineland.

On the establishment of the kingdom of Westphalia Böhmer returned to Germany as a Justice of the Peace at Schlandstädt bei Oschersleben and Commissar General of Police in the *département* of Harz and Leine. After the end of the French occupation he was commissioned to compile the law catalogue at Göttingen University library, and became a lecturer at the university in 1816. During this last period of his life he published a number of works on the law and legal history (*Literatur des Criminalrechts*, 1816; *Über die authentischen Ausgaben der Carolina*, 1818; and *Über die Ehegesetze im Zeitalter Karls des Grossen und seiner Regierungsnachfolger*, 1826).

Although not one of the most important figures in the Mainz Republic, Böhmer made a significant contribution to the republican cause. During the occupation of Mainz he was keen to win over the local population to the French and the ideas of the French constitution. He was active as a propagandist in support of the republic in Speyer, Worms and the surrounding villages. Like Matthias Metternich (q.v.) he was an advocate of the argument that the best chance for democracy in the Rhineland lay in the area's annexation by France and incorporation into the Republic. During his exile in France he worked actively in support of such a policy, and in 1796 wrote a number of pamphlets emphasising the advantages of French annexation, which were subsequently published as a collection entitled *La rive gauche du Rhin, limite de la République Française*.

Otherwise, Böhmer wrote little apart from his speeches, perhaps the most famous of which is *Die Aristokraten am Rheinstrom bei der eingebildten Flucht eines verräterischen Königs oder Erinnerung des 23, 24, 25 Novembers 1791. Eine Rede in der Gesellschaft der Konstitutionsfreunde zu Mainz 1792* (Mainz, 1792). A useful source of primary material on the Mainz republic and the Jacobin Club, of which Böhmer was a member, is a collection of documents edited by Heinrich Scheel, *Die Mainzer Republik. Protokolle des Jakobi-*

nerklubs (Berlin, 1975). Böhmer's biographical details are in the third volume of the *Allgemeine Deutsche Biographie* (Leipzig, 1876). T.C.W. Blanning, *The French Revolution in Germany. Occupation and Resistance in the Rhineland 1792–1802* (Oxford, 1983), describes the political and military background to Böhmer's activities in the Rhineland.

TIM KIRK

BONNEVILLE, Nicolas de (1760–1828)
French journalist and social reformer of the revolutionary period, early supporter of the abolition of the property qualification

Bonneville was born in Evreux into an old and respected Normandy family; his father, Pierre Jean de Bonneville, was a *procureur*. Little is known of his early years or education, but he is reputed to have had a lively imagination and his use of it, to defend Rousseau's views on deism at a school prize-giving ceremony, led to his leaving Evreux in his late teens to settle in Paris. There he benefited from the patronage of D'Alembert, read widely in the classics, studied both Rousseau and the Bible, and taught himself fluency in both English and German. From an early stage he showed a concern to reconcile the principles of early Christianity with the democratic ideals of Rousseau. In 1782 he collaborated with the German author, Friedel, on a twelve volume translation, *Nouveau théâtre allemand, ou Choix des pièces dramatiques qui ont eu le plus de succès sur les Théâtres de l'Allemagne*, and four years later published an anthology of translated German short stories. He visited England in 1786, and began work on a translation into French of Russell's *Letters on Modern Europe*. However, he soon tired of this and started work instead on his own *Histoire de l'Europe moderne* (3 vols. 1789–1792), which used Russell as a base but was marked by his own anticlericalism, an admiration of the institutions of Anglo-Saxon England, and hostility towards monarchy. In 1787 he first came into contact with the Illuminist masonic

sect in Bavaria, and was attracted by its ideas of cosmopolitan fraternity, social harmony and human progress, which fitted in well with his own Biblical and Rousseauist views. In 1788 he published an anti-Jesuit work *Les Jésuites chassés de la maçonnerie et leur poignard brisé par les maçons* which, again permeated by anticlericalism, alleged that the Jesuits had infiltrated masonry to become its invisible masters, and recommended their immediate expulsion.

In the spring of 1789 he was a second degree elector for the Carmes-Déchaussés district in the elections to the Estates General in Paris and, on 25 June, recommended to the Parisian Electoral Assembly the establishment of a *Garde bourgeoise* to keep order in the capital: '. . .the bourgeois guard will prevent internal troubles, the dearth of foodstuffs, and that blind enthusiasm which might lead our ardent youth astray. . .if you fear for your persons, your wives, your children, set up the bourgeois guard.' The idea was taken up by the Electoral Assembly on 10 July, and lay at the root of the creation of the National Guard three days later. In September Bonneville was elected to the Assembly of Three Hundred, created to draw up a constitution for the capital, and was quickly noted as belonging to its democratic wing. In January 1790, with the help of the abbé Fauchet (q.v.), he founded the *Cercle Social*, as a small group of élite democratic activists dedicated to monitoring the reforms of the National Assembly and to preparing the masses for the exercise of political power. It had its own newspaper, the *Bouche de Fer* which Bonneville edited with Fauchet, and on October 13, 1790 opened its doors to a wider public under the name of the *Confédération des Amis de la vérité*, with the avowed aim of working for 'l'union de tous les peuples et de tous les individus qui habitent la terre en une seule famille de frères ralliés par la tendance de chacun au bien général'. The organisation and ideology of the Confederation was unmistakably masonic, but Bonneville was also attracted by the spirit and ideology of the

Cordeliers Club, and opened the columns of the *Bouche* to articles from its members too. In his paper, and in the Confederation, he opposed the censitary suffrage of the 1791 constitution, and advocated direct democracy, with the use of referenda on major issues. Strongly anticlerical, he proposed the adoption of a civic religion, similar to that of Rousseau, based on civic virtues and the idea of an all-powerful Supreme Being, and in 1791 published a book, *De l'Esprit des Religions* which, drawing on articles already published in the *Bouche de Fer*, praised the spirit of early Christianity, and argued the need for radical social change. In particular he deplored inequality, advocated the implementation of social welfare measures to alleviate the plight of the destitute, and criticised primogeniture, suggesting adjustments to the inheritance laws in order to ensure a more even distribution of property. In response to critics, however, he denied any sympathy with the more radical concept of the *loi agraire*.

In late June 1791, after Louis XVI's flight to Varennes, Bonneville was prominent in the republican agitation that led to the massacre of the Champ de Mars. He founded a Société Républicaine in early July, with Tom Paine, Condorcet (q.v.) and others, and launched a newspaper, *Le Républicain*, to publicise its views. He was prominent in debates on the king's fate, both at the Federation and at the Cordeliers Club, and helped in the drafting of the petition that was signed at the Champ de Mars on 17 July. In the regression that followed, both the Confederation and the *Bouche de Fer* closed down, and Bonneville informed his readers that he needed time to reconsider his position. The summer of 1791 nevertheless proved to be the high point of his radical activity, and henceforward his concern for social harmony proved stronger than his interest in democracy. In November 1791 he returned to journalism as one of a large editorial team for a monthly review, the *Chronique du Mois*, writing its accounts of Assembly debates. He also became increasingly favourable towards the Girondins, mixing socially with

their political leaders, and finally left the *Chronique* in early September 1792 as a protest against the September massacres. His political interests remained, however, for through Roland, Minister of the Interior, he was appointed as commissaire to restore order in Rouen after food disturbances in the city, between 5 and 26 September, working with Jean-Réné Loyseau.

On his return to Paris he continued to contribute occasional articles to the *Chronique du Mois*, but in January 1793 launched his own daily paper, the *Bulletin des amis de la vérité* with contributions from Condorcet and Paine, to campaign for non-partisan republican democracy: 'No Mountain, no Plain, no rocks, but a single Convention as indivisible as the Republic itself. . .'. However, it was not a commercial success, and closed down in the spring through lack of money. On May 18, 1793 he was arrested, but later released, after being denounced by Marat (q.v.). Arrested again during the summer, he spent the Terror in prison and was only released in the weeks following Robespierre's (q.v.) fall. He then returned to Evreux briefly, but was back in Paris by 1797, when he lived at no. 4 rue du Théâtre Français, with his wife and three sons, and with Thomas Paine, whom he had first met while working on the *Chronique du Mois*, as a family guest for the next five years. In September 1797 Bonneville launched another newspaper, the *Bien Informé*, which specialised in reports on overseas news and foreign policy. Its publication was twice suspended by the Minister of Police, but despite financial problems it lasted until the spring of 1800. Then an article comparing Bonaparte to Cromwell led to its permanent closure.

Bonneville returned to Evreux to live with his father, under police surveillance, and in 1802 his wife and family moved to the United States, where they were supported by Paine until his death in 1809. Bonneville himself remained in France until 1815, when he finally rejoined his family in New York. Four years later he returned, with his wife, to set up as a *bouquiniste*, with a small shop on the rue des Près Saint-Jacques in Paris. He died there, in abject poverty and failing mental health on November 9, 1828. His wife returned to the United States in 1833 and died in St Louis in 1846. One of his sons, Benjamin, was later a general in the United States army.

Bonneville's ideology was often obscured by his enigmatic use of language and symbolism. Yet there were several significant strands to his thought which influenced contemporaries and link him to more prominent activists such as the Enragés or Babeuf (q.v.). From Illuminism and the masonic ideal he developed the concept of an enlightened élite, working to change society for the benefit of all, realised in the work of the *Cercle Social* and taken up later in the ideas of Babeuf. From Rousseau he picked up the interest in radical democracy which saw him active in the Cordeliers Club during the early revolution and a leading republican in the summer of 1791. From a combination of Rousseau and early Christianity he developed a conviction of the role of a rational religion in creating social harmony: 'To separate religion from government is to detach the head and root from the tree of political and civil liberty'. From them too he developed several of the early ideals of socialism, most notably those of abolishing property inequality through modifications to the inheritance laws, and of relieving poverty through the state provision of social welfare. Like many of his contemporaries, he envisaged wealth as synonymous with land, ignoring both mercantile and industrial capital, but his ideas and those of the *Cercle Social* were to have an important influence on the development of socialism after his death.

Bonneville wrote extensively. His major pre-revolutionary works include *Nouveau théâtre allemand ou Recueil des pièces qui ont paru avec succès sur les théâtres des capitales de l'Allemagne* (10 vols., Paris, 1783–5); *Les jésuites chassés de la maçonnerie et leur poignard brisé par les maçons* (2 vols., London, 1788); *Histoire de l'Europe moderne, depuis l'iruption des peuples*

du Nord dans l'Empire romain jusqu'à la paix de 1783 (3 vols., Geneva, 1789–1792). During the revolution he edited three periodicals with Claude Fauchet, the *Bulletin de la Bouche de Fer* (Jan.–July 1790), the *Cercle Social* (1790) and the *Bouche de Fer* (Oct. 1790–July 1791); he was also later editor of the *Bien Informé* (Sept. 1797–April 1800). Among his other publications during the revolution the most significant are *Le Tribun du peuple* (1789), *Le Tribun de Peuple, ou Recueil des Lettres de quelques électeurs de Paris, avant la Révolution de 1789* (1789), *De l'Esprit des Religions* (1791), *Le Nouveau Code conjugal, établi sur les bases de la constitution et d'après les principes de la loi....* (Paris, 1792), and *L'Hymne des combats, hommage aux armées de la République* (Paris, 1797). The only full length biography is Philippe Le Harivel, *Nicolas de Bonneville, Pré-Romantique et Révolutionnaire 1760–1828* (Strasbourg, 1923). For his early revolutionary activity, see R.B. Rose, 'Socialism and the French Revolution: the Cercle Social and the Enragés', *Bulletin of the John Rylands Library* (1958), pp. 139–66; and for his mission to Rouen in 1792, P. Caron, 'La mission de Loyseau et Bonneville à Rouen, septembre 1792', *La Révolution française*, t. 85 (1932).

HUGH GOUGH

BOURBOTTE, Pierre (1763–1795)
French revolutionary, member of the National Convention

Bourbotte was born at Vault-de-Lugny (Yonne) into a middle-class family. From the outset he was an enthusiastic supporter of the revolution and became an administrator in the Yonne department. In 1792 he was elected to the Convention, where he sat with the Mountain. In the trial of Louis XVI he voted against an appeal to the people and for the death-penalty without reprieve.

He was sent on mission to Orléans, Tours, and then to the Vendée where he led the resistance to the rebels. In the battle of Saumur his horse was killed under him and he was only saved by the timely arrival of a group of soldiers. He was present at the Mans massacre of Vendéens in December 1793 and at the recapture of the Ile de Noirmoutiers in January 1794. By this stage, however, he was ill from fatigue and asked Barère (q.v.) to recall him. After a month's leave in Paris he returned to Nantes from where he led a division of the army of the West to join the army of the Rhine. He was present at the capture of Trèves on 21 Thermidor (August 8, 1794) and of Bingen, and at the surrender of the fort at Rheinfelds.

Following Thermidor he was recalled to Paris, resumed his place on the side of the Mountain, and played a major role in the events of Prairial Year III. He was one of the four members (along with Duquesnoy, Duroy and Prieur de la Marne (q.v.)) of the Commission set up to replace the Committee of General Security. With the defeat of the insurrection, Bourbotte was arrested, along with Goujon, Romme (q.v.), Duquesnoy, Duroy and Soubrany, and imprisoned in the Château du Taureau. On 22 Prairial they were brought back to Paris, tried by a military commission and sentenced to death. In his last letter Bourbotte wrote, 'O Liberty, I have lived only for you and by you', and at the moment of his execution cried, 'Vive la République!'

An ardent defender of the principles of the revolution, Bourbotte displayed great courage in opposing both internal and external resistance to the dissemination of those principles even in their most radical form. Indeed it was just such a principled resistance to the Thermidorian reactionaries that cost him his life.

There is no biography of Bourbotte, but biographical sketches appear in A. Kuscinski, *Dictionnaire des Conventionnels* (Paris, 1917), and J. Robinet et al., *Dictionnaire historique et biographique de la Revolution et de l'Empire 1789–1815* (Paris, 1899).

D. NICHOLLS

BRISSOT DE WARVILLE, Jacques Pierre (1754–1793)
French revolutionary journalist and politician

Born in Chartres, the tenth son of a moderately prosperous hotelier, Brissot was educated locally and, at the age of fifteen, was apprenticed to a local *avocat*, Horveau. Through a friendship with Horveau's son he gained access to the family's large library and read voraciously, teaching himself Spanish, Italian and English and abandoning the deep Catholic faith of his family upbringing to become an admirer of Rousseau. It was at this time too that he added the words 'de Warville' to his surname—the anglicised form of Oarville, a small village some twenty-three kilometres outside Chartres, where his father held land—thereby following a local tradition of adopting the name of the village where, as an infant, he had been put out to wet nurse.

In 1774 he moved to Paris to work as *clerc* to a *procureur* to the parlement of Paris, Nolleau, for 400 *livres* per annum. However he soon met Linguet, editor of the *Journal de Bruxelles*, was attracted by the prospect of a literary career, and within three years had abandoned law for full time writing. His first two pamphlets, which were critical of the legal profession, caused a *lettre de cachet* to be issued for his arrest, which he evaded by going into hiding. In 1778 he published a *Testament politique de l'Angleterre* which criticised British policy in the American War of Independence. Banned in France, it was published in Neuchâtel and attracted the attention of an English publisher, Swinton, owner of the London-based *Courrier de l'Europe*, which contained a digest of the English press. Swinton employed Brissot to act as his French editor. Brissot had already become interested in journalism through his meeting with Linguet, and he worked on the *Journal de Bruxelles* for a little over a year, until the French government objected to him adding his own editorial comment. He returned to Paris, where he published a *Théorie des lois criminelles* which he dedicated to Voltaire, but which, because of its criticism of the legal profession, ensured that the career was closed to him forever. He won prizes from the *Académie des sciences* of Châlons-sur-Marne for two essays—again on legal topics—and became interested in science too, following courses in chemistry and meeting Forcron and Lavoisier. He also became a friend of Jean Paul Marat (q.v.), supporting his unorthodox theories on the nature of fire and electricity, and sharing his hostility to the scientific establishment.

In 1782 he decided to set up a *lycée* in London which would help spread new scientific ideas through meetings and a newspaper, the *Correspondance philosophique et politique*. He spent much of that year negotiating with potential collaborators and patrons, and while in Geneva met the financier Etienne Clavière, with whom he formed a lasting friendship. In July 1782 he moved to Neuchâtel with Clavière, then to London where he again worked for Swinton, this time as a literary columnist for the *Courrier de l'Europe*. However, his attempts to launch the *lycée* rapidly ran into financial difficulty, while the *Correspondance philosophique et politique* attracted few subscribers, and was banned from circulation in France. Brissot soon found himself deeply in debt and his problems increased when Swinton persuaded Cox, printer of the ailing *Correspondance*, to imprison him for his debts. Friends rallied round to redeem them, but Brissot still owed 15,000 *livres* which he had borrowed to help establish the *lycée*, and when he returned to Paris was imprisoned in the Bastille on suspicion of writing and circulating libels against the queen. The accusation was false, and Brissot was released within four months, possibly on the basis of agreement with the Paris *lieutenant de police*, Lenoir, that he supply secret reports on the activity of the literary underworld. He probably did this for the next year.

Between 1783 and 1787 Brissot's activity was based on Paris. In 1785 he became secretary to the Marquis du Crest, friend and chancellor to the Duke of Orléans, who was ambitious to gain ministerial office and used Brissot as a paid pamphleteer to attack the financial policies of Calonne and Brienne. Between 1785 and 1789 he also wrote a number of pamphlets on financial matters for Clavière, both under his own and under assumed names, to aid Clavière's financial speculation and his ambitions of influencing French policy towards Geneva. However, one of these, published in late 1787, *Point de banqueroute, ou Lettres d'un créancier de l'etat*, prompted the government into issuing a *lettre de cachet* against him and he took refuge in England in November. Clavière joined him and they came into contact there with the Society for the Abolition of the Slave Trade. On their return to France in February 1788 they formed a French equivalent, the *Société des amis des Noirs* which counted amongst its founder members Lafayette, Carra (q.v.), Clavière, Mirabeau and Condorcet (q.v.).

During the summer of 1788 Brissot went to the United States, on financial business for Clavière, but returned in the spring of the following year. In April and May he made two unsuccessful attempts to launch a newspaper in defiance of government censorship, and failed to get elected to the Estates General. However in July he secured election to the first Paris Municipality and finally succeeded in launching his newspaper the *Patriote Français*, which he edited until the autumn of 1791. Journalism suited his literary talents and the *Patriote* rapidly built up a substantial circulation, providing an excellent platform for his political campaigns. His views reflected the radicalism of his pre-revolutionary career, and made him frequently critical of the reforms of the National Assembly. He opposed the granting of the royal veto, criticised the *marc d'argent* decree and censitary suffrage and advocated instead universal male suffrage and more emphasis on direct democracy, through the delegation of powers to local authorities and the use of referenda. On social questions, he advocated measures to alleviate poverty, including bread subsidies, the sale of

Church lands in small lots and restriction on inheritance rights in order to break up large estates, but like many other radicals he was reluctant to interfere in the rights of property and resolutely defended free trade in grain and other foodstuffs. His ideal, like Robespierre's (q.v.), appears to have been that of Rousseau: a society of small and independent property-owners. However, one of his most consistent preoccupations during these years remained the campaign against the slave trade, which he continued in the columns of the *Patriote Français* and in the debates of the Paris Jacobin Club, attracting a great deal of hostile opposition.

After the king's flight to Varennes in June 1791 Brissot supported the creation of a republic and helped to organise the petition presented at the Champ de Mars on 17 July. His prominence in this made him the main target of a press campaign, led by two court financed gutter press journals, the *Chant du Coq* and the *Argus Patriote*. Yet he remained a member of the Jacobin Club after its split on 16 July, and played a major role in rebuilding it during the autumn months of 1791. In September he was elected for Paris to the Legislative Assembly, and handed over editorial control of the *Patriote Français* to a close friend, Girey-Dupré, continuing nevertheless to contribute regular articles to it, and to a monthly review, the *Chronique du Mois*. A mediocre speaker, with a weak voice and little capacity to improvise on his feet, he made less impact on the floor of the Assembly than he had through the columns of his newspaper. Nevertheless he became a member of the Assembly's *comité diplomatique* and devoted much of his attention to foreign affairs, which he always, quite wrongly, regarded as his major strength. In five major speeches in December 1791 and January 1792, at the Jacobin Club and in the Assembly, he urged the declaration of war on the émigrés and Austria, convinced that French victories would swiftly end their threat to the revolution, encourage revolution elsewhere in Europe, and resolve the country's internal difficulties.

Robespierre opposed him, and an irreparable rift opened up between them which widened in March 1792 when some of Brissot's friends—notably Clavière and Roland—accepted office in the first Girondin ministry. After they were dismissed in June, Brissot hoped that a compromise ministry might be patched together and, fearing the growth of sans-culotte radicalism, resisted mounting demands for the king's removal from office. Yet, once insurrection had achieved this on 10 August, he accepted it enthusiastically.

By now, however, he regarded popular radicalism and Robespierre's influence among the sans-culottes as a major threat to the stability of the republic. On 1 September Robespierre denounced him to the Paris Commune and, on the following day, its *comité de surveillance* ordered his arrest. But the order was never carried out, saving him from what would have been certain death in the prison massacres which followed. Instead he was elected to the National Convention for three departments, opting for his home base of the Eure-et-Loire, and once again became a member of the *comité diplomatique*, as well as of the *comité de défense générale*. He played a subdued role in the conflict between Girondins and Montagnards that dominated the Convention's first nine months, but was convinced that the best strategies for checking radicalism lay in wooing Danton (q.v.) away from the Mountain and concentrating criticism instead onto the unpopular figure of Marat. However, most of his political allies were less discriminate, alienating Danton by their attacks, and Brissot's past prominence inevitably dragged him into an increasingly bitter conflict. On 12 October he was struck off the membership lists of the Jacobin Club. In the king's trial he voted for reprieve, and in May 1793 published a pamphlet, *A Mes Commettants*, which called for the closure of the Jacobins and the suspension from office of the Paris Municipality.

After the insurrection of 2 June the Convention ordered his arrest, but he left Paris secretly and headed south, only to be recognised and arrested at Moulins. Sent back to Paris, he was imprisoned at the Abbaye, where he wrote his memoirs while awaiting trial. Found guilty of treason by the revolutionary tribunal on 30 October, he was guillotined the same evening. He left behind him a wife, Félicité Dupont, whom he had married in 1783.

Brissot played an important role in the French Revolution, and few careers offer as striking an example of two important features of the late eighteenth-century life: the magnetic attraction of a literary career to young and ambitious provincial bourgeois in the last decades of the Ancien Régime, and the fame that journalism could bring once revolution broke out in 1789. It was the latter which brought him to public attention, secured his election to the Legislative Assembly and Convention, and gave him political influence. His social and political ideas were deeply influenced, on the one hand by Rousseau, and on the other by his frustrations as a writer before 1789. From both he acquired a commitment to social and political reform, based on the belief that the Ancien Régime was morally corrupt. Yet his ambition, his enthusiasm and his loyalty to friends were seriously to compromise him when revolution began. Persistent rumours that he had worked for Lenoir as a police spy after his release from the Bastille in 1784 surfaced during the revolution, to cast doubts over his honesty. His choice of friends and colleagues—most notably that of Girey-Dupré to whom he entrusted the *Patriote Français* from October 1791 onwards—embroiled him in the kind of bitter personal polemics that finally sealed his fate. An unfounded belief in his own competence in diplomacy led him to completely miscalculate the political and military impact of war in 1792: the most serious political error of the entire decade. Like many other revolutionary activists too, he lacked political consistency, dropping much of the radicalism that he voiced in the early part of the revolution when he himself came close to the levers of power in the summer and autumn of 1792. Yet, with all his faults, his talents as a publicist

and his political influence were considerable and they were matched by generosity towards friends and a complete disregard for financial affairs, which left his publisher to reap the massive profits from the *Patriote Français* and his wife penniless on his death.

A full list of Brissot's works can be found in A. Martin and G. Walter, *Catalogue de l'histoire de la révolution française*, tome 1 (Paris, 1936), pp. 316–24. Of his pre-revolutionary works, see *Moyens de prévenir les crimes en France* (Châlons-sur-Marne, 1781); *Théorie des lois criminelles* (Paris, 1781); *Bibliothèque philosophique du législateur, du politique, du jurisconsulte* (10 vols., Berlin, 1782–5); *Journal du lycée de Londres, ou Tableau des sciences et des arts en Angleterre* (1784); *Point de banqueroute, ou Lettres à un créancier de l'Etat* (London, 1787). With the revolution his major work was the daily newspaper, *Le Patriote Français* (1789–1793); but see also *Mémoire aux Etats-Généraux sur la nécessité de rendre dès ce moment la presse libre* (Paris, 1789); *Discours prononcé au district des Filles Saint-Thomas, le 21 juillet 1789, sur la constitution municipale à former dans la ville de Paris* (Paris, n.d.–1789); *J.-P. Brissot. . .à tous les Républicains de la France, sur la Société des Jacobins de Paris* (Paris, 1792); *J.-P. Brissot, député du département d'Eure-et-Loire, à ses commettants, sur la situation de la Convention Nationale, sur l'influence des anarchistes et les maux qu'elle a causés* (Paris, 1793). A starting point for biographical study is his own, somewhat unreliable *Mémoires (1754–1793), publiés avec Etude critique et Notes par Claude Perroud* (3 vols., n.d.). See also, E. Ellery, *Brissot de Warville* (New York, 1915); N. Hampson, *Will and Circumstance. Montesquieu, Rousseau and the French Revolution* (London, 1983); P. Laborie, *Etude sur le Patriote Français* (Toulouse, 1959–60); and for evidence of his work for the police prior to 1789, R. Darnton, 'The Grub Street Style of Revolution: J.P. Brissot, Police Spy', *Journal of Modern History*, 40 (1968).

HUGH GOUGH

BRUNNER, Joseph (1759–1829)
German priest, Jacobin writer and publicist

Joseph Brunner was born on May 7, 1759 in Philippsburg. His father, Johann Michael Brunner, was a garrison schoolmaster, and his mother, Maria Barbara Franziska Brunner, was a Jewish convert to Roman Catholicism. Brunner attended the Cathedral school in Speyer, and studied Roman Catholic theology both there and in Heidelberg. He belonged to the order of the Illuminati under the pseudonym Picus Mirandolanus, and worked on the Enlightenment journal *Oberdeutsche Allgemeine Literaturzeitung*. He was ordained a Roman Catholic priest in 1783, but expelled from Heidelberg after a conflict with the ex-Jesuits, who attacked his lectures and writings.

From 1767 he was a parish priest in Tiefenbach and in Eichelberg bei Odenheim. In his sermons he demanded equality with Catholics for Jews, Anabaptists and Lutherans. He was a close friend of E. Schneider (q.v.), who dedicated a long autobiographical poem to him, of Blau and J.G.N. Nimis, who were priests in Mainz, and later Jacobins, and Bohl (q.v.) author of the Jacobin satire *Die Zölibat ist aufgehoben*. Brunner was at the centre of an oppositional group and in 1794 was taken by the authorities of the bishopric of Speyer to be the author of the satire about celibacy. His papers were seized and he himself was imprisoned.

After his release from prison, Brunner made contact with the Jacobin émigrés from Mainz who were living in Paris. On November 7, 1796, the *Pariser Zuschauer* published a letter from Brunner, which reported that in Germany 'the fire of revolution' was burning everywhere: 'The heart of the nation (Der Kern der Nation) is almost entirely on the side of freedom. We are working silently to remove the yoke of slavery from the shoulders of the people.'

In 1796 Brunner published *Freimütige gedanken über die Priesterweihe der kath. Geistlichkeit*, and in 1802 *Die letzte akten-mäßige Verketzerungsgeschichte unter der Regierung des Herrn Fürstbischofs von Speyer August Grafen von Limburg-Stirum*. From 1803 to 1806 he was a member of the church committee and school board at Bruchsal, and from 1807 to 1813 a member of the government committee on the ecclesiastical and educational reorganisation of Baden, and an acting priest alongside his administrative work. From 1814 to 1826 he was dean in Karlsruhe. His *Gebetbuch für aufgeklärte katholische Christen*, published in 1801, ran to twenty-three editions by 1870. In his will, written in 1827, he left a sum of money each for distribution to poor Catholic, Protestant and Jewish schoolchildren in Karlsruhe.

Chiefly to be remembered for his involvement with the Mainz Jacobins, Brunner's radicalism was essentially directed against religious conservatism rather than being concerned with overtly political issues.

Further details on Brunner are to be found in *Eudämonia*, vol. 3 (Frankfurt, 1793), pp. 503–513; Gerhard Steiner, *Jakobinerschauspiel und Jakobinertheater (Deutsche revolutionäre Demokraten*, vol. 4) (Stuttgart, 1973).

W. GRAB

BUONARROTI, Filippo Michele (1761–1837)
French revolutionary, communist, and Italian patriot

Buonarroti was born in Pisa on November 11, 1761 and belonged to a noble Florentine family. Educated at the University of Pisa, he graduated Doctor of Laws in 1782 and began a career as a journalist in Florence. Exiled in 1789 for his enthusiastic welcome to the French Revolution, during 1790–1792 Buonarroti worked to consolidate the revolution in Corsica as an administrator and journalist, and to expand its influence to Sardinia and to Italy. Forced to leave Corsica for Paris he associated himself with Robespierre's (q.v.) following and was made a French citizen in 1793. A protégé of the Corsican Saliceti and of Robespierre's brother Augustin, in 1794 he was appointed National Agent to administer French-occupied territories centred on Oneglia in north Italy. He sought to make Oneglia a model for an Italian revolution by pursuing a Jacobin policy of social welfare and educational indoctrination, until he was recalled to Paris in March 1795 for 'excesses' and imprisoned. After his release in November 1795 Buonarroti became, with Babeuf (q.v.), one of the organisers of the communist Conspiracy of the Equals in Paris. Meanwhile he maintained contact with Dutch and Italian revolutionaries and attempted to persuade the French Directory to follow an Italian policy based on the encouragement of local popular uprisings and the ultimate creation of a republican and united Italy, thus linking the cause of Italian nationalism with that of social revolution. The successes of Bonaparte's armies in Italy during the first half of 1796 however made this policy unnecessary, and it was rejected.

After the Conspiracy of the Equals collapsed in May 1796 Buonarroti was arrested and sentenced to deportation. He was imprisoned until the end of 1802 and continued under close surveillance for another four years. In 1806 he went to Geneva, where he chiefly resided until 1823, before moving to Brussels. Buonarroti strove to make Geneva the capital of an international revolutionary opposition to the Napoleonic Empire and subsequent régimes, relying on a series of quasi-masonic secret societies: the *Philadelphes* (c. 1804–9), the Italian *Adelphi* (c. 1807–9), and the *Sublimes Maîtres Parfaits* (c. 1809–1823). Buonarroti himself established the *Sublimes Maîtres Parfaits*, its successor, the *Monde* (1823–?1830) and the *Charbonnerie démocratique universelle* (c. 1830–7). Some historians regard these organisations as direct continuations of the attempt by Weishaupt's *Illuminati* in the 1780s to infiltrate masonic orders and divert them to radical political ends. However, while masonic influences are unquestionable, contemporary conditions of repression, dating from Thermidor (July 1794) also led revolutionaries inevitably to adopt parallel principles of secret organisation, and it is not necessary to postulate the hidden hand of an occult order.

Until its collapse in 1823 the *Sublimes Maîtres Parfaits* maintained connections with the Italian Carboneria and Buonarroti continued to exercise an influence on Italian revolutionary nationalism even in the 1830s, but he rapidly lost ground to Mazzini's more independent 'Young Italy' movement.

In 1828 Buonarroti published his account of the 1796 conspiracy. The *Conspiration pour l'égalité*, translated into English by Bronterre O'Brien in 1836, was a vindication of both Jacobin radicalism and Babouvist communism, and demonstrated that Buonarroti's fundamental objectives remained those of the conspirators, and had not changed over three decades: a communist order based on the complete equality of labour and goods, and the bureaucratic control of production and distribution. This was to be achieved by the conquest of political power and the more-or-less long-lasting dictatorship of an enlightened élite.

Buonarroti was strongly influenced by the works of Rousseau, Mably, and Morelly, and was both a Deist and a Utopian. His special individual contribution to both the reality and the tradition of the Conspiracy of the Equals was an emphasis on the moral organisation of the projected community. He envisaged an essentially agricultural and rural community on a 'Spartan' model, held together by civic festivals, public virtue and a hierarchy of age and wisdom. Unlike the Saint-Simonians he did not recognise, or rejected as irrelevant, the new possibilities of material progress opening up as a result of the developing Industrial Revolution; nor was he concerned, like Fourier and Robert Owen, with a basic restructuring of the mode of economic production. He sought instead a universal affective return to the spirit of equality and fraternity he believed had been manifest in Robespierre's 'Republic of Virtue' of 1794.

This vision remained the ultimate goal of the inner circle of each of Buonarroti's secret societies, but, especially after 1815, their conceived role as the organisers of immediate insurrection increasingly gave place to that of faithful custodians of dangerous and secret truths in a hostile world. At the same time interim reformist policies became acceptable, so that, after 1830, when Buonarroti returned to Paris, and until his death in 1837, he supported public agitation for such limited objectives as universal manhood suffrage and a single, graduated income tax, and generally helped to create the democratic and socialist opposition to Louis Philippe's reign. The renewed contemporary emphasis of Blanqui, Barbès and others on the revolutionary seizure of power by a conspiratorial coup d'état did not therefore mark a direct continuation of Buonarroti's influence so much as a return to the common inspiration of the 1790s.

Buonarroti's influence on radical thought was ambiguous. Praising Robespierre as a true democrat, at heart an enemy of private property, and minimising the differences between the Jacobins of 1793–4 and the Equals of 1796, he did much to create the powerful Robespierrist myth around which radical democrats and socialists united after 1830. At the same time his history of the Conspiracy of the Equals kept alive the rival tradition of Babouvist communism which attracted its own adherents among the radical opposition to Louis Philippe, was recognised by Marx and Engels, and formed a significant stream in the developing socialist and communist movement.

Buonarroti's account of the Babeuf conspiracy is available in two volumes: *Conspiration pour l'égalité dite de Babeuf* (Paris, 1957), while further information on his life can be obtained from the following secondary sources: *Dizionario biografici degli italiani* (1972) XV; A. Saitta, *Filippo Buonarroti* (2 vols., Rome, 1950–55); P. Onnis Rosa, *Filippo Buonarroti e altri studi* (Rome, 1971); E.L. Eisenstein, *The First Professional Revolutionist: Filippo Michele Buonarroti* (Cambridge, Mass., 1959); R.B. Rose, *Gracchus Babeuf: the first Revolutionary Communist* (Stanford,

1978); J.H. Billington, *Fire in the Minds of Men* (London, 1980); A. Lehning, 'Buonarroti and his International Secret Societies', *International Review of Social History*, 1 (1956); and A. Lehning, 'Buonarroti's ideas on Communism and Dictatorship', *International Review of Social History*, 2 (1957).

R.B. ROSE

BUTENSCHÖN, Johann Friedrich (1764–1842)
German Jacobin, publisher of radical journals and supporter of the French Revolution

Butenschön was born in Bramstedt in Holstein into a poor family. After studying at the *Christineum*, Altona's scholarly academy, he went to the University of Jena in 1785, and then to Kiel. In 1786 he moved, on the invitation of the blind poet, Konrad Gottlieb Pfeffel, to the latter's school in Alsace, where he worked as a teacher and translator. He then lived for a while in Zürich and Heidelberg, spent the early days of the revolution in Strasbourg, and then worked for three years as a teacher in Stuttgart. In 1792 he returned to Jena to finish his studies in history and philosophy, and made contact there with Schiller and Reinhold.

While many of the friends of the revolution were alienated by the social radicalisation of the revolution, Butenschön became a convinced Jacobin in the autumn of 1792, who, in his own words, sought to 'spread the noble ideals of freedom and equality' in Germany. 'Fearlessly I defended the honour of France and did not allow myself to be blinded by princely splendour, aristocratic arrogance and clerical artifice.' With cosmopolitan enthusiasm he described himself as a 'Danish sansculotte' and at the same time 'French in body and soul', and went in January 1793 to Strasbourg, where he arrived on the day of Louis XVI's execution. He immediately joined the Jacobin Club. He became a close friend of Schneider (q.v.) and worked with him on the Jacobin newspaper *Argos*, *oder der Mann mit hundert Augen.* In May 1793 he went to the Vendée to defend the revolution, fought against the rebels there, and returned to Strasbourg. With the Jacobin reform of the Strasbourg municipality he became a town official on November 5, 1793, and after Schneider's arrest took over the publication of the *Argos.* Like all the other German Jacobins in Strasbourg he too was arrested, on December 29, 1793. While in prison he continued to write articles for his paper and to publish the *Argos* until June 16, 1794. During the 'Great Terror' he was taken to Paris, where he was imprisoned in the Conciergerie, along with Friedrich Cotta (q.v.). After his release on October 30, 1794 he went to Colmar, where he taught history and geography at the Central School there. He married a Strasbourgeoise, defended the memory of Schneider in the journal *Klio*, edited the *Straßburger Neue Zeitung*, and identified himself with 'the great nation of the Franks', as is clear from his republican speech of December 20, 1797 on the occasion of the Treaty of Campo Formio.

In 1803 Butenschön moved to Mainz, where he taught classics, English, German, history and geography at the Lyceum. In 1809 he became an inspector, and in 1812 rector of the Lyceum, a position which he held until the end of the French occupation. Transferring to the Rhine-Hessian education department in 1814, he was for a while a subordinate of J. Görres (q.v.), inspected the schools and became a district school councillor in 1815 in the newly-established protestant Consistory-General in Worms. He was director of primary and secondary education in the Palatinate, and editor of the *Speyerer Zeitung* from 1816–1821. After the death of his first wife he married a second time at the age of 57. In 1825 he was relieved of his official duties and he finally retired in 1833. Butenschön brought up his children in the spirit of freedom; his son Friedrich Eugen, who was a lawyer in Frankenthal, successfully objected to the banning of the Hamburg Festival in 1832. The death of this son was a severe blow to Butenschön's health and he died six years later.

Butenschön was therefore both a publicist and an activist in the cause of French revolutionary ideals, which he continued to support even in the most radical phase, and to which he remained attracted to the end of his life.

Details of Butenschön's life are to be found in *Neuer Nekrolog der Deutschen*, Vol. 20 (Weimar, 1842). Further information is contained in Hermann Schreibmüller, 'Der pfälzische Konsistorial- und Kreisschulrat Friedrich Butenschön (1794–1842)', *Pfälzischer Protestanten-vereinskalendar* (1917), pp. 18–40; Roger Jacquel, 'Les jacobins allemands d'aprés la revue *Klio*', in *Alsace et la Suisse à travers les âges* (Strasbourg, 1952), pp. 307–26; Hans Hahn, *Johann Friedrich Butenschön, Ein Lebensbild aus Revolution, Empire und Restauration* (Diss, Mainz, 1952); W. Grab 'Eulogius Schneider. Ein Weltbürger zwischen Mönchszelle und Guillotine', in G. Mattenklott and K. Scherpe (eds.) *Demokratisch-revolutionäre Literatur in Deutschland, Jakobinismus* (Kronberg, 1975), pp. 61–138; and Friedrich Müller, 'Johann Friedrich Butenschön', *Jahrbuch des Instituts für deutsche Geschichte*, Vol. 15 (1986), pp. 193–230.

W. GRAB

CAMBON, Pierre Joseph (1756–1820)
French revolutionary, member of the Legislative Assembly and the National Convention, organiser of the Republic's finances

Cambon was born at Montpellier (Hérault), the son of a wealthy textile merchant. He took over his father's business in 1785, but in 1788 turned to politics. On 9 April 1789 he was elected to the Third Estate and signed the Tennis Court Oath. He returned to Montpellier in January 1790, was elected to municipal office, and founded the local *Société des Amis de l'Egalité*, which was affiliated to the Paris Jacobins. As President of the Montpellier Jacobins he sent, in June 1791, an address to the Constituent Assembly urging it to proclaim a republic.

In September 1791 he was elected deputy for the Hérault to the Legislative Assembly. He was not a great orator, but he quickly established a reputation for his business acumen and knowledge of financial matters. He presided over the reformed Finance Committee through which he advocated reform of the national debt, the sound management of national finances, and control over the issuing of assignats. But he also intervened in the debates on other issues – he opposed Neufchâteau's attempt to abolish the civic oath for priests; he moved that the statue of tyrants be melted down for cannon; and he supported Ruhl's (q.v.) proposal to order the German princes to disperse groupings of émigrés. However, and despite his republican sentiments of June 1791, his attachment to constitutionalism was revealed at this time by his acknowledgement of the king's right to veto his proposals.

The events of August 10, 1792 ended any such moderation. On August 22 he proposed that nonjuring priests be deported to Guyana and, four days later, argued that, if property-owners were not prepared to defend their own property, then it would be necessary to take their weapons and arm the sans-culottes. Indeed, he added, it was necessary to attach to the revolution the masses who had nothing – to make them property-owners by a redistribution of the *biens communaux*. From mid-September he presided at the Legislative Assembly until the end of the session.

In September 1792 Cambon was elected by the Hérault to the National Convention where he again took charge of the Finance Committee. While he sided with the Girondins in their conflicts with the Paris Commune, he separated from them in his attacks in November-December 1792 on Dumouriez' financial management of the Belgian campaign. Moreover, at the trial of Louis XVI he voted for the death-penalty without reprieve.

His major achievement in the Convention was, however, the reorganisation of the national finances in the extreme conditions of revolutionary war and terror. In October 1792 he proposed the issue of 400 million assignats whose value would be guaranteed by the wealth of the *biens nationaux*. In January 1793 he centralised financial control by abolishing a range of special funds and making the Treasury the centre for all receipts and expenses. He simplified the Treasury's accounting system and made the information readily available to the Committee of Public Safety, to which he had himself been elected in April 1793.

Cambon was increasingly caught in the middle of the factional feuds that characterised the Convention. He failed in his opposition to the creation of the Revolutionary Tribunal but managed to secure immunity for Treasury officials from arbitrary arrest by it. He clashed first with the Girondins over financial questions and then with Bouchotte over his connections with the popular uprisings of May-June. In the event he failed to gain re-election to the Committee of Public Safety but was given the task of supervising the Treasury on its behalf.

From July 10, 1793 to 9 Thermidor Cambon was the master of the Republic's finances. The majority of financial reforms emanated from him and were adopted often in the face of Jacobin hostility. On August 15 he outlined his proposals for a *Grand Livre*, a single account book which incorporated republican debts with the old royal debts, thus making it difficult for creditors to distinguish between revolutionary and counter-revolutionary causes. He further proposed to increase Treasury resources by taxing chattels along with land and by raising a loan. By these and other measures he succeeded in placing the Republic's finances on a sound footing.

Yet Cambon was never close to the extreme Jacobins and he came to play an unpremeditated part in Robespierre's (q.v.) downfall. At the Convention on 8 Thermidor Robespierre attempted to reassert his authority over that body by attacking the mismanagement of the nation's finances, but Cambon's defence blunted this manoeuvre. He wrote to his father later that day: 'Domain, de Robespierre ou de moi, l'un des deux sera mort.' His relationship with the Thermidorians, however, soon deteriorated and he was subjected in the winter of 1794–95 to attacks in the Convention from Tallien (q.v.) and others. On 13 Germinal Year III Tallien accused Cambon of complicity in the *journée* of that month and demanded his arrest. He managed to elude capture and was in any case amnestied in Brumaire Year IV.

Cambon retired to his estate near Montpellier. During the Directory he wrote a *Lettre sur les finances* defending his financial reforms and his reputation against accusations of malversation. On 25 Thermidor Year V he escaped an attempt on his life. He reappeared briefly on the political scene during the Hundred Days when he was elected as a deputy for the Hérault. But with the Restoration his property was seized and he was forced as a regicide into exile in Belgium where he died in 1820.

Cambon was an administrator *par excellence*. He eschewed political factions preferring to devote his skills to the routine management of revolutionary finances, and in this respect he was the archetypal bourgeois and precursor of the modern state manager. But in these apparently mundane roles, his contributions to the promulgation of the war and the terror, and thereby to the success of the revolution, should not be underestimated.

In addition to the biographical sketches of Cambon in A. Kuscinski, *Dictionnaire des Conventionnels* (Paris, 1917); J. Robinet et al., *Dictionnaire historique et biographique de la Révolution et de l'Empire 1789–1815* (Paris, 1899); and S. Scott and B. Rothaus (eds.), *Historical dictionary of the French Revolution 1789–1799* (2 vols., Westport, CT; 1985); there is an old study by F. Bornarel, *Cambon et la Révolution française* (Paris, 1905).

D. NICHOLLS

CARNOT, Lazare Nicolas Marguerite (1753–1823)
French military officer, Jacobin, member of the Committee of Public Safety, 'Organiser of the Victory'

Lazare Carnot was a native of Nolay, Burgundy, and the son of a royal notary and judge. He was a captain in the royal artillery on the eve of the French Revolution. Under the Old Régime the army would most probably have denied him further promotion because he was a commoner. Carnot had conceived plans before the revolution to open the ranks of the officer corps to commoners on the basis of merit in order to create a more national army. Such a policy, of course, would have also advanced the careers of men like himself.

In 1791 Carnot was elected to the Legislative Assembly from St Omer and in the following year he was elected to the National Convention. As a *conventionnel* he was interested chiefly in military affairs, going on mission in the spring of 1793 to supervise the defence of besieged garrisons. In mid-August he joined the Committee of Public Safety whose members felt his military expertise was needed there. During his long tenure he was concerned almost exclusively with the problem of organising and supplying the revolutionary armies that were defending the frontiers and repressing counter-revolution.

During the crucial period from August 1793 to the spring of 1794, Carnot implemented the *levée en masse*, the first mass conscription of citizen soldiers by a modern nation. The troops had to be assembled, equipped and infused with revolutionary ideals. To the last of these ends Carnot saw that the conscripts were constantly exposed to revolutionary literature, slogans, symbols and exhortations from officers and deputies on mission. He purged officers whose competence and loyalty were doubtful. These were mainly nobles, but he refrained from a wholesale dismissal of aristocrats from the officer corps. He retained and promoted those (including Napoleon) who were trustworthy and able. In this respect he anticipated Napoleon's policy of careers open to talent.

To supply the armies Carnot established government-controlled munitions workshops in Paris and some provincial locations. He condoned the requisitioning of food and property needed by the armies. When Belgium was finally occupied in the summer of 1794, he called for the confiscation of wealth from the well-to-do for the purpose of maintaining the French forces. In these actions, Carnot was motivated by the needs of the armies, not by any notion that they were socially just or equitable. He was not a social reformer and he believed that public management of economic affairs 'in general does not suit the interests of the republic'.

Carnot was not an innovator in military tactics. As a military engineer trained in the traditional manner, he favoured defensive warfare based on fortifications and garrisons. The use of mass armies taking the offensive was an idea of others to which Carnot yielded. An idea that had intrigued him since pre-revolutionary days was the use of hot-air balloons as observation posts. Such a balloon was used at the battle of Fleurus, but without decisive importance. He remained open to ideas suggested by others including the able Minister of War, Bouchotte, with whom he worked closely. One result was the implementation of a semaphore system to relay news from the front to Paris in a matter of hours.

Carnot was a loyal republican and member of the Jacobin Club, but by nature apolitical. He almost never attended Jacobin meetings. In the final months of the terror, he quarrelled with Robespierre (q.v.) and Saint-Just (q.v.) whose rigid idealism was not compatible with his more pragmatic approach to the revolution. He gave his support to the factions who effected Robespierre's removal in the crisis of Thermidor (July 1794). Because he remained aloof from factional infighting and because his administrative skills were essential to the armies, he survived the general purge of Jacobins that followed, retaining his seat on the Committee of Public Safety until it was dissolved (August 1795) and then serving as one of the original five members of the Executive Directory.

Carnot opposed the coup of Fructidor (September 1797) and had to flee to Switzerland when it was successful. He returned to serve briefly as Napoleon's Minister of War (1801) and in the Imperial Tribunate. He disagreed with Bonaparte's assumption of a hereditary crown and with his expansionist policies, retiring from politics when the Tribunate was abolished in 1807. Motivated by patriotism, Carnot served the emperor again as Minister of the Interior during the Hundred Days. The second Bourbon restoration brought permanent exile for Carnot who died in Magdeburg in 1823. By that time his reputation was obscure, but it was revived by later republican régimes. The Carnots became a republican dynasty; Lazare Carnot's son was a minister in the Second Republic and his grandson president of the Third.

Carnot was not a radical by nature or intellect. He was concerned with increasing military efficiency rather than social restructuring. Nevertheless the *levée en masse* which he implemented and supported by force of the terror and property requisitions was a radical innovation. Within the army it served to level class distinctions and it moulded particularistic peasants and sans-culottes into a national army inspired by the concepts of national fraternity and careers open to talent. The *levée* showed the way to modern mass conscription. More immediately, it saved the revolution from foreign and domestic enemies in the crisis of 1793–94. It thus permitted the Jacobin Republic to introduce measures such as the Maximum and the Law of Ventôse which would become part of Europe's radical heritage. By 'organising the victory', therefore, Carnot helped prepare for the radical and revolutionary transformation of Europe in the nineteenth century.

For Carnot's own account of his role in

the revolution, see the *Mémoires sur Lazare Carnot* (Paris, 1861–63), edited by his son, H. Carnot. There are a number of biographies: Huntley Dupré, *Lazare Carnot: republican patriot* (1940; repr. Philadelphia, 1975); Marcel R. Reinhard, *Le grand Carnot* (2 vols., Paris, 1950–52); and Sidney J. Watson, *Carnot* (London, 1954).

JOEL S. CLELAND

CARRA, Jean Louis (1742–1793)
Radical journalist of the French Revolution, representative on mission, member of the Convention

Born in the Burgundian town of Pont-de-Veyle, (department of the Ain), Carra was the eldest of six children. His father, Claude Carra, who was a seigneurial dues commissaire, died when Jean Louis was two years old, and his mother, Marie-Anne Calas, when he was sixteen. He was educated at the Jesuit College in Mâcon but, in 1758, shortly before completion of his studies, was arrested on a charge of stealing 2,500 *livres* worth of clothing from a shop in the town. He took refuge in Thoissy, across the border in the principality of Dombes, but was sent back to Mâcon and imprisoned for two and a half years, finally being released without any formal charges being brought. He moved to Paris where, by 1768, he was secretary to the Marquis D'Argenson, but left this position shortly afterwards and in 1770 was in Iverdon working on a pirate edition of Diderot's *Encyclopédie*. In 1771 he moved to Geneva and in the following year to Bouillon, working on a counterfeit edition of the *Encyclopédie*. While there he made his debut as a journalist, writing articles for Pierre Rousseau's *Journal Encyclopédique*. In 1772 also he published a novel, *Odazir*, and a philosophical work, the *Système de la raison ou le poete philosophe*. After leaving Bouillon in the summer of 1772, he travelled in England, Germany, Poland and, in 1775, Russia, where he worked in Jassy as a tutor for two and a half years, before returning to Paris in 1777. He then published an *Histoire de la Moldavie et de*

la Wallachie and a philosophical work, the *Esprit de la morale et de la philosophie*. In the latter work he condemned nobility and kingship and claimed the American Revolution to be the beginnings of a new era in human history in which men would regain their natural rights. He became secretary to the Cardinal de Rohan, probably through the intervention of D'Alembert, but in 1779 moved to Vienna and worked with the printer von Trattner. He returned to Paris two years later. By now Carra had developed an interest in science and published a four volume *Nouveaux principes de physique* (1781–83) which purported to update Newton by proving the existence of an omnipotent fluid in the universe. He also published an *Essai sur la nautique aérienne* (1783) on the means of propelling balloons, but it was rejected by the Paris Academy of Science. Rejection appears to have embittered Carra, and he became involved in mesmerism, publishing in 1785 an *Examen physique du magnétisme animal* in which he endorsed Mesmer's views, but offered his own modified explanation of the workings of the fluids that lay at the centre of the theory. This explanation led him to link the physical world with the psychological, and to the assertion that, just as unjust legislation could harm health, so too could physical events, such as astronomical change, give rise to political change. Much of his writing at this time also shows that Carra was convinced that some kind of revolution was imminent.

In April 1784, through the influence of Loménie de Brienne, he was made a secretary at the *Bibliothèque du Roi* but disagreed with the reforms being introduced by the Head Librarian, Lenoir, and published a pamphlet critical of him in 1787, accusing him of neglect and maladministration. In that same year, on the eve of the meeting of the First Assembly of Notables, he published a strident attack on Calonne, *Un petit mot en réponse a M. Calonne*, which played an important part in undermining Calonne's authority. Over the next two years he published several more critical pamphlets, and in 1789 he was also a founder member of the *Société des amis des noirs,* with Brissot (q.v.), Clavière, Mirabeau and others.

Carra's talents as a pamphleteer, and connections in patriot circles brought him to the attention of the publisher François Buissan who launched the *Annales patriotiques et littéraires* on October 3, 1789. He also contributed to other newspapers, such as the *Mercure national* during the early months of 1790, but it was in the *Annales* that he published his major articles and made his reputation. He specialised in articles on foreign affairs, in which he claimed a particular expertise. He campaigned for the abolition of the slave trade and, during the winter of 1791–2, was one of the most prominent campaigners for war against Austria, denouncing Louis XVI and the activity of the *comité autrichien.* He was also involved in speculative land-purchasing, forming a syndicate with his fellow journalist Gorsas in November 1790, for the joint acquisition of lands in the Loire-Inférieure and the Finistère.

During the summer of 1792 he was a member of a clandestine committee plotting the overthrow of Louis XVI and, on the night of 9 August, personally visited the *fédérés* from Marseilles to encourage them to join the insurrection which took place on the next day. He was subsequently rewarded with the post of joint head librarian in the *Bibliothèque Nationale,* at an annual salary of 4,000 *livres.* Because of his political activity he rarely appeared there and was finally dismissed on 16 August, 1793. On 19 August he was sent on a mission to the armée du Nord by the Minister of War, Servan, returning before the end of the month. There is no record of his having participated in the September massacres and, although certain of his articles in the *Annales patriotiques* during mid-August can be seen in retrospect to have encouraged popular violence, he quickly condemned them subsequently. In early September he was elected as deputy to the Convention by no less that eight departments, a figure matched by no other deputy, and chose to sit for the Saône-et-Loire. He went as a deputy on mission to

the armée du Centre, returning at the end of October and, in mid-November, was elected secretary of the Convention. On December 21, 1792 he was expelled from the Jacobins, but was readmitted on January 9, 1793 and, in Louis XVI's trial, voted for his execution. In the increasingly bitter conflict between Girondins and Montagnards, he attempted to stay neutral, as did the the *Annales patriotiques,* but his known social links with Roland – who had secured him his post at the *Bibliothèque Nationale* – as well as with Dumouriez and other leading Girondins, led to denunciations of the *Annales patriotiques* at the Jacobin Club. On 12 March he went as a representative on mission to the Vendée, and on 30 April to the armée de la Rochelle. But he quarrelled with his fellow representatives and was recalled from Blois, returning to Paris in June, where he found himself under suspicion. On 28 July the Convention ordered his arrest on charges of conspiracy against the government and of royalism. Condemned to death on 30 October, along with other leading Girondins, he was executed on the following day. He had married Anne Bouyn in Paris on April 28, 1777. There were no children, and his property was confiscated by the state at the time of his execution.

Carra's career, like that of Brissot and Marat (q.v.), progressed from obscurity in the Ancien Régime literary world, through journalism, to active politics. His execution as a Girondin, and reluctance to endorse the economic and social demands of the Parisian sans-culottes, has obscured his contribution to the political radicalism of the revolution, notably on issues such as the abolition of slavery, political reform and foreign affairs. The wide circulation of the *Annales patriotiques* among provincial Jacobin clubs ensured that his views reached a wide audience.

Carra was a prolific writer on historical, philosophical, scientific and political subjects. A full list of the political pamphlets he published during the revolution can be found in G. Walter and A. Martin, *Catalogue de l'Histoire de la Révolution française,* vol. 1 (Paris, 1936); among the most significant, however, are: *Cahier de la déclaration des droits du peuple* (1789); *Considérations, recherches et observations sur les Etats-généraux* (1789); *L'Orateur aux Etats-généraux pour 1789*; *L'Orateur aux Etats-généraux. Seconde partie* (Paris, 1789); *Projet de cahier pour le tiers-état de la ville de Paris* (1789); *Précis de la défense de Carra contre ses accusateurs* (n.d. – 1793). As for his journalism, he contributed many articles during 1790 to the *Mercure National ou Journal d'Etat et du citoyen*, but his main activity lay with the *Annales patriotiques* between October 1789 and July 1793. On his early life, see M.L. Kennedy, 'The development of a political radical. Jean-Louis Carra, 1742–1787', *Proceedings of the Third Annual Meeting of the Western Society for French History* (1977); and A. Vidier, 'Le Noir, Bibliothécaire du Roi, (1784–1790). Ses demêlés avec Carra', *Bulletin de la Société de l'Histoire de Paris et de L'Ile de France* (51e année, 1924), pp. 49ff. For his journalism during the revolution, see M.L. Kennedy, 'L'Oracle des Jacobins des départements: Jean-Louis Carra et ses *Annales patriotiques*', *Actes du Colloque Girondins et Montagnards* (Paris, 1975). The details of his arrest and trial are in Archives Nationale F7 4634 d.l, and W292, no. 204.

HUGH GOUGH

CARRIER, Jean Baptiste (1756–1794)
French Jacobin and terrorist

Carrier was born at Yolet (Cantal), the son of a respectable peasant farmer. A lawyer and business agent at Aurillac in Auvergne before 1789, he is still thought to be personally responsible for the *noyades* at Nantes in 1793–4 in which as many as 2000 people, including priests, women and common criminals as well as peasant counter-revolutionaries, were drowned by crowding them into boats which were then sunk at the mouth of the Loire. Yet Carrier is best understood as a man whose limited talents were incapable of managing the local revolutionaries in a time of civil war.

Elected to the Convention in 1792 as representative of the department of the Cantal, he was shy and so an undistinguished orator but, as a regicide, found favour with the Committee of Public Safety. After purging the local administration at Caen and Rennes which had protested the expulsion of the Girondins on May 31–June 2, 1793, he was appointed one of several deputies to supervise military operations against the Catholic and royalist counter-revolutionary rebellion known as the 'Vendée'. He focussed his activities on repression outside Nantes and on securing its food supplies. This allowed the cabal of extremist revolutionaries who controlled the interlocking institutions of the club, surveillance committee, revolutionary tribunal and revolutionary army (known as the 'Compagnie Marat') to acquire great influence. These men were directly responsible for the *noyades*. Although they were brutal and self-serving, their actions were the product of the fear of combined internal and external conspiracies that were common throughout the revolutionary period. On December 23, 1793, the republican armies smashed the Vendéan army at the Battle of Savenay. So long as the other Vendéan armies remained to besiege the city, however, and so long as the British cruised off the coasts to supply them, the Jacobins feared the thousands of prisoners were a potential fifth-column which could spread disease or break out anytime and massacre the inhabitants of the city, as they had massacred those of Machecoul in March 1793. The *noyades* were thus a defensive panic, a prison massacre like those of the Midi in 1792–3 or in Paris in September 1792. The fact that the *noyades* were taking place was reported in the Paris press shortly after they began (seven have been documented, the first on 16 November when it was feared Angers was under attack) and no one objected, least of all the Paris Jacobin Club which gave Carrier a thunderous welcome upon his return in February 1794. No one in Paris knew, and Carrier seems not to have known, that at least half the *noyés* had not been tried by any military commission or revolutionary tribunal. Yet this had nothing to do with his recall by the Committee of Public Safety. With his brooding silences and unpredictable fits of temper, he soon quarrelled with the local Jacobins who eventually accused him of favouring the counter-revolution. He concluded at the same time the government did that his mission was no longer serving any purpose and asked to be recalled. Upon his return, he threw himself into the 'hébertiste' agitation against 'neo-moderation' but was spared in the purge of March 1794. His trial in October 1794 was the first great anti-terrorist show trial and although he was not convicted on any of the counts in the original indictment, he was executed anyway. Far from appeasing the anti-terrorists, the trial enflamed them more, led to the closing of the Paris Jacobin Club and contributed to the anti-Jacobin prison massacres of 1795. In an ironic way, therefore, his mission did contribute to counter-revolution.

Although Carrier's mission was not substantially different from many others – there were countless executions without trial at Angers and Toulon and he was as anti-clerical and as hostile to the rich as many other representatives on mission – it has become a symbol of mindless atrocity and so a source of embarrassment to historians sympathetic to the revolution. Aulard ignored him, Mathiez, Lefebvre and Soboul dealt with him in a few lines, almost without comment. So, in a sense, Carrier is outside the European radical tradition. Yet the experience of Carrier and the men around him showed how the mentality of pitiless vengeance which was the hallmark of a certain variety of Jacobinism in 1793–4, could, in the circumstances of fear and civil war, lead to the loss of any sense of common humanity. In provincial France, that too was one of the legacies of the French Revolution and helps to explain why counter-revolutionaries acquired popular support.

Among the biographical studies Gaston Martin, *Carrier et sa mission à Nantes* (Paris, 1924) is best, while A. Lallié, *J.-B. Carrier, représentant du peuple à la Convention* (Paris, 1910) is useful despite the author's hostility to the revolution.

There are vital documents in F.A. Aulard (ed.), *Receuil des actes du comité de salut public* (28 vols., Paris, 1889–1951), vols. vii–ix for Carrier's letters; and Ch.–L. Chassin, *La Vendée patriote, 1793–1795* (4 vols., Paris, 1895), vol. iv for extracts from local and national archives. E. Lockroy (ed.), *Une mission en Vendée, 1793* (Paris, 1893) gives a partial account of Carrier's recall and quarrels with other Jacobins.

D. SUTHERLAND

CASTELLA, Jean Nicole (1739–1807)
Swiss radical, leader of the revolt in Fribourg and participant in the Helvetic Republic

Castella was born on December 2, 1739 in the canton of Fribourg. He left his homeland at an early age, going to Paris where he studied law, becoming a *notaire* in 1760. He later returned to Fribourg and in 1781 became involved in the great uprising in that canton which had started in his own home territory of Gruyère. At that time effective power was monopolised by the seventy-one 'heimliche Burger' families who excluded from that power not only the peasants and urban poor but also the so-called 'petty Burgers' who made up the mass of the bourgeois class and the entire titled aristocracy. The revolt which began in Gruyère arose originally out of protest against a reduction of the number of feast days and was a peasant movement led by Pierre Nicolas Chenaux, a mule dealer. As the revolt progressed and came under the influence of Castella and others, it became more widely-based and acquired a more revolutionary tone. The uprising was crushed by forces sent from Berne and after further disturbances a compact was made between the nobility and urban patriciate to the exclusion of the lesser burgers. Castella had been condemned to death on July 12, 1781 and was forced to flee, first to Savoy then to Paris.

During his time in France, Castella was active among the circle of Swiss émigrés living in Paris and he became the head of the Helvetic Club which acted as the forum and medium for La Harpe (q.v.) and Ochs (q.v.). In 1798, with the establishment of the Helvetic Republic, he returned to Switzerland where he played an important part in the politics of his own country, becoming a judge and sub-prefect of Gruyère until his death there in March of 1807.

The central features of Castella's political views, which make it possible to speak of him as a radical rather than a reformer, were his commitment to universalist notions of political rights and his support for direct action to realise these, rather than working within the system, something which he had rejected from the time of his participation in the Gruyère revolt.

Accounts of Castella's career are limited. The best starting place is the brief entry in the *Dictionnaire historique et biographique de la Suisse* (Neuchatel, 1924–29), and the entry in the same work for Gruyère. Otherwise one has to rely on the standard histories of Switzerland of which the most useful is C. Gilliard, *A History of Switzerland* (London, 1952).

S. DAVIES

CERACCHI, Giuseppe (1751–1801)
Italian Jacobin

A talented artist who achieved recognition in Europe and the newly-formed United States, Ceracchi never abandoned the ideals of the French Revolution. He came from a middle class family of prosperous Roman artisans – his father and grandfather were goldsmiths – a social group which especially in Rome was becoming increasingly restive and discontented.

In 1771 a prize from the Academy of St Luca where he had studied sculpture launched his career. For the next twenty years he travelled throughout Europe, as a growing reputation brought him many commissions. During his six years in London Ceracchi exhibited at the Royal Academy and numbered Reynolds, West, and Copley among his friends. In Vienna the Austrian Chancellor Kaunitz and the Empress Maria Theresa were among his patrons and he was offered the directorship of the academy of sculpture, a position he refused preferring his independence and freedom. Similar success greeted him in Holland, Prussia, and Bavaria. In 1790 he decided to visit the newly-established United States, where he worked until 1792. In Philadelphia the American Philosophical Society elected him to membership and he met Washington, Hamilton, Jefferson, and Adams. Failing to get a commission from Congress for a giant statue of liberty, Ceracchi returned to Europe, arriving in Rome at the end of 1792 after stops in Amsterdam, Munich, and Vienna.

In Rome, he met with suspicion from the pontifical authorities. His many sojourns in protestant Holland, his contacts with American republicans, and his open sympathies for the French Revolution singled him out for surveillance. After the assassination in January 1793 of the French ambassador, Bassville, to whom he had been close, Ceracchi was banished from the papal states. His radicalism made him equally unwelcome among his former patrons in Europe. Thus, in 1794 Cerachi decided to return to the United States. Here too his pro-French leanings and his friendship with Fauchet, the French republic's envoy in Philadelphia, alienated his friends. Leaving what had become an inhospitable country, Ceracchi embarked for France, arriving in Paris in the summer of 1795.

From 1795 to 1801 Ceracchi became deeply involved in the politics of France and of Italy. His fame as an artist and his known support of revolutionary France opened all doors for him. He had no difficulty gaining access to the men of the Directory, whom he wished to advise on Italian and especially Roman affairs and to whom he addressed a number of memoranda outlining the policy France should follow in Italy. He urged the French to invade Italy, enclosing a plan for the military campaign. The moment was propitious, he insisted. There was unrest throughout the peninsula. At first, Ceracchi's memoranda found no response, but when an invasion of Italy began to be considered the Directory called upon Ceracchi for advice. The young general Bonaparte seemed to have been impressed by him and a close friendship developed between the two men. When Ceracchi was on trial for his life six years later, his lawyer informed the court that Ceracchi, together with Carnot (q.v.) and Bonaparte, prepared the campaign that had assured the success of French arms and the freedom of Italy.

In 1798 Ceracchi returned to Rome. Like so many Italian Jacobins, however, he discovered that France under the Directory had abandoned radicalism in favour of middle-class moderation. In Rome, the French-inspired republic distrusted Jacobinism, and Ceracchi encountered the same suspicion in government circles which he had experienced from papal authorities in 1792. One of the French commissioners wrote to Paris denouncing Ceracchi as a dangerous anarchist. Meanwhile, Ceracchi left Rome. The defeat of the French forces in Italy found him once again in Paris, urging renewed action in Italy.

Napoleon's coup against the Directory, his emergence as First Consul and virtual dictator of France turned Ceracchi into a bitter enemy of the man whom he accused of betraying the revolution. Together with other disillusioned Italian and French revolutionists, Ceracchi plotted to assassinate Napoleon on October 11, 1800 at a performance of the Paris Opera. The conspiracy was betrayed. Ceracchi and his fellow conspirators were arrested and quickly brought to trial. Four of the ringleaders, including Ceracchi, were condemned to death. On January 31, 1801 Ceracchi was guillotined in the Place de Grève.

A man of conviction, Ceracchi never abandoned his revolutionary beliefs. Like many others, he remained faithful to the Jacobin ideology even after France discarded it. Among Italians he represented a radical persuasion that refused accommodation with the new conservatism personified first by the Directory and then by Napoleon. Precursor of the revolutionists of the nineteenth century, he sacrificed a life of ease and comfort for principles that became increasingly unpopular after 1795.

There is no full-length biography of Ceracchi but details of his life are available in the following: S. Vasco Rocca and M. Caffiero, 'Giuseppe Ceracchi', *Dizionario biografico degli italiani* (Rome, 1979), XXIII, pp. 645–50; Renzo De Felice, 'Giuseppe Ceracchi', *Italia giacobina* (Naples, 1965), pp. 61–130; V.E. Giuntella, 'Gli esuli romani in Francia alla vigilia del 18 brumaio', *Archivio* (1953), pp. 225–39; U. Desportes, 'Giuseppe Ceracchi in America and his busts of George Washington,' *The Art Quarterly*, XXVI (1963), pp. 141–79.

EMILIANA P. NOETHER

CHABOT, François (1756–1794)
French Jacobin, ex-Caputin monk, deputy to the Legislative Assembly and the Convention, one of the first clerics to swear the oath to the Civil Constitution of the Clergy.

Chabot was born at Saint-Geniez on October 23, 1756. He graduated from the collège of Rodez where his father, Etienne Chabot, worked as a cook. Progressive ideas frequently surfaced in his early writings, and his bishop ordered him not to preach provocative ideas. When the revolution began, Chabot was a principal figure on the left. In 1790 he founded the Société des Amis de la Constitution in Rodez. Soon he left Rodez for Saint-Geniez where his mother and sister were living. In Saint-Geniez Chabot gave moral instructions and explained the decrees of the National Assembly to the public. On September 2, 1791 he was elected as a deputy to the Legislative Assembly from the department of the Loir-et-Cher (Averyon). He joined the Jacobin Club of Paris in October 1791.

On May 28, 1792, while his colleague and friend Basire was accusing the king's bodyguards of conspiring to help Louis XVI escape from the Tuileries, Chabot declared that he had one hundred and eighty-two documents proving the existence of a plot to dissolve the assembly. Robespierre (q.v.), convinced of the intrigues of the Girondins, asked Chabot to go to the Faubourg Saint-Antoine on the evening of June 19, 1792 to persuade the people to submit a simple petition sanctioning the decrees of the Legislative Assembly. Chabot went and addressed the public in the Church Enfant-Trouvées for about three hours and claimed to have calmed the masses. No evidence of his participation in the uprising of June 20, 1792 exists and it would appear other individuals induced the people to arm themselves after he left.

After the publication of the Duke of Brunswick's manifesto on August 1, 1792, all but one of the sections of Paris advocated dethroning the king. The Jacobin Club of Paris remained non-committal about the dissolution of the monarchy, but Chabot supported it and he was an architect of the 10 August insurrection. On 11 August the Convention was summoned and Chabot was re-elected. Commenting on the massacre of September 2, he told the Convention on September 4, 1792 that the enemies of liberty were engaged in diatribes against it in order to sow discord and distrust among the citizens and create division among patriots. He claimed that the Convention should declare, publicly and plainly, its aversion to royalty. On 5 September he appealed to the Convention to stifle the voices of the enemies against the republic: 'Let us swear that we have a horror of kings and royalty.' As a member of the Convention, he voted for Louis XVI's death.

Chabot served as a member of the Committee of General Security. In the party strife of the Convention he sided with the Montagnards and testified against Brissot (q.v.). He asserted that Brissot and his followers had conceived a plan for recalling the dismissed ministers, Roland, Clavière and Servan.

Chabot's influence took a sharp downturn on September 14, 1793 when he was expelled from the Committee of General Security on a charge of corruption brought against him by the anti-Austrian faction. He was suspected of having accepted bribes amounting to 200,000 *livres* from two banker brothers – Junius and Emmanuel Freys (née Schonfeld). They were Austrian Jews who later became Christians and joined the revolution. Chabot was engaged to their sixteen-year old sister, Léopoldine. This relationship with an Austrian developed at an inopportune time when all foreigners were suspect and the involvement became a liability to Chabot's political career and might have even contributed to his untimely death. Recognising his influence as a member of the Committee of General Security, bankers and speculators often curried favour with Chabot. His association with members of financial groups therefore put him in a vulnerable position.

Chabot apparently accepted a bribe of 100,000 *livres* to make advantageous modifications to the text of a decree for the liquidation of the East India Company. He and his friend Bazire, anticipating that a charge of bribery against them was about to be made public, tried to blunt the imminent charges by revealing in a meeting with Robespierre on November 14, 1793 that their enemies had themselves been involved in financial intrigues and had schemed the charge of bribery against them. Chabot claimed that certain deputies (Delaunay, Julien of Toulouse, d'Espagnac) profited from their political influence by blackmailing bankers and trading companies by threatening punitive legislation against them. Chabot further claimed in this meeting with Robespierre that Hébert (q.v.), and extremists in the War Office, the Commune, and the Revolutionary army were engaged with the royalist baron de Batz in a counter-revolutionary plot. Robespierre, who recorded Chabot's visit, noted that Chabot had apparently participated in the financial scheme in order to expose the plotters. Robespierre advised Chabot to reveal all he knew to the Committee of General Security. But the Committee was reluctant to act on the information given by Chabot, and he threatened to expose both the financial and political plots on the floor of the Convention. As a result, on November 18, 1793 Chabot and ten other individuals, including Basire, Batz, Julien and Delaunay, were arrested following a joint-meeting of the Committee of Public Safety and the Committee of General Security.

In his defence, Chabot maintained that Delaunay had approached him with a plan to make money out of the East India Company and with the information that fellow deputies Cambon (q.v.), Ramel, Danton (q.v.), Delacroix and Fabre d'Eglantine (q.v.) were also involved in various forms of speculation. Chabot was then instructed to buy Fabre's collaboration in the deal by offering him 100,000 *livres* in assignats. Fabre appeared to have been obstructing those who were exploiting the Company, presumably to raise his own price in the deal, but he finally signed the false decree for liquidation, a fact which was unknown to Chabot. A memoir by the Company's directors (written in 1795) denounced Fabre, Amar (q.v.), Julien and Delaunay as the men who had held them to ransom in 1793 and supports Chabot's claim of innocence of the charge of bribery and involvement in the East India Company.

It is difficult to prove Chabot's claim of a counter-revolutionary plot involving Hébert, Batz, and Pitt. The full story of the 'Batz Plot' is not yet known. So far the evidence suggests that the revolutionary government either disbelieved Chabot's charges against Batz or had its own reasons for ignoring them. Some of Batz's agents had received such favourable treatment as to suggest that they enjoyed some kind of protection. Some may have feared the exposure of their own speculation; others like Robespierre did not want to expose the weakness of the Jacobins and the Convention. Later on when the government reversed its policy, persons accused of being Batz's agents were tried and executed.

To save himself from the charges of corruption, Chabot had exposed a financial scandal of which the government seemed to be unaware. He had also revealed the counter-revolutionary plot which threatened the security of the Republic. His revelations played an important part in determining the policies of the terror, even though they struck him a fatal blow. Unfortunately for Chabot he failed to convince either Robespierre or the Committee of General Security that his role was that of a patriot trying to unearth the plots of enemies of the Republic. On March 19, 1794 the Assembly voted for the trial of Chabot and he was executed on April 5, 1794.

As one of the first clerics to swear the oath to the Civil Constitution of the Clergy, and as the founder of the Société des Amis de la Constitution in Rodez, Chabot revealed his radical leanings in the early part of the revolution. He viewed the wealthy as the greatest threat to the Republic and he advocated that they be deprived of their wealth so that social order and justice be firmly retained. In November 1793 he demanded that all the deputies should have the right to defend themselves in the Convention. He was therefore a firm protagonist of radical principles who unfortunately fell victim to the counter-revolutionary purges which followed the outbreak of war.

Not much information on François Chabot is available in English. In his *Le Procès des Dantonistes: d'après les documents* (Paris, 1879). Dr Robinet published Chabot's statement on his own defence at the Committee of General Security. J-M-J de Bonald's *François Chabot: membre de la Convention 1756–1794* (Paris, 1908) and A. Mathiez (ed.), *François Chabot réprésentant du peuple à ses concitoyens qui sont les juges de sa vie politique* (Paris, 1913) are the best sources of information on Chabot's life and activities. M.J. Sydenham's *The Girondins* (London, 1961) mentions Chabot's accusations against the Girondins. Marc Bouloiseau's *The Jacobin Republic 1792–1794* (Cambridge, 1977) mentions Chabot's relationship with the Jacobins. Norman Hampson's *Danton* (London, 1978) discusses Chabot's relationship with the Dantonists. Norman Hampson's article. 'François Chabot and his plot', *Transactions of the Royal Historical Society*, (London, 1976), pp. 1-14 provides the best account of Chabot's alleged involvement with the East India Company and the counter-revolutionaries. See also, Bernard Edeine, 'Le citoyen Chabot, député du Loir-et-Cher à la Convention, devait-il être assassiné par une amie de Charlotte Corday (Julie Calvo).' *Bulletin Société Arts, Histoire, Archeologie Sologne*, 2 (1984), pp. 11-13.

N. CHAUDHURI

CHALIER, Joseph (1747–1793)
Lyonnais ultra-Jacobin

The son of a notary, Chalier was born at Beaulard near Briançon. Like many Savoyards and Dauphinais he migrated at an early age to Lyon, where he tried teaching and dabbled in painting, philosophy and architecture before entering a firm of silk merchants. He represented them in the Levant, Italy, Spain and Portugal where he later claimed to have been struck by the contrast between 'despotism, tyranny and abuses of all kinds' and the 'great days of Athens and Rome'. Nineteenth-century biographers, perhaps seeking anticipations of his revolutionary career, maintained that his expression of such opinions obliged him to flee Lisbon in 1783. But reliable documentation of his career before 1790 is lacking and this and similar stories need to be treated with caution, particularly in view of the intense hatred concentrated on him in 1793 by the partisans of Lyon's revolt against the Convention.

Chalier was in Paris for part of 1789 and on his return to Lyon towards the end of the year he wrote a letter to the *Révolutions de Paris* (XXX, January 30–February 6, 1790) denouncing in his usual ungainly style not only the aristocratic spirit which reigned in Lyon but the city itself, 'ungrateful city, perfidious city which contains in its bosom more than all the others the sworn enemies of the happiest as of the most astonishing of revolutions'. He had by now worn out his welcome amongst the mercantile bourgeoisie but his super-*patriotisme* won him support amongst partisans of the revolution and in February 1790 he was elected thirtieth of forty-two *notables* on the first General Council of the Commune of Lyon. He became allied with the *patriotes* who, led by J.-M. Roland and Louis Vitet, took over control of the Municipal Council in December 1790 and held it for two years with the support of the Lyonnais popular societies. In the elections of November 1791 he received 3,652 votes, nearly four times as many as the year before, and was the third Municipal Officer elected. Unfortunately, Chalier was made a member of the *comité de surveillance*, a role which fed his pathological suspiciousness and led to his suspension from office on 25 January, 1792 by the *feuillantin* Departmental Directory of Rhône-et-Loire for abuses of power during investigations into two imaginary counter-revolutionary plots.

He went to Paris to clear his name before the Legislative Assembly and to air the Municipality's manifold grievances against the departmental administration. He did not obtain his vindication until after the fall of the monarchy but when it came it was full vindication: the Assembly's decree of 15 August not only reinstated him 'with honour' but destituted the entire departmental directory. While in Paris Chalier defined clearly, and for the first time in print, his diagnosis of what he saw as Lyon's inherent counter-revolutionary tendencies: 'Immensely populous, Lyon was always divided between a great number of the privileged and oppressive rich, and an even greater number of the poor poor, crushed by the weight of taxes, degraded by that of humiliation. The former were indignant that others dared to contemplate the *declaration of the rights of man and the citizen;* hatred of equality was the source of Lyon's troubles...[which] exist still because of the desire to reestablish the old regime' *(Adresse de Joseph Chalier, officier municipale de la ville de Lyon à l'Assemblée Nationale* [sic] (Lyon, n.d. [1792]), p. 2). Chalier also began to suspect the patriotism of his municipal colleagues and particularly of Roland, who had spent most of 1791 in Paris and whose house was frequented by the Brissotins.

Soon after his return home, Chalier began to mobilise the poor for the regeneration of Lyon. 'The day before yesterday', wrote Vitet to Roland on 25 August, 'Monsieur Chalier mounted the tribune of the *Club central* and said that the municipality, the new district and the new department should be surrounded and during this time the people should be made to exercise all its sovereignty by cutting off the heads of the refractory priests and all the aristocrats: it is only by seeing impure blood flowing everywhere that you will acquire tranquillity, safety and happiness' (*Archives Nationales*, F⁷3686⁶, dossier 8). Like most of the information we have on Chalier this letter was the work of an enemy, but the account it gives of his intentions is consistent with his behaviour over the next nine months. He may not have been directly responsible for the prison massacres of 9 September and October 26, 1792, as his detractors claimed, and he denied organising an attempt to form a revolutionary tribunal at a secret meeting of the *Club central* on February 6, 1793, but he did advocate the elimination of an 'incalculable' number of Lyonnais counter-revolutionaries in speeches and placards full of striking images, notably in the *Serment des Trois Cents Romains* of April 1793, a vision of the Rhône transformed through the Midi before emptying itself into the 'terror-stricken seas'.

Chalier encouraged popular action to carry out the necessary acts of revolutionary justice but the Lyonnais Jacobins did not have sufficient control of the popular movement to achieve their ends. Although the elections of November-December 1792 won them the municipality, Chalier was defeated in the mayoral elections by the Rolandin Nivière-Chol and received fewer votes (3,578) than he had the previous year, despite the introduction of universal suffrage. He had to be content with the presidency of the district tribunal. What was worse, from early December 1792 the popular societies began to split, with some of them remaining loyal to the Rolandins, defying the Jacobin-dominated *Club cen-*

tral and resisting purges of supporters of the *appel au peuple*. Increasingly Chalier and his supporters turned to the methods of Jacobin centralism. There is evidence that as early as January 1793 he considered replacing the existing decentralised network of thirty-one popular societies with a single, politically homogeneous Jacobin Club and in March this was attempted, resulting in further dissension. By 6 May more than half the clubs were anti-Jacobin. The Jacobins came to see themselves as a tiny minority of patriots isolated in 'this Sodom' and increasingly they turned to the Montagnards to reinforce their tenuous hold on the city. But the Representatives on Mission sent out in March disappointed them ('I proposed several measures of reform to Bazire the *muscadin*, to Rovère the artful, to Legendre the viper', wrote Chalier, '... nothing, nothing, nothing' (*Fonds Coste, Bibliothèque de la Ville de Lyon,* ms 4315)). When a new set of deputies from the Convention, led by Dubois-Crancé, provided them with a Revolutionary Army in May, it was already too late: anti-Jacobins controlled most of the sections and their national guard battalions. On 29 May they besieged the town hall and captured it after several hours' fighting.

Chalier seems to have played no part in the defence of the town hall but he was arrested in his bed the next morning. The 'federalist' authorities which now controlled Lyon held him responsible for the deaths which had occurred and after an inadequate trial in July he was condemned to death for incitement to murder. It appears from accounts of his execution on 16 July that by this time popular feeling was strongly against him. The rejoicing was somewhat abated as a result of a maladjustment of the guillotine, which took four drops to decapitate him. Since the Convention had expressly forbidden the 'federalist' authorities at Lyon to harm any of the officials they had deposed, Chalier's death was a major step on the road to the civil war which broke out in August between Lyon and the Convention. And since Chalier had established a firm reputation in Paris as a *patriote*, the killing was classified with that of Marat (q.v.) as a revolutionary martyrdom. Chalier thus joined Marat and Le Peletier (q.v.) to form the trinity of republican saints, a canonisation confirmed by the Convention's decree of December 22, 1793 ordering that his remains be placed in the Panthéon.

Chalier's position was somewhere between Robespierre (q.v.) and the enragés, but he was rather closer to the former than has usually been thought. Like several of the Lyonnais Jacobins he was well acquainted with Robespierre and admired him. Robespierre in turn praised him warmly, most notably in a speech to the Paris Jacobins on July 11, 1794 which credited him with having been the first to expose Roland's perfidy. He was more inclined than Robespierre to extol spontaneous violence and acts of popular justice as revolutionary weapons but he was not so much an enragé as to defy the Convention – the Lyonnais Jacobins complained when their attempts to set up a sans-culotte revolutionary tribunal were frustrated by the decree of 15 May, but they submitted. Chalier's intransigence, his extreme hostility towards the *aristocratie du commerce* and his emphasis on violence reflect the sharpness of social antagonisms in Lyon in the late eighteenth century. But although he saw the revolutionary struggle there as one between rich and poor, what was at stake for him was the fate of the revolution, not the shape of the social order. His excoriations of the *classe mercantile contre-révolutionnaire* anticipated the language of class warfare but there is no evidence apart from some allegations by his enemies that he advocated redistributing property except in the Robespierrist sense of making the rich pay for the defence of liberty. Again, although he advocated the maximum on grains there is no evidence that he shared the plans of his fellow-Lyonnais Rousseau Hidins for nationalising the grain trade. His speeches are said to have included lamentation over the plight of the Lyonnais weavers and their oppression by the silk merchants but as

with Robespierre economic questions usually came second to political ones. Chalier's downfall, too, parallels Robespierre's. Popular disillusionment with the Jacobins' failure to deal with economic grievances and resistance to their centralist tendencies left him and his supporters isolated in the face of a hostile bourgeoisie. Even more clearly than Thermidor the defeat of Chalier illustrates the fragility of the Jacobin alliance with the *menu peuple*.

The main holdings of Chalier's writings are in the *Fonds Coste* of the Bibliothèque de la Ville de Lyon, for which see Aimé Vingtrinier, *Catalogue de la bibliothèque Lyonnaise de M. Coste* (Lyon, 1861). During the weeks before Chalier's trial the 'federalist' Guerre published a collection of documents entitled *Histoire de la Révolution de Lyon* (reprinted G. Guigue (ed.) *Registre du Secrétariat-Général des Sections de la Ville de Lyon Août 2–Octobre 11, 1793* (Lyon, 1907)). This contains many letters attributed to Chalier but they should be treated with extreme caution. Other writings and supposed writings of Chalier are scattered in a variety of sources to which the best guide is A. De Francesco, 'Montagnardi e sanculotti in provincia: il caso lionese (agosto 1792-maggio 1793)', *Studi Storici*, 19 (1978), pp. 600-626, which also contains useful discussion of Chalier's ideas. Takashi Koi, 'Les "Chaliers" et les sans-culottes lyonnais (1792-1793)', *Annales historiques de la Révolution française*, 50 (1978), pp. 127–31 credits Chalier's social ideas with more originality and significance than the present writer thinks warranted. The best biographical study remains Maurice Wahl, 'Joseph Chalier. Etude sur la Révolution française à Lyon', *Revue historique*, 34 (May-August 1887), pp. 1–30.

BILL EDMONDS

CHASLES (a.k.a. Châles), Pierre Jacques Michel (1753–1826)
French revolutionary democrat, member of the National Convention

Chasles was born at Chartres (Eure-et-Loir), the son of a master joiner. He was educated at the Collège du Plessis in Paris. He entered the priesthood, taught the children of the comte d'Estaing, and then took up a teaching post at the Collège de Chartres. A work he published in 1785, *Timante ou Portraite fidèle de la plupart des écrivains du XVIIIe siècle*, led to his appointment as canon and personal secretary to the archbishop of Tours. At the outset of the revolution he contributed to *L'Ami du roi*, then founded, with his brother, *Le Correspondant*, which became the leading 'patriotic' journal in the Eure-et-Loir. He took the oath to the Civil Constitution of the Clergy, became principal of the Collège de Nogent-le-Rotrou and, in November 1791, mayor of that town.

In September 1792 Chasles was elected by the Eure-et-Loir to the National Convention where he sat with the Mountain. In the same month he joined the Jacobin Club, and in November opposed Manuel's (q.v.) proposal to abolish the Civil Constitution of the Clergy, regarding it as unnecessarily provocative. In the Convention he was one of the first to demand the requisitioning of grain held by speculators. In the trial of Louis XVI he opposed an appeal to the people and voted for the death-penalty without reprieve. In the spring of 1793 he and Guffroy were sent to oversee army recruitment in the departments of the Seine-et-Oise and Eure-et-Loir. On his return he became involved in the struggles against the Girondins and, after Marat's (q.v.) assassination, urged the Jacobins to acquire his presses and continue his journal.

On August 1, 1793 Chasles was sent as representative on mission to the army of the north. He was seriously wounded at the battle of Hondeschoote in September, and taken to Lille, where he abandoned the priesthood and joined with the ultra-revolutionaries. His activities earned him the admiration of the workers of Lille and the reputation of 'scourge of the rich', but alienated the middle class of Lille and his fellow representatives, Hentz and Guiot, who sought to have him recalled. He was eventually recalled by the Convention on

27 Nivôse Year II (January 16, 1794) but he used his injuries as a pretext to stall his departure. The Convention, at its meeting of 12 Pluviôse, issued a further decree ordering him to return within eight days. When he appeared before the Jacobin Club a fortnight later Levasseur and Collot d'Herbois (q.v.) rose to defend him against his critics. Moreover, the Committee of Public Safety agreed to bear the cost of the treatment for his war injuries.

After the fall of Robespierre (q.v.), Chasles was prominent in opposing the Thermidorian reaction. On 29 Fructidor he began, in collaboration with Lebois (q.v.), to publish the sans-culottic journal *L'Ami du peuple*, but abandoned it after sixteen issues following a disagreement with Lebois. In the paper he had staunchly defended the Constitution of 1793 and used the language of class struggle against the privileged and on behalf of the 'fourth estate'. When the paper was denounced in the Convention by right Thermidorians, Chasles responded by reprinting the sixteen editions under the title *Chronique scandaleuse de l'aristocratie française....*

Following the *journée* of 12 Germinal Year III (April 1, 1795) Chasles was arrested and imprisoned, until released under the general amnesty of October 26. He was one of the old Jacobins automatically arrested at the time of the Babeuf (q.v.) conspiracy, but he was quickly released. He returned for a time to teaching and later set up a tobacconist's shop in Paris in his wife's name. Although he had not signed the *acte additionel* he was harassed at the time of the second Restoration and there is good reason to believe that he chose to exile himself for a while in London. He died in Paris on June 21, 1826.

Chasles was a revolutionary democrat who remained faithful to the principles of 1793. He sought to maintain the alliance between the Jacobins and the sans-culottes and to prevent the rightward drift of the revolution after the fall of Robespierre. At Chasles' funeral, his son honoured his father's commitment to his class with this epitaph: 'Né plébéien, il s'est constamment et invariablement le défenseur de la classe plébéienne.'

In addition to the short biographical details in A. Kuscinski, *Dictionnaire des conventionnels* (Paris, 1917), and J. Maitron (gen. ed.), *Dictionnaire biographique du mouvement ouvrier français. Part One: 1789–1864* (3 vols., Paris, 1964), there is the standard biography by C. Pichois and J. Dautry, *Le conventionnel Châsles et ses idées démocratiques* (Aix, 1958).

D NICHOLLS

CHAUMETTE, Pierre Gaspard ('Anaxagorus') (1763–1794)

Procureur of the Paris Commune, dechristianiser and ultra-revolutionary.

Chaumette was born in Nevers on May 24, 1763. His father, Pierre Gaspard, was a shoemaker. In early 1789 he was in Paris as a medical student. With the outbreak of the revolution, Chaumette emerged as a leader of lower middle-class consciousness. He first appeared as a revolutionary on July 17, 1791 on the Champ de Mars where he organised a popular movement to draft a petition urging the dethronement of Louis XVI. This event became the nucleus for a united movement against the monarchy and prompted the 'massacre' of Champ de Mars. Chaumette became the principal organiser of the Paris sections and of the insurrectional Commune. He was responsible for the successful attack of August 10, 1792 on the Tuileries.

As president, and later an elected *procureur* of the Commune, Chaumette became a major figure in Parisian political and religious movements in 1793. It was at this time that he rejected his Christian name and chose instead the name of the Greek philosopher, Anaxagorus. He was passionately egalitarian and he used the general Council of the Commune to express his own brand of egalitarianism. When the Convention was deciding on the king's fate and the city of Paris was experiencing food shortages, Chaumette in a speech to the General Council, claimed that prices would remain high and food shortages would continue to exist as long

as Louis and his royalist friends went unpunished. He proposed the criminal prosecution of hoarders and profiteers. He also presented a scheme to create a large scale public works programme 'to ease the distress of the aged and the infirm and to find some way of employing the destitute so that there would be no more begging in Paris and that the suffering of humanity might be alleviated'. In support of this project he stated that 'the rich must be forced to play their part and made to contribute whether they liked it or not, towards the happiness of all citizens'.

The Parisian poor strongly favoured price control on commodities. Chaumette, along with the mayor of Paris, brought the issue of the fixed price or maximum to the Convention. The Convention initially ignored the proposition, but the General Council of the Commune, on a motion from Chaumette, declared that 'it would remain in a state of revolution' until food supplies had been assured. The Convention reversed its earlier decision, and on May 4, 1793, it imposed the Law of General Maximum and created a Revolutionary army which, as an agent of the terror, was supposed to guarantee food supplies to Paris.

In alliance with the Hébertists, the Commune, under Chaumette's direction, initiated an intensified dechristianisation campaign. In August-September 1792, at his insistence, the Commune established a secularisation programme. This programme included the oppression of religious orders and the closing of their premises, spoliation of churches, and termination of church control of public welfare, parish registers, education and acceptance of divorce. Chaumette advocated the overthrow of the constitutional church and wanted to foster a *culte de la patrie*, which created altars to the nation. He took his campaign of secularisation to the provinces. While visiting his ailing mother in Nevers, Chaumette urged the local representative on mission, Fouché, to promote dechristianisation.

His aversion to church authority did not abate. On November 10, 1793 Chaumette appeared with the Commune at the Festival of Liberty at Notre Dame where a large crowd gathered. At this festival Chaumette declared that the people wanted no more priests: 'No other gods than those whom Nature offers us. We, the people's magistrates, have verified its decision; we bring it to you from the Temple of Reason.' Chaumette demanded that the Church of Notre Dame should henceforth be called the Temple of Reason. A decree to that effect was immediately passed. To celebrate the occasion Chaumette organised the Festival of Reason at Notre Dame. Many other celebrations also took place in the Paris sections and in the provinces, accompanied by mock religious ceremonies and vandalism in the churches.

The establishment of the Cult of Reason was the hallmark of Chaumette's triumph against the Church. Dechristianisation was at its height in 1793. On November 24, 1793 Chaumette pressured the Commune to pass a resolution on the subject. This resolution noted that the people of Paris had declared their unwillingness to accept no religion other than that of Truth and Reason. It went on to order, in the name of the Council General of the Commune, the closure of all churches and temples of every religion which existed in Paris and to hold all priests and ministers responsible for any religious disturbances which might break out. Furthermore, the resolution declared that individuals demanding the re-opening of churches or temples would be liable to arrest, that the revolutionary Committees would be asked to keep a close watch upon all priests and that the Convention should be petitioned to decree the exclusion of priests from the exercise of public duties and from all employment in national manufacturing concerns.

Dechristianisation lost its impact in 1794 when Robespierre (q.v.) replaced the Cult of Reason with the Cult of the Supreme Being which emphasised the existence of God as well as the doctrine of the immortality of the soul. The issue of religion prompted a major conflict between Chaumette and other dechristianisers and Robespierre. Chaumette was denounced as a corrupter of morality whose atheistic policies discredited France. Accused as an aristocrat and traitor to the Republic he was guillotined on April 13, 1794.

Chaumette maintained that one of the duties of government was to protect citizens from starvation. As a measure against non-availablity of goods and high inflation he suggested a controlled economy which the Jacobins were reluctant to follow. By promoting the issue of price contol and persuading the Convention to impose the Law of General Maximum, Chaumette championed the cause of the proletarians of the Paris sections. He also campaigned intensively for dechristianisation and helped the Commune to establish a secularisation programme. By the advocacy of major changes in the existing economic and religious structures of eighteenth-century French society, Chaumette secured his position among the European radicals.

A biography of Chaumette in English is yet to be written. F.A. Aulard's *The French Revolution; a political history, 1789–1804* (4 vols., tr. Bernard Miall, New York, reissued 1965) is the best source of information on Chaumette's activities in English. The best French sources are: F.A. Aulard, *Mémoires de Chaumette sur La Révolution du 10 aôut 1792* (Paris, 1893), and F. Braesch (ed.), *Papiers de Chaumette* (Paris, 1907). Albert Adrien, 'Chaumette et la commune de 93', *La Revue Socialiste*, Vol.XI, (1890), and R. André-Simon, *Dénonciations contre Gaspard Chaumette* (Paris, 1932) also provide some important information on Chaumette's activities in the Commune and on his trial.

N. CHAUDHURI

CHÉNIER, Marie Joseph Blaise de (1764–1811)
French Jacobin poet and playwright

Son of the French consul in Constantinople and brother to the poet, André, Chénier was born in Constantinople but came to France the following year. He was educated at the Collège de Navarre in Paris. At 17 he entered the army, becoming an officer at Niort, but resigned two years later and began a literary career. His first two plays, produced in 1785 and 1786, received a hostile reception, but the third, *Charles IX*, staged in November 1789, was a great success thanks to its attacks on the Court and the clergy. A stream of patriotic plays followed, together with revolutionary poems and songs, notably *Le Chant du départ*. Chénier was elected to the Convention in 1792, and sat on the left. He served on the Committee of Public Instruction, and voted for the execution of the king. In Thermidor he turned against Robespierre (q.v.), and subsequently attacked other members of the Committee of Public Safety. In 1795 he was elected to the Committee of General Security, and under the Directory he served as a member of the Conseil des Cinq Cents, with two terms as president. He supported Bonaparte initially, and became a member of the Tribunate, but soon joined the opposition. Together with Constant, Daunou, J.B. Say and others, he was expelled when the Tribunate was purged in 1802. Chénier then obtained a post as inspector-general of education, which he held from 1803 to 1806.

His play *Cyrus*, staged in 1804 just after the coronation of Napoleon, offended the emperor with its thinly veiled attacks on the suppression of democratic institutions, and led to the banning of all Chénier's plays. In 1806 he published a *Letter to Voltaire*, an attack on despotism which lost him his job. Henceforth, until his death in 1811, he devoted himself to writing and teaching, working on the dictionary of the French Academy, of which he was a member, and on a history of French literature since 1789, a work interrupted by his death.

Chénier welcomed the revolution and became an outspoken critic of royal (and later imperial) despotism. He was a republican by 1792, and a staunch Jacobin, but his continued opposition to excessive executive power won him the disfavour of both Robespierre and Napoleon. He was always a vigorous anticlerical, even before the revolution attacking religious intoler-

ance, and during his term on the Committee of General Security pursuing the former clergy. Education remained a major interest, and during both the revolution and the empire he attempted to improve the efficiency of primary education in France.

There are brief details of Chénier's life in two collections of his works: *Théâtre de M.J. de Chénier, précédé d'une notice et orné du portrait de l'auteur* (3 vols., Paris, 1818); and M.J. Chénier, *Poésies* (ed. C. Labitte, Paris, 1844). The political content of his writing can be gauged from the following: the plays *Azémire* (1786), *Charles IX* (1788), *Henri VIII* (1791), *La Mort de Calas* (1791), *Caius Gracchus* (1792), *Fénélon* (1793), *Timoléon* (1794), *Cyrus* (1804). *Philippe II, Tibère*, and *Nathan-Le-Sage* were published posthumously. See also his *Fragmens de littérature* (1818); *Tableau historique de l'état et des progrès de la littérature française depuis 1789* (1815); *Epître sur la Calomnie* (1795); *Epître à Voltaire* (1806); and *Poésies* (1844).

D. GARRIOCH

CLAUER, Karl (? – 1794)
German Jacobin and revolutionary democrat

Little is known about the early life of Karl Clauer, one of the first German Jacobins. Contemporary accounts begin only with those events immediately preceding his move to Strasbourg in 1791, and even here there seems to be some disagreement on details. However, the sources agree that he was born in Schleiz, the son of a barber; that he studied law, and practised as a lawyer in Dresden; and that when he left Dresden he was a widower with children. He remarried – it is uncertain whether in Prague or Vienna – and moved to Strasbourg in 1791. There he was a member of the Jacobin Club, and his writing appeared as a supplement to the journal *Geschichte der Gegenwärtigen Zeit*.

After returning to Germany, and spending some time in Mainz, where he was an affiliated member of the Mainz Club, he was appointed a Commissar in Buchsweiler, in the *département* of the Lower Rhine. Alsace, Lorraine and part of the Palatinate had become French after the Thirty Years' War, but real power continued to reside with the local German aristocracy. In July 1789 there had been a peasants' revolt in the Buchsweiler area, and local people had marched into the town to present the council with a list of demands. Clauer's appointment was part of a general policy to replace moderates with radicals following the Jacobin victory in Paris, and his task was to prepare the canton for defence against the approaching Austrian army. However, the townspeople, particularly the better off, had become increasingly unsympathetic towards the revolution, and Clauer was eventually forced to leave under the protection of French troops in the autumn of 1793.

Following his return to France he was appointed an extraordinary commissioner, and later a district administrator, by the Committee of Public Safety in Strasbourg. He had been ill for some time when the persecution of German Jacobins in Alsace began. Both Schneider (q.v.) and Cotta (q.v.) had already been arrested when the authorities turned their attention to him. His abduction from his sick-bed was prevented only by the intervention of his doctor, and he died shortly afterwards.

Clauer's political importance stems not only from his active participation in the events of the early 1790s and his relatively minor administrative positions, but also from his theoretical contributions to the debate on the French constitution and human rights. In a polemical exchange in the *Berliner Monatsschrift* in 1790, Clauer took issue with the conservative historian Justus Möser, challenging his assertion that property was the basis of all law, and effectively defining the Third Estate as the entire French nation. In certain respects his radicalism exceeded that of many of his contemporaries. Going beyond Kant (q.v.), who sought to rely on persuasion for the implementation of political change, Clauer asserted the right to resist tyrannical authority.

Following his move to Strasbourg Clauer warned against intervention against France; his *Kreuzzug gegen die Franken*, which appeared in June 1791, was one of the most important tracts of the time to put forward this argument. He warned of the danger of unrest in Germany if during a counter-revolutionary war, French troops should make incursions into German territory. However, the *Kreuzzug gegen die Franken* is on the whole an appeal for the reform of the existing order by German rulers so as to avoid a possible uprising. However, his *Sendeschreiben an alle benachbarte Völker Frankreichs, zum allgemeinen Aufstand* goes further and argues that a people has the right to rebel if the ruler breaks the terms of the original 'contract' with his subjects to govern in accordance with the general will of the people. He appeals to the people to rise up against their rulers, to 'take what the French have done as an example'.

Although he was neither one of the greatest theoreticians nor one of the most important activists of the period, Clauer, like many of his contemporaries, nevertheless made a contribution by developing the ideas of the revolution and defending them against conservative contemporaries.

Karl Clauer, 'Der Kreuzzug gegen die Franken', is available in Jost Hermand (ed.), *Von deutscher Republik 1775–1795. Texte radikaler Demokraten* (Frankfurt am Main, 1968). For biographical details and an assessment of Clauer's work, see Hans Werner Engels, 'Karl Clauer. Bemerkungen zum Leben und zu den Schriften eines Jakobiners', in Helmut Reinalter (ed.), *Jakobiner in Mitteleuropa* (Innsbruck, 1977). Heinrich Scheel, *Die Mainzer Republik. Protokolle des Jakobinerklubs* (Berlin, 1975) is a useful source of material on the Jacobin Club, of which Clauer was a member.

TIM KIRK

CLOOTS, (a.k.a. KLOTZ), John Baptiste du Val de Grâce, baron de ('Anarchasis') (1755–1794)
German-born President of the Paris Jacobin Club, member of the Convention and dechristianiser

Cloots was born in 1755 into a very wealthy Prussian family. He went to Paris at the age of twenty-one in order to improve himself, and wanted to become a philosopher like his hero Voltaire. Disappointed by life in France he travelled abroad and returned, at the age of thirty-four, to the announcement of the fall of the Bastille. He immediately became involved in politics, and put himself at the service of the revolution. He adopted the name Anarchasis after the Barthélémy novel *Les voyages du jeune Anarchasis* which appeared in 1788. In March 1790 he was to be found among the ranks of the Jacobins and claimed to have been one of their first members. He accorded himself the title of orator or ambassador of the human race and immediately became the representative of foreigners come to Paris on 'pilgrimages of freedom'. After becoming a French citizen he stood for election to the Convention and was successful in 1792. The Jacobins elected him president of the club, a position he held from November 11–30, 1793.

Cloots' flamboyant character caused him problems throughout the revolution. The first major blow was dealt by Camille Desmoulins (q.v.), when the Convention under Robespierre (q.v.) affirmed its support for religious freedom. Robespierre criticised Cloots for being noble, Prussian and rich, and finally managed to discredit him. Cloots had in fact kept in touch with his bankers, who were counter-revolutionaries, and had even tried to protect them from French law. Robespierre reproached him with betraying France by defending the human race rather than the French nation. He was imprisoned following the decree on the expulsion of foreigners of December 26, 1793. He was guillotined on March 24, 1794.

Cloots started out a close ally of the Girondins; he was in favour of war and revolutionary expansion. He was hostile towards Robespierre and feared popular movements. He then followed the tide of opinion, acknowledged the necessity of the September massacres and distanced himself from the Girondins. When the Convention was re-established this development became more marked, and he left in November 1792. Cloots realised the importance to the revolution of a popular alliance, and moved towards the Mountain, despite his dislike of Marat (q.v.) and Robespierre. In the name of the Universal Republic, a term he coined himself, he became a fervent publicist for the cause of revolutionary expansionism. On April 25, 1793 he put before the Convention the constitutional bases of the Republic of the Human Race, and announced the imminence of universal human unity. He considered himself a sans-culotte, but used this expression in its political rather than its social sense. For him the sans-culotte movement united the middle class and the working class against the aristocracy. Cloots took sides against the Agrarian Law and proved himself to be a staunch defender of property. He took up the same position on the issue of slavery in the colonies and was against the granting of political rights to free men of all colours. He did not think it necessary to redistribute land among the peasants or to make independent farmers of them. The existence of a dependent working class was for him the prerequisite of a stable bourgeois economic order. His was not a plebeian internationalism then, but a bourgeois cosmopolitanism, and it was in this context that he considered the annexation of the left bank of the Rhine a necessary precondition for peace. On the other hand he was extremely anti-clerical and worked for the triumph of the cult of reason; he was one of the principal architects of dechristianisation.

Cloots therefore appears to have been a committed revolutionary. If his thinking on property and the working class was flawed in this respect, he was by no means alone. He fell victim to his own fanatical character and his continuing connections with his bankers. When French policy on foreigners became tougher he quickly fell under suspicion, while other Germans such as Forster (q.v.) or Hofmann (q.v.) retained the Convention's confidence, and were even entrusted with missions of diplomatic secrecy. Cloots shared the fate of those such as von der Trenck (q.v.) or Schneider (q.v.), who served the French Revolution only to end up on the guillotine.

Cloots' own writings are available with a preface by Albert Soboul in A. Cloots, *Oeuvres* (Munich, 1980). The nineteenth-century biography of Cloots has been re-issued: G. Avenel, *Anarchasis Cloots. L'orateur du genre humain* (1865; repr. Paris, 1976). See also, H. Jung, 'Jean Baptiste Cloots, ein gescheiterter Weltverbesserer', in *Aus dem Antiquariat* (1980), 3, pp. 121–23.

M. GILLI

COLLOT D'HERBOIS, Jean Marie (1749–1796)
French Jacobin, member of the Committee of Public Safety, terrorist

Jean Marie Collot ('d'Herbois' was a *nom de théâtre*) was born to a struggling artisan family in Paris on June 19, 1749. Brought up in straitened circumstances and probably with little formal education, he entered the acting profession at the age of eighteen and, for fifteen years, toured France playing leading roles in all its important provincial theatres – such as Bordeaux, Nantes, Rouen and Lyon – and in those of Belgium and the Netherlands. Collot was a gifted and successful actor and, by the 1780s, had reached the top of the profession. In this period, he wrote a dozen plays of which some were short, occasional pieces marked by extravagant adulation of the monarchy and the old order and others serious attempts at dramatic composition in the sentimental and declamatory style of late eighteenth-century French dramaturgy. There is little to suggest a radical disposition in any of Collot's pre-revolutionary plays. In the 1780s, as manager-director of the theatres

of Geneva and Lyon, he demonstrated administrative and organisational ability in trying circumstances and formed fruitful connections with the governmental and social élites of the latter. Successful professionally and financially – he enjoyed a stipend of 6,000 *livres* per year at Lyon – Collot cannot be counted among such Jacobins as Brissot (q.v.) and Billaud-Varenne (q.v.) whose revolutionary radicalism has been attributed to their exclusion from high literary society before the revolution.

In Paris soon after the insurrection of 14 July, Collot wrote and produced a series of plays for the revolutionary theatre between 1789 and 1791. For the most part, these works were innocuous political celebrations of the new order but a number of them, especially *La Famille Patriote* and *Le Procès de Socrate* (both 1790), enjoyed great popularity and established Collot's name in the revolutionary movement. It was also in the revolutionary theatre that Collot forged connections with Marie Joseph Chénier (q.v.), Desmoulins (q.v.) and others in the Dantonist group which led to his joining the Jacobin Club in late 1790. His rapid rise to a position of leadership of the Jacobins, membership of the Commune of 10 August, presidency of the Electoral Assembly of Paris and election to the Convention as the third deputy for Paris after Robespierre (q.v.) and Danton (q.v.) (September 1792) can be explained not, as is traditionally held, by any involvement in the sections and popular movement but entirely in terms of his activity at the club. He spoke frequently and volubly on a wide range of subjects, was constantly involved in the club's bureaucracy as vice-president, secretary and member of committees, led the important and popular Jacobin campaign for the release of the Château-Vieux soldiers and took a leading part in the opposition to La Fayette. On contentious issues such as the war-question and republicanism, he adopted a position of cautious neutrality, advocating the war only after its declaration (May 1792) and, like Robespierre, adhering to the republican movement only weeks before the fall of the monarchy (July 1792). Collot's political ideas at this time were of the vaguest and those that he espoused publicly conformed with what can reasonably be called Jacobin orthodoxy. It was his ambivalence on divisive issues, championship of popular causes, frequent appearances at the tribune and universally acknowledged oratorical skill which accounts for his ascendancy at the Jacobin Club.

A partisan of Robespierre since mid-1792 and a leader of the Montagnards in the Convention, Collot played a substantial role in their feud with the Girondins and, for political reasons, advocated political and economic emergency measures demanded by the popular movement. In the Convention and at the Jacobin Club he made an apology for the September massacres (November 1792), defended the revolutionary role of Paris against Girondin attacks (November 1792–March 1793), sponsored the law against hoarding (July 1793) and called for rigorous suppression of suspects (September 1793). In three missions in 1793 to the departments of the Nièvre and Loiret (March–May), Oise (August–September) and to Lyon (November–December), he was a reliable but harsh enforcer of national policies and an effective agent of governmental centralisation. These missions were marked by purges of the local authorities, the early establishment of the machinery of the terror, the suppression of dissident elements and the implementation of radical economic controls. Collot can be counted among the most severe advocates and practitioners of the official terror in the departments. Shortly before the promulgation of the law of suspects, four hundred had been arrested in the Oise as a result of his mission and at Lyon, his conscientious application of the Convention's policy of brutal repression resulted in the execution of approximately 1,700 people condemned as participants in the rebellion of 1793.

Collot was elected to the Committee of Public Safety in September 1793 and his application to its onerous administrative work and his consistent defence of its policies at the Jacobin Club made him one of its most assiduous, loyal and useful members. He was not a creator of policy but he was a reliable and forceful defender and enforcer of policies adopted by the committee. He defended its policies on religion, social issues, the war, the terror and governmental centralisation. He had a leading part in the committee's destruction of both the moderate and extremist factions and of the section movement between February and May 1794. Collot has traditionally been classified as a personal associate and a representative on the committee of the radical Cordeliers group but no evidence has ever been produced in support of this contention; in fact, he was instrumental in their elimination. His campaign against the Indulgents (December 1793–March 1794) was the result not of political or personal connections with their Hébertiste enemies but of the need to defend his mission to Lyon and those who had collaborated with him. Partly for the same reason, Collot was the committee's most important advocate of the maintenance of the terror between his return from Lyon and the Thermidorian reaction and as such his power and influence at the Jacobin Club and on the committee came almost to rival that of Robespierre. It was this rivalry as well as internal personal conflict in the committee and Robespierre's objections to certain aspects of Collot's mission to Lyon – particularly the latter's defence of Fouché (q.v.) – not any disagreement over the continuation of the terror or any other policy, which accounts for Robespierre's alienation from Collot and the latter's participation in the conspiracy of 9 Thermidor. Soon after, Collot left the committee, was repeatedly denounced as a terrorist and condemned to deportation to Guyana where he died in 1796.

Unlike such Jacobin colleagues as Billaud-Varenne, Saint-Just (q.v.) and Robespierre, Collot's radicalism is to be found not in theoretical disquisition but in political action in the field. Furthermore, it was a radicalism directed not to forging a new order but to protecting an established (if nascent) one. What distinguished Collot from the majority of the Montagnards was his greater willingness to employ radical, practical strategies for the sole purpose of strengthening the Republic against subversion within and invasion without. His radical action was therefore the product of external circumstances rather than a response to an ideological imperative. For this reason, Collot's missions rather than his political activity in Paris provide the key to the definition of his place in revolutionary politics. Faithful to the Jacobin antipathy to economic regulation before his mission to the Nièvre, his observations there, not any association with the Parisian sans-culotte movement, resulted in his advocacy of war taxes on the rich and the draconian law against hoarding. His implementation in the Oise of a radical interventionist programme of price control and forced requisitions was aimed merely at securing the provisionment of Paris and the armies. The repression of Lyon was directed not, as has been alleged, at the eradication of the 'merchant aristocracy' but at the destruction of the political enemies of the Convention. The famous 'revolutionary tax' imposed by Collot and Fouché, often interpreted as a definite stage in a new social revolution, was merely a war tax of which part would be employed for piecemeal assistance to the indigent at the expense of the rich; it was not at all an attempt to effect a redistribution of wealth from one social group to another. Even the radical *Instruction* of Collot's and Fouché's Temporary Commission of Lyon, described as a 'communist manifesto' by Babeuf (q.v.), Jaurès and some modern historians, was, as its wording demonstrates, the product of an emergency situation and cannot be interpreted as prescribing socialism. There is no evidence to justify Collot's description as a 'proto-socialist' or a 'leveller'; all his social and economic initiatives were motivated entirely by the pressing local and national circumstances in which he was operating.

The crucial point is that the political action of Collot d'Herbois was performed in execution of specific defensive policies of the established government in an emergency. He can be classified as a radical only insofar as he was prepared to go to extreme lengths, farther than most French revolutionaries, to achieve his and the government's immediate aims. His radicalism was, then, one of means rather than ends. In terms of French revolutionary politics, Collot's importance was not, as is commonly but erroneously held, as a link between the popular movement and the Committee of Public Safety but as a pillar of the Revolutionary Government and one of the most powerful proponents of its policy of organised terror as a political weapon in extreme circumstances.

None of Collot's important plays, pamphlets and published speeches have been translated into English. Those most useful for an assessment of his political ideas and strategies are the following, all held by the British Library:

Discours prononcé à la tribune de l'assemblée électorale du département de Paris, le 3 septembre 1792 (Paris, 1792); *Projet de décret sur l'emprunt forcé d'un milliard, présenté à la séance du 9 juin* (Paris, n.d. – 1793); *Rapport fait au nom du Comité de salut public, sur la situation de Commune–Affranchie. . .Le l Nivôse* (Paris, An II – 1793); *Rapport sur les accapareurs. . .* (Paris, 1793); *Instruction adressée aux autorités constituées. . .par la Commission Temporaire de Surveillance Républicaine* (Lyons, An II – 1793); *Réponse à l'inculpation dirigée par le représentant Clausel contre Collot. . .* (Paris, An III – 1795); *Eclairsissements nécessaires sur ce qui s'est passé à Lyon. . .* (Paris, An III – 1795); *Défense de J.M. Collot. . .* (Paris, An III – 1795); *Réponse de J.M. Collot. . .à la pétition des Lyonnais* (Paris, An III – 1795); *Discours fait à la Convention nationale,. . .prononcé le 4 germinal an III* (Paris, An III – 1795).

There is no published authoritative study of the political career of Collot d'Herbois. The following provide information on him but with the exception of Fuchs' article, they are hostile to Collot and should be read critically:

A. Bégis, *Curiosités révolutionnaires.
Billaud-Varenne membre du Comité de
Salut public. Mémoires inédits et corres-
pondance accompagnés de notices biographiques sur Billaud-Varenne et Collot
d'Herbois* (Paris, 1893); V. Fournel, 'Les
comédiens révolutionnaires. Collot d'Her-
bois acteur et auteur dramatique', *Le
Correspondant. Religion – Philosophie –
Politique – Sciences – Littérature – Beaux-
Arts*, vol. 172 (Nouvelle série, vol. 136),
pp. 50–83; A. Aulard, 'Collot d'Herbois',
Les Orateurs de la Convention (Paris,
n.d.), vol. 3; M. Fuchs, 'Collot d'Herbois
Comédien', *La Révolution Française.
Revue d'histoire moderne et contemporaine*,
vol. 79 (1926), pp. 14–26, 112–39; E.
Herriot, *Lyon n'est plus*, vol. 3 (*La
Répression*) (Paris, 1937); R. Palmer,
*Twelve Who Ruled. The year of the terror
in the French Revolution* (Princeton, 1941);
D. Guérin, *La Lutte des Classes sous la
Première République. Bourgeois et bras
nus 1793–1797* (Paris, 1946); R. Cobb,
*L'Armée Révolutionnaire Parisienne à
Lyon et dans la Région Lyonnaise (frimaire
– prairial, an II)* (Lyon, 1951).

PAUL MANSFIELD

COMPAGNONI, Giuseppe (1754–1833)
*Italian Jacobin sympathiser, journalist
and publicist*

Born into a family of modest means,
Compagnoni was directed to the priesthood
by his father. Having finished his studies
in theology, he was ordained. In 1786 he
moved to Bologna to become editor of the
Memorie enciclopediche, a literary weekly.
Thus began a career as journalist and
publicist which Compagnoni pursued all
his life. In 1787 he left his native Romagna
for Venice, becoming editor the next year
of the *Notizie del mondo*. An admirer of
the reforms of Joseph II, Compagnoni
revealed a sympathy for enlightened despotism, a sentiment that later inspired him
to support Napoleon. Assured of a more
congenial livelihood, he seems to have left
the priesthood at this time. Meanwhile,
news from France disquieted European
conservatives, and Compagnoni's impartial

and balanced reports on French developments in the *Notizie del mondo* alarmed
the state inquisitors in Venice, but he
managed to allay their suspicions.

In 1794 Compagnoni relinquished the
editorship of the *Notizie del mondo*, and
two years later started a new journal, the
Mercurio d'Italia. Influenced by French
revolutionary ideas, Compagnoni shifted
from moderate conservatism to a progressively radical position. He was not alone
in his growing sympathy for Jacobinism.
Impressed by the changes in France, Italian
intellectuals were becoming increasingly
radicalised. The new doctrines seemed to
offer hope for the regeneration of Italy.
Thus, despite the disillusionment caused by
the Peace of Campoformio, many Italians
continued to see in France the bellwether
of progress and to support Napoleon
through his various incarnations, from
general of the French army in Italy to
consul to the king of Italy and emperor of
France.

Compagnoni's political conversion was
marked by increased political activity. For
the next two decades he filled important
offices in French-dominated Italy. He distinguished himself in the different assemblies convened to deliberate Italian affairs,
particularly at the Congress of Reggio
Emilia, where on January 7, 1797 he
proposed and persuaded the delegates to
accept the white, red, and green tricolour
as the flag of the newly-organised Cispadane Republic. This flag remained the
standard of French Italy and after 1860
became that of united Italy. Recognising
Compagnoni's skill and knowledge, Napoleon charged him with many responsibilities. Compagnoni thus participated in the
elaboration of the new penal, military, and
commercial codes promulgated in Napoleonic Italy.

The fall of Napoleon marked the end of
Compagnoni's public career, and during
the next two decades he lived by his pen.
Among the writings of his later years,
the many volumes of *Storia dell'America*,
published between 1820 and 1822 most
clearly reflected his continuing support for
what the American and French revolutions

had represented. Avoiding censure by the Austrian administration of Milan, he lived quietly until his death on December 29, 1833.

More reformer than revolutionist, Compagnoni belongs among the advocates and supporters of change. Influenced by the ideas of the Italian Enlightenment, of men like Pietro Verri, Cesare Beccaria, and Gian Rinaldo Carli, Compagnoni contributed to the end of the old régime in Italy and the formation of a national spirit. Realistic in his appreciation of French hegemony over Italy under Napoleon, he tried to exploit it to foster reform in his country.

Among Compagnoni's own publications the most useful for assessing his political views are G. Compagnoni, *Memorie autobiografiche. . .* (ed. A. Ottolino, Milan, 1927); and G. Compagnoni, *Storia dell'America in continuazione del compendio della Storia universale del sig. Conte di Segur. . .* (28 vols., Milan, 1820–22). There are biographical details in G. Gullino, 'Giuseppe Compagnoni', *Dizionario biografico degli italiani* (Rome, 1982), vol. XXVII, 654–61; and Delio Cantimori (ed.), *Giacobini italiani* (Bari, 1956–64), Vol. I, 23–96.

EMILIANA P. NOETHER

CONDORCET, Marie Jean Antoine Nicolas de Caritat, Marquis de (1743–1794)
French mathematician, Enlightenment reformer and writer, member of the Legislative Assembly and the National Convention

Condorcet was born at Ribemont, in the department of the Aisne, into an old noble family, originally from Orange, that had settled in the Dauphiné. The family had a long tradition of military service from the French crown, but Condorcet broke from that tradition by becoming a mathematician, social scientist and politician, spending most of his adult life in Paris. His early education was at home, under the close control of a pious mother, then at the Jesuit college in Rheims. From there, in 1758, he went to the University of Paris and, at the Collège de Navarre, fell under the influence of a gifted mathematics teacher, Girault de Kéroudou. He pursued his interest in mathematics at the Academy of Sciences and, through the patronage of the philosophe d'Alembert, was elected a member in 1769, assistant secretary in 1773, and permanent secretary three years later. In this capacity he was effectively the official spokesman on scientific matters in France until the suppression of the Academy in 1793. D'Alembert also introduced him to salon society, where he became a friend of Turgot and convinced supporter of the Enlightenment. He supported Turgot's activities as controller general of finances in the early years of Louis XVI's reign, 1774–1776, with a series of pamphlets advocating social reform and economic freedom.

With Turgot's fall from power in May 1776, he returned to mathematics, constructing a theory of the calculus of probabilities which, in an *Essai sur l'application de l'analyse à la probabilité des décisions rendues à la pluralité des voix* (1785), he argued to be applicable to the problems of political representation and decision making. Meanwhile his interest in politics remained, and in 1787–88 he published a number of pamphlets supporting the reforms of Calonne and Brienne, particularly those providing for elected local assemblies. Initially an opponent of the decision to call an Estates General, through fear that it would be controlled by the nobility and clergy, he was a member of the Society of Thirty during the winter of 1788–1789, which distributed model *cahiers* and pamphlets in support of the Third Estate. In the spring of 1789 he drafted the *cahier* of the nobility of Mantes and took part in the electoral assembly for Paris, but failed to get elected to the Estates General and gained his first practical experience of politics when elected to the second Paris Municipality in September 1789. He became a journalist, writing articles for the *Moniteur, Feuille villageoise* and *Journal de Paris*, and was also a founding member of the *Société de 1789*, established early in 1790 to counteract the growth of political radicalism in the Jacobin Club. Yet slowly his views became more democratic: he opposed the *marc d'argent* decree, which limited eligibility for deputies to the very wealthy, and through his experience on the Paris Municipality abandoned the idea of a censitary franchise as unjust and unworkable. In July 1791, after Louis XVI's abortive flight to Varennes, he then openly aligned himself with Brissot (q.v.) and Thomas Paine in calling for the abolition of monarchy and the establishment of a republic, and was elected to the Legislative Assembly for Paris. There he joined the Girondins in calling for war as a solution to the country's political problems, and during the spring and summer of 1792 shared their belief that popular agitation and crowd violence could be used to pressurise the king into accepting the reforms of the revolution. However he opposed the attack on the Tuileries on 10 August, and bitterly opposed the subsequent growth of radical influence in Paris. Elected to the National Convention for the Aisne in September 1792, he was president of its constitutional committee and, on its behalf, presented the draft for a new constitution on February 15, 1793. But it rapidly became embroiled in the conflict between the Gironde and the Mountain and was superseded by the more radical constitution of 1793. On 2 June the leading Girondins were arrested, and Condorcet responded with a pamphlet, *Aux Citoyens Français*, which prompted the Convention to order his arrest on 8 July. He went into hiding in Paris, and worked on an analysis of the history of human progress which was published posthumously in 1795, as *Esquisse d'un tableau historique des progrès de l'esprit humain*. However, on March 13, 1794 he was outlawed and, fearing arrest, left Paris to seek refuge with former friends in Fontenay des Roses. They refused him shelter, and he was arrested on 27 March at Bourg-la-Reine. Two days later he was found dead, probably from exhaustion, although contemporaries alleged suicide.

Condorcet's intellectual interests were wide, and he was the leading member of the second generation of *philosophes* to survive into the revolution. Through his study of mathematics he was convinced that reason could establish laws of moral and political science similar to those established by Newton for the physical world. Because of this he shared Turgot's belief in the need for fundamental reform in the structures of French society and politics. He admired the political principles behind American independence, and did much to spread an awareness of the constitutional debates there to the French public. In *De l'Influence de la révolution d'Amérique* (1786), he argued that any constitution should guarantee three basic human rights of property, freedom and equality before the law. Political power, according to his *Essai sur la constitution et la fondation des Assemblées provinciales* (1788), should then be exercised by the propertied classes in a seriues of assemblies, building from municipal to national level. Radical in the last years of the *ancien régime*, these beliefs made him a political moderate in the context of the revolution. He was, for example, a reluctant convert to universal suffrage, and, despite a brief flirtation with mass democracy in the summer of 1792, remained fundamentally opposed to popular radicalism. On the other hand, he was one of the few politicians in the revolution to call for the extension of the vote to women and was the first leading *philosophe* to declare openly in favour of a republic, in July 1791. Throughout his adult life he campaigned for the abolition of slavery and, throughout the 1780s, for religious toleration. The *Esquisse* which he left behind him after his death was a classic statement of the eighteenth-century belief in human progress which profoundly influenced Saint-Simon and Comte in the nineteenth century.

The standard edition of Condorcet's works is the *Oeuvres de Condorcet* (12 vols., Paris, 1847–9), edited by François Arago and A. Condorcet-O'Connor. The most comprehensive and recent analysis of his ideas is Keith Michael Baker, *Condorcet. From Natural Philosophy to Social*

Mathematics (Chicago and London, 1975), which also contains a comprehensive bibliography. There is also useful information to be gained from Léon Cahen, *Condorcet et la Révolution française* (Paris, 1904), and from Hélène Delsaux, *Condorcet journaliste (1790–1794)* (Paris, 1931).

HUGH GOUGH

COTTA, Friedrich Christoph (1758–1838)
Franco-German Jacobin, journalist and political agitator

Cotta came from a family of Württemberg booksellers and publishers who had lived in Tübingen or Stuttgart (his birthplace) since the seventeenth century; his social background was that of the protestant bourgeoisie. During his law studies at Tübingen and Marburg he specialised in German imperial and state law, and began his writing career with works on the court history of Württemberg, and on topical political themes. During the late eighties he edited the *Stuttgarter Hofzeitung* for his father's publishing house, and taught at the Karlsschule in Stuttgart. At the *Konföderationsfest* in June 1790 he became a corresponding member of the Strasbourg Jacobin Club, and emigrated to Alsace in October 1791, where he took the French oath of allegiance. As an émigré Cotta published the *Straßburger politisches Journal*, best known of all exile publications sympathetic to the revolution to be directed at a German audience during this period.

In November 1792 Cotta joined the French Rhine army and was an active political agitator in the Mainz Republic. In February and March 1793 he was Vice-President and President of the Mainz Jacobin Club. As postmaster general in Mainz he ensured that communication lines were secured for the French occupation army. In the autumn of 1793 Cotta worked in Strasbourg's revolutionary town council, and participated in the persecution of the opponents of the revolution in the *département* of Bas-Rhin; he also worked with surveillance committees. As a member of the German group within the Strasbourg

Jacobin Club he was arrested in connection with the events surrounding the fall of Eulogius Schneider (q.v.) and imprisoned in Paris from January to September 1794. He was released after the 9 Thermidor.

From 1795–1799 Cotta, as a member of the circle around Georg List (q.v.), took an active and politically conspiratorial part in the plans for the foundation of a south German republic. The Directory saw him as a potential member of the government of such a republic, along with List, Linck, Jägerschmidt and others. After attempts at agitation from Basle he returned to Germany with the French army in 1796 and took part in the civil administration of the occupied areas under Haussmann, the government commissar.

After the failure of the occupation he returned to Strasbourg and in December 1796 married Sarah Stamm, the former wife of Eulogius Schneider. They had two children. He continued his republican agitation during trips to southern Germany, and made contact with the opposition in Reutlingen and Esslingen. He opposed the establishment of the Napoleonic system of government in Alsace during the years 1799 and 1800. He returned first to Wissembourg, and then, in 1810, to Germany. In 1815 he took part in the civil administration of the allied occupation armies in Alsace and the Palatinate. From that time until his death in 1838, Cotta lived in Landau and Trippenstadt; he held no more official positions, and effectively played no further part in politics.

As a consequence of his experience of the revolutionary movements in western Europe in 1789, Cotta developed from a publicist with moderate Enlightenment sympathies into one of the foremost critics of the Ancien Régime. In 1790 he planned to found a *Journal für Menschenrechte* as a forum for public criticism of the government in Germany. His Strasbourg contacts influenced him in favour of early French Jacobinism, and in exile he followed the developments in Jacobin ideology, accepting and promoting the ideas of the radical phase (1793). He was an adherent of the neo-Jacobinism which followed the fall of Robespierre (q.v.), but an opponent of Babeuf's (q.v.) left-wing radicalism, and of Napoleon's system of government. Cotta managed to unite journalistic agitation with practical politics. His principal aims were the securing of the republican social and political structure of 1792–1793 in France, and the radicalisation of Germany, even if this was to be through French military rule.

Of Cotta's own writings, the following are the most useful: *Einleitung in das natürliche Staatsrecht mit Anwendung auf das Reich und teutsche Staaten* (Diss., Heidelberg, 1786); *Teutsche Staatsliteratur* (Tübingen/Strasbourg, 1790–1792); Straßburgisches Politisches Journal (Strasbourg, 1792; reprint 1976); *Handwerker- und Bauernkalender des alten Vaters Gerhard* (Mainz, 1793); *Rheinische Zeitung* (with M. Metternich, Strasbourg, 1796); *Eulogius Schneider's Schicksale in Frankreich* (Strasbourg, 1797; reprint ed. by C. Prignitz, 1979.) His correspondence with Schiller was published in a collection edited by W. Vollmer, *Briefwechsel zwischen Schiller und (Joh. Fr.) Cotta* (Stuttgart, 1876), see pp. 379ff; and there are details of his life in volume 4 of the *Allgemeine deutsche Biographie* (Leipzig, 1876). For more recent studies, see C. Träger (ed.), *Mainz zwischen Rot und Schwarz* (Berlin, 1963); H. Scheel (ed.), *Die Mainzer Republik* (2 vols., Berlin, 1975/1981); M. Neugebauer-Wolk, 'Der Bauernkalender des Jakobiners Friedrich Christian Cotta, Realität und Idylle der Mainzer Republik', *Jahrbuch des Instituts für deutsche Geschichte Tel Aviv* (1985); M. Neugebauer-Wolk, Das '*Journal für Menschenrechte*'. Pressepolitik im deutschen Reich 1790/1791', *Das achtzehnte Jahrhundert und Osterreich* (1986).

M. NEUGEBAUER-WOLK

COUTHON, Georges Auguste (1755–1794)
French Jabobin, member of the Committee of Public Safety, terrorist

Couthon was born in Orcet in the Auvergne, the son of a notary and became a lawyer in pre-revolutionary Clermont-Ferrand. He was active in the masonic lodge, the local literary society and in politics, serving as deputy to the Auvergne provincial assembly of 1787. By the time of the revolution Couthon was crippled in both legs by meningitis. Inspired by events in Paris, however, he sought and won election in 1791 to the Legislative Assembly from the department of Puy-de-Dôme (of which Clermont was the capital) and in the following year to the National Convention. In Paris he became an active member of the Jacobin Club and sat with the radical Jacobins who in the Convention became known as the Mountain. On May 31, 1793 it was Couthon who moved the arrest of twenty-two members of the rival Girondist faction, an action supported by the milling crowds who surrounded the Convention. Three days later he was selected to serve on the Committee of Public Safety.

Although a member of the committee, Couthon returned to Clermont as a deputy on mission in late August. His tasks were to subdue nascent rebellion in the surrounding department and raise a military force to participate in the attack on nearby Lyon which was held by Girondist and royalist forces. In both tasks he succeeded, taking command of the Jacobin forces besieging Lyon in time to direct the final assault on October 9. He was directed by the Committee of Public Safety to carry out extensive executions and destruction of rebel property. Instead Couthon took token acts of revenge and tried to repress spontaneous acts of terrorism. He requested and received permission to be relieved of his mission, leaving to other agents of the committee (Collot d'Herbois (q.v.) and Fouché (q.v.)) the task of mass executions.

Couthon returned to Clermont to attempt the transformation of the once recalcitrant department into a miniature Jacobin republic. By and large this took the form of a dechristianisation campaign. Couthon dismissed all members of the clergy including constitutional priests, confiscated gold vessels and other items of wealth still in possession of the Church, ordered the replacement of Sunday worship by the observance of revolutionary *décadis*, and oversaw the destruction of religious relics. He sought moral regeneration in the department on the basis of republican values which would be disseminated through education, publications and various forms of public festivity. To finance the campaign he imposed a special tax on the rich. To improve the condition of the poor and ensure their support for the revolutionary government, he rigidly enforced the Law of the Maximum and regulated the sale of grain.

Much of the work done by Couthon was not in accord with the ideas of Robespierre (q.v.), chief spokesman of the Committee of Public Safety. He was reprimanded by his colleague for his leniency in Lyon. And while Couthon was trying to dechristianise Puy-de-Dôme, Robespierre in Paris was denouncing dechristianisation as a foreign plot. After returning to the capital in November, Couthon adopted Robespierre's view that an overly zealous attack on organised religion was not in the interest of the revolution and supported his colleague's effort to establish a Cult of the Supreme Being.

Although not a Robespierrist in the factional sense, Couthon came to be identified (along with Saint-Just (q.v.)) in the minds of Robespierre's opponents with a Robespierrist triumvirate. Couthon was the speaker who introduced into the Convention the Law of 22 Prairial (June 10, 1794) which dispensed with the remaining legal formalities in the Revolutionary Tribunal. He also played a large part in overseeing the General Police Bureau created in the final months of the terror. Robespierre's enemies in the Committee and the Convention viewed both these acts as a threat to themselves. As a consequence, Couthon was arrested along with Robespierre and Saint-Just on 9 Thermidor (July 27, 1794) and guillotined the next day.

Like Robespierre, Couthon was a stern republican and believer in Jacobin virtue. He believed, as did his more famous colleague, that the future of the republic lay in moral regeneration rather than redistribution of property. Nevertheless, he was also motivated by sincere humanitarian concerns and was more capable than Robespierre of seeing the people as flesh and blood individuals. He worked therefore to alleviate economic distress through price controls and requisitions on the rich.

As a terrorist Couthon was not vindictive. In the three months when he was in personal charge of affairs at Lyon and Clermont, he authorised the execution of only two persons and later he urged mass pardons for peasants who had participated in the Vendéan revolt. He nevertheless introduced the Law of Prairial into the Convention and helped to supervise the terroristic General Police Bureau. Couthon thus bears a share of responsibility for the reign of terror.

Couthon left no writings of importance and his personal actions were not particularly consequential for the revolution. His contribution to the radical tradition is thus largely subsumed in the collective work of the Committee of Public Safety. His correspondence has, however, been published – see F. Mege (ed.), *Documents inédits sur la Révolution française: Correspondance de Georges Couthon* (Paris, 1872), *Le Puy-de-Dôme en 1793 et le proconsulat de Couthon* (Paris, 1877), and *Nouveaux documents sur Georges Couthon* (Clermont-Ferrand, 1899). There is no reputable full biography of Couthon in French or English. The best secondary sources are Robert R. Palmer, *Twelve who ruled: the year of the terror in the French Revolution* (New York, 1969); and G. Bruun, 'The evolution of a terrorist: Georges Auguste Couthon', *Journal of Modern History*, 2 (1930).

JOEL S. CLELAND

DAENDELS, Herman Willem (1762–1818)
Military leader of the Dutch Patriot Movement

Herman Daendels was born in Hattem,

Gelderland, the eighth child of Burchard Johan Daendels, a former mayor of the town. He was educated at the Harderwijk High School and submitted a doctoral dissertation in 1783. His initiation into politics came in 1786 when the burghers of Hattem, together with their contemporaries in several other nearby towns, repudiated the Stadholder's right to make local appointments. Daendels made a name for himself by organising and rallying the morale of the town's two hundred militiamen against the two infantry regiments, sixty cavalry and seventy artillery pieces sent to oppose them. While the defence of the town proved an impossible task, with the defenders fleeing to Kampen and Zwolle, Daendels' military career had begun. A year later he commanded a Gelderland brigade against the Duke of Brunswick's forces during the Patriot Revolt. His conduct and contribution to the revolt was more than enough to make exile imperative when the Stadholder was restored in 1787. He was tried in absentia by the Courts in Gelderland and sentenced to perpetual exile on pain of death should he decide to return.

As a result of his experiences, Daendels became an implacable enemy of the House of Orange and the Dutch aristocracy. Much of his exile was spent in St Omer where he set up in business with a fellow countryman, importing goods into France. At this stage, Daendels was firmly convinced that the only way to bring change to the Republic was with French military help. To this end, he was instrumental in the formation of a Dutch battalion. Known as the 'Free Foreign Legion', it fought alongside General Dumouriez' troops in the ill-fated invasion of 1792. Even in defeat, Daendels' characteristic single-mindedness was evident in the impromptu sortie carried out against the town of Dordrecht with a mere 800 infantry and 100 cavalry.

After the disaster, Daendels continued to press the French to mount a second campaign and acted as intermediary between the French authorities and Patriot interests inside the Republic. The second

invasion under General Pichegru, with Daendels as General commanding the Northern Army, took place in 1794 and met with more success. Daendels took a great deal of credit for the successful besieging of 's-Hertogenbosch but then angered his French allies by issuing a strongly anti-aristocratic manifesto to the people of Gelderland and Overijssel, urging them to take up arms to free the country. The manifesto offended the French mainly because it called on the principles of liberty and freedom – principles which the invading French were perhaps unwilling to concede to an occupied Netherlands.

Daendels was far too impetuous and outspoken for the more conservative French generals. Pichegru even tried to have him transferred to the French Army of the Pyrenees but when this failed, made sure that he was posted to the operations against Holland rather than to the front adjacent to his native Gelderland. After the French victory and the establishment of the Batavian Republic, Daendels as a lieutenant-general was involved in the formation of a republican army under French tutelage and helped to plan expeditions to Germany and to Ireland – neither of which came to fruition.

In 1798 he was instrumental, together with French agent Delacroix and General Joubert, in bringing the extreme unitarist faction of the Patriots to power in the bloodless coup of 22 January. The short-lived Directory of Five soon alarmed both Daendels and its French supporters. In turning against the Directory, Daendels may have been upset by the lack of recognition given to his military exploits but was also undoubtedly appalled by the activities of the purging commissions in the provinces. On 16 May he made his criticisms of the Directors and Delacroix public before fleeing to France. Once there, he was able to engineer Delacroix' dismissal and then returned to the Netherlands via Antwerp. On arrival in The Hague, he was greeted by cheering crowds and by 12 June, the Directory had effectively been deposed.

Daendels continued his military career with the Republic, again serving under French command. A good deal of his popularity disappeared after the Anglo-Russian invasion of North Holland in 1799, and in 1800 he received two years leave. Two years later, he was given an honourable discharge from the army but returned to serve Louis Napoleon as governor of East Friesland and then as governor of the Dutch East Indies. Returning to France in 1811, he fought in Napoleon's Russian campaign before being captured by Russian forces. Soon afterwards, he managed to ingratiate himself with the Prince of Orange who appointed him governor of the Guinea Coast – where he died in 1818.

Daendels was by no means a great theorist of the Patriot movement, yet his espousal of the twin principles of liberty and freedom against the authority of the Stadholder made him an essential part of the movement. His habit of 'acting first and thinking afterwards' made him an impetuous ally and colleague, but his firm opposition to the Stadholderate and military prowess was largely instrumental in bringing about the French invasion of 1794 and the establishment of the Batavian Republic. Moreover, he was to play the leading role in the establishment and later the dissolution of the unitarist Directory of 1798. Thus his part in the crucial events of the Batavian Republic make him a key figure in the development of Dutch political radicalism in the latter part of the eighteenth century.

Information on Daendels' life is available in a number of old Dutch secondary sources: I. Mendels, *Herman Willem Daendels, voor zinje benoeming tot Gouverneur-Generaal van Oost-Indië 1762–1807* (The Hague, 1890); H.T. Colenbrander, *De Patriottentijd, hoofdzakelijk naar buitenlandsche bescheiden* (The Hague, 1897–98); H.T. Colenbrander, *De Bataafsche Republiek* (Amsterdam, 1908); and P.J. Blok and P.C. Molhuysen, *Nieuw Nederlandsch Biografisch Woordenboek* (Leiden, 1911–37). The best and most recent account of the Dutch Patriot movement is S. Schama, *Patriots and liberators* (New York, 1977).

BOB MOORE

DANTON, Georges Jacques (1759–1794)
French revolutionary leader, popular orator, deputy to the National Convention, and member of the Committee of Public Safety

Danton was born in Arcis sur Aube, Champagne. His grandfather had been a farmer, but his father, who died when Danton was only three, was a lawyer of some substance. Danton himself, on the eve of the revolution, had the appearance of being a well-established lawyer, thanks mainly to his marriage to Gabrielle Charpentier. Danton trained as a lawyer, went to Paris in 1780, but received his lawyer's certificate at Rheims. In 1787 he bought the office of *avocat aux Conseils du Roi* for 78,000 *livres* – the first of many financial transactions that would later take on suspicious overtones. Shortly after this he married Gabrielle.

Little is known of Danton's activities in 1789. He did not bask in a classical education like so many other future revolutionaries, although he was well-educated in the writings of the philosophers and many British writers. Nor does Danton appear to have been consumed with ambition, being apparently satisfied with his prospects of a successful law career in Paris. Like so many other provincials of middle-class origins, however, he could not remain unmoved by the events of July 1789. On 16 July he led a company of National Guards from the Cordeliers to the Bastille, and by the end of the year he had established himself as a popular leader in what was to be the most radical of the Paris districts, the Cordeliers. It was here that Marat (q.v.), on the run from the Paris Municipality, sought protection, and where Danton resisted Lafayette and 3,000 National Guards who came to arrest Marat on January 22, 1790. In March, Danton was in turn arraigned for this, but escaped unharmed while his reputation received a further boost. When the Cordelier district was broken up by the creation of the

Sections in the middle of 1790, partly to destroy its power, the activists of the former District founded the Cordelier Club. However, the new club lost some of its leverage through being part of the Paris administration, and could only act as a pressure group. Danton retained his links with the Cordeliers where he had created a most responsive political machine, but in the meantime he had joined the Jacobin Club and it was here that he was more frequently to be found, usually attacking Lafayette and Sieyès (q.v.). Later in the year, after humiliating defeats in the elections for the Paris mayoralty and Paris Commune, Danton was elected to the Department, in theory superior to the Paris municipality and which also took under its jurisdiction part of the surrounding countryside.

The king's flight in July 1791 brought its own crisis for Danton. Until then he had sought to maintain his reputation as a popular leader without frightening the more powerful bourgeois through whom his personal ambitions could be realised. Now he tried to maintain his power base in the Cordelier Club which favoured tough action against the king, even calling for the Republic, and in the Jacobin Club, which wanted to retain the king and the constitutional monarchy and so sought to overlook the king's perjury and treachery. Ultimately, however, Danton sided with the Cordeliers and the radical Jacobins. But friends among the conservative Jacobins (Duport and Lameth) who were about to break away and found the Feuillant Club, warned him of the approaching showdown with the radicals. Thus, when the petitioners on the Champ de Mars were massacred by Lafayette's National Guard, Danton was on his way to his native Arcis and from there, possibly, to England.

Danton was unsuccessful in the elections for the Legislative Assembly in September 1791, did not contest the position of Mayor of Paris won by Pétion (q.v.) shortly after that, failed to get elected *procureur* to the Paris Commune in November 1791, but the following month he was successful in the election as one of Manuel's (q.v.) deputies on the Paris Commune. It was in the crisis leading up to the dethronement of the king in August 1792, but more particularly in the defence of Paris in the weeks following this event, that Danton was to come into his own. Danton's actual participation in the organisation of the insurrection of 10 August is not clear, but it must have been significant, for within twenty-four hours of the successful attack on the Tuileries, Danton was appointed Minister for Justice. In this role he directed the search for royalists which swelled the prisons and raised fears of a break-out at a time when the Prussian army was marching on Paris. Such fears lay behind the September massacre that broke out on September 2, the same day Verdun fell. No more than any other Paris administrator could Danton have stopped the bloodshed, but more than most did he accept the insult or threat of *buveur de sang*. Although he was officially Minister for Justice, Danton was equally involved with the war ministry. It was he, more than any other individual, who roused the patriotism that sent thousands of young Parisians off to join the army. The massacre of prisoners who might have escaped to attack Paris when it was emptied of all its young men (who had left for the war front) was a secondary consideration. On the day the massacres began, Danton made his famous call to arms: 'The tocsin that will ring is no signal of alarm; it is sounding the charge against the enemies of the nation. In order to defeat them, Messieurs, all that we need is audacity, more audacity, and still more audacity, and France will be saved.' The advance of the Prussians was halted at Valmy and, according to Goethe, a new episode had been written into the history of mankind.

Danton now took his seat with the Mountain in the newly-convoked National Convention. From the start he was accused of forming a triumvirate with Marat and Robespierre (q.v.), but all he shared with them was a passionate commitment to keep the revolution safe from its enemies: he shared neither the wild hatreds of Marat nor the cold logic of Robespierre. In the faction fights against the Girondins he frequently tried to effect a compromise, but they made this impossible. In particular the old charges of corruption were brought up again.

On November 30, 1792 Danton was sent to Belgium to investigate and report on the army. On January 31, 1793 he was sent there again, a trip cut short by the death of his wife in early February, but after a few days in Paris he returned to the army under Dumouriez. On 5 March he was sent back to Paris by the Commission of the Representatives, with Delacroix, to request urgent measures. Danton, unaware or unconcerned about Dumouriez's royalism, expressed his complete confidence in him. On March 12 Dumouriez sent a letter to the Convention expressing his discontent with the revolution, and threatening to march on Paris. Danton and Delacroix were sent to Dumouriez to demand a retraction. In the meantime the general's letter had been made public to be followed by his desertion to the enemy on April 5, 1793. Danton made a speech on 27 March demanding every Frenchman be given a pike at the expense of the rich; that anyone preaching counter-revolution be made an outlaw; and that the revolutionary tribunal be installed immediately. He thus tried to deflect from himself criticisms about his association with Dumouriez, but the Girondins attacked him for failing to denounce Dumouriez and demanded that he account for all his expenditure in Belgium. In his great speech of 1 April he made his final break with the Girondins as he faced the Mountain and admitted that they had judged their adversaries better than he had. He sat down to a great ovation, having weathered the storm, but some more mud had stuck.

On 10 March Danton had called for the creation of a revolutionary tribunal, and the following day he advocated that the Convention be allowed to choose its own ministers, insisting at the same time that he would never accept such a position for himself. On 7 April he entered the first Committee of Public Safety. A week later

he opposed a proposed decree offering assistance to any people that wanted to resist the oppression of its tyrants, proclaiming his belief that it was more important that the Republic be consolidated in France before it went off to help revolutions in China or elsewhere. If France was to win people over to liberty and reason it should do so by its example and its own energy. Danton's good sense carried the day.

In May Girondins approached Danton for his help, but he did not trust them. He did nothing to assist them in the insurrection of May 31/June 2, 1793. Just as on the eve of the Champ de Mars massacre Danton had wanted to keep in touch with the popular base in the Cordeliers and the more reactionary bourgeois, but was forced by the former to side with the latter, so he was forced by the Girondins to align himself unequivocally with the Jacobins.

With the suppression of the Girondins the national government faced two major problems; first to bring the rest of France to accept the coup of June 1793; and second to halt and reverse the worsening military situation. On the first Danton was well placed as a man of the centre to inspire confidence; but his methods of conciliation and a willingness to buy off opposition rather than crush it with military might did not always appeal to the ideologues. He met similar problems when it came to the war effort, where he sought conciliation and compromise rather than *guerre à outrance*. In the meantime his contact with Great Britain whom he thought could be bought out of the Coalition and the possible use of Marie Antoinette as a card to gamble with in his dealings with Austria, added to the suspicions of his enemies without in any way helping the war effort. In the end all he managed was an insignificant treaty of peace with Sweden. Danton's policies on the Committee of Public Safety were a failure; revolts in the provinces worsened and the major powers in the coalition were not to be bought off. Salvation could only come from an alliance with the radicals, and Danton was not yet prepared for this.

This is not to say that Danton had spurned any appeals to the people. Thus he enthusiastically supported delegates from the primary assemblies when, on the occasion of the anniversary of the fall of the monarchy on August 10, 1793, they came to the Convention to decree the *levée en masse* and the arrest of suspects. He declared that, 'the delegates of the primary assemblies have come to exhort us to instigate terror against our internal enemies. Let there be no amnesty for any traitor. Let us mark popular vengeance by bringing down the sword of the law on the conspirators of the interior. . .'. Immediately after this the decree of the *levée en masse* was passed. Danton approved the measures taken at Marseilles when Carteaux's army entered the rebel town, then as a member of a commission set up to bring about a law of subsistence he proposed a nationwide maximum price of fourteen *livres* per quintal on wheat. He also supported the appeals for the formation of a Revolutionary Army, although again the rhetoric of his oratory masked the impracticability of his suggestions, and hence its more apparent than actual radicalism. On September 4 he decreed that arm-makers work day and night until every sans-culotte in the Republic had his own musket; that an end be made to the lethargy of the revolutionary tribunal; and that every day an aristocrat or a criminal pay with his head for his crimes.

Despite this the revolution was heading in a direction that did not please Danton. Sick in body and uneasy in mind, he sought leave from the Convention and retired to his native Arcis. There he stayed from 12 October to 21 November, while the machinery of the terror tightened and the enemies of the revolution broadened to include those who were not fanatical enough in their revolutionary expression. Danton returned to the fray, but his absence from the centre of affairs left him at a disadvantage. His final campaign was to end in his death.

In this last episode in his life Danton seems to have been firmly committed to a policy of moderation and conciliation, without any demagogic outbursts to keep in favour with the radicals – indeed it was not until the day before his execution that the great voice had to be silenced for fear of its power in evoking the support of the people. The main organ of Danton's appeal for clemency for the innocent victims of the terror, particularly of the law of suspects, was Camille Desmoulins' (q.v.) *Vieux Cordelier*, which opened its short but illustrious career with the support of Robespierre and a scathing attack on the 'new Cordeliers', Hébert (q.v.) and his faction. Unfortunately Danton's past obscured his motives, and his friendship for colleagues who were simply swindlers brought suspicions on himself. He was right to bewail the personal disputes that racked the Convention when the enemy was at the door and the pointlessness of the dechristianisation campaign, but his defence of Philippeaux (q.v.) was for a man whose conduct in the Vendée was suspect, while his defence of Fabre d'Eglantine (q.v.) on January 13, 1794 was for a friend who was inextricably involved in the East India Company scandal. In reply the Hébertistes, or 'ultras', attacked Danton, warning him of the fate of those who stood beside Fabre or were his dupes. In these disputes Robespierre supported Danton, but when the Hébertistes were purged (March 24, 1794) that support ended. Now Robespierre supplied Saint-Just (q.v.) with the notes that he incorporated into his speech calling for the arrest of Danton and his faction. The trial and death of Danton have been described many times. He was guillotined on 16 Germinal Year II.

Danton's role in the revolution was almost entirely that of activist, and as such he has left behind little in the way of letters, diaries, speeches or newspaper articles. His lust for life and the powerful figure he cut in the clubs or the assemblies, with his huge voice and pockmarked face, made him a popular figure at the time and also in the eyes of biographers and, more recently, film-makers. At the same time the characteristics that made him a popular leader roused suspicion in the minds of the colder idealists who wanted everyone to conform to their ideals of the pure society. Certainly Danton loved life too much to hold hatreds too closely, and his friendships did not always have the seal of revolutionary approval; above all he allowed his friendships to affect his behaviour in political situations and he did not scrutinise too carefully the use made of revolutionary funds by friends who were outright crooks. He might even have allowed some of this money to find its way into his own pockets. He probably accepted money from the court, but if he was paid he certainly was not bought. Whatever the facts of his personal life, whatever the motives that led him to seek the escape of the queen in June 1793, and whatever one thinks of the timing and motives behind his attacks on the terror in late 1793, Danton emerges from the French Revolution as one of the truly great leaders of the people.

Most of what has been written on Danton has centred around the disputes of the two great academics of the French Revolution, Aulard who took his defence, and Mathiez who uncovered every scrap of evidence that could be used against him. The best survey of Danton's motives and venality is in Norman Hampson's biography, *Danton* (London, 1978). There have been many other biographies in English, but no other serious studies. See, however, L. Madelin, *Danton* (1914; tr. London, 1921), L. Barthou, *Danton* (Paris, 1932), and H. Wendel, *Danton* (1932; tr. London, 1936). A collection of some of his speeches has been translated and published in the series 'Voices of Revolt', vol. V: *Speeches of Georges Jacques Danton* (New York, 1928).

BILL MURRAY

DESMOULINS, Lucie Camille Simplice (1760–1794)

French radical journalist, Cordelier, and Montagnard

Desmoulins was born at Guise in the Aisne Department into a comfortable family where his father held a high position in the law. He retained throughout his life a close attachment to his family, although they were often to be embarrassed by the extreme radicalism of much of what he wrote. From his earliest days at the Louis-le-Grand College, where he shared classes with Robespierre (q.v.), Fréron (q.v.) and other revolutionaries to be, and was a close friend of the future counter-revolutionary, François Suleau, Desmoulins combined precocious talents with a burning ambition to make a name for himself, in conscious imitation of the Roman heroes he read about and studied. He left Louis-le-Grand in 1784, after having won several prizes, but a speech defect limited his ambitions in the legal field, and he turned to writing.

It was as a revolutionary agitator, on July 12, 1789, that Desmoulins made his first significant entry on to the revolutionary stage. It was he who is said to have leapt on to a table in the Palais-Royal and harangued the crowds gathered there about the fate of the newly proclaimed National Assembly and the people of Paris, presaged by the dismissal of Necker by the king. He urged the patriots to defend themselves, taking green ribbons (or leaves from the trees) to distinguish themselves. To the cries of: 'Aux armes, citoyens!' thousands took off in the search for arms which led to the Invalides and from there back to the Bastille, which capitulated on 14 July. Much myth has grown up around that event, but Desmoulins' role, much though he may have embellished it, was significant. Having played his part as a street-agitator Desmoulins returned to that for which he was much better fitted, pamphleteer and journalist, a role which he carried out brilliantly.

Even before the events of July, Camille had written *Free France*, a pamphlet noted for its strong anti-monarchical passages. It did not appear until a few days after the fall of the Bastille, however, but when it did it brought him immediate popularity and to the attention of some of the leading revolutionaries. In September he followed this with his *Speeches from the Streetlamps to the People of Paris*, evoking in the title the image of the public facility that had served as the instrument of popular justice in the punishment of counter-revolutionaries. Less successful than his first pamphlet, it nevertheless laid the foundation for Desmoulins' career as a journalist, and from the end of September until just after the Champ de Mars massacre he brought out his weekly *Révolutions de France et de Brabant*. This paper had an immediate success, expressing the most extreme revolutionary ideas with a wit, satire and scurrility that could be matched only among the journalists of the right. In his attacks on the monarchy Desmoulins was in advance of his time, complaining frequently about the lack of support he had from fellow revolutionaries in this regard. He had more support for his attacks on the other less democratic aspects of the Constitution being written by the National Assembly, particularly the franchise restrictions.

At this time Desmoulins became a leader among the Cordeliers, making friends with Danton (q.v.) in particular. He was involved in the events following the flight of the king and, unlike many other radical journalists, he did not have to retract anything he had said about the monarchy. He was one of the many journalists forced into hiding after the Champ de Mars massacre, as a result of which he brought his newspaper to a close, advising his subscribers that he had passed over their subscriptions to the *Révolutions de Paris*. In April 1792 he returned to journalism when he brought out in association with Fréron, the *Tribune des patriotes*, of which, however, only four issues were published.

In the National Convention, to which Desmoulins was elected by the electors of Paris, he sat with the Mountain, but again his only significant contributions were in writing. Two of his pamphlets were violent tracts against the Girondins: *Jean-Pierre Brissot Unmasked* and *A Fragment from the Secret History of the Revolution*. When the Girondins were executed Desmoulins' reaction was fairly typical: he wept and uttered his *mea culpa*, at the same time regretting his uncontrollable rush to print

and revealing an over-exaggerated opinon of the effect of such writings. His next major excursion into literature, however, was more carefully considered, and remains as one of the great gestures of the revolution: his *Vieux Cordelier* heavily influenced by Danton is as much a monument to his courage as his literary gifts. Six numbers of this paper appeared in Desmoulins' lifetime, and the first two, issued with the approval of Robespierre, were directed mainly against the Hébertists. The famous No. 3, however, was an appeal to relax the terror, under the guise of a translation from Tacitus. This theme was followed up in the next number, but No. 5 returned to an attack on Hébert (q.v.) and included explanations of Desmoulins' attitudes. By this time he was too deeply embroiled in the politics of the 'Ultras' and the 'Citras' acting as a major spokesman for the Dantonist 'appeasers'. As such he shared their fate and was guillotined in 1794.

Desmoulins was one of the most prominent of the radicals from the early days of the revolution, but he was not an activist, nor did he develop any clear revolutionary policies. His role was that of journalist and watchdog of the enemies of the revolution, most notable of whom were the bourgeois reactionaries attacked with equal fervour, if with less skill, by Marat and Fréron (q.v.). As one of the first exponents of republicanism, however, Desmoulins deserves a special place. For the most part, however, he was the outlet for other people's ideas.

Further details of Desmoulins' life can be found in J. Claretie, *Camille Desmoulins, Lucile Desmoulins. Etude sur les Dantonistes* (Paris, 1875; trans. as *Camilles Demoulins and his wife*, London, 1876); and J. Janssens, *Camille Desmoulins, le premier républicain de France* (Paris, 1973).
BILL MURRAY

DIRNBÖCK, Georg Franz (1766–?)
*Radical Josephinian civil servant and
democratic agitator; adherent of the
ideas of the Enlightenment and natural
religion*

Georg Franz Dirnböck was born in 1766
in Altenmarkt in Untersteyer, and underwent a Roman Catholic school education.
He went on to study law and philosophy
at Graz under Franz Xavier von Neupauer,
professor of canon law at the university,
and a man with progressive ideas about
religion. Following his graduation in 1788
he became an adherent of the group around
the professor. He then went on to Stift St
Paul in Carinthia and Warasdin in Croatia.
In 1788 he became syndic (secretary to the
magistrates) of Knittelfeld, a small town
in Styria, at a time when there was
considerable agitation on the part of both
the peasants and the small town burghers of
the province against the local aristocracy.
Dirnböck himself, like many other Josephinian civil servants, did all he could to
prevent the aristocracy making greater
demands on the peasants.

In Knittelfeld he became a good friend
of the mayor Joseph Wenninger (q.v.),
whom he had also known in Graz. Wenninger was a leading figure in the popular
agitation of the period, and had taken the
grievances of the Styrian burghers and
peasants to Vienna, and presented them
in a petition at court. It was through
Wenninger that Dirnböck became involved
with a group of Styrian Jacobins who were
based in Knittelfeld and had connections
in Vienna.

During the early 1790s Dirnböck undertook two journeys to Vienna (in 1793 and
July 1794), where he made contact with
Viennese Jacobins. The Styrian and Viennese groups discussed politics and found
that they had much in common. Among
the Viennese group was a young doctor,
Ignaz Menz, a Styrian by birth who, like
Dirnböck, had studied philosophy at Graz,
and only recently moved to Vienna to take
up medicine. Menz was one of the more
enthusiastic of the democrats, and had,
with others, devised an oath of loyalty

to the principles of nature, reason and
freedom. During Dirnböck's second trip
to Vienna members of both groups made
an excursion to the Brühl, near Mödling,
south of the city. Here they held an oath-
taking ceremony, which seems to have
been a unique occasion. As word of the
ceremony spread among radicals in Vienna
the participants came under the suspicion
of the authorities, who managed to extract
a confession and the names of all the
other participants from one of the younger
members. All the Viennese members of
the group were arrested immediately.
Dirnböck was arrested on March 27, 1795,
along with Thadäus Wipplinger, a Knittelfeld merchant who had also taken part in
the oath, and taken to Vienna to be
questioned and stand trial.

Despite claims from some of the participants, including Dirnböck himself, that the
oath had been a joke, the authorities were
convinced that it was meant seriously and
was an indication of the democratic and
even revolutionary intentions of those
involved. (Dirnböck himself had mentioned the possibility of revolution.)
Dirnböck was charged with participation
in the ceremony and the dissemination of
seditious material. He made a voluntary
and repentant confession, which implicated
others, including Wenninger, and was sentenced to thirty years in prison; thereafter
he disappears from the record.

Dirnböck was a radical from his days at
Graz university. He settled well into the
intellectual and political atmosphere of
Upper Styria, where the church was losing
its grip and local people were organising
against the province's aristocracy and
against the war with France. He was a
keen participant in political discussion and
popular agitation both in Styria and Vienna.

Biographical details of the leading Styrian radicals are contained in Elisabeth
Führer's doctoral thesis, *Jakobiner in der
Steiermark* (Phil. Diss., Vienna 1965),
which also gives a thorough account of the
events surrounding the 'Styrian complicity'
and the 'oath in the Brühl'. These events
are placed in the wider context of reform

and radicalism in the Habsburg empire by Ernst Wangermann, *From Joseph II to the Jacobin Trials. Government Policy and Public Opinion in the Habsburg Dominions in the Period of the French Revolution* (Oxford, 1959). Also useful is Helmut Reinalter (ed.), *Jakobiner in Mitteleuropa* (Innsbruck, 1977).

TIM KIRK

DOLIVIER, Pierre (1746–?)
French curé whose writings advanced proto-socialist ideas

Dolivier was born in Neschers in the Puy-de-Dôme, where his father was a notary. In 1777 he was forced to leave his diocese in the Auvergne because of a speech he had made 'on the abuse of popular devotions'. This was published in 1788 (*Discours sur l'abus des dévotions populaires*). On the eve of the revolution he was active in producing brochures from his diocese near Paris (Mauchamps) where he had been a curé since 1785. In these brochures he advocated the abolition of the three orders. It was not until April 1792, however, that his fame spread beyond local confines, with his petition to the Jacobin Club and the Legislative Assembly – *Petition from forty citizens of Mauchamps (and the communes close to Etampes) who had the good fortune not to be in any way mixed up in the unfortunate affair*. The 'affair' referred to was a significant incident in the unrest sweeping over the countryside around Paris in the early months of 1792, as adherents of liberal economic policies tried to maintain their principles in the face of ruinous rises in the price of essential foodstuffs. On March 3, 1792 Simmoneau, the mayor of Etampes, in an attempt to resist popular price fixing, during which he twice called on troops to fire on the demonstrators, was himself beaten to death. The government sent in troops to restore order, but met with many difficulties in trying to bring the culprits to trial, in part because of the sympathy of the locals for the murderers, in part because of the fear of reprisals. The Legislative Assembly itself inaugurated a Festival of Liberty to honour the mayor of Etampes (April 1792) which had a qualified success, and initially at least the Jacobin Club and other radical leaders showed little sympathy for Simmoneau's killers. For this reason Dolivier's petition was passed over or dismissed at the time, particularly since it espoused the notions of direct democracy that would constitute a threat to Jacobin rule over a year later, and which, moreover, set forth ideals that anticipated a radical change in property relations.

Dolivier depicted Simmoneau, the murdered mayor, as a 'hero to the grain merchants, who died a victim of their inhuman and selfish speculations' and tapped popular beliefs about hoarders and speculators, who were, he said, supported by officials who 'couldn't care less' about ordinary folk. From this traditional belief in the right to subsistence, Dolivier went on to claim that: 'The benefits of society ought principally to fall to the man who contributes to society the most laborious and constant services.' For him then, working men were the heart of any society, while rich speculators were parasites, against whose greed the poor had to be protected. From 'consumers' rights' he went on to proclaim that a society that excluded sections of the population from political participation could not expect those excluded to abide by the system of justice set up by that society: for justice to be accepted by all it had to be 'absolutely universal'. Dolivier, then, was advancing beyond 'moral economy' arguments to a plea for the poor to exert a positive force in their political destinies. From this he went further to attack existing property relations. He claimed that the nation was the only true owner of its terrain, and so could not accord rights to proprietors which in turn deprived those without property of such rights. Property could only be held in private hands if it had the approval of society as a whole. This could only be done in a society where all the citizens of France who had made the revolution created a new set of institutions for their self-government. In conclusion he reminded his listeners of Rousseau's aphorism that *whoever eats bread that he has not earned steals that bread* but then, no doubt aware that he might be stretching the patience of his bourgeois audience, ended with a plea to bring to an end the terror the central government was waging against the people of Etampes. By that time the government was at war with Europe and the Legislative Assembly was divided between those who saw the real threat as coming from beyond France's borders and those who continued to see it as coming from within, an issue that was only partly resolved by the insurrection of August 10, 1792.

Dolivier married Marie Chausson on November 12, 1792 and had one child by her. He served the government during the Convention and in 1793 published an *Essay on primitive justice, to serve as the essential principle for the only social order that can assure all the rights of man and all the means by which he can achieve happiness*. This essay, which was in the possession of Babeuf (q.v.) when he was arrested, proclaimed that the earth belonged to all people in general and none in particular, that each person had the exclusive right to the fruits of his labour, which he was free to dispose of as he wished, and that the only property that could be passed on was personal property. He became a teacher during the Directory, published the occasional brochure, and although he distrusted military might, he voted for the Constitution of the Year VIII. Thereafter little is known of him, including the year of his death.

Dolivier is chiefly to be remembered for his defence of the assassins of the mayor of Etampes in 1792 and the fact that he not only defended the need for controls on prices but went on to challenge existing property relations and to advocate a social order essentially based on proto-socialist principles.

There is no full biography of Dolivier, but in addition to the short entries in the standard biographical dictionaries of the revolution, see David Hunt, 'The people and Pierre Dolivier: Popular uprisings in the Seine-et-Oise Department (1791–1792)', *French Historical Studies*, XI, No. 2, (Fall 1979), pp. 184–214.

BILL MURRAY

DORSCH, Anton Joseph (1758–1819)
German Jacobin and revolutionary democrat

Anton Joseph Dorsch was born in Heppenheim in 1758 of a family of civil servants. After studying theology he became a priest and went to Paris in 1783 to continue his studies. His name is to be found on the list of Illuminati in 1784, and at this time he belonged to the party of Enlightenment reformists. Following a journey to England in 1786, from which a prolific correspondence with Johannes von Müller remains, he became a lecturer in philosophy at Mainz University. Along with Wedekind (q.v.) and Blau he was persecuted as an Illuminatus and had difficulties with the orthodox because he taught the philosophy of Kant (q.v.).

In 1791 he went with his wife to Strasbourg, probably at the request of Eulogius Schneider (q.v.). Here he taught ethics at the Seminary, addressed the Jacobin Club, and occupied himself with questions of educational organisation. Following the occupation of Mainz by the troops of General Custine he was invited to return to the city as president of the General Administration. After arriving in Mainz on November 3, 1792 he clashed with several of his former colleagues, and experienced difficulties with the more virtuous and less opportunist Hofmann (q.v.). After the Convention elections Hofmann gained preference because of his integrity and Dorsch played a more modest part. On 30 March he left Mainz again for Paris, from where he was sent to Switzerland to negotiate that country's incorporation into the Republic. When Switzerland was divided into four *départements* he was given the important post of Commissar of the Directory. He became Under-prefect [*Sous-préfet*] at Cleves in 1800, director of taxes at Finisterre in 1805, and director of taxes at Münster under King Jerome in 1811. He felt so strongly tied to France that he returned after the defeat of Napoleon, but he was no longer happy there. He died in 1819.

His firm adherence to Kant's philosophies led to difficulties in Mainz; he was defrocked and married his mistress, which earned him a bad name and resulted in rumours of all kinds. However, he did distinguish between liberty and dissoluteness in his philosophy. He explained that obedience to the law and the idea of freedom were compatible if the laws were made by the representatives of the people. In his speeches he sought to persuade his audience by argument, for he believed that the strength of an administration rests on public opinion. The real enemies were those tyrants who wanted war because they were not prepared to tolerate the triumph of a revolution based on popular rights. The uprising of a down-trodden people was dreadful for the oppressors. The French had seen that monarchy was a poisonous plant in the soil of liberty and had uprooted it. Soon all enlightened nations would welcome the fall of kings. He sought to convince his audience that the 'Francs' had saved Mainz and that it was now important to assist in the establishment of liberty. In France the people's societies had been most effective and Dorsch expected the Jacobin Club to serve the same function and enable freedom to be established once and for all. From the outset he was in favour of the incorporation of the left bank into the French Republic and defended the idea of rivers as natural borders. In 1797 he again defended the annexation against Rebmann (q.v.) and Goerres (q.v.), who wanted to establish an independent republic on the left bank.

This Rhineland Jacobin was therefore a truly unambiguous revolutionary democrat. He wanted a German revolution on the French model and had no reservations about the course of events in France. His great adaptability and opportunism enabled him to serve under all the régimes in France, even after the fall of Napoleon.

Yet in spite of his opportunism he was never tempted to compromise with the German princes.

Dorsch's political opinions are evident in a number of his own writings most notably: A.J. Dorsch, *Anrede an die neue gebildete Gesellschaft der Freunde der Freiheit und Gleichheit in Mainz* (Mainz, 1792); *Bekanntmachung an die Bürger und Bewohner wegen Abstellung aller Menschen und Bürger erniedrigen Ausdrücke in Bittschriften, Vorstellungen und Berichten an irgendeine Verwaltung des Erzbisthums Mainz und der Bisthümer Worms und Speier* (Mainz, 1792); *Antrittsrede zu seiner Ernennung zum Präsidenten der Zentralverwaltung* (Mainz, 1794); 'Rede bei der Gedächtnisfeier der Hinrichtung Ludwigs des sechzehnten', *Aachener Zuschauer*, No. 10 (1795), p. 79. See also the short biography by H. Mathy, 'Anton Joseph Dorsch (1756–1819). Leben und Werk eines rheinischen Jakobiners', *Mainzer Zeitschrift*, 62 (Mainz, 1967).

M. GILLI

DROUET, Jean Baptiste (1763–1824)
French Jacobin, member of the National Convention, famous for apprehending Louis XVI at Varennes.

Drouet was born at Sainte-Menehould (Marne), the son of a wood merchant. He studied at the collège de Châlons and served in the army from 1779 to 1784. He was postmaster at Sainte-Menehould at the time of Louis' attempted flight from France, and he recognised the king from his likeness on the currency. Drouet hurried ahead of the royal party by an alternative route to Varennes where he alerted the authorities and secured the king's arrest. As a result he was fêted in Paris, achieved national fame, and was launched on a political career. The National Assembly voted him a reward of 30,000 *livres*, but there is some dispute among his biographers as to whether he accepted the money.

In September 1791 he was elected as an alternate deputy for the Marne to the Legislative Assembly but never actually sat there. A year later, however, he was elected by the same department to the Convention and sat with the Mountain. He joined the Jacobin Club and became a member of the Committee of Public Safety. At the king's trial he voted against an appeal to the people, for the death-penalty and against a reprieve.

In March 1793 Drouet was sent on a recruitment mission to the Marne and the Meuse. On his return to the Convention he took a leading role in the factional struggles against the Girondins. In September he was sent on mission to the army of the North and was trapped in the siege at Maubeuge. In leading a daring attempt to break-out, his horse was killed and Drouet was taken prisoner by the Austrians. He was recognised as the captor of Louis XVI and badly treated during his imprisonment. But, true to character, he attempted on July 6, 1794 to escape from the fortress at Spielberg by making a parachute out of sheets and jumping from his cell window. Unfortunately he broke his leg and was recaptured. He was released with other prisoners in November 1795 in exchange for Louis' daughter.

Drouet was elected to the Council of 500 for the Nord, and did not attempt to conceal his Robespierrist sympathies. He tried to establish links between his Montagnard colleagues and the Babouvistes and was arrested on 21 Floréal Year IV (May 10, 1796). The move against Drouet was by no means popular and it seems likely therefore that the government, through the agency of Barras, engineered his escape on 1 Fructidor (August 18). He travelled first to Switzerland and then overseas. He was tried in absentia by the High Court of Vendôme and acquitted. He returned to France from the Canary Isles in October 1797.

He re-joined the left Republicans and organised them into the Society of the Manège in Messidor Year VII. On 2 Thermidor (July 20, 1799) he was appointed commissioner of the Directory to the department of the Marne. Later he became subprefect of Sainte-Menehould, held this post until the first Restoration, and was named to the Legion of Honour

in 1807. Napoleon is alleged to have told him: 'Monsieur Drouet, you have changed the face of the world.' He was again decorated in 1814 for organising resistance to the invasion in the Argonne. In the Hundred Days he was elected deputy for Sainte-Menehould. In 1816 he was exiled as a regicide but assumed a false identity and settled in Mâcon where he died in 1824.

Although it was chance that thrust Drouet on to the national stage, he thereafter performed his revolutionary role with zeal and panache. He was no political thinker but an activist with a capacity for leadership and daring that made him a popular figure and something of a folk hero – 'un homme du peuple', as his biographers dubbed him.

The standard biographies are G. Benoit-Guyod, *Qu'est devenu Drouet, l'homme de Varennes?* (Paris, 1946); and H. Manèvy and R. Vailland, *Un homme du peuple sous la Révolution* (Paris, 1947). See also A. Kuscinski, *Dictionnaire des conventionnels* (Paris, 1917); and S. Scott and B. Rothaus (eds.), *Historical dictionary of the French Revolution 1789–1799* (2 vols., Westport, CT, 1985).

D. NICHOLLS

FABRE D'EGLANTINE, Philippe François Nazaire (1750–1794)
French poet, playwright, actor and journalist; author of the Republican calendar

Born in Carcassonne in the south of France to a merchant-draper, Fabre was a brilliant student whose talents took him into the life of the more frivolous literary society of pre-revolutionary France, particularly the ambulatory world of the theatre. Out of this period, however, came two songs that were to outlast any of his productions produced during the revolution: 'Il pleut, il pleut bergère' and 'L'hospitalité'. In 1789 he was living in the Cordelier district of Paris where he became a friend of Marat (q.v.) and Danton (q.v.). Prior to the revolution he had taken no part in the revolutionary agitation, but now he became a member of the Cordelier Club when it was set up in mid 1790, was appointed secretary, and replaced Loustalot (q.v.) as principal writer for the *Révolutions de Paris*, when that highly regarded journalist came to a premature death at the beginning of September 1790. Like Loustalot and other journalists who contributed to the extraordinary success of Prudhomme's newspaper, Fabre wrote anonymously, so that his precise contribution is unknown. Fabre also became a member of the Jacobin Club, and in the midst of his political activities continued to write for the theatre: his *Le Philinte de Molière*, played on February 22, 1790 at the Théatre Français, was a great success, with its revolutionary undertones. Despite the success of his theatrical works Fabre was constantly in financial trouble. This led him to the Court, whose case he promised to present at the Jacobin Club in return for financial subsidies. The aura of venality was to taint his whole career as a revolutionary.

The revolution of August 10, 1792 opened up a new era for Fabre, mainly through his friend Danton. He was appointed secretary by Danton when the latter became Minister for Justice the day after the revolution, on a salary of 1500 *livres* per month – but with access to secret funds. With these funds Fabre produced a placarded newspaper *Account rendered to the sovereign people*, in which his language surpassed that of Marat and in which he prepared the way for the September massacres. About this time Fabre was engaged in the activities that further clouded his reputation, being involved in the traffic of military supplies and entering relations with Dumouriez.

On 5 September, Fabre was elected to the National Convention by the electors of Paris. He sat with the Mountain, but did not play a prominent role, preferring to act in the shadows. As a journalist he continued to write for the *Révolutions de Paris*, in which he put forward his ideas for a new revolutionary calendar. This brought together his poetic and revolutionary talents in what some would see as his major triumph. This calendar, 'decimali-

sed' and based on 'nature', was to free the new society from the religious superstition of the past, with holidays celebrating the great days of the revolution instead of the holy days of the Christians. Its picturesque nomenclature, however, could not make up for its inconveniences, and France's neighbours were neither convinced of the beauty of the new system, nor conquered. Nevertheless it survived through to year XIII of the Republic, which, however, had then become an empire. Fabre's calendar was evoked briefly during the Commune of 1871 (Year 79).

As a revolutionary Fabre's talents were more often used by others than by himself. He campaigned for the Mountain against the Girondins in the *Gazette de France*, and for Robespierre (q.v.) against the Hébertists, but at the end of 1793 Robespierre learned of his role in the East India Company scandal, and for this, and his association with the Dantonists, he was condemned to death, and guillotined on April 5, 1794.

Fabre's chief contribution to the revolution was his revolutionary calendar and his radical plays and articles which expressed the iconoclastic spirit of the early 1790s.

Fabre's writings can be studied in C. Vellay (ed.), *Oeuvres politiques de Fabre d'Eglantine* (Paris, 1914). For his biography, see L. Jacob, *Fabre d'Eglantine, chef des "Fripons"* (Paris, 1946).

BILL MURRAY

FAUCHET, Claude (1744–1793)
French revolutionary pioneer of christian democracy and the theology of revolution

Claude Fauchet was born in 1744, at Dornes, a village in the Nièvre, and belonged to a bourgeois family. Educated for the Church at the Sulpician Seminary at Bourges, he was ordained in 1769 at Besançon. Thanks to the patronage of the Bishop of Nevers, about 1764 he was appointed tutor to the nephew of the Cardinal Archbishop of Besançon, a member of the influential Choiseul family, who became Fauchet's patrons. About 1770 he moved to Paris, where he served as a supernumerary priest in the Saint-Roch parish. Fauchet's intellectual and oratorical talents were notable, and he was in demand during the 1770s as a preacher on important public occasions. He preached before the Assembly of the French Clergy and before the French Academy. By 1778 he was established as a court chaplain at Versailles and enjoying a substantial royal pension.

In 1785 Fauchet was appointed Vicaire-général of Bourges, but he remained in Paris and played no part in the affairs of the Diocese. On the eve of the revolution, Fauchet, at 44, was thus a highly successful cleric, with an income of about 20,000 *livres* a year. Only the Bishop's mitre, reserved in practice for candidates of noble origin, continued to escape his grasp.

Fauchet's sermons were already political in the 1770s, and he was briefly interdicted for publicly supporting Turgot's reforms. Preaching before the Court, he constituted himself the scourge of the conscience of the rich and powerful, and the advocate of the poor. He attempted to combine *philosophie*, the secular wisdom of the age, and religion.

At the time of the convening of the Estates-General in 1789 Fauchet published *La Religion Nationale*, a plan for the extensive reform of the French church which urged the elevation of the status of parish priests and their election by their congregations, the end of sinecures, and stringent reform of the monastic orders. Subsequently Fauchet was one of the leaders of the Parisian clergy who rallied to the Paris electors of the Third Estate when they took control of Paris during the uprising of 14 July. He became a member of the insurrectionary committee, and came under fire at the Bastille. Soon afterwards, Fauchet was elected to the General Council of the Paris Commune, on which he served for a year.

During 1789 and 1790 Fauchet undertook a programme of popular preaching in Paris, officiating at many public ceremonies at Notre Dame and in the parish churches, and proclaiming the compatibility of the Catholic religion and the revolution. He justified the 14 July uprising theologically: the revolution was the work of Providence; the will of the people was a higher authority demanding obedience than the will of kings; the Catholic Church gives its sanction to the ideas and actions of people fighting oppression. True Christianity, he maintained, demanded a revolutionary approach to politics, while revolutionary politics would be meaningless without the religion to provide the immanent moral sanctions of the new just order to be constructed.

In practice, Fauchet was one of the first revolutionaries to advocate a system of direct democracy, with the ultimate approval of the laws vested in the primary assemblies of the active citizens, who comprised the majority of the adult male population. He also defended progressive taxation, to redistribute the surplus of the rich for the benefit of the impoverished.

In the winter of 1790–1791 Fauchet delivered a series of twenty-five public lectures in the gardens of the Palais Royal, under the aegis of a radical political club, the Cercle Social. Before audiences of several thousands he presented a synthesis of Jean Jacques Rousseau's *Social Contract*, gospel christianity, and freemasonry. Exposition of fairly commonplace notions of the implications of the 'social contract' led to Fauchet's being accused of preaching 'The Agrarian Law' or the forcible redistribution of property to redress inequality. In fact, Fauchet derived from Rousseau, on the one hand, the right of all men to enough land to live on, and on the other, the superior right of society to regulate the conditions of the individual tenure of property. Although Fauchet denied any practical intention of using such arguments to redistribute property, the resulting controversy gained him a reputation as an extreme revolutionary radical.

When the schism occurred in the French Church, Fauchet adhered to the revolutionary faction and was elected Constitutional Bishop of Calvados, in Normandy. He took up his duties at Bayeux in May 1791 and during the next five months strove to reconstruct the church in his diocese around a combination of Catholic orthodoxy and political democracy. For this he relied heavily on the support of the local Jacobin Clubs, particularly of Bayeux and Caen. Although he was again accused by his Norman enemies of preaching the Agrarian Law, there is no evidence that he did so, or that he encouraged attacks on property.

At the same time he did support a democratic revision of the Constitution of 1791 and continued to offer a political and social message in his sermons. His combination of religious and political roles made Fauchet a charismatic popular figure, and in 1791 he was elected deputy for Calvados to the Legislative Assembly with overwhelming support. In 1793 he was again elected by Calvados to the Convention. Although retaining his bishopric Fauchet never returned to Calvados after 1791, and took only a marginal interest in the administration of his diocese, preferring the arena of national politics.

Fauchet's record in the Legislative Assembly was that of an able committeeman rather than of an original thinker or leader of opinion. While concerning himself with the defence of the Constitutional Church and the suppression of its enemies, he built nothing further upon the political and social insights of the first years of the revolution. In the Convention Fauchet attracted the hostility of Robespierre (q.v.), Marat (q.v.) and the Montagnards, partly as a close associate of the Girondin leaders, and partly for his advocacy of clemency for King Louis XVI.

In his journal, the *Journal des Amis*, he attacked Jacobin terrorism and defended freedom of worship against the gathering challenge of dechristianisation. His opposition to clerical marriage cost Fauchet support among the Jacobins of Calvados, his political base. Finally, the involvement of many of Fauchet's political and religious followers in the Federalist uprising in Calvados led to his arrest, trial, and execution in November 1793, although his personal participation remains problematic. According to Catholic sources he abjured his errors and reconciled himself to the Roman Church before his death.

Fauchet's attempt to found a democratic church failed, and he left behind no political or religious disciples. His espousal of the heretical Constitutional Church placed him outside orthodox Catholic tradition, so that the rebirth of Catholic political and social radicalism associated with Lamennais, Buchez and Lacordaire in the 1830s and 1840s took place without reference to Fauchet's example or teachings.

Marx paid tribute to the role of the Cercle Social in the development of modern communism, and this theme has been explored by modern Marxist scholarship, but it was not until the 1960s that a renewed interest in the reconciliation of religion and revolution led to a revived interest in Fauchet among historians of religion. It is in this context that he has been presented as a precursor of modern christian democracy and of the theology of revolution.

For the development of Fauchet's religious and political views, see his *De la religion nationale* (Paris, 1789); *Discours sur la liberté française* (Paris, 1789); *Second discours sur la liberté française* (Paris, 1789); *Troisième discours sur la liberté française* (Paris, 1789); *Eloge civique de Benjamin Franklin* (Paris, 1790); *Sermon sur l'accord de la religion et de la liberté* (Paris, 1791); and *Journal des Amis* (Paris, 1793). The old standard biography is J. Charrier, *Claude Fauchet, evêque constitutionnel du Calvados* (2 vols., Paris, 1909). For more recent appraisals, however, see N. Ravitch, 'The Abbé Fauchet: Romantic Religion during the French Revolution', *Journal of the American Academy of Religion*, vol. xlii, no. 2 (June 1974), pp. 247–62; H. Maier, *Revolution and Church* (Southbend, 1969); B. Plongeron, *Conscience religieuse en révolution* (Paris, 1969); and V. Alexeiev-Popov, 'Le Cercle Social, 1790–91', *Recherches Soviétiques* (1956–7), no. 4, pp. 89–150.

R.B. ROSE

FIJNJE, Wybo (1750–1809)
Dutch journalist and leader of the Patriot movement

Born in Zwolle, the son of Jan Wijbes Fijnje and Johanna Seye, Wybo Fijnje was registered as a student at Leiden University in 1771. Three years later, he graduated with a dissertation entitled *Theoriae Systematis Universi specimen philosophicum* (L.B.1774). During a short period as a Mennonite teacher in Deventer, he became a virulent supporter of the Patriot movement. Soon afterwards, he moved to Delft and took up the editorship of the influential radical periodical, the *Hollandsche Historische Courant*. As secretary of the 'geconstitueerden' in the city, he emerged as one of the most influential leaders of the movement and played a major part, together with Pieter Vreede (q.v.), in the drawing up of the Patriots' programme of July 1785, the Leiden Draft (*Leidse Ontwerp*). The publication of this document effectively marked the split between the Patriots and the Regents in the city, but it was not until the summer of 1787 that the Regents were finally expelled from office to be replaced by Fijnje and Gerrit Paape. Their period of power, however, was to be short-lived, and the city fell to the Orangists on 19 September of that year, forcing Fijnje to flee to Amsterdam, the last Patriot stronghold.

After the final capitulation of the Patriot forces to the Orangists on 10 October, Fijnje was forced into exile at St Omer. After the French invasion of Belgium, he moved to Antwerp and was active in planning a revolution against the Dutch Republic. The revolution of 1795 brought him back to the Netherlands as Chairman of the Provincial Council of Representatives for Holland, a position which enabled him to devote a good deal of time to the establishment of a union of political societies for the whole country. Based in Amsterdam, he became associated with the Jacobin society, *De Uitkijk* and allied himself with the most radical of the Jacobin groups at the two National Assemblies and took a central role in their deliberations.

Fijnje was heavily implicated in planning, with French help, the coup of January 22, 1798 which overthrew the National Assembly and brought to power an Executive Directory of Five, including Fijnje, Vreede, and van Langen. This triumvirate, with Fijnje very much to the fore, was effectively responsible for the running of the country until they were themselves overthrown by the second coup of June 12, 1798. Under the Directory, the Netherlands introduced a new constitution. The results of months of deliberation during the period of the National Assembly, the Agreed Constitutional Points represented a victory for the unitarist over the federalist Patriots.

Having alienated even the moderate unitarists by his behaviour while in power, Fijnje was forced to flee from the Directory building when the régime was overthrown by Daendels' (q.v.) troops. Although effecting an escape, he was later captured and accused of financial mismanagement and fraud during his period in office. Put on trial for his crimes, the proceedings were halted in November 1798 by a general amnesty brought in by the French authorities anxious to protect their own popularity in the country.

Although his pension as a Director was not paid until after his death, Fijnje continued to earn a living as a journalist but eschewed further involvement in active politics. He later came to prominence again under Schimmelpenninck and King Louis as editor of the official *Bataafsche Staatscourant*, afterwards the *Koninklijke Staatscourant* and finally the *Koninklijke Courant en Moniteur van Amsterdam*, retaining this position until his death in 1809.

Simon Schama lists Fijnje among the true revolutionaries of the period. The Leiden Draft of 1785 perhaps best represents his ideas. Written in conjunction with Pieter Vreede, it was a systematic attack on the Stadholderate as a form of government but went further in advocating, among other things, the primacy of popular sovereignty, the responsibility of elected representatives, the abolition of inherited and venal offices, and free speech as 'the foundation of a free constitution'. While by no means a unique document, the Draft did form the basis of Fijnje's thinking, both in and out of power. Although an attempt to bring together a consensus based on principles of democracy, the Draft did not address what was to be the main point of contention for the Batavian Republic, namely the structure of the state. Thus during his period as a Director, Fijnje found it impossible to mediate between federalists, moderate unitarists and the radical unitarists such as himself. His refusal to compromise led to the alienation of these other groups and his unswerving, and perhaps rather naïve belief that a new social order would emerge merely through the destruction of the old, effectively brought about his downfall.

Apart from Fijnje's thesis at the University of Leiden, there is also his *Bveknopt tijdrekenkundig begrip der algemeene geschiedenis* (vol. 1, 1783), and a collection of his letters can be found in H.T. Colenbrander, *Gedenstukken der algemeene geschiedenis van Nederland van 1795 tot 1840* (10 vols. in 22 parts, The Hague, 1905–22), esp. vol. 2. For details of his life and the movements with which he was associated, see S. Schama, *Patriots and liberators* (New York, 1977); P.J. Blok and P.C. Molhuysen, *Nieuw Nederlandsch Biografisch Woordenhoek* (Leiden, 1911–37); A.J. Kronenberg, 'Wybo Fijnje, Een Misdadiger?', *Nijhoffs Bijdragen* IV, 191; VI, 290; H.T. Colenbrander, *De Bataafsche Republiek* (Amsterdam, 1908); P. Geyl, *De Patriottenbeweging 1780–87* (Amsterdam, 1947); P. Geyl, 'De Bataafsche Revolutie', *Studies en Strijdschriften* (Groningen, 1958); and A. Kroes-Ligtenberg, *Dr. Wybo Fijnje* (Assen, 1957).

BOB MOORE

FONVIZIN, Denis Ivanovich (1745–1792)

Russian dramatist and satirist, best known for his plays The Brigadier *(1768) and* The Minor *(1782), who urged reform from above*

Fonvizin was born into a well-to-do noble family, and at ten years entered the Gymnasium attached to the newly-founded Moscow University. Here he went on to study foreign languages and philosophy. In 1762, at the start of Catherine II's reign, Fonvizin embarked on a civil service career and served for six years as secretary to cabinet minister I.P. Elagin, a literary dilettante who was subsequently director of the court theatre. Fonvizin was then appointed to the staff of the remarkable Minister for Foreign Affairs, Count Nikita Panin. As Panin's personal secretary, Fonvizin, until his resignation in 1782 (the year of Panin's death), enjoyed a position of great confidence and influence in the realms of diplomacy and Russian foreign policy.

At university he acquired knowledge of Latin, French and German and became familiar with the theories of German natural law and neo-Stoicism. His first literary essays were translations from Voltaire and other French writers. In the 1760s, Fonvizin was involved in a circle of young intellectuals led by F.A. Koslovsky, whose philosophical orientation was anti-clerical and 'free-thinking', and who were close to the empress. Fonvizin's anti-clericism is readily apparent from his verse-satire first printed in 1769, *Epistle to my servants Shumilov, Vanka and Petrushka*. His interest in political matters led him to translate and expand a treatise by the German political theorist, J.G. von Justi, entitled *A brief explanation of the freedom of the French nobility and of the advantage of the third estate*. Fonvizin drew the following conclusions about its application to the Russian context: 'In a word, there should be in Russia: 1) a nobility entirely free; 2) a third estate, entirely emancipated; and 3) a populace occupied with agriculture, although not entirely free, yet having at least the hope of being so.'

In his mordantly comic plays he assailed moral delinquency and social uselessness. A strong believer in both the privileges and the responsibilities of his class, Fonvizin sought a commercially and socially useful role for the nobility which formed the butt of much of his criticism for its laziness, parasitism and abuse of serfs. It was the contrast Fonvizin perceived between an idealised 'true nobility' and the selfish, ignorant, provincial, variety which formed the central theme of his plays and essays. Special targets were the manners and values of the Francophile Russian nobility which for Fonvizin were essentially symptomatic of the basic political and social deficiencies of his day. He stressed the central importance for political stability of a code of 'unalterable state laws' designed to curb the unbridled power of ruler and ruled alike. He insisted that it was from such laws rather than sheer force that the ruler should derive his authority. This idea was formulated in the document he drew up with Nikita Panin, by now incapacitated during what was to be his final illness, entitled *A Discourse on permanent laws of state*. Dating from the 1780s, the document may represent Panin's views, but more recent scholarship attributes it to Fonvizin. At any rate, they shared the conviction that Russia stood urgently in need of institutional safeguards against the arbitrary actions of its rulers and the negative effects of government through influential and powerful favourites. It was intended as political advice to Grand Duke Paul on his eventual accession to the throne and comprised a manifesto of eighteen articles setting out the goals of Paul's reign (1796–1801). There is some doubt as to the extent of its impact on Paul or even as to whether he ever saw it, but when it eventually came to the attention of Tsar Nicholas in 1831 he characteristically had it locked up out of harm's way.

The *Discourse* proceeded from the declared premise that Russia should have 'a monarchical government with unalterable fundamental laws'. It warned against the evils of autocracy, and argued the need for the constitutional rule of law as the surest means of outlawing tyranny, pointing out that the people would be fully entitled to remove power into their own hands if it was abused by the monarch. Although it contained no specific call for the emancipation of the serfs, the author stressed that the country's welfare depended on the limitation by law of the power of the landlords. In a ringing passage he observed that the state's 'supreme authority is a soulless machine set in motion by the arbitrary will of the sovereign', and declared that 'one cannot speak of democracy in a country where the common people, steeped in abysmal ignorance, drag without complaint the cruel yoke of slavery'. The treatise was described in contemporaneous police files as 'one of the most outrageous works of its age', while a modern assessment deems it 'one of the most penetrating documents of eighteenth-century Russian political thought'. It had some influence on members of the Decembrist conspiracy (1816–25) in Petersburg thanks to one of its members, General M.A. Fonvizin, the author's nephew. Although Herzen published it in London in 1861, it was not published in Russia until after the 1905 Revolution.

For his day Fonvizin was undoubtedly a man of independent views who showed himself prepared to challenge the authority of Russian absolutism. However, a precursor of Radishchev (q.v.), his position was that of the 'repentant nobleman's' moral revolt rather than that of an outright political opponent of Catherine's régime.

Further information on Fonvizin can be found in the following sources: W. Gleason, *Modern Encyclopedia of Russian and Soviet History*, vol. 11 (Gulf Breeze, 1979), pp. 196–99; M. Kantor, *Modern Encyclopedia of Russian and Soviet Literature*, vol. vii (Gulf Breeze, 1984), pp. 237–48; W.E. Brown, *A History of Eighteenth-Century Russian literature* (Ardis, 1980); G. Makogonenko, *Denis Fonvizin. Tvorcheskii put'* (Moscow, Leningrad, 1961); M. Raeff, 'Les Slaves, les allemands et les "Lumieres",' *Revue canadienne d'études slaves*, i (Hiver, 1967), pp. 521–51; David L. Ransel, *The Politics of Catherinian Russia. The Panin Party* (Yale, 1975). The text of the *Discourse* in English translation may be found in W. Gleason (ed.), *The Political and Legal Writings of Denis Fonvizin* (Ann Arbor, 1985).

P.J. O'MEARA

FORSTER, Johann Georg Adam
(1754–1794)
German Jacobin, writer and
revolutionary activist

Forster was born on November 27, 1754 in Nassenhuben near Danzig (Gdansk), the eldest of seven children. His father Johann Reinhold Forster (1729–1798) was a minister, his mother, *née* Nicholai, was the daughter of a shopkeeper. His ancestors came from Scotland.

In 1764 Forster made his first journey to Russia. His father was sent to the recently settled country along the Volga to study conditions there, and took young Georg, who was ten at the time. On returning home after the journey the father found that his position as minister was no longer available and that the family had emigrated to England. Georg as a young man had to earn his living doing scientific work and translating. He studied science with his father, and was a self-educated man. Between 1772 and 1775 Forster travelled round the world with his father as part of Cook's second voyage. His father was prevented from writing a 'philosophical description' of the voyage by a dispute with Cook and the Admiralty. Georg wrote the text instead and translated it into German. This work made him famous.

From 1778 to 1784 he lived in Kassel. He was appointed Professor of Biology at Kassel's Collegium Carolinum and became a friend of Jacobi. In 1779 he entered the Rosicrucians. Here he practised alchemy and got into debt. His scientific work distanced him more and more from the Rosicrucians and he left the circle. In debt and disappointed with life in Germany, and also afraid of reprisals from the Rosicrucians, he accepted a post at the Polish University of Vilna. In 1784 he became engaged to the daughter of a teacher from Göttingen, Thérèse Heyne.

From 1784 to 1787 he lived in Poland. He quickly became aware that despotism was more intolerable in Poland than in Germany. He vehemently criticised political and social conditions and the unashamed exploitation of the peasants; he claimed the country and its inhabitants were backward. Men treated like animals would not work, but took to drink. The place was filthy and Forster found both living and working conditions intolerable. He feared for his existence as a scientist and left Vilna with his family in 1787.

In 1788 he became a librarian in Mainz, at the request of the Prince-Elector, who was anxious to make Mainz a seat of learning. In March 1790 he embarked on a journey to the Lower Rhineland, England and France with Alexander von Humboldt. He used his diary of this journey to write his most important work, *Ansichten vom Niederrhein* (1790).

Forster's major political activity began with the outbreak of the Revolutionary Wars. On October 21, 1792 General Custine entered Mainz with French revolutionary troops. The Prince-Elector and the majority of the nobility fled. After a period of deliberation Forster joined the 'Society of Friends of Liberty and Equality' on 5 November because, he said, one could not sit on the fence. He participated actively in the revolutionary events and was in turn, a member of the Mainz Club, vice-president of the General Administration, president of the club and, finally, vice-president of the Rhineland National Convention. He also founded a newspaper, *Die Neue Mainzer Zeitung*, and was involved in amateur theatre.

He wanted to win over public opinion to the ideas of the revolution, show that the Germans were no different to the French, and that the revolution had positive consequences for everybody. He argued for a French annexation of the Rhineland, and developed the theory of a natural border along the Rhine. As president of the club in January 1793 he sought to reduce divisions and tried to make of it an organ which could shake the general apathy of the masses. As vice-president of the General Administration he showed tireless energy in solving the city's problems. He made preparations for elections, especially in the country, informed and educated, explained the role of the mayor and the Convention and so on.

After deciding to demand the annexation of the Rhineland by the French Republic, Forster and a small delegation (Lux and Patocki) were sent to Paris to present this demand to the French Convention. Shortly after their departure, on March 25, 1793 counter-revolutionary troops surrounded Mainz and they were unable to return; a price was put on Forster's own head. While in Paris Forster was entrusted with two diplomatic missions. One was in northern France and involved negotiations over prisoners with England; the other was at Pontarlier, where he was able to see his wife and family again. His wife had left Mainz at the end of 1792 to go first to Strasbourg and then to Neuchâtel with her lover, Forster's friend Ludwig Ferdinand Huber (q.v.). In November he returned to Paris and wrote his most important political works. But the separation from his family affected his health and in September 1793 he fell ill. He died alone on January 10, 1794 aged thirty-eight.

In his philosophical description of his voyage around the world, *Reise um die Welt* (1789), the first German-language account of a scientific expedition, Forster covered many topics. At each stage of his journey he studied the land's resources both for the native and the traveller, the flora and fauna, meetings with the inhabitants, their physical and psychological make-up, and relations with them. Such a detailed study of the 'savages' had never before been undertaken in so exhaustive a fashion. It demanded complete freedom from prejudice. Thus he introduced the idea of the 'good savage' in Germany in a concrete way and his work was an important contribution to anthropology and science. A disciple of Linnæus, Forster was ahead of those scholars of his day who sacrificed empirical fact to hypothesis. Struck by the social injustice on the boat, by despotic régimes and by slavery, his political conscience started to take shape. He denounced the exploitation of man and British colonial policy. *Reise um die Welt* had a wide impact across Europe.

Forster went on to write a series of scientific and anthropological works. He drew up a work on natural history, characterised by his preference for concrete and precise scientific observations at a time when science was still very speculative. He tried to reconcile Linnæus and Buffon and became embroiled in a controversy with Kant (q.v.) (*Etwas über die Menschenracen* (1786)), which distanced him from Rousseau and Buffon. The journey round the world was therefore a fundamental experience which determined the basis of his activity until his death. Two dominating factors in his thinking were a respect for reality and a deep-rooted optimism.

The Rosicrucian experience occupies a relatively small place in his work. In Kassel he wrote little as his time was taken up with alchemy. The only positive result was that he accepted the theory of the unity of nature, which he developed in *Ein Blick in das ganze der Natur* and *De la félicité des êtres physiques*. The latter led him towards pantheism, about which he was briefly enthusiastic. He severed his connection with Rosicrucianism, however, and sought the truth in experience and verifiable experiments: in *Über Leckereyen* physiological materialism, in *Leitfaden zu einer künftigen Geschichte der Menschheit*, he affirms that the material world in its entirety and the development of mankind, is independent of any higher force, and shows himself to be a precursor of Darwin. Materialism is implicit along with an expression of the dialectical development of mankind in the direction of progress.

Ansichten vom Niederrhein (1790) was the product of his second long journey, in which he dealt again with a wide variety of subjects. However in this book there are two central themes: aesthetics and politics. He held that art is not a true representation of nature but the transformation of nature by the imagination. His historic conception of art claimed that it depended on the circumstances of the country where it flourished. Greek art was thus the result of the prevailing favourable factors in Greece, and English art and literature though less perfect, were nevertheless products of a people living in a free country with a democratic constitution. He developed this theory in *Geschichte der englischen Literatur* (1789–1790) and in the introduction to his translation of *Sakoutala*, an Indian work which he wanted to promote.

In *Ansichten vom Niederrhein* Forster also analysed political events. He criticised despotism in the name of man's natural rights, and he criticised religion in the service of despotism, particularly in the Catholic states such as Cologne, where the clergy were superstitious. He also criticised the despotism of reason and the tendency to want to impose one's own opinions, and made a plea for tolerance and individual freedom. Finally, in the field of economics he criticised the tyranny of the guild system and was in favour of commercial and industrial freedom. But his position with regard to the constitution of Aachen, that of enlightened despotism, was ambiguous. He criticised Joseph II for the introduction of radical change to the Netherlands without due respect for tradition and custom and for wanting to govern all his territories according to a single blueprint. However, he praised Frederick II for his toleration of a certain degree of freedom of religion, thought, press and conscience and conceded that enlightened despotism might on occasion be progressive.

On the subject of revolutions he concluded that the causes were oppression and intolerable tyranny. Given these conditions revolution was bound to follow swiftly, if a people was not already too down-trodden. Revolution was a natural right, a force of nature with an irresistible impetus. Revolution therefore was violent, destructive and regenerative. Forster emphasised above all the destructive aspect, and his sympathy lay with the people in revolt, for he considered their action to be legitimate self-defence. Despite this, elsewhere in *Ansichten vom Niederrhein* Forster's opinions remain very moderate.

In his Mainz speeches and *Darstellung der Revolution in Mainz*, Forster declared that his aim was the establishment of freedom. Freedom alone would allow man to achieve perfection. This concept became clearer in the revolutionary context of Mainz. Until 1792 freedom meant the abolition of despotism. Then freedom became obedience to the laws laid down by the people. It was important to have the most libertarian constitution possible; everything should be sacrificed for freedom. Mistakes were inevitable in the early stages, but freedom alone could ensure the establishment of an acceptable régime. Forster classed popular sovereignty with reason. Equality interested him less at first. In Mainz he distinguished between natural inequality and legal inequality. His development was influenced by reading Fröhlich (q.v.) and Godwin, and by the policies of Robespierre (q.v.): he considered social equality the basis of political equality. Private property must be abolished for the good of the nation. Contact with the most underprivileged citizens of Mainz made him realise the consequences of economic liberalism and revise his ideas about the economy. Liberalism benefitted only the bourgeoisie and bred pauperism. His thinking was in advance of that of his colleagues in Mainz, who wanted to protect private property. For the revolutionary theorists of Mainz, the question of an equal distribution of property did not arise, and equality, for them, did not rest on economics. Forster himself had progressed from liberal to democrat.

Forster had attended the celebration at the Champ de Mars on July 14, 1790. He was filled with enthusiasm by the participation of the people, their altruism, their maturity, and the solidity of the movement. He witnessed the beginning of a radical renewal, and understood what was meant by popular sovereignty. This experience determined his theoretical thinking. Then, during his stay in Paris, he observed events and was left with contradictory conclusions. On the negative side, he found that the revolutionaries were carried away by their emotions, but that they lacked energy; and that the spirit of factionalism and egotism was prevalent. But these were reflections on the men and not on the revolution itself. Forster was convinced that the revolution was not a lost cause and that it would triumph.

He noted the benefits of the republican constitution and the end of the Vendée revolt. The situation in France was better than that of her enemies. He regretted the elimination of the Girondins but preferred the Montagnards, whose more solid political doctrine was the leading force of the revolution in the Jacobin Club. He put himself above all the in-fighting, and thought that the stability of the Republic was threatened more by war than by political differences.

While in Paris Forster wrote *Parisische Umrisse, Darstellung der Revolution in Mainz*, and *Über die Beziehung der Staatskunst auf das Glück der Menscheit*. He defined the revolution as an inevitable and natural phenomenon whose function was purification and elevation, a force which eluded human reason. Public opinion was the engine of the revolution and the guarantee of democracy; it had prepared the fall of the authorities and permitted the people's representatives to govern the country free from contradiction. The deepening of the revolutionary consciousness was an important factor for success. The role of Paris was important because it was there that public opinion was determined. Forster praised the financial policies of the Convention: the abolition of luxury, simplicity and respect for equality. He approved of those measures limiting economic freedoms which promoted inequality. To render wealth unusable would lead to its being scorned. He agreed with Robespierre's policies: the fixing of prices; prohibition of speculation; the attack on private property. The nation was to become the trustee of all wealth.

The goal of the revolution was the conquest of political freedom, a precondition of spiritual freedom. Material wellbeing was necessary for the elevation of the spirit and for happiness. Forster held that the exploited man is unhappy and cannot improve himself, and that social inequality is responsible for popular ignorance; that despotism corrupts men; that a people unused to liberty sinks into vice; that it was necessary to reconquer human dignity, to liberate mankind, to make no compromise with tyranny, which found its legitimation in the immaturity of a people; that the cultural and moral condition of man depended on social conditions. The French Revolution had changed the world and the rule of reason would allow people to improve themselves.

Forster can be distinguished from those German 'liberals' such as Klopstock, Wieland, Herder, Schiller, Humboldt etc, who had rapidly turned away from the revolution because they had remained individualists and rejected popular sovereignty. He belongs in the mainstream of German revolutionaries and was less isolated than has been claimed. German revolutionaries, including Forster, have long been misunderstood, forgotten or discredited by history. Forster was denounced by such writers as Goethe, Schiller, Heinse and Humboldt. His reputation has suffered at the hands of historians who have treated him as a traitor to the Prince-Elector and to his country because he argued for the annexation of the Rhineland at a time when nationalism was practically non-existent in Germany, although soon afterwards the king of Prussia ceded the whole of the left bank to France.

Forster would never have regained his reputation had it not been for the 1843 edition of his works, but more especially the work of the Berlin Academy of Sciences after 1958. He was a true revolutionary in word and deed. His thinking was similar to that of the Montagnards, and he is one of the few German revolutionary writers to have experienced such important political activity. Facts were important to him, but he could also clearly analyse abstract concepts such as liberty and equality. Forster's ideas were the most advanced of their time in Germany, and only by living abroad could he remain a true revolutionary. His was a tragic destiny – that of a man who could only realise his ideals by leaving himself open to criticism for living in exile.

Forster's works have recently been republished in an edition which also includes letters, diaries, and miscellaneous writing: G. Steiner (ed.), *G. Forsters*

Werke, sämtliche Schriften, Tagebücher, Briefe (13 vols., Berlin, 1968+). G. Steiner has also edited a four-volume edition of Forster's works: *Forster, Werke* (4 vols., Frankfurt am Main, 1967). Further information on Forster can be found in the following: Arthur Chuquet, 'Le révolutionnaire Georges Forster', *Etudes d'histoire* (Paris, 1903); Kurt Kersten, *Ein europäischer Revolutionär. G. Forster 1754–1794* (Berlin, 1921); Ludwig Uhlig, *G. Forster. Einheit und Mannigfaltigkeit in seiner geistigen Welt* (Tübingen, 1965); Marita Gilli, *G. Forster. L'Oeuvre d'un penseur allemand réaliste et révolutionnaire (1754–1794)* (Lille, 1975); Helmut Peitsch, *Georg Forsters 'Ansichten vom Niederrhein'. Zum Problem des übergangs vom bürgerlichen Humanismus zum revolutionären Demokratismus* (Frankfurt am Main, 1978); Thomas P. Saine, *Georg Forster* (New York, 1972); Gerhard Steiner, *Georg Forster* (Stuttgart, 1977); Edith Shirock, *G. Forster und die französische Revolution* (Phil. Diss, Freiburg im Breisgau, 1972); Gerhard Pickerodt and Peter Koch (eds.), *Georg Forster in seiner Epoche* (Berlin, 1982); Hans Hübner and Burchard Thaler (eds.), *Georg Forster (1754–1794). Ein Leben für den wissenschaftlichen und politischen Fortschritt* (Halle, 1981); Gerhard Steiner, *Freimaurer und Rosenkreuzer. G. Forster's Weg durch Geheimbünde* (Berlin, 1985).

M. GILLI

FOUCHÉ, Joseph (1759–1820)

French Jacobin, member of the National Convention, and holder of ministerial offices during the revolutionary and Napoleonic periods

Fouché was born in Nantes, the son of a sea captain. From 1782–1792 he was a college professor. As a one-time president of the Jacobin Club of Nantes, he was elected to the Convention in September 1792, where he became a member of the relatively obscure committees of Public Instruction and later, Colonies. He took no part in the great debates between Montagnards and Girondins and his committee reports were rare, dry and brief. There is no convincing evidence that his vote for the death of Louis XVI represented a switch of allegiance to the winning side, as is often said. In fact, as a member of one of the more radical provincial clubs, it is likely that he always had supported harsh measures against the counter-revolution – in the case of Nantes, against much of the local clergy – and supported the club's policy of a lightning war against Austria and the German princes to remove foreign support for domestic counter-revolution. Be that as it may, he made his reputation outside the Convention as one of its more capable representatives on mission. His first mission to the department of the Loire-Inférieure to supervise recruiting for the levy of 300,000 men for the army in March 1793 is particularly important because the lessons he drew from it had a powerful influence on his more famous missions to Nevers and to Lyon later in the year. He narrowly escaped serious injury or perhaps death near Rennes from Catholic and royalist peasants who had rebelled against conscription and he later helped organise the defence of Nantes. Like many of his contemporaries, he blamed the risings on the 'softness of the [local] administrations [which] have lost everything . . . by a false system of moderation and tolerance, they have betrayed their country'. Also, the risings were the result of 'ignorance and fanaticism, having become the blind instruments of the aristocracy which work with it to annihilate the cities . . .'. The solution to the dual problem of administrative weakness and peasant superstition was authoritarian control and dechristianisation.

That the risings in the west were more critical in the emergence of Fouché as a radical Jacobin than an opportunistic conversion to the Montagnards at the time of the king's trial is evident from an examination of his views on the role of religion. Whatever his private beliefs, in November 1792 he foresaw an important place for the teaching orders in a regenerated system of national education and spoke of 'the necessity' of religious sentiments. After the risings, he denounced the clergy wholesale and advocated a system of 'public instruction . . . inspired by the revolutionary and clearly philosophical spirit [which alone] can offset the odious influence of religion'. Since he believed that 'misled and ignorant men abandoned to themselves seem to run the risk of false and dangerous ideas . . . [that] education is necessary to the establishment of the Republic', eliminating religion from the curriculum presented the problem of what substitute could inculcate civic virtues among a populace so easily led astray. Although he never articulated it clearly, the result was the dechristianisation campaign of the autumn of 1793, at once an inspiration to the sans-culottes and a prophylactic against spreading counter-revolution.

After relatively unimportant missions to Troyes and Dijon, Fouché was posted to the departments of the Allier and Nièvre to mobilise local resources against Lyon where anti-Jacobin federalists had rebelled against the Convention in May 1793. The traditional start of the dechristianisation campaign is generally held to be Fouché's inauguration of a statue of Brutus in the cathedral of Nevers. This was quickly followed by his *arrêté* of 10 October forbidding outdoor religious ceremonies and the wearing of clerical garb in public, secularising funerals and ordering the slogan 'Death is an eternal sleep!' posted before every cemetery. The *arrêté* electrified Jacobins and sans-culottes alike. Other representatives on mission from the Pyrenees to the plains of Picardy used it as a basis for their own dechristianising measures and Chaumette (q.v.), procurator of the Paris Commune, took the campaign to the capital where it led to the forced resignation of Archbishop Gobel and the rededication of Notre Dame to 'Reason'. Since the dechristianisation campaign spread as rapidly as it did, Fouché was clearly representative of a current of opinion among the revolutionaries, not an innovator. Indeed, measured by the

proportion of priests who resigned or by the number of secularised place-name changes, dechristianisation in the Allier and Nièvre was relatively superficial and of short duration. None the less, Fouché was proud of his work. He reported that 'the aristocracy was struck with astonishment and dread and religious fanaticism thunderstruck; they are crushed'.

Despite Robespierre's (q.v.) revulsion for dechristianisation, the Committee of Public Safety posted Fouché to Lyon which had fallen to the Convention's forces in October because the reputation he had acquired for ruthlessness was thought more appropriate than the relatively fair-minded approach of Georges Couthon (q.v.). His work in Lyon was arguably the most experimental of the entire revolutionary period. Along with Collot d'Herbois (q.v.), he organised a grandiose ceremony to commemorate the memory of Joseph Chalier (q.v.), the local Jacobin whose crazed threats had done much to bring about his execution by the federalists. This was a substitute fête which illustrated much of the mawkish sentimentality and religiosity of dechristianisation as a whole (the demagogue's head was shipped to the Convention as a relic). However, dechristianisation was less prominent in Lyon because Fouché agreed with the general Montagnard line that the city's problem was 'the rich' and that the solution was a pitiless and thorough repression. The revolutionary tribunal he and Collot established condemned 1,667 people to death, 268 of them in a mass execution on 4–5 December. The prisoners were chained together on the plain of Les Brotteaux, mowed down by cannon fire and grape-shot, and finished off by visibly retching soldiers. Many of these unfortunate victims were quite ordinary working people too and Fouché's attitude to Lyon, along with that of the other conquerors, was almost colonial. 'We are sceptical of the tears of repentance,' the representatives wrote, 'nothing can disarm our severity . . . indulgence is a dangerous weakness, liable to rekindle criminal hopes . . . The demolitions [of the major buildings] are too slow . . . The explosion of mines and devouring flames alone can express the total power of the people . . .' Yet dramatic social measures were ordered to benefit native working people. Following similar steps in the Nièvre, Fouché levied a revolutionary tax, graduated to fortunes and political opinions, on the rich, to lodge, clothe and feed the indigent and to buy tools for the able-bodied. The recalcitrant rich were to be interned as suspects and the property of all suspects was to be sequestered for the duration of the war. Significantly, even the Paris Commune found these measures too radical and adopted only those articles requiring the baking of a single type of bread, *le pain de l'égalité*. In many respects, these measures anticipated and went beyond St Just's (q.v.) much more famous Ventôse laws. Like many of the schemes before and after 1789, however, it did not allow for the mobility of the poor (indeed tried to restrict it), prescribed imprisonment for mendicants and 'the lazy', assumed small-scale industry based on independent artisans and never envisaged co-operation or economic growth as devices for solving poverty and unemployment. For all the democratic and levelling rhetoric, it was still a long way from the 'socialism' of Babeuf (q.v.), let alone that of the Second Republic.

The reaction to Fouché's imperious rule taught him the guile he later needed to serve every régime between 1795 and 1816. His power base in Lyon was the republican army, detachments of the sans-culotte Paris revolutionary army and bureaucrats recruited from outside. He soon quarrelled with the powerless local Jacobins who had their own scores to settle, over the scope and direction of the repression. They accused him of being a moderate, he retaliated by closing the club and each denounced the other as traitors to the Convention. Since he had also tended to ignore government directives, he was recalled. Robespierre, who had developed an immoderate hatred of him for his denial of the immortality of the soul in the dechristianisation campaign, had him expelled from the Paris Jacobin Club and

was certainly preparing to have him executed. Fouché retaliated by spreading rumours among the other deputies that Robespierre was preparing a vast purge. The panic this engendered certainly played a role in Robespierre's overthrow. For over a year after the fall of the revolutionary government in July 1794, he managed to evade numerous cries for his arrest. Between the amnesty of October 1795 and his diplomatic career, he developed contacts with royalists which he never dropped and managed to acquire a modest fortune in private business which continued to swell from skimming profits of gambling houses while back in office. Although he never shook his reputation as a man of the left because of his continued hostility to the clergy, as Minister of Police of the Directory, he prepared the way for Bonaparte's coup in November 1799, only to betray him during the Hundred Days in 1815. In the meantime he served Napoleon as his Minister of Police (1799–1802, 1804–10, 1815), Minister to the Illyrian Provinces (1813), and as a Senator (1802–14). In 1809 he was created Duke of Otranto. Like his imperial master, the viciousness of revolutionary politics enhanced the authoritarianism of his character and produced a disillusioned cynic with an elastic conscience. Towards the end of his life he denounced those who wished to govern men by 'pompous formulas' and 'abstract principles'. He had travelled far from the young deputy who had demanded the union of liberty and education 'to bring perfection to human nature'.

Fouché is, however, dismissed too easily as a self-serving rascal, capable of trimming his views to suit the whims of the successive régimes of the revolutionary era. As a member of the Convention, he was typical of many extreme Jacobins – a democrat, an authoritarian, an egalitarian, and an anti-Christian. His metamorphosis from radical into policeman was rare for the Jacobins of his generation but was foreshadowed in his willingness to use physical force to preserve the values of the revolution against their enemies during the radical phase from 1792 to 1794.

The basis of all subsequent biographies is Louis Madelin's *Fouché, 1759–1820* (2 vols., Paris, many editions) but since Madelin had no sympathy for his subject as a radical, recourse should be had to E. Herriot, *Lyon n'est plus* (4 vols., Paris, 1937–40). Amazingly, there is no adequate study of the mission to the Allier and Nièvre so one must rely on Fouché's own reports in F.-A. Aulard, *Receuil des actes du comité de salut public* (28 vols., Paris, 1889–1983), especially vols. viii–x which are also useful for Lyon. M. Vovelle, *Religion et révolution. La déchristianization de l'An II* (Paris, 1976) is an important first step towards re-opening the study of dechristianisation.

D. SUTHERLAND

FRÉRON, Stanislas Louis Marie (1754–1802)

French revolutionary journalist, member of the National Convention, terrorist, but subsequently leader of the reactionary jeunesse dorée

Fréron was born in Paris, and went to school at the College of Louis-le-Grand (1771–79), where he was a friend of Desmoulins (q.v.) and a colleague of Robespierre (q.v.). His father was the founder and editor of the *Année littéraire*, celebrated organ of the anti-philosophes. Fréron loved his father, who died in 1776, but inherited his malice without his talent. He claimed early in the revolution that his father would not have opposed it; but he detested his step-mother and her brother, the abbé Royou, teacher at the Louis-le-Grand. Mme Fréron eased him out of his rights to the *Année littéraire* and then founded her own newspaper during the revolution, the *Ami du Roi*, edited by Royou, a paper which despite the young Fréron's special pleading, rightly saw itself as the 'successor to Fréron' in its violent opposition to the revolution.

By that time Fréron had become a journalist himself, writing under the name Martel in the *Orateur du peuple*, a daily that began its uneven career on May 22, 1790. This newspaper shared Marat's (q.v.) violence and the same enemies; it also shared the *Friend of the People*'s persecutions, and like Marat, Fréron was frequently driven underground. When the king tried to flee France on June 20, 1791 Fréron demanded his execution and the public humiliation of his wife. He was also prominent, through his paper, *Labenette*, in the agitation that preceded the Champ de Mars massacre. Driven underground again he nevertheless continued his paper through to November 1791. Fréron was also associated with Desmoulin's *Révolutions de France et de Brabant*, and founded with him the *Tribune des patriotes* in April 1792.

Fréron was elected as deputy for Paris to the National Convention on September 14, 1792, where he shared the sympathies of the Mountain, but was frequently absent on mission in the provinces. From March to May 1793 Fréron accompanied Barras in recruiting missions in the Upper and Lower Alps, and then was sent to Nice to assist Barras who had been sent as deputy on mission to the army in the Var. From there he acted with the utmost severity against the rebels of Marseilles and Toulon. When Toulon was taken he changed its name to Port-la-Montagne, boasted of having twelve thousand masons to raze the town, and took pleasure in seeing 200 Toulonnais executed each day. After the suppression of the Marseilles revolt he and Barras set up a revolutionary tribunal which sentenced more than four hundred people to death, ordered the destruction of the houses of the rebels and changed the name of the port city to Ville-sans-nom. He had several fine buildings destroyed but the entire order was not carried out.

Fréron was recalled to Paris on January 28, 1794, where he was denounced by Hébert (q.v.) as a 'muscadin'. The Committee of Public Safety demanded a justification for the 800,000 *livres* that he and Barras had allocated to themselves, but the fall of Robespierre, in which Fréron played a key role with Tallien (q.v.), brought that enquiry to a close. From that time on Fréron became as wild in his abuse

of the Jacobins as previously he had
been towards the royalists, but after the
unsuccessful royalist insurrection of Vendémiaire he came back to the Mountain.
He lost his influence thereafter, although
he continued to hold government positions
and attract to himself accusations of corruption and fraud. Bonaparte finally got
rid of him when he sought to marry Pauline
Bonaparte: he sent him to Santo Domingo
as sub-prefect. Fréron left his wife and
children behind and died there of yellow
fever.

Fréron's radicalism was evident in his
work as a journalist during the early 1790s,
when he put forward anti-royalist views,
and in his defence of the revolution against
its enemies as a representative on mission.
In this latter role, however, he displayed an
excessive enthusiasm for arbitrary violence
which alienated other Jacobins but which
in Fréron's view was entirely justified in
the service of the revolution.

Some of Fréron's correspondence has
been published – E. Poupé, *Lettres de
Barras et de Fréron* (Draguignan, 1910).
In addition to the short entry on Fréron's
life in A. Kuscinski, *Dictionnaires des
conventionnels* (Paris, 1917), see R.
Arnaud, *Journaliste, sans-culotte et thermi-
dorien. Le fils de Fréron* (Paris, 1909).

BILL MURRAY

FRÖHLICH, Carl Wilhelm
(1759–1828)
German utopian socialist

Fröhlich was born in December 1759 at
Landsberg an der Warthe, son of Caspar
Fröhlich, army chaplain in a Prussian
regiment, and then a farmer at Gross-
Rosenburg, a village situated near to two
communities belonging to the Herrnhuter.
In 1788 Carl Wilhelm became a law student
at Halle, where he was influenced by
the Sturm und Drang movement and the
American war of independence. In 1789
he became a secretary for the postal service
in Berlin. He married Friederica Henrietta
Rauthe, a writer. In 1792 he settled at
Scharfenbrück, where he had bought property, and published his *Über den Menschen*

und seine Verhältnisse, a book which was
immediately prohibited, and one which in
any case enjoyed little success on account
of its utopian character. He now occupied
himself with his estate and led an intense
intellectual life at Scharfenbrück. He tried
to realise his proposals for popular education by, for example, creating Sunday
schools for the peasantry. In 1801 he edited
*Thierarzneibuch für den Landmann und
Oekonomen*, and in 1802 *Gemälde nach
der Natur*. In 1813 he returned to Berlin
with his family, and sold his estate following the manifest failure of his attempt to
live among the peasants according to his
ideas. Together with his brother, he
founded a museum of literature and art,
which opened in 1814 and acquired a
French and German lending library. In
1820 Henrietta published *Virginia oder die
Kolonie von Kentucky*, a work jointly-
written. The family's financial situation
grew worse and Carl Wilhelm died in
poverty on May 23, 1828. Their eldest son
looked after Henrietta until she too died
in Berlin on April 5, 1833.

Fröhlich's work was a lively critique of
the established order written under the
influence of Rousseau, and above all of
Mably, Morelly, and the Herrnhuter. He
departs from the theory of natural law to
elaborate a utopian scheme for a society
without private property. He wanted to
free mankind from the bonds of selfishness
and submission to base interests and to
prepare man's inner liberation. His work
remained essentially utopian, for he had
no sense of historical change. In *Virginia*
he dealt with emigration to North America,
land of freedom. Fröhlich was in favour
of a radical agrarian law and took up
the communist ideas of Babeuf (q.v.). A
republican, he took an interest in the
wishes and reactions of the people, and
proselytised the improvement in the standard of living which would come from a
republican régime. He insisted on the
bonds which must exist between government and people. In *Virginia*, philosophical
and educational ideas were expounded in
an epic fashion. The heroine's aim in the
book is to collaborate in the establishment

of a republic, where there is no more private property. The highest goal is peace, liberty, truth, justice and a material life without cares or poverty. In *Virginia* this ideal is closely linked to recent political events; the ideas and experience of the French Revolution are present, but nonetheless it remains a social utopia.

Fröhlich, therefore, did not belong to the mainstream of revolutionary democracy, but rather to that of utopian socialism. Together with F.H. Ziegenhagen (q.v.), he considerably enriched the lively German school of utopian socialism in a period of political difficulties in continuing the tradition of Mably and Morelly, and to this extent he is an important link in the development of socialism.

Fröhlich's writings can be studied in modern editions: C.W. Fröhlich, *Über den Menschen und seine Verhältnisse* (Berlin, 1960), and H. Fröhlich, *Virginia oder Die Kolonie von Kentucky* (Berlin, 1963). For further critical and biographical information, see E.S. Paris, 'Un communiste allemand inconnu', in J. Jaurès (ed.), *Histoire socialiste de la Révolution française*, vol. 4 (1971), pp. 274–85; G. Steiner, *Der Traum von Menschenglück* (Berlin, 1959); G. Steiner, 'Un utopiste allemand du 18e siècle: Carl Wilhelm Fröhlich', *Annales historiques de la Révolution française*, no. 166 (October–December, 1961); A.W. Gulyaga, *Der deutsche Materialismus am Ausgang des 18. Jahrhunderts* (Berlin, 1966), pp. 253–67; and M. Gilli, 'L'utopie dans la condition de l'homme de C.W. Fröhlich, est-elle au service du peuple?', *Affrontements de classe et création littéraire* (Annales littéraires de l'Université de Besançon, Les Belles Lettres, Paris, 1973), p. 47.

M. GILLI

GALDI, Matteo Angelo (1765–1821)
Italian Jacobin, revolutionary activist, and educational reformer

Galdi was born into a socially well-connected but not wealthy family in Coperchia, province of Salerno. With Giuseppe Abbamonti (q.v.) and other reformers, he participated in the conspiracy of 1794 against the Bourbon government and was forced into exile. He was in France during the early years of the revolution and in 1796 he enlisted in Bonaparte's Army of Italy. He had contacts with Piedmontese Jacobins and helped them organise the Alba insurrection. In Milan, he contributed to the radical newspapers *Effemeridi repubblicane* and *Giornale dei patrioti italiani*. After the founding of the Repubblica Cisalpina, he was appointed envoy to the pro-French government in The Hague and wrote a treatise on Dutch politics and on the economy. He returned to Naples in 1808 and was put in charge of a reform of the educational system. His treatise *Pensieri sull'istruzione* attracted the attention of the Bonapartist government because it advocated a national system of public education and emphasised education for citizenship.

Galdi's career did not end with the Bourbon restoration. He remained active in the educational and judicial affairs of the Kingdom of Naples. In 1820, he joined liberal elements of the Neapolitan army in pressing for constitutional government and was elected president of parliament in the short-lived liberal revolution. He died in Naples in 1821.

More moderate than most of his political associates, Galdi made two important contributions to the revolutionary period: he demonstrated that intellectuals and political leaders from various regions of Italy could work together towards common goals and he promoted vigorously the importance of literacy and civic education for all.

In addition to his own writings cited in the text, details of his life and background can be found in Stuart J. Woolf, *A History of Italy* (London, 1979), and Carlo Zaghi, *Potere, chièsa et socièta* (Naples, 1985).

CLARA M. LOVETT

GERMAIN, Charles (1770–?)
French revolutionary agitator and Babouvist

Charles Germain was born at Narbonne on September 20, 1770. His father was a minor royal official, keeper of the royal hunting rides at Versailles. Germain was brought up in the Calvinist reformed church. He made some progress in studies at the Paris *collèges* before enlisting in the army at seventeen. Promoted lieutenant in the hussars in late 1793 he was stripped of his rank and briefly imprisoned in 1794 for a speech in a popular society. Released, but not reinstated, Germain was again gaoled as a militant in 1795. He was sent to Arras where, though the two men were in different prisons, he and Babeuf (q.v.) were able to conduct an extensive correspondence, lasting more than six months. It was in the course of this correspondence that Babeuf and Germain discarded 'the agrarian law' (the egalitarian redistribution of landed property) for pure communism, the complete abolition of property.

In his letters, and later, during the trial of the Babouvist conspirators at Vendôme in 1797 Germain paid tribute to Christ 'the sublime Nazarene legislator' and to the Essenes as precursors of the 'Equals'. Germain also showed a knowledge of the history of the Gracchi and of the communistic Anabaptists of the sixteenth century. He cited the inspiration of a number of leaders of the Enlightenment, notably Helvétius, Raynal (q.v.), Rousseau, Diderot and Volney.

Writing to Babeuf, Germain envisaged a two-stage revolution: first, the redistribution of land among individuals, and then the merging of such individual holdings into 'the common domain', with cultivation directed for the good of all, and the ultimate aim complete equality through the equal distribution of commodities. As for the revolutionary method, Germain argued for a sudden, apocalyptic and universal explosion, carefully planned and timed. Ironically, Babeuf at this stage argued against such a central coup d'état and advanced instead the notion of a plebeian Vendée, a local uprising with communism spreading gradually outward as the people were won over. Yet in the end, the Conspiracy of the Equals was closer to Germain's model than to Babeuf's.

Released from gaol in the autumn of 1795, Germain remained Babeuf's devoted disciple. Active in the Panthéon political club until its closure, he then became one of the secret military agents of the Conspiracy, and worked on the Police Legion, the élite corps guarding the Directory, with particular success.

Arrested in May 1796 Germain was tried with the other accused conspirators at Vendôme in 1797 and sentenced to deportation: he was eventually shipped to Cayenne. Captured in turn by the British some years later, Germain did not return to France until 1814, after which date he disappears from the record.

A minor leader of the Conspiracy of the Equals, Germain had some importance as an original thinker, as a foil for Babeuf's developing ideas in 1795 and as an effective agitator.

There is no biography of Germain but details of his activities can be found in M. Dommanget, *Sur Babeuf et la conjuration des égaux* (Paris, 1970); R.B. Rose, *Gracchus Babeuf, the First Revolutionary Communist* (Stanford, 1978); and R. Legrand, *Babeuf et ses Compagnons de Route* (Paris, 1981).

R.B. ROSE

GIOANNETTI, Giuseppe (1768–1843)
Italian Jacobin activist, playwright and educator

Gioannetti was born in Bologna on December 25, 1768. Following his early education in a college for nobility in Bologna, he was persuaded by his cardinal uncle, Andrea Gioannetti, to pursue a career in diplomacy in Rome. Abandoning this goal, however, in order to study pedagogy in Livorno, Venice and Genoa, Giuseppe Gioannetti, along with his brother, Rodolfo, became an active Jacobin. The democratic zeal which he expounded on entering a contest in 1796 displeased the local Bolognese aristocracy and governing senate. When the French occupied Bologna, he joined the civic guard and in October 1796 was instrumental in impelling the communal government to plant a tree of liberty. Perceived by Napoleon and the French general staff as too radical, he was sent in February 1797 to Milano as a way of defusing Bologna as a Jacobin centre. Back in Bologna by May, he participated as leader of a demonstration on 11 June which destroyed all symbols of papal rule, burned the *Libro d'oro* (the symbol and record of Bolognese ennoblement) and ordered the arrest of Bolognese bankers. Gioannetti was arrested on 25 June and condemned with his brother for conspiracy, but received a jail term of only four months.

In December 1798, seeking to amplify the means of public education, he organised the *Teatro Nazionale*, designed to instruct the poor, and published a collection of didactic dialogues. Arrested by the Austrians on June 29, 1799 with the collapse of the Republic, he remained in various jails in Parma, Milano and Bologna until his release in October 1800. Thereafter he reorganised the national guard and devoted his time to pedagogical studies. When anti-French demonstrations occurred in 1802, Gioannetti was arrested but released since proof of his complicity was lacking. Though present at Napoleon's coronation in Milano in May 1805, Gioannetti returned to his writings on pedagogy in Bologna. Details of his activities are lacking for the later years. In the atmosphere of Carbonari activities in Bologna in the restoration period, his name was linked with conspiracies of 1817–18 and in December 1821, but he was quickly released by the authorities. He appears to have played no part in the revolutions in Bologna in 1831. He died in Bologna on November 21, 1843.

As a radical Jacobin with a fervent belief in democracy, Gioannetti's writings, especially his earlier written dialogues, attacked the rich, the speculators, and above all the entrenched Bolognese nobility and the clerics. Concerned about the cost of living and unemployment, Gioannetti addressed the needs of artisans and peasants. By organising banquets for the peasantry in the name of brotherhood, he created occasions for instructing the

peasantry on their duties as well as their rights. Both his dialogues, designed to be read by itinerant Jacobins in the countryside, and his plays, written for his people's theatre, were filled with moral instruction. As with many Jacobins of the 1796–1799 period, Gioannetti saw education as the means toward his democratic goal, but he often resorted to active demonstrations against any convenient symbols of obstacles to democracy. While expressing a vehement anti-clericalism, at no time did Gioannetti express anti-religious feelings, and his written dialogues saw no contradiction between religion and his democratic aspirations.

For Gioannetti's place within the Italian Jacobin movement, see Delio Cantimori (ed.), *Giacobini italiani*, Vol. II (Bari, 1964); and F. Cristofari and A. Emiliani (eds.), *I giacobini a Bologna* (Bologna, 1966).

M.S. MILLER

GIOIA, Melchiorre (1767–1829)
Italian Jacobin, economist and journalist

Gioia was born in Piacenza on September 20, 1767, the son of a silversmith. Although educated in theology at the Collegio Alberoni in Piacenza, Gioia's exposure to Jacobinism forced him to leave the priesthood in 1796 and face an early arrest by the Duke of Parma in March 1797. Receiving the news in jail of his success in winning a contest on the theme 'Which form of free government is most fitting for the happiness of Italy' in which he expounded the idea of the unitary state, he was freed by Napoleon and immediately went to Milano in November 1797 and there embarked on a brief editorial career. Following the Treaty of Campoformio in October 1797, he joined Ugo Foscolo in renouncing French policy and in editing the *Monitore Italiano* between January 20, 1798 and April 13, 1798 and subsequently *Il Censore* which lasted for only four issues in 1798. Pursuing now an active life as a journalist and writer, his *Quadro politico di Milano* in 1798, an open attack on the French Directory, brought a brief exile. Back in Milano in 1799, he founded the short-lived journal, *Gazzetta nazionale della Cisalpina*, and then the *Giornale filosofia-politico*. After further arrest and imprisonment during the Austrian-Russian intervention, he became the official historiographer of the Italian Republic in April 1801, publishing *Sul commercio dei commestibili e caro prezzo del vitto* (1802), and *Nuovo Galateo* (1802) and also a book on divorce (1803). The latter appeared at the time of Napoleon's Concordat with the church and cost Gioia his job as historiographer. However, he was reconciled to the imperial Napoleon once the Italian Republic became the Kingdom of Italy, and was named a professor of economics at the University of Padua and director of the office of statistics in 1806. Criticised by the Minister of Interior for the methods used in compiling his *Tavole statistiche*, Gioia lost his position and was jailed following the publication of a resentful satirical work, *La scienza del povero diavolo*. Freed in 1811, he worked as a private citizen for the office of statistics. In the early years of the restoration and Austrian occupation of Lombardy, Gioia wrote widely on economics, including *Nuova prospetto della scienze economiche* (1818–19), *Manifatture nazionali* (1819) and *Filosofia della statistica* (1826). He collaborated with two major journals, *Biblioteca italiana* and *Annali universali di statistica*. Suspected of liberal sympathies through his association with the periodical *Il Conciliatore*, and momentarily jailed between December 1820 and July 1821, he nevertheless died reconciled to catholicism in Milano on January 2, 1829.

Surviving the various political régimes of his lifetime, Gioia's early Jacobinism, including a persistent anti-clericalism, became greatly modified after 1800 as he became at times a part of Napoleonic officialdom. While seeking to shun abstractions, Gioia was influenced in his early years by French empiricism and Condillac's theories of sensation. The new revolutionary realities in the 1790s, in which he perceived the connections between the American and French revolutions, and France's invasion of Italy provoked his advocacy of Italian unity and abandonment of the historic idea of communes and republics. Opposed to absolute monarchy and aristocratic régimes, Gioia at the time of the Cisalpine Republic expounded the rights and duties attached to liberty, and supported the idea of popular sovereignty and the institution of a two-house legislature. An earlier utilitarian element in his philosophy, expressed in his concept of happiness based upon social well-being, was later reinforced by the theories of Jeremy Bentham and the English utilitarians. As Gioia's economic ideas developed, the influence of the eighteenth-century economist, Pietro Verri, became apparent, and by 1802 Gioia was advocating the free circulation of grain and, abandoning the ideal of the small landed proprietor defended by many Jacobins, was urging instead the more efficient cultivation of the larger landed estates. As statistician and laissez-faire economist concerned with demography, production, prices and free competition, he addressed more and more the interest of the growing commercial and professional middle classes, thus anticipating the changing social scene of the nineteenth century. Seen by Silvio Pellico, author of *Le mie prigioni*, as the coming economist of the post-1815 period, Gioia also contributed to the methodology of modern statistics, especially in his *Logica statistica* (1808). What distinguished Gioia from other contemporary economists in Italy was his fervour for industrialisation and the development of urban life.

Gioia's political and economic ideas can be studied through his own writings cited above. They are, however, synthesised in the following: Piero Barucci, *Il pensiero economico di Melchiorre Gioia* (Milano, 1965); Carlo Morandi, *Idee e formazione politiche in Lombardia dal 1748 al 1814* (Torino, 1926); Stuart Woolf, *A History of Italy 1700–1860* (London, 1979); and Kent Greenfield, *Economics and liberalism in the Risorgimento: a study of nationalism in Lombardy, 1814–1848* (rev. ed. Baltimore, 1965).

M.S. MILLER

GOERRES, Joseph (1776–1848)
German journalist, republican and Jacobin

Joseph Goerres's adherence to French republicanism in the 1790s was only the first stage in a long career during which he identified himself successively with the romantic movement, the German reaction against Napoleon, the liberal resistance to Prussian bureaucratic conservatism during the Restoration, and finally with the Catholic Church. Goerres's father was a lumber merchant in the small episcopal capital of Koblenz; his mother came from Italy. Before the French Revolution, Koblenz, under the enlightened administration of the Bishop of Trier, was open to the influence of the German Aufklärung. Although Goerres's parents had no intellectual interests, his teachers at the local Gymnasium introduced him to Kant (q.v.) and other contemporary thinkers and imbued him with a strong moral idealism characteristic of German thought during this period. The teenage student enthusiastically adopted the ideals of the French Revolution, and in 1792 he is known to have visited the Jacobin Club in Mainz established by Georg Forster (q.v.) and others during the first French occupation of the Rhineland.

Goerres's active participation in pro-revolutionary politics and journalism began in late 1795, after the second French thrust into German territory. He published his first article in Biergans's journal in October 1795, and completed his first major work, 'Universal Peace, an Ideal', inspired by Kant's well-known essay, around the same time, although it was not published until 1798. In his essay, Goerres urged republican France to become the protector of a universal federation of free republics. He called for the strict subordination of the Church to an enlightened secular state, but showed more interest in moral issues than in social ones.

Like almost all of the German republicans, Goerres found the experience of French occupation after 1794 disillusioning. Despite their promises of liberation, the French subjected the Rhineland to an imported administration with little sympathy for the local population and imposed heavy financial demands to support their armies. The small group of German republicans nevertheless needed French support to promote what they saw as the common cause of mankind in the face of the population's indifference or hostility; at the same time, they recognised that the conduct of the French was undermining any possibility of generating a broad-based republican movement. Despite his youth, Goerres saw this dilemma as clearly as any of the German Jacobins, and his political activities until 1799 were all efforts to resolve it. He first became prominent among the Rhineland republicans through his participation in the shortlived movement for a Cisrhenan republic in the summer of 1797. Fearing that Bonaparte's arrangements with the Austrians at Leoben in the spring of that year would lead to a French withdrawal from the Rhineland in exchange for territories in Italy, Goerres and his group hoped to establish an autonomous republic on German soil. The project had the backing of the French general Hoche, but his death in September 1797 crushed whatever prospects the plan might have had.

Goerres, who had helped to draft a manifesto for the Cisrhenan movement, shifted after Hoche's death to advocacy of a French annexation of the Rhineland, which he hoped would give the German territories representation in the assemblies of the Directory and the right to claim constitutional protections against the French armies and administrators. He promoted his programme in a club in Koblenz, but he had his greatest impact through his journal, the *Röthe Blätter*, founded in February 1798 during the period of republican reinvigoration that followed the French coup d'état of Fructidor. Through his journal, Goerres pursued a dual programme: on the one hand, he sought to dissolve loyalties to the old régime and promote republicanism among the local population, while on the other hand he launched an outspoken campaign against the abuses of the French administration and the exclusion of the Rhineland republicans from political responsibility. His well-documented accusations against certain French officials inevitably led to complaints against him, and he had to suspend publication after a few months. He soon founded a new magazine, the *Rübezahl*, in which he resumed his campaign, particularly after the coup d'état of 30 Prairial VII brought a lifting of press restrictions in France and a revival of the neo-Jacobin movement there. Goerres's journals were only one among a number of republican periodicals published in the Rhineland, and probably had little influence outside of Koblenz and its region, but they stood out from the rest of the press thanks to their author's vivid and forceful prose. Inspired by the pre-revolutionary German journalist Wekhrlin and the German republican Rebmann (q.v.) more than by French journalism of the revolutionary period, Goerres produced lively satires and exhortations to his countrymen that showed a vitality and originality sadly lacking in the French republican press of the Directory.

The conflict between the German republicans and the French administration in Koblenz came to a head in October 1799, when the local military commander dismissed the city administration. Goerres, who had already suspended publication of the *Rübezahl*, was chosen as part of a delegation sent to Paris to plead the local republicans' case. He experienced the full measure of the distrust between the French authorities and his own group when he found himself imprisoned for three weeks in Mainz en route. He arrived in Paris just after Bonaparte's seizure of power on 18 Brumaire VIII and quickly realised that any hope of implementing his republican ideals had vanished. Concluding that the French Revolution had betrayed its own principles and demonstrated that the French were not ripe for freedom, he returned to Koblenz in April 1800. He

expressed his bitter disillusionment in an eloquent account of his mission; after making his break with the French public, he withdrew from public life until the end of the Napoleonic period.

Although the Jacobin phase of Goerres's career had ended, he continued to play an important role in German cultural life for four more decades. After 1800, he turned to teaching; his interests ranged from the natural sciences to German history and folkways. As professor at Heidelberg from 1806 to 1808, he contributed to the revival of German national consciousness associated with the romantic movement. When that consciousness took political form after the French defeats of 1813, Goerres made a spectacular reappearance with the founding of a new journal, the *Rheinische Merkur*, in January 1814; it was quickly recognised as the most outspoken and influential of the many press-organs directed against the crumbling Napoleonic Empire. In its columns, Goerres campaigned for a German constitution that would combine liberty with a respect for the organic institutions of the German past. The Prussian bureaucratic administration installed in the Rhineland after 1815 failed to satisfy him. After abandoning the *Merkur* in January 1816, he became identified with the liberal opposition, finally being driven into exile in 1820. While living in Switzerland and France, Goerres drifted away from liberalism and returned to the Catholic Church. An appointment to teach at Munich in 1827 allowed him to return to Germany, and his pamphlet *Athanasius*, published in 1837 in connection with the conflict between the Catholic Church in Cologne and the Prussian government, became the manifesto of the modern German Catholic political movement. Goerres died on the eve of the revolutions of 1848.

The 'Jacobin' ideas Goerres espoused in the 1790s were similar to those of other German republicans; what set him apart was his extraordinary writing style and his extreme youth, which made it easier for him to abandon republicanism and identify himself with the romantic movement. His participation in so many of the intellectual currents of the nineteenth century saved him from the oblivion that descended on most of the other German Jacobins, but it also posed a major problem for the understanding of his personal development. To many conservative scholars well into the twentieth century, Goerres's Jacobinism was simply a youthful aberration. Goerres himself, though disavowing his republicanism and admiration for France, never sought to bury this earliest phase of his career and maintained that he never abandoned the love of freedom that had led him to embrace the revolution.

The major studies of Blanning, Grab, and Scheel contain relatively little specific information on Goerres, who seems to be somewhat neglected in the current revival of interest in the German Jacobins, no doubt for the same reasons that he was more prominent in the historiography up to 1945. The most useful sources of information are, therefore, Max Braubach, 'Der Junge Görres als "Cisrhenane" ', *Diplomatie und Geistiges Leben im 17. und 18. Jahrhundert* (Bonn, 1969), and H. Raab, *Joseph Görres: Ein Leben für Freiheit und Recht* (Paderborn, 1978). The latter contains a full bibliography. For Goerres's own political writings, see Joseph Goerres, *Politische Schriften der Frühzeit (1795–1800)* (ed. Max Braubach, Köln, 1928) (Vol. 1 of Goerres, *Gesammelten Schriften*).

J. POPKIN

GOGEL, Isaac Jan Alexander (1765–1821)
Dutch merchant, member of the Patriot movement and minister in the Batavian Republic

Gogel was the son of a German officer in government service and born in Vugt near 's-Hertogenbosch in Brabant. He went to Amsterdam in 1791 to train as a merchant and there became influenced by the Patriot movement. As a result of the movement's connections with the French Republicans, Gogel, together with Willem van Irhoven van Dam was sent to persuade the French Army and representatives of the Convention to invade the Dutch Republic as soon as possible. The result of these discussions was the abortive revolution of October 1794 when a Patriot uprising in Holland failed to receive the necessary French military assistance and was swiftly crushed. Evading the authorities, Gogel was able to take refuge in Bremen.

Before the failure of the uprising, Gogel had become one of the most zealous members of the Patriot's Revolutionary Committee, and after the successful revolution of 1795 he returned to become president of the *Societeit voor Een- en Ondeelbaarheid* and one of the main advocates of financial reform and a switch to direct taxation. After 1795 he held a number of official positions including Agent for Finance during the Directory of January to June 1798. He also held this post in the succeeding régime, and became Minister of Finance under Schimmelpenninck in 1805. Later, he became Intendant-General of Finance for Napoleon's government in Paris, a post he held until 1813. His work in reforming the taxation system of the country was widely appreciated when the Dutch authorities took over from the French in 1814. Having retired from public service in 1813, Gogel bought a dye factory in Overveen and in 1821 was appointed Privy Councillor by King Willem I before dying in March of that year.

Gogel was acknowledged as the great financial talent of his age, but his accomplishments in this area were combined with his views on the nature of Dutch society. Too young to have been involved in the Patriot movement of the 1780s, he became convinced that a revolution from within was impractical and that real change could only come through French intervention. To an extent, his views had been coloured by the failure of the Patriots to consolidate their gains in the years 1785–7 and the ideological divisions within the movement. After the formation of the Batavian Republic in 1795, Gogel became prominent as joint editor, with Anthonie Ockerse, of the periodical *De Democraten*. His views were based on the fear that if the privileges of provinces and cities were allowed to remain, this would give the opportunity for the Stadholderate to reassert its authority. Thus he saw the federalists as counter-revolutionary and became closely associated with the more radical of the unitarists.

While Gogel held radical political views, his reaction to the coup of January 1798 was somewhat muted. While espousing the cause of democracy, he became concerned by the opportunism of some Jacobin leaders in distributing public office – one of the very reasons for his opposition to the Orangists. Moreover, he became disillusioned with the type of people brought to the fore by the revolution, seeing a political danger in the potential for mob rule and also an economic danger to the financial structure of Amsterdam if the 'social' revolution was put into operation. In effect, Gogel was happy to uphold the principles of democracy, but his social position combined with a belief in self-help, meritocracy and liberty of thought made him somewhat wary of that democracy in action. Thus even as Agent for Finance under the Directory, Gogel was isolated from the likes of Fijnje (q.v.) and Vreede (q.v.), likening them to 'a small band of anarchists. . . (working) steadily to create disorder and to win office for themselves'. His attempts to get the French authorities to intervene met with little success, but the coup of June 1798 unseated the first Directors, leaving Gogel to continue his work with the country's finances.

While remembered primarily for his work in reforming the taxation system of the country, Gogel's contribution to the Patriot movement should not be underestimated. Having come to the movement through his opposition to the Orangists and the Stadholderate, he represented the intellectual wing of the movement which based its thinking on a rejection of corruption in the interests of efficiency. Thus when the Patriots themselves indulged in the sins which Gogel had condemned among the Orangists, he had no qualms about opposing them also. His later career, although still centred on the republican ideal, became almost exclusively concerned with economic, financial and taxation matters.

Two old sources are J.M. Gogel, *Memoriën en Correspondentiën betrekkelijk den staat van 's Rijks geldmiddelen in den jare 1820 door I.J.A. Gogel* (Amsterdam, 1844); and J.A. Sillem, *De Politieke en Staathuishoudkundige Werkzaamheid van I.J.A. Gogel* (Amsterdam, 1864). See also, P.K. Blok and P.C Molhuysen, *Nieuw Nederlandsch Biografisch Woordenboek* (Leiden, 1911–37); L.G. Verberne, *Gogel en Uniteit* (Nijmegen, 1948); and S. Schama, *Patriots and liberators* (New York, 1977).

BOB MOORE

GORANI, Giuseppe (1740–1814)
Italian Jacobin

Gorani was born in Milan to a fairly prosperous family of the lower nobility and pursued a military career with the Habsburg armies. Following the Seven Years' War, when he was captured by Prussian forces, he travelled extensively throughout Europe. He became a freemason and member of an international network of European intellectuals interested in political reform and hostile to monarchy and established religion. While living in Noyon, Switzerland, he introduced the work of Pietro Verri and other Milanese reformers to intellectuals from other countries. In 1770 he published a political treatise, *Il vero dispotismo*, and in 1773 he proposed to Victor Amadeus III, Duke of Savoy, a plan for the liberalisation of his government and eventually of all of the Italian governments. The plan, however, was not well-received, and Gorani resumed his wanderings. He fought with the forces of Pasquale Paoli in Corsica before moving on to Portugal where he served the government of the Marquis de Pombal.

In August 1792 Gorani was among the first European radicals to become an honorary citizen of the French Republic, whose principles he endorsed enthusiastically. In his *Lettres sur la révolution française*, he expressed the hope that agrarian and educational reforms would be introduced and that the democratic and unitary ideals of the French Revolution would be adopted in his native Italy. However, disillusioned with the excesses of the terror and, later, with the return to monarchical government under Bonaparte, he returned to Switzerland, where he died in 1819.

Gorani's radicalism therefore was most evident in his consistent opposition to monarchy and his determination to further the cause of political reform throughout Europe. In his younger years, he was an advocate of very radical causes, questioning private property, championing the rights of women, and advising the despotic rulers of the 1770s to build a base of support among the masses. Later in life, probably as a result of having witnessed the terror in France, he adopted more moderate views.

The principal source of information is Gorani's own *Mémoires* (4 vols., Paris, 1944). But see also, Marc Monnier, *Un aventurier italien du siècle dernier: le comte Joseph Gorani* (Paris, 1884); and Stuart J. Woolf, *A History of Italy* (London, 1979).

CLARA M. LOVETT

GOUGES, Olympe de (1748–1793)
French playwright, pamphleteer, political activist, and early feminist

Olympe was born Marie Gouze near Montauban in 1748. Her father, Pierre Gouze, was a butcher and her mother, Olympe Mouisset, was a trinket peddler. Information about her early years is lacking. She was married in 1765 to Louis Yves Aubry, a restaurant owner and less than a year later she had a son, Pierre. The marriage was shortlived because either Louis Yves died or Marie left him. She adopted her mother's name Olympe and she also changed 'Gouze' to de Gouges. She came to Paris in the early 1780s and began her career as a courtesan from which she made a considerable fortune.

Soon Olympe found her new talents as a playwright, and a career that placed her in the limelight in some circles of the theatre-going French public. In 1784 she wrote her first play, *Zamore et Mirza ou*

l'Heureux Naufrage which showed her opposition to slavery. Comédie Française considered this play for performance in December 1789 under the title of *L'Esclavage des noirs*. It was performed on December 28 at the Théâtre de la Nation. In spite of the timeliness of the topic and roles being played by popular actors of the time, the play was not favourably received either by the critics or by the audience. Olympe then revised the play, but the actors refused to accept the revised version and went ahead, despite her opposition, with two further performances of the original play in front of small audiences.

In 1788 she turned her energies to politics. In her first political tract, *Lettre au peuple, ou Projet d'une casse patriotique* (1788), Olympe suggested that only voluntary tax paid by the members of all three orders could remedy the deficit of the French treasury. In *Remarques patriotiques* (1788–89) she proposed establishing a luxury tax. She insisted that people should pay tax on the number of horses, carriages and armories they owned. Groups oppressed in society were often primary focal points in her writings. Revolted by the deplorable state of widows, orphans and the aged, she recommended vast social reforms in *Remarques patriotiques*. She suggested building homes for old people, abandoned children, and widows whose husbands were killed in work-related accidents.

Olympe believed that women were the most exploited group under the French economic, social and political systems. She urged women to assume greater responsibility in society to free themselves from their opprobrious state. With the coming of the revolution, changes in the political system were in the offing and Olympe found a ray of hope of bringing concomitant changes in the condition of women in society. One of the most pressing problems of the country, which the Constituent Assembly had to face, was the overwhelming national debt. Assuming that the financial crisis would bring a halt, and even total rejection, of social and political reforms, she conceived of a plan where women could help to ease the national debt. Olympe appealed to women in her pamphlet of 1790, *Action héroique d'une Française ou la France sauvée par les Femmes*, to donate their gold and valuable possessions to help reduce this debt.

The belief that women should enjoy the same civic rights in society as men was foremost in her feminist philosophy. A major accomplishment of the revolution was the *Declaration of the Rights of Man and Citizens*, adopted in August 1789. Lamenting that the rights under this *Declaration* were not extended to women, Olympe wrote, 'Oh! My poor sex, Oh! women, you have gained nothing in this revolution.' In 1791 she drafted her own *Declaration of the Rights of Women (Les Droits de la Femme)*. She addressed this pamphlet to the queen hoping that Marie Antoinette could be convinced to take up the fight for political rights for women. Olympe was convinced that the goals of the revolution would not be attained until all women were freed from their deplorable lot and given back the basic rights they had lost in society. While pleading with women to fight for their own rights and end once and for all the imbalances between the sexes in the enjoyment of the basic human rights, she challenged men by asking: 'Men, are you capable of being just? Tell me, what has given you the power to oppress my sex? Your strength? Your ability?' Pointing to the harmony and cooperation of the sexes in nature, she rejected men's claim to command despotically 'a sex which has all the intellectual faculties'. She declared in *Les Droits de la Femme* that 'woman is born free and lives equal in rights to the man'. She emphasised that 'all the citizens, including men and women being equal in its eyes, should be equally admissible to all public dignities, places and employment according to their capacity and without distinctions other than those of their virtue and talent'. Women were as much a part of the nation as men; she therefore maintained that the 'principle of all sovereignty resides essentially in the nation which consists of women as well as men'. She further maintained that 'Law ought to be the expression of the general will: all the *citoyennes* and the *citoyens* ought to contribute to its formation. . .'.

Her idea of emancipation of women not only rested on political equality, but also dealt with reformation of the social customs such as the institution of marriage and family responsibility. Claiming that marriage should be a social contract between a woman and a man, she wrote in her *Le Contrat Social de l'Homme et de la Femme* (a segment of *Les Droits de la Femme*): 'We,. . . . . .and . . . . ., moved by our own will, unite ourselves for the duration of our lives, and for the duration of our mutal inclinations. . .'. She propounded that the contracting parties were to hold their property in common, with the reservation that it could be divided in favour of their children and those for whom they might have a special attachment. Both husband and wife should agree that their property belonged to their children without any sex distinction. The children should have the right to bear the names of their mother or their father.

Knowing that the claim of rights for women would bring demands for their assuming many responsibilities, Olympe de Gouges asserted that women as individuals should be responsible for their own actions. She wrote in *Le Philosophe Corrigé* (1787): 'I think that both sexes regardless of wealth, rank or marriage, should equally become masters of their own destinies and actions.' Moreover, Olympe envisaged that women would be able to defend the nation. She even advocated military training of women. Three of the heroines were portrayed as female soldiers in her *L'Entrée du Dumouriez à Bruxelles* (1793) and women with military training had a place in her novel *Le Prince Philosophe* (1792).

Olympe was both an ideologue and an activist. On October 28, 1789 she led a deputation of women to present to the National Assembly a programme of feminist reforms bringing complete sexual equality and equitable economic and social customs before the law. On May 20, 1792 she attended the Fête of Federation where she was at the head of a body of fully-armed women. In 1793 Olympe, along with Théroigne de Méricourt (q.v.) and Etta Palm d'Alders, established the Club des Citoyennes Republicaines Révolutionnaires, which, during its short existence, was extremely active in promoting women's causes. She favoured the idea of having a women's journal and of having a second national theatre exclusively for women.

Calling the attention of the Convention to the fact that 'heroism and generosity are also possessed by women' on December 15, 1792, Olympe volunteered to defend Louis XVI who was on trial. Her defence of the king was simple: acknowledge the difference between the king and the man. When she became convinced that the king was a traitor, Olympe apparently was sympathetic to the republican form of government. However, with the changing political climate she gradually became disillusioned with the political mood of the country. On October 29, 1792 Olympe posted a placard entitled *Pronostic sur Maximilien Robespierre, par un animal amphibie*. Blaming Robespierre (q.v.) for the September prison massacre she wrote: 'You wish to assassinate the last Louis in order to deprive him of legal trial; you wish to assassinate Pétion, Roland, Vergniaud, Condorcet, Louvet, Brissot. . ., in one word all the luminaries of the republic and of patriotism.' Her constant criticism of the Jacobin government and its terror made her an enemy of Robespierre. To her 'Robespierre was an ambitious person without soul. . . who would sacrifice the entire nation to become a dictator.' She now advocated in her pamphlet, *Les Trois Urnes, ou le Salut de la Patrie*, a popular vote to determine the form of government for France. The Convention considered this tract seditious and arrested Olympe. Charges were brought that besides writing inflammatory pamphlets such as *Les Trois Urnes, La France sauvée, ou le Tyran détrôné*, and *Olympe de Gouges au Tribunal Révolutionnaire*, Olympe repeatedly undermined the constitutional authorities. Pointing to a letter she had written to

Hérault de Séchelles (q.v.), the prosecutors indicted her for supporting federalism. The Revolutionary Tribunal found her guilty and she was condemned to death. Olympe now declared that she was pregnant. The appeal, had it been accepted, would have delayed the sentence until the birth of the child. The court ordered a medical examination which established that it was a hoax. Her appeal was denied and she was guillotined on 13 Brumaire (November 3, 1793).

Olympe de Gouges was an early and forthright exponent of feminism who sought to broaden the political and social programme of the revolution to embrace women's rights. Between 1784 and 1793 she wrote at least ten plays, a novel and countless pamphlets in which she not only criticised discrimination against women but rooted this criticism in a critique of the socio-economic and political problems of French society. In this ability to link the feminist issue with a comprehensive view of social and economic inequality even after the political changes of 1789, lay the essence of her radicalism.

Little information on de Gouge's life and activities is available in English. Her pamphlet *Les droits de la femme* has been translated by Nupur Chaudhuri with Karen Offen in Susan G. Bell and Karen M. Offen (eds.), *Women, the family and freedom: the debate in documents* (Stanford, 1983). Accounts of Olympe's trial can be found in Darline Gay Levy, Harriet B. Applewhite and Mary D. Johnson (eds.), *Women in Revolutionary Paris 1789–1795* (Urbana, 1979). A.N. W.293, dossier 210 contains materials regarding Olympe's imprisonment and trial including *Les trois urnes* and *Olympe de Gouges au Tribunal Révolutionnaire*. To date the best biography of de Gouges is Olive Blanc's *Olympe de Gouges* (Paris, 1981). M. Cerati's *Le Club des citoyennes républicaines révolutionnaires* (Paris, 1966) and L. Lacour, *Les origines du féminisme contemporain: Trois femmes de la Révolution, Olympe de Gouges, Théroigne de Méricourt, Rosa Lacombe* (Paris, 1900) also contains some useful information. Marvin Carlson, *The theatre of the French Revolution* (Ithaca, N.Y., 1966) contains some information on de Gouge's plays.

N. CHAUDHURI

GRÉGOIRE, Baptiste Henri (1750–1831)
French constitutional bishop, egalitarian and republican

Grégoire the son of an artisan was born in Vého, a small village in ducal Lorraine. Educated by Jesuits, but perhaps more influenced by his mother's Jansenism, Grégoire was ordained in 1775. He was never an abbot in spite of the appellation 'Abbé' commonly used in historical texts. By the outbreak of the revolution Grégoire was an advocate of greater equality within the church hierarchy, toleration for non-Catholics and civil rights for the Jewish population of France.

The liberal *curé* was elected as a delegate for the First Estate for the *baillage* of Nancy, but at Versailles he joined the Third Estate in its successful endeavour to form a National Constituent Assembly. He became an influential voice within that body. He helped frame the Civil Constitution of the Clergy and legislation extending civil equality to Jews including the culturally unassimilated Ashkenazim of Alsace and Lorraine. Joining the *Amis des Noirs*, a club favouring rights for blacks and mulattos, he worked for admission of West Indian mulattos to the Assembly and abolition of slavery in the French colonies.

In 1791 the diocese of Blois elected Grégoire its constitutional bishop. He took the oath required of the clergy by the Civil Constitution and worked to gain public support for the constitutional church. As the revolution became more hostile to organised religion, he attempted to maintain a consistent course by remaining faithful to Catholic doctrine, opposing the persecution of non-juring clergy and speaking out against the Hébertist Cult of Reason. Robespierre's (q.v.) Cult of the Supreme Being received Grégoire's approbation, but after Thermidor he attempted to revive the constitutional church. Secular

liberals and radicals on the left and conservative Catholics on the right frustrated his efforts. Rather than accept Napoleon's Concordat with the Papacy in 1801, he resigned his bishopric, but remained a member of the clergy until his death.

Grégoire evolved quickly as a republican. He favoured a more democratic constitution than that produced by the National Assembly in 1791 which distinguished between active and passive citizens. The king's flight to Varennes confirmed his distrust of monarchy. Electors of Loir-et-Cher sent him to the National Convention in 1792 where he sat with the Plain but joined in the call for abolition of the monarchy and trial of the king. He was away from the Convention when the vote on Louis' death-penalty was taken, but issued a public statement opposing it.

Although the Jacobins in the Convention heeded Grégoire's call for the abolition of slavery (which was re-instituted under Napoleon), Grégoire's personal influence diminished. After the Convention disbanded, he was elected successively to the Council of Five Hundred (1795–98), the Legislative Body (1800) and the Senate (1802) until his objections to Napoleonic policies led to retirement. A bid to return to political life was blocked by the Bourbon monarchy in 1819. He refused to endorse the Orléanist Monarchy in 1830 because he favoured a republic. He died the following year.

Grégoire believed in political and civil equality for persons of all races and faiths. He proposed to extend public instruction and vocational training, build public libraries and inscribe monuments in French as means by which all minorities could be integrated into the national culture. But beyond these measures he had no political programme to speak of. His belief that an egalitarian and humane Church could take the lead in the battle against injustice did not appeal either to conservatives or to the secular left. He had no convictions on crucial economic and social issues generated by the growth of capitalism and industrialisation.

Grégoire was intolerant of those whose

idealism fell short of his personal standards and he lacked practical abilities as a political organiser. As a propagandist, he enjoyed only a brief period of prominence in the early years of the revolution. His influence was probably more lasting in the Americas where he was recognised for his efforts to abolish slavery than in Europe where his moral crusades were largely forgotten by the time of his death.

The large collection of Grégoire's writings, Henri Grégoire, *Oeuvres de l'abbé Grégoire* (14 vols., Paris, 1977) contains a foreword by Albert Soboul and a chronology of the life of Grégoire. In addition to Paul Grunnebaum-Ballin, *Henri Grégoire, ami des hommes des toutes les couleurs* (Paris, 1948), there is a biography in English by Ruth F. Necheles, *The Abbé Grégoire, 1787–1831: the odyssey of an egalitarian* (Westport, Conn., 1971).

JOEL S. CLELAND

GRENUS, Jacques (1751–1804)
Swiss radical and leader of the Genevan revolution of 1782

Born in Geneva in 1751 into a professional/middle-class family Grenus, like so many of the radicals of that time, was trained as a lawyer, rising eventually to the rank of advocate. The first thirty years of his life were peaceful and unmarked by controversy but from 1780 onwards he published several works all violently critical of the ruling 'patrician' oligarchy of his native city. Members of the Oligarchy, termed 'citizens', were distinguished from the mass of burghers who had social privileges but no power and the great majority of the population who had neither, the latter being further subdivided into 'natifs' and 'habitants'. In his works Grenus criticised the existing state of affairs both as a denial of natural rights and justice and as a violation of traditional Helvetic liberty – a combination of philosophical and historical critique which was typical of the intellectual climate of the Swiss Confederation at that time. He became an important member of the *Representant* faction which advocated reform, as opposed to the *Negatifs* who

upheld the status quo. His moment came with the anti-patrician uprising of 1782 which overthrew the oligarchy's power in favour of the so-called 'natifs' following an initial split in the ranks of the 'citizens'. Grenus was made a member of the reconstituted Council of State but the failure of the new régime to sustain itself in the face of intervention by France, Sardinia and Berne led to his being sentenced to death in absentia and his seeking refuge in France where he maintained himself by practising law in Paris. He became at this time a close associate of his compatriot and fellow exile Clavière, like himself a leader of the 1782 revolt.

In 1789 he returned to Geneva and soon became involved once more in subversive activity. He now sought to involve the 'subject' class of Geneva's dependent territories in the movement for reform, creating a new party known as the '*Egalisateurs*' which advocated substantially more radical changes than those proposed by the *Representant* party. His agitation had results leading to the uniting of *Négatifs* and *Representants* and the passing of limited reforms. Grenus himself was soon recognised as a dangerous radical, being named as the leader of a popular uprising in the subject lands of Mandement De Penay. As a result he was exiled again in 1791, returning to France. Almost immediately he became involved once more in French politics, becoming a deputy to the National Assembly. He survived the terror and the purge of his erstwhile Girondin associates and later became the Commissioner for the Army of the Alps. An advocate of the union of Geneva and France in 1798, he played a much less prominent role after the creation of the Helvetic Republic. As with many Swiss of that time his commitment to Switzerland as an entity was very lukewarm and in many ways he was a figure of French rather than Swiss politics. Like his compatriots Ochs (q.v.) and LaHarpe (q.v.) he seems to have despaired of an indigenous transformation of Swiss society and so looked rather to France as the external agency which could bring about change. He played an important part in the connection of Swiss and French radicalism and his career serves to remind us of the international nature of radical and revolutionary politics in the age of the French Revolution.

There is no life of Grenus in English but a full picture of his career can be gleaned from the standard histories of the period. Particularly useful are J. Godechot, *France and the Atlantic Revolution of the Eighteenth Century* (London, 1965) and R.R. Palmer, *The Age of the Democratic Revolution* (2 vols, Princeton, New Jersey, 1958–64). For Grenus' part in the 1782 Geneva revolt see E. Chapuisat, *La Prise D'Armes De 1782 à Genève* (Geneva, 1932). Also essential is J. Godechot, *Les Commissaires Aux Armées Sous Le Directoire* (Paris, 2 vols, 1938).

S. DAVIES

GROSSMANN, Gustav Friedrich (1743–1796)
German playwright and director, anti-feudalist and French revolutionary sympathiser

Grossmann was born in Berlin, the son of a clerk. He enjoyed a good education and was interested in the theatre from his early youth. He took up the position of Prussian legation secretary in Danzig in 1767. His first (unfinished) play was *La Prison*. In 1772 he left his post and returned to Berlin, where he translated *Minna von Barnhelm* into French. On the way to Prague in 1774 he made the acquaintance of Abel Seyler's theatre company in Weimar. He became an actor, appearing first in Lessing's plays and then working on those of Shakespeare. In 1778 he became a theatre director in Bonn, where the production of J.A. Leisewitz's *Sturm-und-Drang* play *Julius von Tarent* led to a complaint from the emperor's ambassador for ridiculing the clergy.

In 1783 Grossmann took over as director of the Mainz theatre and in 1784 founded a theatre company in Frankfurt. In 1785 he put on Beaumarchais' anti-feudal comedy *The Marriage of Figaro*. He had connections with G.A. Bürger and A. von Knigge

(q.v.) and tried to present on stage his ideas about the necessity of the emancipation of the bourgeoisie. His main attack was directed at the privileges of the nobility, and he realised that absolute monarchs were only interested in the enlightenment ideas so long as they served their own ends. He experienced difficulties with censorship even before the French Revolution, which he welcomed enthusiastically. In 1791 he translated the French play *Papa Harlequin, King and Son of Harlequin, Crown Prince*, which had a revolutionary effect when it was transferred to a German setting. The play was prohibited by the censor and Grossmann fell into financial difficulties. In 1792 he turned to the public with a request to send donations to J. Campe for a memorial to Lessing.

Grossmann, who became increasingly radicalised politically, and bitter about the behaviour of the nobility, lost control on 3 February 1795 during a theatre production in Hanover, when he began to extemporise, and compared the King of England with a donkey in the presence of his sister, Amalie, Duchess of Brunswick. He was arrested and imprisoned, but refused at first to apologise publicly for the insult. Finally, however, in November 1795, when he was financially ruined and physically in ill health, he wrote to the Lord Chamberlain, begging him not to take away his company's licence, But he never recovered his health, and died several months later.

Grossmann's importance was chiefly as a populariser of anti-monarchical and anti-feudal ideas in Germany through the theatre company, and as a disseminator of the ideas of the French Revolution in Germany.

There is no biography of Grossmann, but for his theatrical activities, see G. Steiner, *Jakobinerschauspiel und Jakobinertheater* (Stuttgart, 1973), pp. 93–135.

W. GRAB

HACKEL, Johann (1750–1816)
Austrian businessman involved in the
'Jacobin conspiracy'

Hackel was born in 1750 in Vienna, the son of a silk merchant. After six years of school he went into his father's business before undergoing three years' further business training in an exchange office in Augsburg. On his return to Vienna in 1770 he became his father's partner and, in 1779 married Anna Katharina Moshammer, the daughter of a wealthy Linz lottery owner. They had two children. In 1785 he took over his father-in-law's silver lottery by court contract and ran it for three years in the Crown lands, particularly in Lemberg, and from 1788 for two years in Vienna. In 1790 the contract expired, and was not renewed by the authorities, an alleged reason for his later dissatisfaction with the government.

In 1783 Hackel was received into the Vienna freemason's lodge 'Zu den drey Adlern', and there made the acquaintance of, among others, Johann Jutz, doctor of law, who was also to be a defendant in the Jacobin trials. It was in Lemberg, however, that he became a friend of the future Hungarian Jacobin Ignác Martinovics (q.v.), who visited Hackel frequently. Hackel wrote down and learnt by heart the *Eipeldauerlied*. It was said of this song that it could 'cause unrest among the common crowd'. Along with his friendship with Martinovics, this was the central point of the charges against him. Martinovics allegedly tried to involve him in his 'conspiracy', and to initiate him into his secret society in Pest. There were no punishable offences, only occasional conversations about revolution, but his involvement with Martinovics led to his arrest and trial.

Hackel was sentenced on the basis of forced confessions elicited by beatings and torture, and without any corroborating evidence. In one of his first confessions he said 'I praised the first French constitution. . . I expressed the wish that here too the nobility might be made more compliant so that the bourgeoisie (Bürgerstand) might rise. I was pleased at the victories of the French over our armies, because I hoped that they would bring peace. . . I may have said that France would be recognised as a republic. . .'.

Hackel lost his citizenship and was publicly humiliated with the inscription 'on account of treason'. He was sentenced to thirty years' imprisonment at Kufstein in the Tyrol, but in 1795 was transferred by military transport and under strict supervision to Munkacs in the Carpathian Ukraine (then in Hungary) because of overcrowding at Kufstein. He property was confiscated at first, but his wife Katharina petitioned the emperor to lift the property confiscation. In 1796 his wife was also granted the right to afford him modest support in his imprisonment at Munkacs. In 1802 he was pardoned by the emperor, but interned at Linz where, after 1812 he lived with his father-in-law, Moshammer. Hackel died of tuberculosis in 1816.

In the criminal investigations it was repeatedly emphasised that the *Eipeldauerlied* served to subvert the lowest class and not intellectuals, and therefore was particularly dangerous. Hackel, of all the defendants and suspects, could be convicted of no other crime than popularising this song. He was sentenced firstly for complicity in Martinovics' treason, secondly for copying down the *Eipeldauerlied* and thirdly for copying out the 'Letter to the Emperor' for Martinovics.

As with the other Austrian defendants there was no evidence of any treasonable activity; they had merely been members of groups of former Josephinians and Leopoldinians who took part in radical discussions. Hackel's house was a meeting place for Enlighteners, former freemasons and Illuminati, and Hackel also seemed dangerous to the authorities because of his connections with the lower classes.

Insufficient is known about Hackel, who was only marginally involved in the 'conspiracy'. There is no biography, but further details of the Viennese Jacobins and the 'conspiracy' can be found in the following: Paul P. Bernard, *Enlightenment and Enlightened Despotism in Austria* (Urbana, Chicago, London, 1971), which is recommended with considerable reservations; Leslie Bodi, 'Enlightened Despotism and Literature of Enlightenment', *German Life and Letters*, vol. 22 (Oxford, 1969); Franz Gräffer, *Kleine Wiener Memoiren und Wiener Dosenstücke* (a selection edited, introduced and annotated by Anton Schlossar and Gustav Gugitz, 2 vols., Munich, 1918); Alfred Körner, *Die Wiener Jakobiner* (Stuttgart, 1972); Joseph Richter, *Die Eipeldauer Briefe* (a selection in two volumes edited by Eugen Paunel, Munich, 1917); Edith Rosenstrauch-Königsberg, *Freimaurerei im Josephinischen Wien. Aloys Blumauers Weg vom Jesuiten zum Jakobiner* (Wien, 1975), and 'Aloys Blumauer – Jesuit, Freimaurer, Jakobiner', *Jahrbuch des Instituts für deutsche Geschichte der Universität Tel Aviv* (1973), pp. 145–171; Friedrich Anton von Schönholz, *Traditionen zur Charakteristik Österreichs, seines Staats- und Volkslebens unter Franz I* (edited by Gustav Gugitz, 2 vols., Munich, 1914); Denis Silagi, *Jakobiner in der Habsburger Monarchie. Ein Beitrag zur Geschichte des aufgeklärten Absolutismus in Österreich* (Vienna, Munich, 1962); Ernst Wangermann, *From Joseph II to the Jacobin Trials* (Oxford, 1959), and (with others) *The Austrian Achievement 1700–1800* (London, 1973).

EDITH ROSENSTRAUCH-
KÖNIGSBERG

HAJNÓCZY, József (1750–1794)
Hungarian Jacobin

Hajnóczy was born in Modor, Hungary (now Modta, Czechoslovakia), the son of a Lutheran pastor. He studied at the Lutheran grammar schools of Sopron and Pozsony, (now Bratislava, Czechoslovakia), then he read law at the Pozsony academy. He became a lawyer-candidate at Eperjes (now Prešov, Czechoslovakia) in 1770 and at Pest (Budapest) in 1772, and qualified in 1774. Not belonging to the noble class and being a Protestant, Hajnóczy could not enter a state position and he also lacked the financial capacity to set up a practice of his own, therefore he accepted the job as private secretary to Count Miklós Forgách in 1774. For four years Hajnóczy worked for Count Forgách, who was an enthusiastic supporter of the ideas of the French Enlightenment and one of the leading figures of the Hungarian national resistance to Vienna. There he became acquainted with the external and internal conditions of the country and in the count's library and archives studied the history of government and public administration. In 1779 he became private secretary to Count Ferenc Széchényi. His employer, later the founder of the Hungarian National Museum and Library, belonged to the reformists of the nobility and was a zealous freemason. By his support Hajnóczy entered the masonic lodge 'Silence' in Pozsony in 1780.

Hajnóczy was a supporter of Joseph II's reformist policy. Through the instrumentality of Széchényi the king appointed him deputy-lieutenant of the County of Szerém. In 1790, when Joseph II's reforms were annulled upon his death, Hajnóczy lost his job. Entering public life, he attempted in his anonymous pamphlets to convince the noblemen deliberating at the national assembly of the necessity of reforms. The pamphlets were written in Latin and some of them appeared in printed form: *Ratio proponendarum in comitiis Hungariae legum* (1790); *Dissertatio . . . de regiae potestatis in Hungaria limitibus* (1791); *De comitiis regni Hungariae* (1791); *Extractus legum de statu ecclesiastico catholico* (1792); *De diversis subsidiis publicis* (1792). In 1792 he was offered a minor position at the Hungarian Royal Treasury in Buda. Unable to persuade the Hungarian nobility to encourage reforms and pushed by the ever more reactionary policy of Francis I (after the death of his father Leopold in 1792), Hajnóczy welcomed the radical endeavours of the French Revolution. One of the most respected personalities among democratic-minded intellectuals, he spread the revolutionary ideas and his conceptions about the democratic and bourgeois transformation of Hungary, through the 'Reading Circle'. These were taken over partly by Martinovics (q.v.) as well. In 1794

Martinovics involved him in the Hungarian Jacobin movement and appointed him one of the directors of the 'Society of Liberty and Equality'. After the disclosure of the underground movement he was arrested by the police in Buda on October 16, 1794, brought to trial, sentenced to death on April 27, 1795 for high treason and beheaded on 20 May.

Hajnóczy was one of the best-educated representatives of radical bourgeois ideas and also one of the bravest propagators of the necessity of social changes. He was an enthusiastic supporter of the French Revolution and helped to spread its ideas into the Russian Empire through pamphlets and underground political organisation. His political beliefs eventually led him to abandon his early support for an enlightened and reforming monarchy as an agency of democratic change.

Examples of Hajnóczy's writings are to be found in *Documents of the Hungarian Jacobins*, edited by K. Benda, Volumes 1–3 (Budapest, 1952–1957). The major secondary works on Hajnóczy's career are K. Benda, 'Histoire des jacobins hongrois', *Annales Historique de la Révolution française (1959) No. 155; K. Benda, 'Menschenfreund oder patriot', in Studien über die Revolution* (Berlin, 1969); and György Bónis, *Jozsef Hajnóczy* (Budapest, 1954).

KÁLMÁN BENDA

HEBENSTREIT von Streitenfeld, Franz (1747–1795)
Austrian philosopher and Jacobin, a leader of the Vienna 'conspiracy' of 1794–95

Franciscus Ignatius Felix Procopius Hebenstreit von Streitenfeld was baptised in Prague on November 26, 1747. His father, Peter Hebenstreit von Streitenfeld (d. 1788), was President of the Faculty of Philosophy and the Humanities at the Caroline University of Prague; his mother was born Barbara von Götz. There were nine children in the family. In connection with the ennoblement of the Hebenstreit family in 1753, Peter Hebenstreit succeeded in proving that his ancestors had

been Freemen of the city of Prague since 1543 and that a Hebenstreit von Streitenfeld had been mayor of the old city of Prague in 1599.

Little is known of the childhood, early school years and family life of Franz Hebenstreit. His early instruction came from tutors, as was the practice in families of his class, and it seems that he owed much of his remarkable learning to this experience. He registered in philosophy at the Caroline University at the age of sixteen in 1763, and his results were very good. In addition he studied the humanities, natural law, civil law and canon law. From 1766 to 1768 he continued his studies at the University of Vienna, where he read finance under the well-known reformer Joseph von Sonnenfels and medicine under Johann Heinrich Nepomuk. On account of his large family Hebenstreit received little financial help from home, and earned his living by clerical work and teaching French.

On July 1, 1768 Hebenstreit entered Joseph II's Sixth Imperial Light Cavalry Regiment, without taking his degree. On January 1, 1772 he was promoted to the rank of corporal. Passed over for further promotions, and feeling that he had been unfairly treated, he deserted on July 21, 1773. He intended to go via Saxony to America. However, after an adventurous flight to the Prussian border he was captured along with his two companions and imprisoned in the fortress at Glatz in Silesia. There he was pressed into the service of the Prussian army (Fouqué regiment). Encouraged by a general amnesty on the part of the emperor during the War of the Bavarian Succession (1778–9), he returned to the Austrian army on August 30, 1778. He was posted to the Staff Dragoons Regiment in Prague and Gaya in Moravia and was sent to Hungary to buy horses. Between 1782 and 1784 he tried in vain to study at the famous School of Veterinary Medicine in Vienna.

On July 1, 1786 Hebenstreit was promoted to the rank of sergeant-major, and on 6 September to adjutant of the regiment. On 1 November his promotion to first lieutenant took him to Vienna. It was there, in December 1792, that he made the fateful acquaintance of Andreas von Riedel (q.v.) and his circle. His intellectual and political influence, even on Riedel, cannot be overestimated. Riedel and Hebenstreit together formed the dual leadership of the group, which owed much to the latter's excellent education, his military status, and to his charismatic leadership.

Since June 1792 Hebenstreit had been composing a 542 line political-philosophical didactic poem in Latin hexameters, *Homo Hominibus*, in which he presented his political faith – the glorification of the original state of society without private property, similar to early Christian communities. In 1793 he co-operated with Captain Carl de Beck of the Deutschmeisterregiment, on the *Eipeldauerlied*, popular for the simplicity of its text and melody and for its rousing rhythm. In 1794 he constructed a model of a war-machine, a sort of mobile stockade (Spanish riders on wheels) for protection against attacking cavalry. Such a model was sold to the Polish insurrectionists under Kosciuszko (q.v.), and another was to be sent to the French National Convention, with a greeting and a copy of *Homo Hominibus*, which was to serve the National Convention as the basis for discussion about a new social order. Before it came to this, however, Hebenstreit was betrayed by the *agent provocateur* Degen. After the preliminary police investigation he was brought before a court martial, where he was charged with the following offences under the Constitutio Criminalis Theresiana of 1769: complicity with failure to report the subversive attitudes of his friends; complicity in a planned military coup with the intention to murder the imperial family; authorship of seditious texts; and construction of a model war-machine and its delivery to the enemy. He and Riedel were seen as the ringleaders.

Although there was an element of truth in most of the charges, the judges exaggerated the facts, combined them with the seditious opinions of the accused, and drew such disproportionate conclusions, that the appearance was given that the state had been seriously endangered. Hebenstreit was sentenced to death by hanging, and publicly executed on January 8, 1795 outside the Vienna *Schottentor*. Although the aim was for the execution to serve as a deterrent, the authorities were afraid of popular unrest and demonstrations of sympathy (a hundred thousand spectators are said to have been present). So special security measures were taken: the military guard accompanying Hebenstreit was reinforced, and one or two dozen drummers were deployed in order to prevent his being heard, should he make a speech. Additional patrols were also deployed in the town, and the place of execution was cordoned off by some 1500 soldiers in order to ensure the maintenance of law and order.

Hebenstreit's political and social opinions were expressed in *Homo hominibus*. This work, written in Latin, was copied down again from memory by Hebenstreit during his imprisonment. There were plans to have it printed in Hungary, but these had to be abandoned when he was arrested. The title *Homo hominibus* is probably an allusion to the tag *homo homini lupus*, whose sentiments Hebenstreit opposed. He argued that man's crimes and moral decay were increasing more and more despite religion and the law. Humanity had moved further and further away from its natural condition, the happiness of the kind which had been present among early Christian groups. The cause of this was the replacement of communal property by individual ownership, which brought with it envy and all other vices. Private property, and the inequality of its distribution, led to the formation of classes, and therefore to exploitation and oppression. Religion and the law existed to strengthen and protect this differentiated social structure in the interests of the ruling class. The original virtues and value systems of the early brotherly communities were thereby destroyed and replaced by an unnatural, and therefore immoral, code of ethics.

In the records of his interrogation Hebenstreit interpreted and explained his work. He also expressed his opinions on the tactics and strategy of revolutionary movements and propaganda. He held that every class society brought about a 'spiral of evil', because private property, the root of all evil, had not been abolished. He reproached both the French Revolution and the Polish rebels with this failure: 'Idols are deposed, only to be replaced by others, and private property always remains, the seed of all evil.' Hebenstreit's solution was a return to communal property and its communal enjoyment – if necessary by revolutionary means. Man's natural equality in his basic functions, birth, illness and death removed all justification for the class social inequalities of life.

Hebenstreit wanted to realise his utopia by a return to a rural, pre-industrial and patriarchal society, in which the nobility lived on the land with the peasants rather than leading a parasitic and dissipated life in the towns. In the country, living among his peasants, the nobleman would have neither need nor opportunity to exploit them beyond his own modest material requirements, and this would bring about an increase in the peasants' own standard of living. Differences in the ownership of property would therefore be relativised; the advantages of communal production (and consumption) would be increasingly recognised, and the peasants' standard of living would rise. From these village cells based on common production there would eventually arise a national community based on collective consumption and production, in which the question of political reform – monarchy or republic – would become secondary.

Although Hebenstreit hoped to realise these revolutionary aims through an alliance of peasants and soldiers, rather than through the urban bourgeoisie, he was also aware that the intellectual and political backwardness of the peasantry made this impossible. Finally, Hebenstreit wanted to avoid 'the enrichment of those working by those not working', and he anticipated an intensification of social inequality following the victory of the bourgeois revolution. The question of the originality of Hebenstreit's views cannot be answered satisfactorily. He was too closely involved with the intellectual developments of his time in the fields of philosophy, and social and cultural criticism. The most probable influences are those of Morelly, Mably and Meslier. Riedel coined the term 'Hebenstreitism' to describe Hebenstreit's system of abstract philosophical and social-critical ideas, introducing the term into German usage for the first time.

In sum it was Hebenstreit who above all worked for a democratic and republican form of government in the Habsburg Empire and for a fundamental reform of property relations. This was to be achieved by preparation for a revolution or through a military coup. And in working for this end, Hebenstreit paid with his own life.

Hebenstreit's *Homo hominibus* was first published, in the Latin original and in German translation, in Alfred Körner's *Die Wiener Jakobiner* (Stuttgart, 1972), Volume 3 of *Deutsche revolutionäre Demokraten*, edited by Walter Grab, and with translation and commentary by Franz-Josef Schuh. The *Eipeldauerlied* was published in the same book. For further details of Hebenstreit's life, see Alfred Körner, *Andreas Riedel. Ein politisches Schicksal im Zeitalter der Französischen Revolution* (Phil. Diss., Cologne, 1969); Alfred Körner, 'Franz Hebenstreit. Biographie und Versuch einer Deutung', in Helmut Reinalter (ed.), *Jakobiner in Mitteleuropa* (Innsbruck, 1977), also in *Jahrbuch des Vereines für Geschichte der Stadt Wien*, Vol. 30/31 (1974/1975) and with slight alterations in *Jahrbuch des Instituts für deutsche Geschichte*, III (Tel Aviv, 1974); and Franz-Josef Schuh, 'Franz Hebenstreit. Jakobiner und Kommunist', in Hans Pelger (ed.), *Studien zu Jakobinismus und Sozialismus* (Berlin, Bonn, 1974). On the Viennese Jacobins in general, see Ernst Wangermann, *From Joseph II to the Jacobin Trials* (Oxford, 1959); and Denis Silagi, *Jakobiner in der Habsburger Monarchie* (Vienna, Munich, 1962).

ALFRED KÖRNER

HÉBERT, Jacques Réné
(1757–1794)
*French revolutionary journalist
and sans-culotte orator*

Hébert's family background was comfortable and bourgeois, a fact which his oponents were later to hold against him. His father was a goldsmith in Alençon, his mother was of noble origin, and one of his cousins became an émigré. After a wayward youth, Hébert struggled to support himself as a writer and journalist in Paris during the early 1780s.

In 1786–8 he obtained a front-of-house job at the Théâtre des Variétés, until the political crisis of 1788 gave him the opportunity, and the audience, for his satirical brochures. In June and July 1790 Hébert established his paper, the *Père Duchesne*, the popular journal through which he became a leading spokesman of the demands and resentments of the Parisian sans-culotterie. The *Père Duchesne* himself was a character taken from popular folklore, a *marchand de fourneaux* (stove dealer), with a thick moustache and a smoking pipe, distinguished by his coarse language, crude jokes and fiery temper. Hébert made his blunt and obscene tongue the medium of attacks against the rich, the Austrians and the royal family. His early targets included Lafayette, Mirabeau, and the Duke of Orléans ('Capet-Bordel'). In 1792 the *Père Duchesne* was virulently anti-monarchical, thundering against 'Monsieur Véto', and Marie Antoinette, 'la garce autrichienne' (the Austrian trollop).

By 1791 Hébert's outspoken journalism had won him a reputation in the capital and he had become a regular attender at the Cordeliers Club. Between April–June 1792, he was the club's president. The revolutionary *journée* of August 10, 1792 consummated the *Père Duchesne's* campaign against the royal family, by overthrowing the monarchy. Hébert was elected a delegate for his section of Bonne-Nouvelle to the general council of the Insurrectionary Commune of Paris. He then became *substitut* to the *procureur du commune*, Chaumette (q.v.).

Hébert's angry articles against the enemies of the revolution may have contributed to the popular fury which exploded in September 1792, when the inmates of several Parisian prisons were massacred, after summary popular trial. The *Père Duchesne*, however, did not relent, and demanded the quick execution of Louis XVI, contradicting those Girondins who wanted a popular referendum on the fate of the king.

Early in 1793 Hébert and Chaumette entered the Jacobin Club, and the 'great wrath' of the *Père Duchesne* was turned on the Girondins, and, in particular, on Roland, Minister of the Interior, and his wife. The unhappy couple were ignominiously caricatured as 'le vieux cocu' and 'Reine Coco'. Hébert defended Marat (q.v.) against the Girondins, and called for the creation of an *armée révolutionnaire* to guarantee food supplies in Paris. In May 1793 the Girondins attempted to silence the oratory of the *Père Duchesne*. Hébert was arrested and interrogated by the Commission of Twelve. His responsibility for the September massacres was raised, and he was accused of incitement to murder and the overthrow of the National Convention. In the Abbaye prison, he continued to write and produce the *Père Duchesne*. Hébert was defended by a deputation from the Paris sections, and the Convention voted his release. This was a clear indication both of the failing authority of the Girondins and of Roland, and also of Hébert's popular following among the Parisian militants.

After the proscription of the Girondin deputies on June 2, 1793, the Montagnard government gave its official support to the *Père Duchesne*. At the War Ministry, Bouchotte gave employment to many sans-culotte agitators and militants, and he ordered the free distribution of thousands of copies of the *Père Duchesne* to the army. Together with the introduction of the Price Maximum, in September 1793, and the creation of an *armée révolutionnaire*, this marked the highest point of

Hébert's influence.

On July 21, 1793 Hébert spoke in the Jacobin Club, shortly after the assassination of Marat, seeking perhaps to assume the right of succession to the martyred *Ami du Peuple*. He denounced General Custine, known to the *Père Duchesne* as 'general Moustache', and Custine was arrested. In Brumaire Year II Hébert testified at the trial of Brissot (q.v.) and Vergniaud, and in October 1793, he made his celebrated appearance at the trial of Marie Antoinette. Assuming the *Père Duchesne*'s habitual contempt for the conventions of public decency, Hébert accused Marie Antoinette of the crime of incest with her own son. Even his most sympathetic biographer found this obscene charge unworthy of Hébert.

The food shortage figured largely in the pages of the *Père Duchesne*, which demanded the harshest penalties against speculators and food-hoarders. These echoes of sans-culotte punitive social justice were potentially embarrasing for the revolutionary government. The Jacobins agreed only reluctantly to abandon economic liberalism and introduce price controls, partly to avoid the wholesale guillotining of merchants and capitalists which agitators like Hébert demanded. Hébert defended the *armée révolutionnaire* of Paris, the sans-culotte militia which scoured the countryside for food supplies, threatening astonished peasants with the guillotine, if they were reluctant to part with their surplus grain, or to embrace the sans-culottes' crude anti-religious or anticlerical views. Hébert's answer to the food shortage was more determined coercion of the peasantry supported by the guillotine.

Hébert, however, was accused of fostering atheism. In 1792 he had shocked many by marrying a defrocked nun in a church wedding; the Paris Commune under Chaumette was suspected of dechristianising tendencies; and the activities of the *armée révolutionnaire parisienne*, which Hébert supported, also seemed violently iconoclastic. Although the *Père Duchesne* responded vigorously to allegations, the combination of the moderates, or the Indulgents, and

the Jacobin government against him was to prove too much for Hébert.

Philippeaux (q.v.) launched an attack on the conduct of the Vendéan War, which inculpated Bouchotte at the War Ministry. In Desmoulins' (q.v.) journal, *Le Vieux Cordelier* (no. 5), Hébert was 'exposed' as a rich man, drawing on generous financial support from the government, and a frequent visitor to a luxury suburban villa owned by the Dutch banker Kock (the father of the famous novelist). Whether true or not, such allegations were extremely damaging for a popular orator complaining of economic hardships.

In Ventôse Year II the government arrested Hébert and his 'fellow-conspirators' in an alleged insurrectionary plot, based in the Cordeliers Club. On trial in the so-called Hébertist plot were an assortment of individuals cynically grouped together by the public prosecutor Fouquier-Tinville, to heap the maximum discredit on the chief accused. Through Hébert, the Jacobin government was aiming at the elimination of a much larger group of revolutionary agitators, including Ronsin, Vincent (q.v.), and Mazuel, the leaders of the Parisian *armée révolutionnaire*. Their presence lent credence to the prosecution's claims that a military coup was being planned.

These accused were joined in the dock by 'les corrompus', bankers and shady financiers like Kock, Proly and Pereyra. These individuals, some of them not of French origin, may possibly have had connections with the obscure and elusive counter-revolutionary conspirator, the Baron de Batz. Their presence in the dock enabled the government to portray the 'Hébertist plot' as a foreign plot. Under the weight of these accusations, Hébert broke down in court. The night before the verdict was delivered, he was reportedly delirious with fear. There was apparently a record number of spectators at Hébert's execution: this was an indication of the fame of the *Père Duchesne*, but not necessarily of enduring popular sympathy for Hébert. The Jacobin government was later to liquidate the Indulgents, like Desmoulins, who had attacked Hébert so bitterly. For the moment, it had removed some of the leading Parisian militants, and made a further call for unity, against the spectres of military coups and foreign plots.

In spite of the allegations about Hébert's personal wealth, he left a modest fortune at his death, and he had not purchased a *bien national*. Although Hébert had demanded the partition of large estates into smaller plots, he cannot be described as a sophisticated or thorough-going socialist. Rather, he voiced, in the pages of his journal, the frustrations of Parisians with the Republic's military leaders, with wealthy merchants and capitalists, with hesitant and hypocritical politicians, and with obstinate peasants who would not part with essential food supplies. For Hébert the guillotine offered a ready and effective solution to the problems of food shortage and social inequality. In his hands the *Père Duchesne* became an enduring figure in the revolutionary tradition, for journals bearing the same name appeared in 1848 and during the Paris Commune, claiming, like Hébert, to represent the authentic cry of Parisians for social justice.

The two standard biographies of Hébert are: Louis Jacob, *Hébert, le père Duchesne, chef des sans-culottes* (Paris, 1960); and Gérard Walter, *Hébert et le Père Duchesne, 1757–1794* (Paris, 1946).

MARTYN LYONS

HEILIGENSTEDT ('Rosentreter'), Gustav Friedrich (1754–1820)
German Jacobin

Heiligenstedt was born in Quedlinburg, the son of a Protestant minister. He broke off his studies in theology for unknown reasons, took the name of Rosentreter, and moved to Altona before the French Revolution. He moved in democratic circles, knew Johann Christoph Unzer (q.v.), befriended Freidrich von der Trenck (q.v.) when the latter came to Altona in April 1792, and made the acquaintance of the French envoy in Hamburg, François. Lehoc, who set up a short-lived reading society with G.H. Sieveking and F.W.

von Schütz (q.v.). Heiligenstedt was a permanent guest in Christian Pflock's inn in the Town-hall Square in Altona, where a Jacobin conventicle met in 1792–1793.

In November 1792 Heiligenstedt went to Berlin to engage in democratic agitation. After about four weeks he was arrested by the Prussian police, who charged him, on the strength of intercepted letters, with 'plotting in the French manner'. He was committed for trial and imprisoned first of all in the Berlin prison and then in the fortress at Spandau. After his return to Altona and the death of Christian Pflock he married the latter's daughter Katharina, and took over the running of the inn. He continued to engage in revolutionary politics and made his public house available for the French and German democratic meetings. On July 14, 1798 the German Jacobins celebrated the anniversary of storming of the Bastille. Heiligenstedt sold the inn in 1802 and became the owner of a vinegar factory in Altona, which traded under the name Pflock and Co., and which he appears to have run until his death in 1820.

Heiligenstedt was therefore a convinced and active member of the Altona circle of Jacobins. However, like his north German companions, he was prevented from continuing radical political activity after 1799 by the reactionary politics of Denmark when Kai von Reventlow was head of the Deutsche Kanzlei and censorship made it impossible to publish anything progressive.

Further information on Heiligenstedt can be found in W. Grab, *Demokratische Strömungen in Hamburg und Schleswig Holstein zur Zeit der ersten französischen Republik* (Hamburg, 1966), pp. 109–112, 220f.

W. GRAB

HÉRAULT DE SÉCHELLES, Marie Jean (1759–1794)
French Jacobin, author of the 1793 Constitution and member of the Committee of Public Safety

Son of a wealthy aristocrat, Hérault was born in Paris where he studied law and practised as a lawyer before being appointed *avocat général* (king's attorney) in the Paris courts. He advocated a measure of reform in 1789, and was present at the taking of the Bastille. In 1791 he was elected to the Legislative Assembly as one of the deputies for Paris. There he emerged as a prominent Jacobin, linked with Danton (q.v.) and the Hébertistes. He was elected president of the Legislative Assembly in September 1792, and of the National Convention on two occasions, in November 1792 and August 1793. Principal author of the 1793 Constitution, he subsequently became one of the twelve members of the 'great' Committee of Public Safety. He seems to have been disliked and mistrusted by Robespierre (q.v.) and St Just (q.v.), both for his aristocratic airs and for his links with the Hébertistes. Accused of plotting with foreign powers, in October 1793 he was sent on a mission to Alsace and never rejoined the Committee of Public Safety. In January 1794 he was arrested and was executed, together with Danton, on April 5.

Before the revolution, Hérault was a keen reader of the *philosophes*. Despite his aristocratic background and flourishing career under the old régime, he welcome the revolution. In 1792 he advocated war against the crowned heads of Europe, and subsequently demanded severe penalties against priests and nobles hostile to the revolution. The Constitution of 1793, for which he was largely responsible, affirmed universal male suffrage and opened public office to all men over twenty-one. The vote was extended to most foreigners living in France. Insurrection was recognised as a right and a duty if the government were to violate the rights of the people. The Constitution also proclaimed the need for universal education and the right to work, and made it the duty of society to provide for those unable to work.

Hérault's mission to Alsace reveals him to have been a keen supporter of dechristianisation. He created a revolutionary army there to stimulate patriotism, formed a revolutionary tribunal and encouraged denunciations, but had very few people executed. As a prominent Jacobin, President of the Convention at the crucial moment of the expulsion of the Girondins, and as a member of the Committee of Public Safety, he played an important part in the consolidation of the revolution and in the progagation of Jacobin ideas.

Hérault's published writings include: *Eloge de Suger* (Paris, 1779); and *Théorie de l'ambition* (Paris, 1802). R.R. Palmer, *Twelve Who Ruled* (Princeton, N.J., 1941), is primarily concerned with Hérault's part in the work of the Committee of Public Safety. Palmer reproduces a portrait (p. 195). A. Mathiez, *Etudes robespierristes* (2 vols., Paris, 1917–18), vol. 2, pp. 222–260, looks at Hérault's ideas and political affiliations during the revolution. An old biography by E. Dard, *Hérault de Séchelles* (Paris, 1907) has now been superseded by two recent works: A. de Contades, *Hérault de Séchelles: ou, La révolution fraternelle* (Paris, 1978) and J.J. Locherer, *Hérault de Séchelles: l'aristocrate du Comité de salut public* (Paris, 1984).

D. GARRIOCH

HIPPEL, Theodor Gottlieb von (1741–1796)
German radical feminist, author of novels, drama, poetry and popular philosophy

The small East Prussian town, Gerdauen, was the birthplace and childhood home of Hippel. Hippel's father was headmaster of the town school, and his mother came from an artisan family in a neighbouring village. His pre-university education was gained largely in the home, and both parents apparently took an active role in it. As an adult, Hippel later praised his father's sensitivity and thoroughness in the son's early academic training which included Hebrew in addition to Latin, Greek and modern languages.

Like many Enlightenment figures, Hippel grew up under the influence of a devout pietism. This was certainly a factor in his decision to undertake the study of theology. In 1756, at age fifteen, Hippel matriculated at the university in Königsberg. Just prior to completing his training, Hippel interrupted his academic career to accompany a friend on a courier mission to the latter's home in Petersburg. This trip to Russia, on which he came into contact with aristocratic society and people of influence in government, was apparently a highly significant experience for the young man. He credited it with his decision to discontinue his enrolment in theology, in order to seek a career in which he could exercise a greater influence in public affairs than an ecclesiastical profession would afford.

Returning to East Prussia, Hippel accepted a position as a tutor for a prestigious local family but soon returned to the university to study law. Upon completing the professional training, Hippel obtained an appointment as an attorney in the municipal court at Königsberg, a stepping stone into a career of rapid advancement in the complex bureaucracy of Frederick the Great's Prussia. He held positions in the royal law court, in the city council, and as director of the criminal court before he joined the influential Law Commission, established in 1780 to advise the monarch upon new legislation prior to the promulgation of Prussia's famous General Law Code (1794). In this role, Hippel participated in the process of synthesising the existing complex of German, Roman and natural law to produce a legal system epitomising the principles of enlightened absolutism. Also in 1780, Hippel gained two other prestigious appointments. He became governing mayor of Königsberg and a War Commissioner. The latter office was a high position in the royal tax bureaucracy.

In 1786, with the ascension of Frederick William II to the throne, Hippel advanced to the position of Privy Councillor, and the new king conferred upon him the titular office, City President, which he held until his death. In 1795 provincial minister von Schroetter commissioned Hippel to preside over the process of integrating West Prussian territory, newly acquired in the aggressive act known as the Second

Partition of Poland, into the Prussian administrative system. One year after his move to Danzig to carry out this responsibility, Hippel contracted a severe infection, causing, among other things blindness in one eye. He returned to Königsberg but never recovered, dying at the age of fifty-five.

This civil servant in an absolutist state enjoyed an illustrious public life, but one that would hardly seem compatible with his career as a novelist and essayist, and even less with his activities as a publicist which would earn him a posthumous reputation as a radical social critic. Hippel was a complex personality. Contemporaries in his home province knew him as a splendid orator. The merchants of Königsberg held him in high esteem, in spite of the fact that in his office as mayor he was answerable to the royal government in Berlin rather than to the local guilds. The monarchs under whom Hippel served granted him honours on several occasions, including a gold medal for his work on the Law Commission. Following these achievements Hippel appealed for 'reinstatement' of a lapsed title of nobility, thus obtaining the coveted 'von' in his name. Rising from humble origins, he amassed a substantial estate. Hippel was a familiar figure among the learned societies and literary circles in Königsberg whose members included Kant (q.v.) and Hippel's lifelong friend, Johann Georg Scheffner. Hippel was at the same time shy and almost reclusive.

Practically unknown to his wide circle of friends and admirers, he led a double life as an author. Prussian civil servants were forbidden to publish their own writings, and Hippel was amazingly successful at carrying on an anonymous literary career by having Scheffner act as intermediary between himself and his publisher, Christian Friedrich Voss, in Berlin. In addition to novels, Hippel wrote comedies, poetry, Protestant hymns, essays on legal and political topics, a popular treatise on marriage, satirical criticism on freemasonry, and the book, *Über die bürgerliche Verbesserung der Weiber* (On Improving the Status of Women). Hippel's most well-known work in terms of literary history are the novels, *Lebensläufe nach aufsteigender Linie* (Biographies in the Ascending Line) (1780–81) and *Kreuzund Querzüge des Ritters A bis Z* (Crusades of the Knight A to Z) (1793–94). These represent landmarks in the development of the modern German novel. Hippel experimented with highly personal, introspective forms of fiction.

Much of Hippel's writing reflects his goal of popularising the cult of reason of the Enlightenment. One of his favourite arguments was that Christianity and reason were not incompatible. He believed religion to be based on rational principles.

It was in his book, *On Improving the Status of Women* (1792), that Hippel stepped outside the bounds of traditional Enlightenment thinking. This work is both a bitter criticism of patriarchy and a radical advocacy of equality among the sexes. The feminist tone of the book is surprising in part because Hippel, who himself never married, had published, also anonymously, a highly popular work, *Über die Ehe* (On Marriage), eighteen years previously. The earlier work was relatively uncritical of existing conventions regarding the relations of the sexes, and it advocated marriage for women. Yet in 1792 Hippel penned a work highly critical of the legal foundations and the social implications of eighteenth-century marriage. (Later editions of *On Marriage* reflected some of Hippel's criticism regarding inequality in marriage.)

Recognisable as an eighteenth-century work, *On Improving the Status of Women* is dedicated to the ideals of equality of all human beings, the right of human freedom, and the goal of emancipating those who lived in subservience. Constructing an argument which rested on two bases, reason and experience, Hippel maintained that women could not possibly be inferior to men. Since women enjoyed the specialised task of bearing human life, it was inconceivable that nature would have assigned this divine responsibility to second-rate beings. Observing that working-class women were often not incapacitated by childbirth like women of higher status,

Hippel surmised that the pain and weakness associated with bearing children were class-related phenomena, not based on nature's laws.

In explaining the existing state of inequality of women, Hippel developed a unique hypothesis about the original, natural state of society. He argued that at one time, both genders had enjoyed equal status, and both were engaged in hunting. Soon, however, a vital separation of gender roles occurred. Being temporarily detained from the hunt during the process of giving birth and the approximate six hours following, females developed skills which allowed them to continue productive work close to home. They domesticated animals and discovered ways to raise crops. This specialisation of labour and important contribution to humanity, the invention of agriculture, ironically led to their decline, for it left males in sole control of weapons. As society became more complex, men formed communities to protect their properties, among which they regarded their wives. Out of this grew the institution of the state in which women were not citizens, but mere wards, confined to the household.

In later times men sought theories to mask their suppression of females and their fear of competition and thus developed the argument that sexual inequality was rooted in nature. Roman law institutionalised the inferiority of women, and in modern times the practice of marriage, unequal education, the ever-popular ideal of female modesty and many other social conventions served to perpetuate women's state of submission.

Hippel's plans for change began, predictably, with the demand that women be granted citizenship. He criticised the revolutionary French constitution of 1791 which abolished feudal institutions but failed to make women citizens of the new age. Citizenship alone, however, would not elevate women out of their retarded position. Like his fiery contemporary, Mary Wollstonecraft, Hippel contended that equality in education was a prerequisite to improvement of women's position. He advocated that boys and girls be educated together until the age of sexual maturity. Girls' clothing should be made more practical so that they were not prohibited from activities which developed strength and self-confidence. Girls must no longer be taught to use polite, submissive language which later put them at a disadvantage in discourse with men.

Finally, Hippel argued that only when women were entitled to enter professions would society enjoy the benefits females were capable of bestowing upon it. Somewhat at variance with his insistence upon equality, Hippel believed that women possessed special talents which were less developed in males. As lawyers and judges women would raise the moral standards in the conduct of law. Their capacity for nurture would suit them ideally for the profession of teaching. They should be admitted to the study of medicine which they had been forced in recent times to practise in secret. In short, the state 'should open to women its council chambers, courts, lecture halls, commercial establishments, and places of employment'.

Hippel's far-reaching demand for women's right to enter the professions places him in a category by himself among eighteenth-century thinkers. Unlike Wollstonecraft, he was able to identify the institution of domesticity as the factor which entrapped women. Women must no longer be tied to the hearth. Significantly, Hippel addressed his treatise to men. It was clear to him that males would have to accept altered roles before women became social equals. For example, they must accept their responsibilities as parents, sharing equally in the rearing of children.

On Improving the Status of Women met with indifference and rejection. It was too extreme to be taken seriously in German-speaking Europe of the 1790s, despite a growing middle class readership which was hungry for writings on female education. Hippel's essay *Über weibliche Bildung* (On Female Education), intended to be incorporated into a revised second edition, saw publication only thirty-two years after the author's death as part of his collected works. The book itself was hardly reviewed in literary and popular journals, unlike Hippel's other works. Hence the radical statement by the mayor of Königsberg slipped almost into oblivion. When his authorship was revealed following his death it sparked great controversy. Some contemporaries were outraged, and others refused to believe that Hippel was indeed responsible for the feminist ideas.

Of all the scholarly interest in Hippel during the last two centuries, there has been relatively little attention devoted to his most important work, *On Improving the Status of Women*. Moreover, the feminist movements of the nineteenth and twentieth centuries, which might have used his work as an ideological cornerstone, largely overlooked Hippel's early criticism of patriarchy. Only in very recent times has the work been rediscovered.

Hippel's thought is remarkable for its focus on domesticity as the key factor prohibiting women from breaking out of inferior status. He wrote in an era when bourgeois capitalism was in an immature stage and the corresponding ideology of domesticity had hardly been articulated. Only after significant structural change in society would Marxist thinkers be able to describe with precision the distinction between male productive activity and female reproductive roles which perpetuated the conditions Hippel found so disturbing. In posing solutions to the problem of inequality, Hippel anticipated the 'social feminism' of the 1848 revolutionary, Jeanne Deroin, who advocated reallocation of political power between the sexes.

Hippel's complete works (*Sämmtliche Werke*) were published in a single edition of fourteen volumes between 1827 and 1839. Two of these volumes contain correspondence. This is fortunate, because any remaining archival material was destroyed in World War II. The complete edition, *Theodor von Hippels Sämmtliche Werke* was reprinted in Berlin, 1978. There are also several new and reprint editions of *Über die Ehe* and *Über die Bürgerliche Verbesserung der Weiber*. The best of the latter is edited with a critical, scholarly introduction by Juliane Dittrich-Jacobi

(Vaduz, 1981). English-speaking readers will welcome the translation by Timothy Sellner published in Detroit, 1979. A reprint of the 1796 edition of *Über die Ehe* (Selb, 1976) is important because it takes into account some of the views Hippel expressed in his more feminist work. A reprint of Hippel's biography/autobiography, originally published in 1801, was issued by Gerstenberg Verlag, Hildesheim, 1977.

Alongside the essay by Dittrich-Jacobi mentioned above, the best secondary work on Hippel's feminist thought is Ruth Dawson, 'The Feminist Manifesto of Theodor Gottlieb von Hippel' in a special issue of *Amsterdamer Beiträge zur Germanistik*, Vol. 10, 1980, edited by M. Burkhard. Dawson also published a short essay, 'Theodor Gottlieb von Hippel und seine Schrift "Über die bürgerliche Verbesserung der Weiber"', in *Akten des VI. Internationalen Germanisten-Kongress* (Basel, 1980).

Standard biographical material can be found in the reference works, *Allgemeine Deutsche Biographie*, *Neue Deutsche Biographie*, and *Altpreussische Biographie*. Modern readers would benefit more from consulting recent works by literary scholars: J. Campe, *Der Programmatische Roman* (Bonn, 1979); H. Beck, 'Hippel and the Eighteenth-Century Novel' (Ph.D. diss., Columbia University, 1980); P. Peterkin, *Gesellschaftliche und fiktionale Identität* (Stuttgart, 1981); and J. Kohnen, *Theodor Gottlieb von Hippel: L'homme et l'oeuvre* (Bern, 1983). With the exception of the latter, these do not address Hippel's feminism. They do give insight into Hippel's personality and writing, Peterkin being especially good in that regard. This author appended some previously unpublished primary source material related to Hippel's life. Kohnen's two-volume work is extensive, and his bibliography is exhaustive. It will lead researchers to all known primary and secondary sources dealing with Hippel.

MARION W. GRAY

HOFMANN, Andreas Joseph (1752–1849)
German Jacobin, revolutionary democrat

Hofmann was born in July 1752 in Zell into a family of civil servants. He was orphaned while young, and was brought up by his uncle, who forced him to study poetry, rhetoric, and then the law. He studied at Mainz, then at Würzburg. In 1777 he went to Vienna to gain practical experience, and came into conflict with the court on account of a frivolous satirical article he wrote for a theatrical journal. He returned to Würzburg in 1783, and successfully applied for a post as a philosophy teacher at Mainz. He gave his courses in German and taught Kantian philosophy. His activity in the Illuminati lodge and at the Reading Club gave rise to his being denounced by the prince-elector in 1792 for having spoken against the Church and clergy during his classes, and in particular for having said that prayer served no purpose. The prince-elector forbade him to repeat the offence and his lessons were subjected to close surveillance. The censorship laws ensured that he wrote little, and he preferred action.

The opportunity for action arose with the arrival of General Custine in Mainz in October 1792. Hofmann joined the Mainz Club several days after its establishment, and quickly became the spokesman of uncompromising radical republicanism. He wanted a republic of virtue and policies based firmly on moral principles. He clashed with Dorsch (q.v.) whom he considered opportunist and vain, and he told the general that his troops were badly behaved. He was elected President of the National Convention, and then President of the Civil Administration when the seige of Mainz forced the Convention to disband. At the time of the surrender of the city (July 1793) he succeeded in leaving Mainz with the French army.

From then on Hofmann's fate was tied to that of the French Republic. With Reubell's support he gained employment at the Ministry of the Interior, a position which was interrupted by a two-year secret mission to England. He resumed his post at the end of 1795, and had to compile a daily report for Bonaparte in his capacity as *Directeur de la Police des étrangers*. Following the Peace of Campo Formio he was promoted to Tax-Collector General in the *département* of Mont-Tonerre, a position which he occupied from 1798 to 1803, when the misappropriation of funds by one of his subordinates forced him to resign.

He continued to work privately, but was no longer very much involved in politics, although he remained a radical Jacobin even under the empire. Following the end of French domination he retired to his wife's estate. He was treated with suspicion, and his property was searched. He suffered at the failure of the 1848 revolution and died in 1849. He was buried without religious ceremony, and his daughter had engraved on his tombstone the epitaph that his life was devoted to truth, right and the struggle against political and religious slavery.

Even before the revolution, Hofmann proved himself to be progressive. He questioned the infallibility of the Church, wanted to popularise science, and do away with Latin in schools. He wrote a treatise to this effect in 1784: *Über die heimliche Lehrart der Alten und die der Neueren in lateinischer Spräche*. His main work was written at the end of 1792 during the events in Mainz: *Der Aristokratenkatechismus*. It is about a dialogue between a revolutionary democrat (who is Hofmann himself) and an aristocrat representing the Ancien Régime. The main aim of this work is to show that people lived happier lives without princes and nobles. The aristocrat who scorns Christian tradition accounts the equality preached in the bible as nothing short of folly; the democrat maintains on the other hand that the barefaced oppression of the people by the nobility is a crime against the rights of man and against Christianity. The whole discussion serves to ridicule the aristocrat and expose his reasoning as totally opposed to moral and religious values, while the democrat's ideal is one of social justice and virtue.

On the whole, Hofmann was a moralist. Rigorous and austere, he would not tolerate weakness of any kind. For this reason he became involved in a controversy with the co-editor of the *Journal de Paris*, Roederer, who inaugurated an open forum with the theme: 'Is it in the interests of the French Republic to extend its borders to the banks of the Rhine?' Hofmann found the issue ridiculous and immoral since the question had long since been answered. He recalled that it was he who had concluded the first treaty of reunion of the first freemen of Germany with the French nation, and that the French nation had accepted the incorporation of the left bank of the Rhine. In his revolutionary activities, Hofmann was squarely on the side of the French.

Hofmann was an unambiguous revolutionary, who never sought compromise with princes. The course of the French Revolution served him as an example. He was a fervent supporter of the movement for a natural frontier at the Rhine, and wanted to see the annexation of the Rhineland by France. Compared with other Rhineland Jacobins, he was distinguished by his austerity and severity. Morally faultless and irreproachable on any grounds, he was elected President of the Convention for precisely these qualities; his fellow citizens knew that he could not be bought and had complete faith in him.

Hofmann's main published works were: A.J. Hofmann, *Der Aristokratenkatechismus. Ein wunderschönes Büchlein gar erbaulich zu lesen für Junge und Alte* (Mainz, 1792); *Gespräche über den Mainzer Freiheitsklub* (Mainz, 1793). For further details of his life and activities, see H. Mathy, 'Andreas Joseph Hofmann (1752–1849). Professor und Präsident des rheinisch-deutschen Nationalkonvents', *Jahrbuch der Vereinigung 'Freunde der Universität Mainz'* (Mainz, 1973), p. 1545; H. Mathy, 'Andreas Joseph Hofmann, der Präsident des rheinisch-deutschen Nationalkonvents von 1793', in *Deutsche Jakobiner, Mainzer Republik und Cisrhenanen 1792–1798*. Vol. 1, p. 235; and K. Reuter,

Erinnerungen an Andreas Joseph Hofmann (Wiesbaden, 1884).

M. GILLI

HORODYSKI, Andrzej (1733–?)
Polish politician, writer, Minister of Foreign Affairs in 1831

Horodyski came from a noble family in Podolia. He studied philosophy in the Austrian University of Lvov. Well-acquainted with the operation of Austrian administration, he was primarily interested in law and economy. He became politically active in the so called Centralizacja, a Polish conspiratorial organisation founded in Lvov, which connected the idea of independence with a moderate social programme. He went on their behalf to Stambul with an instruction and money in 1797.

After the Centralizacja had been disrupted, Horodyski took refuge in Warsaw in 1798, and here co-organised the Society of Polish Republicans, soon becoming the successor to its president, the deceased Colonel E. Mycielski. Initially, the Society counted on help from France, but at the turn of 1800, because of the international state of affairs, it was resolved that Poland had to win independence by means of an uprising without any foreign help. Horodyski wrote an instruction in which he stressed the leading role of conspirators, but set aside the question of regaining independence and delivered an unclear social programme. He became an exponent of the right-wing in the Society of Polish Republicans. Instructed by the society, he entered in 1801 into a correspondence in code with the imprisoned H. Kollątaj (q.v.), later to become one of his close friends.

After the Society of Polish Republicans had been suspended, Horodyski gave up conspiratorial politics and became co-founder of a business firm in Odessa which was involved in Black Sea trade. Though the trading business was far from successful, it enabled the ex-republicans to spread their political influence to Podolia and the Ukraine. In 1803 Horodyski became a member of the Society of Friends of Sciences in Warsaw where he gave lectures on history, statistics and philosophy. In the following year he was engaged in translating into Polish the Prussian civil law, and in 1807 he corrected the Napoleonic code.

At the beginning of the Duchy of Warsaw, Horodyski set his hopes on Napoleon. In 1807 he became a member of the Warsaw department authorities, then stayed in Dresden in the company of the Duke of Warsaw. He also took part in publicity campaigns in favour of French legislation and improvement of the status of peasants, as well as participating in translating into Polish, C.C. Rulhière's *L'Histoire de l'anarchie de Pologne*. In February 1807, as a deputy of the Society of Polish Republicans which was revived in 1806 in Podolia, Volhynia and Ukraine, Horodyski delivered proclamations which suggested instigating uprisings in these provinces to the ministers Maret and Talleyrand.

During the first years of the Duchy of Warsaw, Horodyski – like other 'Jacobins' who came from the Society of Polish Republicans – enjoyed the support of a French resident, J. Serra, who sought to promote him to a higher post. But the plan failed, and in January 1809 Horodyski became merely an advisor in the Supreme Financial Division. His role increased during the Austro-Polish war of 1809 when at Serra's request he was appointed one of the administrators of the capital. Although he attempted to plot against the commander-in-chief of the Polish army, Duke Josef Poniatowski, he joined the commander's entourage when military operations were successful and exerted considerable influence on the organisation of provisional authorities in regained Galicia. Now a powerful figure, he summoned several of his political friends to Cracow, among them Kollątaj, who was the actual author of the second reform of Cracow University (Horodyski only signed the plan).

By the end of 1809 Horodyski's importance had decreased. He was refused promotion to the post of the prefect of Cracow department, and his plan of revising the Duchy Constitution which was considered by the 'Jacobins' and by the Saxon Minister of Foreign Affairs, Sbefft von Pilsach, failed. In July 1810 he handed in his resignation from his post in the Supreme Financial Division. He collaborated with the opposition during the 1811 Diet in order to force the government to revise the constitution. After the Russian campaign had failed at the beginning of 1813, Horodyski left for Cracow and then for Dresden along with the rest of the government. From there he criticised the conduct of the withdrawing authorities, Duke J. Poniatowski in particular, and propounded the necessity of raising an insurrection in Poland.

He returned to Warsaw in the same year and joined Duke A.J. Czartoryski, leader of the pro-Russian faction. Horodyski's step facilitated the project of an anti-French and pro-Russian and pro-German plot which had been devised by republicans at the end of 1810. Horodyski became one of the closest advisers of Czartoryski, drafted projects for a new political system, and in 1815 helped write the final draft of the Kingdom of Poland's constitution. As far as the peasantry was concerned, he argued that peasants should own land in the course of time, provided that 'the proprietors' rights are not violated in the least'. Other opinions expressed by Horodyski on the peasant question also show his compliance with the conservative tendencies of other politicians. From 1813 to 1817 he held a few minor posts in the state administration. His own property concerns then led him to abandon his political career. For the next few years he was active in the Warsaw Society of the Friends of Sciences, and from 1816 was honorary member of the Cracow Society of Science.

Horodyski returned to politics during the uprisings of 1830 and 1831 when, as a friend of a group of conservatives and of General J. Skrzynecki – an incompetent commander in chief – he became commissioner of the government at the general's side on February 28, 1831. As commissioner he helped Skrzynecki make a foreign policy which was independent of the government; he drafted letters, instructed political agents and communicated with the Austrian consul. On March 23, 1831 he became President of the Financial Division and on 17 May, vice-Minister of Foreign Affairs. According to unanimous testimonies by his contemporaries he was not well-suited to the latter post.

It was Horodyski who on Skrzynecki's behalf suggested to the leftist Lelewel that he resign from the National Government. When Skrzynecki was deprived of command, Horodyski encouraged General H. Dembiński to assume the 'anti-Jacobinic' dictatorship. He thus drifted far away from his youthful views. Horodyski did not go into exile, and for the next few years he probably stayed in Galicia. In 1843, at the request of the Russian authorities who were attempting to expose connections between plots in the Kingdom of Poland and Galicia, he was summoned to Warsaw but after a short investigation was released. Horodyski died between 1847 and 1857.

Apart from his political activities, Horodyski wrote a number of plays which were staged in Lvov and in Warsaw. In 1799 *Hamlet*, translated by Horodyski from a rearranged piece by J.F. Ducis, was performed for the first time in the capital. He translated from German (Kotzebue, among others), Italian (Goldoni, among others) and French. He also put forward his views on philosophy, and was probably Polish editor of the translated works of Turgot.

Horodyski was a key figure in the development of Polish nationalism and an active participant in the modernising reforms of the early nineteenth century. From being radical in his early years he moved to a more conservative position later, but retained an enthusiasm for reform, albeit through the means of enlightened leaders and administrators introducing rational change from above. Horodyski must also be credited with introducing many radical ideas into Poland through his writings and translation work.

Further information on Horodyski's life

and times can be found in W. Tokarz, *Ostatnie lata Hugona Kołłątaja* (The last years of Hugon Kołłątaj) (Krakow, 1905), Vols. I–II; M. Handelsman, *Napoleon et la Pologne (1806–1807)* (Paris, 1909); M. Handelsman, *Rozwój narodowości* (The Growth of Modern Nationality) (Warszawa, 1924, repr. 1973); K. Krzos, *Z księciem Józefem w Galicji w 1809 roku* (With Duke Jozef Poniatowski in Galicia in 1809) (Warszawa, 1967); B. Grochulska *Księstwo Warszawskie* (The Duchy of Warsaw) (Warszawa, 1967); B. Grochulska, 'Lewica wobec Napoleona w świetle "Korrespondecji w materiach obraz kraju i narodu rozjasniajacych"' ('The Left before Napoleon in the light of "Correspondences explaining the condition of the Country and the Nation"') in *Francja – Polska XVIII–XIXw* (France – Poland XVIII and XIX Century) (Warszawa, 1983), pp. 62–9.

LUKASZ KĄDZIELA

HOURWITZ, Zalkind (?1751–1812)
French revolutionary, Jewish anti-clerical

The precision of Zalkind Hourwitz's death is matched by vagueness concerning his birth. Although traditional accounts give the year 1740, a census of 1809 provides the more likely date of 1751. Abandoning his native Poland (Lublin?) where he lived in 'ignorance' and 'poverty', Hourwitz travelled to Berlin and then to France, first going to Nancy, Metz and Strasbourg before arriving in the capital in 1774. Once settled on the rue St Denis, this aspiring intellectual sought support from wealthy Jews while often wandering the streets of Paris hawking used clothing. An autodidact in all matters secular, Hourwitz entered a competition sponsored by the Metz Royal Society of Arts and Sciences on the question of making the Jews useful and happy citizens (1788). Publication of his prize-winning *Apologie des Juifs* (April 1789) helped to bring him the post of curator of oriental manuscripts in the Bibliothèque Royale. Inspired by revolutionary events, he joined the National Guard, donated one quarter of his small annual salary to the revolution (even before the rights of citizenship were awarded to Ashkenazic Jews), and became one of the more prolific contributors to the revolutionary journals. Unable to resist commenting on a multitude of disparate and usually controversial issues, he affixed his by now famous signature – Zalkind Hourwitz, Juif polonais – to articles ranging from diatribes against the King, the Church and duelling, to impassioned pleas for the enfranchisement of the Jews, the construction of fire escapes, and a transformation of the city map of Paris.

Dismissed from his post at the Bibliothèque during the ministry of Roland (all 'honorific' positions were abolished), Hourwitz remained in Paris as a teacher of languages. He was noticeably absent from the Napoleonic Assembly of Jewish Notables (1806) and Sanhedrin (1807); his well-known disdain towards the rabbis and Jewish leaders made their presence in Paris unlikely if he were among the deputies. The answers proposed by the Assembly and sanctified by the Sanhedrin, however, reflect his influence and suggest that he was, in fact, surreptitiously consulted. Living in a garret with little more than a straw mattress and a substantial library, Hourwitz completed three monographs (*Polygraphie, Origine de Langues* and *Lacographie*), before his death from apoplexy on February 8, 1812.

Hourwitz had no use for what he believed to be an archaic religious past, nor did he seriously advocate a purified Judaism. In articles and letters, often written for other purposes, he conveyed his antipathy to rabbinic Judaism, his annoyance with the economic and religious control of the Jewish masses by their leaders, and his concern lest the 'superstitions' and 'particular interests' of these leaders convince them to sacrifice the future well-being of the Jews. Much to the chagrin of the Jewish leadership, he advocated destruction of the Jewish quarters and relegation of the rabbis' influence to moral suasion. He simultaneously demanded (all this before the revolution) that the Jews be permitted to acquire property, exercise all professions and attend public schools. Hourwitz disapproved of the traditional and particularist welfarism advocated by the Jewish establishment and suggested instead schools for teaching the Jews various trades. Self-improvement also lay behind his proposal to establish chairs in Hebrew studies in those cities in which there were Jews.

While critical of the Jewish leadership, Hourwitz was no less vehement in his attempts to obtain equal rights and citizenship for the Jews. It is astonishing, he wrote on January 24, 1791, that 'the National Assembly has adjourned the business of Jews of all colours and men of colour of all religions, while it lets the directors and secretaries of gambling casinos enjoy all the rights of citizenship. To be a citizen and even a legislator in this country of equality and liberty, it suffices to be the owner of a white foreskin and to have just enough honesty to avoid being hanged'. Hourwitz's sarcasm knew few if any boundaries; his satiric pen, however, inspired radical and often successful measures.

Although he rejected what he believed to be the 'moral superiority' implicit in enlightenment ideology – 'It is not the Jews whom one must regenerate', he told the Metz Academy, 'but rather the Christians whom one must restore to justice and humanity' – Hourwitz never lost faith in the Enlightenment and especially in the role he assigned to education. Consider his project for a new map of Paris first proposed in the *Journal de Paris* of January 23, 1799. Paris would form a detailed map of Europe, a vast gallery of gods and goddesses and famous men, a veritable library. Principal streets were assigned the names of countries, secondary streets the names of capitals. Seas, forests, islands, mountains were all recorded. Sewers, to be painted in red, were named after tyrants, such as Caligula and Nero. It will be sufficient, Hourwitz wrote, for a stranger to know that someone lived at Cicero to be sure to find it on the rue de

Rome. Children of seven and eight years old who amused themselves by looking at the statues and who knew the streets of their *quartier* would be for this alone better historians and geographers than many 'pedants' of the day.

In three extraordinary monographs, Hourwitz proposed a remedy for the evils resulting from the diversity of languages, sought to explain the origin and nature of languages as well as their irregularities, similarities and differences and outlined a method of writing as quickly as one spoke. In each of these works, he explored, in a startling and often sophisticated way, an area which twentieth-century scholars of linguistics are only now rediscovering.

A philosophe of consequence, a Polish Jew of much notoriety and great integrity, a committed and outspoken revolutionary, Zalkind Hourwitz was simultaneously feared, courted, insulted and consulted. From his fellow revolutionaries he often elicited surprise that a Polish Jew expressed himself with such 'intelligence' and 'wit'. For many of his co-religionists, he continues to present the discomforting example of an anti-clerical iconoclast whose 'indiscretion' and 'zeal' nevertheless brought to public attention the oppression and strength of the Jewish people.

Hourwitz's articles appeared in *Le Journal de Paris*, *La Chronique de Paris*, *Le Courrier de Gorsas* and *L'Amis des Lois*. His publications include *Apologie des Juifs* (Paris, 1789), *Polygraphie* (chez l'auteur, An 9), *Origine des Langues* (Paris, n.d.), and *Lacographie* (Paris, 1811). He has been the subject both of a small and critical biographical sketch by his contemporary Michel Berr in *Biographie Universelle Ancienne et Moderne* and of a more generous study by the nineteenth-century Jewish historian Léon Kahn in *L'Annuaire des Archives Israélites* (1895), and in *Les Juifs de Paris pendant la Révolution* (Paris, 1898). See also Robert Anchel *Napoléon et les Juifs* (Paris, 1928); *Les Juifs de France* (Paris, 1946); David Feurwerker, *L'Emancipation des Juifs en France* (Paris, 1976); and Frances Malino, 'Zalkind Hourwitz – Juif Polonais', *Dix-huitième Siècle* (1981).

FRANCES MALINO

HUBER, Ludwig Ferdinand (1764–1804)
German republican reformer and political writer

Huber was born in Paris of a French mother and a Saxon father. Both parents regarded France as their true home, and although they returned to Leipzig when Huber was two, they raised their son to feel similarly. In 1784 Huber attended Leipzig University, where he became friends with a young professor, Christian Körner, and through Körner with Friedrich Schiller. The influence of these men confirmed Huber in his ambition to be a writer. Most of his energy over the next few years was devoted to poetry and literary criticism, the latter being more successful. In 1788, however, he became a member of the Saxon legation in Mainz, a position that brought him face to face with the French Revolution.

Huber's stay in Mainz coincided with a general decline in his productivity as an artist and critic, which was made worse because of a personal breach with Körner and Schiller. The intellectual stimulation that these two had provided was soon made up, however, after Huber made the acquaintance of Georg Forster (q.v.), the librarian at the local university. Forster turned Huber's attention toward the study of history and political economy, interests that were reinforced by the unfolding drama in France. Like Forster, Huber admired the revolution as the victory of rationality over mere custom and prejudice. He had no doubt that the organising principles put forward by the French Constituent Assembly could be applied elsewhere with relative ease. Huber's position as a member of the Saxon delegation made it impossible for him to take a public stand on this question, however, and although he remained in Mainz after the rest of the mission left in 1790, he never joined the Revolutionary Club (i.e. the Society of the Friends of Liberty and Equality). With the arrival of a French army in October 1792, however, Huber also fled. He returned briefly the following year out of concern for the safety of Forster's wife, Theresa, with whom he was already in love, and whom he would marry after Forster's death in January 1794.

Huber's ambiguous conduct in Mainz and his close connection to a famous revolutionary like Forster were sufficient to oblige Huber to give up his diplomatic post – a decision he seems not to have regretted. Early in 1794 he and Theresa moved to Neuenberg, Switzerland, where he devoted himself exclusively to writing, mainly political and historical essays, which appeared anonymously in a variety of periodicals, and were subsequently collected under the title *Friedens-Präliminarien, herausgegeben von dem Verfasser des heimlichen Gerichts* (10 vols., Berlin, 1794–96). In 1796–98 he was editor of *Neue Klio*, a monthly devoted to French affairs that appeared in Leipzig. In the spring of 1798 he moved to Tübingen, to assist in the editing of J.F. Cotta's (q.v.) new daily newspaper, the *Allgemeine Zeitung* (originally entitled *Neueste Weltkunde*). When E.L. Posselt (q.v.), the first editor-in-chief, was dismissed for political reasons the following September, Huber took his place. His appointment tended to reassure some of the paper's early critics, who found Huber's treatment of events less openly partisan than Posselt's had been. When the paper was forced out of Württemberg in 1803 it was in fact the French who had come to find the *AZ*'s coverage insufficiently sympathetic – a clear reflection of the illiberal drift of French policy under Napoleon. Huber and the *AZ* then moved to Ulm, where Cotta arranged for his editor to receive a post in the Bavarian school administration as a kind of unofficial subsidy. It was, financially and professionally, the most congenial position Huber had ever occupied, but it did not last long. In December of 1804, during a trip to Leipzig, he fell ill, and died unexpectedly on Christmas night.

Ludwig Huber was drawn to politics,

and specifically to radical politics, by a general cultural sympathy for things French (inherited from his parents), and by an equally general impatience with the irrationality and obscurity of traditional German institutions. Both feelings were common among educated Germans in 1789, but in most cases, for instance that of Huber's friend Schiller, they did not survive the fall of the French monarchy. In Huber's case they did. Although he was not himself a revolutionary, he never made the mistake of attributing the violence of the revolution to the desire for change per se. From the start he viewed the revolution as an international phenomenon, which would reproduce itself spontaneously across Europe in response to the French example. As editor of the *Allgemeine Zeitung* he paid particular attention to developments of this kind in southern Germany and in Switzerland, at a time when French policy was less and less interested in encouraging indigenous revolutionary movements. Although he was finally unable to protect the *AZ* from the anger of the French, his conduct in an increasingly difficult situation went a long way toward establishing that paper's reputation for intellectual sophistication and political independence, and certainly contributed to the willingness of other states to give the *AZ* a home.

For a long time the only significant source of information on Huber's life was a biography written by his wife, included in his *Sämtliche Werke seit dem Jahre 1802, nebst seiner Biographie* (2 vols., ed. Theresa Huber, Tübingen, 1806). His role in the history of the *Allgemeine Zeitung* is discussed briefly in Eduard Heyck, *Die Allgemeine Zeitung, 1798–1898* (Munich, 1898). There is now a biography in English: S.D. Jordan, *Ludwig Ferdinand Huber (1764–1804): His life and works* (Stuttgart, 1978), which contains an excellent bibliography.

DANIEL J. MORAN

JAGOT, Grégoire Marie (1750–1838)
Member of the Committee of General Security in the French revolutionary terror

Jagot was born in Nantua (Ain), where his elder brother became *président du district*. He became successively *marchand, juge de paix*, and a member of the Legislative Assembly, where he sat on the *comité de surveillance* until August 10, 1792. For this, Desmoulins (q.v.) was to denounce him as an ex-Brissotin in *Le Vieux Cordelier*, no. 7.

In November 1792 he was sent *en mission* to Nice and Savoy, to supervise the creation of the new departments of Mont-Blanc and Alpes-Maritimes. As a result, he was absent from Paris when the vote was taken in the Convention on the fate of Louis XVI: not the only time that Jagot was absent when a vital vote was taken. He sent a letter, however, voting for the king's death.

On September 19, 1793, he was elected secretary to the Convention for a month, and on 13 October, he joined the Committee of General Security. He was responsible for the areas of the Alps, Provence, the Pyrenees and the South-west. The committee's agent, Sénart, described Jagot as one of the 'radicals' of the committee, distinguished by his brutality, and the peremptory way in which he despatched suspects to prison.

On 9 Thermidor Year II Jagot was again absent from the Convention at a crucial moment. Although he gave ill-health as an excuse, he was almost immediately denounced as an Hébertist and a Robespierrist (an unlikely combination). He was expelled from the Committee of General Security a few days after the fall of Robespierre (q.v.). In Prairial Year III he was arrested, but under the Directory he re-emerged as a departmental administrator in the Ain. After 18 Brumaire he retired to Toul, where he died at the age of eighty-eight.

Jagot's strategic absences from crucial debates in the National Convention make it difficult to characterise his radicalism, or to assess how far his actions justified his undoubted radical reputation. In the Year II he was a dedicated supporter of the terror. Under the Directory, his republicanism was flexible enough to allow him to hold an important local office; but he would not compromise with Bonapartism.

There is no biography of Jagot, but for further information, see A. Kuscinski, *Dictionnaire des Conventionnels* (Paris, 1917).

MARTYN LYONS

JASIŃSKI, Jakub (1761–1794)
Polish general, politician, engineer and poet

Born on July 24, 1761 in Greater Poland to a nobleman's family, Jasiński received a careful primary education, and by eleven knew Latin, French and German. From 1773–83 he studied in the Cadet School in Warsaw where he also became an instructor. In 1785–87 he was a tutor to the sons of Piotr Potocki who later became Polish envoy in Istanbul. Jasiński had to leave the home when a conflict developed between him and his employer's family over the modern methods of education which he propagated and because of his ignoring of lessons on religion. He returned for a short time to the Corps of Cadets.

During the Four Years' Diet he became a commander of a Lithuanian engineers' corps in 1790 thanks to the support he obtained from the Potockis. Since his immediate superior, the Duke K.N. Sapieha – one of two speakers of the Four Years' Diet – was busy in political life, Jasiński organised unaided a corps and an engineers' school in Vilnius. In the Russo-Polish War of 1792 he commanded the engineers' staff in the Lithuanian army. It was probably he who pinpointed a wrong place for a camp near Mir, but in the critical moment of the battle (June 11, 1792) saved the army by indicating the proper way of retreat. From July 19 to 23, 1792 he fortified and prepared Brześć Litewski for street clashes, and was the author of a plan which brought about victory in a battle fought at that town. Consequently Jasiński was awarded a decoration.

After the king had acceded to the pro-Russian Conferation of Targowica, Jasiński did not resign together with a numerous group of officers. He remained in the army, won the confidence of the leaders of the Confederation in Lithuania, and on their behalf was a member of the supreme authorities of the army administration. In the summer of 1793 he joined the Vilnius conspiracy. The conspirators saw in him the future commander of the Vilnius garrison. Jasiński was the author of the rules of the conspiracy published under the disguised title of 'Selections from the Books on Morality by Good the Great, a Hindoo philosopher' which were rooted in masonic organisation and symbolism as well as in the Enlightenment ideology of the rights of man. In mid-April 1794 Jasiński organised a convergent march of Lithuanian troops on Vilnius, took command of a few hundred civilians and soldiers, and on the night 22 to 23 April captured the town, taking more than a thousand Russians prisoner. On the next day he became a member of the Lithuanian Supreme Council and made a major contribution towards the decision to hang the leader of the Targowica Confederation in Lithuania, Szymon Kossakowski.

On 3 May the Council promoted him to the command of the Lithuanian armed forces, but he did not have full power and commanded only in the region of Vilnius. He was not very successful in major battles, but achieved triumphs in the organisation of guerilla excursions. Jasiński wished to seal the insurrection in Lithuania with an explicitly revolutionary stamp. This desire made some members of the Lithuanian Supreme Council intervene by appealing to Kościuszko (q.v.). In effect, another general was made commander in Lithuania, whereas Jasiński, was promoted to the command of one of the three divisions which were operating in the province. He fought a few more battles and then, alleging ill-health, left for Warsaw. Kościuszko managed to persuade Jasiński to assume command of a sector which linked Lithuania with the Kingdom of Poland. Jasiński was charged mainly with the organisation of the troops. In September, disillusioned with the condition of the army, he asked to be dismissed, but on Kościuszko's insistent demand again took command of a Lithuanian division and led it to Warsaw. It was believed that he conceived the idea of killing the king and prisoners of war in order to enforce insurgents to the utmost effort in resisting the enemy. With Suvorov's army approaching, he volunteered to defend the Praga suburb of Warsaw. He was entrusted with the northern sector, where he died in battle on November 4, 1794.

Jasiński was a man of extensive education but uneven personality. He was capable of a momentary effort, but in general lacked perseverance. As an officer he proved unable to take unaided command of any major military unit. Ideologically he inclined to Jacobin radicalism and was influenced by the works of J.J. Rousseau. As a poet he began by writing sentimental personal lyrics, but his later libertine and deistic poems reveal the explicit influence of Voltaire. His last works are filled with patriotism and desire for social justice, Jasiński being aware of the relationship between the two ideas. He has rightly been seen as a forerunner of Romanticism.

For further details of Jasiński's life, see *The Cambridge History of Poland*, vol. II (Cambridge, 1941, 1951); *A History of Poland* (Warsaw, 1968, 1979); O. Halecki, *A History of Poland* (London, 1978, 1983); N. Davies, *God's Playground. A History of Poland*, vol. 1 (Oxford 1961, 1982, 1983); B. Lesnodorski, *Les Jacobins polonais* (Paris, 1965); H. Mościcki, *General Jasiński i powstanie kościuszkowskie* (General Jasiński and Kościuszko's Insurrection) (Warsaw, 1917); H. Mościcki, *Jakub Jasiński* (Kraków, 1948); and Z. Sulek, *Sprzysiężenie Jakuba Jasińskiego* (The Conspiracy of Jakub Jasiński) (Warsaw, 1982).

LUKASZ KĄDZIELA

JEANBON SAINT-ANDRÉ, André (1749–1813)
French Jacobin, member of the National Convention and the Committee of Public Safety, organiser of the Revolutionary navy

Jeanbon was born at Montauban (Tarn-et-Garonne), the son of the owner of a fulling mill. Although his parents were Calvinist, he was baptised in a Catholic church and sent to a Jesuit college, though his father withdrew him when his teachers suggested he join their society. The Catholic-sounding 'Saint-André' was attached to his name – perhaps to assuage potential persecutors and to demonstrate his desire for religious toleration. He entered the merchant marine in 1765, attained the rank of captain, but left after suffering a shipwreck on a return voyage from Saint-Domingue. In 1771 he went to Lausanne to study theology, was ordained a Calvinist minister in 1773 and became pastor at Castres. He was an able preacher but several conflicts with his consistory led him to resign in 1782. He resumed the ministry at Montauban in 1788 having, in the intervening period, written his *Considérations sur l'organisation civile des églises protestantes*. Religious troubles at the outbreak of the revolution forced Jeanbon to leave Montauban in May 1790, first for Toulouse and then for Bordeaux, where he came to know several of the future Girondins. He returned to Montauban in December, joined the Société des Amis de la Constitution, failed in his attempt to be elected to the Legislative, but succeeded in November 1791 in standing for municipal office in Montauban. He was sent by the municipality to Paris in March 1792 to try to secure a lycée for Montauban and while there spoke at the Jacobin Club.

In September 1792 Jeanbon was elected to the Convention for the Lot. At first he sat with the Girondins whom he had met two years earlier, but was quickly alienated by their hostility to the Paris Commune and went over to the Mountain. On November 2 he was elected president of the Jacobin Club. Shortly before the trial of

Louis XVI, Jeanbon published his *Opinion sur cette question: Louis XVI peut-il être jugé?* He answered his own question thus: 'A king, by the fact alone that he is king, is guilty towards humanity. because royalty itself is a crime.' He therefore voted against the appeal to the people and for the death-penalty without reprieve. And it was on his motion, on March 1, that the Jacobin Club excluded from its meetings all those deputies who had voted for the referendum. On March 9, 1793 he was sent with Lacoste on mission to the Lot and the Dordogne to organise military recruitment which, because of resistance, he had to enforce with strict measures: sequestrating émigré property, disarming suspects, and sending refractory priests to Bordeaux for deportation. On his return to the Convention on May 27 he participated in the last stages of the conflict between the Montagnards and the Girondins. With the victory of the former he was elected, on July 10, to the Committee of Public Safety with responsibility for naval affairs. The following day he was elected president of the Convention, his first task in that capacity being to announce the assassination of Marat (q.v.). When Gasparin resigned from the C.P.S. on July 27 it was Jeanbon who proposed that Robespierre (q.v.) replace him. In August he was sent with Prieur de la Marne (q.v.) to reorganise the armies of the Nord, Ardennes, and Moselle.

On August 23 Jeanbon resumed his place on the Committee of Public Safety and it was now that he began to play the role in the revolution for which he is chiefly remembered – the reorganisation of the navy. In the wake of the naval defeat at Toulon and the mutiny at Quiberon Bay Jeanbon was sent, again with Prieur, to Brest to restore order in and to re-build the Atlantic fleet. In the space of two months he transformed the situation: incompetent aristocratic officers were replaced by men of bourgeois birth, better wages and conditions were introduced for sailors and dockyard workers, republican ideas were disseminated among the ranks (for example, naval chaplains were replaced by teachers), new ships were commissioned and old ones repaired.

In the middle of November he was sent to the Vendée and then to Cherbourg, where he became involved in local religious disputes. He returned to Brest in mid-December to find similar religious discord. When the Committee of Public Safety despatched Laignelot to set up a revolutionary tribunal to restore order Jeanbon, who was opposed to this, returned in bad humour to Paris. However, on 28 Pluviôse (February 16, 1794) the Committee ordered him back to Brest in order to prepare the fleet for an invasion of the Channel Islands, though he only went on condition that Laignelot was recalled. On 27 Floréal (May 16) Jeanbon sailed with the fleet to escort a convoy of merchant ships carrying 24 million pounds of much-needed flour from the United States through a British blockade. In the major engagement that followed on June 1, the French fleet was defeated but Howe's ships were so badly damaged that they were forced to return to port and the convoy was able to get through. Although the battle revealed the inexperience of Jeanbon's new navy, the zeal with which it fought was a tribute to his reforming skills. On July 6 the Committee entrusted him with the task of constructing a new fleet at Toulon. Jeanbon had learned from the battle of June that greater training and discipline were necessary. A marine artillery corps was re-formed, officers were no longer to be elected by their men, and naval recruitment was stepped up. With the fall of Robespierre, Jeanbon lost his seat on the C.P.S. and his position came under attack, but the new Committee recognised the need for his reforming abilities and he was allowed to continue at Toulon. When he was finally recalled to Paris on 10 Pluviôse (January 29, 1795) he left behind a powerful Mediterranean fleet.

Back in the Convention he supported (10 Germinal) the motion of Cambon (q.v.) and Cambacérès for the implementation of the Constitution of 1793, and upheld (16 Floréal) the freedom of the press. Criticism from the Thermidorian right mounted and, although he was not involved in the *journée* of 1 Prairial (May 20, 1795), he was denounced as a Robespierrist and arrested and imprisoned in the Quatre-Nations.

Jeanbon was released under the general amnesty of 4 Brumaire Year IV (October 27, 1795) and on 28 Brumaire was appointed consul to Algiers. Two years later he was appointed consul general to Smyrna but had barely taken up his post when relations between France and Turkey deteriorated, and Jeanbon was flung into prison (November 17, 1798). He was in jail for three years during which time he wrote a *Récit de ma captivité*. He returned to France in October 1801 and was appointed by Napoleon prefect of Mont-Tonnerre and *commissaire général* for the four new departments on the left bank of the Rhine. He served Napoleon well though without abandoning his republican views, and he proved a popular and capable administrator. He became a member of the Legion of Honour and was created baron de Saint-André in January 1810. In 1813, when Mainz was filled with the sick and wounded of Napoleon's Grand Army in retreat from Moscow, Jeanbon contracted typhus and died.

Like Carnot (q.v.), Jeanbon's main contribution to the revolution was to make the Republic militarily sound in the face of the serious external threat of 1793–94. Although rightly remembered primarily as an efficient naval reformer, his political radicalism, developed in the early days of the Convention, helped to shape those reforms – in particular in the opening up of the navy to men of talent rather than birth. His value as an administrator to the revolutionary French state was especially demonstrated by the decision of the Thermidorian government to allow him to continue his work at Toulon in 1794, and by his retention of positions under the Directory and Napoleon when other terrorists had long since been swept aside.

For further details on the life of Jeanbon, see L. Lévy-Schneider, *Le Conventionnel Jeanbon Saint-André* (Paris, 1901); M. Nicolas, *Jeanbon Saint-André, sa vie et ses*

écrits (Montauban, 1848); R.R. Palmer, *Twelve who ruled. The year of the terror in the French Revolution* (Princeton, 1941); N. Hampson, *La Marine de l'An II* (Paris, 1959); A. Kuscinski, *Dictionnaire des Conventionnels* (Paris, 1917); and S. Scott and B. Rothaus (eds), *Historical Dictionary of the French Revolution, 1789–1799* (2 vols., Westport, CT, 1985).

D. NICHOLLS

KANT, Immanuel (1724–1804)
German philosopher sympathetic to the ideas of the French Revolution

Kant was born on April 22, 1724 at Königsberg. He came from a family of artisans; his mother was a Pietist. In 1732 he entered the Collegium Fridericianum, and in 1740 the University of Königsberg, where he studied philosophy, mathematics and theology. In 1746, on the death of his father, he was left without means and became a private tutor to earn his living. Following his *Habilitation* in 1755 he became a junior lecturer and then, from 1770, Professor of Logic and Metaphysics at the University of Königsberg. He was no longer financially embarrassed and started writing his philosophical works. Kant was a sickly individual who lived according to a strict timetable. Only the reading of a new book by Rousseau, or the news of the French Revolution could alter the time and course of his daily walk. The only significant political event in his life was his clash with the censorship of Frederick William II in 1793 on the publication of *Die Religion innerhalb der Grenzen der blossen Vernunft*. From 1798 he considered himself released by the king's death from the promise he had made not to deal with religious questions. He returned to the question in *Der Streit der Fakultäten*. His life was one dedicated to education and research and unmarked by milestones other than those of the publication of his works. He retired from his chair at the university in 1797 and died at Königsberg on February 12, 1804.

The first period of his philosophy can

be placed between 1763 and 1770. Under the influence of Newton and Leibnitz he was particularly interested in the natural sciences. Then, under the influence of Locke and Hume, he developed an interest in the theory of knowledge. A large part of his courses dealt with mathematics, physics, the art of fortifications and physical geography. The methods which he acquired in the natural sciences enabled him to become a critic in philosophical matters. He introduced the idea of evolution. Then he went on to logic and metaphysics, interested from now on not so much in the history of the subject, as in the human mind. In 1781 he published the *Kritik der reinen Vernunft* which constituted a veritable revolution in philosophy. He criticised dogmatic philosophy, the metaphysics of Plato and Descartes. The multiplicity of metaphysical systems caused him to doubt; metaphysics cannot be a science because it uses pure non-verifiable ideas. The world of appearances is apprehended by our senses, and our intelligence is determined by them. The very essence of a thing, the thing itself, cannot be known to us. But in the *Kritik der praktischen Vernunft* (1788), Kant considered that if we cannot know a thing itself we can think it, and he thereby rehabilitated God, freedom and immortality. He saved metaphysics by faith in order that morality might have some meaning. The Christian religion remained fundamental to his thinking: 'radical evil' is an emanation of original sin.

Kant's philosophy contains so many revolutionary ideas that it is impossible to call him a liberal. Initially an adherent of the Enlightenment and enlightened despotism, he showed great interest in the French Revolution. The *Declaration of the Rights of Man* seemed to him to be the first practical application of his system, and he was to excuse the excesses of the revolution in his letters and did not think a revolution possible without violence. In 1798 he said that the general and lasting progress achieved by the French Revolution was more important than temporary problems. But he did not want to enter politics, and

despite encouragement from Paris, preferred to stay on the sidelines.

In all that he wrote on the French Revolution, Kant was certainly influenced by Rousseau and the great principles of the revolution itself, but also by the texts of Grotius and Pufendorf on natural law. The idea of the social contract and the theories of natural law constitute a framework in which Kant is easily integrated. In *Die Religion innerhalb der blossen Vernunft* (1793), Kant turned his attention to the problem of freedom. Contrary to classical German thinkers, Goethe, Humboldt or Schiller, he declared that one could only become mature enough for freedom by being free. To refuse man liberty was to encroach on the privileges of the deity himself, who created man for liberty. This text brought Kant the reputation of being a Jacobin. He was to reformulate his ideas in *Zum ewigen Frieden* in 1795. At that time the majority of German thinkers considered the 'horrors' of the French Revolution a consequence of the moral and political immaturity of the French people. As with many other concepts, Kant recognised that the concept of the idea of eternal peace was a concept which went beyond experience, and for that reason could not but perceive of a systematic unity. Man had a duty to find the path which leads to this end. Unlike Rousseau, Kant thought that happiness was not to be found in nature at all: the natural state was one of rivalry and hostilities, of general war, and it was necessary to leave it in order to live in an ethical community. The state of peace must therefore be instituted. The natural state founded on force and instinct was opposed to the natural state founded on reason. Natural law was achieved in the state by joining with rational law, which presented freedom as human freedom. Freedom and the state were founded on a reciprocal basis. The state could be considered the result of a contract. Participation in civil society and in relations between the men who constitute it is a duty. Linked to this duty, the concept of law proceeded from freedom. Law was nothing more than the limitation on individual freedom imposed by respect for the freedom of others. Every member of society must be free as an individual, equal as a subject, and independent as a citizen. External freedom was man's opportunity to develop civic virtues, and the possibility of not obeying laws other than those to which he had given his consent. It fell to the citizen to abide only by those laws in whose creation he had assisted. No other law was worthy of application than that which was created by a free will acting rationally.

Thus Kant reaffirmed the principle of popular sovereignty; but in practice he admitted the existence of a long transitional period during which the monarch would have the duty of governing in a republican fashion. The most important principle was this: act in whichever way you might wish in order to make your maxim a general law, the realisation of peace derives from this principle.

All the principles put forward here are clearly compatible with those of the French Revolution. It is only with regard to the fundamental problem of the right to rebel that ambiguities are to be found in Kant's thought. Although he had watched with approval as his own conception of freedom became reality in the French Revolution, and had concluded, unlike most of his contemporaries, that it was ridiculous for man to be ready for liberty without first giving it to him, he did not admit a right to rebellion. Nevertheless he agreed that a revolution could change the rights of a citizen. In *Der Streit der Fakultäten* (1798), he argued that mankind is constantly progressing towards good, and he cited the French Revolution despite the evils it entailed. The experience of the French Revolution was of interest to the whole of mankind as a stage on the path to a state of law and justice. In saying this Kant recognised, at least implicitly, the right to rebel, but did not want to express it explicitly. He recognised that the question did arise as to whether men should rebel if the state committed injustices. But, like Pufendorf, he considered that if authority went beyond the limits assigned to it by

the constitution then one must assume that it is acting only in the interests of the state, and might only oppose it within the law. To admit a right to resistance would be to remove the foundation of the state, since all opposition would be justified *a priori*. In according the right of resistance the French revolutionaries did not escape this contradiction. But if a revolution succeeded and a new constitution was established, it must be obeyed despite the illegality of its establishment. Against authority man only has freedom of thought. There was then an ambiguity in his judgement on the French Revolution: although it inspired irresistible sympathy no one would want to start it again, the sympathy having no other cause than the general moral disposition of mankind. On a philosophical level this meant that a critical politics is impossible. It Kant wanted absolutely to put a brake on freedom, it was because for him it had always been freedom for evil. For him, man was an animal in need of a master, and he feared the rise of the masses which seemed to him to threaten individual freedom. There was an insoluble contradiction between the principle of equality and this élitist and individualist point of view. So he welcomed the arrival of the Directory which, according to him, saved the revolution. He thought the political problem in the shadow of evil, and that is why, in the terms of his dialectic, the political problem is confused with the ethical problem and is formulated on the ideal rather than on the conceptual level.

Should one conclude that Kant argued against the revolution? In fact he only denied the right to rebel; but he was well aware that there might be times when the law was no longer respected. This is what happened during the French Revolution, which represented progress. The optimism of *Zum ewigen Frieden*, and his hope of seeing one day true peace are based on the French Revolution, a decisive stage in human progress. But he remains laconical on the path which leads to the ideal state. The Germans have retained above all his idea that there can be no freedom outside moral law. They turned this idea against revolutionary France, which had instituted freedom without preparing the nation to enjoy it. Kant's thought has often been interpreted in a counter-revolutionary way which is alien to it.

Kant's major philosophical works are: *Kritik der reinen Vernunft* (1781); *Kritik der praktischen Vernunft* (1788); *Die Religion innerhalb der Grenzen der blossen Vernunft* (1793); *Zum ewigen Frieden* (1795); *Der Streit der Fakultäten* (1798). Recent secondary works dealing with Kant's philosophical and political ideas are: A. Philonenko, *Théorie et praxis dans la pensée morale de Kant et de Fichte en 1793* (Paris, 1976); Zwi Batscha, 'Bürgerliche Republik und bürgerliche Revolution bei Immanuel Kant', in J.H. Schoeps and I. Geiss (eds.), *Revolution und Demokratie in Geschichte und Literatur* (Duisburg, 1979), p. 133; G.L. Fink, 'La dialectique du despotisme éclairé selon Kant', *Recherches Germaniques*, 7 (1977), p. 29; E.R. Sandvoss, *Immanuel Kant* (Stuttgart, 1983).

M. GILLI

KÉRALIO, Louise Félicité Guinemont de (1758–1822)

French journalist, early feminist and social reformer

Louise was the daughter of a minor noble from Brittany, who assigned to himself her education. With him she first became involved in politics when they co-edited the *Journal de l'état et du citoyen* in 1789. This newspaper gained greater fame when it ceased to come out twice weekly and instead came out as the weekly *Mercure national*, probably the first paper to advocate republicanism. Associated with Kéralio on this paper were Carra (q.v.) and Robert (q.v.), whom she married and who became co-editor with her on the paper.

The two were prominent in the politics of the Cordelier district and were associated with Danton (q.v.) and Prudhomme, owner of the best selling radical paper the *Révolutions de Paris*. In particular they were among the main organisers of the popular clubs in the first months of 1791

and in 1792: they believed that these clubs should be open to all classes and both sexes. The Roberts were instrumental in ousting Dansard from the *Société fraternelle des deux sexes* (Fraternal Society for Both Sexes) and injecting it with a more pronounced political activism. Louise herself urged the other popular societies to follow the example of the *Fraternelle* and eliminate all titles such as Madam, Monsieur and Mademoiselle in favour of frère and soeur. More important she hoped to establish these societies in every part of Paris and then throughout every town and village in France. She saw these clubs as political education centres, not just for criticising the constitution, but for instilling in the minds of the people that they were part of the General Will and as such had taken part in it and did not just obey it. She agreed that France had adopted the representative form of government, but did not believe that because of this the people had forfeited their rights to the deputies: on the contrary the people had to watch over their every move and reject what they did not approve. This was one of the main tasks of the popular societies. Louise also claimed that the wealth of the rich was based on the exploitation of the poor, whom she tended to idealise. She claimed that the rich could well benefit from a visit to one of the societies for the poor, such as the *Société des indigents*, where those who were well-dressed and spoke in polished accents might learn a great deal about the virtues of ordinary folk whose formation came straight from nature.

With the Republic Louise's career seems to have fallen into the shadow of her husband's. She died in Brussels in 1822, having been deported with François in 1815.

Louise Kéralio was therefore one of the major feminists of the revolution, and is generally regarded as being superior in intellect and understanding to her husband. But her radicalism lay not just in her early support for women's rights but also in her belief in a radical republicanism that would make representatives more directly accountable to ordinary people. She was a supporter of social equality, champion of the poor, and a critic of the more restricted reform currents which emerged during the revolutionary period.

For further details of Kéralio's life, see: L. Antheunis, *Le conventionnel belge François Robert (1763–1826) et sa femme Louise de Kéralio (1758–1822)* (Wetteren, 1955).

BILL MURRAY

KERNER, Johann Georg (1770–1812)
German revolutionary democrat

Kerner was born on April 9, 1770 at Ludwigsburg, son of Christian Ludwig Kerner, a senior official in the service of Karl Eugen, Duke of Württemberg. His education was spartan, his father beat him, and he wanted to leave home. On June 14, 1779 he became, like Schiller, a pupil of the military academy at Stuttgart and an intimate friend of Johann Gottfried Reinhold. He wished to study medicine in order to be able to travel as a military doctor. On July 14, 1790 he took part in the celebration of the fall of the Bastille at the school and burned the letters patent of nobility of his family. He went to Strasbourg, where he visited the houses of the poor and the prisons, thus revealing his interest in social institutions. He wore the tricolour rosette. He completed his studies in May 1791, became engaged to Auguste Breyer, but drawn by the 'land of liberty', settled in Strasbourg. Here he joined the Jacobin Club in June 1791.

In November of 1791 Kerner travelled to Paris where he lived in poverty. He met the Germans whose enthusiasm for the revolution had brought them to France. Forster (q.v.) wrote of him 'Der kleine Schwabe Kerner sprüht Freiheit wie ein Vulkan' (The little Swabian Kerner spouts freedom like a volcano). Following the fall of the Gironde, he came under suspicion and fled to Switzerland, where he worked as an agent of the French Republic. Returning to Paris in 1794, he was entrusted with a mission to the north of England. In 1795 he returned to Paris and wrote *Lettres de Paris* for the journal *Klio*.

In September 1795 he left for Hamburg, with his friend Reinhold, by whom he was employed as secretary. In 1797 he founded the Philanthropic Society whose aim was to propagate the ideas of the French Revolution, but which was banned the following year. In 1797 he wrote *Briefe über Frankreich, die Niederlande und Deutschland*, and founded the journal *Nordstern*, which was also quickly banned. Disappointed at these setbacks he devoted himself to medicine and the care of the poor. He died at the age of forty-two during a typhus epidemic.

Kerner was an enthusiastic supporter of the French Revolution at its outset, and considered Karl Eugen a wretched despot. But, like many idealists he was disappointed by events in France, though he still thought that France would bring freedom to the world. He considered the Jacobin dictatorship a relapse into despotism, and for him the insurrection of May 31, 1793 marked the beginning of the counter-revolution. However, he still preferred the cause of France to that of the tyrants of Europe and hoped for a French victory. He thought that a counter-revolutionary victory would be a blow not only to France, but to the whole of Europe. In Hamburg he was touched by the misery he found, and by the plight of the peasants. This reinforced his hatred of monarchy. During a journey to Italy in 1797, he witnessed corruption and speculation, and expressed his first doubts on the mission of the French army. He reproached Bonaparte for his personal ambition. Despite these disappointments, he remained an enemy of tyrants, of monarchy and of aristocracy, and hoped for the victory of the republican cause. He did not understand the period 1793–1794, because he had distanced himself from the mass of the people, but this did not affect his deepest convictions. Devoting himself to the poor, he never betrayed his ideals.

J.G. Kerner was one of those revolutionary democrats who, despite their criticism of the terror and their reservations about the policy of Bonaparte, remained loyal to their revolutionary ideals and devoted their lives to the spread of such ideas. He was convinced that the French Republic would emerge victorious from its battles and its deviations.

Something of Kerner's ideas can be gleaned from his *Briefe über Frankreich, die Niederlande und Deutschland* (Altona, 1797). The main sources on his life and ideas are, however, Hedwig Voegt (ed.), *Georg Kerner, Jakobiner und Armenarzt. Reisebriefe, Berichte, Lebenszeugnisse* (Berlin, 1978), and Adolf Wohlwill, *Georg Kerner* (Hamburg und Leipzig, 1886).

M. GILLI

KNIGGE, Adolph Freiherr von (1752–1796)
German political novelist and moderate reformer

Knigge came from a noble family of Lower Saxony; his father, Philipp, was a landowner and Hanoverian officer. He was born on October 16, 1752 and was brought up on his father's estate at Bredenbeck near Hanover. His father died a debtor in 1766 and the estates were sequestered. Three years later Knigge went to study law at Göttingen, and in 1771 he was appointed to an official position at the court in Kassel, where he married Henriette von Baumbach in 1773.

From 1780 to 1783 he lived in Frankfurt am Main where he became involved with Adam Weishaupt's order of Illuminati. From 1783 to 1787 he was in Heidelberg but, not for the first time, financial difficulties forced him to move on, and he returned to Hanover to try and secure the inheritance of his father's estate. He remained here until 1790 and was appointed a chief magistrate in Bremen in 1791. He was already ill when he moved to Bremen and died there in 1796.

Although primarily a writer of fiction and author of several successful novels in the 1780s, Knigge wrote a number of essays and other discursive pieces, including *Über den Umgang mit Menschen* (1788) which gained him widespread recognition as a writer in the Enlightenment tradition.

Knigge's sympathy for the French Revolution and opposition to the old régime in Germany is clear from his later satirical novels (*Benjamin Noldmann*, 1791, *Schaafskopf*, 1792, and *Wurmbrand*, 1792). *Benjamin Noldmann* contains important political passages, and repudiates the idea of reform from above as a possible way of transforming society. The book contains a detailed description of a republic based on freedom and equality which he intended to send to the French National Convention.

Although he opposed the political order of his day, Knigge remained an élitist in many respects; his writing was aimed at the upper classes and his practical political activities were restricted to his work with the Illuminati. Nevertheless he was firmly opposed to the prevailing social and political conditions in Germany and frequently came into conflict with the conservative and counter-revolutionary defenders of the old régime, notably with Leopold Alois Hoffmann, editor of the *Wiener Journal*. He was an aristocrat who could trace his family tree back to the twelfth century, and his defence of Enlightenment and republican ideas provoked accusations from some of the rather more recently ennobled, such as Johannes Georg Zimmerman, a doctor in Hanover, that he had betrayed his class. However, his radicalism was of a qualified sort. Although a proponent of social and political change, he concentrated his attention almost exclusively on the emancipation of the bourgeoisie, and considered excessive enlightenment for the majority of the population both unnecessary and unhelpful.

Knigge's writings have been published as Adolph Knigge, *Schriften* (12 vols., Hanover, 1804–1806); Adolph Knigge, *Der Traum des Herrn Brick. Essays, Satiren, Utopien* (edited by Hedwig Voegt, Berlin, 1968). Secondary works on Knigge are: Wolf Kaiser, '"Welcher Art von Revolutionen in den Staats-Verfassungen zu erwarten, zu befürchten, oder zu hoffen sey?" Zur politischen Publizistik Adolphs Freiherrn Knigge', in Gert Mattenklott and Klaus R. Scherpe (eds), *Demokratische-revolutionäre Literatur in Deutschland:*

Jakobinismus (Kronberg, 1975); Inge Stephan, *Literarischer Jakobinismus in Deutschland* (Stuttgart, 1976); W.E. Yuill, 'A genteel Jacobin, Adolph Freiherr von Knigge', in *Erfahrung und Überlifering* (1974).

TIM KIRK

KOLLATAJ, Hugo (1750–1812)
Polish clergyman, reformer of the educational system, politician, writer and philosopher

Born on 1 April in Volhynia to a family of poor nobility, Kołłątaj went to school in Pińczów; from 1761 he stayed in Cracow, and probably attended the Cracow University. He took holy orders before 1764. Between 1771 and 1772 he stayed in Vienna where he undoubtedly studied law; and from 1772 to 1774 he was in Rome. The place where he obtained his D. ClL. and D.D. is unknown. It was possible for him to have made a career in the Curia, close to Clement XIV. While in Italy he made several Polish acquaintances and those connexions helped in his later career. By the end of his stay in Rome he had obtained the Pope's recommendation for the cathedral canonry in Cracow, a post which he took over a year later in a dispute with K. Sołtyk – the Bishop of Cracow.

He began striving for participation in public life and for improving his financial status. In Warsaw, supported by Michal Poniatowski, the Bishop of Płock (brother of the king and later primate), Kołłątaj joined the Society for Elementary Books in 1776 where he distinguished himself with his diligence in giving opinions on handbooks for the educational system then under reform by the National Education Commission. He was soon charged by the Commission with the task of reforming Cracow University (1777).

Although Kołłątaj's plan of turning the university into a modern establishment composed of five academic departments failed (he was opposed by the nuncio, T. Archetti), the university was slowly and gradually reorganised into two colleges: an excellent Natural Philosophy College and

inferior Moral one. Kołłątaj emphasised the development of the Medical School and contributed to imposing on towns a duty of sending barber-surgeons to study there. He also set in order the archives of the university and the library, took care of the finances of the university, and was partly successful in secularising some monastic property. The Commission approved of those of Kołłątaj's projects which referred to school hierarchy – subordinating primary and secondary schools to a main school and university, in each province – and to setting up a separate 'academic estate'. However, his proposal to laicise the whole teaching staff was not appreciated. From 1783 to 1786 Kołłątaj was rector of the university. His reform remained uncompleted. It nevertheless brought the university to the level of the west European schools and it represented the idea of civic education according to the spirit of opposition to the Jesuits.

During his time in Cracow, Kołłątaj was greedily accumulating prebends as well as villages which could be purchased. He founded schools and charity brotherhoods based on mutual aid in those villages. He also favoured adopting new scientific and technological methods in agriculture. Primarily, however, he strove to increase his profits from trade in corn and timber with Danzig (Gdańsk), from the exploitation of mineral resources (limestone, salt), and from the development of industry. He spent money on a comfortable life, on collecting books, paintings, coins, and on supporting his family.

In 1786 Kołłątaj settled down in Warsaw and bought the office of the Lithuanian referendary the following year. He tried to be neutral in the contention between the court and the magnate-opposition, taking the role of mediator and keeping in touch with representatives of both parties. In foreign policy he was an advocate of armed neutrality which meant opposition to the king's project of a Russo-Polish alliance. He intended to use the favourable state created by the Turkish-Russian war to reject the Russian empress's warrants and to carry out in Poland a 'mild revolution' (G. Filanghieri's term). An important role in political debates was played by Kollątaj's *Letters of an Anonymous Writer to the Speaker of the Diet* (parts I–III: August 1788 – May 1789) which were addressed to S. Małachowski, the Speaker of the Four Year's Diet. In these letters he displayed a view of a new social order based on a compromise between the gentry-freeholders and owners of urban property with some of the teachers, clergymen and officers. He suggested that the middle-class be admitted to the Diet which meant opposition to the idea of strengthening the king's power, and he supported the development of the otherwise weak administration in Poland, which in turn meant subordinating it to the parliament. He wished that the Polish Church could be to a greater extent free from Rome and more strongly tied to the state.

Writers and publicists connected with Kollątaj and gathered in the so-called 'Kollątaj's Forge' followed him and began publishing numerous pamphlets. These publications contributed to moving the matters of argument from the conference room of the Diet to the streets. This circle of people suggested the setting up of the first political club in Warsaw. Kollątaj was also one of the organisers of a congress and author of a proclamation which was handed to the king on December 2, 1789 by the representatives of the towns (the so-called Black Procession).

Kollątaj simultaneously joined the work on the new constitution. Initially, he arranged information and projects for I. Potocki and S. Małachowski, and from the time of their rapprochement with the king (1790), he served as a mediator and advisor, preparing compromise versions of the document. These versions became the foundation for the final form of the Constitution of 3 May. Kollątaj played an important part on the day when the constitution was resolved; he had organised a demonstration of the townsmen in the conference room of the Diet and on the streets of Warsaw. In the coming months he became one of the most important personages in Poland. Appointed deputy chancellor of

the Kingdom of Poland (May 17, 1791) he became occupied with the realisation of the resolved municipal reform; with preparing a similar one which referred to the Jews, and with the codification of the civil and criminal laws. He was also one of the main organisers of a political club named the Society of Friends of the State Constitution which was to continue the reforms. He organised armed formations of Warsaw townsmen in order to activate the reforms and to resist the opponents of the constitution.

In spring 1792 Kollątaj drafted, with the French envoy M. Descorches, a project of Polish-French alliance. It was supposed that Kollątaj wanted to play the role of Prime Minister at the side of Stanisław-August, although the king himself was ill-disposed towards him. In February 1792 Kollątaj became coadjutor with the right of succeeding to the rich Cracow bishopric.

During the Russo-Polish war of 1792, Kollątaj was a member of the Council of War, organised volunteers, but at the same time aimed at negotiations. He deceived himself that at the cost of appointing Grand Duke Constantine, the grandson of Catherine II, to the Polish throne, part of the Diet reforms of 1788–92 could be preserved under the second protectorate. During the famous meeting of July 23, 1792 he proclaimed himself in favour of the idea that the king should join immediately the pro-Russian Confederation of Targowica. Kollątaj then abandoned his accession to the Confederation in Warsaw and left for Leipzig where, for the next six months, he waited to see whether the king would be able to come to an agreement with Russia and the Confederation.

Kollątaj was the co-author of a book *On the Creation and Fall of the Constitution of 3 May*, which praised reformatory works and attacked the king as a traitor. Together with I. Potocki, he was also making preparations for Kościuszko's (q.v.) mission to Paris, contacting French representatives in Leipzig, and ideologically tending towards the ideas of the French Revolution in its pre-Jacobinic phase. He supervised preparations for the uprising, although he did not believe that the home conspiracy was ready yet. On April 17, 1794 he arrived at Kościuszko's camp. The Act of Insurrection, composed in Leipzig, was of collective authorship, whereas Kołłątaj was the sole author of the Manifesto of Połaniec, and joint-author with I. Potocki of the resolution concerning the Supreme National Council. Kościuszko left the decision respecting membership of the Council to them. The two authors of the resolution then left for Warsaw.

Kołłątaj's arrival in the capital – preceded by the return of his confidants (such as T. Maruszewski (q.v.)) – was enthusiastically greeted by the Jacobins and the people. From July 6, 1794 he performed the duties of president of the Treasury of the Supreme National Council, but was active in many other interior and international matters relating to the insurrection and its propaganda. One of his most important, though late, moves was his proposal to grant land 'for perpetual heritage' to peasant-soldiers and to children of those killed in the war (October 20, 1794). Kołłątaj also played a part in instigating state terror and popular riots in Warsaw on 9 May and 28 June. According to most recent works he was not the actual leader of the Jacobins (though he protected them), but treated them as a pressure-group in order to maintain unity among the insurgents. Before the insurrection collapsed Kołłątaj attempted to revive the Jacobin Club under the name of the Assembly for the Support of Revolution and of the Act of Cracow, a step which went in opposition to the majority of the leaders of the insurrection.

He left Warsaw immediately after Praga (a suburb of the capital) was attacked on November 4, 1794. Austrian authorities, at the request of the Russians, arrested him near Przemyśl on 6 December because of a denunciation by one of his former associates. He was found to be carrying a considerable amount of money and valuables, most of which came from the treasury of the insurrection. This led to accusations of embezzlement. From 1794 to 1802 he remained in the Austrian prisons of

Ołomuniec and Josephstadt during which time he was strenuously questioned about his participation in the uprising and his relations with revolutionary France. Several interventions aimed at freeing Kołłątaj from prison failed; but, finally, Tsar Alexander I's pleading to Francis II, undertaken at the suggestion of A.J. Czartoryski (who hoped to resolve the Polish question by collaboration with Russia) was successful. Kołłątaj was freed when he undertook not to return to Galicia, which made him lose his benefices and the estates he had inherited.

Ill, icily received by many of his former associates from the time of the Four Year's Diet, and whole-heartedly rejected by the Republicans, he left for Volhynia. He busied himself with educational and administrative organisation of the Polish Lyceum (secondary school) of Krzemieniec which was being set up by T. Czacki. In 1803 he drafted a plan of organisation of the secondary and popular schooling in three south-westerly provinces of the Russian Empire. He remained, from 1804, under discreet police supervision and after Napoleon had marched into Poland, and when unrest intensified in Volhynia, Kołłątaj was arrested and transported to Moscow (January 1807 – May 1808) where he was well-treated and where Alexander I even granted him a salary.

Kołłątaj was asked to come to the Duchy of Warsaw for the first time as early as 1806 by the Republicans who acted in consultation with Napoleon. But his delay in complying increased Napoleon's resentment against him. Besides, the emperor treated Kołłątaj as one of the Jacobin leaders in Europe whom he disliked. When, later, Kołłątaj came to Warsaw, his candidature for the post of Minister of the Interior was met with the ill-will of Polish politicians and with Napoleon's categorical objection – both of which proved stronger than Marshall Davout's support for him. The result was that he did not obtain a place in the government. Before the 1809 Diet, when the Republicans were gathering their forces, Kołłątaj wrote a pamphlet entitled *Nil desperandum*. Despite his friends' advice the text was an apologia for Napoleon, the Grand Empire and the Duchy of Warsaw.

In mid-1809, through the mediation of A. Horodyski (q.v.), Kołłątaj tried to move closer to Duke J. Poniatowski, the commander-in-chief of the Polish army. When his attempts failed, he began plotting against the duke with support from Dresden. He continued writing political tracts at that time, in which he departed from his republican ideas towards changing the authoritarian monarchy in the Duchy into a fully constitutional order. He proposed also the reduction of the clergy's influence on the cultural and educational life of Poland. From 1809 to 1810, encouraged by Horodyski, Kołłątaj accomplished a second reform of Cracow University, again based on proposals from the National Education Commission. He created a scientific society under the name of the Academic Institute. He visited Dresden to have the educational system in the Duchy reorganised, but failed in his attempts to subordinate primary education to the university. He was, however, given back part of his confiscated property.

In his Austrian prison Kołłątaj had begun working on philosophy. In his works, he propagated the materialistic philosophy of the Enlightenment and the physiocratic doctrine which he reconciled with the theories of Adam Smith. He repudiated Kantian ideas which were spreading then. He also worked on a Polish history of 1750–1796, having in mind a multi-voluminous 'memoir' which would consider socio-economic, legal, cultural, moral and political matters, and which would link contemporary history with his own recollections. However, he only completed the first volume.

Kołłątaj's active mode of life affected his health. Imprisonment ruined him for good and changed the psyche of this persistent and ambitious, though revengeful, unforgiving and malicious politician. By the end of his life his conflict with the world increased and so did his sense of wrong, solitude and menace. He died in Warsaw on February 28, 1812, his funeral being attended by a small group of his friends. For one-and-a-half centuries Kołłątaj was called both the 'Polish Robespierre' and father of Polish democracy. It seems that the last word on him has not been pronounced yet.

For further information on Kołłątaj the following can be consulted: *The Cambridge History of Poland*, Vol. II (Cambridge, 1941; repr. 1951); O. Halecki, *A History of Poland* (London 1978; repr. 1983); N. Davies, *God's Playground. A History of Poland* (Oxford, 1981, 1982, 1983), vols. I–II; N. Davies, *Heart of Europe. A Short History of Poland* (Oxford, 1984); W. Tokarz *Ostatnie lata Hugona Kołłątaja* (The Last Years of Hugo Kołłątaj) (Kraków, 1905); M. Janik, *Hugo Kołłątaj* (Lwów, 1913); N. Jabloński, *Sąd Kryminalny Wojskowy w r. 1794* (The Army Criminal Court in 1794) (Warszawa, 1935); B. Leśnodorski, *Les Jacobins polonais* (Paris, 1965); K. Krzos, *Z księciem Józefem w Galicji w 1809 roku* (With Duke Józef Poniatowski in Galicia in 1809) (Warszawa, 1967); H. Hinz, *Filozofia Hugona Kołłątaja* (The Philosophy of Hugo Kołłątaj) (Warszawa, 1973).

LUKASZ KĄDZIELA

KOŚCIUSZKO, Andrzej Tadeusz Bonawentura (1746–1817)
General of American and Polish armies, commander-in-chief of the 1794 uprising in Poland, politician and social reformer

Kościuszko was born on 4 February 1746 in Polesie to a family of lesser nobility. From 1755 to 1760 he was educated in a Piarist school, then continued his education from 1765–68 in the Cadet School – the recent foundation of King Stanisław-August Poniatowski – where he also was an instructor in 1767. The years 1769–74 he spent in France studying in the Academy of Painting and Sculpture in Paris. Though refused admission to the École de Génie in Mézières as a foreigner, he went through its course with tutors. He was open at the time to the influences of the political climate of France which was then maturing to revolution. He read J.J. Rousseau and also absorbed the ideas of humanitarianism and religious indifferentism. After returning home he settled matters concerning his estate, and then, on being refused permission to marry his beloved by the young lady's parents, he again left Poland in October 1775 for Saxony where he hoped to find a job either in the army or in the civil service.

His plans failed, and he left for France where, probably through the mediation of P.A. Beaumarchais, he enlisted on the side of America in the War of Independence. As early as autumn 1776 he co-operated in drafting plans to fortify Billingsport; in winter that year he was strengthening Philadelphia; in spring he began, under General H. Gates, constructing field defences which were a decisive contribution to the victory of Saratoga on 17 October 1777. From 1778 to 1780 he was busy fortifying West Point where he became head of the engineers' staff, and in 1781–82 he took an active part in the blockade of Charlestown. He was promoted to Brigadier-General, became a member of the Society of the Cincinnati, and won himself the appreciation of Congress. He left America equipped with the abilities of military engineer, builder of fortifications, and quartermaster, as well as with the experience in organising militia and improvising a standing army. Moreover, American democratic ideas had strengthened Kościuszko's social criticism.

He came back to Poland in 1784. For the next five years he unsuccessfully tried to manage his inherited estate. The reasons for this failure lay in Kościuszko's uneconomical management and in his reducing by half, on humanitarian grounds, the villein service of his peasants. In his private letters of that time he wrote that the essential evil of Poland lay in serfdom and in the indifference of the peasantry. He pointed to the necessity to polonize the Ruthenian peasantry by the Church. Kościuszko became interested in public matters by the political revival which took place during the Four Years' Diet (1788–92). He drafted

a project concerning the organisation of militia which was to include the gentry, the burghers and peasants. Though the project was not carried into effect, Kościuszko entered active service following a resolution which increased the size of the standing army. From 1789, in the rank of Major General, he organised and instructed the military. He took part in skirmishes in the Ukraine and Volhynia during the Russo-Polish War of 1792, in defence of the Constitution of 3 May, and he independently and successfully commanded at the battle of Dubienka on 18 July 1792.

Although holding a decoration and promoted to a higher rank, he resolved to leave the army towards the end of the fighting when the king and the troops joined the pro-Russian Confederation of Targowica. Many patriotic officers and politicians went into voluntary exile and Kościuszko followed in their footsteps, leaving Poland at the beginning of October 1792. As a result of holding consultations with the political leaders of the emigration, I. Potocki and H. Kollątaj (q.v.), Kościuszko left for Paris in January 1793. In political terms Kościuszko's mission demonstrated that the Polish exiles had become reoriented to France. The aim until then had been to establish a modus vivendi with Catherine II. In social terms the mission to France meant explicit radicalisation as compared with the programme of the Four Years' Diet. Kościuszko failed, however, to obtain any definite promises of support either from the Girondins or from the Jacobins, and in August 1793 he returned to Leipzig. Soon, after holding negotiations with the representatives of the home conspiracy, he agreed to be the commander-in-chief of the prospective uprising. However, he delayed the outbreak of the insurrection because of insufficient preparations. Eventually, the decision to rise was made under the pressure of a threatened reduction in the strength of the army by the government on 15 March 1794.

Initial clashes took place in Mazovia under the command of Brigadier-General

A. Madalinski. Soon afterwards, on 23 March, Kościuszko arrived in Cracow taking advantage of the fact that Russian troops had left the town. Here, on the next day, he took the famous oath in the Market Square. Absence of the emigrant politicians was used by Kościuszko to strengthen his dictatorial power and introduce a significant change in the oath-taking ceremony: he took the oath before the gathered people – as the symbolic source of power – and not, as it had been planned, before the circle of conspirators in the king's castle on Wawel. On his arrival in Cracow he also sent orders to the troops, and announced a conscription of all males of the region of Cracow aged eighteen to forty years (after the American model). Despite that, the insurgents' forces were weak and this was the reason why the war was to be confined solely to Russia. Kościuszko marched off bound for Warsaw and on 4 April 1794 he fought a victorious battle at Racławice; the battle's result was determined by an attack of a column of peasant scythe-bearers, a deviation from the rules of linear tactics. Kept in check by the Russians, Kościuszko picked a camp near Połaniec and from there promulgated the essential reforms of the uprising: concerning the peasant question and organisation of the supreme authorities. These documents were drafted by H. Kołłątaj and I. Potocki, and signed by Kościuszko.

Kościuszko's dictatorial duties intensified when communication was established with some regions of the country as well as Warsaw, which on 17 and 18 April 1794 was cleared of the Russian troops by the insurgents. He was prepared to make temporary compromises in order to secure the mobilisation of forces needed in the war. He made certain that the king, though debarred from power, was informed of important decisions made by the leaders of the insurrection. Kościuszko appointed a new general to the post of commander-in-chief in Lithuania in order to outweigh the undue radicalism of J. Jasinski (q.v.) which was complained of by other commanders of the uprising. On 28 June Kościuszko sent his troops to Warsaw to put down rioting there, and to secure order in the rear of his army before the enemy's attack took place. He took personal command at the battle of Szczekociny where he faced the overwhelming forces of Russia and Prussia on 6 June 1794. Then he fortified Warsaw and prepared the army and the city for the siege. On 25 August at a critical point of the siege, Kościuszko decided to begin the insurrection in Greater Poland, which was under Prussian administration. As a result, the Prussian troops withdrew and the siege of the city was raised on 6 September. The successful defence of Warsaw was Kościuszko's greatest victory, a triumph of military skill. At the same time his willingness to compromise with the Jacobin left in order to stir the masses to their utmost effort revealed his political talents.

During September Kościuszko reorganised the army in the Kingdom of Poland as well as in Lithuania. From mid-September he was attempting to prevent the union of two forces: the Russian troops which had been fighting the insurgents, and the corps under Suvorov (the future conqueror and perpetrator of the slaughter of Praga, the Warsaw suburb) which was approaching from the Ukraine. The outcome was the battle lost by the Polish at Maciejowice. Seriously wounded, Kościuszko was taken prisoner. Prussian propaganda falsely attributed to him the exclamation: 'Finis Poloniae'.

From 13 October to 10 December Kościuszko was taken from Kiev to St Petersburg where he was confined in the Petropavlosk fortress. Two days after his arrival he underwent a cross examination concerning the recent events, but unlike some of his fellow prisoners, he betrayed nobody. It was only when Catherine II died on 17 November 1796, that Kościuszko's predicament changed. Paul I, her successor, decided to set free the Poles under the condition that their commander-in-chief would take an oath of allegiance to the emperor. Kościuszko did so and was given twelve thousand roubles by the tsar and granted a thousand peasants. Soon afterwards he travelled via Finland and

Sweden for London, and on 17 July 1797 set sail from Bristol to America. Although he was greeted here with enthusiasm by the crowds, the Federalists, then in power, received him with distrust being reluctant to endorse the republican traditions of freedom which he represented. While in America, he availed himself of the opportunity to obtain his army arrears' payments and renew some old acquaintances and establish some new friendships – for example, with Jefferson. In a will composed in America he bequeathed some funds to the cause of the freedom and education of the negroes.

In mid-July 1798 Kościuszko arrived back in Paris. In August he sent back to Paul I the gift of twelve thousand roubles with a letter renouncing his oath of allegiance. He declined to accept command of the Polish Legions which had been organised alongside the French army in Italy in 1797 arguing that he would take their lead only when they began to march off to Poland. He did not want to become dependent on foreign governments. Nevertheless, since the Poles considered him their leader, he represented their interests to the French government. At first he remained under the influence of the moderate faction of the Polish exiles – the proponents of the Constitution of 3 May. Later, under the influence of Alojzy Orchowski (q.v.), who arrived from Warsaw as an emissary of the Society of Polish Republicans, he joined that faction and from then on he proclaimed himself in favour of the republican form of government. He was the inspirer of a pamphlet by J. Pawlikowski *Whether the Poles can win their independence?* (1800) which gave reasons for carrying out an uprising without any foreign help, and argued the necessity of freeing the peasants and creating a strong national government. Though criticised, the tract went through many editions (also in German) and played an important part in the Polish uprisings of the nineteenth century.

Kościuszko's relations with Napoleon were not fortunate. Bonaparte tried to gain the general's support when he visited Kościuszko after his return from Egypt. Despite this Kościuszko distrusted him; and after the 18 Brumaire regarded him as the 'grave-digger of the Republic'. In the face of the First Consul's successes, Kościuszko withdrew to a country seat near Fontainebleau. Napoleon tried to reach an agreement with him again after the battle of Jena when he was facing war with Russia. However Kościuszko demanded in February 1807 that the emperor make good a public promise to rebuild the Polish government modelled on the English system and to restore the Polish state with its former frontiers. Once again, then, Kościuszko was apt to sacrifice his republican views for temporary gains, but Napoleon declined these demands and called him a fool. Kościuszko did not, therefore, influence the creation of the first modern Polish state – the Duchy of Warsaw. After the fall of Napoleon in 1814 he appeared in Tsar Alexander I's lodgings during the Congress of Vienna, after the decision to establish the Kingdom of Poland had been made. The tsar wanted Kościuszko back in Poland because his return would symbolise the final solution of the Polish question. Kościuszko imposed, however, certain conditions which referred to social and political reforms, and to the reconstitution of Poland to her pre-partition historical boundaries. These demands were rejected, and Kościuszko left for Switzerland. Nevertheless, in 1816 he sent a sum of one thousand francs for the raising of the triumphal arch for Alexander I in Warsaw. The following year he freed from serfdom and enfranchised peasants from his ancestral village and wrote out his last will. He died in Solura on 15 October 1817.

Of poor health, impatient and suspicious, Kościuszko was nevertheless capable of great physical efforts. He suffered from depression, which occasionally led him to contemplate suicide. His character was shaped by the heroic readings in the Piarist school and by the philosophy of the Enlightenment. He came across the practical realisation of the idea of freedom and democracy in America. He gradually matured to his political role of 1794 by reconciling himself to ideological compromises in order to achieve better results from his activities. Personally brave, bold in operations, he believed in the tactics of fortifications and artillery which made ill-trained and ill-equipped soldiers useful at war. He was an innovator in using revolutionary means of fighting which were simultaneously introduced by commanders of the armies of revolutionary France.

Kościuszko became one of the best known Poles in the world, whose name was given to mountain peaks, towns, islands, institutions and military units. In Poland he was acknowledged during the following centuries as a patron of democrats of various shades. His reputation also became subject to interpretations by researchers from different schools of thought who brought out different aspects of his radicalism.

Further details of Kościuszko's life can be found in the following secondary works: *The Cambridge History of Poland*, Vol. II (Cambridge, 1941; repr. 1951); O. Halecki, *A History of Poland* (London, 1978; repr. 1983); N. Davies, *God's Playground. A History of Poland* Vols. I–II (Oxford, 1981, 1982, 1983); N. Davies, *Heart of Europe. A Short History of Poland* (Oxford, 1984); M. Haiman, *Kościuszko. Leader and Exile* (New York, 1946; repr. 1977); M. Haiman, *Kościuszko in the American Revolution* (New York, 1943); H. de Monfort, *Le drame de Pologne. Kościuszko 1764–1817* (Paris, 1945); B. Leśnodorski, *Les Jacobins polonais* (Paris, 1965); T. Korzon, *Kościuszko. Biografia z dokumentów wysnuta* (Kościuszko. A Biography Deduced from Documents) (2nd edition, Krakow, 1906); A. Skałkowski, *Kościuszko w świetle nowszych badań* (Kościuszko in the Light of Recent Research) (Poznan, 1924); J. Pachoński, *Kościuszko w niewoli carskiej 1794–1796* (Kościuszko in the Tsarist Captivity) (Krakow, 1947); J. Pachoński, *Kościuszko w Krakowie* (Kościuszko in Cracow) (Krakow, 1952); J. Pachoński, *Legiony Polskie 1794–1807* (The Polish Legions 1794–1807), vols. I–IV (Warszawa,

1969–1979); J. Pachoński, *Kościuszko na Ziemi Krakowsiej* (Kościuszko in the Region of Cracow) (Krakow, 1984); J. Kowecki, *Uniwersal połaniecki i sprawa jego realizacji* (The Manifesto of Polaniec and a Problem of its Fulfilment) (Warszawa, 1957); M. Kukiel, *Od Wiednia do Maciejowic* (From Vienna to Maciejowice) (London, 1965); R.F. Arnold, *Tadeusz Kościuszko in der deutschen Literatur* (Berlin, 1898).

LUKASZ KĄDZIELA

KRECHETOV, Fedor Vasilevich (?–?)
Russian enlightener, writer and publicist, well-known to Soviet historiography for his dissident ideas

Only the sketchiest biographical data have survived: he was born in the early 1740s and disappeared from the historical record after his amnesty in 1801, though his precise dates are unknown. He was most probably not of noble birth and nothing is known about his education, save that he became among the best read men of his day. His career was unspectacular: he occupied a series of minor clerical posts in military and civil service (working for two years under A.I. Radishchev's (q.v.) command) and attained the modest rank of lieutenant, on the tenth grade of the Table of Ranks.

An irascible, impetuous and volatile individual, he espoused with greater passion and vigour than was good for him a surprising number of forward-looking causes: the abolition of autocracy (to be replaced by a system of constitutional monarchy); thoroughgoing legal reform (considerably influenced by his reading of the English jurist Blackstone in S. Desnitskii's translation); freedom of speech (he apparently behaved as though this already existed); equal rights for all classes and, most unusually, for both sexes; radical expansion of education not only in Russia but throughout the world (he recognised the dangers inherent in granting political and social liberty to uneducated masses and regarded education as the indispensable prerequisite for such free-doms); and an end to war (the army was to be disbanded in the new order).

In 1785 he founded a secret society ('The National Society freely established for Good Works') to promote enlightenment in Russia, chiefly by founding schools financed by its members, who were some forty in number. The following year he initiated publication of a journal devoted to the same cause, quirkily entitled *Not Everything and Not Nothing*. It was sup-pressed following the first issue. He submit-ted detailed proposals for educational and legal reform to Catherine, convinced that she had no intention of implementing the reforms outlined in her *Nakaz*, but to no effect. Among his most original suggestions was for the establishment of a travellers' society which would pool information on Russia's topography and natural resources, in fact amounting to the first scientific survey of the Russian Empire. But this idea, too, met with official indifference. In 1789 after numerous difficulties with the censor, he eccentrically petitioned the Petersburg nobility to allow his society, subject to the empress's approval, to become the sole agency of censorship.

In 1793 Krechetov was arrested following denunciation by a government spy for slandering Catherine and her reforms, the senate and the synod, and incitement among troops and serfs to revolt. After investigation, during which he made no attempt to deny his radical views, he was sentenced to indefinite incarceration in the Peter-Paul Fortress. Closer examination of his papers revealed him to be an even greater danger to the state than had first been supposed and so he was moved to the maximum security of the Schlusselburg Fortress (to share the fate of his more illustrious contemporary, Radishchev) where he suffered a harsher régime and total isolation until he was amnestied in 1801 on the accession of Alexander I.

His personal papers amounted to over fifty different essays and articles, written in a highly idosyncratic, opaque style which, it is thought, must have posed their readers considerable difficulties. These,

and his all too ready, fiery eloquence, revealed him to be unusually radical for his day, although it is hard to detect any coherent, consistent strain running through his political and social views. He was strongly influenced by religious belief and his writings are punctuated with frequent references to the scriptures and by strident calls for the establishment of a universal and egalitarian brotherhood in Christ, to be brought about by revolutionary force if need be.

Further details of Krechetov's life can be found in the following sources: L.B. Svetlov, 'F.V. Krechetov', *Modern Encyc-lopedia of Russian and Soviet History*, vol. 18 (Gulf Breeze, 1980), pp. 57–58; P.N. Berkov, *Istoriia russkoi zhurnalistiki. XVIII v.* (Moscow, Leningrad, 1952); N. Chulkov, 'F.V. Krechetov, zabytyi radi-kal'nyi publitsist XVIII veka', *Literaturnoe nasledstvo* (Moscow, 1933), vols. 9–10; G.P. Makogonenko, *Radishchev i ego vre-mya* (Moscow, 1956); Isabel de Madariaga, *Russia in the Age of Catherine the Great* (London, 1981).

P.J. O'MEARA

LACOMBE, Claire (1765–?)
French revolutionary women's leader

Claire Lacombe was born in 1765 at Pamiers, close to France's Spanish border, the daughter of Bertrand Lacombe and Jeanne Marie Gauché. Their occupations are not known. By the outbreak of the French Revolution she had become, at twenty-four, a popular and successful actress in the south of France. Her open revolutionary sentiments are said to have led to difficulties in her profession, and in March 1792 Lacombe moved to Paris and became involved in Jacobin politics, taking part in the campaign that led to the uprising of 10 August. In July she delivered a patriotic address before the Legislative Assembly in which she asked to be allowed to enrol to fight in person against the invading counter-revolutionary armies. On 10 August itself Lacombe joined a detach-ment of *Fédérés* in the attack on the Tuileries, and was subsequently awarded a civic crown by the *Fédérés*. She appears to have kept in touch with the military volunteer organisation, which provided an important radical pressure group in Paris in 1793, and defended its interests. At the time of Dumouriez' treachery in April 1793 she reminded the Jacobin Club of the importance of keeping 'patriots' under arms in Paris, while sending 'aristocrats' to serve at the war front; the same address advocated holding the families of aristocrats as hostages.

The formation of the Society of Revolutionary Republican Women during May is sometimes attributed to Lacombe, but there is no evidence for this, and she did not begin to play a leading role in the society until mid-August. Nor does Lacombe figure as a participant in the uprising of 31 May – 2 June, although she allegedly sheltered the Enragé leader Théophile Leclerc (q.v.) immediately prior to the revolt, and was accused of being his mistress.

From about 18 August to the closing down of the Society of Revolutionary Republican Women on 30 October, Claire Lacombe was the society's leader most in evidence. She thus bore the prime responsibility for the final phase of the society's activity: the campaign for the replacement of the Convention and the immediate introduction of the Constitution of 1793, the campaign for the enforcement of the laws against speculation and hoarding, and the campaign for the generalisation of the wearing of the revolutionary cockade. She also bore the brunt of governmental and Jacobin hostility toward the society, and was personally attacked by a rioting crowd mobilised against the members on 28 October.

After the closing of the women's society on 30 October Lacombe appears to have withdrawn from active politics, and she had arranged to return to the stage in the spring of 1794 when she was arrested in the general purge of Hébertist sympathisers. Imprisoned for more than a year in various Paris prisons, Lacombe was released in August 1795. She was acting at Nantes in 1796, and in Paris, at the Odéon in 1797–8,

where her salary was 5,000 *livres* in specie. After 1798 Lacombe found jobs hard to get, and she is last heard of living in poverty in 1799.

Like Pauline Léon (q.v.), Claire Lacombe did not advance any coherent feminist programme. Her significance lies rather in her role as a symbol of martial patriotic womanhood in the service of the revolutionary cause, and in her leadership of the most important women's political organisation during the revolution. As such she acted as a focus for the hostility of orthodox Jacobins and others who sought to exclude women from public affairs, and for the ambiguous attention of later historians.

Details of Lacombe's life and political activities are available in: R.B. Rose, *The Enragés: Socialists of the French Revolution?* (Sydney, 1968); Marie Cerati, *Le Club des Citoyennes Républicaines Révolutionnaires* (Paris, 1966); and Darline Gay Levy, Harriet Branson Applewhite and Mary Durham Johnson (eds.), *Women in Revolutionary Paris* (Urbana, 1979).

R.B. ROSE

LA HARPE, Frédéric César de (1754–1838)
Swiss radical and leader of the Helvetic Republic

Born at Rolle on 6 April 1754 into an old Vaudois family, La Harpe was to play as active a part as anyone in the politics of Switzerland throughout his life as well as playing only slightly less prominent a part in the wider politics of revolutionary Europe. The most important figure, along with Ochs (q.v.), in the Helvetic revolution of 1798, he is generally regarded as the 'founder' of Swiss liberalism. He was not the only member of his family to play an active part in the turbulent events of the times: his cousin, Amadée de La Harpe, having taken part in the abortive uprising of 1791 in Vaud, fled under sentence of death to France where he joined the army and had a distinguished military career under the Republic, rising to the rank of General before being killed in action at

Codogno in 1796.

Although the family of La Harpe was an old one of noble and armigerous status, its members did not enjoy the privileges and perquisites commonly associated with that social position in Ancien Régime Europe. This was because the Vaud was a subject territory, under the rule of Berne, and its inhabitants therefore lacked all political and civil rights, regardless of social rank.

Frédéric César de La Harpe was trained as a lawyer, becoming an advocate in 1778. He then acquired employment in Italy as secretary to Prince Lanskoi who was sufficiently impressed with his abilities to recommend him to the tsarina Catherine the Great. In 1784 the empress entrusted La Harpe with the education of her grandson, the future Tsar Alexander I so beginning a lifelong and intimate friendship. La Harpe sought to imbue his charge with the philosophy and ideas of the Enlightenment, of which he was an ardent partisan, and hoped to turn him into a model 'enlightened despot', a project in which he can be said to have enjoyed only the most limited success. When revolution broke out in France he soon became known as a strong supporter of the new régime and in 1795 he went to live in Paris where he became active in the Helvetic Society set up in 1790 by other Swiss émigrés such as Grenus (q.v.) and Dumont. At this time he published a series of polemical works, mainly directed at the Bernese oligarchy, culminating in 1797 in his major work, the *Essai sur la constitution du pays de Vaud.* In this work he presented a general political argument on the nature of sovereignty and more particular theses regarding the legal and historical position of the Vaud with respect to its Bernese overlords. This led La Harpe into a more active and controversial phase of his career. On 9 September 1797 he submitted a paper to the Directory, based upon the thesis of his *Essai,* arguing that the Treaty of 1564 made between France and Berne entitled France to intervene to protect the liberties of Vaud which she had guaranteed. He then made contact with Ochs, in Paris as ambassador for his native Basle, and on 31 October 1797 La Harpe wrote to Ruebell urging that France should intervene in the affairs of Switzerland and again arguing that the actions of the Swiss, and particularly the Bernese, authorities amounted to a breach of neutrality. Following the secret meeting of December 8 between Ochs and Reubell, La Harpe, along with Ochs and some thirty other signatories, presented a formal petition to the Directory asking them to intervene militarily in the affairs of Switzerland on the putative grounds of the violation of the treaty of 1564. This document was adopted by the Directory as the formal basis for the invasion of Switzerland by Brune in the spring of the following year which led to the creation of the Helvetic Republic on 12 April 1798. Initially Brune planned to create three separate republics out of the territory of the Confederation but La Harpe and most of the other émigrés strongly opposed this and he was able to use his influence with Reubell to ensure the adoption of Ochs's unitary constitution. This was modelled very closely on the then French constitution, with a unitary state divided into twenty-three administrative cantons and an executive Directory of five elected by the Great Council as in the French model.

Following the French invasion Swiss politics were in a state of great confusion with the invaders and the new régime warmly welcomed in some areas such as Vaud, bitterly resisted in others such as the forest cantons and the Valais. The Directory in Paris felt the need to have a completely loyal government in Switzerland and so, on 16 June 1798, the Army Commissioner, Rapinat, forced the Swiss Directory to accept Ochs and Dolders as new members. On June 29 the Great Council replaced Dolders by La Harpe who, it was hoped, would be acceptable to the French yet less committed to their interests than either Ochs or Dolders. From that time La Harpe was the dominant member of the Directory and, while struggling with horrendous financial and other problems brought about by the war and the presence of French troops, put through in very short order a wide range of reforms including the abolition of all feudal remnants, the abolition of tithes, and the introduction of true religious toleration as well as a sweeping reform of the law. However the problem of relations with France became steadily more acute. The treaty of alliance of 19 August 1798 had effectively made the Helvetic Republic a satellite and Rapinat in particular saw Switzerland mainly as a milch-cow which could be used to replenish the coffers of France. La Harpe became increasingly estranged from Ochs whom he saw as excessively devoted to the interests of France and on 25 June 1799 he succeeded in having Ochs removed from the Directory. However his own success was short lived for on 7 January 1800 he was himself replaced and the Swiss Directory was then dissolved.

La Harpe then retired to Lausanne but was arrested on suspicion of plotting against Bonaparte and taken to Berne. However, he managed to escape and went to France where he lived in retirement at Plessis-Picquet apart from a brief visit to Tsar Alexander in 1801. In 1814 he was stirred into activity by the threat of the re-annexation to Berne of his beloved Vaud and was able to put his friendship with the tsar to good effect, securing Russian support for the continued independence of the Vaud. At the Congress of Vienna he was one of the Swiss representatives and is often credited with using his influence with the tsar to ensure both the survival of Switzerland as an independent state and the preservation of some of the reforms of the revolutionary period. Although he certainly sought to use his influence in this direction, as his correspondence shows, he would probably not have been successful had such a policy not also suited the interests of Russia. In 1816 he became a member of the Vaudois Grand Council and, along with Usteri (q.v.) and Zschokke (q.v.), he became a leading figure in the liberal opposition to the restoration régime. In 1830 he and the others were successful in effecting a major revision of the constitution: by this time he was

generally recognised as the nearest approach to a national liberal leader. He died on 30 March 1838 at Lausanne.

The life and career of La Harpe display several pronounced ambiguities. A mild-tempered and kindly man, he was not averse to the use of ruthless action and force when the occasion required. Although a convinced democrat he also looked throughout the earlier part of his career to the idea of a transformation of the political order by a beneficient autocrat or outside force. This was apparent both in his relationship with Alexander I and in his willingness to use outside intervention to reform the government of Switzerland. There were limits to this aspect of his politics however; he refused to have anything to do with Napoleon whom he despised as the worst sort of despot. Perhaps the most pronounced ambiguity can be seen in his attitude towards the constitutional arrangements of Switzerland itself. Although not as thoroughgoing a centralist as Ochs, he supported the establishment of the 'one and indivisible' republic in 1798. Yet he remained throughout his life a Vaudois patriot and the fate and government of the Vaud was always his main concern. Perhaps all of this amounts to no more than to say that he was a politician, forced to adjust to circumstances and events. However, the tensions and ambiguities of La Harpe's career and thought perhaps also reveal the various conflicts inherent in the politics of revolutionary liberalism in late eighteenth century Europe, particularly those between individualism and the idea of the general will, between the support for local liberties and the idea of the nation, and most acutely between the notion of individual rights and the need to use force to achieve reform or in other words the frequent conflict between ends and means.

The best way to an appreciation of La Harpe's ideas and his engaging personality is through his massive correspondence. This is now in course of publication in two separate series. The first is the already printed *Correspondance de Frédéric César de La Harpe et le Tsar Alexandre I* (3 vols., Neuchâtel, 1978–80). Secondly there is the *Correspondance de Frédéric César de La Harpe sous la République Helvétique*. Volume I, *La révolutionnaire* (Neuchâtel, 1982) covers the period between 16 May 1796 and 4 March 1798. Volume II, *Le Chargé d'affaires à Paris* (Neuchâtel, 1984) covers March to July 1798. Volumes III and IV, *Le directeur helvétique* and *L'exile* will cover the years 1798 to 1800 and 1800 to 1803 respectively once they appear. Accounts of La Harpe's career can be found in most works on the general history of Europe for this period. Particularly useful are: R.R. Palmer, *The age of the democratic revolution* (2 vols., New Jersey, 1959–64); J. Godechot *La grande nation* (2 vols., Paris, 1956). For a work arguing that La Harpe and the other émigrés had only the most marginal influence on French policy, see J. Feldman, *Propaganda und diplomatie* (Zurich, 1957). For a contrary view see E. Chapuisat, *La Suisse et la révolution française* (Geneva, 1945) and A. Rufer, 'La Republique Helvétique', in *Dictionnaire historique et biographique de la Suisse* (Neuchâtel, 1928). La Harpe's *Mémoires* were printed in Jakob Vogel (ed.), *Schweizergeschichtliche Studien* (Berne, 1864).

S. DAVIES

L'ANGE, François Joseph
(c. 1743–1793)
French democratic socialist

The birthplace of L'Ange is uncertain but it was probably in Alsace, and the Munster where he was brought up was probably the small town in the present-day department of Haut-Rhin, not the Westphalian city. His parentage is unknown. He went to Paris at fifteen before settling in Lyon at an unknown date. He described himself sometimes as an *artiste*, sometimes as a *peintre*, and probably was a cloth designer in the silk-weaving industry, a job much more prestigious and better paid than other manual work. His first publications were inspired by the Montgolfiers' balloon ascents at les Brotteaux near Lyon. One

of his pamphlets discussed methods of aerial navigation, another envisaged an air force of balloon-borne *pyronautes*. During the French Revolution L'Ange combined a minor political career with publishing plans for a more rational and democratic hierarchy of powers (he opposed the property qualification) and for eliminating social problems by controlling the cost and reorganising the distribution of basic necessities. He was elected a Municipal Officer in December 1791 and *juge de paix* of the wealthy canton of la Fédération in December 1792, at the same time as the ultra-Jacobins grouped around Joseph Chalier (q.v.) took control of the Municipality. He collaborated with the anti-Jacobins who seized control of Lyon during the 'federalist' rebellion, 29 May – 9 October 1793, was condemned to death by the *Commission de Justice populaire* on 14 November 1793 and guillotined the next day.

L'Ange's socialist projects were all based on controlling the distribution of grain by a federation of thirty thousand *centuries*, groups of one hundred families who were to share and maintain common granaries (*greniers d'abondance*) containing sufficient wheat to meet their needs for at least a year. There were co-operative elements in the plan – the *centuries* were responsible for reporting on the *pourvoyeur national* who managed their purchasing and for maintaining not only the granary but a police force, a school, a prison, a hospital and a chair of moral philosophy. But the central role was played by the state. In the name of the French people shares worth sixty thousand *livres* were to be issued for each *centurie* to start the scheme off with 'funds to provision one hundred families with grain, flour and vegetables for two years' (*Remède à tout ou Constitution invulnérable de félicité publique* (Lyon, 1793), Chapter VII, Article 1). The cost of transporting food was paid out of public funds and the prices of flour and grain (and also, in the *Remède à tout*, L'Ange's last version, meat) were fixed permanently at a just level which L'Ange specified for the main cereal products on the basis of a crude labour theory of value. A role was envisaged for private capital but it was not to be employed in a capitalistic manner. In L'Ange's view the specified prices guaranteed ample returns to attract investors but speculative gains were of course eliminated for both the merchants involved in the scheme and the farmers. (For the latter, the only advantages were guaranteed prices and a scheme of insurance against natural disasters. L'Ange's was very much a townsman's utopia.) In addition there was to be a cadastral survey to determine the value of land not only for taxation purposes but in case of sale, with criminal sanctions provided to deter vendors from seeking a higher price. Similarly, rents were to be fixed to provide 4% annual return on the assessed value of land and buildings. There were to be minimum wages and elaborate charitable mechanisms. All this was to be established by the use of the revolutionary assemblies' constituent powers and the triumph of the *centuries* was to be achieved not by force but by their inherent economic rationality.

The radicalism of L'Ange's approach to private property consisted not in any systematic rejection of it but in his willingness to subordinate it to the requirements of equality and social justice. Unlike the revolutionary constitutions of 1791 and 1793 his draft constitutions omitted property from the list of the rights of man and his increasingly elaborate schemes encroached substantially on the freedom to dispose of property in land and its products. L'Ange's plan amounted to a programme for the socialisation of consumption. While it had something in common with the sans-culotte remedies of price maxima and coercion it went beyond them not only in its elaboration but in its extensive use of the powers of the democratic state to establish social justice, its use of a labour theory of value to justify the price-fixing procedure and the cooperative character of its primary organisational units, the *centuries*. L'Ange's lack of interest in the organisation of production reflects his pre-industrial outlook. Never-

theless he belongs in the tradition of democratic state socialism, for which his proposal to the President of the National Assembly dated November 1789 is one of the earliest schemes.

It was long believed (notably by Jean Jaurès) that L'Ange was a proto-Fourierist and even that Fourier (who spent a lot of time in Lyon) had been influenced by his work. But this was based on a nineteenth century misreading of the 'lost' *Remède à tout* which is in fact only a more elaborate version of the system first sketched in 1789 and outlined in several other pamphlets. Fernand Rude effectively discredits this myth in his excellent summary of the *Remède à tout*, 'Du nouveau sur le socialisme de L'Ange. La découverte du "Remède à tout"', *Cahiers d'Histoire*, 15 (1970), pp. 223–242.

There is an edition of L'Ange's work edited by Paul Leutrat, *Oeuvres* (Paris, 1968). The proposal of November 1789 is reproduced in A. Iaonnissian, 'La première ébauche du Plan de Lange', *Annales historiques de la Révolution française*, 38 (1966), pp. 15–18.

BILL EDMONDS

LA REVELLIÈRE-LÉPEAUX, Louis Marie (1753–1824)
Member of the executive Directory of the first French Republic

Revellière-Lépeaux was born into a bourgeois family of Anjou, where his father was mayor of Montaigu. He was educated at the Oratorian college of Angers, studied law, and left for Paris in 1776 to continue his legal studies. He was never committed, however, to a legal career, and when he married, he returned to the west to live at Sablons. His wife's inheritance relieved him of the necessity of finding gainful employment. Revellière learned Italian, developed a lifelong passion for botany, and suffered a physical disability: he was hunchbacked.

He was involved in the democratic movement from the outset of the revolution. In 1789 he published two pamphlets, *Lettre à un seigneur d'Anjou*, and the *Adresse à la noblesse et clergé*, which rebutted Montesquieu's defence of aristocratic forms of government. Revellière was a member of the pro-revolutionary bourgeoisie, in a part of France that was fiercely clerical and conservative. His political ideas, as well as his personal tastes, owed much to the influence of J.J. Rousseau. He contributed to the writing of model *cahiers de doléances* distributed in Anjou, favouring regular meetings of the Estates-General, voting by head and by acclamation, a tax on real estate, a free press, and the abolition of seigneurial hunting rights. The demand for the marriage of Catholic clergy in these *cahiers* perhaps foreshadowed Revellière's later anticlericalism. He was elected deputy to the Estates-General for the Third Estate of Anjou.

He signed the Tennis Court Oath and was a member of the democratic Club Breton. He joined the Committee of Thirty, appointed to draft a constitution. He spoke against the power of royal veto (1789), and, in a Rousseauist vein, argued against the re-election of deputies after the dispersal of the Constituent Assembly. He supported the election of judges, and the Civil Constitution of the Clergy. During the period of the Legislative Assembly (1791), Revellière returned to the west as an administrator of the department of Maine-et-Loire, where he perhaps came to realise the strength of the clerical opposition to the revolution.

In July 1791 Revellière had left the Jacobin Club, regarding it as a dangerous faction, but as a member of the National Convention his position was ambiguous. On the one hand, he voted against a referendum on the trial of the king, and approved the death sentence for Louis XVI, without reprieve. On the other hand, he was closer to the Girondin viewpoint in attacking the Paris Commune, and the danger of 'Cromwellism', in other words, of dictatorship. Although he also favoured the trial of Marat (q.v.), he was not purged with the Girondin deputies in June 1793. Nevertheless, the Committee of General Security ordered Revellière's arrest in August 1793, and he went into hiding during the revolutionary terror.

There were personal as well as political reasons why Revellière was never to be reconciled to the government of the Year II: his brother was guillotined during the terror, his family house was looted in the course of the Vendéan war, his property was burned and razed to the ground. In the Year III, however, Revellière was reinstated as a deputy of the Convention, whose president he became, working again on a new constitution. He became member of the new Conseil des Anciens, and he topped the poll in the elections for the new five-man executive Directory. Revellière was an honest and upright politician, tedious at times, but always sincere, and he had made few enemies. The most important and most constructive period of his political career was about to begin.

Within the Directory, Revellière disapproved of the corrupt Barras, and generally supported Reubell against Carnot (q.v.) and Barthélémy. His main responsibility was in educational and artistic affairs. He was to give the funeral oration for General Hoche, celebrating the pacification of his native west. Together with his friend Ducis, the French translator of Shakespeare, he designed the new republican marriage ceremonies. He inaugurated the *Institut*, and took chief responsibility for establishing the new Odéon as a national theatre and drama school. He was instrumental in providing government assistance for intellectuals such as Raynal (q.v.), Bernardin de St Pierre and Benjamin Constant, and he supervised the transfer of looted art treasures from Italy to Paris.

Revellière was a firm republican, and supported the 'purge' of the legislature which occurred in Fructidor Year V. He was the Directory's president at the time of this 'coup'. This republican victory was celebrated by a speech of Revellière made 'in blissful contemplation of his state of oneness with the ruler of the universe who had snatched France from the edge of the precipice'. This kind of Rousseauist rhetoric annoyed colleagues like Barthélémy, a victim of Fructidor, who described Revellière's speeches as 'boring, metaphysical platitudes'.

In Prairial Year VII, Revellière was forced to resign from the Directory, as the government came under heavy fire in the legislature for France's military defeats. As a firm republican and contributor to the Constitution of the Year III, Revellière could not be expected to be sympathetic towards ideas of constitutional revision canvassed by Sieyès (q.v.). He retired to his country house at Andilly, and his circle of friends at the Institut. He did not approve of either the Consulate or the Empire, and lost his chair at the Institut accordingly, in 1804. He wrote his memoirs, and on his death, was buried in the Père Lachaise cemetery in 1824.

Revellière's influence on the Directory's foreign policy was aimed at defending republicanism in Europe. He opposed the imperialist or centralist view, rejecting for example the annexation of Rousseau's Geneva, and favouring the development of satellite republics allied to France. He felt that Bonaparte had betrayed the Directory at the peace of Campoformio by not guaranteeing the existence of a Venetian Republic. Campoformio, however, had to be accepted, according to Revellière, because opinion in the legislature supported it, and because the Directory took Bonaparte's advice that the army was not fit to continue campaigning. Revellière also argued that the Directory did not deliberately send Bonaparte to Italy to be rid of him, and he emphasised that an army of 40,000 was not to be risked that lightly.

The distinguishing feature of Revellière's political life, however, was his anticlericalism and his apparent support for the short-lived cult of Theophilanthropy. Revellière's religious views were summarised in his *Refléxions sur le culte*, published and read to the Institut in 1797. Revellière wanted a simple form of worship, based on two main truths: the concept of a deity who rewarded good and punished evil, and the immortality of the soul. These principles were very similar to those of Theophilanthropy. In his memoirs, Revellière described Catholic confession as a kind of prostitution and self-humiliation. He criticised the hierarchy of the Catholic Church, its pomp, ostentation and exclusiveness. In addition, he had serious doubts about child baptism, declaring that an infant should not be brought to a sacrament, like a packet to be registered at the customs. He acknowledged Protestant influences on his ideas, and claimed that a Calvinist service had once reduced him to tears.

As far as Theophilanthropy was concerned, however, Revellière should be regarded as a sympathiser and a remote patron, rather than as an inspirer or founder of the cult. He never in fact attended a service, even if he gave the cult government support and permission to use Parisian churches like Notre Dame, and even if the English press dubbed him 'the French Mahomet'. Theophilanthropy had no elaborate rules, and no permanent priesthood; it was based on religious toleration, and the simple dogmas of the existence of God, and the immortality of the soul. In 1798 it held services in many Parisian churches, where the congregations heard readings from the Koran, Socrates, Seneca, Confucius and Pascal, in the eclectic spirit of Theophilanthropic toleration. They would sing patriotic hymns like the 'Chant du Départ', led by an officiator in a tricoloured tunic. Theophilanthropic societies were also formed in provincial cities like Dijon, Mâcon and Troyes, and the cult also had support in the Yonne, an area where the dechristianisation campaigns had earlier evoked a positive response.

The cult, however, was shortlived. It appealed briefly to the republican intelligentsia, but it was too abstract to draw a truly popular following. In 1799 it went into decline, and by 1801 Theophilanthropy was dead. The historian Mathiez argued that Revellière had withdrawn his support from Theophilanthropy, because the Directory was afraid of radical or Jacobin influences in the cult. Mathiez, however, could not fully substantiate this claim, suggesting merely that it was true because Revellière had not mentioned it in his memoirs (because he allegedly did not have the courage to do so). At any rate, Revellière could not protect Theophilanthropy from the encroachments of rival forms of republican worship, such as the *culte décadaire*.

Revellière was therefore a dedicated anticlerical, and a stubborn member of the republican intelligentsia, which briefly took power during the period of the Directory. In his ideas about democracy, and civic religion, he was a Rousseauist, as he also was in his love of botany. On his death, the Jardin des Plantes, where he had often strolled for relaxation after political work, went into mourning. True to the fashion for *sensibilité*, he named his son Ossian, after the popular (but fictitious) Celtic bard. Revellière's honesty and domestic virtues were not sufficient to make him a great statesman, and his attempts to institutionalise republican morality may now appear bizarre or ridiculous. As a radical, however, he represented the unswerving anticlericalism of the 'blue' bourgeoisie of the Vendée.

La Revellière-Lépeaux's own account of his role in the revolution can be read in his *Mémoires* (Paris, 1895). The standard biography in English is Georgia Robison, *Revellière-Lépeaux: Citizen Director 1735–1824* (Columbia, N.Y., 1938; repr., New York, 1972). For his involvement with Theophilanthropy, see Albert Mathiez, *La Théophilanthropie et le culte décadaire, 1796–1801* (Paris, 1904).

MARTYN LYONS

L'AURORA, Enrico Michele (?1764–?1803)
Italian Jacobin and patriot

Very little is known about L'Aurora's early years, and in 1803 he disappeared without leaving any trace. His public life, which can be reconstructed from existing records, covers the period from 1796 to 1803, when he was active on Italy's changing political scene.

He seems to have been born in Rome around 1764. Orphaned at an early age he was brought up by an uncle in Nice. Entering the family business, he travelled extensively in Europe, north Africa, Mexico, and may have been in France during the revolution. In 1796 he appeared in Italy with the general staff of the French army. His reports to the Directory in Paris reveal growing disenchantment with the policies and conduct of the French in Italy. Gradually he elaborated a political programme that he explicated in his reports. To ensure future stability he urged the dissolution of the Holy Roman Empire, which he blamed for the unhappy state of Europe, the exclusion of Austria from all of Italy, and the abolition of papal rule in the states under the control of the Church. Increasingly, he advocated the independence and unity of Italy, based on popular sovereignty. His ideas found little sympathy in France and French authorities expelled him from Lombardy.

At the beginning of 1798 he was in Rome. Openly critical of the French, he organised a secret society, the 'Emuli di Bruto'. As a result the French exiled him from Rome, but the next year found him attached to General Championnet's army with which he entered Naples. When the French abandoned the Neapolitan Republic, L'Aurora stayed on to participate in its defence. Imprisoned with the Jacobin leaders when they surrendered, he remained in a Bourbon gaol for twenty-three months. Finally released after the French victory at Marengo, he was assigned to the army of the second Cisalpine Republic.

Again he seemed to have been active in anti-French agitation, for at the beginning of May 1802 he was accused of participation in a masonic conspiracy against Napoleon. He was arrested and brought to trial. Lacking conclusive evidence on the extent of his role in the plot, the court sentenced him to life exile from the Italian Republic. Given the opportunity to choose his place of exile, L'Aurora chose the Republic of Lucca. Released from confinement on 13 May 1803, he was escorted to the borders of Lucca, where he arrived after two-and-a-half days of travelling. After this time no trace of him appears in any archive in Italy or France.

L'Aurora personified the disillusionment and frustration of those Italian patriots who had hoped to achieve independence and unity for at least part of Italy with French support. Inspired by Jacobin revolutionary ideals, they clung to them after the Directory had discarded them. As it became clear that France had no sympathy for Italian aspirations, they turned against the French and particularly against Napoleon who came to personify French arrogance and aggrandisement and plotted against the new masters of their country. Many, like L'Aurora, evolved an early nationalism which the men of the Risorgimento inherited and expanded to include all of Italy.

Two short accounts of L'Aurora's political career are available: Pietro Nurra, 'Emilio Michele L'Aurora e la politica francese verso l'Italia (1792–1803)', *Nuova rivista storica*, 31 (May–December 1947), pp. 294–312; and Delio Cantimori, 'Enrico Michele L'Aurora', in *Utopisti e riformatori italiani* (Florence, 1943), pp. 53–76.

EMILIANA P. NOETHER

LAVICOMTERIE, Louis Charles de (1732–1809)

Pamphleteer and French revolutionary terrorist, member of the National Convention and the Committee of General Security

Lavicomterie was born in Tovigny (Manche), where his father was a *procureur du roi*. Little is known of his early life, except his authorship of an *Eloge de Voltaire* in 1779. Lavicomterie is reputed to have always kept a letter from Frederick the Great, thanking him for sending a complimentary copy.

Lavicomterie was an energetic publicist. His *Les Crimes des Rois de France depuis Clovis jusqu'à Louis XVI*, published in Paris in 1791, attacked royal powers of arbitrary arrest and the bloodshed caused by French monarchs. Three new editions appeared in 1792, and the work was to be re-issued in 1833. In 1792 Lavicomterie repeated the formula from an anticlerical stance in *Les Crimes des Papes depuis St Pierre jusqu' à Pie VI*, which was to give him a reputation as a dechristianiser. His other works were a pamphlet of 1790, which contained an early advocacy of republicanism, and *Les Empereurs d'Allemagne depuis Lothaire Ter jusqu' à Léopold II* (1794).

The popularity of *Les Crimes des Papes*, and membership of the Jacobin Club were enough to secure Lavicomterie's election to the Convention as a deputy for Paris. He was an adamant enemy of Girondism, opposing the persecution of Marat (q.v.), and voting for the death of Louis XVI without reprieve. He was a member of the Committee of General Security from 16 June 1793, and president of the Jacobin Club in Ventôse Year II. On the police committee he was responsible for the Paris region, and for interrogations, but the committee's agent, Sénart, described him as a moderate. He never attended the joint meetings of the C.S.G. and C.S.P., apparently for fear of encountering Robespierre (q.v.).

He was absent from the Convention on the night of 9 Thermidor Year II, and was almost immediately removed from the Committee of General Security. On 9 Prairial Year III he was arrested, but went into hiding, until the amnesty of Brumaire Year IV. He lived miserably in Paris, until the Directory gave him a post in the *administration du timbre* with a mediocre salary of 1200 *livres* per annum. He died in obscurity, aged 77.

Lavicomterie's main claim to radicalism therefore rests upon his activity as a publicist of anti-monarchical, anticlerical and republican ideas.

There is little biographical information on Lavicomterie, but see Martyn Lyons, 'The 9 Thermidor: motives and effects', *European Studies Review*, 5 (1975), pp. 123–46.

MARTYN LYONS

LEBAS, Philippe François Joseph (1764–1794)

Regicide and French revolutionary terrorist, member of the National Convention and the Committee of General Security

Lebas was born at Frévent in the Pas-de-Calais, the department he later represented in the National Convention. The son of a *notaire*, he was educated in Paris, and became *avocat* to the Parlement in 1789.

In 1792 Lebas was elected to the National Convention. He voted for the death of the king, and on 14 September 1793 was elected a member of the Committee of General Security. On October 22, however, he was sent *en mission* with St Just (q.v.) to the army of the Rhine which they proceeded to purge of its incompetent officers and to restore discipline. This was followed in January 1794 by a similar mission to the army of the Nord, where Lebas ordered the arrest of all nobles. Because of these absences from Paris, he rarely attended committee meetings until the end of Ventôse Year II, but he was present for the arrest of the Dantonists, and was elected president of the Jacobin Club in Floréal Year II. On the 10 Floréal he was entrusted with a further mission in the Nord. On his return he was appointed one of the administrators of the new School of Mars, set up by the Committee of Public Safety to provide military training for boys of sixteen and seventeen.

On 9 Thermidor Year II the Committee of General Security arrested Lebas as a Robespierrist, and within twenty-four hours, he had committed suicide in the hôtel de ville, by shooting himself in the head.

Lebas's career was remarkable for the complete loyalty he showed towards St Just and Robespierre (q.v.). He married the daughter of Duplay, Robespierre's landlord, and freely chose to share the fate of the 'Incorruptible' on 9 Thermidor. Most of Lebas's contribution to the revolution was outside Paris, as the government's representative to the armies. In 1793 and 1794 he worked in the shadow of Robespierre and St Just, to whom he was devoted.

There is no biography of Lebas, but details of his life and political activities are mentioned in Martyn Lyons, 'The 9 Thermidor: motives and effects', *European Studies Review*, 5 (1975), pp. 123–46; R.R. Palmer, *Twelve who ruled: the year of the terror in the French Revolution* (Princeton, 1971); and S. Scott and B. Rothaus (eds), *Historical Dictionary of the French Revolution, 1789–1799* (2 vols., Westport, CT, 1985).

MARTYN LYONS

LEBOIS, René François (?–?)

French revolutionary Jacobin and journalist

Little is known of Lebois' early life, but he was probably born in Paris and, by 1789, was a printing worker, living in the rue de la Parcheminerie on the left bank of the Seine. During the summer of 1789 he was politically active in the District Assembly of Mathurins and later claimed to have taken part in the assault on the Bastille. He enrolled in the National Guard battalion in the Mathurins District, participated in the march on Versailles on 5–6 October, and wrote many polemical radical pamphlets. However, in September 1790, he was dismissed from the unit for publishing criticism of Lafayette's role in the Nancy massacre in a pamphlet, *Les Bassesses de l'Assemblée ou conduite exécrable du général Lafayette par un de ses soldats* and moved to the rue des Noyers, where he found work, first as director of the press of the radical daily newspaper, the *Journal universal*, and subsequently in other printing shops too. He was a member of the Cordeliers Club and on 15 December 1790, at a time when radical *sociétés fraternelles* were being formed in some parts of the city, successfully proposed that the club urge every section in Paris to set up 'assemblées gratuites d'instruction pour le peuple', in which both active and passive citizens could participate. Secretary of the Cordeliers in November 1790, he was its president in the following August during

the difficult weeks that followed the massacre of the Champ de Mars. He re-joined
the National Guard, this time in the *section
du Luxembourg*, and took part in the
assault on the Tuileries on 10 August 1792.

During the early months of the National
Convention he supported the Mountain
against the Gironde and published two
violently anti-Girondin pamphlets in the
spring of 1793, gaining a position on the
comité révolutionnaire of the Beaurepaire
section by early June. He lost this later in
the month when moderates in the section
launched a counter-offensive, but in September, when they were finally ousted, he
became a member of the section's *comité
civil* and secretary of its *assemblée générale*.
Not for long, however, for on 29 October
he was arrested, for reasons which remain
obscure, and he remained in the Lazare
prison for almost ten months, until his
release on 17 August 1794.

Shortly after his release on 29 Fructidor
Year II (15 September 1794) Lebois
launched a newspaper, the *Ami du Peuple*,
which was edited at first by the Montagnard
deputy, Chasles (q.v.). By now he was a
printer on his own account, for in July
1793 he had established a print shop, the
Imprimerie de l'Ami des Sans-Culottes.
However, the co-operation with Chasles
did not last long, for, after a quarrel
in the following Frimaire (mid-December
1795) Chasles left the paper and Lebois
continued it alone. The title was a deliberate evocation of Marat's (q.v.) *Ami du
Peuple* and Lebois used the paper to
denounce the conservative social and political policies of the Thermidorian reaction.
He defended the constitution of 1793,
denounced the misery caused by inflation
during the winter of 1794–5, and was
arrested on 17 Ventôse Year III (7 March
1795) as an accomplice of Babeuf (q.v.).
Detained first in Paris, then in the Baudets
prison in Arras, where he shared captivity
with Babeuf, he wrote manuscript copies of
his *Ami du Peuple* for circulation amongst
fellow prisoners. Released on 2 Brumaire
Year IV (24 October 1795), he resumed
publication of the *Ami du Peuple*, was
a founder member of the neo-Jacobin

Pantheon Club, and produced wall posters
and pamphlets condemning the harsh
effects of the Directory's economic policies
on the poor. For this he was arrested
briefly in Frimaire of Year IV on a
charge of advocating the redistribution
of property, or the *loi agraire*. He was
acquitted, but arrested again in the summer
of 1796 on a charge of threatening state
security and of advocating the implementation of the constitution of 1793. After
three months in prison, he was finally
acquitted on 9 Vendémiaire Year V (1
October 1796), but arrested briefly again
in the following Nivôse (23 December 1796
– 3 January 1797). The Ministry of the
Interior also attempted, unsuccessfully, to
implicate him in the Babeuf plot. This
accentuated his opposition to the Directory
and, during the winter of 1796–7, despite
his personal and political differences with
Babeuf, he gave a great deal of publicity
in the *Ami du Peuple* to the trial at
Vendôme, condemning the final verdict.
In Thermidor of Year V (July–August
1797) he briefly ceased publishing the *Ami
du Peuple*, producing a daily *Eclaireur du
Peuple* instead, but after the Fructidor coup
he resumed it briefly until 24 Vendémiaire
Year VI (15 October 1797). For the next
eighteen months his activity remains
obscure, but with the revival of Jacobinism
during the summer of 1799 he returned to
journalism, editing first *Le Défenseur du
peuple faisant suite à l'Ami du peuple* and
then *Le Père Duchesne*. He was also a
member of the neo-Jacobin Manège Club,
but with the coup d'état that brought
Bonaparte to power, the *Père Duchesne*
was closed down and, in 1801, Lebois was
deported to Cayenne. He was still there
in 1806, and his date of death remains
unknown.

Although Lebois shared Babeuf's opposition to the social and political conservatism of the Directory, he was rarely on
good personal terms with him and did not
share his views on property and revolution.
He was essentially a radical Jacobin
throughout the revolutionary decade, committed to the democratic and social aims
of the 1793 constitution, but also to the

Rousseauist ideal of the small independent property-owner and to constitutional politics. His journalism during the early Directory helped to keep those ideals alive.

Lebois' main activity was as a journalist, as editor of the *Ami du Peuple* (29 Fructidor Year II – 24 Vendémiaire Year VI) and *L'Eclaireur du Peuple, Journal politique et littéraire* (24 Thermidor – 12 Fructidor Year V), and as contributor to *Le Défenseur de la Patrie, faisant suite à l'Ami du Peuple* (7 Messidor – 6 Fructidor Year VII) and *Le Père Duchesne* (Messidor Year VII – Brumaire Year VIII). Yet he was also a prolific pamphleteer: see, for example *La Chasse aux monopoleurs sur le pain* (Paris, n.d. – 1789); *Boniface Culture, laboureur, ex-militaire, à Jérôme Moustache, son neveu, grenadier aux gardes-françaises et qui a coopéré à la prise de la Bastille, avec promesse aux Parisiens de leur envoyer du pain* (Paris, n.d. – 1789); *Brissot, Pétion, Buzot, Louvet, Gensonné, Barbaroux, Gorsas, Guadet, Vergniaud, Lasource. . . enfin toute la bande du Marais, qui voulez que la Convention nationale aille tenir ses séances à Versailles, rendez-nous nos dix-huit francs et foutez-nous le camp bien vite. . . ou gare le Tribunal criminel révolutionnaire et l'aimable guillotine* (Paris, n.d. – 1793); *Grande victoire remportée par les patriotes de la Montagne, cassation des complots, liberté rendue à Hébert* (Paris, n.d. – 1793); *Détails de l'assassinat commis. . . sur la personne de Marat* (Paris, n.d. – 1793); *R.-F. Lebois au prêtre Châles et ses concitoyens* (n.d. – 1795); *Le Directoire exécutif traîté comme il mérite par le peuple malheureux* (Paris, n.d. – 1796); *Mise en jugement de R.-F. Lebois (l'ami du peuple) au tribunal criminel du département de la Seine. . .* (Paris, n.d. – 1796).

There is no adequate biographical study of Lebois, but see Henri Welschinger, 'Le journaliste Lebois et "l'Ami du Peuple" (an III – an VIII)', in *Le Livre*, 10 Decembre 1885; this is almost wholly based on Lebois' own manuscript account of his life ('Conduite révolutionnaire de Réné-François Lebois'), written in late 1793, in Archives Nationales F7 4771(21). Useful references to him can also be found in C. Pichois and J. Dautry, *Le conventionnel Châles et ses idées démocratiques* (Aix, 1958), chapt. VII; and R. Legrand, *Babeuf et ses compagnons de route* (Paris, 1981).

HUGH GOUGH

LE BON, Guislain François Joseph (1765–1795)
French revolutionary, member of the National Convention and the Committee of General Security, terrorist

Le Bon was born at Arras, the son of a minor official in the municipal magistracy. He was educated at the college of the Oratorians, became a novitiate in 1783, and began teaching philosophy at the college of Beaune the following year. While there he developed an interest in the writings of the philosophes, especially Rousseau. In 1789 he was ordained. In 1790 he joined the Society of the Friends of the Constitution at Beaune and left the Oratorians. He retired briefly to Ciel before his appointment as constitutional curate at Neuville-Vitasse in July 1791. The insurrection of 10 August 1792 sharpened his radicalism, and the following month he abandoned the priesthood. He became mayor of Arras and then a member of the administrative council of the Pas-de-Calais. He was also elected an alternate member of the Convention and eventually took his seat there on 1 July 1793 when Magniez resigned.

On August 9 Le Bon replaced Chabot (q.v.) on mission to the Somme. He broke up a counter-revolutionary grouping near Saint-Pohl and, on returning to Paris, was appointed to the Committee of General Security on September 14. The Committee sent Le Bon in October to the Pas-de-Calais to suppress local counter-revolutionary movements. His main function in the revolution was thus established, and thereafter he was engaged in a series of terrorist activities. He concluded one letter from Calais to the Committee of Public Safety in December 1793 with a sentence that might well stand as his watchword: '*Vite, vite, vite* une bonne mesure qui fasse tomber les têtes des contre-révolutionnaires. . ..' The work of the revolutionary tribunals was extended, first to Arras (February 1794) and then to Cambrai (May 1794). Le Bon's methods were described in some detail by A.J. Paris in 1864 – they included the opening of mail at Calais, the packing of the tribunal at Arras with his own relatives, the increase in the arrests of nobles and non-juring clergy and the re-trial or re-imprisonment of many who had been acquitted, and, of course, a high incidence of executions.

The Convention was inundated with complaints against Le Bon's excessive measures. The prisons in his departments were overflowing and he sought permission to transfer some of the prisoners to Chantilly in order to make room for more. The Committee on this occasion refused his request. But while Robespierre (q.v.), who understood well the problems of his native Arras, remained in control, Le Bon's excesses were tacitly approved. Indeed, in a report to the Convention on 21 Messidor (2 May 1794) defending the need for such terrorism in the face of counter-revolution, Barère (q.v.) made the classic understatement that Le Bon's methods were sometimes 'un peu acerbes'! However, the next day the Committee of Public Safety ordered the termination of the tribunals of Arras and Cambrai.

Le Bon's fate was tied up with Robespierre's. On 10 Thermidor he was recalled to Paris and arrested. He was imprisoned for several months while evidence was assembled against him. He was tried by the criminal tribunal of the Somme, condemned to death and guillotined at Amiens on 16 October 1795.

The revolutionary careers of terrorists like Carrier (q.v.) and Le Bon have posed problems of assessment for historians. If violence is the midwife of revolutionary change, then men like Le Bon have a radical role to play in such cataclysmic events. It must not be forgotten that the terrorists were the instruments of policies determined in Paris. Indeed, such was the recognition of the extent of counter-revolution in the Pas-de-Calais and the Nord, threatened as they were by invasion, that when the provincial revolutionary tribunals were suppressed in Germinal Year II, the Committee of Public Safety agreed to perpetuate that at Arras. Moreover, it was Saint-Just (q.v.) and Lebas (q.v.) who instructed Le Bon to extend its work to Cambrai. In this way Le Bon was an agent, if willing one, of national policy and played an essential part in the most radical phase of the revolution.

Le Bon's son published his letters to his wife in 1845 and a biography of 1861 which sought to rehabilitate his father's reputation. See also, L. Jacob, *Joseph Le Bon, 1765–1795: La terreur à la frontière* (2 vols., Paris, 1933); A.J. Paris, *La terreur dans le Pas-de-Calais et le Nord* (Arras, 1864); A. Kuscinski, *Dictionnaire des conventionnels* (Paris, 1917); and S. Scott and B. Rothaus (eds), *Historical dictionary of the French Revolution, 1789–1799* (2 vols., Westport, CT, 1985).

D. NICHOLLS

LECLERC, Jean Théophile Victor (1771–?)
French revolutionary journalist and advocate of revolutionary terror

Théophile Leclerc was born near Montbrison, not far from Lyon, in 1771, one of five children of Grégoire Leclerc, an engineer in service of the royal government. During the early years of the revolution Leclerc styled himself Leclerc D'Oze, indicating pretensions to nobility. The Leclerc family had trading interests in the West Indies, and in 1790 and 1791 Leclerc was in Martinique, where he became involved in local revolutionary conflicts and was arrested. Sent back to France he enrolled in the National Guard at Lorient, before moving to Paris at the beginning of 1792. In Paris he made a name for himself at the Jacobin Club by taking up the cause of a detachment of Grenadiers sent home from the West Indies in disgrace by royalist authorities, and attacking Narbonne, the War Minister. A fiery republican address to the Jacobins on April 1 led to further notoriety and to Leclerc's arrest, but he was almost immediately recruited for a secret espionage mission for the French government in Baden.

In February 1793, attached to the headquarters of the Army of the Alps at Lyon, Leclerc was plunged into the middle of a savage revolutionary struggle in which he joined forces with the leaders of the Jacobin extremists at Lyon, Chalier (q.v.) and Hidins. In May he returned to Paris to lobby support for the creation of a revolutionary tribunal and a republican militia or 'Revolutionary Army' that would entrench the terror at Lyon, and attracted the condemnation of Robespierre (q.v.) for the unashamed bloodthirstiness of an address to the Jacobin Club. At Lyon Leclerc had suggested throwing six thousand 'aristocrats' into the Rhône; now he advocated a 'Machiavellism of the people' to banish 'all that was impure' from the surface of France.

Leclerc joined in the preparations for the Paris uprising of 31 May – 2 June, in which he played an active part. Denounced by Hébert (q.v.), one of the Commune's leaders, for his violent extremism during the uprising, Leclerc formed links with the Enragé group in the Cordeliers Club (particularly Roux (q.v.) and Varlet (q.v.)), who shared a common disappointment with the relative moderation of the results.

On 20 July Leclerc launched the first number of his journal L'Ami du Peuple, in an open attempt to capture the sansculotte readership of Marat's (q.v.) newspaper following the latter's assassination. L'Ami du Peuple appeared regularly for about three months during the summer of 1793, combining in its columns all the main themes of contemporary Enragé agitation: price-control on all commodities, death to food speculators, a strict purge of the army command, a round-up of suspects, including ex-nobles, ex-priests and speculators, and the formation of a Revolutionary Army of dedicated terrorists to enforce these measures, with the sacrifice, if necessary, of 'a hundred thousand scoundrels' to the revolution.

From the beginning of August the Ami du Peuple became increasingly anti-government in tone. While eschewing open and direct criticism of Robespierre, Leclerc attacked the burgeoning dictatorship of the Committee of Public Safety and called for the immediate introduction of the suspended new Constitution of 1793, and for elections to replace the Convention. In this campaign Leclerc worked in close liaison with Pauline Léon (q.v.) and Claire Lacombe (q.v.) of the Society of Revolutionary Republican Women. Robespierre, Danton (q.v.) and the Jacobin Club reacted sharply to this challenge, and by mid-September 1793 the Ami du Peuple had been closed down and Leclerc silenced. In November he married Pauline Léon and soon after left Paris on military service. He was nevertheless arrested for complicity in the alleged Hébertist conspiracy of the spring of 1794, and spent almost five months in gaol before the fall of Robespierre released him. He rejoined the army in September 1794, disappearing thereafter into obscurity. In 1804 Pauline Léon then living in Paris, referred to herself as 'femme Leclerc', indicating that her husband was still alive.

A militant agitator and journalist rather than a profound thinker, Leclerc linked a Rousseauistic interpretation of the collective and equal right to subsistence with a clear class analysis of the revolution. The aristocracy of nobles and priests, he wrote in the Ami du Peuple, had been succeeded by the aristocracy of merchants and bourgeois. At first favourable to the revolution, which raised it up to the same level as the former aristocracy, this new ruling class now faced an enlightened and aroused people demanding equality through the Republic, and had become the revolution's cruellest enemies.

Karl Marx was familiar with Leclerc's writings, and linked him with Roux as a protagonist of communism in the revolutionary era, and he has received some attention from Marxist historians. In addition to Leclerc's contributions to L'Ami du Peuple (1793), see R.B. Rose,

The Enragés: Socialists of the French Revolution? (Sydney, 1968); A. Mathiez, *La Vie Chère et le Mouvement Social Pendant la Terreur* (Paris, 1927); and J.M. Zacker, *Dveshenye 'Beshenyih'* (Moscow, 1961).

R.B. ROSE

LEHNE, Friedrich Franz (1771–1836)
German Jacobin

Friedrich Lehne was born on 8 September 1771 in Gernsheim and studied history and the arts. He was a friend of the Jacobin dramatist Nikolaus Müller (q.v.) and of Johann Georg Forster (q.v.). Following the occupation of Mainz by the French revolutionary army, Lehne became a member of the Mainz Club on 29 November 1792. He was an enthusiastic Jacobin and composed a number of revolutionary and polemical poems which were published together with those of Müller.

Lehne's literary works were published in five volumes in Mainz between 1836 and 1839. His writings include a description of Mainz following the capitulation of the Republic. However, his main contribution was to the theatre. He was one of a number of radical playwrights, actors and theatre managers active in Mainz during the Republic. He wrote for the *Allgemeines Theater-Journal*, which was published by Heinrich Gottlieb Schmieder (q.v.), including an essay entitled *Thaliens Rede an die Eingweihten ihres deutschen Tempels* (1792), which argued for the moral renewal of the theatre and which echoed some of the ideas expressed by Friedrich Schiller in his poem *Die Götter Griechenlands*. Lehne believed strongly in the didactic value of drama, and that one of the tasks of theatre was the dissemination of enlightened ('virtuous') ideas. Like Forster he looked forward to a drama based on the ideas and achievements of the Enlightenment.

However, Lehne's interest was not exclusively in the theatre. Following Napoleon's retreat from Moscow he turned his attention to the preservation of French institutions and the defence of civil rights in the province of Rheinhessen, which had become part of the Grand Duchy of Hesse-Darmstadt. In particular he was keen to see religious tolerance; preference given to local men in appointments to public office; the encouragement of trade; freedom from interference by the military in civilian life; fair taxation; and the restoration of public education. His ideas were part of a general attempt by liberals in southern and western Germany to preserve what they could of the benefits of the previous twenty years.

Although Lehne was by no means one of the most important of the Mainz Jacobins, he was an enthusiastic and committed republican, making his contribution in his own profession. The durability of his radical commitment is illustrated by his concern for the constitutional future of the Rhineland and in particular his attempt to salvage what he could of the French liberal heritage after the Napoleonic wars.

Lehne's work has not been reprinted and, as far as is known, the last edition of his writings was published in the mid-nineteenth century: Friedrich Lehne, *Gesammelte Schriften* (Collected Works) (Mainz, 1836–39). However, short extracts from his work appear in Hellmut G. Haasis, *Morgenröte der Republik. Die linksrheinischen deutschen Demokraten 1789–1849* (Frankfurt am Main, 1984), a selection of contemporary documents relating to the history of radicalism on the left bank of the Rhine with a useful commentary. Further details of Lehne's life, and in particular of his contribution to the theatre, may be found in Gerhard Steiner, *Jakobinerschauspiel und Jakobinertheater* (Stuttgart, 1973).

TIM KIRK

LÉON, Anne Pauline (1768–?)
French revolutionary women's leader

Pauline Léon was born in Paris in 1768, the daughter of a chocolate maker of modest means. At the outbreak of the revolution she was living with her widowed mother and a large family and helping to run the chocolate business. By her own account Léon was a revolutionary from the very earliest days, when she helped to throw up the barricades in July 1789. In February 1791 she led a party of women rioters to the sack of the house where the Royalist journalist, the Abbé Royou, was living. About the same time she began to attend meetings of the Cordeliers Club and of the *Société Fraternelle des deux Sexes*, which admitted women to equal membership. In March 1792 the *Société Fraternelle* sent Léon on a delegation to the Patriotic Society of the Luxembourg Section, of which she became a prominent member, serving on the committee during the autumn of 1792. In the meantime, in February 1792, Léon had won the support of the popular society of the Minimes for a projected legion of armed and trained women. More than three hundred women signed a petition in support of the legion, and Théroigne de Mericourt (q.v.) appears to have become involved, for she too addressed the Minimes Society on the need for arming and organising a force of women a few weeks later.

The legion may never have been formally constituted, but armed women were occasionally present at popular festivals in 1792, while on 10 August Léon presented herself, pike in hand, ready to serve with the Fontaine de Grenelle Section detachment at the storming of the Tuileries. Unlike Claire Lacombe (q.v.), however, she was dissuaded from marching with the men.

A few months later, in May 1793, Léon played an important part in the founding of an exclusively feminine political organisation, the *Société des femmes républicaines révolutionnaires*, which met at first under the same roof as the Jacobin Club and the Société Fraternelle, but ultimately had its headquarters in the Church of Saint-Eustache, close to the Halles centrales. Léon at first represented this enterprise to the Jacobin Club as an attempt to recruit women volunteers to fight against the insurgents of the Vendée. The rules of the Revolutionary Republican Women however left the bearing of arms optional, and in the event its activities were confined to Paris, and were, from the first, frankly political.

Claiming a wildly exaggerated membership of 4000, the society could probably muster a couple of hundred regular supporters. Although described as 'quasi-proletarian' by one historian, the membership, as far as can be judged, appears to have been drawn predominantly from a typical sans-culotte milieu of professionals and small-traders, with a sprinkling of wealthier bourgeoises. During the summer of 1793 the Revolutionary Republican Women closely aligned themselves with the campaigns of Roux (q.v.), Varlet (q.v.) and Leclerc (q.v.) for a purge of aristocrats and suspects, and for economic terror against speculators and profiteers, while armed members took part in the uprising of 31 May and 2 June.

In the autumn of 1793 the energies of the society were directed particularly in support of the Enragé campaign for the replacement of the Convention by the immediate introduction of the 1793 constitution, towards enforcing anti-hoarding legislation, and to imposing on Parisian women, often violently, such outward badges of republican loyalty as the tricolour rosette and the red cap of liberty.

Pauline Léon continued to play a leading role in the society at least until mid-August 1793, when she appears to have begun to be overshadowed by Claire Lacombe. Shortly after the Convention closed down the society at the end of October 1793, Léon married Théophile Leclerc and retired from active politics. She was nevertheless arrested, together with Leclerc, in the general purge of Hébertist sympathisers in April 1794. Released in August, she disappears from the historical record until 1804, when she sought clemency for a brother exiled for anti-Bonapartist agitation. Léon was then a schoolteacher, living in Paris with her mother and her son. There is no evidence that Pauline Léon ever advocated a specifically feminist programme of marital, legal and educational reforms such as that put forward by Etta Palm. Nor did she or the Society of Revolutionary Republican Women ever explicitly demand equal formal political rights. There was, nevertheless, both a practical and a symbolic feminist content to Léon's revolutionary militancy.

Active membership of popular societies itself vindicated women's contested right to emerge from the domestic sphere, while the constitution of an exclusively feminine club was a demonstration of feminine self-confidence, competence, and political significance. Moreover, the insistence on the arming of women in 1792 needs to be seen in the context of a contemporary and successful campaign to extend full citizen rights to all men under arms. By a similar logic it was publicly argued, in 1793, that if women were fit to wear the revolutionary colours, they should enjoy the vote and receive equal consideration with men for government appointments. For the most part these implications remained latent. Pauline Léon, and the Revolutionary Republican Women's chosen mode was participation in political life in the Enragé style of direct democracy. The same combination of martial enthuasiasm and direct action would re-emerge in feminist manifestations in 1848 and 1871.

There are details of Léon's political activities in: R.B. Rose, *The Enragés: Socialists of the French Revolution?* (Sydney, 1968); R.B. Rose, *The Making of the Sans-culottes* (Manchester, 1983); Marie Cerati, *Le Club des Citoyennes Républicaines Révolutionnaires* (Paris, 1966); Darline Gay Levy, Harriet Branson Applewhite and Mary Durham Johnson (eds.), *Women in Revolutionary Paris* (Urbana, 1979); and M.D. Sibalis, 'Un sans-culotte Parisien en l'An XII: François Léon, Frère de Pauline Léon, *Annales Historiques de la Révolution française*, no. 248 (Avril-Juin 1982), pp. 294–8.

R.B. ROSE

LE PELETIER de SAINT-FARGEAU, Louis Michel (1760–1793)

French revolutionary and educational theorist, deputy to the National Assembly and the National Convention, the 'first revolutionary martyr'

Son of Michel Etienne Le Peletier de Saint-Fargeau, president in the Parlement of Paris, Louis Michel Le Peletier was a member of one of the most famous, extensive and aristocratic dynasties of the pre-revolutionary nobility of the robe. He received a 'strong education' closely supervised by his father, and entered the parlement in 1779, becoming a president in his turn in 1785. On 16 May 1789 he was elected to the Estates General as a deputy for the nobility of Paris, but voted with the liberal minority of his order. He was president of the National Assembly from 21 June to 5 July 1790, and in May 1790 moved retention of the death-penalty for serious crimes. In 1792 he was president of the electoral assembly of the Yonne department, which returned him as a deputy to the Convention. Here he voted with the Montagnards for the death of Louis XVI and no prior appeal for popular endorsement; but on 20 January, the day before the king's execution, he was assassinated by a former royal bodyguard incensed to see a nobleman prepared to condemn his king. He was buried with elaborate ceremonial in the Pantheon, and many plaster busts of his prominent features were produced to adorn Jacobin Clubs alongside those of later martyrs such as Marat (q.v.) and Chalier (q.v.). In October 1793 the Paris section *Quatre-vingt douze* renamed itself *Lepeletier* in his memory.

His importance was therefore largely symbolic; but among his papers after his death was found a plan for a national education system which was read to the Convention by Robespierre (q.v.) on 13 July 1793. It involved compulsory attendance of all children at national primary schools paid for by education rates. At five all would be sent to state boarding schools to undergo republican indoctrination under a Spartan regime of plain fare. There would be instruction in basic skills but no religion, and only a small minority would go on after the age of twelve to advanced education in *lycées*. This scheme was adopted, with some amendments, on 13 August 1793, but revoked without ever being implemented on 20 October following.

There is an old biography by A. Wattinne, *Un magistrat révolutionnaire, Michel Lepeletier de Saint-Fargeau (1760–1793)* (Paris, 1913); while Le Peletier's educational plan is discussed in H.C. Barnard, *Education and the French Revolution* (Cambridge, 1969), ch. 8.

W. DOYLE

LINDET, Jean Baptiste Robert (1746–1825)

French revolutionary legislator, deputy to the Legislative Assembly and the National Convention, and member of the Committee of Public Safety

Lindet was born on 2 May 1746 at Bernay, in Lower Normandy, the second son of Thomas Lindet, a wood merchant, and Marie-Anne Jouvin. Trained as a lawyer, Lindet served as an *avocat* before the parlement and as a *procureur du roi* in Bernay prior to 1789. He made his reputation during the revolution chiefly as an elected official, serving in local administrations in 1790–91 before gaining election in August 1791 as a deputy from the department of the Eure to the Legislative Assembly. A year later he won re-election to the National Convention. Lindet sat with the Mountain and was assigned to prepare the formal charges against Louis XVI in late 1792. He later voted for the death of the king without reprieve, and in April 1793 was among the first deputies named to the Committee of Public Safety, a post he retained until after Robespierre's (q.v.) fall. Lindet and Barère (q.v.) alone among the deputies served on the Committee with both Danton (q.v.) and Robespierre.

Lindet earned a reputation as a capable administrator and political moderate during his eighteen-month tenure on the Committee on Public Safety. His political moderation, at least within the context of 1793 and the Year Two, is apparent in his performance as a representative on mission to the departments in the spring and summer of 1793. Sent to Lyon in early June, Lindet wrote back to Paris that there were many good republicans in the city and that misunderstandings had inspired the Lyonnais' resistance to the new Montagnard régime. His conciliatory attitude contrasts sharply with the harsh repression launched by Fouché (q.v.) and Collot d'Herbois (q.v.) against Lyon later that year. Lindet left Lyon in mid-June 1793, before the city broke into open rebellion, and was sent on mission to Evreux and Caen, where federalist rebels posed a more immediate danger to the capital. Accompanied now by a republican army, Lindet again showed restraint in punishing the rebel leaders in Caen. He and his colleagues dismissed from office all those implicated in the revolt, imprisoning those who did not flee, but ordered no executions, despite pressure from Paris. When Lindet himself stood accused before the National Convention in May 1795, the citizens of Caen would come to his defence for the leniency he had shown them in 1793.

Lindet returned to Paris in October and over the next year assumed chief responsibility on the Committee of Public Safety for military provisioning and food supply. He worked closely with the Subsistence Commission, established in October 1793, and in that position guided the economic policies of the revolutionary government. In the spring and summer of 1794 Lindet remained aloof from the political struggles that led up to the fall of Robespierre. Alone among the members of the Committee of Public Safety, Lindet refused to sign the indictment against Danton. Although not a supporter of Robespierre, Lindet tried to mediate the differences within and between the two great Committees, and did not join in the coup of 9 Thermidor. He left the Committee of Public Safety in October 1795 in the course of the normal rotation.

Lindet's political radicalism, apparent in the indictment of Louis XVI and in his later report defending the arrest of the proscribed Girondin deputies, became clearest in the period after Thermidor. In March 1795 he defended, without success, his former colleagues on the Committee of Public Safety, Billaud-Varenne (q.v.), Collot d'Herbois, and Barère. Two months later Lindet, too, came to trial for supporting the uprisings of April and May, and escaped condemnation only by virtue of the general amnesty voted by the National Convention on 24 October 1795. In 1796 he apparently joined in efforts to revive the outlawed Jacobin Club in Paris. Subsequently accused before the high court of complicity in Babeuf's (q.v.) Conspiracy of Equals, Lindet was acquitted for lack of evidence in May 1797.

In 1798 Lindet married A.E. Mesnil, daughter of one of the Caen federalist leaders. The following year he accepted appointment as minister of finance, a position he held until 18 Brumaire. He refused public service under Bonaparte's régime and resumed a private law practice. Even as the restoration of the monarchy appeared imminent, Lindet refused the entreaties of Jacobin friends to support Bonaparte's government, and for this was spared exile as a regicide after 1816. Robert Lindet died in Paris on 16 February 1825 and is buried in Père Lachaise cemetery.

Lindet's stature as a radical, perhaps questionable due to his relative moderation during the Year II, is substantiated by his posture and his actions both before and after that period. Although slow to join the Montagnard camp, at the trial of Louis XVI he had played a major role and in the period after Thermidor he consistently supported participatory democracy broadly defined. He was a man of principle and integrity, a committed Jacobin long after it had ceased to be fashionable. The First French Republic might have endured rather longer had more men such as Robert Lindet assumed positions of leadership.

In addition to the old biography by Amand Montier, *Robert Lindet* (Paris, 1899), and the information in R.R. Palmer, *Twelve who ruled* (Princeton, 1941), see Huntley Dupré, *Two brothers in the French Revolution: Robert and Thomas Lindet* (Hamden, CT, 1967).

PAUL R. HANSON

LIST, Johann Georg (1753–1806)
German Jacobin revolutionary

Johann Georg List was born in Karlsruhe. His father was a counsellor-in-secret and surgeon to the Marquis of Baden; he was also co-owner of a porcelain factory, which his wife took over when he died in 1757. The young Georg List studied medicine and was then sent by his mother to Lausanne for a training in commerce. In 1777 he returned to Karlsruhe and took up an important position in the business. In 1781 he married Charlotte Rupp, and in 1789 he took over as manager of the firm Battier in Basle. The town was an active centre of revolutionary propaganda, and List became one of the leaders of the revolutionary movement in southern Germany. He was in contact with the French ambassador, the Committee of Public Safety and the French Foreign Minister in Paris.

Together with his friend Ernst Alexander Jägerschmidt, List organised a revolutionary society. From 1794 he undertook espionage missions on the Austrian army, entrusted to him by Reubell. He was under close surveillance, and encountered difficulties which forced him to move to Strasbourg, where he set himself up as a pharmacist. In 1797, following the institution of *cercles constitutionels* after the coup of 4 September, he joined such a group, which was then dissolved on 2 October with the arrival of General Augerau. Again he found his position difficult, and had to escape – this time to Switzerland – where he assùmed a false name. He took up his political activities again when the Jacobins in the south started to prepare a new uprising. Accused of spying on behalf of Austria, he was forced to leave Switzerland at twenty-four hours' notice, and was arrested and imprisoned by the French. His friends in France managed to secure his release, and he went to live in Mainz, where he continued to work on his project for revolution. He worked in the service of the French as a hospital inspector, and died in 1806.

List was a man of action. He wrote very little and was more interested in practice than theory. He wanted to see a revolution in Germany, and worked towards this aim. However, he did take part in a competition organised by the *Journal de Paris* on the theme: 'Is it in the interests of the Republic to extend its frontiers to the banks of the Rhine?' (7 August 1795). Along with many other Rhineland Jacobins he declared himself a supporter of a natural frontier on the Rhine. The Germans could see no secure future without the incorporation of the left bank into the Republic. It was also in the interests of the French to extend their border so far as the Rhine, and the French revolutionaries did not hesitate to conduct an annexationist policy. While developing these arguments, however, List did not lose sight of the fact that the ultimate goal was the establishment of a democratic bourgeois society within the framework of an independent national German state.

List was unquestionably an active revolutionary who did not hesitate in the cause of the revolution, even at the risk of his own life. He served the French Revolution to the end of his life.

List's essay of 1795, G.F. List, 'Est-il d'intérêt de la République française de reculer ses limites jusqu'aux bords du Rhin?' is reprinted in J. Hansen (ed.), *Quellen zur Geschichte des Rheinlands im Zeitalter der französischen Revolution* (Bonn, 1935), vol. III, p. 573. For further details of his life, see H. Scheel, *Süddeutsche Jakobiner. Klassenkämpfe und republikanische Bestrebungen im deutschen Süden Ende des 18 Jahrhunderts* (Berlin, 1962); E. Dittler, 'Johann Georg Friedrich List', in *Ekkart-Jahrbuch 1970 der 'Badischen Heimat'* (Freiburg im Breisgau, 1970); and E. Dittler, 'J.G.F. List (1753–1806)', in *Deutsche Jakobiner. Mainzer Republik und Cisrhenanen 1792–1798* (Mainz, 1981), vol. 1, pp. 229–234.

M. GILLI

LOFTHUUS, Christian Jensen (1750–1797)
Norwegian peasant leader

The illegitimate son of a sea-captain and a farmer's daughter, Lofthuus came into possession of the Lofthuus farm in southern Norway on the death of his mother's childless brother in 1773. Lofthuus was an enterprising farmer, operating a sawmill and engaging in maritime trade. His combative attitude towards officialdom and the urban merchants of Arendal resulted in heavy fines from the courts, reducing him to bankruptcy in 1783.

In June 1786 Lofthuus presented a series of complaints against the tax extortions of the local crown bailiffs and the usurious practices of the merchants of Arendal to Frederik, the crown prince of Denmark-Norway. Advised by the crown prince to seek further evidence, Lofthuus toured the Nedenes region, collecting signatures. His activities, which he claimed were sanctioned by the crown prince, aroused the ire of local officials, but attempts to arrest him failed. A meeting attended by two hundred farmers at Lillesand on 2 October 1786, demanded passports for Lofthuus and his companions to go to Copenhagen to present their grievances. Though the local sheriff agreed to issue passports, he also sought the government's permission to arrest Lofthuus as a dangerous agitator. On 21 October, the government issued the warrant for his arrest, and Lofthuus fled north. In speeches in Telemark and his home district, Lofthuus sought to rouse the peasantry. The seriousness of the situation eventually persuaded the government in Copenhagen to rescind the order for his arrest, and to appoint a commission to investigate the grievances of the peasantry. The commission met in Kristiansand in February 1787, and heard evidence from Lofthuus and his followers. As a result, two officials were dismissed, but an order for the arrest of Lofthuus was also issued. He was detained in Lillesand on 15 March, and a peasant uprising to free him was put down by the army. Lofthuus was sentenced to life imprisonment in chains in 1792, and died in the Akershus fortress five years later.

Lofthuus was a man of considerable character, with the ability to arouse and retain the loyalty of the farming population of southern Norway, long oppressed by the burden of heavy taxation and indebtedness to the privileged urban merchants. He acquired a reputation for standing up to local officials, and exposing their malpractices. Lofthuus urged the peasants to be ready to persuade authority to 'do right in the land, so that the farmer could have justice according to the laws of God and the king', and he hoped to secure redress from the crown. He was in no sense a rebel against the crown, though he proclaimed himself to be a patriot, speaking on behalf of the oppressed of Norway.

The peasant unrest in southern Norway prompted the government in Copenhagen to institute a number of economic reforms after 1788; but the connection between the two kingdoms, already under strain, was further weakened by long periods of virtual separation during the Napoleonic wars. In May 1814, a constituent assembly meeting at Eidsvoll proclaimed the kingdom of Norway to be free, independent and indivisible; and although the Norwegians were compelled to accept union with Sweden, as sanctioned by the Treaty of Kiel (January 1814), they retained their constitution. The independence movement was led by high officials, landowners and entrepreneurs, though it made much of the peasantry as the foundation of Norway's national existence. Lofthuus, whose deeds had found their way into folk tradition, began to attract the attention of Norwegian writers such as Wergeland and Ibsen from the 1840s onwards, and in national literature he appeared as a patriotic popular leader who had suffered martydom for his cause.

Lofthuus' leadership of the peasantry is given due space in H. Koht, *Norsk bondereising* (Oslo, 1926). Koht also contributed the biography of Lofthuus to the *Norsk biografisk leksikon* (vol. VIII).

DAVID KIRBY

LOUSTALOT, Elysée
(1761–1790)
Radical journalist of the French Revolution

Born in the town of Saint-Jean d'Angély, (Charente-Maritime), Loustalot came from a respected bourgeois family that had converted from protestantism a century previously. His father and uncle were *avocats* at the parlement of Bordeaux, his grandfather and uncle *lieutenants du roi*, and his godparents bourgeois of Niort. He himself was educated first at the college of Saintes, where he acquired the sound grounding in the classics that marked his later journalism, then at the faculty of philosophy at Poitiers. Next he studied law at Bordeaux, where he was received as an *avocat* in 1783. Four years later, however, he was suspended for six months after publishing a pamphlet critical of a judge in the seneschal court of Saint-Jean d'Angély and went to Paris. There he worked as a *surnuméraire* at the Paris bar until the revolution broke out. It has been suggested that he may have written pamphlets during the political crisis of the pre-revolution, but, if so, none has survived. By the summer of 1789, however, his political involvement is certain for he became involved in agitation at the Palais Royal and, in late June, acted as defence lawyer for eleven members of the *Gardes Françaises* imprisoned at the Abbaye prison by their commander for insubordination and sympathy with the revolution. It was probably this that brought him into contact with the publisher Louis Prudhomme, who launched a weekly newspaper, the *Révolutions de Paris*, in mid-July. Loustalot first contributed to the fourth number, in mid-August, and from October onwards was the chief editor for almost a year. His long editorial articles became a feature of the paper, and a major reason for its financial success. He lived with Prudhomme and his family, on the rue Jacob, was a member of the Cordelier and Jacobin Clubs, and a founder member of the *Société des amis de la liberté de la presse* in July 1790. He died prematurely on 11 September 1790 after a short illness, brought on, it was alleged by grief at the Nancy massacre. The Jacobin Club and the *Société des amis de la liberté de la presse* went into mourning for three days, but the *Révolutions de Paris* continued until February 1794, with Prudhomme taking over as his own chief editor.

Loustalot's importance lies almost exclusively in his activity as a journalist in one year of the revolution, 1789–1790. He brought to this the debating skills of a lawyer, the culture of a classical education and the logic of Enlightenment rationalism. He was less interested in reporting events than in arguing a case, and saw his function as that of an educator and leader of radical opinion. On economic matters his views were essentially orthodox, for he defended both free trade and private property, differing little from fellow radicals and future Montagnards, such as Robespierre (q.v.). His views, like theirs, might well have evolved in later years under the pressure of events. His political views, however, were strongly critical of the Ancien Régime and he was an implacable opponent of the right-wing in the National Assembly. He also opposed many of the Assembly's reforms, most notably the *marc d'argent* decree, the division of citizens into active and passive, and the legislative veto conceded to Louis XVI. Instead he campaigned for universal suffrage – excluding women and executioners – and supported direct democracy, wanting deputies to be revocable by their electors, major political issues to be decided by plebiscite, and both jury members and army officers to be elected. He also opposed the municipal reform of 1790 which dismantled the sixty districts of Paris and replaced them with forty-eight sections, endowed with more restricted political autonomy. Finally he was an implacable critic of Necker, Lafayette and Mirabeau, and shortly before his death increasingly hostile to Louis XVI.

Loustalot's career is a striking illustration of the power of the press and of journalists during the French Revolution and, had he

lived longer, he would almost certainly have been as influential politically as other journalists, such as Brissot (q.v.), Carra (q.v.), Desmoulins (q.v.) or Marat (q.v.). As it was, his ideas had a substantial influence because of the large circulation of the *Révolutions de Paris* – up to 200,000 readers during its early months – and helped to shape the development of both Parisian radical thought and the later beliefs and action of the Parisian sans-culottes.

Loustalot's only published work is his journalism in the *Révolutions de Paris* between July 1789 and September 1790. Basic biographical information, and some of his newspaper articles can be found in ch. 1 of Marcellin Pellet, *Elysée Loustalot et les Révolutions de Paris (Juillet 1789–Septembre 1790)* (Paris, 1872), while there is useful information too in G.V. Villaceque, *Les Révolutions de Paris, Journal patriote 1789–1790* (Diplôme d'études supérieures, Toulouse 1961: unpublished). Camille Desmoulins delivered a eulogy at the Jacobin Club on his death, published in *Révolutions de France et de Brabant*, no. 45, pp. 253–267, which reflects something of the impact that he had on contemporaries, as does a hostile pamphlet, *Précis sur la vie du fameux Loustalot* (Paris, n.d.).

HUGH GOUGH

MAILLARD, Stanislas Marie (1763–1794)
Leader of the Parisian crowd during the French Revolution

Maillard, the son of a *petit bourgeois*, was a discharged soldier from Gournay (Seine-Inférieure) who served for a time as a court attendant in Paris but never really established himself in a stable occupation. He emerged to prominence at the storming of the Bastille. There exists an engraving showing Maillard crossing a plank over the Bastille moat to accept terms of surrender through a crack in the still-closed drawbridge. Whether he was actually the performer of this feat is uncertain, but Maillard did become known as the hero of the occasion and he was one of those who arrested B. de Launey, the commander of the fortress. It was Maillard who drew up one of the still extant lists of *Vainqueurs de la Bastille* approved by the Constituent Assembly.

Early on 5 October 1789, Maillard was in the streets as captain of a band of Bastille volunteers who had been sent to pacify some disorderly workers. They returned only to find a greater disturbance as demonstrators invaded the hôtel de ville, threatened the city authorities, and then marched to Versailles. Maillard helped restore order at the hôtel de ville and then led the women's march to Versailles, where he acted as their spokesman when they invaded the National Assembly. We have it from Barnave that he spoke crudely and emotionally but seemed sincere in demanding bread for Paris, apologies from the king's bodyguard for insulting the tricolour, abolition of aristocratic distinctions, and liberty for the nation. After a delegation from the women had visited the king and been promised food deliveries, Maillard returned to Paris with the delegates in carriages provided by the court. He was therefore not a participant in the disorders of that night or the royal procession to the city the next day.

As the revolution progressed Maillard seems to have enjoyed minor celebrity in the streets and cafés. Marat (q.v.) accused him of spying for the moderate Lafayette faction, but retracted in January 1791. In July, after the aftermath of the king's aborted flight, Maillard was among the petitioners on the Champ de Mars where crowds gathered and were fired upon by Lafayette's National Guards. During the September massacres in 1792, Maillard was sent by city officials to set up a tribunal at the Abbaye Prison at Saint-Germain-des-Prés, where priests and other suspects were being killed by uncontrolled crowds. When Maillard arrived he improvised a people's court, interrogated the remaining prisoners one by one, and while delivering more than half of them to the volunteer executioners, saved the lives of the rest. As in the case of the women's march in 1789, Maillard was to some extent tempering a bad situation, although again his motives and his place in the network of political relationships remain obscure.

During the period of the National Convention Maillard was employed briefly for police work by the Committee of General Security. He made arrests in the city and its environs as leader of a troop known as *tape-durs*, but he was also a member and for a time president of one of the popular societies, the *Défenseurs de la République*. In his police work Maillard reported to Hanriot, who also combined service to the national leadership with neighbourhood ties. During the winter of 1793–4 Maillard seems to have been caught up in the rivalry between Hanriot's National Guards and Ronsin's Parisian Revolutionary Army, one of the terror agencies, a product of initiatives in the sections (and not to be confused with France's regular armies). In his actions and propaganda against Ronsin's forces Maillard found himself cooperating with the Dantonist Fabre d'Eglantine (q.v.), who considered Maillard to be an ultra-revolutionary like Ronsin and succeeded in getting them both arrested. Maillard was in fact twice arrested and twice freed as the Convention's leaders manoeuvred between moderate and ultra-revolutionary tendencies. When, finally, the Committee of Public Safety in March and April 1794 eliminated both the Hébertists and the Dantonists, Maillard escaped the great purges but did not live to experience the next phase of the terror. Ill with tuberculosis, he died on April 14.

The revolution became Maillard's career. He was a bold and decisive leader, and his oratorical gifts enabled him to emerge at the head of the Parisian crowd at decisive moments – the taking of the Bastille, the women's march to Versailles, and the September massacres.

The main biographical sources are A. Sorel, *Stanislas Maillard, l'homme du 2 Septembre 1792* (Paris, 1862); G. Walter, 'Maillard (Stanislas-Marie)', in G. Walter (ed.), *Michelet, Histoire de la Révolution française*, vol. 2 (Paris, 1952); and P. Caron 'Indications biographiques', *Révolution française*, 85–86 (1932–33). Further background and information can also be found in R. Cobb, *Les Armées révolutionnaires, instruments de la Terreur dans les départements, avril, 1793 – Floreal An II* (2 vols., Paris, 1961, 1963); J. Egret, *La Révolution des notables. Mounier et les monarchiens 1789* (Paris, 1950); G.Rudé, *The Crowd in the French Revolution* (Oxford, 1959); and A. Soboul, *Les Sans-culottes parisiens en l'An II. Mouvement populaire et gouvernement révolutionnaire 2 juin 1793 – 9 Thermidor An II* (2ᶜ edition, Paris, 1962).

PAUL H. BEIK

MANUEL, Louis Pierre (1751–1793)
French revolutionary, procureur-syndic *of the Paris Commune, and deputy to the National Convention*

Manuel's father worked as porter at the Collège des Doctrinaires in Montargis, department of the Loiret. After coming to Paris, Manuel became a private tutor for the son of a Parisian banker. Later he became a *commis* to a book dealer before taking up a career as a writer. In 1783 he published *Essais historiques, critiques, littéraires, et philosophiques*, and in 1786 a brochure entitled *Lettre d'un garde du roi* which ridiculed Cardinal Rohan and J. de Luz, Comtesse de la Motte, for their involvement in the affair of Marie Antoinette's necklace. In the same year, after publishing his *Coup d'oeil philosophique sur le règne de Louis*, Manuel was arrested and imprisoned in the Bastille for three months.

During the tumultuous period of the late 1780s he often criticised the priests and the princes who separated themselves from the people and 'belittled the majesty of the communes'. In a letter to his fellow citizens Manuel claimed that 'it is within the communes that Spartacists may be found'. However, fearing the consequences for political and religious reforms, Manuel cautioned the people in August 1789 that they should fear anarchy because 'it can do more damage than a tyrant'.

In September 1791 in spite of the recommendation of the Société des Amis de la Constitution of Avallon, Manuel was not appointed deputy to the Legislative Assembly. After Louis XVI's abortive flight to Varennes on 20–21 June 1791, Manuel began calling the king *Louis-le-perjure* and insisted that sovereignty belonged to the people, not to the monarch. On 2 December 1791, with support from the Jacobins, Manuel stood successfully for election as the *procureur-syndic* of the Paris Commune. He was a member of the Commune's *conseil de ville* and of its police administration. In January 1792 he wrote a letter to Louis XVI stating, 'Sire, I have no liking of kings. They have done so much evil in the world. . .'. But he was willing to extend to the king, whom he disliked, the full rights under the constitution. He wrote: 'since the constitution which has made me free has made you a king, I must obey you. . .'. Like the Girondins, Manuel was in favour of declaring war against Austria.

Louix XVI's continued reluctance to sanction popular policies brought renewed waves of attacks on the Court in June 1792 and Manuel was in the forefront of those who mounted this criticism. After the Tuileries insurrection of 20 June 1792, in which he played an active role, he was suspended from his duties as the *procureur* on 6 July. But he was reinstated one week later. He supported the imprisonment of the king in the Temple and, as the *procureur* of the Commune, accompanied the troops that moved Louis XVI and his family there from Manège. En route he ordered the coach to halt in the Place Vendôme so Louis could see the overturned beheaded statue of Louis XIV.

The massacre of 2 September 1792 deeply disturbed Manuel. Following the genocide, he proposed the creation of a tribunal 'to maintain order in Paris, to track down the guilty and to do justice swiftly'. On 5 November 1792 at the Jacobin Club, he claimed that people as evil as the king had wished to have their own St Bartholemew's Day massacre on 2 September. He stated that the sight of the dead had awakened an awful doubt in his mind, and he raised the question: 'Is it better to dream of Liberty than to possess it?' Shortly after this, on 26 December 1792, he was excluded from the Jacobin Club.

Meanwhile, in September 1792 he had been elected as a deputy to the National Convention. Addressing the Convention on the subject of whether that body had the right to try Louis, he declared that only slaves could question if the king was judgeable. When the Girondins insisted that the rule of law must be preserved and Louis' trial must have an unquestioned foundation in legal procedures, Manuel called for submitting the decrees which would abolish the monarchy and establish the republic to the people. He insisted that the question of the abolition of royalty should be the first question for the members of the Convention to decide. Manuel considered Louis XVI guilty as a king. He retained his mistrust for royalty, and denounced the varied roles of kings with appropriate allusions to classical times. He stated that: 'We ought all to swear an oath, and I will swear it first: In whatever position I find myself placed, all my efforts will be directed toward this important end – to purge the earth of the pest of royalty.'

He served as the secretary of the Convention during the king's trial. In the process of counting the votes on the motion to execute the king, he abruptly left the table and tried to escape through the exit on the Jacobin side. He was stopped when a fight broke out on that side; he then escaped from the Girondin side. The next day he resigned from the Convention claiming that 'it is impossible for the Convention, the way it is composed, to save France. . .'. He retired to his native Montargis. His departure on 17 January 1793 set off an enormous disturbance in the Manège. The Jacobins demanded Manuel's arrest. Chateauneuf-Randon moved that Manuel be recalled by the President. Mercier claimed that Manuel had tried to steal some votes favourable to the unfortunate king, and he was almost killed when he tried to escape from the Convention hall. Although he believed Louis XVI guilty and indeed 'perfidious',

Manuel favoured forgiving the king of his vices and the ills of his birth and hoped to re-educate him. He stated that 'a dead king is no less a man' and he should be left to live 'in order to inspire disgust with royalty'. To him the Convention was 'an assembly of philosophers, occupied with preparing the happiness of the world' and ought not to take such a reactionary path as murdering the king.

Following his disillusionment with the Convention, Manuel went back to Montargis where he hoped to continue his literary career. He was arrested in August 1793 by the local revolutionary tribunal as a Girondin for not voting for Louis XVI's death. He was condemned and guillotined. The sources differ as to the date of his death, but it was either 24 or 27 Brumaire Year II (11 or 14 November 1793).

Although politically moderate by the standards of the Mountain, Manuel remained an opponent of royalty and a champion of the liberties won by the people in the early stages of the revolution. He was a strong proponent of a secular state, and had wanted to abolish the Civil Constitution of the Clergy in 1792. Above all, he was an opponent of censorship, and a champion of the freedom of the press.

Aside from the account in the *Dictionnaire des Conventionnels* by A. Kuscinski, there is no biography of Manuel. Manuel's own writings: *La police dévoilée* (2 vols., Paris, 1790); *Les Lettres de P. Manuel, l'un des administrateurs de 1789, sur la Révolution, recueilliés par un ami de la constitution* (Paris, 1791); and *Opinion de P. Manuel sur la première question: pour le jugement de Louis XVI* (Paris, 1792) are important for his political views. M.J. Sydenham's *The Girondins* (London, 1961) deals with Manuel's relationship with the Girondins. Alison Patrick's *The Men of the First French Republic* (Baltimore, 1972) not only provides Manuel's voting records in 1793 but also describes Manuel's actions during Louis XVI's trial. In his *The King's Trial: The French Revolution vs. Louis XVI* (Berkeley, 1979),

David P. Jordon describes in detail Manuel's role in Louis' trial.

N. CHAUDHURI

MARAT, Jean Paul (1743–1793)
French revolutionary journalist, member of the National Convention

Born in Boudry near Neuchâtel, (then Prussian territory), Marat was the oldest of six children. His father, who was a doctor of Sardinian origin, had settled in the town in 1741, a convert from Catholicism to Calvinism; his mother, Louise Cabrol, came from Geneva. The family circumstances were modest, but he studied at college at Neuchâtel before leaving, at the age of sixteen, to study medicine and work as a private tutor in Bordeaux. He finished his studies in Paris during the early 1760s, spending short periods in Utrecht and Amsterdam, and between 1765 and 1775 practised medicine in Britain, at London and Newcastle. In 1775 he bought the honorary degree of Doctor of Medicine from St Andrews University. During these years he also wrote a novel, *Les Aventures du comte Potowsky* (published posthumously in 1847), and published a number of philosophical works, including an *Essay on the Human Soul* (1772), *A Philosophical Essay on Man* (1772) and *The Chains of Slavery* which was published on the eve of the 1774 British election and contained a lengthy attack on despotism. He later published a French edition of it in 1792, during the revolution.

By 1776 he had returned to France and was appointed doctor to the household troops of the count of Artois, with a free apartment and salary of 2,000 *livres* per annum. He acquired a reputation for his diagnostic ability but, at the same time, took up scientific research, which was intellectually fashionable in Paris during the late 1770s and early 1780s, publishing *Recherches physiques sur le feu* (1780), *Découvertes sur la lumière* (1780), and *Recherches physiques sur l'éléctricité* (1782), in which he claimed to have destroyed all of Newton's theories and shown that fire and electricity were derived from igneous and electrical fluids. The rejection of these views by contemporary scientific opinion, and more significantly by the Paris Academy of Sciences, merely convinced him that the scientific establishment was uniting to reject him and stifle scientific innovation. This rapidly became an obsession and, according to his own claims (*Le Publiciste*, 19 March 1793), fired him with that determination to destroy all privilege, that characterised his political career after 1789. In 1783 he left his position in Artois' household, but failed to gain the post of director of a scientific academy in Madrid in 1785, and spent the next four years in some poverty, continuing to publish his scientific theories on electricity and optics. He had also, in 1780, published a *Plan de législation criminelle* which was re-published in a new edition in 1790 and relied heavily on the work of Beccaria to argue the need for a reform of the criminal code.

The events of 1789 attracted him to politics. In February he published an *Offrande à la Patrie* which praised Louis XVI and Necker, drawing on Montesquieu to argue the need for a constitution based on the separation of powers. This had little impact, and neither did a supplement to it which he published in April, which was more critical of royal policy. He wrote to Necker and several deputies to the Estates General, offering his services to the country, and on 23 August published a *Project de Déclaration des Droits de l'Homme et du Citoyen* which had little impact on public opinion but contained both a defence of constitutional monarchy and a recognition of the duty of the state to provide for the welfare of the poor. However, on 12 September he turned to journalism, which was to transform his career, launching a daily paper *Le Publiciste Parisien* – which changed its title four days later to *L'Ami du Peuple*. It was a paper of comment rather than news in which he mounted campaigns on political events and prominent personalities, claiming the right to exercise surveillance on behalf of the people. His style was marked by violent polemic and exaggerated denunciation of politicians, administrators, speculators and hoarders, while the ideology was that of radical democracy. However, its most significant features were his advocacy and justification of violence, and his insistence on the need for a popular dictatorship. Inevitably such views brought him into conflict with the law. On 8 October 1789 the provisional Paris Municipality prosecuted him for criticism of the work of their subsistence committee, but he went into hiding, in Paris and Versailles, before finding refuge in the radical Cordeliers District. When an attempt was made to arrest him there on 21 January 1790, he escaped to England returning in the following May. Shortly after his return, in late July, he published a pamphlet *C'en est fait de nous*, which led to another attempted prosecution – this time on the orders of the National Assembly itself – while an offended reader's attempt to sue for libel in the following December only failed because Marat's supporters filled the courtroom and intimidated the plaintiff from appearing.

After the massacre of the Champ de Mars, publication of the *Ami du Peuple* was interrupted for three weeks (21 July – 10 August) as Marat went underground to avoid prosecution, and several of the September numbers were written from addresses in Picardy. In mid-December, having urged on his readers the need to execute up to six thousand people – 'mais fallut-il en abattre vingt mille, il n'y a pas à balancer un instant' – he crossed to England again to avoid possible prosecution, returning to Paris to resume publication on 12 April 1792. On 3 May the Legislative Assembly ordered his prosecution, after he had recommended a purge of several deputies, but although his presses were impounded two weeks later, he continued publication from hiding throughout the summer. He shared Robespierre's (q.v.) opposition to war with Austria and, during the summer of 1792, came out in favour of a republic. He played no direct role in the insurrection of 10 August but, between 21 August and 13

September was made an unofficial member of the Commune's *Comité de surveillance*, and was given a press from the confiscated stock of the *Imprimerie Nationale* on which to print the *Ami du Peuple*. Both in it, and at the *Comité de surveillance*, the violence of his language helped contribute to the atmosphere that led to the September massacres; on 2 September he was formally co-opted onto the *Comité de surveillance* and published a circular urging all departments throughout the country to imitate the Parisian example. In mid-September 1792 he was elected from Paris to the National Convention and sat with the Mountain, but his bizarre physical appearance and dress, his exaggerated language, and his reputation for violence acquired during the September massacres, made him a prime target for Girondin attacks, and a source of frequent embarrassment to other members of the Mountain, including Robespierre. He treated all criticism with contempt and relentlessly pursued his campaign of denunciations both in his paper – renamed *Journal de la République Française* (25 September 1792 – 11 March 1793) – and from the rostrum of the Convention. He defended the September massacres, voted for the execution of Louis XVI without reprieve or appeal to the people, attacked the Girondins for attempting to save him, and because of his repeated denunciation of hoarders and speculators was believed to be partly responsible for encouraging the raids on grocery shops which broke out in Paris on 25 February. Denounced in the Convention, he defended himself from the rostrum by claiming the right to freedom of expression and derided his critics; as a result no action was taken against him. During March, however, he continued his denunciation of Girondin leaders and by the end of the month had concentrated his criticism on Dumouriez. Elected president of the Jacobin Club on 5 April, he signed a circular to provincial clubs alleging that counter-revolution was supported by several members of the Convention and recommending a new insurrection. Denounced by Guadet for this in the

Convention on 12 April, he refused to recant – 'C'est vrai. Les principes que contient cet écrit, je les avoue.' – and was sent for trial before the revolutionary tribunal. On 24 April he was acquitted and escorted back to the Convention through the streets of Paris by cheering crowds. In his paper, now renamed *Le Publiciste de la République Française*, he encouraged plans for the insurrection of 31 May – 2 June, but played no direct part in it and subsequently appeared only rarely at the Convention, hampered by illness and an aggravation of his long-standing acute eczema. The eczema required daily baths and it was while in his bath, on 13 July, that he was fatally stabbed by Charlotte Corday, a young girl from Caen, who was convinced that his death would bring an end to Jacobin power. His funeral took place on 16 July, organised by Jacques-Louis David, who later painted a celebrated portrait of his death. His body was interred in the gardens of the Cordeliers Club, then removed in September 1794 to the Pantheon. His heart was hung from the roof of the Cordeliers Club where, over the following months, it became an object of republican veneration. Busts of Marat were produced in large quantities and displayed in public places, but during the Thermidorian reaction opinion changed abruptly and they were ceremonially smashed; his body was removed from the Pantheon in December 1795 and transferred to a common grave.

Marat represented a political style more than a fixed ideology. He owed much to Rousseau, notably his support for democracy, his admiration of rural simplicity, his suspicion of wealth and his sympathy for the poor. But he was also marked by the frustrations caused by the failures of his pre-revolutionary career, which instilled in him a bitter resentment against the cultural and political establishment. He was never a consistent thinker, and in practice his political activity was marked by exaggeration, megalomania, and the apparently sincere conviction that he possessed a unique political vision, alone capable of guiding the revolution. Consistent denunci-

ation ensured that he was occasionally correct in his many allegations, and gained him substantial support from sans-culotte radicals, but it also made him an object of suspicion and ridicule amongst many moderate Jacobins. Consequently he was, for much of the revolution, a political maverick within the broad strand of Jacobin radicalism, an outsider who revelled as a critic. He once justified this in a response to an offer of co-operation from Fréron (q.v.) and Desmoulins (q.v.) which might serve well as his epitaph: 'The eagle goes alone; only turkeys in flocks.'

Marat's pre-revolutionary works include *The Chains of Slavery, a work wherein the clandestine and villainous attempts of princes to ruin liberty are pointed out, and the dreadful scenes of despotism disclosed* (London, 1774); *De L'Homme, ou des Principes et des loix de l'influence de l'âme sur le corps et le corps sur l'âme* (3 vols., Amsterdam, 1775–6); *Découverte sur le feu, l'électricité et la lumière* (Paris, 1779); *Découvertes sur la lumière* (London, 1780); *Recherches physiques sur le feu* (Paris, 1780); *Recherches physiques sur l'électricité* (Paris, 1782); *Notions élémentaires d'optique* (Paris, 1784); and *Mémoires académiques, ou Nouvelles découvertes sur la lumière* (Paris, 1788). During the revolution most of his energy went into his newspapers, *L'Ami du Peuple* (12 September 1789–15 September 1792); *Le Junius Français* (June 1790); *Journal de la République française* (26 September 1792 – 11 March 1793); and *Le Publiciste de la République Française* (14 March – 13 July 1793). But he also published a number of pamphlets, including several in 1789 when he was attempting to establish a reputation: *Offrande à la patrie, ou Discours au Tiers-Etat de France* (Paris, 1789); *Supplément de 'l'Offrande à la Patrie', ou Discours au Tiers-Etat, sur le plan d'opérations que ses députés aux Etats-Généraux doivent se proposer* (Paris, 1789); *Projet de déclaration des droits de l'homme et du citoyen, suivi d'un plan de constitution juste, sage et libre* (Paris, 1789). In the summer of 1790 came the controversial *C'en est fait de nous* (Paris, 1790), followed by *L'Affreux réveil* (Paris, n.d.) which dealt with the Nancy massacre, and *Les Charlatans modernes, ou Lettres sur le charlatanisme académique* (Paris, 1791).

There are several biographical studies of Marat, the best of which are L.R. Gottschalk, *Jean-Paul Marat: A Study in Radicalism* (1927; repr. New York, 1967); G. Walter, *Marat* (Paris, 1936), and N. Hampson, *Will and Circumstance: Montesquieu, Rousseau and the French Revolution* (London, 1983). See also C. Vellay (ed.), *La Correspondance de Marat* (Paris, 1908), and C. Vellay (ed.), *Les Pamphlets de Marat* (Paris, 1911).

HUGH GOUGH

MARCHENA, José (1768–?)
Spanish Jacobin, poet and writer

Marchena was born in Andalusia in 1768. He studied moral philosophy at the Reales Estudios de San Isidro, Madrid, and later attended the University of Salamanca where he took a bachelor's degree in civil and canon law in 1788. A gifted linguist, he read and admired the work of the *philosophes* and considered Rousseau his favourite philosopher. He also translated into Spanish verse *De rerum natura* of the Roman naturalist poet Lucretius. His own poetry greeted the outbreak of the French Revolution. In the spring of 1792 he appeared in Saint-Jean-de-Luz in the French Basque region where he was admitted 'by acclamation and unanimously' to the Club des amis de la Constitution de Bayonne. His impromptu acceptance speech contained the heart-felt cry 'I come from the land of slavery, the land of religious and civil despotism. . . I come to the country of Liberty'. Such an impact was his speech said to have had that the Club des amis decided to publish it. (See *Inpromptu d'un Espagnol, admis par acclamation et à l'unanimité, au Club des Amis de la Constitution de Bayonne*, Bayonne, 1792.) This latter document passed into the hands of the Inquisition who claimed that Marchena was helped by the Jews (a copy of speech plus appended comment is in Archivo Histórico Nacional, *Inquisición*,

legajo 4429, No. 27). Marchena later produced a propaganda sheet for circulation in Spain, entitled *A la nación española* (Bayonne, 1792), said to be the first tract printed by the French for a Spanish readership. It purported to be an address by a French citizen to the Spanish nation. Its main theme was to call for religious liberty south of the Pyrenees and the need to destroy the Inquisition which persecuted men of talent. Hence Spain lacked a Voltaire or a Rousseau. Spaniards were invited by the club to carry out their own revolution and were promised armed support. Five thousand copies of the tract are thought to have been printed and sent off for distribution in Spain.

Reaction in Spain to the revolution was limited compared with events in France's other neighbouring states. It is in this context, therefore, that the few sympathetic voices – such as Marchena's or that of the republican conspirator Picornell – take on their particular significance. These generally uncoordinated radical responses paved the way for the more specific liberal programme of the Cortes of Cadiz in 1810 and mark the origins of the Spanish radical tradition.

In addition to Marchena's own political writings cited above, the following secondary sources provide additional information on his career: A. Morel-Fatio, 'José Marchena et la propagande révolutionnaire en Espagne en 1792 et 1793', *Révue Historique* (1890); and M. Menéndez Pelayo, *El Abate Marchena* (Buenos Aires, 1946). R. Herr, *The eighteenth-century revolution in Spain* (Princeton, 1958) is an excellent introduction to the political context.

JOSEPH HARRISON

MARÉCHAL, Pierre Sylvain (1750–1803)
French revolutionary, atheist, socialist and journalist

Born in central Paris, the son of a wine merchant, Maréchal avoided the commercial career that his father intended him to follow and qualified instead as a lawyer.

A serious stammer prevented him from ever practising, however, and instead he developed an interest in literature, reading extensively in the classics and in the works of the eighteenth-century philosophes. In 1770 he published a short book of poems, *Bergeries*, on the strength of which he was appointed an assistant in the library of the *Collège des Quatre-Nations*. He lived in an attic-flat there for the next fourteen years, making use of its extensive library. He was strongly influenced by Rousseau, on whose death he published *Tombeau de J.-J. Rousseau* (1779), and also, somewhat contradictorily, disavowed the devout Catholicism of his youth in favour of militant atheism. He published *Fragmens d'un poème moral sur Dieu* anonymously in 1781, which denied the existence of a deity, and *Le Livre échappé au Déluge* (1784) which parodied the psalms of the Old Testament. This caused his dismissal from the *Collège des Quatre Nations*, and forced him to make his living by writing. During the mid-1770s he had already become a freemason, joining the lodge *La Céleste Amitié* in 1785, but he shared none of masonry's religious views and, in 1788, published an *Almanach des Honnêtes Gens* which differed from traditional almanachs in ignoring the Christian calendar and traditional saints' days entirely, thus anticipating the reforms brought in during the terror some five years later. Instead he placed the beginning of the year on 1 March, renamed eight of the twelve months, lengthened the week to ten days and dedicated individual days to an ecumenical selection of 'benefactors of mankind', including Voltaire, Rousseau, Coligny, Jesus Christ and Spinoza. Condemned by the parlement of Paris for atheism and blasphemy, the almanach was publicly burnt in January 1788, and Maréchal imprisoned at the Saint-Lazare for three months.

In addition to atheism, Maréchal's pre-revolutionary writings also reveal a commitment to republicanism and socialism. In *Le Livre de tous les ages* (1779), he criticised the institution of monarchy and at the end of 1788, in *Premières leçons du fils aîné d'un roi* argued that it was both

immoral and obsolete, urging the dauphin to abdicate in the interests of his people. In it he also amplified some of the social ideas that had appeared in earlier works, condemning the enslavement of the poor to the rich and forecasting the use of a general strike to compel the wealthy to share out their land with the poor.

He supported the revolution enthusiastically and, in the spring of 1790, moved to the rue du Paon in the heart of the radical Cordeliers district, joining the Cordeliers Club and the National Guard. Nevertheless his stammer and timidity precluded an active political career and drew him instead towards pamphleteering and journalism. He published two short poems celebrating the fall of the Bastille in 1789 and, in the spring of 1790, a newspaper, *Le Tonneau de Diogène ou les Révolutions du Clergé* which was sufficiently anticlerical to prompt a police prosecution for being 'attentatoire au respect dû à la religion'. The case was dropped, but Maréchal penned a number of anticlerical brochures under cover of anonymity over the summer of 1790 and, after the death of Loustalot (q.v.) in September, became the chief contributor to Prudhomme's *Révolutions de Paris* for the next three years until its closure in the spring of 1794. Here he continued his anticlerical campaign, particularly focussing on non-juror priests who refused to accept the civil constitution of the clergy, and his criticism of monarchy, proposing in December 1790 the recruitment of a *bataillon des tyrannicides* to defend the revolution against its enemies. In 1791 he published a brochure, *Dame Nature à la Barre de l'Assemblée Nationale* which returned to the social question and, rejecting violence as a means of securing change, urged the wealthy instead to voluntarily redistribute their land to the poor.

During the spring and summer of 1792 he shared Robespierre's (q.v.) opposition to war, welcomed the dethronement of Louis XVI and defended the prison massacres of early September. However he failed to take a clear stand in the conflict between Girondins and Montagnards during the winter of 1792–3, seeing faults in both sides, and wrote several articles for Bonneville's (q.v.) *Bulletin des Amis de la Vérité* between January and April 1793. Nevertheless, with the advent of the terror he threw himself into propaganda work, and published a collection of atheist poems, *Dieu et les prêtres*, in November 1793, which received subsidies from the Paris Commune and the Provisional Executive Council. He also turned his hand to the theatre, writing *Le Jugement Dernier des Rois* which was performed at the *Théâtre de la République* in October 1793 and enjoyed substantial success in both Paris and the provinces. Although an atheist, he opposed dechristianisation in the latter weeks of 1793 because of its effects on the political loyalty of the peasantry, and supported Robespierre's Cult of the Supreme Being in the following summer as the first step towards a more gradual destruction of religious belief.

He was never an enthusiastic supporter of Robespierre, however, and after Thermidor voiced his dissent in a pamphlet, *Crimes de la Révolution*, which alleged that revolution had so far only benefited the wealthy peasantry and bourgeoisie. In the early months of 1793 Gracchus Babeuf (q.v.) had written to him in search of employment and Maréchal had found him a post on the *commission des subsistances*. During 1795 he met Babeuf, subscribed to the *Tribun du Peuple*, and became involved in the Conspiracy of Equals in the spring of 1796. His name was among those designated by Babeuf to be added to the Convention when the insurrection had been carried out, and in March 1796 he joined the Secret Directory of Public Safety with Babeuf, Felix Lepeletier and Antonelle. It was he who wrote the Manifesto of Equals, defining the purpose of the insurrection, and composed the *Chanson nouvelle à l'usage des faubourgs* for more popular consumption. Yet his stutter prevented him from taking an active part in the discussions of the Secret Directory, and the police informer Grisel was unable to identify him as one of the participants. As there was no written proof of his participation, he was therefore never

arrested when the conspiracy was broken.

In the aftermath he returned to writing, and in his latter years lost none of his anti-religious enthusiasm. His *Lucrèce français* (1798) criticised the theophilanthropic cult, while the *Culte et Loix d'une Société d'Hommes sans Dieu* (1798) mapped out a means of establishing pilot communities of atheists within existing society. Most outspoken of all, his *Dictionnaire des Athées* (1800), drew on the ground work for many of his publications since the *Fragmens* of 1781, and from previous similar works by Jesuit priests, Garasse and Hardouin in the seventeenth and eighteenth centuries, to list no less than 1,057 'atheists', or writers who had expressed views favourable to atheism. It attracted a storm of criticism, some of it from people such as Mercier who were offended by their own inclusion. Yet he did not totally ignore politics, for he was a vigorous opponent of Bonaparte, publishing *Correctif à la gloire de Bonaparte* (1797) which accused him of arrogance and incompetence, and *Voyage de Pythagore* (1798) which contained more oblique criticism. He also wrote simple and brief histories of the world and of Russia, and entered the debate on women's education in a pamphlet of 1801, *Project d'une loi portant défense d'apprendre à lire aux femmes* which, as its title implied, recommended that women's education should be domestic rather than intellectual.

Throughout his career he had been on close terms with many literary figures and political activists, including Desmoulins (q.v.), Chaumette (q.v.), Prudhomme and Babeuf. On 28 April 1792 he married Marie Ann Nicholas Despres, daughter of a merchant from Dijon. He died after a long and painful illness in 1803 – still a committed atheist; but in deference to his wife's religious beliefs he had a Christian marriage and burial.

Maréchal was more a writer than a man of action, his one brief incursion into active politics being his participation in the Conspiracy of Equals in 1796. Already an atheist, socialist and republican prior to 1789, his radicalism was nevertheless tempered by pragmatism. In particular, although a theoretical supporter of the equal distribution of land, or the 'agrarian law', he disavowed the use of violence to achieve social change and looked instead to the altruism of the wealthy (*Dame Nature à la barre de l'Assemblée Nationale*). On the religious question too, his atheism was held in check during the terror by an awareness of peasant sensibilities. Yet his ideas, although tempered by pragmatism, were both important and influential. His socialism, typically for the eighteenth century, was utopian and agrarian, rooted in a moral revulsion against the extremes of wealth and poverty, and the belief that land was the source of wealth. He ignored the growth of industry and, apart from his references to a general strike in the *Premières leçons* (1788), and his brief involvement with Babeuf, envisaged no means of social change other than the voluntary surrender of wealth by the landed classes. His atheism, although a product of the eighteenth century too, was outspoken even by the standards of the age, and the *Dictionnaire des Athées* was to be republished in 1833 and later read by Gambetta and the anticlerical propagandists of the early Third Republic. Moreover, both his socialism and atheism were permeated with a strong individualism, and a rejection of institutional constraints, which made him of interest to the anarchist and syndicalist writers of the early twentieth century.

A comprehensive list of Maréchal's works can be found in A. Martin and G. Walter, *Catalogue de l'Histoire de la révolution française*, tome III (Paris, 1940). Among his pre-revolutionary publications, the most significant are *Le Temple de l'Hymen, dédié à l'Amour* (Paris, 1771); *Le Tombeau de J.-J. Rousseau* (Ermenonville, 1779); *Almanach des Honnêtes Gens* (Paris, 1781); *Fragmens d'un poème moral sur Dieu* (Paris, 1781); *Mélanges tirés d'un petit portefeuille* (Avignon, 1782); *Livre echappé au déluge, ou Psaumes nouvellement découverts* (Paris, 1784); *Apologues modernes à l'usage du Dauphin* (Brussels, 1788); and *Almanach des Honnêtes Gens*

(Paris, 1788). During the revolution he was editor of *Le Tonneau de Diogène* (Jan.–March 1790) and a regular contributor to the *Révolutions de Paris* between September 1790 and February 1794. Among his many other works are the anticlerical *Dieu et les Prêtres* (Paris, 1790); *Dame Nature à la barre de l'Assemblée nationale* (Paris, 1791); *Dictionnaire des honnêtes gens. . .pour servir de correctif aux Dictionnaires des grands hommes* (Paris, 1791); a one act opera *La Fête de la Raison* (Paris, Year II); *Hymne sur l'éternel* (Paris, n.d.); *Hymne pour les trente-six fêtes décadaires. . .suivis d'un calendrier pour l'an III de la République* (Paris, n.d.); *Manifeste des Egaux* (Paris, 1796); *Culte et Loix d'une société d'hommes sans Dieu* (Paris, Year VI); *Correctif à la gloire de Bonaparte, ou lettre à ce général* (Venise, Paris, Year VI); *Voyage de Pythagore. . .suivi de ses lois politiques et morales* (Paris, Year VI); and his play *Le Jugement dernier des rois, prophétie en 1 acte, en prose* (Paris, Year II). For his latter years, see especially *Dictionnaire des athées anciens et modernes* (Paris, Year VIII); *Crimes des empereurs russes, ou Histoire de la Russie réduits aux seuls faits importants* (Paris, Year X); *Histoire universelle en style lapidaire* (Paris, 1800); *Pour et contre la Bible* (Paris, 1801); *Mythologie raisonnée à l'usage de la jeunesse* (Paris, 1802); *Projet d'une loi portant défense d'apprendre à lire aux femmes* (Paris, Year IX).

The two fullest accounts and assessments of Maréchal's life are M. Dommanget, *Sylvain Maréchal. L'Egalitaire. L'Homme Sans Dieu. Sa Vie. Son Oeuvre 1750–1803* (Paris, 1950), and M. Nettlau, *Der Vorfrühling der Anarchie* (Berlin, 1925).

HUGH GOUGH

MARTINOVICS, Ignác József (1755–1794)
Head of the Hungarian Jacobin movement

Martinovics was born in Pest (now Budapest), Hungary on 22 September 1755. His family had moved from Serbia to Hungary at the end of the seventeenth century, where they became Catholics. His father, Mátyás Martinovics, was a soldier and from 1749 an inn-keeper in Pest. His mother, Anna Mária (née Poppini) was the daughter of a Pest bourgeois family. In 1791 Vince Martinovics, captain of the hussars, was raised to Hungarian noble rank together with his five brothers, including Ignác József. His father died in 1770 and Ignác József, upon the request of his mother, entered the Franciscan Order at the age of sixteen. Finishing the Franciscan school he studied at Pest University from 1775. Ordained in 1778, he became a doctor of theology and philosophy in 1779. However, he was mainly interested in mathematics and the sciences from the beginning. From 1779 he worked as a teacher at the Franciscan grammar school in Buda, but he had great difficulties obeying monastic rule and therefore conflicts with his superiors for which he was transferred to the monastic school of Brod (in present-day Yugoslavia) in 1780. Without permission he left the place in 1781 for Bukovina which then belonged to the Habsburg Monarchy. With the help of his uncle, Major Poppini, he became the army chaplain of an infantry regiment and, under pressure from the military, the Franciscan Order officially released him in 1782. Martinovics entered the masonic lodge of Lemberg (now Lwow) and, according to a later statement of his made before the court (no further data confirm it), he travelled with Count Potoczki in western Europe for several months in 1783.

In October 1784, upon the recommendation of his high-born friends, Emperor Joseph II appointed Martinovics professor of experimental physics at Lemberg University. In those years his first scientific works were published: *Dissertatio Physica de iride et Halone* (1781); *Dissertatio de micrometro* (1784); *Dissertatio Physica de altitudine atmospherae* (1785); *Praelectiones physicae experimentalis* (two volumes, 1787). Martinovics constructed a threshing-machine and made experiments with balloons. In his philosophical work *Mémoires philosophiques, ou la nature dévoilée* published in 1788, he professed atheist views. After the death of Joseph II in 1790 he issued an anonymous pamphlet in which, in the form of a parliamentary address, he attacked the power of the Hungarian clergy and noble privileges with the arguments of the Enlightenment (*Oratio ad proceres et nobiles regni Hungariae*). Martinovics resigned his Lemberg professorship and desired an appointment either to Vienna or Pest University or to some position with the Hungarian government. However, his attempts were unsuccessful. In order to attract the attention of the new sovereign, Leopold II, in 1791 he became a court secret agent (a police-spy). Leopold II, to whom he suggested through his reports reforms of a liberal and bourgeois character and whom he defended against the Hungarian nobility in an anonymous pamphlet, *Oratio pro Leopoldo rege* (1792), appointed him Chemist of the Court and conferred the title of Abbot of Szászvár on him, for the sake of appearances.

After the death of Leopold (1 March 1792) Francis I dismissed Martinovics from service, although he was ready to support the completely reactionary course of the court. Therefore he turned against the court in 1793, joined the discontented bourgeoisie in Hungary and organised the Hungarian Jacobin movement. Martinovics founded two secret societies and laid down the basic principles in secret catechisms. The 'Society of Reformers' included the reformists of the nobility and its aim was to detach Hungary from the Habsburg Empire by armed revolt and to establish an independent state. The 'Society of Liberty and Equality', the society of the Jacobins, would then have come to the front in order to accomplish a bourgeois revolution. The movement started in the spring of 1794 and in two months had about 150–200 members from all parts of the country, mainly from among the intellectuals. On 23 September 1794 Martinovics was arrested in Vienna, suspected of participation in the Austrian

Jacobin movement. Before the board of inquiry he disclosed the Hungarian conspiracy and in October arrests were begun in Hungary as well. In December fifty persons were brought to trial accused of high treason. Martinovics was also transferred to the Hungarian court, and was sentenced to death. On May 17 he was degraded from his holy office in the Buda castle church and on May 20 he was beheaded, together with the four directors of the conspiracy.

Despite his opportunistic character, Martinovics emerged as the organising force behind Hungarian Jacobinism and helped to spread French revolutionary ideas into the Habsburg Empire. He helped to stimulate Hungarian nationalism and to expose the authoritarian nature of the Habsburg dynasty. His conspiratorial tactics set a pattern for other anti-imperial movements and seriously alarmed the conservative forces at the centre of Habsburg politics.

Further information on Martinovic's life and political activities can be found in the following secondary sources: Kálmán Benda (ed.), *A magyar jakobinusok iratai* (Documents of the Hungarian Jacobins), vols. 1–3 (Budapest, 1952–57); Vilmos Fraknói, *Martinovics élete* (Life of Martinovics) (Budapest, 1921); Kálmán Benda, 'Die ungarischen Jakobiner', in Walter Markov (ed.), *Maximilien Robespierre, 1758–1794. Beiträge zu seinem 200. Geburtstag* (1958; 2nd edition, Berlin, 1961), pp. 401–434; and in Helmut Rinalter (ed.), *Jakobiner in Mitteleuropa* (Innsbruck, 1977), pp. 271–290; Denis Silagi, *Jakobiner in der Habsburger Monarchie* (Wien and München, 1962), pp. 65–176; Charles Kecskemétic, 'Les jacobins hongrois', in *Actes du 87. congrès national des Sociétés Savantes* (Paris, 1963), pp. 335–362; Zoltán Szökefalvy Nagy, 'Ignac Martinovics, Eighteenth-century chemist and political agitator', *Journal of Chemical Education*, 41 (Aug. 1964), pp. 458–460; and Kálmán Benda, 'Les jacobins hongrois', *Annales Historiques de la Révolution française*, 155 (1959), pp. 38–60.

KÁLMÁN BENDA

MARUSZEWSKI, Tomasz
(1769–c.1834)
Polish Jacobin

Maruszewski came from the region of Piotrków of a wealthy middle-class family. In 1788 he was a student at Cracow University, where he made friends with the future Jacobins, and came under the influence of Kołłątaj (q.v.). He was raised to the rank of nobility during the Four Years' Diet. He also assisted in the organisation of the movement of towns during this period.

Under the rule of the pro-Russian Confederation of Targowica he was in secret contact with Kołłątaj, then an exile, who – knowing Maruszewski's abilities – charged him with the responsibility of maintaining contact between Poland and the émigrés. After his stay in Leipzig in the first half of 1793 he went to Warsaw where he joined an organised plot headed by moderate politicians. Together with the Rev. J. Mejer he constituted the left-wing of the conspiracy. At the beginning of 1793 he went again to Saxony in order to inform émigrés in the name of the conspirators that Poland was ready to rise regardless of the exiles' attitude. He came back to Warsaw after arrests had been made (4 March 1794) and the conspiracy had been crushed. Maruszewski is unanimously credited with the reorganisation of the conspiracy under the name of the Revolutionary Association (trade guilds and junior officers of the garrison participating) and preparing the outbreak of the Insurrection in Warsaw on 17 April 1794.

Following the moderates' takeover of power in the Warsaw uprising, Maruszewski, together with other radicals, organised a club of 'citizens who, for the sake of their homeland, offer their help and service to the national authorities', named the Club of Jacobins (19 April 1794). Although Maruszewski did not perform any formal duties, he maintained contact on the club's behalf with Kościuszko (q.v.) and Kołłątaj who were staying outside Warsaw. He went to see both men several times in order to hand them the club's complaints against the moderate authorities of Warsaw. Maruszewski was mostly likely one of the organisers of the executions of Targowica politicians on May 9 which were demanded by the mob. He was also probably involved in preparing the lynching riots of 28 June 1794. On 22 June 1794, when the dominance of either the left or the right of the Insurrection was about to be determined, Maruszewski announced the Jacobins' domestic programme. In it he stressed the importance of propaganda; he recommended the propagation of the Manifesto of Połaniec in order to arouse the peasants; he asserted that Poland could count on nobody but herself and, consequently, advocated conscription; he warned against the king's influence; he demanded that political trials be held, and that the number of foreign trips by the rich be limited. In the same month he was appointed to a minor committee which was engaged in revising the Russian Embassy documents captured in Warsaw. When the situation on the front became difficult, the Jacobins were entrusted with the judiciary, and Maruszewski, commissioned Major of the National Cavalry for this purpose by Kościuszko, became a member of the Army Criminal Court. This nomination demonstrated Kościuszko's appreciation of Maruszewski's abilities. The latter attended every session and passed uncompromising sentences.

After the end of the uprising Maruszewski went, at the beginning of 1795, to Venice, a point of arrival for many Polish exiles. At first he belonged to the émigré left and was among the initiators of the radical faction of the exiles, the so-called Deputation. However, on becoming familiar with the progress of the revolution in France, he relented in his radicalism and severed his connections with this group. Maruszewski visited Poland on several occasions as emissary of the émigrés and thus participated in the beginnings of the Polish Legions in Italy. His prudence and discretion, however, make a comprehensive reconstruction of his activities difficult. He stood, for sure, at the head of an organisation composed of forty persons which was ideologically close to the Society of Polish Republicans, though it constituted no part of the Society. The two associations came close when joint attempts were made to release Kołłątaj from an Austrian prison. Maruszewski was particularly active in the cause. When Kołłątaj was released, Maruszewski invited him to live on his estate, and assisted him financially and in the renewal of old connections (for example, with I. Potocki).

From 1802 he rented an estate in the region of Czestochowa formerly belonging to a monastery, where he assembled an excellent library. During the Duchy of Warsaw Maruszewski was a member of the Kalisz department which designated him to draft a plan for constructing waterways to improve river navigation. He collaborated with the Warsaw Society of the Friends of Sciences and established a foundation for their benefit. It was stated as late as 1818 that Maruszewski was a freemason but he had probably joined sometime between 1788–94. He re-emerged on the political scene following the uprising of November 1830. In his proclamation directed to the National Government on 19 February 1831 he warned against dictatorship of an individual and pointed out that the uprising could count only on itself. However, he did not himself return to public life. The exact date and place of his death remain unknown.

Maruszewski was one of the most important Polish Jacobins. His contribution to this group was as a politician rather than an ideologue. Although he postponed his public activities during the Napoleonic era he never denied the ideals of his youth.

There is no biography of Maruszewski but details of his life can be found in W. Tokarz, *Ostatnie lata Hugona Kołłątaj* (The last years of Hugon Kołłątaj), vols. 1–2 (Kraków, 1905); S. Askenazy, *Napoléon et la Pologne* vol. 1 (Brussels, 1925); B. Leśnodorski, *Les Jacobins polonais* (Paris, 1965); B. Leśnodorski, 'Les Jacobins polonais (1794)', *Annales historiques de la Révolution française*, XXXVI (1964), pp. 329–47.

LUKASZ KĄDZIELA

MERLIN DE DOUAI, Philippe Antoine (1754–1838)

French revolutionary, deputy to the Estates General and the National Convention

Merlin was born in Arleux, the son of a farmer. He studied law and became an *avocat* in the parlement of Flanders in 1775. At the outbreak of the French Revolution the electors of Douai sent Merlin to Versailles as a delegate of the Third Estate. He participated in the debates of the National Constituent Assembly where he demonstrated his legal expertise, and was responsible for drafting the legislation which abolished primogeniture and other feudal privileges.

In 1792 Merlin was elected by the department of the Nord to the National Convention. He sat with the Jacobin Mountain, voted for the execution of the king and was the primary author of the Law of Suspects. This piece of legislation, setting out broad definitions of anti-revolutionary behaviour, provided a legal basis for the Jacobin terror.

The coup of Thermidor did not end Merlin's career. He served on the reconstituted Committee of Public Safety and was instrumental in arranging the return of surviving Girondist deputies to the Convention. He wrote much of the Convention's criminal code which survived until 1811 when it was incorporated into Napoleon's criminal code. Although elected to the Council of Ancients in 1795, he gave up his seat to become minister of justice. Under the Directory he co-authored (with Daunon) constitutions for the satellite republics of Batavia (the Netherlands), Helvetia (Switzerland) and Rome. Merlin became a Director following the coup of Fructidor (4 September 1797) when the republican majority on the Directory overturned royalist electoral victories and ousted the two conservative directors, but he was forced to resign after the coup of 30 Prairial (18 June 1799) when the conservatives turned the tables.

Under Napoleon Merlin served as *procureur général* of the Court of Cassation (1801–1814). The emperor promoted the jurist to the Council of State and to the rank of count in 1810. During the Hundred Days Merlin rallied to Napoleon and was forced into exile following Waterloo. He lived in Holland and Belgium until 1830 when the July Monarchy allowed his return to France. He died in Paris in 1838.

In sum, Merlin was a man of considerable legal talent with flexible political convictions. This combination enabled him to serve every régime of the revolutionary era and to re-shape radically the French legal system.

The old biography of Merlin by L. Gruffy – *La vie et l'oeuvre juridique de Merlin de Douai* (Paris, 1934), should be supplemented by R. Falco, 'Philippe-Antoine Merlin de Douai', *La Révolution française*, 17 (1939), and A. Cocâtre-Zilgien, 'Merlin de Douai et le droit public de la monarchie française', *Revue historique de droit français et étranger*, 38 (1960).

JOEL S. CLELAND

METTERNICH, Matthias (1741–1825)

German Jacobin, member of the Rhineland Convention, and publicist of French revolutionary ideas

Metternich was born at Steingrenz, near Limburg on 8 May 1741. He studied mathematics at the university in Mainz, and gained a doctorate there before moving to Göttingen, where he became a student of Kästner. He subsequently returned to Mainz to teach, and was appointed professor of mathematics and physics in 1785. In 1789 he was awarded a prize by the Jablonski Society of Leipzig.

Metternich was an active participant in the revolutionary movement of the early 1790s, and occupied important administrative positions in the Mainz Republic. He was a founding member of the Mainz Club, whose inaugural session took place on 23 October 1792, shortly after the defeat of the armies of Mainz and Austria by Custine and the occupation of the city by the French. He was vice-president of the club in the first month of its existence, and president the following year (February 1793). He was also a member of the club's Correspondence Committee, and of its Education Committee.

There was disappointment in Mainz when elections were not immediately held, and feudal dues not immediately abolished. On 19 November 1792 Custine instituted the General Administration, in which Metternich served, and which provoked opposition in the city. Metternich repudiated criticism of the Administration in the journal *Der Bürgerfreund*, which he edited from October 1792 to April 1793. Metternich himself had also expected early elections, and when they eventually did take place in February 1793, he was both an election commissar and a candidate, and was duly elected to the Rhineland National Convention, which sat from 17 to 31 March 1793. Following the siege and fall of the city and the withdrawal of the French, Metternich was arrested and imprisoned at Petersburg near Fulda. On his release he emigrated to Paris. He returned to Germany in 1797, and from the following year was chief of police and head of the so-called *Denominationsbureau* in Mainz, and was active in the municipal administration until he returned to teaching mathematics, this time at the *Zentralschule*, where he remained for the rest of his life. During this last period of his life he seems to have no longer taken an active part in politics, but published a mathematical treatise, *Parallelentheorie*, in 1815.

During the Mainz Republic, Metternich was a prolific publicist on behalf of the French and the ideas of the revolution. Apart from editing *Der Bürgerfreund* he published a number of essays and pamphlets, including *Der Aristokrat auf Seichtheiten und Lügen ertappt*, and *Untersuchung der Frage, wie kann der rheinisch-deutsche Freistaat in seiner freien Verfassung erhalten*, both published in the *Mainzer Zeitung* in 1793.

Following the incorporation into France of the territory between Rhine, Lauter and Nahe in 1797, he returned to the fray, attacking certain municipalities for their lack of commitment in the journal *Politische Unterhaltungen am linken Rheinufer*. In October of the same year he suggested founding new clubs, and people's societies (*Volksgesellschaften*) and Constitution Circles (*Konstitutionskreise*) sprang up in Speyer, Zweibrücken, Alzey and Neustadt.

Metternich opposed the establishment of an independent republic on the left bank of the Rhine, considering such an experiment unworkable if the rest of Germany remained under the old régime. He listed nine advantages of such a course, including: the right of the Rhinelanders to elect their own officials, like the French; the abolition of feudal dues, tithes etc; the opportunity to own their own land instead of working as day-labourers for the nobility and clergy; free trade; and protection against future wars.

Metternich who, like Cotta (q.v.), belonged to the generally somewhat older and less radical faction in the club, was a collaborator and supporter of the French and the ideas of the revolution rather than an original radical thinker in his own right. His contribution was that of a capable administrator – both during the short-lived Republic, and later during the French occupation of the late 1790s – and a tireless publicist.

The following writings by Metternich are available in the Mainz City Library: *Der Aristokrat auf Seichtheiten und Lügen ertappt* (Mainz, 1793); *Beschwerde des Landmannes über die langsame Entschließung der Bürger zu Mainz* (Mainz, 1792); *Untersuchung der Frage, wie kann der rheinisch-deutsche Freistaat dauerhafte Sicherheit in seiner freien Verfassung erhalten* (Mainz, 1793). A further piece has been reprinted: 'Neun Gründe für einen Anschluß an das revolutionäre Frankreich', in Jörn Garber (ed.), *Revolutionärer Vernunft. Texte zur jakobinischen und liberalen Revolutionsrezeption in Deutschland 1789–1810* (Kronberg Taunus, 1974). For further details of Metternich's life, see *Allgemeine deutsche Biographie*, Vol. 21

(Leipzig, 1885). See also Helmut G. Haasis, *Morgenröte der Republik. Die linksrheinischen deutschen Demokraten 1789–1849* (Frankfurt am Main, 1984), and Heinrich Scheel, *Die Mainzer Republik. Protokolle des Jakobinerklubs* (Berlin, 1975).

TIM KIRK

MEYER, Georg Conrad (1774–1816)
German political journalist

Meyer was born in Flensburg in Schleswig, the son of a customs officer, and he grew up in poor circumstances. He began to study law at Kiel University in October 1792. An enthusiastic supporter of the ideals of the revolution he took part in a demonstration of sympathy with Professor C. F. Cramer, who had been dismissed from his teaching post on 6 May 1794 as a result of the efforts of reactionary circles. On 20 September 1794 Meyer, who was known as the 'apostle of unconditional equality' and a sans culotte, was sent down. He returned home without a degree and remained a 'candidate of law' (i.e. one studying for a degree) to the end of his days.

In the autumn of 1796 he began to publish a weekly, *Der neue Mensch*, one of the most radical revolutionary organs on the right bank of the Rhine. In verse and prose Meyer propagated the ideas of popular sovereignty, constitutional rights, the separation of powers, the abolition of the guilds, commercial freedom, the abolition of class privileges and monopolies, the emancipation of the Jews, and equality of the sexes. Meyer, who signed some of his essays with the pseudonym 'Sincerus Gallus', emphasised the legitimacy and necessity of the execution of Louis XVI, and was close to the ideas of the circle of Gracchus Babeuf (q.v.) in his demands for social and economic equality. Reports from Paris which he published in his paper seem to indicate that he was in contact with the Babouvistes. He was also in contact with H. C. Albrecht (q.v.) and members of the North German Jacobin circle around the *Verlagsgesellschaft von*

Altona (Altona Publishing Society), and wrote sympathetic reviews of the work of Rebmann (q.v.) and Schütz (q.v.). He was filled with sorrow and concern when realising that the French Directory departed more and more from the original emancipatory principles of the revolution. When he accused the conservative pastor Nikolaus Johannsen of St. Nicholas' church in Flensburg, of filling the 'heads of the unenlightened masses' with 'devilry' and indulging in 'the crassest sixteenth-century dogma', he came into conflict with the authorities. The pastor complained to the high court that Meyer was spreading anti-monarchist ideas. In the autumn of 1797 Meyer was compelled to close down his paper, of which forty-one issues altogether had appeared. The following year he emerged as an actor with an amateur theatre company in Flensburg. The ending of the freedom of the press in Denmark at the end of 1799 made the continued existence of a democratic press impossible. A new publication of Meyer's *Der Feind Englands*, which appeared during the Anglo-Danish conflict of 1801, called for the defence of the fatherland; however, only five issues appeared.

From 1810 Meyer suffered from consumption and spent the last years of his life in the Flensburg hospital. There he composed moralising epigrams, which appeared shortly before his death in 1816 under the title *Versuche in Grabschriften*.

Meyer was among the most radical of the north German Jacobins – his ideas being not dissimilar to the most democratic produced in revolutionary France. And, from the preface to the collection of epigrams and poems published on the eve of his death, it is clear that he never abandoned the libertarian ideas of his youth.

Further details of Meyer's life are to be found in D. L. Lübker and H. Schröder, *Lexikon der schleswig-holsteinischen, lauenburgischen und eutinischen Schriftsteller von 1796 bis 1828* (Altona and Schleswig, 1829–1831), p. 368. See also: F. Valjavec, *Die Entstehung der politischen Strömungen in Deutschland 1700–1815*

(Munich, 1951), p. 424f; R. Erhardt-Lucht, *Die Ideen der französischen Revolution in Schleswig-Holstein* (Neumünster, 1969), pp. 151–158; Walter Grab, *Demokratische Strömungen in Hamburg und Schleswig-Holstein zur Zeit der ersten französischen Republik* (Hamburg, 1966), pp. 184–191; Walter Grab, *Leben und Werke norddeutscher Jakobiner* (Stuttgart, 1973), pp. 66–72 (a selection of Meyer's writings appears on pages 249–281); Walter Grab, 'Der Flensburger Jakobiner Georg Conrad Meyer und seine Zeitschrift "Der Neue Mensch", in *Grenzfriedenshefte*, vol. 4 (Flensburg, 1982), pp. 193–202.

W. GRAB

MOMORO, Antoine François (1756–1794)
French revolutionary, Cordelier and dechristianiser

Born in Besançon of an old Spanish family, Momoro came to Paris as a young man where he became a skilled printer and successful book dealer. When the revolution broke out he joined the Cordeliers and became secretary of the Club and editor of its journal. On 10 June 1791 he was elected secretary of his section's primary assembly (Théatre-Français, then Marat), and on July 2 he became an elector.

After the massacre of the Champ de Mars he attacked Lafayette and was imprisoned as a result. Upon his release from prison, 15 September 1791, he remained bitter and resented both his imprisonment and his loss of livelihood. After the overthrow of the king, Momoro was elected to the administration of the Paris department. On 11 May 1793 he was sent to the Vendée as a National Agent and supported General Rossignol against Leonard Bourdon and Goupilleau de Fontenay who, as representatives on mission, had removed Rossignol from command.

In May 1793 Momoro examined the rights of property in connection with his exposition on the need for a maximum on grain. His brochure on the subject – *Opinion sur la fixation du maximum du prix des grains dans l'universalité de la République française*–was written in the form of questions and replies in an effort to prove that it was both necessary and workable. He argued, essentially, that products of the soil belonged to society rather than to individual owners. When popular societies came under attack by the Jacobins he made the sensible reply that although it was true that in some sections intriguers had abused the privileges accorded to popular clubs the right to meet in these bodies was sacred.

On 14 Ventôse Year II (4 March 1794) the Cordeliers had veiled the Declaration of the Rights of Man in protest against the policy of compromise with the Jacobins of the right (the 'Indulgents' as Mathiez termed them). This was followed by some threatening remarks from Carrier (q.v.) and Hébert (q.v.) calling for a 'holy insurrection' and supported by Momoro, Vincent (q.v.), and others. The government became alarmed and the Jacobins sent a delegation led by Collot d'Herbois (q.v.) in an effort to heal the breach between the two popular societies. When Collot asked to see the *procès-verbal* of the meeting at which threats of insurrection had been made, Momoro, who presided, was evasive. Instead, he offered the excuse that several amendments had been made during the session and were not yet incorporated into the minutes. That his own sentiments were far from conciliatory may be gleaned from a document found among his papers after his arrest. In it he denounced 'the perfidious system of cowardly men who because they lack vigour, make it a crime for those who have it. . . .'

Momoro was arrested during the night of 23–24 Ventôse (13–14 March) and his premises were searched the following day, but nothing of a suspicious nature was found. The denunciations received by the Revolutionary Tribunal accused him of conducting the general assembly of his section despotically whenever he presided and of threatening those who opposed him. Others claimed that during the session of 15 Ventôse of the section Marat, when a motion for insurrection had been made, a member who recognised the danger of such a proposal attempted to shunt aside the discussion. It was then that Momoro as chairman of the session attacked him for wanting to turn away the discussion from 'the larger objectives' of the meeting. Momoro aware that he was doomed, took his farewell in a letter to his wife who had also been arrested. He was executed with the leading Cordeliers on 4 Germinal Year II (24 March 1794).

Momoro represented the more radical current of the French Revolution in the 1790s and through his writings on the question of economic organisation and the maximum showed himself to be an early supporter of economic equality and social ownership as the necessary corollaries to political democracy. As such he anticipated later developments in the European radical tradition.

Among Momoro's pre-revolutionary writings is his treatise on printing: *Traité élémentaire de l'imprimerie ou le manuel de l'imprimeur* (Paris, 1786; repr. 1796). His revolutionary publications are available in the Bibliothèque National: *Rapport sur l'état politique de la Vendée* . . . (Paris, s.d.), B.N., 8° Lb⁴¹ 3389; *Rapport sur les événements de la guerre de la Vendée* . . . (Paris, s.d.), B.N., 8° Lb⁴⁰ 2388; and *De la Convention nationale* . . . *Déclaration des droits* (Paris, s.d.), B.N., 4° Lb⁴¹ 2978. See also, Albert Mathiez, *Le club des Cordeliers pendant la crise de Varennes et le massacre du champ de Mars* (Paris, 1910), and *Annales historiques de la Révolution française*, vol. 3 (1926), pp. 484–492 (three discourses of Momoro in Ventôse Year II presented by Albert Mathiez).

MORRIS SLAVIN

MONGE, Gaspard (1746–1818)
French revolutionary scientist and administrator

Son of a lesser merchant, Monge was born at Beaune (Côte-d'Or) in 1746. From his earliest years, he demonstrated great intellect, showing especially strong interest in mathematics and science. His education

at the Oratorian college at Beaune and then the collège de la Trinité in Lyon furthered his intellectual development. Admitted to the Royal Engineering School at Mézières in 1765, Monge demonstrated considerable skill in draughtsmanship and the construction of model fortresses, introducing descriptive geometry into designs. By 1775 he had secured the rank of royal professor of mathematics and physics at the school, where he taught until 1784. His experimental work in geometry and mathematics brought his admission to the Academy of Sciences in 1780, a position he filled with distinction. Monge also turned his attention to the study of chemistry and established a laboratory at the Royal Engineering School. In addition to his academic responsibilities, he became an inspector of naval schools, a post that he retained from 1783 to 1792 and one that enabled him to visit all major coastal installations. During these years he collaborated with the noted scientists Lavoisier, Vandermonde, and Berthollet in various experiments.

Monge supported the changes resulting from the French Revolution. But if he joined such political clubs as the Patriotic Society in 1789 and the Patriotic Society of the Luxembourg in 1791, he played no important role in the political events of the day, preferring to continue his purely scientific work. His reputation for learning led to his appointment to the Central Commission on Weights and Measures, an offshoot of the Academy of Sciences. The body proposed fundamental reforms in the complicated national system of measures, one based on 'natural' phenomena.

The scientist entered the political arena shortly after the monarchy was overthrown. On 12 August 1792 Monge was unexpectedly nominated by Condorcet (q.v.) to be Minister of the Navy and overwhelmingly approved by the Legislative Assembly. In his new position, one made critical by the war then raging against Austria and Prussia, and soon to involve Great Britain as well, Monge worked with dedication. During his eight months in office, he sought to reorganise the fleet, weakened by the emigration of aristocratic officers, and to provide it with adequate guns and ammunition. But this heavy burden undermined his health and political attacks from radicals eventually forced him to resign.

But Monge's contributions to the success of the revolution had only begun. Mobilised with other noted scientists to serve the war effort, he utilised his abilities wholeheartedly in the struggle. As a member of the Committee on Arms from October 1793 to November 1794, he developed a process for forging confiscated church bells into bronze for cannons. He helped to invent methods for producing high-quality steel and to refine saltpetre taken from the cellars of homes into an ingredient of gunpowder. Monge also designed balloons for military observation. Besides contributing these technical skills, he strove to improve methods of training engineers. In March 1794 he was nominated to serve on a commission that established a Central School for Public Works, the direct ancestor of the Ecole Polytechnique. For several months Monge lectured on descriptive geometry in its 'revolutionary' classes. He also taught at the Ecole Normale in early 1795, training teachers for the nation's secondary schools.

In March 1796 Monge was called to serve on the Commission of Sciences and Arts in Italy. The body was instructed to inspect and protect works of artistic and scientific value confiscated by the republican armies led by Bonaparte during his lightning campaigns in the peninsula. As a commissioner, Monge travelled widely in Italy, visiting Rome, Florence, and Venice. During his stay from 1796 to 1797 he made the acquaintance of Bonaparte, who already knew of his scientific accomplishments. When the Peace of Campoformio was concluded in October 1797, Monge returned to Paris bearing the text of the treaty as well as carts of confiscated treasure.

Back in the capital Monge returned to teaching and also assumed the directorship of the Ecole Polytechnique. But, after only three months, he was again named to carry out a mission to Italy. This time he served as a political commissioner whose task it was to investigate the murder of the French representative to Rome, General Duphot. Arriving in the Papal States, he helped to organise the Roman Republic in 1798. But he concerned himself chiefly with creating a scientific society and selecting works of art to be shipped to France.

While in Italy, he was elected to the Council of Elders and to the Council of Five Hundred by several departments. Before he could take his seat in the legislature, however, Bonaparte persuaded him to participate in the expedition to Egypt. Monge spent twenty months in the Near East, carrying out scientific missions such as the creation of the Institute of Egypt. With Bonaparte he returned to France in the autumn of 1799 and resumed his place as director of the Ecole Polytechnique.

Monge benefited considerably from his friendship with the Corsican general. During the Consulate and Empire the scientist was named to the Conservative Senate and later became its president. He was elected to the Legion of Honour in 1804. Four years later Napoleon elevated him to comte de Pélouse. Although he was left undisturbed at the First Restoration in 1814, Monge compromised himself during the Hundred Days when he accepted a peerage from the returned Napoleon. With the Second Restoration of Louis XVIII, Monge fled to the Netherlands, only to return to Paris a few months afterward. His pro-Bonapartist behaviour resulted in his expulsion from the Institut and dismissal from the Ecole Polytechnique. Ill and disillusioned, he died in October 1818.

The contributions that Monge made to the success of the French Revolution were neither political nor ideological. Rather, he placed all his great scientific talents in its service, just as he had done under the Old Régime and would under Napoleon. Unquestionably loyal to the Republic and its ideals, the scientist enabled it to survive the onslaught of foreign invaders. Convinced that education was essential for France's development, he laboured to found the Ecole Polytechnique and the Ecole Normale, guiding them through their difficult first years. In this way he implanted the idea of material progress in the minds of a new generation. By his scientific missions to Italy and Egypt in Bonaparte's wake, he brought valuable knowledge to his country, helping to make it the intellectual capital of Europe in the nineteenth century. Few other revolutionaries proved as selfless and as successful as Gaspard Monge. But few possessed the same genius and good fortune.

Monge's scientific, naval and educational ideas can be studied through his own writings: *Compte-rendu à la Convention Nationale de l'état de situation de la marine de la République* (Paris, 1792); *Lettre du Ministre de la Marine à la Convention Nationale, du 11 mars 1793 l'an II de la République française* (Paris, 1792); *Description de l'art de fabriquer les canons* (Paris, 1793); and *Développemens sur l'enseignement adopté pour l'Ecole centrale des travaux publics* (Paris, 1794). The most useful secondary sources on Monge's life and work are: C. Richard, *Le Comité de salut public et les fabrications de guerre sous la Terreur* (Paris, 1922); R. Taton, *L'Oeuvre scientifique de Gaspard Monge* (Paris, 1951); and P. V. Aubry, *Monge, le savant ami de Napoléon Bonaparte, 1746–1818* (Paris, 1954).

J. FRIGUGLIETTI

MONNET, Denis (1750–1793)
French weavers' leader and political activist

Born at Aix-en-Provence of unknown parentage, Denis Monnet had some early legal training but by the mid-1780s he was a master-weaver living at Lyon in the poor quarter of Port Saint-Paul. His arrest in November 1786 is the first of the circumstances which make him one of the very few leaders of the labouring poor in late eighteenth-century France about whose life and ideas we have some detailed knowledge. Between August and September 1786 there had been a series of popular disturbances in Lyon, beginning with protests over the *banvin* (indirect tax on wine) and spreading into industrial troubles involving various trades, particularly the largest, silk weaving. Strikes and demonstrations by the weavers had forced the *consulat* (City Council) to concede temporarily their main demand, an increase of two *sous* in piecework rates. On 13 September, however, after the troubles had abated, all regulation of the rates was abolished. The authorities alleged that Monnet was 'un point de ralliement' of the disaffected weavers and that he attempted to renew their strike by distributing hand-written appeals for a general cessation of work. Monnet admitted only to writing the handbills found in his possession but the *Prévôt des Marchands* regarded the arrest as a great coup likely to deter Monnet's followers from further action. Monnet was imprisoned for two months without trial and the silk-merchants continued his punishment by blacklisting him.

As David Longfellow has pointed out, the Lyonnais master-weavers were better placed than most French textile workers to organise in pursuit of their goals because their industry had remained largely concentrated in Lyon rather than being dispersed into its hinterland. They quickly seized the opportunities presented by the upheavals of 1789 to re-establish the control over their corporation, the *Grande Fabrique*, which they had lost to the silk-merchants during the previous century. Monnet played a prominent role in the year of well-organised agitation which developed out of the preliminaries to the Estates-General. On 28 February 1789 he was elected by a rowdy meeting of more than 3,300 master-weavers as one of thirty-four weaver delegates to the assembly of the Third Estate of Lyon. By an administrative manoeuvre the *Consulat* prevented him and other militant weavers from taking part but in April he was again active as the weavers' spokesman at Versailles, pressing their case with Lyon's deputies to the Estates-General. The master-weavers continued to press their main demands for equal representation with the merchants amongst the *maîtres-gardes* of the *Fabrique* and for a general *tarif* regulating piecework rates adjusted regularly to the cost of basic necessities. Monnet was probably the author of their main manifesto of 1789, the *Mémoire des électeurs fabricants d'étoffes en soie de la ville de Lyon* (Lyon, 1789). Although in April 1790 they won the support of the newly formed Municipal Council for their *tarif*, the weavers found the silk merchants unwilling to abide by it and in May, having elected Monnet president by acclamation, another large meeting effectively established a new silk-weavers' corporation from which the merchants were excluded. Monnet was elected one of four *maîtres-gardes*. In 1790, however, the Allarde and Le Chapelier laws which abolished the gilds and prohibited all forms of labour organisation, wrecked these efforts to redress the weavers' grievances by collection action. They were reduced to lobbying successive Municipal Councils for support and patronage, but in a worsening economic climate they had little evident success apart from the temporary employment of many weavers in the apparatus of the repression after Lyon's rebellion of May–October 1793.

There are superficial contradictions in the remainder of Monnet's career but they can be resolved by taking account of the peculiarities of popular politics in Lyon, and in particular the unique role played by its popular societies between late 1790 and early 1793. In 1790 Monnet was not only a weavers' leader but a radical *patriote*. Later in the year he achieved local fame for exposing the royalist *conspiration de Lyon*, one of whose instigators had approached him in an attempt to win over the weaving community, and he became secretary-clerk of the *patriote juge de paix* François Billemaz. In August 1791 he was president of his section's club and in November he was elected to the municipality as a *notable*. Like Billemaz and the other *patriotes*, both artisans and bourgeois, who filled such posts in Lyon in increasing numbers between 1790 and 1793, Monnet almost certainly owed his

election to the support of the clubs. These had a genuinely popular membership, particularly in the weaving areas, and there was one of them in each of the city's thirty-one quarters and *faubourgs* by January 1791. Through their *Club central* they seem to have coordinated their electoral activities earlier and far more effectively than their counterparts elsewhere, maintaining the *patriotes* securely in power until the latter split into Rolandin and Jacobin factions soon after the establishment of the republic. We lack evidence on the process which made Monnet an active anti-Jacobin but it seems probable that it was connected with personal feuds (one of the Jacobins, Laussel, had denounced him and Billemaz as speculators in the *Journal de Lyon*), with Monnet's own preference for the orderly forms of government practised by the municipality before the Jacobins took it over in December 1792 (a letter he wrote on 2 June 1793 (Rhone Departmental Archives, 42L39) equated Jacobinism with anarchy) and with the attempt made in March 1793 to replace the decentralised, federated network of popular societies with a single, politically-hygienic Jacobin Club on the Parisian model. Although the Jacobins had made vague promises to better the lot of the labouring poor they were unable to implement them during their five months in office or even to prevent food shortages and sharp price rises. It is not difficult to understand Monnet's preference for the anti-Jacobins who invoked, some of them disingenuously, the popular democratic principles of sectional permanence and autonomy against Jacobin 'despotism'.

Like other eighteenth- and early nineteenth-century artisans faced with increasingly threatening *laissez-faire* legislation, Denis Monnet aimed to revive and strengthen traditional forms of government regulation of conditions in his industry rather than to question prevailing assumptions about the ownership and control of the means of production. His activities thus provide an important point of reference in the history of French working-class radicalism. Despite the intensity of the struggle within the *Grande Fabrique* and the rapid acceptance of democratic political ideas amongst the *menu peuple* of Lyon, the weavers' most articulate spokesman was unable to transcend traditional ways of thinking about the organisation of production. He was, however, a radical critic of the free labour market which placed the master-weaver in a condition little different from the *compagnon*, and 'delivers [him] entirely into the hands of the merchant, and thus reduces [him] to the salary which it pleases the merchant to fix, with the understanding that the former, forced by the imperious law of simple need, will soon be obliged to submit to the one who imposes it on him'. He expressed the extreme hostility which united masters and *compagnons* against the merchants and he played an important role in the masters' attempt to replace the traditional gild with an independent weavers' organisation, an attempt which anticipated later struggles of organised labour against capital. In revolutionary history he is the best known of the Lyonnais artisans who used the clubs to democratise municipal politics and whose attachment to sectional autonomy brought them into conflict with Jacobin centralism in 1793.

Details of Monnet's activities and writings on behalf of the weavers between 1789 and 1791 may be found in Louis Trénard, 'La crise sociale lyonnaise à la veille de la Révolution', *Revue d'histoire moderne et contemporaine*, 2 (1955), pp. 5–45, and David L. Longfellow, 'Silk Weavers and the Social Struggle in Lyon during the French Revolution, 1789–94', *French Historical Studies*, 14 (1981), pp. 1–40 (from which the translation of the above excerpt from the *Mémoire* of 1789 was taken). See also W. Edmonds, 'A Case-Study in Popular Anti-Jacobinism: the Career of Denis Monnet', *French Historical Studies*, 13 (1983), pp. 214–251.

BILL EDMONDS

MÜLLER, Nikolaus (1770–1851)
German poet, playwright and artist who used his art to advance the ideas of the French Revolution

Müller was born in Mainz on 14 May 1770, and was the ninth of seventeen children of a merchant. While still a schoolboy he published poems and had plays performed, and at the age of sixteen was a member of the Mainz theatre of which Grossman (q.v.) was a director. In the same year his first book, a collection of poems entitled *Poetische Versuche*, was published. He studied philosophy at Mainz University under Dorsch (q.v.) until 1788, and then went on to study anatomy under Samuel Thomas Sömmering. However, he did not abandon his connections with the theatre during his studies; he continued writing and had a comedy performed (*Die Hämosrosen*). He became a friend of August Wilhelm Iffland (1759–1814), an actor, playwright and theatre director, and of H. W. Seufried and Johann David Beil, also actor-directors. He helped with the painting of the sets, and became an assistant to the theatre painter. On leaving university he attempted to live off his earnings as a painter.

Following the French occupation of Mainz, Müller became a member of the Jacobin Club, where he belonged to a group of radical young Mainzers. Müller took an active part in the politics of the Mainz Republic. He was a member of two of the club's committees; directed political festivals and plays; worked as an interpreter; and frequently made speeches and wrote poems celebrating the ideas of the revolution, which were published together with those of Johann Friedrich Lehne (q.v.).

When the city returned to German control he managed to escape in the uniform of a French soldier. He made his way to Paris, where he studied art for a time, before returning to Germany. When Mainz was re-occupied by the French in 1798 he returned there and made his living by giving drawing lessons. He also wrote and painted for the theatre, and in 1802 was appointed to a teaching position at the *Lyceum*. In 1805 he became curator of the city's art gallery. He continued to hold both these positions when Mainz came under the control of the state of Hesse.

In his later life Müller diversified his interests and undertook studies in mythology and philology. In 1802 he published a study of Indian art, science and religion (*Glauben, Wissen und Kunst der alten Hindus*) and in 1831 *Mithras*. He died in Mainz on 14 June 1851.

Müller wrote a number of plays with a Jacobin slant, but only two have survived. *Der Aristokrat in der Klemme* is an unsophisticated comedy very largely based on a contemporary French play, which mocks the problems of an aristocrat who finds it difficult to come to terms with the revolution. *Der Freiheitsbaum* is a didactic drama which shows how the planting of a 'liberty tree' in a German village on the French border reveals political tensions in the countryside, and the play touches on problems the Mainz Jacobins themselves faced. Müller also made a number of contributions to dramatic theory, including an open letter to Iffland: *Über das Fortschreiten des Drama-Dichters mit dem Geiste der Zeit*, which deals with the relationship of the playwright to the intellectual climate of the time, and *Über die Bühne als Sittenschule*, an essay on the 'stage as school of morals'.

Müller was a young radical whose contribution to the Mainz Republic was to convey the revolutionary ideas of the time through the medium of his art. He also served in a number of minor offices both during the republic itself, and in the period between his return from Paris and the reoccupation of Mainz by French troops. Politically he belonged to the opposition in the club, rather than to Cotta's (q.v.) faction.

Further details of Müller's life and work are to be found in the *Allgemeine Deutsche Biographie*, Vol. 22 (Leipzig, 1885) and in Gerhard Steiner, *Jakobinerschauspiel und Jakobinertheater* (Stuttgart, 1973).

TIM KIRK

NOVIKOV, Nikolay Ivanovich (1744–1818)
Russian enlightener

Scion of an old noble family, Novikov was born on the ancestral estate of Avdot'ino near Moscow and was one of the first students at the Moscow University Gymnasium established in 1756. A member of the Izmaylovksy Guards regiment that led the palace revolution which brought Catherine II to the Russian throne, he was appointed to serve as minute-taker in Catherine's Legislative Commission 1767–9. In 1769, prompted by the empress's example, Novikov produced a year's run of a moral weekly *Truten'* (The Drone) succeeded by *Pustomelya* (The Tattler) (1770) and *Zhivopisets* (The Painter) (1771–3). These journals, modelled on Addison and Steele's *Spectator*, castigated the obscurantism of conservative backwoodsmen and promoted the image of a meritocratic 'truly noble man'. To a great extent they illustrated views proposed in Catherine's *Nakaz* (Instruction) to her Legislative Commission. The 1770s saw Novikov making a significant contribution to the development of book printing and publishing by encouraging the formation of independent 'companies'. His 'Society for the Printing of Books' was intended as private support for the official 'Society for the Translation of Foreign Books'; but, despite state subventions, this venture did not prosper since a readership for the European classics promoted by the Translation Society did not yet exist in Russia. At the same time, however, Novikov showed that he was aware of the requirements of the growing reading public in publishing on his own account books of more popular appeal. His concern for Russian culture showed itself in his *Opyt istoricheskogo slovarya o rossiyskikh pisatelyakh* (Essay at an Historical Dictionary of Russian Writers) (1772), in his collection and editing of historical records, with the encouragement and support of Catherine II, *Drevnyaya rossiyskaya vivliofika* (The Ancient Russian Library) (1773–5), and in a periodical which examined the Russian

national character *Koshelek* (The Bag)
(1774). In 1775 Novikov entered a masonic
lodge and subsequently became a leading
figure in Russian freemasonry. An early
masonic philanthropic venture, linked with
his publishing, was the support gained
through the journal *Utrenniy svet* (Morning
Light) (1777–80) for two charity schools in
St Petersburg. Masonic connections with
Kheraskov, curator of Moscow University,
enabled Novikov to obtain a ten-year lease
on the University Press in 1779. Although
his move to Moscow removed him from
the support enjoyed at the St. Petersburg
court, it allowed him to benefit from the
patronage of the highly-placed masons in
the older capital. Moscow University Press
dominated Russian publishing under Novikov's direction in the years 1779–89 which
were called by Klyuchevsky 'Novikov's
decade'. Among his periodical publications, apart from the semi-official
Moskovskiye vedomosti (Moscow News),
were *Ekonomicheskiy magazin* (The Economic Magazine) (1780–9), three successors
to *Utrenniy svet* (Morning Light) – *Moskov-
skoye yezhemesyachnoye izdaniye* (The
Moscow Monthly) (1781), *Vechernaya
zarya* (Evening Light) (1782) and *Pokoy-
ashchiysya trudolyubets* (The Diligent at
Repose) (1784–5), the miscellany *Gorod-
skaya i derevenskaya biblioteka* (The Town
and Country Library) (1782–6) and Russia's first children's magazine *Detskoye
chteniye dlya serdtsa i razuma* (Children's
Reading for Heart and Mind) (1785–9).
He helped in founding student societies at
the university and created the Typo-
graphical Company, a large independent
publishing concern, which flourished until
its dissolution in 1791. He responded to
the succession of poor harvests after 1787
by organising extensive famine relief at his
home estate in Avdot'ino. During the
1780s, however, Novikov was subjected to
police surveillance and his publications
were assessed for orthodox rectitude by
Archbishop Plato in 1786. The lease of
Moscow University Press was not renewed
to Novikov in 1789, and in 1791 following
an investigation into his publishing by
Moscow's police authorities and interrog-

ation by Sheshkovsky, Catherine's chief
inquisitor, Novikov was sentenced to fifteen years' imprisonment in the Schlüssel-
burg fortress. Although released within
four years on Paul's accession, Novikov
made no attempt to return to a prominent
position in Russian public life and was
content to live on his estate, occupied with
agricultural improvement and the copying
of spiritual texts in manuscript until his
death in 1818 when his name was already
eclipsed.

It is the fact of his imprisonment that
ensured Novikov's standing as a martyred
radical. It was Novikov and Radishchev
(q.v.) whom Plekhanov cited as the first
martyrs to figure in his projected study
of Russian writers incarcerated for their
writings. The supposed clash between the
empress and her oppositionist subject,
Novikov, was used by Dobrolyubov and
other radicals from the 1860s onwards as
a paradigm of their own opposition to
tsarist rule. The appreciation of Novikov's
contributions to Russian culture has suffered from this teleological approach. Were
it not for his harsh sentence in 1792,
Novikov would be viewed as a man who
had endeavoured in many ways to spread
the moderate, Christian enlightenment of
Northern Europe within Russia. It is evident that as journalist, historian and publisher he acted in response to imperial
initiatives and consequently received hand-
some court subsidies. Nevertheless the
fifteen-years' incarceration in the Schlüs-
selburg fortress was a signal that Novikov's
activities could not in the end – and
particularly in the period of reaction following the French Revolution – be toler-
ated by the state. The exact reasons for
his punishment are not clear: the possible
subversive nature of some of the philosophe writings published by him and
jealousies aroused by his philanthropy
undoubtedly contributed to the oppro-
bium. What gave deep offence to the
presumptions of the traditional state tutelage of Russia, however, were the private
initiatives and the formation of influential
groupings at which Novikov had proved
adept and which were often contiguous

with masonic fraternities. This was the radicalism that proved his undoing. Furthermore, links had been forged, through freemasonry, between Novikov's societies and sympathisers outside Russia's borders, particularly in Prussia: this activated Russia's latent xenophobia. Most reprehensible, for the police authorities, was his attempt to implicate Grand Duke Paul in these private initiatives. The imprisoning of Novikov was a reassertion by the absolutist Russian state that no private expression of views, however moderate and loyal, and no independent action were ultimately tolerable.

There are several biographies of Novikov in Russian. See, for example, G. P. Makogonenko, *Nikolay Novikov i russkoye prosveshcheniye XVIII veka* (Moscow, Leningrad, 1952); A. V. Zapadov, *Novikov* (Moscow, 1968); and I. F. Martynov, *Knigoizdatel' Nikolay Novikov* (Moscow, 1981). Two recent studies – one in French, the other in English – are possibly more accessible. They are: André Monnier, *Un publiciste frondeur sous Catherine II: Nicolas Novikov* (Paris, 1981); and W. Gareth Jones, *Nikolay Novikov: Enlightener of Russia* (Cambridge, 1984).

W. GARETH JONES

OCHS, Peter (1752–1823)
Swiss Jacobin and leader of the Helvetic Republic

Ochs was born in 1752 at Nantes in France where his father was living as representative of the family banking firm. Although born into a leading bourgeois family of Basle and despite his living in Switzerland for the greater part of his life, he remained strongly, even intensely, francophile throughout his life. In 1769 he returned to Basle and in 1776 he qualified as a lawyer. After further study at Leyden to 1778 he returned to Basle where he soon began a rapid rise to public prominence. He became a senior judge in 1780, secretary to the council in 1782, a deputy to the Diet in 1786, chancellor in 1790, a member of the Grand Council in 1794 and in 1796 Uppergildmaster (*Oberstzunftmeister*).

Between 1776 and 1798 his views on politics and society became steadily more radical, a process which can be clearly traced in his voluminous correspondence. There was no 'road to Damascus' experience however, rather a continuing development of views already held. Thus, in his dissertation submitted at Basle in 1776, he argued for a doctrine of natural rights antecedent to society; his later development was essentially a working out of the implications of this view. By 1790, although still apparently a respectable bourgeois, Ochs had become a committed radical.

As well as being strongly francophile, Ochs soon revealed his radical political views and sympathies with the revolutionary régime in France and by 1792 was recognised throughout Switzerland as the leading French sympathiser in the country. In both 1792 and 1795 he played a major part in ensuring continued Swiss neutrality and in 1791 took part in an embassy to Paris. Here he made contact with leading French revolutionaries and with the circle of Swiss exiles settled in Paris. In 1796 he had covert discussions with members of the Directory on the possibilities of French intervention in support of a revolution in Switzerland. Following this he drew up a draft constitution for a 'single and indivisible' Helvetic Republic and in 1797 made contact with La Harpe (q.v.) and the circle of exiles. Following La Harpe's first memorandum to the Directory in September 1797 a secret meeting took place between Ochs, Reubell and Napoleon at Reubell's house on 8 December of that year. This led directly to an appeal to the Directory to intervene in Switzerland, drawn up jointly by Ochs and La Harpe and presented the following day. With the invasion of Switzerland he became in short order president of the national assembly of Basle and then, on 12 April 1798 at Aarau, proclaimed the establishment of the Helvetic Republic. At first the French commander, Brune, sought to divide the territory of the Confederation into three parts but after successful appeals by Ochs and La Harpe this was reversed in favour of Ochs' original design for a single,

unitary state. Ochs became president of
the Helvetic Senate and then, after the
intervention of Rapinat, on 16 June 1798
a member of the executive Directory.
Although by far the most able and admi-
nistratively competent member of the
Directory he became increasingly
estranged from his colleagues and particularly from La Harpe who brought about
his fall from office in June of 1799.

After his departure from the wider stage
Ochs returned to Basle, serving as a
representative in Paris in 1802–3 and, after
the Act of Mediation, as a member of the
Small and Great Councils of Basle and
latterly the Council of State. He was vice-
Burgomaster of Basle from 1813 to 1818.
He died at Basle in 1821. A man of
outstanding intellect and ability, he also
wrote several poetic and dramatic works
and an eight-volume history of Basle.
Besides his activities while leader of the
Helvetic Republic, Ochs was also responsible for composing the *Basler Landesord-
nung* in 1813, the first part of Basle's penal
code in 1821 and for the reorganisation of
his alma mater, the university of Basle, in
1813 and 1818. In comparison to La Harpe,
Ochs has been harshly treated by Swiss
historians, as an unpatriotic francophile
and as an opponent of the principle of
federation, the paramount doctrine of the
Swiss constitution. Yet the achievements
of the Republic which he created were
considerable, particularly when one bears
in mind the obstacles faced by the Swiss
Directors. In less than two years the reform
programme put through in France between
1789 and 1794 was also put into effect in
Switzerland and although the short-term
impact of some reforms such as the abolition of tithes was drastic, the old order
was fatally weakened and could never be
fully restored. Most notable were the
changes brought about in education,
reflecting the influence of Pestalozzi. The
political scheme of Ochs failed firstly,
because of the international situation and,
secondly, because of his disregard of, and
profound contempt for, the principle of
local autonomy which in Switzerland was
still a powerful political force. A more

thoroughgoing and radical revolutionary
than La Harpe or Usteri (q.v.), Ochs in
retrospect seems to fit clearly into the
category of 'Jacobin' rather than, as in
their case, 'liberal', in his commitment to
the idea of the single and indivisible nation,
his support for the use of state power as
a means of reform, and his desire for a
total and radical break with the past in all
areas of political life.

There is no conveniently available life
of Ochs. The best starting place is his
entry in the *Dictionnaire historique et
biographique de la Suisse* (Neuchâtel,
1924–29) and the book-length entry by
Rufer in the same work on the Helvetic
Republic. The main source for his life is
G. Steiner, *Korrespondenz des Peter Ochs*
(3 vols., Basle, 1927–37). For his time as
an active revolutionary, in addition to the
above, one should consult R.R. Palmer,
The age of the democratic revolution (2
vols., New Jersey, 1959–64) and the various
works of J. Godechot, in particular *La
grande nation* (Paris, 1956), *France and the
Atlantic revolution of the eighteenth century*
(London, 1965) and *Les commissaires aux
armées sur le directoire* (Paris, 1941). It
is also worth consulting H.B. Hill 'The
constitutions of continental Europe
1789–1813', *Journal of Modern History*
(1936), pp. 92–94, and E. Chapuisat *La
Suisse et la révolution française* (Geneva,
1945).

S. DAVIES

OELSNER, Konrad Engelbert (1764–1828)
*German republican reformer and
political writer*

Oelsner was born in Goldberg, Prussian
Silesia, on 13 May 1764. He attended the
Gymnasium in Frankfurt am Oder and the
University of Göttingen, before taking a
job as tutor and companion to a young
nobleman, whom he accompanied on frequent travels around Europe. The outbreak of the French Revolution found him
in Vienna, where he took leave of his
patron and moved to Paris. There he

joined the circle of German radicals who were congregating around the Abbé Sieyès (q.v.), a group that included Georg Forster (q.v.), Gustav von Schlabrendorf, and Karl Reinhard (q.v.). Oelsner was one of the first journalists to supply first-hand reports on the revolution to the German press; his essays in Johann von Archenholtz's (q.v.) *Minerva* (Hamburg) certainly contributed to the wide-spread sympathy with which educated Germans viewed the events of 1789. After war broke out in 1792 he began following French armies into the field, a most remarkable procedure at the time. His reports on Dumouriez's campaign in the Champagne district, published in the *Minerva*, are among the first examples of the war correspondent's craft.

During the reign of terror Oelsner fled Paris. He returned sometime after 1794 as the representative of the city of Frankfurt am Main and several surrounding principalities. Under the Directory Oelsner's connection with Sieyès once again put him close to the centre of affairs. He declined, however, to be drawn into direct service to the French régime, preferring to remain an observer and interpreter of events – a decision that represented a considerable financial sacrifice. After 1798 he supplied regular reports on France to J. F. Cotta's (q.v.) *Allegemeine Zeitung*, an important new venture in German journalism that Oelsner had helped to encourage when Cotta had been in Paris a few years before.

Politically Oelsner was squarely on the side of constitutional reform. His enthusiasm for France had always been an extension of his enthusiasm for representative institutions, and after Napoleon's seizure of power on 18 Brumaire (9 November 1799) his support for French conduct in Europe became less pronounced. During the Napoleonic period he was in some respects a man without a country. His reluctance to forsake France altogether forced him to forego a financial legacy that he badly needed, but which he could only receive if he returned home to live. Yet he was still viewed with suspicion by Prussian authorities, and during a trip to Silesia to visit his mother he was briefly arrested as a French agent.

After 1815 Oelsner returned to Germany to help promote the new German Federation, whose Diet would meet in Frankfurt. Oelsner believed that parliamentary institutions should be extensions of public opinion, and in 1817 he launched a new periodical called the *Bundeslade*, which was supposed to publicise the work of the Diet, and if possible aid its evolution into a true national assembly. But it soon became apparent that the Federation would be of scant political consequence, and after two issues the *Bundeslade* folded. By then, however, Oelsner had acquired a new circle of influential friends among the Prussian reformers, including the chancellor, Hardenberg, who gave him a post in the Prussian Legation in Paris. Oelsner remained in this position for seven years, during which the conservative drift of Prussian policy made him feel increasingly like 'the fifth wheel on a wagon.' He retired on a pension in 1825, and spent the last three years of his life in Paris, where he became involved in the utopian socialist movement inspired by the ideas of Henri de Saint-Simon. He died on 20 December 1828, at the age of sixty-four.

Oelsner's political life was given its shape by his personality, which all observers found exceptionally sensitive and unpretentious. Most of what he wrote appeared anonymously, less out of fear than out of modesty. His unwillingness to put himself forward clearly disposed him to remain an observer rather than an actor on the political stage – a distinction that admittedly loses some of its usefulness in the case of a political writer. Oelsner never satisfactorily solved the problem that his status as a political expatriot posed for him. A career like Karl Reinhard's, wholly in the service of a foreign government, was to Oelsner unacceptable. But there were not many German institutions that he could support unreservedly. He never shared the enthusiasm of the War of Liberation, probably because, having witnessed the 'nationalisation' of the French Revolution close up, he recognised that patriotism was only a part of politics, not a substitute for them. Like most of the Germans who went to Paris during the early 1790s, Oelsner had not gone to stay. Rather he hoped to prepare himself to spread the gospel of republicanism in his native land. After 1815 he believed that the opportunity to do so had finally presented itself. But in fact it did not, and there was nothing for him to do but to return to the city that had, against his wishes, become his true home.

Konrad Oelsner is known to posterity mainly through the reports of his friends and correspondents, especially Friedrich von Staegemann and Karl August von Varnhagen von Ense. Oelsner's correspondence with the first has been published by Dr Wilhelm Dorow (ed.), *Briefe des Königl. Preus. Legationsraths Karl E. Oelsner an den wirkl. Geheimen Rath Fr. Aug. von Staegemann aus den Jahren 1815–1827* (Leipzig, 1843); with the second by Ludmilla Assing (ed.), *Briefwechsel zwischen Varnhagen von Ense und Oelsner, nebst Briefen von Rahel* (Stuttgart, 1865). Most of what is known of Oelsner's life is in the editor's introductions to these volumes. For his early years in Paris there is *Briefe des nachmaligen Königlich Preussischen Legationsraths Karl Ernst Oelsner an den herzoglich Oldenburg Justizrath Gerhard Anton von Halem von Paris aus geschrieben in den Jahren 1790–92* (edited by Dr. Merzdorf, Berlin, 1858). The best study of his political career is K. Deinet, *Konrad Englebert Oelsner und die Französische Revolution* (Munich and Vienna, 1981). A volume of Oelsner's anonymous essays was published by his son, Dr Oelsner-Monmerque, entitled *Politische Denkwürdigkeiten* (Bremen, 1848).

DANIEL J. MORAN

OPIZ, Johann Ferdinand (1741–1812)
Czech enlightener

Opiz, the son of a secretary at the court of appeal in Prague, was born on 11 October 1741. He attended Jesuit schools and entered an order in 1757. From 1761 he studied philosophy in Olmütz, and was a private tutor for noble families. From 1767 he was in the service of Prince K.E. Füstenberg, with whom he remained, until 1773, in Wetzlar. Here he began to write poems and published a literary journal. He lived in Tschaslau from 1775 until the end of his life.

His extensive written legacy comprises several volumes of notes and correspondence, and his correspondents included Casanova, Lamberg, Mittrowsky and Cornova. He was a radical enlightened chronicler of his time, well versed in Enlightenment philosophy and an admirer of Rousseau. His initial admiration for the reforms of Joseph II and Leopold II later gave way to revolutionary ideas. First of all he supported constitutional monarchy, and then Jacobinism, although he never really understood the latter. He saw a danger to the Habsburg monarchy in the long revolutionary war. After contact with the popular movement he rejected his earlier thoughts on revolutionary upheaval. A reformer in his later years, he occupied himself with the dissemination of ideas and popular education. Through his letters he influenced a number of people who otherwise had no opportunity to educate themselves in current affairs. These people then propagated revolutionary ideas among the ordinary people around them, from whom Opiz, despite his sympathy for the French Revolution, kept his distance. He provided his correspondents with literature and urged them to pass it on.

Opiz' correspondence affords an insight into the otherwise unknown opinions of representatives of the most diverse social groups, and is an important source for the history of Bohemia and the French Revolution. By the standards of the French Jacobins, Opiz was clearly a moderate, but it is by comparison with his Czech contemporaries that he deserves to be considered a radical reformer.

His publications – e.g. *Beschreibung der Haupstadt Prag* (Prague, 1774); *Der Köcher. Ein Rezept für mein krankes Vaterland* (1782); *Die Bücherfreiheit* (Brno, 1794) – are insignificant. Further information on his life and work is to be found in J.F. Opiz, *Autobiographie* (ed. K. Kraus, Prague, 1909), and G. Casanova, *Briefwechsel mit J.F. Opiz* (Berlin, Vienna, 1922).

K. MEJDRICKA

ORCHOWSKI, Jan Alojzy (1767–1847)
Polish lawyer, politician, journalist and writer

Born in Łuck, Volhynia, to a poor noble-man's family, Orchowski was educated in Łuck, then became a barrister at the Crown Tribunal in Lublin where, in 1792, he composed some verses to celebrate the first anniversary of voting under the Consti-tution of May 3. He joined the conspiracy which planned the 1794 uprising. When, on 17 and 18 April 1794, Warsaw was captured by the insurgents, Orchowski was active in a radical club. He tried but failed to join the artillery because of poor sight. In June 1794 he became a member of the local insurgent authorities in Volhynia. In July he submitted to the Supreme National Council a project to grant land to those peasants who were taking part in the uprising, and to those who sent their sons to the army. He recommended that the landed property of traitors and exiles be given to peasants in return for compulsory military service. Orchowski's project did not find the approval of the Council, and though Kołłątaj (q.v.) intended to make use of it, the plan was never implemented. Some years later Kościuszko (q.v.) told Orchowski that he would have carried the project into effect if he had known of it.

On the defeat of the uprising Orchowski joined the clandestine City Club in Warsaw which had been founded by a moderate conspiratorial political group, the so-called Centralizacja Lwowska. In the club he came across a poor nobleman, a land-surveyor, Franciszek Gorzkowski, who was agitating among the peasants of Podlasie and preparing them for the next uprising. Orchowski was one of the founders of the Society of Polish Republicans, co-author of its programmatic proclamation, and in 1798–1801, was one of the five leaders of the Society. In 1799 he went to Paris on behalf of the Society in order to persuade Kościuszko to join the organisation, get in touch with the Directorate, and bring about some unity among the divided Polish émigrés. Orchowski obtained Kościuszko's accession, became for a time the General's secretary, but refused to put his name to a radical social pamphlet written by J. Pawlikowski and approved by Kościuszko entitled 'Whether the Poles can win their independence?' Orchowski did not want to act without consulting the leaders of the Society of Polish Republicans in Warsaw. After the pamphlet had been printed he considered its publication as a premature disclosure of the political plans of the Society. In 1800–02 he was active in the Polish Legions in Italy and the Danubian Legion where he devised plans for forcing the Legions' way to Turkey and, after reaching Podole, stirring up an uprising in Poland and proclaiming freedom for the peasants. He spent some years in France in an institution organised for dismissed Legion officers in Châlons-sur-Marne. He was publishing articles in French magazines at that time and reconciled himself with Kościuszko.

Orchowski came back to Poland in 1805 in answer to a call of his political friends who were then planning to instigate an uprising in Volhynia and Podole. Through the mediation of Horodyski (q.v.), he became a general secretary of the pro-visional government of the Duchy of War-saw, but as a Jacobin, lost his post after only a month (January 1807). He became an attorney and took part in a campaign which advocated legislation modelled on France, the abolition of serfdom, the gradual enfranchisement of the peasants and the development of industry. He published also some historical writings, a play, and was co-translator of C.C. Ruhière's *L'Histoire de l'anarchie de la Pologne*. He was rejected in the Diet elections of 1809, probably because he declared that he would put forward a proposal to abolish serfdom. He announced a similar project in 1810 when he was participating in an anti-Napoleonic conspiracy of the Polish Jacobins which aimed – with the knowledge of the Saxon minister of foreign affairs, Senfft von Pilsach – at an armed uprising. Also at this time, Orchowski, as an attorney, distinguished himself in political trials.

In 1813 Orchowski withdrew before the Russian army to Göttingen. Here, and later in Kassel, he published for the next few years works in German and French on Polish literature and history, then took up philosophy. During the uprising of 1830–31 he acted as an agent of the National Government in Germany where he helped to shape public opinion by his political speeches. Because of these activities he could not return to Poland after the uprising failed. In 1833 he moved to France, where he found shelter in an émigré's house in Châteauroux (Indre), and lived in poverty. In the last years of his life he published his memoirs in Polish émigré newspapers, where he revealed that his views had become conservative. He criticised the Constitution of May 3 and condemned the insurrection of 1794. He died on 27 March 1847 in Châteauroux.

Orchowski belonged to the first generation of radical Polish intelligentsia who firmly related ideals of independence with those of social reform. He was a person active in politics and a man of letters who – travelling around Europe with a case full of books – was one of the first writers who was engaged in politics, the type of literary figure who became popular in the history of Poland in the nineteenth century.

There is no biography of Orchowski but details of his life and activities can be found in M. Handelsman, *Rozwój naredowości nowoczesnej* (The growth of modern nationality) (Warsaw, 1924; repr. 1973); S. Askenazy, *Napoléon et la Pologne* (Brussels, 1925), vol. 3; B. Leśnodorski, *Les Jacobins polonais* (Paris, 1965); and B. Leśnodorski, 'Les Jacobins polonais (1794)', *Annales historiques de la Révolution française*, XXXVI (1964), pp. 329–47.

LUKASZ KĄDZIELA

PACHE, Jean Nicolas (1746–1823)
French revolutionary, mayor of Paris

Jean Nicolas Pache was born on 5 May 1746 at Verdun to Swiss parents who worked as *concierges* at the hôtel of Marshal de Castries. De Castries took a liking to Jean Nicolas, allowed him to tutor his own children, and later helped Pache to secure his first administrative post, secretary to the ministry of marine. Pache subsequently held positions as a naval intendant in Toulon, as director of naval provisions, and as comptroller of the king's household. Before the convening of the Estates-General in 1789, Pache took his family to Switzerland, returning to France only in 1792 after the death of his wife.

Upon his return to Paris Pache met Jean Marie Roland, who gave him a post in the ministry of the interior. The Rolands in turn introduced him to Servan, Minister of War, who also found work for Pache during this period. Pache lost these posts when the Girondin ministers were dismissed from office in June 1792. After 10 August Pache returned to favour, went on a brief mission to Toulon, won election as a *suppléant* to the National Convention from the Paris section Luxembourg, and in October was named Minister of War. In the next months Pache's views diverged from those of the Girondins. He quarrelled with Dumouriez over questions of military supply and split with Roland, his former patron. When Roland fell from office in January 1793, the Girondin deputies secured the dismissal of Pache from the war ministry. Pache was now embraced by the Montagnards, who supported him as candidate for mayor of Paris in February.

Pache served as mayor of Paris until April 1794, and it was in this period that his political radicalism emerged. Although hampered somewhat in his actions by the independent authority of the Paris sections, and the National Convention's suspicion of both the sections and the Paris Commune, Pache did succeed in using his office to exert influence on national affairs. He has been accused of denying troops and supplies to Dumouriez and other generals believed to be sympathetic to the Girondins during the important campaigns of late winter 1793. In early March Pache supported the creation of the Revolutionary Tribunal, and later joined with Chaumette (q.v.) in calling for a special revolutionary tax. Although he did not lead the 31 May insurrection that brought the proscription of twenty-nine Girondin deputies from the Convention, Pache did support the uprising. Late in June, when federalist rebels in Caen made plans to cut off grain supplies to the capital, Pache wrote eloquently to the Caen district council of the dangers of anarchy and the duty of loyal republicans. His plea fell on deaf ears, but similar letters to Robert Lindet (q.v.), then on mission to Normandy, did help to secure special shipments from Le Havre that averted a serious grain shortage in Paris in the summer of 1793.

Since Hébert (q.v.) had been substitute *procureur* in Paris during his tenure as mayor, Pache himself came under accusation when the Hébertists were tried in March 1794. Robespierre (q.v.) may have taken a personal role in protecting Pache. The former archivist of the Revolutionary Tribunal later testified that the president of the Tribunal had excluded witnesses ready to testify against Pache and others and had also removed written denunciations from the files. Pache was finally arrested in May 1794, but did not come to trial for a year. Never convicted, he finally gained release by the general amnesty of 26 October 1795. Pache was implicated under the Directory in the Babeuf (q.v.) conspiracy, though never tried, and responded to these charges with a pamphlet entitled *Sur les factions et les partis*. Shortly thereafter he retired to his estate near Charleville and remained there in relative obscurity until his death on 18 November 1823.

Pache's reputation as a political radical rests chiefly on his actions while mayor of Prais, particularly his support for the Revolutionary Tribunal, his role in the insurrection of 31 May, and his contribution in the summer of 1793 to the struggle against the federalist rebels in

Normandy. Pache never abandoned the Jacobin political principles he had espoused while mayor of Paris, as demonstrated by his later involvement in the Conspiracy of Equals with Babeuf.

Further biographical details can be found in: L. Perquin (ed.), *Mémoires sur Pache* (Charleville, 1900); and A. Sée, *Le procès Pache* (Paris, 1911). See also, Norman Hampson, *The life and opinions of Maximilien Robespierre* (London, 1974).

PAUL R. HANSON

PAGANO, Francesco Mario (1748–1799)
Italian philosopher, jurisconsult, writer, and politician

Born in Brienza (Lucania) into an educated and established family which had produced both functionaries and priests, Pagano studied under the tutelage of his priest-uncle at Naples, and had Giovanni Spena, a disciple of Giambattista Vico, as his first teacher of Greek and Latin grammar. At the University of Naples he was influenced by the old but still dynamic Antonio Genovesi, who held the first chair of political economy there. Genovesi inspired Pagano's patriotism as well as his earliest philosophical work, *Disegno del sistema della scienza degli ufizi* published in 1769. A year earlier Pagano had published his first juridical work *Politicum universae Romanorum nomothesiae examen* in which he tied juridical problems to philosophical and political ones.

In 1769 Pagano sought a university post by public competition but was unsuccessful; in 1770, however, he was made a lecturer at the University of Naples. In 1775 he was assigned the chair of criminal jurisprudence as well. During the decade from 1770 to 1780 Pagano played an active part in the intellectual life of Naples, the most open, vibrant, and cosmopolitan in the whole of Italy. He continued to write on a broad range of topics. In the decade between 1782 and 1792 he wrote a number of dramas including *Gli esuli tebani* (1782) which extolled patriotism and condemned tyranny, and *Gerbino* (1787) and *Agamennone* (1787), which were inspired by the same sentiments. *Corradino* (1789) attacked papal interference in the affairs of the Kingdom of Naples and in 1792 he concluded his theatrical activity with the comedy *L'Emilia*. These works were bitterly attacked by the noted Neapolitan critic Pietro Napoli-Signorelli.

During these years Pagano also wrote on political and philosophical issues publishing his *Saggi politici* in 1783–1785. Following the example of Gaetano Filangieri he contributed to the renewal of penal studies and criminal legislation with the publication of his *Considerazioni sul processco criminale* (1787). The lectures he delivered from his chair of criminal law at the university were published posthumously under the title *Principii del Codice penale* (1803). In 1789 he was made public advocate of the Admiralty Tribunal and in 1794 named a justice of the same court.

After 1789 he was influenced by the events of the French Revolution and espoused increasingly liberal ideas, especially following the visit of the French fleet to Naples in 1792. In 1794 when a number of Neapolitan Jacobins were arrested, he undertook their defence. For this action, as well as his known liberal sentiments, he was denounced before the inquisitorial junta in 1795. He was deprived of his chair at the university and imprisoned in February 1796. Released in July 1798 he left for Rome and then Milan. He returned to Naples when the Parthenopean Republic was proclaimed in January 1799.

Pagano was actively involved in the provisional government of the Republic in Naples and introduced the legislation to confiscate the land and property of those who had fled to Sicily with Ferdinand I. He played a major part in the elaboration of the constitution of the Republic which he modelled upon the French constitution of 1793. Vincenzo Cuoco considered the project too French and not sufficiently Neapolitan and a drastic departure from the past of the people it was supposed to serve. When the Republic faced the sanfedist onslaught led by Cardinal Fabri-

zio Ruffo, Pagano took up arms to defend it. Following its collapse he was interned on the British ship the *Audax* before being turned over to the Neapolitans who condemned him to death. He was hanged with a number of other republicans on 29 October 1799.

In many ways the most influential work of Pagano is his *Saggi politici* (1783), whose principal theme is the origin and formation of societies as well as their progress and decadence. In it Pagano traces the entire evolution of human society and seeks to integrate the thought of Vico with some of the more contemporary conclusions. He maintained that the philosophical idea of order led to the notions of equality and justice. Pagano's equality differs somewhat from that of Rousseau with the first asserting that the latter based his claim on the social contract, and thus on property. If such were acknowledged, noted Pagano, then the non-possessors would be *ipso facto* excluded. The Neapolitan argued that before the formation of this or that society there existed the society of the human species, so that the idea of order had not only a historical but a natural validity.

The *Saggi politici* provoked both support and condemnation in Italy and abroad. The work was attacked on two planes: in the name of orthodox religion and by those who claimed that in attempting to integrate Vico's work with other enlightened thought, Pagano had misinterpreted the master. In response to the first criticism which accused Pagano of pantheism, naturalism, and impiety, the author responded that he had made his inquiries as a historian and philosopher and consequently theological condemnations were irrelevant. Concerning his interpretation of Vico, Pagano found his critics' observations off the mark. The polemic was prolonged.

Pagano's *Considerazioni sul processo criminale* (1787) established his Italian and European-wide reputation. In it he continued the work of Beccaria and Filangieri seeking to reform the penal code and render its application more progressive by deriving its basic principles from the laws of nature. He argued that a penal system based upon these common underlying principles would make possible a code that would be applicable to all nations and peoples. While he read the works of the French sensory school and encyclopedists, his philosophy was not simply a reflection of their thought. He was equally inspired by Genovesi and expressed the views of enlightened Neapolitans. He shared with this latter group the desire to see scientific findings applied to the civil order as well as their belief in the perfectibility of man.

There is little written about Pagano in English. For some basic information the interested reader might refer to Edmund E. Jacobitti, *Revolutionary Humanism and Historicism in Modern Italy* (New Haven, 1981); Emiliana P. Noether, *Seeds of Italian Nationalism* (New York, 1951); and Antonio Pace, *Benjamin Franklin and Italy* (Philadelphia, 1958). Articles on Pagano with good, though largely dated, Italian bibliographies are to be found in the *Enciclopedia Italiana* and the *Dizionario Storico della Letteratura Italiana*.

FRANK J. COPPA

PAULUS, Pieter (1754–1796)
Dutch lawyer and leader of the Patriot movement

The son of Joseph Paulus, mayor of Axel, Pieter Paulus spent a number of years at Utrecht University but did not register there as a student. At the age of nineteen, he wrote an influential work, *Over het nut der stadhouderlijke regering, aangetoond bij gelegenheid der geboorte van Willem Frederik, erfprins van Oranje* (Leiden 1772–3) in which he defended the position of the House of Orange but called upon the stadholder to undertake some long overdue political reforms. Soon afterwards, he moved to Leiden, taking a degree from the university in 1775. His dissertation, *Verklaring der Unie der Utrecht* (Utrecht 1775–7) was a lengthy treatise on the authority of the Union of Utrecht and it established him as a lawyer of some renown.

He set up his practice in The Hague and became solicitor for the poor-law board,

and in 1785, Admiral-Fiscal of the Maas. Dismissed from office in February 1788, Paulus returned to private practice but in 1793 wrote his most seminal work, the 'Treatise on Equality' (*Verhandeling over de vrage: In welken zin kunnen de Menschen worden Gelijk to Zyn*). This work put Paulus in the forefront of Patriot thinking and after the Batavian Revolution of 1795 he was seen as the natural leader for the movement in Holland. He became chairman of the 'Provisional Representatives of the People of Holland' in January 1795, a body which effectively usurped the powers of the States of Holland. In the same year, Paulus was one of four representatives chosen to negotiate a peace treaty with the French. Although the terms were extremely detrimental, the delegates had little room to negotiate given the overwhelming military advantage of the French, and the treaty came into force in May 1795.

In the following months, Paulus devoted a great deal of time to the formation of a National Assembly, organising equal electoral districts, and trying to ensure the participation of all the other provinces. At this stage, he had to work against federalist tendencies in areas which were unwilling even to participate in such a gathering, let alone abrogate any rights to it. The first meeting of the National Assembly took place on 1 March 1796 where Paulus, having been returned as a representative for The Hague, was unanimously elected as chairman. Unfortunately, as a result of attending the opening ceremony of the Assembly, Paulus contracted a cold which rapidly developed into pneumonia. His death on 17 March was almost universally mourned.

Paulus was by no means an early convert to the Patriot movement. His defence of the House of Orange in 1772 was followed only a few years later by an assertion that the principles of government laid down by the Union of Utrecht took precedence over standholderian authority. His 'Treatise on Equality' (1793) was a contribution to the debate on the rights of man and provoked severe criticisms from the orthodox *predi-*

kanten but its significance lay in Paulus's statement of a Christian base and justification for the doctrine of equality. Sometimes termed 'Jacobinism in Christian dress', this type of Christian democracy drew together the political ideals of the Patriot movement with the Christian rhetoric and popular religion common to broad sections of the Dutch population. Although a profoundly held belief, Paulus was also aware that this type of appeal would draw a much wider support from the Dutch urban population than the French version which involved the rejection of Church and Christian values.

This treatise, which gave a Christian authority to the creation of equality and the overthrow of governments based on aristocracy or privilege, effectively made Paulus the leader of the Dutch democrats. His espousal of Christian values and the idea of revolution in the cause of democracy gave him a large following and made him an acceptable candidate for all sections of Patriot opinion. This, combined with his intellectual stature and an ability to mediate between the various factions of the movement, virtually ensured his preeminence in the foundation of the National Assembly and the Batavian Republic before his untimely demise at the age of forty-two.

For the development of Paulus's political opinions, see his *Het Nut der Stadhouderlijke Regering* (Alkmaar, 1772–73); *Verklaring der Unie der Utrecht* (4 vols., Utrecht, 1775–77); and *Verhandeling over de Vrage: In welken zin kunnen de Menschen Gezegd worden Gelijk te Zijn? en welke zin de Regten en Pligten, die Daaruit Voordvloein?* (Haarlem, 1793). Details on his life and activities can be found in: S. Schama, *Patriots and Liberators* (New York, 1977); P.H. Surinagar, *Biographische Aanteekeningen betreffende Mr. Pieter Paulus* (Leiden, 1879); P. Geyl, *La Révolution Batave 1783–98* (trans. J. Godard, Paris, 1971); and I.L. Leeb, *The Ideological Origins of the Batavian Revolution. History and Politics in the Dutch Republic 1747–1800* (The Hague, 1973).

BOB MOORE

PÉTION DE VILLENEUVE, Jerome (1756–1794)

French revolutionary, mayor of Paris, and president of the National Convention

Pétion was born in Chartres (Eure-et-Loir). He was destined by his father, himself a lawyer, for a career at the bar, and on the eve of the revolution he was sub-delegate of the intendant of Orléans at Chartres. He was elected to represent the Third at the Estates-General, and when that body became the National Assembly he consistently voted with the extreme left, supporting the unicameral legislature, opposing the franchise restrictions and Martial Law decree, and the granting of a suspensive veto to the king. When the royal family made their abortive flight to Varennes, Pétion was nominated by the Assembly to accompany them, with Barnave, back to Paris, in the process becoming infatuated with the king's sister, Mlle Elisabeth. His popularity survived the next two months, however, and when he retired from the Constituent Assembly he succeeded Jean Sylvain Bailly (q.v.) as the second mayor of Paris. He still held this position when the demonstrators invaded the king's palace, the Tuileries, on 20 June 1792, incurring the wrath of the royalists for refusing to take action against the invaders. La Fayette, enraged by the news, rushed back from the frontier to Paris, on which Pétion doubled all security regulations around the Assembly and the Jacobin Club. For this he was suspended from his functions along with Manuel (q.v.), *procureur* of the Commune, by the directory of the Department and the king gave his sanction to this decree. The Assembly, however, reversed this decision with cries of 'Vive Pétion!' and the king had to sanction the new decree. A couple of days later the king had to suffer the further humiliation of standing beside Pétion at the Bastille Day celebrations on the Champ de Mars while the crowd gave Pétion a tremendous ovation. On 3 August Pétion headed a delegation from the Sections to the Legislative Assembly calling for the fall of the monarchy. When the insurrection broke out that ended in the violent overthrow of the monarchy, Pétion was the target of some royalists seeking a hostage to hold against the safety of the king. During the September massacres, Pétion, still mayor of Paris, was powerless to prevent them and, like so many other individuals in positions of authority at this time, neither praised nor denounced them.

Pétion did not seek the support of the people of Paris in the election for the National Convention, and was elected instead by his home district of Eure-et-Loire. He was first president of the Convention, presided at the Jacobins from 24 September to 8 October, but from then on he became embroiled in the faction disputes, siding with his friend Buzot against Robespierre (q.v.). Nevertheless, on 4 October 1792 he was overwhelmingly re-elected mayor of Paris without seeking the post, but declined in any case, without, however, expressing any illwill against the people of Paris. Indeed, while he became associated with the Girondins, he remained a neutral (unlike Buzot, for example) and never went back on his revolutionary principles. At the king's trial he voted for the appeal to the people, for the king's death, and for his reprieve. He denounced Marat (q.v.) in the Convention, but be abstained from the vote on his arrest. After the coup of 31 May–2 June 1793 Pétion's arrest was ordered on 9 June, whereupon he fled with Guadet to Caen. From there the fugitives passed through Brittany to the Gironde, where, contrary to their expectations, they encountered a hostile reception. Hunted and friendless Pétion committed suicide, with Buzot, and their bodies when found were half eaten by wolves.

Pétion had reached the height of his fame at the close of the Constituent Assembly in September 1791 when, with Robespierre and Buzot, he shared the adulation of the people for the way in which he had defended their rights. Thereafter, his association with the Girondins led to a decline in his reputation as a radical. Pétion represents the classical case of a man who was carried by the tide of events to a position that his talents did not merit, and who suffered in consequence.

For further information on Pétion's life, see his *Mémoires inédites* (Paris, 1866), and the entry in A. Kuscinski, *Dictionnaire des conventionnels* (Paris, 1917).

BILL MURRAY

PHILIPPEAUX, Pierre (1754–1794)
French revolutionary legislator, member of the National Convention

Philippeaux was born on 9 November 1754 at Ferrières in the Ile-de-France, the son of Pierre Philippeaux, a leather-dresser, and Marie Magdeleine Belière. Trained as a lawyer, Philippeaux held the position of *avocat* before the *présidial* court of Le Mans before 1789.

Philippeaux's activities in the early years of the revolution are unknown, but in 1792 he gained election to the National Convention from the department of the Sarthe. He took an active part in debates before the Convention and voted for the death of Louis XVI. It was after the proscription of the Girondin deputies, however, that Philippeaux played his most prominent role in revolutionary politics.

During the summer of 1793 the Committee of Public Safety sent Philippeaux to the Vendée to reorganise local administration. While there he introduced the successful strategy of mobile columns in combatting the Vendée rebels. Philippeaux clashed, however, with the Saumur army staff and because of this was recalled to Paris in the autumn of 1793, a decision for which he apparently harboured resentment against the Committee of Public Safety. In November 1793 Philippeaux called in the National Convention for an investigation into the wealth of all deputies, a proposal that the deputies seriously discussed but ultimately defeated. In December he denounced the Hébertists and published a pamphlet detailing his version of the September disasters in the Vendée, placing particular blame on the sans-culotte generals Ronsin and Rossignol, political allies of Hébert (q.v.). Philippeaux accused them of negligence, ignorance, and treason and charged the government (particularly Bouchotte, Minister of War) with incompetence and irresponsibility for failing to take action against them. In late December 1793 Philippeaux made his charges before the Paris Jacobin Club, which formed a committee to investigate them. On 5 January that committee presented its report, censuring Philippeaux for stirring up trouble against loyal patriots and expelling him from the club.

Philippeaux thus cast his lot with the critics of the revolutionary government in the winter of 1793–94. Although not particularly close to Danton (q.v.), he was tarred with the brush of political moderation and labelled a vocal troublemaker. Arrested along with Danton, Desmoulins (q.v.), Hérault-Séchelles (q.v.), and Lacroix and quickly convicted as a traitor, Pierre Philippeaux died on the guillotine on 5 April 1794. After 9 Thermidor another erstwhile critic of the Committee of Public Safety, Merlin de Thionville (q.v.), did much to rehabilitate Philippeaux's reputation.

Philippeaux's position among the radicals of the revolution is somewhat tenuous, then, but arguably his break with the Committee of Public Safety and the Jacobins grew more out of personal disappointment, perhaps bitterness, than out of principled disenchantment with the politics of the revolutionary government. His main grievance with the government obviously grew out of the handling of the campaign against the Vendée, a military more than political matter, although certainly with political ramifications. Philippeaux's arrest along with Danton and the others, in any case, would seem to have owed more to convenience than anything else, and his early contribution to the struggle against the Vendée may be enough to warrant a reputation as a radical.

There is no biography of Philippeaux, but see Norman Hampson, *The life and opinions of Maximilien Robespierre* (London, 1974); and Wilfred B. Kerr, *The Reign of Terror, 1793–94* (Toronto, 1927).

PAUL R. HANSON

PIMENTEL, Eleonora de Fonseca (1752–1799)
Italian poet, journalist and revolutionary

Born of Portuguese parents in Rome, Pimentel moved to Naples with her family in 1760 when her father entered the service of the Bourbon monarchy. Given the opportunity to study she mastered Greek and Latin. At an early age she revealed a talent for poetry, excelling at improvisation, a skill much appreciated in the eighteenth century. With recognition came acceptance by the intellectual élite of Naples and favour with the Neapolitan monarchs. Called the 'queen of the muses' or the 'muse of the Tagus' (a reference to her Portuguese ancestry), she became a member of the major academics of Italy and of one of the many masonic lodges then active in Naples. Correspondence with Metastasio, court poet at Vienna, enhanced her prestige abroad. Neither marriage in 1777, nor motherhood distracted her from her studies, as she turned to mathematics and the natural sciences. Her interest in economics produced an essay proposing the establishment of a national bank in Naples. She also wrote defending the rights of the Neapolitan kingdom against the continuing feudal encroachments of the Church. In 1790 King Ferdinand rewarded her with a commendation and pension.

Nine years later this same king ordered her execution. It was events in France that changed Pimentel from a supporter of the monarchy into a republican revolutionary. In Naples, the moderate programme of reforms which had marked the royal administration since the reign of Charles III came to an abrupt halt. Ferdinand and his queen, Maria Carolina, sister of France's Marie Antoinette, adopted repressive reactionary policies. Clerical influence increased at court and throughout the kingdom. As a result Neapolitan intellectuals turned against the monarchy. The masonic lodges became centres of republican agitation. How and when Pimentel joined the anti-monarchical agitation is not known, but in 1794 her name appeared among those suspected of Jacobin sympathies. She was not arrested, however, until October 1798, when Naples was at war with the French. Two months later the court precipitously left the city for refuge in Sicily under the protection of the British navy. With French forces under General Championnet at the gates of the city, Pimentel and other political prisoners were released from jail. They organised a Central Committee and on 22 January 1799 proclaimed the Neapolitan, or Parthenopean, republic, 'one and indivisible'. Pimentel recited her 'Hymn to Liberty'. Quickly the republicans took over the responsibilities of government.

Pimentel, one of the few women to have participated prominently in the republic's founding, became editor of the Jacobin paper, *Monitore napolitano*. She seems also to have been the paper's sole contributor, for no other name was ever listed as collaborator. The first issue appeared on 2 February 1799. Thereafter, it came out regularly twice a week until the Republic's demise. The last issue is dated 8 June 1799, as Cardinal Ruffo's Sanfedisti (Army of the Holy Faith) advanced victoriously from the south and the French left the city. The pages of the *Monitore* reflect the dreams, achievements, and failures of the Republic. Nothing escaped Pimentel's attention. In the *Monitore* she exposed the Republic's shortcomings, proposed measures for better government, and did not spare French policies in Naples. Read by the queen in Sicily, its republicanism sealed Pimentel's fate. In the royal mind she became identified with the Jacobin republic, guilty like all its leaders of treason and rebellion and condemned to death.

In June 1799, abandoned by the French and attacked by the Neapolitan plebs who had never accepted the republic, the republican leaders surrendered to Cardinal Ruffo. He promised them safe conduct to France in return for their signed oath promising never to return to Naples. Meanwhile they were imprisoned. Pimentel was among those who chose exile in France. The arrival of Admiral Nelson in Naples changed the situation. Ruffo's promises were countermanded on orders of the king and queen. About 1500 Jacobins had opted to go to France, but only some 500 were actually allowed to do so. The rest remained in jail, to be brought before kangaroo courts and sentenced either to death or to long prison-terms. Pimentel was among those singled out for execution. Condemned to death on 17 August 1799, she was executed three days later.

The *Monitore napolitano* remains witness to Pimentel's republican faith. Among the leaders of the Parthenopean Republic she was one of the first to identify the failure to win over the Neapolitan masses as a major weakness of the republic. A true exponent of the eighteenth-century faith in progress and rationality, she supported revolution as a viable alternative to a discredited monarchy and paid with her life.

Pimentel's writings can be read in *Il Monitore napoletano, 1799* (ed. Mario Battaglia, Naples, 1974). See also, Benedetto Croce, 'Eleonora de Fonseca Pimentel e il *Monitore napoletano*', *La rivoluzione napoletana del 1799. Biografie, racconti, ricerche* (3rd rev. ed., Bari, 1912); and B. Croce, *History of the Kingdom of Naples* (trans. Frances Frenaye, Chicago, 1970).

EMILIANA P. NOETHER

PNIN, Ivan Petrovich (1773–1805)
Poet, publicist, social critic, and leading Russian enlightener

Pnin was the illegitimate son of Fieldmarshal Prince N.V. Repnin, from whose surname he inherited the last two-thirds. He was born either in Germany or Holland where his parents were temporarily resident until their return to Russia in 1774. Educated at the Free Noble Boarding School attached to Moscow University from 1782 to 1787, followed by two years in Petersburg at the Artillery-Engineering Academy for Noble Cadets, Pnin entered military service in 1789 and resigned his commission seven years later, aged twenty-three.

In 1797 he commenced publication of the *St Petersburg Journal* with the collaboration of A.F. Bestuzhev. It aimed at promoting the ideals of the European Enlightenment during the bleak, though mercifully brief reign of Tsar Paul I. Pnin's association with the journal made him a well-known figure in the capital's intellectual and literary circles.

On the popularly-acclaimed accession of Alexander I in 1801, Pnin entered government service, first in the newly-established State Council and then (from 1802) in the Ministry of Public Enlightenment. Illness resulting from tuberculosis brought about his early retirement in 1805 and, a few weeks later, his premature death at the age of thirty-three.

In his poems and essays, Pnin challenged the accepted values of the Russian nobility and promoted a concept of civic duty and moral responsibility akin to that of his more famous acquaintance, Alexander Radishchev (q.v.). The two met in 1801, shortly before Radishchev's death, and Pnin was strongly influenced by him. Pnin became a member of the 'progressive' Free Society of Lovers of Literature, Sciences and Arts, formed at the start of Alexander's reign to advance the cause of enlightenment in Russia.

The political treatise for which Pnin is chiefly remembered was entitled *On Enlightenment in Russia*. In it, Pnin identified education as the key to the gradual, peaceful transformation of Russian society. Although it was moderate and reasoned in tone, it was suppressed shortly after its publication in 1804. It urged social and political reform and denounced serfdom but was broadly in favour of retaining the existing hierarchical social structures, with autocracy giving way to constitutional monarchy. Pnin had every confidence that an 'enlightened ruler', as Alexander I was widely supposed to be, would himself initiate reform. He acknowledged the 'div-

ine right of property', and saw in it a key to social stability, arguing that once peasants themselves became property-owners they would have an individual stake in the maintenance of law and order. The emancipation of the serfs, in Pnin's view, was in any case a logical consequence of the enlightenment in Russia. Influenced by Montesquieu and inspired by England's example, he wished to see in Russia a well-ordered society based on the rule of law.

Pnin was a radical only to the extent that anyone who embraced enlightenment ideals in nineteenth-century Russia was by definition officially so-regarded. But in fact, like other Russian thinkers of his age who were alarmed by the excesses of the French Revolution and the rise of Napoleon, Pnin sought improvements in social justice which would not involve the disruption of political and social stability. In the tradition of the French philosophes, especially Jean Jacques Rousseau, he entertained the hope that education would transform social values and eliminate the notion of social inferiority by laying stress on the equality of respect and honour due to all men regardless of social status.

Pnin has often been seen as a link between Radishchev and the Decembrists because of his stance on serfdom, his insistence on the rule of law and his hostility to censorship. But while he admired Radishchev and shared many of his views, he was more moderate in his outlook and has been identified by some commentators with such conservative figures as Karamzin or even Shcherbatov. Nevertheless, his commitment to the enlightenment of Russia is not in doubt, while his fate as a publicist and social critic is illustrative of the problem of a constructive relationship being established between autocracy and intelligentsia in Russia.

There is a short biography of Pnin by S.C. Ramer in *Modern Encyclopedia of Russian and Soviet History*, vol. 28 (Gulf Breeze, 1982), pp. 138–39. See also, S.C. Ramer, 'The traditional and the modern in the writings of Ivan Pnin', *Slavic Review* 3 (1975), pp. 539–59; M. Raeff, 'Filling the gap between Radishchev and the Decembrists', *American Slavic Review* iii (1967), pp. 395–413; I.K. Luppol and V.N. Orlov (eds.), *Ivan Pnin. Sochineniia* (Moscow, 1934); V. Orlov, *Russkie prosvetiteli 1790–1800kh godov* (2nd edn, Moscow, 1953). The text of *On Enlightenment in Russia* in English translation may be found in M. Raeff (ed.), *Russian Intellectual History. An Anthology* (New Jersey, 1966).

P. J. O'MEARA

POGGI, Guiseppe (1761–1842)
Italian Jacobin and journalist

Poggi was born in Piozzano on 21 August 1761 into a noble family. His early studies in Piacenza were in mathematics. As a son of nobility he transferred to Rome to study theology at the *Accademia dei nobili ecclesiastici* where in 1785 he became a subdeacon. Influenced at the time by a Jansenist circle in Rome, he moved to Florence and Pistoia where he was the friend and guest of the Tuscan Jansenist, Scipione De'Ricci, and authored (under the name Colombano) the *Lettere Transpadane*, which were published in Pavia in 1790 in volume one of the *Biblioteca ecclesiastica*, the three volumes of *Delle emende sincere* (1789–91) and his *Saggio sulla libertà dell'uomo* (1789). Critical of the worldliness of the church, the writings were both anti-Jesuit and anti-curial. Returning to Piacenza, Poggi momentarily engaged in ancient epigraphy, an interest acquired in Rome, and planned a collection of inscriptions found in the excavations of Velleia.

As Jacobinism spread in Italy, Poggi became a devoted francophile, fled to Milano after announcing his support for the Cisalpine Republic, and appealed by manifesto for the unity of the Italian people. Influential as director of the *Società d'istruzione pubblica* and its journal, which was suppressed in 1797 when it became too independent of the control of the Directory, he became a collaborator in the official journal of the Cisalpine Republic, *L'estensore Cisalpino*, which also came to be viewed as too independent of French views. His evangelical Jacobin zeal found expression in the journal, *Il repubblicano evangelico*, which served as a propaganda instrument under a religious cloak for democratising the countryside. Granted an annulment of his vows by Pius VI in 1798, Poggi went to France with the collapse of the Republic. Shedding his Jacobinism, he expressed support for Napoleon in a poem, *Fastes de Napoleon*, and became a deputy for Taro in the emperor's legislative assembly from 1811 to 1814. He remained in France after the restoration and represented the ex-empress Marie-Louise, now Duchess of Parma, in her affairs with the French government, both as councillor and as chargé d'affaires. Returning to his earlier interest in ancient Roman history, Poggi devoted much of his later life in France to the study of Roman writers, especially Lucretius. He died in Reubelle-Montmorency on 19 February 1842.

Recent scholarship qualifies the Jansenist aspects of Poggi's career, perceiving these as a transitional phase through which he could express his discontent with curial despotism, aversion to Jesuitical aspects of the Roman church and the popular superstitions propagated by the priesthood. Expressing his evangelical views in *Il repubblicano evangelico*, he sought a return to the simple and democratic origins of Christianity where both charity and brotherhood existed. Perceiving as natural the right to worship by simple prayer individually and privately within one's household, Poggi also defended freedom of conscience and religious toleration. His later writings in *Il repubblicano evangelico* added the right to livelihood to the principles of liberty, equality and fraternity. Poggi's evangelicalism, which existed prior to his Jacobin stance, permeated his democratic political ideas on elections and progressive taxation.

In addition to Poggi's own writings cited above, there is an old study of him by Ettore Rota, *Giuseppe Poggi e la formazione psicologia del patriota moderno* (Piacenza, 1923). See also, Renzo De Felice, *Italia giacobina* (Napoli, 1965); and

Ernesto Codignola, *Illuministi, giansenisti e giacobini nell' Italia del settecento* (Firenze, 1947).

M. S. MILLER

POSSELT, Ernst Ludwig (1763–1804)
German reformer, political writer and editor

Posselt was born in Durlach, Baden, into a family whose background was divided between public service and trade. After preparation at the Gymnasium in Karlsruhe he attended the University of Göttingen, where he studied law and ancient history; he also studied briefly at the University of Strasbourg, and took his doctorate in law there in 1783. From 1784–96 he served as professor of history and rhetoric at the Gymnasium in Karlsruhe, and as private secretary to the ruling Margrave of Baden. During these years he published a number of works of legal and historical scholarship, including *Geschichte der deutschen Fürstenvereine* (1787), a two-volume *Geschichte der deutschen Stände*, and a popular series of *Taschenbücher für die neueste Geschichte*, which appeared irregularly until 1800. He also edited two quarterly reviews, the *Wissenschäftliche Magazine für Aufklärung* (1785–88) and the *Archiv für ältere und neuere, vorzüglich Deutsche Geschichte, Staatsklugheit und Erdkunde* (1790–92), which, despite their pedestrian titles, provided welcome vehicles for reform-minded writers in south-western Germany.

In 1795 Posselt became involved in a more significant project, as editor of a new monthly journal called *Europäische Annalen*, published by the Tübingen book dealer J.F. Cotta (q.v.). The *Annalen* quickly became one of the most respected and sophisticated pro-French periodicals in Germany, and provided Posselt with an ideal vehicle in which his analysis of the emerging geo-political conflict between the 'Republican South' [France] and the 'Barbarian North' [Russia] could be fully aired. Three years later, having given up his official post in return for a pension and an appointment as historian to the Badenese court, Posselt also became co-founder and editor of Cotta's daily newspaper, *Neueste Weltkunde*. In this more popular format, however, advanced political ideas were not welcome, and in September of 1798 protests by the Austrian and Russian governments led to Posselt's dismissal as editor. He remained a major contributor, however, and this newspaper (renamed *Allgemeine Zeitung* after his departure) and the *Annalen* were his principal publishing outlets from then on.

With the rise of Napoleon Posselt's enthusiasm for France began to decline. His feeling that the revolution had been betrayed gradually gave rise to general personal depression, which was substantially deepened by the trial for treason of the French General Jean Victor Moreau in 1804. Posselt had known and admired Moreau since Moreau's Swabian campaign of 1796, and feared that this personal connection might implicate him in the general's difficulties. In the end his anxiety seems to have become unbearable, and on 11 June 1804 he died of a fall from the third floor of his house in Heidelberg, apparently a suicide.

The basis of Posselt's political vocation can be found in the historical training he received at Göttingen, where he was exposed to an evolutionary, implicitly reformist view of the past that was most unusual at the time. Posselt's most important teacher was Johann Pütter, a scholar of German constitutional history. Pütter's emphasis on local tradition and on the organic development of common law is usually regarded as conservative in its implications. But his insistence that legal theory must take account of the reality of constant change, often from outside or from below, amounted to a radical rejection of contemporary legal practice. At the same time Pütter taught his students to believe that the future might well be qualitatively different from the past, a vision whose political implications could only be explored by younger men, like Posselt, whose task it would be to assimilate and interpret the French Revolution.

Almost equally significant for Posselt's later development was the example of August Schlözer, the leading figure among the Göttingen historians, and the most important political journalist of his generation. Schlözer was a distinguished practitioner of so-called 'historico-political' journalism, a characteristic enterprise of the late Enlightenment, which aimed to educate the public by means of periodicals that discussed recent events in the light of historical precedents and processes. Posselt's work as a journalist can fairly be described as an extension of this tradition into the revolutionary era, and into a new format, newspapers, to which, in practice, it was only imperfectly suited.

Like Schlözer, Posselt always viewed political action in educational terms. His chosen audience was the literate middle class, which seemed to him irresponsibly apolitical and complacent, not yet prepared to play a leading role, such as its counterpart had recently assumed in France. Posselt was not a revolutionary. He distrusted the masses, believing that they were too ignorant and too loyal to the aristocracy to be of any use politically. His enthusiasm for France was partly a romantic fascination with the power and drama of what he often described as 'the new Rome'. But unlike most Germans who found the ideas of 1789 sympathetic, Posselt did not lose heart when the revolution turned to war and terror to pursue its ends. His willingness to face (though not to advocate) the violence that had become part of the political discourse of his age set him well outside the mainstream of German political writing. It also made him suspect in the eyes of more purely literary intellectuals, many of whom declined to contribute to Cotta's newspaper because of Posselt's prominent role.

There are no works about Posselt in English. The only reliable biography is Emil Vierneisel, 'Ernst Ludwig Posselt, 1763–1804,' *Zeitschrift für die Geschichte des Oberrheins*, n.s. 49 (1936), pp. 243–71; 51 (1938), pp. 89–126; and 52 (1939), pp. 444–99. A selection of Posselt's letters to Cotta may be found in Maria Fehling (ed.),

Briefe an Cotta, vol. 1: Das Zeitalter Goethes und Napoleons, 1794–1815 (Stuttgart, 1925), pp. 399–435. There is an excellent analysis of Posselt's importance as a journalist in Ingeborg Salzbrunn, 'Studien zum deutschen historischen Zeitschriftenwesen von der Göttingen Aufklärung bus zur Herausgabe der "Historischen Zeitschrift" (1859)' (Ph.D. Dissertation, Munster, 1968), pp. 130–66.

DANIEL J. MORAN

PRANDSTETTER, Martin Joseph (1760–1798)
Austrian Jacobin

Prandstetter was born in Vienna on 5 October 1760. His background was upper middle class, and his education and early career similar to that of the other Vienna conspirators. His father, Johann Ferdinand Prandstetter was an assistant judge in a court of law. He attended the Jesuit school in Vienna and went on to study philosophy, law and, later, aesthetics at the university. He became a freemason in 1782 and entered the Viennese lodge 'Zum heiligen Joseph'. Later, however, he joined another lodge, 'Zur wahren Eintracht', of which Alois Blumauer (q.v.) was a member. Prandstetter published speeches, poems, epigrams and short stories, and freemasonry enabled him to meet other writers. After failing to obtain a teaching appointment at the university, Prandstetter became secretary to the city council in 1783, and later became a councillor himself.

Prandstetter's early adulthood was spent, therefore, in the Vienna of Joseph II and Leopold II, whose reforms – despite restrictions on freedom towards the end of Leopold's reign – inspired a generation of 'Josephinian' administrators. However, Leopold's death in 1792, and the accession of Francis I, spelled the end of hopes for further reform in the Habsburg Monarchy at a time when there were possibly more sympathisers with the ideas and events of the French Revolution in Vienna than in any other central European city other than Mainz. On the whole the former

'Josephinians' with their common background and common experience in the
Habsburg bureaucracy, were to form the
centre of opposition to the new emperor.
Martin Prandstetter was one of a number
of such administrators who were drawn
into the circle around Andreas Riedel
(q.v.). It was this association rather than
specific individual acts of treason with
which Prandstetter was charged following
the arrest of the leading Jacobin 'conspirators' in Vienna during the night of 24 July
1794. (His conduct had already attracted
the attention of his superiors when in 1793
he was taken to task by Hofrat Beer after
he had criticised the emperor in public.)
Along with almost all the other Viennese
Jacobins he was charged with aiding and
abetting a conspiracy (the charge of planning the revolt fell largely on Hebenstreit
(q.v.) and a handful of others); he was also
charged with complicity in other activities,
such as the publication of subversive texts,
and specifically with the communication of
an idea for a war-machine to the French
government. The trials of the Jacobins –
apart from Hebenstreit, who was court-
marshalled and hanged – dragged on for
a year. All received long prison sentences;
Prandstetter himself was sentenced to
thirty years but died in prison after only
three.

Prandstetter was one of the minor figures
in the Vienna Jacobin conspiracy.
Although he himself was a writer, it was
rather the fact that he was a holder
of state office than the composition of
seditious literature that was chiefly held
against him at his trial. Prandstetter, like
his friends, had been a loyal subject under
Joseph and Leopold. His later radicalism
stemmed from disillusionment with the
reactionary policies of the government of
Francis I. It extended no further than his
involvement with members of Riedel's
circle and his collaboration with their
activities.

Further details and material relating to
Prandstetter are to be found in Alfred
Körner, *Die Wiener Jakobiner* (Stuttgart,
1972); Helmut Reinalter (ed.), *Jakobiner
in Mitteleuropa* (Innsbruck, 1977). Prand-

stetter's role in the 'conspiracy' is discussed
in Ernst Wangermann, *From Joseph II to
the Jacobin Trials. Government Policy and
Public Opinion in the Habsburg Dominions
in the Period of the French Revolution*
(Oxford, 1959). Prandstetter is the only
one of the minor Austrian Jacobins of
whom an individual study has been undertaken: Franz Haderer, *Martin Joseph
Prandstätter (1760–1798) Magistratsrat,
Freimaurer, Dichter und Jakobiner* (Ph. D.,
Vienna, 1968 (unpublished manuscript)).
TIM KIRK

**PRIEUR DE LA CÔTE D'OR, Claude
Antoine (1763–1832)**
*French revolutionary, member of the
Legislative Assembly, the National
Convention, and the Committee of
Public Safety*

The son of a minor tax official, Prieur was
born in Auxonne in Burgundy on 22
December 1763. He was educated at a
private school which emphasised the sciences and in December 1781, after passing
an entrance examination, he was admitted
to the royal school of military engineering
at Mézières just before the Edict of 1781
would have barred lowly nobles of the
robe like himself from the officer corps.
Commissioned as a second lieutenant in
1784, Prieur was assigned to various posts
in eastern France but managed for the next
few years to spend most of his time
on leave, particularly in Dijon where he
participated in the intellectual life of that
city and conducted experiments under the
guidance of an eminent chemist, Guyton-
Morveau.

At the outbreak of the revolution Prieur
was on duty at Belfort and, while he
did not play a visible role in provincial
revolutionary politics, he did attempt to
convince fellow officers to support the new
constitution. In 1791 the department of the
Côte d'Or elected Prieur to the Legislative
Assembly. He was not a conspicuous
member of that body, preferring committee
work to parliamentary debate. When the
monarchy was overthrown on 10 August
1792 he was sent, along with other deputies

with military experience, to ensure support of the revolution in the Army of the Rhine.

In September, he was elected to the National Convention. During his first year as a deputy he was away from Paris much of the time inspecting the country's defences in the east and in Normandy and Brittany. On 14 August 1794 he joined the Committee of Public Safety and began the work of organising and mobilising the nation's production of arms and munitions. Recruiting patriotic scientists, many of whom were his friends, Prieur established a proving ground at Meudon where, among other devices, hot-air observation balloons were tested; he set up workshops for what he termed 'the revolutionary production of weapons and explosives,' according to methods taught in special courses; he worked at the improvement of mining and tanning; and he contributed to the development of Chappe's telegraph.

After the fall of Robespierre (q.v.) in Thermidor (27 July 1794) Prieur continued his specialised work until he was removed from the Committee on 6 October 1794. For the rest of his active career, both during the waning months of the Convention and for three years as a member of the Directory's Council of Five Hundred, Prieur devoted himself once more to committee work, especially on education and the metric system. Retiring from the army in 1801 at an insultingly low rank, he established a wallpaper manufactory in Paris and was repeatedly rebuffed by Napoleon's administration when he applied for military or bureaucratic positions and petitioned to be admitted to the Legion of Honour. He spent his last years making wallpaper and conducting valueless scientific experiments. He died in his native Burgundy at Dijon, 11 August 1832.

In one taxonomy of the 'great' Committee of Public Safety Prieur appears as one of the 'experts', that is, as a military technocrat and not a political tactician, influential orator or radical visionary. This is both correct and misleading. Prieur was not eloquent; he did not intervene in parliamentary debate; he was probably not even a member of the Jacobin Club.

But there can be no doubt either of his contribution or his commitment to the Jacobins' attempt to establish the radically egalitarian, democratic republic envisioned by more articulate revolutionaries with oratorical and literary gifts such as Robespierre. In the first place, Prieur's indefatigable labours as a military expert with scientific training and connections with French scientists were essential to the Convention's defeat of its enemies within France and at the frontiers. Secondly, from the earliest days of the revolution Prieur referred to himself as a 'democrat', and consistently voted with the left. Moreover, in his own special domain he proved himself not merely an expert but a radical ideologue. From 1791 he concerned himself both with improving the effectiveness and supply of French armaments and with the radical 'regeneration' of the military, that part of French society in which, he wrote, the 'vices of the Ancien Régime were most profoundly rooted'. He insisted that candidates for military schools prove their 'knowledge of the Constitution' as well as their competence. He was one of the founders of the short-lived 'School of Mars', a radical if ill-conceived training encampment at Paris designed to turn young Frenchmen into heroic soldiers in the Spartan mould and paragons of 'Roman' republican virtue.

After Thermidor Prieur denounced Robespierre as a tyrant. As the machinery of the 'Revolutionary Government' was dismantled, he managed to escape the vengeance of the Thermidorian reaction. In the weeks before Thermidor, however, he had been one of the most active of the members of the Committee. Along with his more 'political' colleagues on the Committee he was thus responsible for both its achievements and excesses.

Prieur's own published writings were on scientific subjects. The standard biography is G. Bouchard, *Prieur de la Côte d'Or, Un organisateur de la victoire* (Paris, 1946), but see the portrait in R.R. Palmer, *Twelve Who Ruled: The Year of*

Terror in the French Revolution (Princeton, NJ, 1941; repr. 1969).

R. BIENVENU

PRIEUR DE LA MARNE, Pierre Louis (1756–1827)

French revolutionary legislator, terrorist and member of the Constituent Assembly, the National Convention and the Committee of Public Safety

Pierre Louis Prieur was born on 1 August 1756 at Sommesous, in Champagne, the son of L.J. Prieur, a local court clerk. Trained as a lawyer, Prieur became an *avocat* before the parlement of Paris and subsequently practised law in Châlons-sur-Marne. He gained election to the Estates General as a delegate of the Third Estate on 24 March 1789, and played a prominent, often leading, role in debates on key issues. Prieur emerged as one of the more radical members of the Constituent Assembly, supporting administrative and judicial reforms, founding the *comité de mendicité*, urging the nationalisation of church lands, and advocating harsh reprisals against émigrés.

Prevented by law from standing for re-election to the Legislative Assembly, Prieur took up a post in local administration at Châlons-sur-Marne and contributed to preparations for local defence before the battle of Valmy in September 1792. That same month he won election to the National Convention from the department of the Marne and became known as Prieur de la Marne, to distinguish him from his colleague Prieur de la Côte-d'Or (q.v.). In the Convention Prieur joined actively in the debate during Louis XVI's trial, voting ultimately for death without reprieve, was in the forefront of opposition to the Girondin deputies, and played a role in the creation of the Revolutionary Tribunal. From the spring of 1793 he spent more time on mission to the departments than in Paris, despite his membership on the Committee of Public Safety from July 1793 until February 1795. During the summer months of 1793 Prieur devoted his efforts to the organisation and

financing of the army, first in Normandy and then in the north-east. In September the Committee sent him to Brest with Jeanbon Saint-André (q.v.) to reorganise the Atlantic fleet. Prieur's revolutionary fervour was ill-suited to that task, however, and he soon travelled south to Vannes, where he spent the remainder of the year organising armies to combat the Vendéan rebels. During this period he formed a Republican Youth group for boys between nine and sixteen years of age, and established the *Commission militaire Bignon*, which went on to sentence more people to death (2,905) than any other revolutionary tribunal in France. Despite his association with that tribunal, over which he did not in fact preside, Prieur was moderate in his exercise of revolutionary justice. Prieur turned his attention in early 1794 to the purging and reorganisation of local administrations in Morbihan and the Loire-Inférieure.

Prieur played little role in the factional struggles of the summer of 1794 or the overthrow of Robespierre (q.v.). Eventually denounced as a terrorist himself, and arrested in May 1795 for his role in the Germinal uprising, Prieur escaped from prison and went into hiding until the general amnesty of October 1795. He withdrew from political life, thereafter earning a modest living as a lawyer in Paris. Exiled as a regicide in 1816, he lived in poverty in Brussels until his death on 30 May 1827.

Prieur's radicalism emerges clearly and consistently throughout his revolutionary career. From his support of the nationalisation of church lands, to his role in creating the *comités de mendicité*, to the founding of the Republican Youth groups in Brittany, one sees a man committed to the cause of the common people. Prieur's fervour in the Vendée and Brittany reveals a man devoted to the principles of the radical revolution.

Prieur's role in the Committee of Public Safety is discussed in R.R. Palmer, *Twelve who ruled* (Princeton, NJ, 1941), and his activities as a representative on mission in P. Bliard, *Le Conventionnel Prieur de la*

Marne en mission dans l'Ouest (Paris, 1906).

PAUL R. HANSON

RADISHCHEV, Alexander Nikolayevich (1749–1802)
Russian enlightener

Born in Moscow, the son of a wealthy nobleman, Radishchev spent his childhood on the family estate in Saratov province before being sent in 1756 to be educated at the newly-established Moscow University Gymnasium. From 1763 he served an apprenticeship in the St Petersburg Court as a member of the exclusive Corps des Pages. When in 1766 Catherine the Great decided to train a future administrative élite by sending outstanding young Russians to the University of Leipzig to study jurisprudence and liberal arts, Radishchev was one of the dozen chosen. During his five years in Leipzig Radishchev was greatly influenced by the party's senior student Ushakov whose personal example in maintaining individual dignity in the face of the bullying of the group's overseer, Major Bokum, was recalled in his *Zhitiye Fedora Vasil'yevicha Ushakova* (Life of Fyodor Vasil'yevich Ushakov) (1789), the first intimate biography to be published in Russia. Ushakov's resistance to the petty despotism and cruelty of Major Bokum was stiffened by the lessons learnt at Leipzig. In their university classes, at the feet of Platner and Gellert, the Russian students were exposed to the moral concerns and benign deism of German idealism, while their extracurricular reading made them aware of the materialism and atheism of French philosophes such as Helvetius, D'Holbach and La Mettrie. Radishchev came to realise that literature's role was the moral education of man.

On his return to Russia he began his literary career with his Rousseauist *Dnevnik odnoy nedeli* (Diary of One Week) (1773) and the free and annotated translation of Mably's second, 1766, edition of *Observations sur les Grecs* which in its examination of state organisation idealised Sparta under Lycurgus and the rule of law. At the age of twenty-three Radishchev, opposed to despotism on psychological and moral grounds, had taken a political stand for the separation of powers and their limitation. While translating Mably, Radishchev was a close observer of the practice of Russian politics. From 1771 he served at the centre of the Imperial administration as a protocolist to the Senate's First Department. In 1773 he transferred to the staff of General-in-Chief Yakov Bryus, commander of the Finland Division, as Ober-auditor to advise him on questions of law in military courts with their power to dispense ferocious justice. Radishchev resigned briefly from military and civil service on his marriage in 1775 to return in 1777 to a more congenial appointment in the College of Commerce where he assumed judicial and administrative functions and won the powerful patronage of Alexander Vorontsov, the department's director. He remained here for a decade, becoming in 1780 deputy to the director of the St Petersburg Customs. He enjoyed the capital's society, was member of a masonic lodge and of the 'Society of Friends of Literature'.

In 1788 he had completed *Puteshestviye iz Peterburga v Moskvu* (A Journey from St Petersburg to Moscow), the work which ensured his subsequent fame but led to his downfall. Not being able to find a publisher despite the approval of the censor, Radishchev had to print the work privately at his house and the *Journey* did not appear on sale until May 1790. Meanwhile the French Revolution had changed the political climate. Catherine II saw the book as 'infected by and full of the French madness' and considered that it endeavoured to 'stir up in the people indignation against their superiors and against the government'. Radishchev was immediately arrested and interrogated: the death sentence of the Criminal Court was confirmed by the Senate in August 1790 but commuted to ten years banishment to Ilimsk in Siberia. The rigours of exile were mitigated by Vorontsov's kindnesses in favour of his protégé, who was able to write for his patron papers on Siberia and the China

Trade as well as composing the first philosophical treatise by a Russian *O cheloveke, yego smertnosti i bessmertii* (On Man, His Mortality and Immortality) which was published posthumously in 1809. Its chief value resides, perhaps, not in any originality or even in its critique of contemporary philosophy but as a moving document of a man in extreme adversity striving to come to terms with his mortality. On Paul's accession in 1796, Radishchev, although not pardoned, was allowed to return to the family estate of Nemtsovo near Moscow where he penned the unfinished *Opisaniye moyego vladeniya* (Description of My Estate) which reaffirmed his conviction that serfdom should be abolished. Alexander I not only granted Radishchev a full pardon but appointed him to his Commission for the Composition of Laws. Although he wrote three memoranda *O zakonopolozhenii* (On Legislation), *Proyekt grazhdanskogo ulozheniya* (Project of a Civil Code) and *Proyekt dlya razdeleniya ulozheniya Rossiyskogo* (Project for the Classification of the Russian Code), Radishchev was soon disappointed in Alexander, realising that serfdom, autocracy and an overweening bureaucracy were to remain in any reconstructed administration and that there were to be no civil rights, no rule of law. In 1802, in a fit of depression, he committed suicide by drinking nitric acid.

Radishchev's reputation rests on the notoriety of his *Puteshestviye iz Peterburga v Moskvu* (A Journey from St Petersburg to Moscow) which remained proscribed until after the 1905 Revolution. Although only eighteen copies of the original edition are extant, the book circulated widely in manuscript copies throughout the nineteenth century and a second edition was published by Herzen in London in 1858. The official Soviet view is that Radishchev was a committed materialist revolutionary and a precursor of the Bolshevik Revolution. Certainly the *Journey* contains passages arguing that a resort to violence is justified to overthrow despotism and Radishchev did not conceal his enthusiasm for the popular revolutions of England and America. Although in the form of a Sternean sentimental travel account and borrowing widely from the classics of contemporary Europe and antiquity, the *Journey* expressed unprecedented conceptions in Russian. The book included Radishchev's *Vol'nost'*, *Oda* (Ode to Liberty), written in 1782, which reviled clerical power and despotism. The *Journey* continually attacks serfdom as a system that had to be abolished in order to avert an inevitable and disastrous peasant rising. A 'Project for the Future', discovered by the sentimental traveller, outlined a programme for gradual serf emancipation, the abolition of the rank system and a call for a free press and an end to censorship. Outraged by the arbitary abuses of absolutism and devoted to personal liberty, Radishchev was an outstanding representative of the European liberal radicalism absorbed during his student years in Leipzig. It was Russian political reality that made him write in the *Journey's* preface those words which Berdyayev recognised as the declaration which gave birth to the Russian intelligentsia, 'I looked around me – and my soul was afflicted with the sufferings of mankind'.

In addition to the studies in Russian of Radishchev – especially Y.L. Barskov and M.V. Zhizhka, *Materialy k izucheniyu "Puteshestviya iz Peterburgga v Moskvu" A.N. Radishcheva* (Moscow and Leningrad, 1935); S.A. Pokrovskiy, *Gosudarstvenno-pravovyye vzglyady Radishcheva* (Moscow, 1956); and G.P. Makogonenko, *Radishchev i yego vremya* (Moscow, 1956); – there are two useful accounts of his life in English – David M. Lang, *The First Russian Radical: Alexander Radishchev (1749–1802)* (London, 1959); and Allen McConnell, *A Russian Philosophe: Alexander Radishchev 1749–1802* (The Hague, 1964). Moreover, his most famous work is available in translation: Roderick Page Thaler (ed.), *Aleksandr Nikolaevich Radishchev: A Journey from St. Petersburg to Moscow* (trans. Leo Wiener, Cambridge, Mass., 1958).

W. GARETH JONES

RANZA, Giovanni Antonio (1741–1801)
Italian democratic intellectual

Ranza was born in Vercelli. A priest, educator and publicist, he came to the attention of Piedmontese authorities in the 1780s for his interest in reform, religious as well as political, and for his organising abilities. In the early 1790s he was forced into exile, at first in Switzerland, then in Corsica, France, and Monaco. After the outbreak of the French Revolution, while he was still in Monaco, Ranza published *Il monitore politico e letterario*, to which other Italian radical exiles contributed. He returned to Piedmont in the mid-1790s and was one of the leaders of a republican uprising in the town of Alba just prior to the arrival of the French army. He became known among fellow republicans for his outspoken anti-semitism, for his distrust of the lower classes, and for his advocacy of civic religion as a substitute for traditional religion. After the Cherasco Armistice, he moved on to Milan and resumed his journalistic career as editor of the radical newspaper *L'amico del popolo italiano*.

Unlike most radical intellectuals who flocked to the Lombard capital, Ranza was suspicious of the competition for the best essay on the question of a future form of government for Italy. While others, including the winner, Melchiorre Gioia (q.v.), viewed the competition as an opportunity to arouse Italian public opinion and secure French support for an Italian movement for reform, Ranza viewed it as Bonaparte's clever ploy to test the political waters and to make Italy completely subservient to French political ambitions. Ranza was an outspoken opponent of the French Constitution in 1799, which he called 'a ladder to monarchism', and he was jailed briefly for his views. His worst fears were confirmed by the Brumaire coup and by the subsequent transition from French Republic to First Empire. Disillusioned with the outcome of the French Revolution and physically frail, he returned to Turin in the latter part of 1800. He died in Turin in 1801.

Essentially an intellectual opponent of authority, Ranza's chief importance lay in his publishing activities and his forthright attacks on the dictatorial tendencies of Bonapartist rule in France and in Italy which were often distinct from the more compromising attitudes of other Italian intellectuals.

There is no biography of Ranza but there are some details on his life in Christof Dipper, 'Aufklärung und Revolution in Italien: Ein Forschungsbericht', *Archiv für Sozialgeschichte*, 23 (1983), pp. 377–438; Stuart J. Woolf, *A History of Italy* (London, 1979); and Carlo Zaghi, *Potere, chiesa e società* (Naples, 1985).

CLARA M. LOVETT

RAYNAL, Guillaume Thomas François (1713–1796)
French anti-colonialist

Born at Lapanouze in Languedoc of a merchant father and noble mother, Raynal was educated at the Jesuit college of Rodez and himself became a Jesuit priest. He taught in Jesuit colleges until 1747, when he left the order and moved to Paris. Here he found various clerical employments, but lost them through simoniacal practices. His literary abilities brought employment as a ghost-writer, and he began supplying a monthly literary newsletter to the court of Saxe-Gotha, selling out to Grimm in 1754. From 1750 to 1754 he was editor of the *Mercure de France*, a sign of his powerful connections; and indeed by this time he knew Rousseau, Diderot, and d'Holbach, was a prominent member of several *salons*, and was earning a comfortable living from literature. Between the late 1740s and 1762 he published various descriptive and historical works, but his name was made in 1772 with the publication (dated 1770) of *Histoire philosohique et politique des établissements et du commerce des Européens dans les deux Indes*. Not until 1780 did Raynal openly admit authorship of this anonymous work, and in fact it was a collaborative effort, much material being supplied by Diderot, d'Holbach and others. It was repeatedly condemned by the government and the courts, and once he claimed authorship Raynal's arrest was ordered. In 1781 he evaded it by fleeing the country, and for three years travelled in England, Germany, the Low Countries and Switzerland, writing further works on the peace of 1783 and the government of Saint-Domingue. In 1784 he was allowed to return to France, but not Paris, and settled in Marseilles. He refused election as a Third Estate deputy in 1789, and although allowed by the National Assembly to return to Paris in 1790, disliked the course of the revolution and denounced its work publicly in 1791. His fortune, largely invested in government stocks, was destroyed by revolutionary inflation, and he died in poverty in Marseilles.

The *Histoire Philosophique* was one of the greatest best-sellers of its time. Constantly revised and amended, it went through three editions and thirty impressions in Raynal's lifetime and was last reprinted in 1880. It was also translated into English and Spanish. Although strongly anti-clerical and hostile to despotism, its main thrust was a comprehensive attack on European colonialism. Raynal never visited the colonies, but he read widely, and was convinced that the arrival of the Europeans had been a disaster for the rest of the world. The Chinese had been right to exclude them, because wherever else they had gone they had brought cruelty, greed and exploitation. He denounced the slave trade and racial discrimination. Only racial mixing could promote stability in colonial territories; enslaved races would one day rise up with savagery against their oppressors. Even colonial settlers were not destined to remain tied to their mother country: Raynal welcomed the American Revolution as an event both natural and entirely desirable. But he offered no practical or consistent programme for ending Europe's exploitation of the rest of the world. Natural evolution would one day bring it about, and even positive action to abolish slavery would need to be spread over several generations. The book sold well because it was luridly written and intended to provoke; but also because it was a

unique compendium of information about overseas territories. Its attacks on the established order brought condemnations not only in France, but throughout the Spanish empire, but these only boosted its fame and sales. When America established its independence, and when the black slaves of Saint-Domingue rose in revolt in 1791, Raynal was hailed as a prophet. Toussaint l'Ouverture, the black leader, was rumoured to have read him. Raynal was certainly regarded as a precursor by subsequent anti-colonial writers, and until his outburst in 1791 was looked upon as one whose works had helped to bring about the French Revolution.

Raynal's *Histoire philosophique et politique des établissements et du commerce des Européens dans les deux Indes* (6 vols., Amsterdam, 1770; third edition, Geneva, 1780), incorporates material reacting to events in America. See too A. Feugère, *Un précurseur de la Révolution, l'Abbé Raynal (1713–1796). Documents inédits* (Angoulême, 1922); H. Wolpe, *Raynal et sa Machine de Guerre. L'"Histoire des Deux Indes' et ses perfectionnements* (Stanford, 1957); A.C. Kors, *D'Holbach's Coterie. An Enlightenment in Paris* (Princeton, NJ, 1976).

W. DOYLE

REBMANN, Andreas Georg Friedrich (1768–1824)
German Jacobin, satirical writer and radical-democratic publicist

Rebmann, the son of an Ansbach civil servant, studied law at Erlangen and Jena and graduated in 1789. He turned first to writing and then to political journalism and published a series of critical letters, *Briefe über Erlangen*, the novel *Heinrich von Neideck*, and a four-volume collection of essays and stories entitled *Nelkenblätter*. In 1792 he settled in Dresden where he edited the journals *Neue Dresdner Merkwürdigkeiten* and later *Der Allgemeine Sächsische Annalist*, which were subject to the strict censorship in force in Saxony, and therefore politically tame.

Following a trip through various German states he published his *Kosmopolitische Wanderungen durch einen Teil Deutschlands*, which vividly depicted the poverty and misery of the urban manual workers. His *Empfindsame Reise nach Schilda; Hans Kiekindiewelts Reisen in alle vier Weltteile und in den Mond*; and *Ludwig Wagehals*, all of which appeared anonymously, were novelistic, partly autobiographical satires on the political and social condition of Germany. In the manner of Adolph von Knigge (q.v.), Rebmann derided the ignorance, narrow-mindedness and patronage of the petty tyrants of Germany, and became one of the most passionate defenders of human rights in central Europe. Interspersed in the two last-named utopian novels are fragments of speeches made by the French Jacobin leader Robespierre (q.v.) in the National Convention and at the festival of the Supreme Being in Paris.

While the overwhelming majority of German adherents of the Enlightenment turned away from the revolution after the execution of Louis XVI and the appearance of the sans-culottes on the political stage, Rebmann's ideas became increasingly radical during the period of Jacobin rule in France. He translated Robespierre's speech on Jacobin foreign policy of 18 November 1793, and published it anonymously a short time later under the title *Neuestes Manifest der Frankenrepublik an alle Völker der Welt*. It was in this speech that Robespierre had declared that his government had no intention of exporting the revolution abroad, and warned the tyrants of neighbouring states that 'now it could be the turn of the people to punish the kings'. Rebmann, who considered this indirect exhortation to revolt 'the most important document of the time', published Robespierre's speech again after the fall of the Jacobins in two improved editions with better commentaries. In the third edition, which appeared in 1797, he emphasised the peaceful aspirations of Jacobin foreign policy in order to 'instruct all nations in the principles of the French Republic and the attacks of its enemies on the general security of all peoples'.

Persecuted as a Jacobin, Rebmann was forced to leave Saxony in 1794 and, after a short stay in Dessau, settled in Erfurt in the electorate of Mainz where, together with the publisher Gottfried Leberecht Vollmer (q.v.), he began to publish the revolutionary journal *Das neue graue Ungeheuer*. This journal which, in Rebmann's words, pilloried 'censorship and restrictions on the press, military despotism, the patchwork of misery and luxury, the rule of mistresses, priests' conspiracies. . .bureaucracy, exorbitant dues, and the abuses of gamekeepers', readily found a readership.

Persecuted by the authorities as an 'adherent and propagator of the rebellious principles of the New Franks', Rebmann fled in December 1795 in order to escape imminent arrest. Chased by dogs, he escaped in disguise to Altona, which belonged to Denmark. Here he found refuge among the North German democrats Heinrich Würzer (q.v.), Friedrich Wilhelm Schütz (q.v.) and their friends. The Jacobin publishing house *Verlagsgesellschaft von Altona*, founded by Vollmer, Rebmann and Schütz in 1794, published more revolutionary writings between 1795 and 1800 than any other publisher on the right bank of the Rhine. Rebmann stayed in Altona for six months and along with a report of his persecution and flight, and a number of short essays, composed *Der politische Tierkreis oder die Zeichen unserer Zeit* which also appeared under the title *Das neueste graue Ungeheuer*, and on which he probably collaborated with J.F.E. Albrecht (q.v.), a theatre director and writer, who also belonged to the circle of democrats. The piece appeared under the pseudonym 'Huergelmer' and constituted a comprehensive and precise presentation of the political ideas of the Jacobins.

When the authorities of the electorate of Mainz demanded his extradition, Rebmann fled in the summer of 1796 via Amsterdam to Paris. He sent J.F. Albrecht his *Briefe auf einer Reise durch Holland und Frankreich*, which the latter published in his journal *Der Totenrichter*. From Paris Rebmann edited the journals *Die Geißel* and *Die Schildwache*, which appeared under the auspices of the *Verlagsgesellschaft von Altona*. Rebmann's dispute with Schütz in the pages of these journals in 1797–1798, as to whether the French armies or the German people should liberate Germany from feudal rule, constituted a high point of Jacobin social criticism. While Schütz had welcomed the French in his *Niedersächsischer Merkur* as liberators from the yoke of despotism in 1792–1793, and was convinced of the impossibility of an autonomous German revolution, Rebmann, in his Paris exile, had seen the French Directory government depart from its original revolutionary democratic ideals. He realised that the French were not interested in a republicanisation of Germany, but in a pact with its traditional rulers. In a fly-sheet entitled *Laterne für die mittlere Volksklasse*, whose four issues also appeared in the monthly journal *Die Geißel*, he called on the German people to rise against their rulers and to erect a 'moderate revolutionary dictatorship'. The new democratic order must be achieved by the people themselves, without the help of the French. 'A people must win its own freedom by its own efforts, not receive it as a gift', Rebmann declared.

After the annexation of the Rhineland by France at the end of 1797 Rebmann, a trained lawyer, was appointed a judge in Mainz. He served as president of the criminal court in the trials of the 'Schinderhannes' robber bands in 1803, and at the trial of Damian Hessel several years later. After Napoleon's accession to power his political journalism became more and more infrequent. Following the fall of Napoleon Rebmann served in the judiciary of the Bavarian Palatinate and died as President of the Court of Appeal in Zweibrücken while taking a cure in Wiesbaden.

A foremost publicist of French revolutionary ideas in Germany, Rebmann never lost faith in the ideals of his youth. He remained convinced that the struggle of the French revolutionaries had been a just one, and that rulers must be subordinate to laws promulgated by an elected assembly of people's representatives.

For further details about Rebmann's life and career see Hedwig Voegt, *Die deutsche jakobinische Literatur und Publizistik* (Berlin/GDR, 1955); Rainer Kawa, *Georg Friedrich Rebmann (1768–1824). Studien zu Leben und Werk eines deutschen Jakobiners* (Bonn, 1980); Walter Grab, *Deutsche Jakobiner, Büchergilde Gutenberg* (Frankfurt, 1984).

W. GRAB

REINHARD, Karl Friedrich (1761–1837)
Revolutionary republican, the only German ever to serve as Foreign Minister of France

Reinhard was born in Schorndorf, Württemberg on 2 October 1761. His father was a Lutheran minister, and as a young man Reinhard also seemed destined for a career in the church. From 1778–83 he attended Tübingen University, first as a stipendiat of the Stift, then as a candidate in theology. Although Tübingen was at that time a bastion of Lutheran orthodoxy, his years there were Reinhard's first exposure to the works of Voltaire, Rousseau, and Kant (q.v.), which were widely admired by his fellow students, and which made a lasting impression on him. Over the next several years Reinhard held a number of insignificant ecclesiastical posts, which he filled without much enthusiasm, preferring to devote his energies to poetry and journalism. One of his essays, a bitterly satirical portrait of the Swabian Protestant establishment, attracted sufficient attention that Reinhard felt obliged to seek his fortune in Switzerland. In 1787 he became private secretary and tutor to an aristocratic Swiss family. In this capacity he was able to travel twice to France, at a time when the political unrest that would finally give rise to the revolution was just beginning to stir. Between 1789 and 1791 he published a number of articles, in Hausleutner's *Schwäbische Archiv* and in Schiller's *Thalia*, hailing the revolution as the triumph of Enlightenment, and urging his countrymen to view events in France sympathetically. In 1791, after vowing to 'remain forever German,' Reinhard moved to Bordeaux; he spent the rest of his life in French service.

In Bordeaux Reinhard affiliated himself with the local chapter of the Friends of the Constitution, a political club dominated by the Girondist party. In September, 1791, he accompanied the club's delegate to the National Assembly in Paris, where he soon became friends with the Girondin leadership, particularly the Abbé Sieyès (q.v.), with whom Reinhard shared a special interest in Kant. When Sieyès's faction came to power in March 1792, Reinhard was rewarded with a post in the Foreign Office, mainly on the basis of his fluency in foreign languages – he spoke half a dozen passably well. In April he accompanied the French Ambassador, the Marquis de Chauvelin, to London, where he served as legation secretary and, informally, as liaison between the embassy and Talleyrand, the dominant foreign policy figure in the Assembly. Following the outbreak of war between France and Great Britain in February 1793, Reinhard was posted briefly to Naples, where he remained until November, despite the fall of the Girondin government in March – an early indication that, politically, the Foreign Service offered a relatively safe harbour, at least for those serving outside the capital. In Paris, however, Reinhard, who became a divisional chief within the ministry, was subject to much closer political supervision. By the spring of 1794 the Foreign Office was entirely under the control of the Committee of Public Safety, which viewed Reinhard with suspicion because of his earlier alliances and his foreign birth. He was finally arrested and condemned on 27 July 1794, the very day of Robespierre's (q.v.) fall, but returned to his post shortly thereafter.

Over the next five years Reinhard held a number of ambassadorial appointments, first to the Hanseatic cities in northern Germany, then, in 1798–99, to the Grand Duchy of Tuscany. Following the invasion of Tuscany in March, 1799, Reinhard served for three months as head of the occupation government, during which he won the good will of native observers through his efforts to minimize plunder. He was unable, however, to control anti-French agitation in the countryside, and in June of 1799, following a successful rising in the Tiber district, Reinhard fled Florence altogether, convinced that the counter-revolution was at hand, and deeply dismayed that the Italians had failed to grasp the gift of liberty that the French had given them. At the start of July he was named ambassador to the Swiss Confederation, but before he could assume that post he was again called to Paris, this time as Foreign Minister. It was, as he himself recognised, a caretaker appointment, for which he was chosen because of his indifference to the party intrigue that would soon bring the Directory down altogether. The end came on 18 Brumaire (9 November 1799), after which Reinhard gave way to Talleyrand, and assumed the ambassadorship to Switzerland he had already been promised.

Despite considerable personal antipathy for the new régime, Reinhard remained in the French diplomatic service throughout the Napoleonic period, serving in Bern (1799–1801), Hamburg (1802–5), Milan (1807), and Westphalia (1808–13), the latter an especially delicate assignment, since it involved keeping tabs on Napoleon's brother, Jerome. After the fall of the Empire he again surfaced in high office, as Chancellery Director in Talleyrand's Foreign Ministry. During the Hundred Days Reinhard fled to Belgium, where he was treated coldly by the other exiles from Louis XVIII's court, and briefly imprisoned by Prussian authorities. After Waterloo, however, he was restored to the good graces of the king. The following year he was made a count, and named French Ambassador to the German Federation in Frankfurt, a post that he held until 1829. In 1831 he was made a Peer of France, and admitted to membership in the *Academie Française*. He died in 1837, at the age of seventy-six.

Overall Reinhard's career presents a somewhat peculiar picture of great distinction and only modest achievement. That he should have survived and prospered under so many governments is a reflection both of his perspicacity and of his lack of personal ambition. Politically he was a committed republican all his life, a conviction that he managed to reconcile only imperfectly with his professional obligation to speak for whoever was in power in Paris. Reinhard was initially drawn to the revolution because it represented the triumph of rationality and justice over intellectual obscurity and social privilege, and he continued to believe that, given the existing alternatives, French influence in Europe remained salutary, even if it had to be exercised at the point of a bayonet. He envisaged himself as a mediator between his spiritual and his hereditary homelands, and there can be no doubt that his German birth aided his acceptance in most of the posts where he served. But his tenure in most of them was short, in part because of the volatile nature of French policy (whose most common outcome, up to 1815, was war), but more generally because he tended to develop close relationships with local political figures, to the extent that his objectivity and reliability might be called into question by his own government. His natural sympathies were with those who sought peace and independence, aspirations that often cut across the goals of his masters in Paris.

His last assignment was probably the one he had envisaged for himself all along: spokesman for France before a German parliament. That such a role might have opened him up to charges that he was simply an instrument of reaction would no doubt have seemed inconceivable to him before 1800. By then, however, he had learned, as he wrote to one friend, that 'politics has nothing to do with the love of mankind'. After Brumaire, he wrote to another, he 'had no illusions left'. What was left was loyalty to the state that the revolution had made, strengthened by the realisation that nowhere else in Europe could the poor son of a German pastor have risen so high so quickly.

There are no significant works about

Karl Reinhard in English. He has been the subject of an impressive biography by Wilhelm Lang, *Graf Reinhard* (Bamberg, 1896) and a number of shorter essays, most notably those in Else R. Gross (ed.), *Karl Friedrich Reinhard, 1761–1837* (Stuttgart, 1961). Quite apart from his political career, Reinhard was a man of universal culture and considerable intellectual penetration, as can be seen from his quarter-century's correspondence with Goethe, published in Otto Heuschele (ed.), *Goethe und Reinhard* (Wiesbaden, 1957).

DANIEL J. MORAN

RIEDEL, Andreas von (1748–1837)
Austrian Jacobin

Maria Andreas Nicolaus Tolentin von Riedel was born on 12 September 1748 in Vienna. His father, Franciscus Antonius von Riedel, was a captain in the Imperial Engineers Corps, and teacher of fortification and arithmetic at the *Theresianische Militärpflanzschule* (cadet school) in Vienna; his mother Eva Rosa Catharina came from Italy. From 1758 to 1764 Riedel attended the *Militärpflanzschule* and from 1764 to 1770 the *Theresianische Militärakademie* in Wiener Neustadt. From 1770 to 1772 he studied under Karl Scherffer, the famous professor of mathematics, at Vienna. During the next two years he took part in an expedition led by the geographer Joseph Liesganig to map East Galicia and the Principality of Moldavia. From 1774 to 1779 he was an engineering teacher at the military academy in Wiener Neustadt, and in September 1779, at the suggestion of Emperor Joseph II and Empress Maria Theresa, he became mathematics teacher at the court of Archduke Leopold, later Leopold II, in Florence. Here Riedel was particularly favoured by the archduke, and they struck up an almost friendly and personal relationship. Both were adherents of the ideas of Montesquieu and later of Paine, and the archduke's constitutional plans for Tuscany seem to have awakened Riedel's interest in constitutional issues. Riedel also took a lively part in the social life of the court and the city. There were considerable disagreements between Riedel and his pupil Francis, later Francis II, an educationally-difficult child. Intrigues with the object of having Riedel removed from Florence foundered when Leopold took his side, and it was probably for this reason that Riedel turned down a chair in physics at Lemberg.

When Leopold became emperor in 1792, Riedel returned with him to Vienna. Here the emperor built up a secret service, but Riedel's planned participation as a colonel came to nothing. However, as a retired captain he supported the emperor's domestic policies in his book *Das Undankbare Wien*. With no real intellectual and political work to do, he pursued a number of other projects. In 1791 he submitted to Leopold a plan for the constitutional reform of the Habsburg Monarchy, probably in line with the emperor's own plans and written with the work of the French National Assembly in mind. Its aim was the transformation of the absolute state into a constitutional monarchy, or even a republic, in which the emperor would be the first citizen of the state. While in Vienna Riedel became a friend of Dr Franz Anton Mesmer, founder of modern magnetopathy and psychotherapy, and he also renewed his acquaintance with Antonie Bernasconi, the most celebrated singer and actress of the eighteenth century, whom he had known in Florence.

Riedel was raised to the nobility in 1778 as 'Edler von Riedel', and was awarded the title of baron on 22 October 1792, probably at the instigation of Leopold. After Leopold's death in March 1792 the Emperor Francis turned down Riedel's offers of co-operation. The new emperor's policies were markedly reactionary in comparison with those of his predecessor, and a response to the radicalisation of the French Revolution. The supporters of the relatively liberal policies of the emperors Joseph and Leopold became deeply disaffected. Riedel soon became leader of a group of politically dissatisfied officers and public servants, who met in his house, held discussions, and read the banned *Moniteur*.

Between July and October 1792 Riedel worked on his revolutionary *Aufruf an alle Deutsche zu einem antiaristokratischen Gleichheitsbund*. In this exhortation to rebellion, 1 November 1792 was proclaimed the appointed day for an armed uprising of the entire people, under the sign of the tricolour. The appeal was ineffective however since only longhand copies could be produced: its effect was to evoke sympathy among intellectuals and instil fear into the aristocracy. The group around Riedel, commonly known as the Vienna Jacobins, were denounced by Degen, an *agent provocateur*, and some thirty or forty persons were arrested for Jacobin conspiracy against the state. The main points of the charges were: complicity in a conspiracy to stage a coup d'état; treason; the composition and distribution of revolutionary literature; the intended abolition of the nobility and murder of the emperor; the formation of a secret society; and public propaganda for the French Revolution. The revenge which the emperor demanded in Riedel's case in particular was refused by the supreme court, but even so there were harsh deterrent sentences. Riedel was sentenced to sixty years' imprisonment. Until 1806 he served his sentence in inhuman conditions, and mostly in chains, in the infamous state prisons at Kufstein, Graz and Munkacz, where he got to know the Hungarian poet Ferencz Kazinczy, also imprisoned for political reasons. In order to relieve the tedium of his solitary confinement he invented a code to use by tapping on the wall, so that he could communicate with his fellow prisoners.

In 1806 Riedel was transferred to the *Minoritenkloster*, a monastery near Brno. In 1809 he escaped and placed himself under the personal protection of Marshal Davout, who had taken Brno. He travelled with Davout's retinue, via Vienna, Linz, Würzburg, Mainz, and Bad Nauheim to Paris, and was the marshal's guest there. All attempts by the Austrian government and police to secure his return, and all attempts to issue warrants against him, failed. Following Napoleon's marriage in

1811 to Marie Louise, one of the daughters of the Austrian emperor, Riedel was afraid of possible extradition to Austria. For this reason he took rooms in a modest Paris boarding house which Davout had found for him, lived meagrely from his pension, gave private lessons and received financial support from Dr Mesmer, whose work was then being widely discussed in France. After the fall of Napoleon he lived under the pseudonym Baldram (or Baldvam) in St Flour (Cantal), and as Donadieu in Aix-en-Provence, before finally moving back to Paris where he lived in extreme poverty. He died there on 15 February 1837.

Riedel was highly-educated, and the intellectual and organisational leader of the Vienna Jacobins. Originally a supporter of the bourgeois reform policies of Leopold, his views and methods were radicalised under Francis. Since the Austrian Jacobins could not rely on popular support in the socially and economically backward Habsburg Empire, political mass action was less important in their case than their theoretical discussions about politics and society. In no other German state – apart from the Mainz Republic of 1792–1793, which had come about as a result of the French occupation – were there more organised adherents of the French Revolution than in Vienna. They were mostly civil servants who had worked on the reformist policies of Joseph II and Leopold II, and had political and organisational experience. Some had even belonged to Leopold's secret group of assistants, and he had allowed them a limited measure of freedom within his own terms.

With the death of Leopold all hopes of reform were frustrated by the intellectual mediocrity and reactionary policies of Francis. As a result the former reformist democrats, with Riedel at their head, became revolutionary radicals. Riedel recognised early that the methods and aims of the French revolutionaries could not be transferred to the Habsburg Monarchy. The comparatively backward social structure of the multi-national state; the lack of a democratic urban bourgeoisie; and the political lethargy of the masses meant that diverse and specifically Austrian, forms of political propaganda and organisation were required. Among the basic subjects under discussion were: the future republican constitution of the Habsburg monarchy; equal rights for the nationalities; changes in property relations and social structures towards a form of production and consumption communism; the essence of a revolution as the moral and intellectual catharsis of the nation; aspirations towards peace and an end to the revolutionary wars in order to relieve the misery of the people and make them more receptive to revolutionary ideas. Simultaneously, there was an attempt to put these revolutionary ideas and theories into practice in an everyday context and on a small scale. This meant that new forms of organisation and communication had to be found. In order to lend clarity and political consciousness to the confused and ill-articulated demands of peasants, artisans, journeymen, day-labourers, soldiers and students, it was necessary to find adequate literary and journalistic forms of expression. The best method of propaganda to emerge under the conditions of illegality was the production of numerous small, handwritten fly sheets, which were easily accessible and quickly passed on. Among the material were poems, dirges, poems in the form of prayers, politicised hymns, folk songs, and political addresses disguised as sermons. The old, well-known forms and melodies were invariably accompanied by revolutionary lyrics. In addition there were political appeals in biblical language, and political catechisms in the well-known dialogue form. The printing of this unique Austrian propaganda, which was both rich in ideas and varied in presentation, was prevented by the extreme stringency and the vigilance of the censorship; as a consequence it was ineffective among the masses, and has remained largely unknown to this day. Riedel's plans to send teachers into the villages to educate the peasants as a substitute for printed material were never realised.

Despite its limited political effectiveness,

which was a product of the objective facts of life in the Habsburg state rather than of the subjective assumptions of the Riedel group, this activity should not be underestimated. Riedel's organisation was the first (and only) interesting illegal attempt by a bourgeois opposition to establish a republican and democratic constitution in the Habsburg state. Riedel was no doctrinaire utopian; he correctly evaluated the political and social situation in the empire, recognised the possibilities and limits of revolutionary action, and avoided simply trying to impose both the content and the strategy of the French Revolution on Austria. He and his friends propagated revolutionary ideas in an intelligent, imaginative and popular way for the first time in Austria. Riedel's work was characterised by the Enlightenment ideal of a mission to educate the people and the social criticism of the French Revolution. As such he was the most significant and consistent pioneer of democracy and republicanism in Austria. In the service of these aims he took upon himself heavy personal sacrifices, in a long life devoted to the ideas of the Enlightenment and revolution.

Riedel's *Entwurf eines Verfassungsprojekts für die Habsburgermonarchie* (1791), is reprinted in Fritz Valjavec, *Die Entstehung der politischen Strömungen in Deutschland 1770–1815* (Munich, 1951). His *Das undankbare Wien. . .* (Vienna, 1790) is a rare pamphlet. It was originally published anonymously, and the places of publication given as Frankfurt and Leipzig. There are probably no extant copies of his *Nicht-Höflichkeit einem Manne gesagt, der mit dem hohen Adel nicht gar freundlich umgegangen ist* (1791, anonymously). Finally, his *Favole Italiene, del medico Andrea Re d'Occimiano*, a collection of fables, is also a rare book. A copy is held at the British Museum. Further information on Riedel is to be found in Alfred Körner, *Andreas Riedel. Ein politisches Schicksal im Zeitalter der Französischen Revolution* (Phil. Diss., Cologne, 1969), and Alfred Körner, 'Andreas Riedel. Zur Lebensgeschichte eines Wiener Demokraten', in *Jahrbuch des Vereines der Stadt Wien*, vol.

27 (1971). Revised versions of the same article are in *Jahrbuch des Instituts für deutsche Geschichte*, III (Tel Aviv, 1974), and in Helmut Reinalter (ed.), *Jakobiner in Mitteleuropa* (Innsbruck, 1977), and an Italian translation in *Critica Storia* Year 10, NS 3 (1973). See also Alfred Körner, *Die Wiener Jakobiner. Deutsche revolutionäre Demokraten 3* (Stuttgart, 1972); Ernst Wangermann, *From Joseph II to the Jacobin Trials* (Oxford, 1959); Denis Silagi, *Ungarn und der geheime Mitarbeiterkreis Kaiser Leopolds II* (Phil. Diss., Munich, 1960); and Denis Silagi, *Jakobiner in der Habsburgermonarchie* (Vienna, Munich, 1962).

ALFRED KÖRNER

RIEM, Andreas (1749–1807)
German Enlightenment writer

Riem, who came from a respected Calvinist family in the Palatinate, studied theology and went in 1774 to Prussia, where he became a minister in Friedrichswalde (Uckermark). His two part novel, *Dorset und Julia* (1774), was one of his earliest attempts at writing. In several works, such as *Vom Einfluß der Religion auf das Staatssystem der Völker* (Berlin 1776), and *Verträglichkeit der Religionen mit der Politik der Staaten* (Berlin 1779), he tried to reconcile the Enlightenment with Reformed Christianity. From 1782 he was the minister at the Berlin Friedrichsspital (hospital) and Reform orphanage. In 1785 he published *Philosophische und kritische Untersuchungen über das Alte Testament und dessen Göttlichkeit, besonders über die mosaische Religion*, and in 1787 *Beiträge zur Berichtigung der Wahrheiten der christlichen Religion. Über Glauben und überzeugung*, which identified him as a neologian and a rationalist. In 1785 he made a trip to France, published a *Gedächtnisrede auf Friedrich den Einzigen* the following year, and in 1787 a number of hitherto unpublished writings of the '*Fragmentist*' Hermann Samuel Reimarus, which were among Lessing's personal papers. A contribution to the history of art, *Über die Malerei der Alten* (1787), which he dedicated to the Prussian ministers Hertzberg and Heinitz, led to his appointment as secretary of the Berlin Academy of Arts.

In his fury at the reactionary edict on religion published by Minister Wöllner, Riem published anonymously in 1788 a fragment entitled *Über Aufklärung. Ob sie dem Staate, der Religion oder überhaupt gefährlich sei? Ein Wort zur Beherzigung für Regenten, Staatsmänner und Priester*, which went into four editions and attracted much attention. He was forced to give up his clerical office, but remained secretary of the Academy of Arts and director of its library. As a contributor to the *Berlinische Monatschrift* and to the *Neues Berlinisches Journal über Gegenstände der Geschichte, Philosohie, Gesetzgebung und Politik*, he welcomed the French Revolution enthusiastically and resolutely opposed the Prussian declaration of war on France in May 1792. In his *Winken über Preußens inneres und äußeres Staatsinteresse* (1792), he demanded a radical change of political course and a close alliance with revolutionary France. In addition he continued to publish theological works in the spirit of the rationalist moral teaching, such as the three-volume work *Das reinere Christentum oder die Religion der Kinder des Lichts* (1789–1794), and *Christus und die Vernunft* (1792).

Riem, who was in contact with republicans and Jacobins such as Theremin and Rebmann (q.v.) welcomed, as a cosmopolitan, and in the name of culture and freedom the incorporation of the Rhineland into the French Republic, and the latter's policy of 'natural borders'. He called upon the Prussian government to conclude a peace with France and take over the political leadership of Germany, and in his two journals, *Europens politische Lage* and *Europa und seine politische und Finanzverhältnisse*, which began to appear after the Peace of Basle in 1795, he propagated the idea of a political alliance with France and a common policy against Britain, Austria and Russia. These demands, along with his vehement condemnation of the destruction of Polish independence, were diametrically opposed to Prussian policy; on 18 November 1795 Riem was arrested, deported and taken over the border into Saxony. He went to Frankfurt and later to Homburg von der Höhe, where a group of people sympathetic to the revolution had gathered around Isaak Sinclair.

In the following years Riem undertook extensive journeys, which he described in his eight-volume work *Reisen durch Deutschland, Holland, Frankreich und England in verschiedener, besonders politischer Hinsicht, in den Jahren 1785, 1795, 1796, 1797* (appeared 1796–1800). Here he proclaimed himself a convinced republican and friend of the revolution, and sharply and passionately condemned Prussian and British policies. He composed a number of memorial addresses for the Batavian Republic, and also wrote three *romans à clef*, which were published anonymously by Vollmer's (q.v.) Jacobin Verlagsgesellschaft von Altona: *Infernale, Geschichte aus Neu-Sodom (1796)*, *Behemoth (1797)*, and *Das Substitut des Behemoth* (1798). Here, like J.F.E. Albrecht (q.v.), he made damning judgements on the immorality and patronage of the Prussia of Frederick William II. Riem's attacks attracted so much attention that the Prussian minister von dem Schulenberg suggested to the cabinet on 6 May 1798 that the 'chief scribbler of the revolutionary party' be bribed to keep quiet. Riem addressed the Rastatt Congress with an *Apologie für die unterdrückte Judenschaft in Deutschland* (two volumes, Leipzig, 1798), in which he called for the emancipation of the Jews, and described the prevalent contempt for, and oppression of, the Jews in Germany as an 'eloquent monument to the barbarity and stupidity' of mediaeval prejudice. In an anonymous piece, *Leviathan oder Rabinen und Juden* (1801), he called on the Jews to give up their traditions, customs and religious laws in order to attain civil equality. Nothing is known of Riem's last years, which were spent in Paris.

Riem was a rationalist thinker and critic of Prussian religious orthodoxy. However his radicalism was also consciously political, welcoming the French Revolution and seeking to spread its ideas into the Rhineland and the whole of Prussia. As a consequence he became one of the fiercest critics of the Prussian state and a supporter of the republican cause in Prussia.

The biographical details in the *Allgemeine deutsche Biographie*, vol. 29 (Leipzig, 1889), p. 756f., are incomplete. Further information on Riem may be found in O. Tschirch, *Geschichte der öffentlichen Meinung in Preußen 1795–1806*, vol. 1 (Weimar, 1933), pp. 127–154, and J. Droz, *L'Allemagne et la Révolution française* (Paris, 1949).

W. GRAB

RIGAS PHERAIOS, (a.k.a. Velestinlis) (c. 1757–1798)
Greek revolutionary, radical publicist, and advocate of armed revolt against the Ottomans

Rigas was born around 1757 in Velestino, the ancient Pherai, a small village of Thessaly (hence his alternative surnames). His father was a rather wealthy landowner and merchant. He received an excellent education at Zagorá, Thessaly, and at about age twenty moved to Constantinople where he served as clerk (γραμματικός) to the prominent Phanariot Aléxandros Ypsilantis. In 1786 he went to Bucharest in the Danubian principalities to work as clerk to Prince Nikólaos Mavroyénis, while continuing his study of foreign languages. He was later appointed subprefect (Kaïmakam) of a small area of Wallachia, was involved in commercial enterprises, and bought some land. In 1790 he went to Vienna, where he appears to have become involved with freemasonry, and perhaps was among the founders of a secret revolutionary society. There, too, he worked as clerk to the baron of Langerfeld, a Greek. Within a year, he was back in Wallachia to look after his land and family. In 1796 he returned to Vienna, where, with the cooperation of two Greek printers, he embarked on an ambitious publication programme connected with his grand plans

for the liberation of the Balkans. His Great Map of the Balkans (Μεγάλη Χάρτα), his picture of Alexander the Great, and revolutionary pamphlets and songs in the Greek vernacular had a tremendous effect on Balkan national feelings. His planned return to Greece to organise and educate the 'pallicars in bondage' was thwarted by the Austrian authorities who arrested him and, after protracted interrogation, delivered him to the Ottoman governor of Belgrade where he and seven of his fellow conspirators were strangled on 24 June 1798 and thrown into the Danube.

Rigas has been called the first martyr (πρωτομάρτυραζ) of the Greek struggle for independence. His heroic figure and fiery personality seemed to represent all the characteristics of contemporary Hellenism. He was most active during the last decade of the eighteenth century, a critical period for Greece. Political and social conditions had begun to improve in the Balkans, particularly after the Russo-Turkish war of 1787–92: new schools were founded, islands such as Hydra, Spetses, and Chios created a Greek merchant marine, commercial enterprises in Thessaly and northern Greece were in direct contact with central Europe. Economic prosperity, the rise of the middle class, widening horizons and better education encouraged the formation and articulation of a Greek consciousness leading to demands for national liberation.

Rigas is central to the history and ideology of modern Greece. He instilled a sense of national consciousness in his fellow countrymen and organised a national movement to overthrow Ottoman rule in the Balkan lands. In this, he was directly influenced and inspired by the doctrines and ideals of the French Revolution. He became an outstanding proponent of nationalism and liberalism, and through his writings and his actions he stimulated the revival of national consciousness which culminated in the Greek war of independence in 1821.

Rigas' central vision was a multi-national state, dominated by Greek culture. Even if the population were largely non-Greek, they would aspire to the higher Greek ideals. This concept was based on three important precedents: Alexander's empire, the Byzantine empire, and the Ottoman empire. This arrangement accorded most closely with the existing demography of the Balkans, where Greeks were dispersed over a large area with isolated pockets of compact settlement. Its attraction lay in the size of the envisaged state, in the possibility for its quick realisation on the assumption that power in the existing Ottoman empire could be taken by Greeks, and in making certain that most of the Greek people would live within one state. This proposal was widely accepted by the Greeks as more realistic than other extant proposals, although many conservative circles, including the church leaders and the old Phanariot families, considered revolutionary agitation premature, dangerous, and outlandish. Thus, a pamphlet by Rigas on *The New Political Administration*, based on the 1793 French constitution, had been attacked by the church, which also issued a patriarchal circular condemning French culture as a symbol of liberalism. In his famous map of the Balkans and the coast of Asia Minor we can follow Rigas' outlines for a possible Balkan federation, but also of the Grand Design (Μεγάλη Τδέα) which implied the unification of all Balkan and Anatolian Greeks within a single Greek state, whose boundaries would include all areas of Greek settlement. This idea remained prominent in Greece until it was demolished in 1922 by the decisive Turkish repulse of the Greek army of Anatolia.

The political philosophy of Rigas was founded on Greek revolutionary tradition and influenced by the political and social ideas of the Englightenment and of the French Revolution. His prolific writings can be divided into three categories: 1. translations of French novels and scientific treatises 2. political philosophy and 3. revolutionary tracts. The revolutionary materials consist of songs, maps, proclamations and treatises on military strategy. The influence of the French Revolution is clear in his *Revolutionary Proclamation, The Rights of Man* and *The New Political*

Constitution of the Inhabitants of Rumeli, Asia Minor, The Archipelago, Moldavia and Wallachia (all of 1797). In these works he speaks of the 'sovereignty of the people', 'the powers of the Republic', and 'the guaranteeing of the rights of the people'. But Rigas is best known for his 'War Hymn' (Θούρειος Ὑμνος), still one of the most celebrated poems of Greek literature: 'Better a single hour of life in liberty/ Rather than forty years' prison and slavery'. Full of exhortations and patriotic fervour, it rang out in the cafés of Vienna and Trieste, sung to the tune of the French 'La Carmagnole', and remained virtually a national anthem until Solomos' 'Hymn to Liberty' replaced it.

The collected works of Rigas have been published only in Greek editions. Excerpts from his political treatises appear in English in Richard Clogg (ed.), *The Movement for Greek Independence 1770–1821* (New York, 1976). The original Greek edition of his political work is Rigas Velestinlis, *Nea Politiki Dioikisis ton Katoikon tis Roumelis, tis Mikras Asias, ton Mesogeion Nison kai this Vlakhobodganias* (The New Political Constitution of the Inhabitants of Rumeli, Asia Minor, The Archipelago, Moldavia and Wallachia) (Vienna, 1797; reprinted Athens, 1971). The *War Hymn*, his revolutionary pamplets and his political treatises have been translated into French by Ap. V. Daskalakis, *Les Oeuvres de Rhigas Velestinlis* (Paris, 1937). The best edition of his collected works (long excerpts), with a scholarly introduction and commentary is Leandros I. Vranoussis, *Rigas* (Athens, 1953), in Greek. Vranoussis' study together with A.V. Daskalakis, *Rhigas Velestinlis, la Révolution française et les préludes de l'indépendence hellénique* (Paris, 1937) include good bibliographies, while the bibliography up to 1962 is covered by A. Manessis in his clear article 'L'activité et les projects politiques d'un patriote grec dans les Balkans vers la fin du XVIIIe siècle', *Balkan Studies*, III, 1, (1962), pp. 75–118.

As there is no recent biography of Rigas, we still rely on the older works of Chr. Perraivos, *Syntomos Viographia touaoid-*

imou Riga Pherraiou tou Thettalou (A short Biography of the famous Rigas Pheraios, the Thessalian) (Athens, 1860) and of S. Lambrou, *Apokalypseis peri tou martyriou tou Riga* (Revelations concerning the martyrdom of Rigas) (Athens, 1892). In English we have A. Edmonds' old *Rhigas Pheraios, the protomartyr of Greek Independence. A biographical sketch* (London, 1890).

A. LILY MACRAKIS

ROBERT, Pierre François Joseph (1762–1826)
French revolutionary, member of the National Convention

Robert was born in Namur, Belgium, became a lawyer and professor of law, and joined the National Guard in 1789. At the beginning of the revolution Robert was also conducting a business in spices and colonial goods, but rose to prominence as one of the editors of the Kéralios' *Mercure national*. He married Louise Kéralio (q.v.) in 1790 and together they threw themselves into the spread of the popular societies in the first months of 1791. Associated with Brissot (q.v.), Danton (q.v.) and Mme Roland, and established in the Cordeliers district, the Roberts' *Mercure national* was one of the first newspapers to support republicanism in France. Robert himself was associated with a pamphlet of October 1789 entitled: *Republicanism adapted for French conditions.* He was an activist as much as a theorist, however, and as well as being a member of the Jacobin and Cordeliers Clubs, was prominent in the *Société fraternelle des Deux Sexes* and the *Société des indigents.* In the labour unrest that marked the spring of 1791 Robert tried to bring together the political societies and the working-men's clubs to fight for better conditions. In this time he supported a strike of building and other workers seeking higher wages. On 11 May he denounced the various masters who had exploited the workers, from kings and aristocrats to the 'rapacity of the contractors'. He pointed out that, at a time when carpenters were seeking a minimum of two-and-a-half *livres* from master joiners, the latter were receiving from three to four-and-a-half *livres*. It was against agitation of this sort that the Le Chapelier Law of 16 June 1791 was passed, dealing a serious blow to the popular agitation of the first half of 1791: the worker's movement had never had the full support of the democrats who were suspicious of the resurrection of corporations if labour unions were permitted, but in any case the repression following the Champ de Mars massacre finished it off.

Robert played a key role in the agitation that stemmed from the king's flight, and on the same day as the flight was announced he called for the Republic at a special meeting of the Cordeliers Club. He was arrested when taking this petition to the Jacobin Club, but was released on the protest of the latter which, however, did not share his republicanism. Robert was a major figure in the drawing up of the Champ de Mars petition of 15 July 1791, and after the massacre there two days later had to seek refuge with Mme Roland. He later broke with her, occasioning some false and harsh stories about him in her memoirs.

Robert also played a role in the events leading up to the overthrow of the monarchy. He was one of the main figures who drafted the Cordeliers Club petition of 15 July 1792 that called for the suspension of the king, the formation of a National Convention and the re-drafting of the constitution. He was elected to the National Convention in September 1792 by the Paris electors, and sat with the Mountain. In voting for the execution of the king he expressed the wish that this be the last, for he was opposed to capital punishment. He was an outspoken enemy of Brissot (q.v.) and his faction, his one time friends, but throughout continued to engage in his trade in colonial goods. His house was invaded in 27 September 1793 and some barrels of rum were seized and he was accused of being a hoarder. He escaped the charge, rum not being among the specified products, but his rum was not returned to him. When the Thermidorians published a list of Montagnards which included the name Robert, François insisted that it was not his. He was sent to Belgium by the Convention, but had to be recalled because of his erratic and high-handed actions. He settled in Belgium after the Restoration, having rallied to Napoleon in the Hundred Days. He died in Brussels in 1826 four years after his wife.

Robert was among the earliest advocates and propagandists of republicanism who gave a lead to the workers in the popular movements of 1791 and 1792. This marked the high-point of his radicalism and he was elected to the National Convention, but thereafter he did not play a prominent part in the revolution.

In addition to the entry on Robert in A. Kuscinski, *Dictionnaire des conventionnels* (Paris, 1917), further information on his life and activities can be found in L. Antheunis, *Le conventionnel belge François Robert (1763–1826) et sa femme Louise de Kéralio (1758–1822)* (Wetteren, 1955).

BILL MURRAY

ROBESPIERRE, Maximilien François Marie Isidore Joseph de (1758–1794)
French Jacobin leader, deputy to the Third Estate, the Constituent Assembly, the National Convention, and member of the Committee of Public Safety

Born in Arras (Pas-de-Calais), Robespierre was the eldest of four children of Maximilien Barthelemy François de Robespierre and Jacqueline Marguerite Carraut. His mother died in 1764 and in the same year his father, a barrister, left Arras, returning occasionally but finally dying in Munich in 1777. From the age of six Robespierre was raised by grandparents, and attended the local Oratorian college in Arras. Then in 1770, with the help of the local bishop, he went to Paris as a scholarshp boy to study at the prestigious college of Louis-le-Grand. He stayed there for eleven years, proved an able pupil and in 1775 was chosen to deliver the school's Latin address to Louis

XVI at the time of his coronation. Among his fellow students were Camille Desmoulins (q.v.) Beffroy de Reigny and Stanislas Fréron (q.v.). In 1781, having qualified as a lawyer, he returned to Arras to practise, and quickly acquired a reputation for honesty, ability and compassion towards the poor. His lifestyle, however, was that of a respectable provincial bourgeois: in 1782 he was made judge in the local episcopal court; on 15 November 1783 he was elected to the Academy of Arras; and in 1784 he won a medal from the Academy of Metz for an essay on the extent to which families shared the guilt for crimes committed by their members. In 1787 he was elected to a select local literary circle, the Rosati, and throughout these years his writings reveal the mind of a serious but moderate reformer, critical of the judicial system and of clerical corruption, careful not to offend local respectable opinion, and with little indication of his future radicalism.

His radicalism, however, was awakened by the events of 1788. He joined local protests against Lamoignon's judicial reforms in the summer of that year and, in the following winter published a pamphlet, *Adresse à la Nation Artésienne*, which praised Necker and denounced the manoeuvres of local conservatives. He followed this up with another, *Les Ennemis de la Patrie Démasqués*, during the spring of 1789, and on 23 March was elected as one of the sixteen deputies for the Third Estate of Artois to the Estates General. He moved to Paris and quickly made a name for himself as one of a small group on the radical left, complementing it with a reputation for personal honesty and incorruptibility. Yet, although a regular speaker in debates, his poor speaking-voice and his radical views ensured that he was never elected to any of the Assembly's powerful committees. Instead he found a more receptive forum in the Paris Jacobin Club which he joined in late 1789 and first presided over in the following spring, rapidly establishing a national reputation for himself throughout its network of affiliated provincial clubs. At both the

Assembly and the Jacobin Club he campaigned on a number of issues, notably against the property-based franchise, and for citizenship for Jews and actors, slave emancipation and press freedom. He also denounced the *marc d'argent* decree which required a substantial property qualification from prospective deputies. He was not, however, an early republican, accepting Louis XVI and monarchy in general as the least dangerous form of executive power, and fearing that a republic would profit either the Duke of Orléans or wealthy patricians such as Lafayette. Thus, after the king's flight to Varennes in June 1791, he remained cautious and dissociated himself from the republican petition at the Champ de Mars. Social issues appear to have interested him somewhat less, for he took little part in the debates on the abolition of feudal dues or on the Le Chapelier law of 14 June 1791. Neither did he make any major contribution to those on the Civil Constitution of the Clergy, save to support proposals for improved salaries for retired clergy.

In the aftermath of the 'massacre' of the Champ de Mars, Robespierre moved into lodgings in the home of a wealthy cabinet maker, Duplay, where he was to stay until his death in 1794. When the Constituent Assembly came to an end (30 September) he was ineligible for re-election, having successfully proposed on 7 April 1791 that no deputies of the Constituent Assembly be eligible for election to the Legislative Assembly. He therefore returned to Artois for six weeks, but by mid-November, was back in Paris where he retained a high profile at the Jacobin Club. He soon became involved in the debate over war in December, and opposed Brissot (q.v.), Carra (q.v.), Gorsas (q.v.) and other leading Girondins over the war issue, arguing, in three major speeches at the club (18 December 1791, 2 and 21 January 1792) that the domestic political situation was too unstable for war, that the army was unreliable and unprepared, and that only the revolution's monarchist or Feuillant enemies would benefit. He was in a minority on the issue, and despite attempts at a reconciliation, a breach opened up between himself and Brissot which widened in March 1792, when several of Brissot's friends accepted posts in the Dumouriez ministry. In its edition of 18 April 1792 the *Patriote Français* suggested that Robespierre was either mad, excessively vain or a secret royalist, and in late April Robespierre decided to defend his reputation by launching a weekly newspaper, *Le Défenseur de la Constitution*.

When the Dumouriez ministry was dismissed on 12 June there was a temporary reconciliation, but it proved short-lived when the Girondin leaders tried to negotiate a compromise political deal with the king, and Robespierre became reluctantly convinced of the need for a republic, urging the election of a Convention by universal suffrage to resolve the crisis. In the event it was a popular insurrection on 10 August which decided the issue, and Robespierre played no part in it, but that afternoon he was elected to the Paris Commune and became a leading figure in the conflict which pitted it against the Girondin-dominated Assembly. While not directly involved in initiating the September massacres, he did make an unsuccessful attempt to have Brissot and other Girondins arrested on the afternoon of 3 September, in the certain knowledge that this would lead to their death. Moreover he subsequently consistently defended the massacres as an essential contribution to the survival of the revolution.

On 5 September 1792 he was elected to sit for Paris in the National Convention and, through skilful manipulation, ensured that the entire Paris deputation was made up of fellow radical Jacobins. From the outset the Convention was split into the radical 'Mountain' (of which this group formed the core) and the more numerous Girondins. As a leading spokesman for the Mountain, Robespierre was accused of complicity in the September massacres and of plotting to establish a personal dictatorship. He defended himself in a new journal which he launched in October, *Lettres à ses commettants*, and in a major speech before the Convention on 5

November, in which he replied to detailed accusations made against him by Louvet a week previously by arguing that illegality could be justified when committed in defence of the revolution. Later that month he supported Saint-Just's (q.v.) demand that Louis XVI be executed without a formal trial, arguing that he had already been tried and convicted by the insurrection of 10 August, and in January 1793 when a trial was nevertheless held before the Convention, voted for his execution, without reprieve. During the early months of 1793, as the Girondin hold on the Convention weakened, he remained their most effective critic, notably after the defeat of Dumouriez at Neerwinden on 18 March. On 26 and 29 March he urged the Convention to order the arrest of Dumouriez and, on 3 April, accused the Girondins of complicity with his treason, singling out Brissot for specific condemnation. Seven days later, again before the Convention, he listed their alleged political errors in a detailed speech in which he claimed that '. . .a powerful faction is conspiring with Europe's tyrants to give us a king', and went on to accuse the Girondins of being the successors of the *Feuillants* and to demand the arrest of Vergniaud, Guadet and Gensonné. This gathered support from thirty-three Paris sections which, on 22 April, petitioned the Convention to expel the leading Girondin deputies, but without success. Within weeks Robespierre had become convinced that only a popular insurrection would remove Girondin influence, and he made an ambiguous call for one in a speech at the Jacobin Club on 26 May, hedging it round with certain reservations. Three days later, with disorder mounting, he urged the Paris Commune to take the initiative, arguing that he himself was too exhausted from four years of continuous political activity: 'I have spoken and have no other duty to perform.'

When the insurrection began on 31 May, he spoke briefly for it on the first day, but then remained silent until it had succeeded on 2 June. However, in the weeks that followed he lent his support to the actions of the Dantonist Committee of Public Safety, and welcomed the new democratic constitution passed by the Convention in late June. He was also notably ruthless in condemning criticisms of the Committee's political and economic policies voiced by the Enragé priest, Jacques Roux (q.v.) in late June. However, on 10 July the personnel of the Committee was radically changed, in response to mounting criticism of its inadequacies, and on 27 July Robespierre was elected to it as a replacement for Thomas Augustin Gasparin. It was his first taste of power at national level, and he was to stay there for exactly a year, but his influence and role on the Committee have frequently been exaggerated. He was only ever one of twelve members, (from March 1794, eleven), re-elected monthly by the Convention. Internal specialisation ensured that several areas of policy were controlled by colleagues with the relevant technical expertise (such as Carnot (q.v.), for military affairs or Saint-André (q.v.) for the navy). Robespierre never covered a specialist area, but instead, because of his prestige at the Jacobin Club and in the Convention, played a major role in elaborating and explaining ideology and policy to both. He was therefore never a personal dictator, although he could be a dominant member in group discussions, and frequently modified his own views in the interest of governmental unity.

During the autumn of 1793 Robespierre was particularly prominent in combating criticism of the Committee within the Convention, rejecting Hébert's (q.v.) demands for the immediate implementation of the 1793 constitution, carrying out a purge of incompetent army commanders, and strengthening the powers of the revolutionary government, with the decrees of 10 October and 4 December. He was, if anything, a moderating influence on the development of the terror, reluctant to see the Girondin leaders executed in late October, and intervening personally in the Convention on 3 October to ensure that seventy-three deputies who had signed a protest against the insurrection of 2 June were not brought to trial. When a dechristianisation campaign hit Paris in November, causing the closure of many of the capital's churches and the laicisation of several hundred priests, he adamantly opposed it at the Jacobin Club and at the Convention, arguing it to be the work of political adventurers, and fearing that it would further alienate the predominantly Catholic peasantry.

By the end of 1793 civil war was almost at an end, and the advance of the First Coalition had been halted. However, political divisions now surfaced between the Indulgent faction, led by Danton (q.v.), which favoured an early return to political normality, and Hébertistes, who demanded an intensification of the terror with the enactment of more radical social measures. Robespierre initially favoured the Indulgents, appreciating the support given to him by Danton in checking dechristianisation, and secretly approving the text of the first two copies of the *Vieux Cordelier*, launched in mid-December by his friend and erstwhile school colleague, Camille Desmoulins, to spearhead the Indulgent campaign. Yet internal pressure within the Committee of Public Safety, most notably the return of Collot d'Herbois (q.v.) from Lyon in late December, persuaded him to draw back in the interest of government unity, and this decision was confirmed in early January by the discovery that several political figures close to Danton were involved in financial and political corruption. At the Jacobin Club on 7 January 1794 he denounced the *Vieux Cordelier*, intemperately recommending that it be burnt, and for the next two months attempted to reconcile the two warring factions. At his suggestion the Jacobin Club was diverted into discussing the alleged crimes of the English government for much of January, while he delivered two speeches there, on 25 December 1793 and 5 February 1794 which attempted to draw the debate onto a higher plane by defining the nature of revolutionary government as being a combination of 'vertu' and terror, each indispensable to the other in a time of war: '. .vertu sans laquelle la terreur est funeste, terreur sans

lacquelle la vertu est impuissante.'

Between 12 February and 10 March illness kept him away from the Committee. But he returned in time to sign the orders for the arrest, and subsequent execution of Hébert and his political allies. Their elimination strengthened the position of the indulgents and, in late March, Robespierre met Danton in an attempt to persuade him to abandon his campaign against the revolutionary government. Danton refused and Robespierre, with apparent reluctance, gave in to pressure from colleagues by signing the order for his arrest on the night of 30–31 March. The elimination of both factions strengthened the Committee and was accomplished by a series of measures, many of which Robespierre helped draft, designed to control the autonomy of the sans-culotte movement and tighten up administrative centralisation. Yet by now the Committee had many secret enemies within the Convention and, during the spring of 1794, was increasingly split by internal divisions and at loggerheads with its sister committee, the Committee of General Security. The Ventôse decrees, providing for the redistribution of the land of convicted traitors to the poor, were tacitly opposed by several members of the Committee of Public Safety, while on 22 and 23 May attempts were made to assassinate Robespierre and Collot d'Herbois which led to the introduction of the law of 22 Prairial which greatly simplified the proceedings of the Revolutionary Tribunal and removed immunity from Convention deputies. Drafted by Robespierre and Couthon (q.v.), it encountered opposition within the Convention, and was disliked by many members of the Committee of General Security who resented provisions which diluted their own powers over the arrest of political suspects. These divisions were further exacerbated by Robespierre's proposals, adopted by the Convention on 7 May, for a Cult of the Supreme Being, designed to replace Christianity, which reflected Robespierre's own deeply held deist convictions. Formally inaugurated in a lavish festival on 8 June 1794 in which Robespierre, as president of the Convention, played a prominent role, it was secretly ridiculed by many deputies, and offended atheists on the Committee of General Security who gained their revenge by publicising the case of a woman visionary, Cathérine Théot, who held secret meetings with known counter-revolutionaries, at which Robespierre was venerated as the herald of a new messiah. On 15 June, when Vadier (q.v.), on behalf of the Committee, described her case to the Convention in ironic terms as evidence of a new plot against the revolution, Robespierre was forced to step in to defend his own reputation and prevent her being sent before the Revolutionary Tribunal.

On 10 Messidor two of his colleagues on the Committee, Collot d'Herbois and Billaud-Varenne (q.v.), accused him of plotting to estabish a personal dictatorship and, for the next twenty-five days, he absented himself from meetings, working on papers in his rooms at the Duplay household. For an even longer period, from 24 Prairial until 8 Thermidor, he made no speech at the Convention, but he did speak regularly at the Jacobin Club where his authority remained unquestioned. On 5 Thermidor his colleagues at the Committee of Public Safety, anxious to retain the façade of governmental unity, persuaded Robespierre to attend a joint meeting with themselves and the Committee of General Security to effect a reconciliation, at which agreement was reached on the implementation of the Ventrôse decrees. But the distrust remained and, on 8 Thermidor, Robespierre took his case to the floor of the Convention in a rambling speech which called for a purge of both committees, but without specifying names. He repeated the speech that evening at the Paris Jacobin Club, but in the meanwhile his opponents grasped the opportunity to co-ordinate their response and, at the Convention on the following day he was denounced and indicted after a long debate, along with his brother Augustin, Couthon, Saint-Just and Lebas (q.v.). The four men escaped arrest and took refuge in the hôtel de ville where, for several hours that evening, an assault on the Convention seemed likely. However, Robespierre procrastinated and was recaptured in the early hours of the following morning, having wounded himself in the jaw in an abortive suicide attempt. Outlawed, he was guillotined without trial on the following evening.

Robespierre is a central figure in the French Revolution because of his early defence of democratic radicalism and his pivotal role in the evolution of the terror. He was a man of many paradoxes: an idealist who proved adept in political compromise and electioneering; a popular politician who dressed and lived fastidiously; a democrat who played a leading role in a ruthless dictatorship. Rousseau was a strong influence on his intellectual development and one which he frequently acknowledged. His views on political democracy, on the primacy of the general will, on the importance of civic 'vertu', on the social harmony of a society of small property-holders, and on deism, were all essentially rousseauist in origin. His attempts to implement and adapt them to the political experience of the revolution make him an important pioneer in democratic and socialist thought. Yet his reluctance to tolerate opposing views and readiness to identify his own beliefs with the interests of the people and the progress of the revolution, reveal an intolerant and élitist side to his thought which found an outlet in the repression of the terror. In this he was not alone, neither was he the most extreme member of the Committee of Public Safety; but he was the most prominent, and the most concerned to justify his evolution in ideological terms. As a result his reputation as a democratic socialist is matched by that as an apologist for revolutionary terror, and the imposition of the élite will of a minority on that of an unwilling majority. Both elements of that reputation have remained live issues in revolutionary theory down to the present day, and make Robespierre an important figure in modern democratic theory.

Robespierre's surviving manuscripts and published works are too numerous to list here, but they have been conveniently brought together in four publications. The papers are in *Rapport fait au nom de la commission chargée de l'examen des papiers trouvés chez Robespierre* (Paris, an III); *Pièces trouvés dans les papiers de Robespierre et complices* (Paris, an III); and *Papiers inédits trouvés chez Robespierre, Saint-Just, Payan etc.* (3 vols., Paris, 1828). The speeches and essays are in *Oeuvres complètes* (Paris, 1910–1967), which also includes the text of his two newspapers. Biographies are numerous, but the most recent, comprehensive and scholarly include: J. M. Thompson, *Robespierre* (2 vols., London, 1935); G. Walter, *Robespierre* (2 vols., Paris, 1936–9); G. Rudé, *Robespierre* (London, 1967); N. Hampson, *The Life and Opinions of Maximilien Robespierre* (London, 1974). All four contain good bibliographies as an orientation for further study.

HUGH GOUGH

ROMME, Charles Gilbert (1750–1795)
French revolutionary politician, deputy to the Legislative Assembly and the National Convention

Born at Riom (Puy-de-Dôme) in 1750, Gilbert Romme was the son of an attorney (*procureur*), who died when the boy was thirteen. He received an excellent education at the college of the Oratorians in his native town, demonstrating a real capacity for mathematics and science. Hoping to pursue a career in medicine, Romme settled in Paris where he absorbed advanced ideas, particularly those of Jean Jacques Rosseau, and associated with free-masons. His scientific interests brought him into contact with educated aristocrats. One of them, count Stroganov, a prominent Russian nobleman, in 1779 appointed him as tutor to his son, Paul. Travelling to Russia with his young charge, Romme observed conditions there and grew sympathetic to the reforms of Empress Catherine II. In 1786 Romme and his maturing pupil set out for Paris, arriving there two years later on the eve of the revolution.
Romme greeted the events of 1789 enthusiastically. He organised two clubs – the Friends of the Law, and the Society of the Tennis Court Oath – to rally public support for the revolution. After Paul Stroganov left France for Russia, Romme returned to Riom where he engaged in agriculture. In September 1791 he was elected to the Legislative Assembly from his department. As a deputy he voted with the moderate centre. Romme devoted most of his energies to work on the Committee on Education, submitting a plan to reorganise France's school system. Along with the Girondins and unlike Robespierre (q.v.), he approved the declaration of war in April 1792. In August he voted to suspend the overthrown Louis XVI.

Elected to the National Convention in September, Romme soon broke with the moderate Girondins. He voted for the death of the king and against any appeal to the people. Active in the Paris Jacobin Club, he became its secretary and an enthusiastic Montagnard. Romme was sent on mission in April 1793 to the army of Cherbourg, was captured by rebelling Federalists, and suffered imprisonment for fifty days. After his release, he resumed his labours as a deputy. A member of the Committee of Public Instruction, he put his scientific ideas to good use. In October 1793 Romme presented a plan for a new, rational calendar. Imposing twelve equal months of thirty days each, a 'week' of ten days, and a day of ten 'hours', the new instrument of time represented a radical depature from traditional Christian practice. Romme's dislike for Christianity was evident from his support of the Cult of Reason instituted by the Paris Commune later that year. Intensely interested in reforming education, he presented two major reports to the Convention in October. One called for the elimination of traditional schools that 'retarded the development of public spirit and the love of country in the developing generation'. The other sought to reorganise education into a four-stage system – primary schools, secondary schools, institutes, and *lycées* – with instruction provided at state expense.

Dispatched on a mission to south-west France in February 1794, Romme remained away from the capital until September. Thus he avoided the intense factional struggles that divided the Convention, the overthrow of the Dantonists, the terror and the fall of Robespierre. Although he personally disliked the Incorruptible, Romme soon became dismayed by the policies of the Thermidorians. Their toleration for Catholicism and repeal of the Maximum especially upset him. He did succeed, however, in having the remains of Jean Paul Marat (q.v.) interred in the Pantheon in October 1794.

Romme played no part in the popular insurrection of 12 Germinal Year III (1 April 1795) and did not participate in the uprising of 1 Prairial (20 May). But he fatally compromised himself when the angry Parisian crowd invaded the hall of the Convention demanding bread and the Constitution of 1793. From the rostrum Romme called for the immediate freeing of imprisoned patriots, permanent meetings of the sections, and improvements in the food supply. After the uprising was quelled, he was arrested along with other outspoken Montagnard deputies, imprisoned, sent before a military tribunal, and condemned to death on 17 June 1795. In a remarkable show of courage, Romme and three colleagues stabbed themselves to death to escape execution. 'I die for the Republic,' were his last words.

A moderate by temperament, Romme moved increasingly towards radicalism as the pace of the revolution quickened. That he identified with the Montagnard faction in the Convention and remained loyal to its principles even after 9 Thermidor demonstrates the strength of his political convictions. His strong interest in science, reason, and natural law were evident from his proposals to transform both public education and the calendar, plans that would have fundamentally altered the nature of French Society and weakened the traditional hold of the Catholic Church. Opposed to unnecessary bloodshed, he differed from extremists such as Robespierre, whose fall he did not regret. But his sympathies for the plight of the Parisian masses ultimately led to his own destruction. His courage in the face of death proves the sincerity of his republican faith and willingness to suffer for the cause of the revolution. Even today historians of the French left still pay homage to the memory of this 'martyr of Prairial'.

Among Romme's most important writings are *Projet de décret sur les spectacles* (Paris, 1792); *Rapport sur l'instruction public considérée dans son ensemble* (Paris, 1793); *Projet de décret sur les écoles nationales* (Paris, 1793); *Rapport sur l'ère de la République* (Paris, 1793); *Tableau de divers projets de nomenclature du calendrier de la République* (Paris, 1793); and *Annuaire du cultivateur pour la 3ᵉ année de la République* (Paris, 1795). There are a number of French biographies of Romme: M. de Vissac, *Un Conventionnel du Puy-de-Dôme, Romme le Montagnard* (Clermont-Ferrand, 1883); D. Strémooukhoff, *Une Education à la Rousseau (G. Romme et P. Stroganoff)* (Paris, 1947); A. Galante Garrone, *Gilbert Romme, histoire d'un révolutionnaire (1750–1795)* (Paris, 1971); *Gilbert Romme (1750–1795) et son temps. Actes du colloque tenu à Riom et Clermont les 10 et 11 juin 1965* (Paris, 1966).

J. FRIGUGLIETTI

ROUX, Jacques (1752–1794)
'Red priest', Enragé, and spokesman of the Paris poor during the French Revolution

Jacques Roux was born at Saint-Cibard de Pransac, near Angoulême, on 21 August 1752 and was the son of a manorial court judge. He entered the Church at fifteen and taught for a while at the Lazarist seminary at Angoulême, before serving as parish priest of a succession of rural parishes in the west of France during the 1780s. In 1790 his parish, Saint-Thomas de Cosnac, was the scene of an agrarian riot which was blamed on Roux' preaching and he was placed under interdict. By November 1790 he had taken refuge in Paris, where he joined the radical Cordeliers Club and began to make a name for himself as an orator and pamphleteer. When the schism developed in the French church over the revolutionary church settlement Roux chose the revolutionary side and in 1791 he was elected *vicaire* of the central city parish of Saint-Nicolas-des-Champs. The heart of the parish was the Gravilliers, a densely populated and impoverished district of artisans and wage-earners.

From the pulpits of the Paris churches, in the Popular Societies and the meetings of the Gravilliers Section, Roux preached a 'political gospel', denouncing speculators and the rich generally, advocating revolutionary terror against aristocrats and refractory clergy, and demanding economic relief for the city poor. He built a strong following of 'jacquesroutins' and was elected to the General Council of the Paris Commune at the end of 1792, but his ambitions for a seat in the Convention were unrealised. The Commune delegated him to accompany Louis XVI to the scaffold.

In 1793 Roux attracted special notoriety as a result of the Parisian grocery riots in February, for which his agitation was held partly responsible. Equally notable was a petition presented to the Convention on 25 June, on the occasion of the celebration of the adoption of the democratic Jacobin Constitution of 1793. Roux caused a scandal by criticising the new constitution for not doing enough for the poor, and in particular for not outlawing currency and food speculation. From this time he was marked out in the politics of the sections and the popular societies as a radical critic of the Montagnard government, a position reinforced after the assassination of Marat (q.v.) in July, when Roux began to publish a continuation of Marat's popular journal as the *Publiciste de la république française*.

Denounced by Robespierre (q.v.) in June, together with other members of the 'Enragé', or extremist party, Leclerc (q.v.) and Varlet (q.v.), Roux had henceforth to struggle against the organised hostility of the Jacobin political machine. Meanwhile he became increasingly isolated in the Commune, whose leaders, the atheists Hébert (q.v.) and Chaumette (q.v.), feared his influence with the Paris poor and distrusted him as a priest. In September Roux was expelled from the Commune and arrested. When he intransigently continued to publish his outspoken journal from prison, it was decided to send him before the Revolutionary Tribunal. Rather than face public humiliation, Roux committed suicide on 10 February 1794.

Jacques Roux was a political activist rather than a profound thinker, and his speeches and writings were concerned with immediate political issues rather than with fundamental analysis. They were also almost entirely secular. The doctrine and traditions of the Church doubtless influenced his condemnation of usury and speculation and his moral denunciation of the selfishness of the rich, but Roux formulated no original social theology. In so far as he presented a theoretical justification for the redistribution of wealth or controls on commerce, it was in terms of a natural rights theory of the kind implicit in Rousseau and Morelly. Because nature had provided abundance for all, all were equally entitled from birth to a sufficiency of the essentials of life. The division of society into two classes, the wealthy and powerful and the wretched and downtrodden, was thus against nature and against God.

The special force of Roux' message lay in his practical illustrations of the way in which the French Revolution itself had falsified the hopes of revolutionaries and actually intensified the division between classes. On the one hand he evoked the plight of the unemployed, of the exploited and starving families of the Paris garrets, and on the other the insolence of the profiteers of the revolution: money-changers who had bought church and émigré lands, petty government contractors who had risen to become the proprietors of great stores and fleets of ships. While Roux demanded the confiscation of the profiteers' property in fierce but vague rhetoric, his practical proposals were limited. They involved the death penalty for money speculators and speculators in foodstuffs and scarce commodities, and strict control of the grain trade and the establishment of public granaries, together with government assistance for widows and soldiers' dependants. Jacques Roux did not, as is sometimes maintained, pioneer the demand for price-control or the maximum, although he eventually endorsed it.

Roux' demands for a reversal of the revolutionary trends towards economic freedom may be seen, and were seen at the time, as backward-looking, recalling the paternalistic policies of the monarchy. In the context of the revolution, however, they had a different significance. For though based on the traditional prejudices and aspirations of the Parisian artisans and wage-earners, they relied not on a paternalistic government, but on democratic political action for realisation. In the same way the demands for the redress of inequality by expropriation were presented as practical politics rather than utopian speculation. Roux' agitation thus formed part of the complex of political pressures that led the Montagnard government to adopt most of the measures he advocated, even as their author was being destroyed politically, in 1793.

There is no evidence for the survival of a 'jacquesroutin' party, or even of a popular 'myth' or memory of Jacques Roux among the Parisian working class. The recognition of the role of Roux and the other 'Enragé' leaders is rather the work of later historians, beginning with Thiers in the 1820s and reinforced by Marx and Engels in *The Holy Family* in 1845, where Roux and Leclerc are presented as primitive precursors of modern communism. Much attention has subsequently been paid to Roux by Marxist historians.

For the development of Roux' political ideas, see his *Discours sur les moyens de sauver la France et la liberté* (Paris, 1792); *Adresse à la Convention Nationale* (Paris, 1793); and *Publiciste du Peuple français par l'Ombre de Marat, l'Ami du Peuple* (Paris, 1793).

Roux has attracted a number of biographers. See especially, W. Markov (ed.), *Jacques Roux, Scripta et Acta* (Berlin, 1969); R.B. Rose, *The Enragés: Socialists of the French Revolution?* (Sydney, 1968); M. Dommanget, *Jacques Roux, Le Curé Rouge* (Paris, 1948); and W. Markov, *Die Freiheiten des Priesters Roux* (Berlin, 1967).

R. B. ROSE

RUHL, Philippe (1737–1795)
French revolutionary and dechristianiser, member of the Legislative Assembly, the National Convention, and the Committee of General Security

Ruhl was born in Strasbourg, into a German Lutheran family, originally from Worms. His father was a Protestant pastor. In 1765 Ruhl was a schoolteacher in the Palatinate, and, in 1769, archivist to the Prince of Linange-Hartenburg. In 1784 he returned to Strasbourg, and in 1789 was elected an administrator of the department of the Bas-Rhin.

He was elected to the Legislative Assembly and, perhaps because of his knowledge of German, sat on its diplomatic committee. He was responsible for confering French citizenship on Schiller. Ruhl was elected to the National Convention for the Bas-Rhin. He was appointed *commissaire* to examine the documents which incriminated the royal family, found in the *armoire de fer*. On 23 December 1792 he was sent *en mission* to the eastern departments, where he quarelled with his colleague Couturier, and fell ill. Ruhl was perhaps suffering from one of his recurrent attacks of dropsy when the vote was taken on the execution of Louis XVI, for he did not register a postal vote.

On 14 September 1793 Ruhl was elected a member of the Committee of General Security, but he was almost immediately entrusted with a mission to the Marne and the Haute-Marne. He returned in Brumaire Year II, but in the following month he was again sent to the Bas-Rhin. These frequent missions, together with ill-health, prevented Ruhl from regularly attending the meetings of the C.S.G. He was present, however, at the overthrow of the Robespierrists on 9/10 Thermidor.

While *en mission* in Rheims, Ruhl assembled a large crowd in front of the cathedral, where he personally shattered the revered relic, the Holy Phial. The phial had reputedly contained a balm brought by a dove to St. Rémi, for the baptism of Clovis, on Christmas Day, A.D. 496. Ruhl proudly sent the fragments back to the Committee of Public Safety.

In the C.S.G., Ruhl was responsible for correspondence, and for the Paris region. He was elected president of the Convention in Ventôse Year II, and translated reports and decrees into German for the benefit of his Alsacien compatriots. He did not sign the warrant for the arrest of Danton (q.v.). After 9 Thermidor Year II he was sent on another mission to Alsace. On 14 Fructidor Year II he resigned from the Committee of General Security. During the last sans-culotte rising of 1 Prairial Year III, after a crowd had invaded the Convention, Ruhl made his final political speech from the tribune. Proceedings were so noisy that hardly anyone heard more than a few phrases in defence of the Jacobin Constitution of 1793. This was enough, however, to include Ruhl in a group of thirteen deputies arrested by the Convention immediately afterwards. At first, Ruhl was put under house arrest, but on 8 Prairial the Convention decided to bring him before the military commission, recently established to try the insurrectionists of Prairial. The news of this decision persuaded Ruhl to commit suicide. He was found stabbed the next day in his apartment in the Butte-des-Moulins, the first of the so-called 'martyrs of Prairial'.

Ruhl was older than many of his Jacobin colleagues and contemporaries, and the radicalism of his generation tended to be more 'Voltairean' than theirs. This was especially clear in the attitude of aggressive dechristianisation he adopted during his mission to the East.

Further information on Ruhl's life is available in three short articles: Michel Eude, 'Le "suicide heroïque" d'un montagnard: Jacques-Philippe Ruhl (1737–1795)',

in *Gilbert Romme et son temps. Actes du colloque de Clermont et Riom, 1965* (Paris, 1966); Gustave Laurent, 'Le Conventionnel Ruhl à Reims: la destruction de la Ste-Ampoule', *Annales historiques de la Révolution française* (1926), pp. 136–67; and Martyn Lyons, 'The 9 Thermidor: motives and effects', *European Studies Review*, 5 (1975), pp. 123–46.

MARTYN LYONS

RUSSO, Vincenzo (1770–1799)
Italian Jacobin journalist

Russo was born in Palma Campania on 16 June 1770 into a middle-class family. Following an early seminary education in Nola, he went to Naples where he joined one of the Jacobin revolutionary clubs, the *Società patriottica*, and on its dissolution in 1794, entered a more radical democratic one. Several arrests led to his flight to Milano by sea in March 1797, then to Geneva and Berne where he studied medicine and was very much influenced by political and social aspects of Switzerland. Returning to Milano in early 1798 and then to Rome in May of that year, he joined and actively participated in the *Circolo costituzionale* and wrote for the *Monitore di Roma* (September to early November 1798). Subsequently he published his *Pensieri politici* in August 1798. With the closing of the Roman circle, he returned to Naples in the French army as a doctor in the 101st regiment, and there published articles in the *Giornale patriottico della repubblica napoletana*. When the office of public instruction opened in February 1799, he was named superintendent and subsequently, on 14 April 1799, a member of the legislative commission of the Parthenopean Republic. Resigning from the latter position on 23 April, Russo was appointed by the Republic to a commission for the organisation of the province of Calabria, but the task could not be accomplished due to the popular uprising led by Cardinal Ruffo. Arrested and imprisoned on 13 June with the fall of the Republic, Russo was hanged in the Piazza del mercato in Naples on 19 November 1799.

Influenced by his sojourn in Switzerland, Russo's republicanism was based on the idea of just distribution. Underlying his dislike of tyranny and feudalism was a social dislike of luxury which translated into an anti-consumerism. Unique among radicals in advocating the abolition of private property, Russo exalted the virtues of life in small villages and towns as he expressed discontent with large cities and especially the commerce and economic growth which led to their development. His projects for agricultural reform would have the republic distribute a parcel of land to each peasant as a means for subsistence, and upon the peasant's death, the land would revert to the republic for redistribution. Russo's egalitarian republican world, then, was an agrarian one, sustained also by domestic industries and limited commerce within a cluster of small villages in which life was one of frugality. A reversion to an earlier Christianity, one of brotherhood without priest or church, was to accompany the austerity of village life devoid of misery and corruption. Under provisional constitutions, education was to serve a vital function of countering individualism and creating a communal mentality prepared to accept a liberal republic governed by direct popular participation. Once achieved, this situation would be preserved through a permanent constitution. Russo's ideal universe, once nations were freed from oppression and wars, would in fact be the small village projected onto a world scale. Vehemently opposed to the concept of private property, his brief identity with the Roman Republic provided him with the opportunity to practise frugality by divesting himself of possessions for the benefit of the *Cassa dei poveri*. Unlike many of his fellow Jacobins, Russo viewed the French role in Italy as a positive one. Aspiring to an ideal of *virtù*, Russo as moralist belongs less to the utopias of the nineteenth century than to a visionary social order of the eighteenth.

For Benedetto Croce, Russo ends an era rather than begins one – B. Croce,

Rivoluzione napoletana del 1799 (Bari, 1912). Russo's *Pensieri politici* (Rome, 1798) is a compendium of his views. See also, Armando Saitta, *La società degli agricoltori filosofi* (Rome, 1946); Marco Cerutti, *Neoclassici e giacobini* (Milano, 1969); and Delio Cantimori (ed.), *Giacobini italiani*, vol. 1 (Bari, 1956).

M. S. MILLER

SAINT-JUST, Louis Antoine Leon de (1767–1794)
French revolutionary leader, Jacobin, deputy to the National Convention

Saint-Just was born in Decize in the Nivernais, where his father, who died in 1777, had been a cavalry officer and *chevalier de Saint Louis*. He was educated at the Oratorian college of Saint-Nicolas at Soissons. In 1786 he was gaoled for running off to Paris with some of the family silver, and he idled the time away in the production of pornographic poems. It seems, however, that by 1789 he had repented his profligate youth, had turned to studying law, and by 1790 was committed to the revolution. He took part in the discussions as to whether Laon or Soissons should be the capital of the new department, Aisne, and represented some villagers seeking the recovery of common lands. He was unsuccessful in his attempt to get elected to the Legislative Assembly in September 1791, in the preparation for which he wrote his first revolutionary treatise – *The Spirit of the Revolution*. The only remarkable feature of this pamphlet, and then only because of the significance it took on due to later events, was the use of the word 'vertu'.

Saint-Just's entry into politics was delayed by only one year, as he was elected to the National Convention in September 1792 by the electors of Aisne. His first speech was printed at the expense of the Jacobin Club, but the first that made his colleagues realise he was not just another deputy was when at the trial of the king he made his declaration that 'kingship itself is a crime'. Less philosophically but equally typically he listed the murders committed by Louis since the beginning of the revolution – Bastille, Nancy, Champ de Mars, Tuileries – and declared that he therefore deserved no pity, no tears. Such clear-cut opinions he carried over to his views on law-making: that 'Long laws are public calamities', and a similar cavalier attitude to facts marked his condemnation of the Girondins. In the faction fighting that racked the Convention before their ultimate expulsion following the 'coup' of May 31/June 2, Saint-Just was not a prominent figure, but on 8 July 1793 he spoke at the tribune on the fate of the thirty-two Girondins arrested in the Convention. In fact this was a fairly moderate speech, especially in comparison with others he was to make, and although his condemnation of the Girondins was more imaginative than sound, it was consonant with his views on the need for a strongly centralised state. He had addressed this subject in a speech of 24 April 1793 criticising Condorcet's (q.v.) proposed constitution, and again on 15 May. He pointed to the United States of America as a country whose safety was constantly at threat because its unity had been sacrificed to federation, and predicted that one day this would result in armed conflict, a prediction that was to prove of some substance in the case of both the United States and France. A few days after that speech he turned his attention more particularly to the threat of Paris being submerged in a multiplication of separate and powerful administrations: 'There has been a desire to divide Paris in order to tranquillise the government, while I think we need an equitable government to tranquillise all of France and reunite all wills under the one law, just as the sparks of the earth come together to form the thunder (foudre).'

Saint-Just played a dominant role in the Committee of Public Safety. He entered the Committee on 10 July, and on 10 October pronounced the speech that declared the government of France 'revolutionary until the peace'. It was as a deputy on mission, however, that Saint-Just played his most dramatic role, when he went with Le Bas (q.v.) to restore morale in the

army in Alsace. When Saint-Just arrived the Army of the Rhine was in a state of disorganisation, waste and corruption, with the department of the Bas-Rhin at the prey of conspiring royalists on the one hand and the revolutionary excesses of Hébertists like Monet and Euloge Schneider (q.v.) on the other. Saint-Just also came into conflict with the nine representatives of the Convention who were already there and who refused to recognise Saint-Just and Le Bas as superior in their powers to them, as indeed the Convention still held itself superior to the Committee of Public Safety. Saint-Just was not to be discouraged. Shortly after his arrival, on 22 October, he and Le Bas issued a proclamation to the troops aimed at restoring their morale and then proceeded to take energetic measures to show that they had come with more than just stirring words. He established an extraordinary military commission to judge and punish all agents in the army found guilty of dishonesty; instituted severe disciplinary regulations and ensured that they were acted upon, on some occasions shooting officers before assembled troops; and reorganised the military hospitals to stop the abuse of hospitalisation papers that encouraged shirking. Discipline in the army was of prime importance and to the Austrians he let it be known that there would be no treaties: 'The French Republic takes from and sends to its enemies nothing but lead.' He decreed extraordinary legislation to ensure that his troops were fed, clothed and armed, imposing a forced loan of 9 million *livres* on the rich citizens of Strasbourg and threatening those who didn't pay within twenty-four hours with a month in prison. After a short visit to Paris, Saint-Just and Le Bas returned to the army, arriving in Strasbourg on 12 December 1793. They immediately took action against the Hébertists. Euloge Schneider, accusateur of the Revolutionary Tribunal at Strasbourg, was arrested, convicted, exposed on the guillotine for four hours daily with a notice hung around his neck saying that he had dishonoured the revolution. Schneider was then sent to

Paris and condemned to death by the Revolutionary Tribunal on 11 Germinal Year II. At the same time Saint-Just prevented the department of the Lower Rhine going the way of Lyon by keeping a tight rein on the ultra-terroristic policies of the representatives on mission, Baudet and Lacoste, who added to their hatred of religion a hatred of all things German. By the end of the year the Austrians had been driven out of Alsace: in a few weeks Saint-Just had restored order and imposed discipline in a region disintegrating amid poor morale and vicious political faction fights. On 22 January 1794 Saint-Just returned to the Army of the Nord, but this was a short visit, although marked once more by vital legislation ruthlessly carried out.

On 1er Ventôse Saint-Just was elected President of the Convention, in time to enter into the crucial machinations that would see the purge of the Hébertists and the Dantonists. Against the 'ultras' he made a speech on 13 March that clearly implicated Hébert and his followers, without naming them: 'If you want to act against the present order of things as the people did against tyranny, you are wicked people who must be unmasked. . .'. A decree was passed by the Convention declaring traitors all those who, among various other offences, had sought to alter the form of the republican government. The government in power was the people, the sovereign. The sovereign was opposed to all factions, who were by definition enemies of the people: 'Every faction is criminal because it tends to divide the citizens; every faction is criminal because it neutralises the power of public virtue'. That evening five Hébertists including Hébert (q.v.) and Ransin, were arrested. More were rounded up over the next few days. They were charged with being part of a foreign conspiracy and executed on 24 March.

Saint-Just next turned his attention to the 'remaining faction', the 'Indulgents', with a speech (31 March 1794) more vicious than that which had attacked the Girondins, and as unrestricted by the truth as his attack on either them or the king, concluding that Danton (q.v.) and his associates had never been patriots, but 'aristocrats more adroit and more guileful than those at Coblentz'. In the end the Dantonists were convicted of being in conspiracy with d'Orleans to restore the monarchy.

On 29 April 1794, again with Le Bas, Saint-Just was sent back to the Army of the Nord. He arrived just as Landrecies had been taken by the Austrians, accompanied by some émigrés who ill-treated and assassinated the patriotic magistrates of that town. Immediately Saint-Just ordered the seizure of the magistrates and nobles of Menin, Courtrai and Beaulieu, who were then taken to Peronne. Soon after this the Army regained the initiative. In June Saint-Just was present as representative on mission when Jourdan reunited under his sole command, on a decision of the Committee of Public Safety, all French armies from the sea to the Rhine. At the siege of Charleroi the garrison sent an officer to discuss terms with Jourdan, only to be told by Saint-Just: 'What I want is not paper but the town'. The town surrendered unconditionally and, a week later, on 26 June, Saint-Just was present at the decisive battle of Fleurus.

Ironically this great military success was instrumental in the downfall of Robespierre (q.v.) and Saint-Just, for the Prairial decrees had tightened the terror at a time when the victory of Fleurus raised hopes that it might be slackened. For ideologues like Robespierre and Saint-Just there could be no relaxation of the terror until the last unclean elements of their version of the virtuous Republic had been established. Not only Tallien (q.v.) and Fréron (q.v.) had reason to fear where the guillotine would strike next, but in their case it was self-interest that motivated their decision to plan the downfall of Robespierre and his fanatical young disciple. Saint-Just stayed by Robespierre to the end, and when the conspiracy to overthrow him came to its climax in the Convention on 9 Thermidor he refused to dissociate himself from his colleague. At the town hall, where Couthon (q.v.) proposed an appeal to the people and the army, Saint-Just argued that this be done in the name of the National Convention, for 'wherever we are that is where it is'. When the Commune was invaded and his colleagues in being arrested were seriously injured around him, Saint-Just remained as cool as ever, and maintained this pose until the guillotine ended his life at 6 o'clock the following evening.

Saint-Just's main contribution to the revolution was in his work as a deputy on mission to the Army of the Nord, but he was also responsible for some memorable epigrams and for the inflexibility of his ideas. In many ways his principles were less developed theories than dogmatic pronouncements, drawn mainly from the example of Sparta which was his ideal state. That state had little time for tradesmen, and there was no worship of the proletariat in Saint-Just's dictum: 'A trade ill befits the true citizen: a man's hand is meant only to till the soil and to bear arms'. Since Rousseau respected the hand that tilled the soil but detested the arm that wielded weapons, such ideas do not come from the author of the *Social Contract*, nor do they come from the eighteenth century, where growing urbanisation and burgeoning industrialisation were upsetting social relations based on agrarian economy.

In Saint-Just's ideal state his 'Republic Institutions' would direct the life of its citizens from the cradle to the grave. Indoctrination was to take the place of education with censorship to back this up. Parents had control over their children until they were five, when their care passed to the state. Boys were then to be brought up in a monastic discipline of silence and rude comforts, on a vegetarian diet. Organised in legions, battalions and companies, they alternated between helping on farms and being taught martial exercises. At sixteen they became workers, at twenty-one soldiers or magistrates. Old age was to be respected, and teachers had to be over sixty. Girls were not included in this training programme, being left to the more tender mercies of their mothers. The new Republic was to be kept under a strict censorship, since the alternative would be to rule by force. An essential feature of this censorship was the patriotic denunciation of those who failed to maintain a proper standard of civic virtue. If Saint-Just's ideal state looked back to Sparta, it also looked forward to some of the régimes of the twentieth century. Where Saint-Just was more original was in his ideas on property. Citizens, he seemed to realise, needed some material encouragement to help them believe in the society that ruled them. He thus wanted to make each member of the Republic a property-holder. 'Opulence is infamy', he cried. 'Beggary must be destroyed by the distribution of national property to the poor.' This was no socialistic redistribution of wealth, but rather insurance against the poor becoming a powerful force that could be used against the established order. He did not want to attack private property, only that of traitors, émigrés or other enemies of the state.

Saint-Just believed in the ideas he proposed. In Alsace he introduced rewards to war-wounded such as having them wear a gold star on their clothing where they had been wounded (if mutilated or wounded in the head they wore the star on their heart); liberated villages in Alsace were to be named after soldiers who distinguished themselves in the fighting. More important, however, were his Laws of Ventôse (March 1794), which decreed that no enemy of the Republic could own property within it, and that land thus sequestered was to be distributed among needy patriots. All the communes of France were to submit lists of indigent patriots who were thus to benefit, but before that could take place Saint-Just was dead.

Saint-Just lived by his own beliefs and wanted magistrates not just to talk like his Roman heroes, but to act like them; he wanted those who lived for glory to rule over those who lived for riches; and preferred the language of blood to the gestures of theatre. He believed that revolutions could not be made by halves and that the only peace for a revolutionary was in the grave. Whether he expected ever to achieve his ideal state can never be known; until then he clearly intended to abide by the ideals he had set out for others and when faced by death did not dishonour the role he had created for himself.

Biographies of Saint-Just in English are rather dated; but see, for example: G. Bruun, *Saint-Just: Apostle of the Terror* (New York, 1932), and J.B. Morton, *Saint-Just* (London, 1939). The most useful of the several works on Saint-Just in French is A. Soboul, *Saint-Just: Discours et rapports* (Paris, 1957). For Saint-Just's own writings, see C. Vellay, *Oeuvres complètes de Saint-Just* (2 vols., Paris, 1907).

BILL MURRAY

SALVADOR, Carlo (1752–1813)
Italian Jacobin and republican, nationalist, journalist, French agent and the public official in Napoleonic Italy

Born in Milan into a middle-class family (his father was a notary), Salvador was one of the first Italian converts to Jacobinism. Little is known of his personal life, except that from youth he was an inveterate gambler. He seems to have been in Paris by the early 1790s and to have lived through the terror. Unconfirmed reports assign him an important role during the September massacres, as judge in a Revolutionary Tribunal, follower of Robespierre (q.v.), and friend and collaborator of Marat (q.v.). What is certain is that he became a French citizen at this time and that these years made an indelible impression on him, giving him a lifelong faith in Jacobinism which he never abandoned. How he survived the fall of Robespierre is not known. He may have been involved in the Conspiracy of the Equals with Babeuf (q.v.) and Buonarroti (q.v.), but when they were arrested in 1796, Salvador was back in Italy.

Correspondence with Charles Delacroix, the Directory's Minister of Foreign Affairs, reveals that Salvador returned to Italy as an agent of the French government, in advance of the French armies. Entering Milan, still in Austrian hands, he began to rally support for Napoleon. After Napoleon occupied the city, Salvador organised the Popular Club, which numbered among its members representatives of the old ruling aristocracy, like Pietro Verri and Gian Galezzo Serbelloni.

French policies in northern Italy soon made clear that France had no intention of satisfying Italian aspirations for independence. Complicating relations between France and its Italian supporters was a growing ideological conflict. Italian francophiles remained Jacobins, while the Directory moved towards conservatism. Salvador belonged to those who became increasingly restive under the French, and he began to give voice to his discontent. On 25 June 1796 he founded the *Termometro Politico della Lombardia*, which lasted until the end of 1798. Consistently Jacobin in its inspiration, the paper, four to ten pages long, came out twice a week. Its programme was to bring about the creation of a democratic, secular, and independent republic in Lombardy as soon as possible, and to extend it to the rest of Italy.

Meanwhile, the Popular Club had ceased its activities, but on 23 July 1796, Salvador organised a new group with himself as president. The Academy for Literature and Public Education was ostensibly a cultural organisation, but it quickly revealed its Jacobinism. As Italian Jacobin discontent grew, Napoleon, in line with official French policy, moved closer to the old Milanese ruling class. Salvador openly criticised this in the *Termometro Politico* and the paper was suspended for several weeks. On 14 October 1796 Salvador and other Jacobins organised a large popular demonstration in front of the Duomo protesting against French policies. For his part in it Salvador was arrested, but released almost immediately.

As Napoleon relied more and more on moderate elements in Milan, Salvador and the Jacobins kept up their agitation for Italian independence and called for a constituent assembly. Meanwhile, the Cispadane Republic was replaced by the

Cisalpine, and Napoleon personally over-saw the writing of its constitution, which established a government closely modelled on the French Directory. Salvador continued his opposition both openly and secretly. But when orders came from Paris for his arrest Salvador did a public about-face, coming out in support of the French and even enlisting in the French army. Paris, however, was not persuaded of his conversion, and Salvador left Milan to avoid gaol.

He turned up in Grenoble, where other Italian Jacobins had found refuge, and started *Le Cri d'Italie*, which became the voice of Italian exiles in France. It criticised the policies of the French Directory and held the moderates responsible for the failures of the Cisalpine Republic. For the next few months Salvador disappeared in the shadowy world of the conspirator. He may have been a member of the secret Society of the Rays, but when Napoleon returned to France, Salvador again joined the French armies in Italy. He served as commissar to Murat and then to Napoleon. Back in Lombardy, Salvador again turned to journalism, founding the *Amico della Libertà Italiana* which made no secret of its Jacobin sentiments and consequently lasted only three months, from June to August 1800.

This marked the end of Salvador's activity on behalf of the Italian cause and Jacobinism. In disfavour, he found no employment other than as police informer, both in Paris and Milan. After the establishment of the empire, Salvador tried repeatedly to get back into Napoleon's good graces. He sent him numerous memoranda and reports on conditions in Italy, and in 1809 published a short pamphlet on the war against Austria which was a paean to Napoleon. Little is known about his last years, except that he played roulette unceasingly losing what little he had, until overcome by debts he ended his life by drowning in the Seine.

Salvador belonged to that first group of Italian Jacobins, converted to the ideas of the French Revolution in the 1790s. They combined its revolutionary principles of liberty, equality, and fraternity with a sense of Italian nationalism and hoped for French support in creating an independent Italian state, republican in form and inspired by the new political creed. The French paid little heed to their aspirations and pursued their own policies in Italy. The ideas and writings of men like Salvador, however, strongly influenced the left during the Risorgimento in the nineteenth century.

There are details on Salvador's life and his journalistic and political activities in the following sources: Giuseppe Gaudenzi, 'Carlo Salvador, un campione del giacobinismo milanese,' *Il Risorgimento*, XXXVII, 1 (Feb. 1985), pp. 28–54; C. Capra, 'Il giornalismo nell'eta rivoluzionaria e napoleonica,' in V. Castronovo and N. Tranfaglia (eds.), *La stampa italiana dal Cinquecento all'Ottocento* (Bari, 1976), pp. 373–537; Renzo De Felice (ed.), *I giornali giacobini italiani* (Milan, 1962); and Giorgio Vaccarino, *Patrioti "anarchistes" e l'idea dell'unita italiana* (Turin, 1955).

EMILIANA P. NOETHER

SANTERRE, Antoine Joseph (1752–1809)
French revolutionary, Jacobin, commandant of the Parisian National Guard

Santerre, the son of a master brewer from Cambrai, was born in Paris and educated there. In 1772 his father bought him a brewery in the Faubourg St Antoine, where he became one of the wealthiest and most prominent citizens. In 1789 he was one of those elected to choose the deputies who would represent Paris at the Estates General. On 14 July 1789 he took a prominent role in the assault on the Bastille, and was subsequently elected commander of the Faubourg St Antoine battalion of the National Guard.

He was a member of the Société des Droits de l'Homme et du Citoyen, together with Marat (q.v.) and Danton (q.v.), and reportedly signed the Champ de Mars petition of July 1791, demanding the removal of the king. He was later accused by royalists of being one of the organisers of the attack on the Tuileries of 10 August 1792, which brought down the monarchy, and he certainly was one of the leaders of the insurrection. The new, revolutionary Commune set up on 10 August named him commander-in-chief of the Paris National Guard.

Santerre held this post until May 1793, commanding the National Guard at the execution of Louis XVI. He resigned in order to lead a division of Parisian volunteers against the Vendée rebels, but after several defeats was recalled to Paris. Arrested and imprisoned, he was released after Thermidor and retired from political life. Following the failure of his business, Santerre managed to obtain a government commission to buy horses abroad, and through speculation on nationalised church and émigré property managed to rebuild his fortune. Under the Consulate he was given a general's pension for his army service. His fortunes apparently again declined in the last years of his life.

Of Santerre's ideas little is known, as he seems to have written nothing. However, as his actions testify, he consistently remained a radical leader in Paris politics, from 1789 right through the most extreme sans-culotte period.

Despite his prominence, Santerre does not seem to have found a modern biographer. There is, however, an old biography by M. Caro, *Santerre, général de la République française* (Paris, 1847), and an article by M. Dommanget, 'Santerre dans l'Oise', *Annales révolutionnaires*, 13 (1921). J. Jaurès, *Histoire socialiste de la Révolution française* (6 vols., Paris, 1968), vol. ii, p. 590 reproduces a letter from Santerre, requesting that petitioners from the Faubourg St Antoine be admitted to the Assembly to express their opposition to the royal veto (20 June 1792).

D. GARRIOCH

SCHMIEDER, Heinrich Gottlieb (1763–1815)
German writer and theatre director

Schmieder was born in Dresden. He studied law and graduated in 1786, but never practised this profession. Instead he served for several years in a Saxon regiment of cuirassiers, before finding jobs as a theatrical writer and director, first in Erfurt, then in Mainz and Mannheim. In 1783 he had already begun to write and publish musical pieces and comedies, biographical sketches, almanacs and theatre calendars. He also translated the libretti of operas and operettas from the French.

When Koch's theatre troop left Mainz following the town's occupation by the French revolutionary army in the autumn of 1792, Schmieder remained there and took charge of the setting up of a *Bürger-National-Theater*, which the Jacobins wanted to be a revolutionary amateur stage. Schmieder published an *Allgemeines Theater-Journal*, to which the Jacobin writer, Friedrich Lehne (q.v.), contributed, and on 22 November made a request to Dorsch (q.v.) to set up the theatre. He also drafted a new 'theatre agenda' which placed a great deal of emphasis on the democratic nature of the plays. Schmieder was director at this Jacobin theatre for some time, then fell out with the other members and left the town before the end of the siege.

He went to Mannheim, where he edited the journal *Rheinische Musen*, and then on to Altona, where he took over a number of important jobs in J.F.E. Albrecht's (q.v.) newly-established 'National Theatre'. He directed and translated and reworked several French operas, including *The Heroine of La Vendée*, and *Raoul Bluebeard*, and wrote tragedies and operas himself, including *Dr. Faust* and *Das Nixenreich*. His plays were produced at the National Theatre. From 1798 to 1801 he also published a *Taschenbuch fürs Theater* and a *Neues Journal fürs Theater und andere schöne Künste*. He was part of the North German Jacobin circle of F.W. von Schütz (q.v.) and J. Evers and became a partner in the Verlagsgesellschaft von Altona. In 1799 he was awarded the freedom of the city of Hamburg.

After he had given up his work as director and manager at the Altona National Theatre, he became manager of the theatre in the Hamburg suburb of St Georg, and in 1804 went to St Petersburg, and found a position at the German theatre there. Plays written by him were performed in Leipzig in 1806, 1807 and 1811, but little is known of him after 1804.

Schmieder's life is illustrative of the role that Jacobin theatre played in the propagation and dissemination of radical ideas in north Germany in the revolutionary era.

Further biographical details are in Hans Schröder, *Lexikon der hamburgischen Schriftsteller bis zur Gegenwart* (Hamburg, 1851–1883), Vol. 6, pp. 622–26; *Allgemeine Deutsche Biographie*, Vol. 32 (Leipzig, 1891), p. 29. See also G. Steiner, 'Theater und Schauspiel im Zeichen der Mainzer Revolution', in H.W. Seiffert (ed.), *Studien zur neuren deutschen Literatur* (Berlin, GDR, 1964), pp. 126ff; and W. Grab, *Demokratische Strömungen in Hamburg zur Zeit der ersten französischen Republik* (Hamburg, 1966).

W. GRAB

SCHNEIDER, Johann Georg ('Eulogius') (1756–1794)
German revolutionary politician and publicist

Schneider, the son of a poor wine-grower, was born in Wipfeld, near Würzburg. He received a church grant and was destined to become a Catholic priest. After the dissolution of the Jesuit school in Würzburg in 1771 he began to study philosophy and law at the university there, attracted by the ideas of the Enlightenment. The withdrawal of his grant compelled him in April 1777 to enter the Franciscan monastery in Bamberg. There he took the monastic name Eulogius. On 23 December 1780 he was ordained a priest in Salzburg, and in September 1784 he was appointed lecturer in philosophy at Augsburg. His hatred of

the Church's asceticism and obscurantism was expressed not only in the poems which he composed in his cell, but also in a public speech of 25 November 1785, in which he attacked 'fanatical clericalism'.

He left the monastery and became minister at the Württemberg court in Stuttgart, where his support of the rights of subjects made him unpopular with Duke Karl Eugen. In spring 1789 he was appointed professor of humanities at the Electoral University of Bonn by Archbishop Max Franz of Cologne. In the same year he greeted the outbreak of the French Revolution and the storming of the Bastille with enthusiasm.

In 1790 he published a volume of poems which echoed the fanfares of the revolution and excited a great deal of interest. When he published a new catechism he was accused by the orthodox of placing reason above revelation and infringing the church's commandments. As the political situation became more tense the Elector gave way to pressure from the conservatives and dismissed Schneider, who fled on 12 June 1791 to Alsace. Appointed curate to the constitutional Bishop of Strasbourg he quickly came to lead the German-speaking Alsatian Jacobins and gathered around him several 'preachers of freedom', for example Dorsch (q.v.), Cotta (q.v.), Clauer (q.v.), and Pape. As a result of the radicalisation of the revolution, Schneider quarrelled with the mayor of Strasbourg, Friedrich Dietrich, who belonged to the right-wing of the Gironde, and drove him and his followers out of the *Klub der Konstitutionsfreunde* on 7 February 1792. Schneider's society called itself from now on the Club of Jacobins and Sans-culottes.

After the beginning of the war, on 3 July 1792 Schneider's journal, *Argos, or the Man with a Hundred Eyes*, one of the most important organs of German speaking Jacobinism, began to appear first twice, then three times, a week. From 14 September to 19 December 1792 Schneider officiated as mayor of Hagenau, Alsace. During this time he translated the Marseillaise into German and spurred on the revolutionary troops under the command of General Custine as they invaded the Rhineland. After the execution of Louis XVI, Schneider observed that 'justice and true politics' had triumphed. On 19 February 1793 he was appointed public prosecutor at the criminal court of the department of the Lower Rhine, and gave up his curacy. The death sentence, which he demanded for three peasants who had made counter-revolutionary speeches and refused military service for the Republic, was carried out in Strasbourg on 31 March 1793.

When affluent citizens, who objected to the social levelling demanded by Schneider, complained to the Paris Convention about the 'vagabond priest', he developed an anti-plutocratic tone in the *Argos*. On 14 August 1793 Schneider and some of his followers paraded through the streets of Strasbourg with a mobile guillotine to intimidate speculators and usurers, and to mobilise the propertyless mass of the people for the revolutionary struggle. His journal welcomed the 'Law of Suspects' of 17 September, which put terror on the agenda. When the French Army of the Rhine suffered a defeat in mid-October Schneider took part in the successful defence of Strasbourg. He was public prosecutor at the newly-instituted Alsatian Revolutionary Tribunal, which published political crimes without a jury, and during his period of office (29 October–15 December 1793) carried out twenty-nine death sentences.

Schneider took an active part in the dechristianisation campaign. His journal took issue with French propagandists who saw all German émigré Jacobins as potential enemies. As spokesman of the sansculottes, he criticised the lenient treatment of those guilty of forcing up prices, and he found himself opposed to the Robespierre (q.v.) government on both national and political grounds. He sought to escape his enemies by marrying on 14 December: a decree of the National Convention forbade the imprisonment of married priests. The next day he was arrested on a threadbare charge on the orders of St Just (q.v.). He was taken to Paris where, from his prison

cell, he tried in vain to persuade Robespierre of his innocence. His denunciation by his opponents in Strasbourg, who alleged that he was a counter-revolutionary conspirator against the freedom of the French people, was sufficient for the Revolutionary Tribunal to sentence him to death; he ascended the scaffold a few days after Jacques Hébert (q.v.).

Radical even before the outbreak of the revolution, Schneider welcomed it and put himself at the head of the German Jacobins of Alsace. There he was an active propagandist, terrorist and dechristianiser, but fell victim to his enemies in the atmosphere of suspicion and counter-revolutionary fears created by the war.

Contemporary accounts of Schneider's career include A.S. Stumpf, *Eulogius Schneiders Leben und Schicksale im Vaterland* (Frankfurt, 1792), and Christoph Friedrich Cotta, *Eulogius Schneiders Schicksale in Frankfurt* (Strasbourg, 1797; reprint Christian Prignitz (ed.), Hamburg, 1978 and 1979). For further information, see also W. Grab, 'Eulogius Schneider. Ein Weltbürger zwischen Mönchszelle und Guillotine', in G. Mattenklott and K. Scherpe (eds.), *Demokratisch-revolutionäre Literatur in Deutschland, Jakobinismus* (Kronberg, Taunus, 1975), pp. 61–138, which has an extensive list of sources and bibliography.

W. GRAB

SCHÜTZ, Friedrich Wilhelm von (1756–1834)
German writer and publicist of French revolutionary ideas

Schütz, who came from an old Saxon noble family, was born near Chemnitz (Karl-Marx-Stadt). He studied law in Leipzig from 1777 to 1779, but did not practise his profession after gaining his degree. Instead he turned to writing. As an enthusiastic freemason he was proposed by Knigge (q.v.) for membership of the order of the Illuminati. As an admirer of Lessing, he demanded, in his *Apologie, Nathan den Weisen betreffend* (Leipzig, 1781), equality before the law for the Jews. His book

Leben und Meinungen Moses Men-delssohns (Hamburg, 1787), was the first biography of the Jewish philosopher. He travelled through Germany, France and Switzerland and settled in Altona in 1787 as a freelance journalist. Here, protected by the Danish law on the freedom of the press, he published the *Archiv der Schwärmerei und Aufklärung* from 1787 to 1791. In this journal he defended the Illuminati, and attacked intolerance, obscurantism and superstition.

After a visit to England he published *Briefe über London* in 1791, which sharply criticised social conditions in England. Attracted by the French Revolution's ideas of freedom and equality, he began, in July 1792, to publish the *Niedersächsischer Merkur* in Hamburg. The journal appeared weekly at first, and then twice weekly from October, and was the most important democratic paper on the right bank of the Rhine.

In his poetry and essays Schütz called on the German people to revolt against privilege and he expected the French armies to liberate Germany without any thought of ulterior motives. He was master of a lodge in the secret association *Einigkeit und Toleranz*, which was the first German lodge to accept Jews. Among the members of the lodge were Heinrich Christoph Albrecht (q.v.) and F.L. Schröder. In order to avoid persecution by the Prussian envoy in Hamburg, Carl Sigmund von Göchhausen, who was spying on him, Schütz accepted the position of secretary to the French ambassador in Hamburg, the Girondist Lehoc, in November 1792, and with him and G.H. Sieveking organ-ised a reading society, whose statutes were based on those of the Mainz Club, founded shortly before. Following the prohibition of the *Niedersächsischer Merkur*, Schütz continued to bring out his journal under the names *Neuer Proteus* and *Manuskript für Freunde* for another ten weeks, and published in it the speeches of the leading Mainz Jacobins.

The defeat of the French army at Neer-winden (18 March 1793) destroyed his hopes of an imminent liberation of Ger-many. Deported from Hamburg, he was enabled by the death of his father to take over the family estate at Stormarn, in Holstein, and not far from Hamburg. When the publisher G.L. Vollmer (q.v.) founded the Jacobin *Verlagsgesellschaft von Altona* in 1795, he took Schütz' step-son, Friedrich Bechtold, as a partner. By 1796, the publishing house had become the centre for democratic literature on the right bank of the Rhine. It published Schütz' *Neues Archiv der Schwärmerei und Aufklärung*, and *Neuer Niedersächsischer Merkur*. In 1797 Schütz entered into a political quarrel with Rebmann (q.v.). While the latter, in his journals *Die Geißel* and *Laterne für die mittlere Volksklasse*, incited the German people to revolution, and stressed that it was not the task of the French to undertake the liberation of Germany, Schütz had given up all hope of an independent German revolution, and appealed to the French to topple the rulers of Germany.

Schütz was a writer and actor at Albrecht's Altona National Theatre, and was also his partner for a time. Between 1798 and 1800 he published a *Theater- und Literaturzeitung*. He was a member of several masonic lodges, for which he com-posed songs, and after the death of the Danish Prime Minister, Peter von Bernstorff, an adherent of the Enlighten-ment, he wrote a biography praising him.

Schütz' disappointment at Napoleon's destruction of the French republic is clear from his *Geschichte des zehnjährigen Kriegs in Europa* (Hamburg, 1802). He lived in Othmarschen, near Hamburg, from 1797 to 1819, where he edited several (unpolitical) journals, and adapted literature for young people. In 1819 he moved to Zerbst, where his eldest son had bought a house and was an active freemason there as well. His *Freie Bekentnisse eines Veteranen der Mau-rerei und anderer geheimer Gesellschaften* (Leipzig, 1824) and his *Maurerische Ansichten* (2 vols., Leipzig, 1825–1827) show that he remained faithful to the ideals of democracy and freedom to the end of his life. He died in Zerbst in 1834.

Schütz used his journalistic and literary

skills to carry the ideas of the French Revolution into Germany. He sought to encourage the German people to achieve a democratic revolution by their own efforts but gradually began to place his faith in French intervention in Germany as the most effective means of radicalising the German population. He remained a convinced democrat and disapproved of Napoleon's crushing of the democratic republicanism of the French Revolution. His later works confirm him as a committed radical and opponent of the conservative reaction of the early nineteenth century.

Further biographical details are to be found in Berend Kordes, *Lexikon der jetzt lebenden schleswig-holsteinischen und eutinischen Schriftsteller* (Schleswig, 1797), p. 304; Hans Schröder, *Lexikon der hamburgischen Schriftsteller bis zur Gegenwart* (Hamburg, 1881–1883), Vol. 7, p. 68; F. Brümmer, *Lexikon der deutschen Dichter und Prosaisten* (Leipzig, 1884), p. 483; W. Kosch, *Deutsches Literaturlexikon* (Berne, 1956), p. 2614. See also, A. Wohlwill, *Neuere Geschichte der Freien und Hansestadt Hamburg, insbesondere von 1789–1815* (Gotha, 1914), and W. Grab, *Demokratische Strömungen* (Hamburg, 1966).

W. GRAB

SIEYÈS, Emmanuel Joseph (1748–1836)
French revolutionary theorist and statesman

Born in Fréjus (Provence) the son of a postmaster, Sieyès was educated by the Congregation of the Christian Doctrine at Draguignan, and was sent in 1765 to the Saint-Suplice seminary in Paris to train for the priesthood. Asked to leave in 1770 as an uncooperative student, he transferred to the Lazarist seminar of Saint-Firmin, where he was ordained in 1772. After several years without a benefice, he became a canon of Tréguier (Brittany), and in 1780 transferred to Chartres, where he was chancellor of the diocese when the pre-revolutionary crisis broke. But he spent much time in Paris intellectual society, and

when the debate over the form of the Estates-General began, he rushed to join it. His name was made between November 1788 and January 1789 with the publication of *Essai sur les Privilèges* and above all the best-selling *Qu'est-ce que le Tiers Etat?*, undoubtedly the most important pamphlet in the whole history of the French Revolution. The notoriety thus gained brought him election to the Estates-General, not for his own order of the clergy, but for the Third Estate of Paris. In June he played a crucial role in the debate over the verification of powers, and it was on his motion (June 10) that the Third Estate decided (in his words) to 'cut the cable' and verify its powers unilaterally. He was active in the debates of the subsequent week over the name to be adopted by the body of verified deputies. He proposed 'Legally verified representatives of the French Nation', but threw his support behind Legrand's simpler 'National Assembly', which was adopted on 17 June. He was prominent, too, in the formulation of the Tennis Court Oath of 21 June in which the Assembly swore never to separate until it had given France a constitution. Throughout the Constituent Assembly (1789–91) he was a member of the Constitutional Committee which drafted the Constitution of 1791, but the limits of his radicalism became clear in his determined advocacy of the distinction between active and passive citizens, and his opposition to the confiscation of church lands. His disdain for political alliances brought him respect but little influence outside the committee, and in the Assembly at large he was an ineffective speaker.

In 1792 Sieyès was elected to the Convention for the Sarthe department and voted for the death of Louis XVI without popular endorsement. But he took no prominent part in the most extreme phase of the revolution, and later boasted that his main achievement during those years was to have survived. He was next prominent in the debates over the constitution of 1795, when, much to his disgust, most of his ideas were rejected. He sat in the Council of Five Hundred until 1798 but

never disguised his contempt for the constitution. In 1799, on returning from an
embassy to Prussia, he was elected a
director and systematically set about undermining it. Realising that any successful
coup would require military support, he
approached General Joubert. When the
latter was killed in action he turned to
Bonaparte, and they were jointly responsible for the overthrow of the Directory in
November 1799. The constitution of the
Consulate, with its guiding principle of
'Authority from above, confidence from
below' was adapted by Bonaparte from a
draft by Sieyès. Under the new régime
Sieyès became president of the Senate,
and in 1808 a count of the Empire. In
1815, at the second restoration, he left
France and lived in Brussels until the
revolution of 1830. His last six years were
spent in increasing infirmity in Paris.

Sieyès' standing as a radical rests on his
ideas, and to a lesser extent his political
role, in 1789. After that he was opposed
to much that was most radical in the
revolution. But he was consistent throughout in the sense that he believed the state
existed to protect, and should be governed
exclusively by those who owned, property.
His attack on the privilege of the old
régime, his scorn for the weakness and
instability of the Directory, and his ultimate willingness to co-operate with the
military dictatorship of Bonaparte all
reflected this overriding preoccupation.
In 1795, 1799 and later it made him a
conservative – though never a royalist. In
1788 and 1789 it made him a radical.
Privilege, he argued in the *Essay*, contra-
vened the fundamental principle of civil
liberty – that everyone had equal freedom
to do whatever did not harm his fellow
citizens. Privilege was parasitic; it created
unearned expectations and groundless distinctions between citizens born equal. The
law should be the same for everybody and
admit of no exceptions. These principles,
so hostile to those underpinning the French
Ancien Régime, were further developed
in *What is the Third Estate?*. Public debate
during the winter of 1788–89 centred on
the relationship and respective powers of

the three orders of Clergy, Nobility and
Third Estate which were to make up the
Estates-General. Sieyès argued that the
separate status and powers of the first two,
or privileged, orders had no moral or
logical justification. The Third Estate was
a complete nation in itself. Three ringing
questions opened the 127 page pamphlet:
    '1) What is the Third Estate? *Every-
       thing.*
    2) What has it been until now in the
       political order? *Nothing.*
    3) What does it want to be? *Something.*'
The Third Estate had been nothing because
the privileged orders had hitherto monopolised the political life of the French nation.
But a nation, Sieyès argued, was 'a body
of associates living under *common* laws
and represented by the same *legislative
assembly*'; and since privileges were by
definition exceptions to the common law,
those who enjoyed them could not form
part of the nation and those without alone
constituted it. Though grossly distorting an
extremely complex situation, these arguments were enthusiastically adopted by all
opponents of a three-chamber Estates-
General, and explain Sieyès' influence in
June 1789. Until the Declaration of the
Rights of Man and the Citizen (August
1789), *What is the Third Estate?* was the
nearest thing to a revolutionary manifesto
produced in France. Rejection of the
structure of Ancien Régime society and a
divided legislature, and endorsement of
national sovereignty and civil equality were
principles which subsequent radicals and
revolutionaries took for granted. In 1789
they were new, or at least untested, and
nobody expressed them more vehemently
and more influentially than Sieyès. This
makes him a figure of central importance
to the history of modern revolution in
general.

There are several full biographies of
Sieyès – see, for example, J.H. Chapman,
The Abbé Sieyès (London, 1912); G.G. van
Deusen, *Sieyès: his life and his nationalism*
(New York, 1932); and P. Bastid, *Sieyès
et sa pensée* (Paris, 1939; new edn. 1970).
Sieyès' major manifesto is available in
English with an introduction by Peter

Campbell: *What is the Third Estate?*, (tr.
M. Blondel, ed. S.E. Finer, London 1963).
Essai sur les privilèges has never been
translated, but can be found printed with
Qu'est-ce que le Tiers Etat? in the most
recent French edition (Paris, 1981).

W. DOYLE

SONTHONAX, Léger Félicité (1763–1813)
French colonial reformer

Sonthonax was born in Oyonnax (Ain) on
17 March 1763, the son of a provincial
merchant. He was educated at the University of Dijon. An *avocat* in the parlement
of Paris, he enthusiastically welcomed the
French Revolution, writing for the *Révolutions de Paris* in support of civil rights
for non-whites in France's sugar colonies.
The Roland ministry sent him to Saint
Domingue (modern Haiti) as civil commissioner to enforce the law of April 4,
1792 that established political equality
between whites and free coloureds. From
September 1792 to June 1794 he struggled
to maintain Republican rule in Saint Domingue against secessionist colonists, royalist
troops, and Spanish and British invaders.
After driving out three successive gover-
nors, he unilaterally freed the colony's half-
million slaves, (proclamation of August
29, 1793, ratified by the Convention, 4
February 1794). Denounced by the colonists, he was imprisoned by the Jacobins on
his return to France but vindicated his
actions before a commission of enquiry
(February–October 1795). In May 1796 he
returned to Saint Domingue with a new
civil commission to organise the war effort.
Forced out in September 1797 by the
black general Toussaint Louverture, he
later sat in the Council of 500. Exiled from
Paris by the Bonapartist régime, he was
kept under police surveillance until his
death on July 28, 1813.

Though embarrassed by the issues of
colonial slavery and racial inequality, France's revolutionary politicians were very
reluctant to tamper with the status quo in
the French West Indies, which accounted
for close to three-quarters of France's

overseas trade. Saint Domingue alone
produced about half of the world's coffee
and sugar. Only when it was partly
destroyed by a slave revolt in 1791 was
equality granted to non-white property-
owners to win their support against the
rebel slaves. Often described as a Jacobin,
Sonthonax was closer to the Girondins and
more particularly to Brissot (q.v.). In
Saint Domingue, he rode roughshod over
colonial prejudices, replacing whites in
public office with free coloureds, deporting
or imprisoning hundreds of colonists, dis-
solving assemblies and municipalities, and
introducing a 25% income tax. He at first
sought to maintain, then to modify, the
slave régime, but the threat of foreign
invasion in 1793 caused him to offer
freedom to the slave rebels and then to
abolish slavery outright. To preserve the
plantation economy, he imposed, with
limited success, a system of profit-sharing
forced labour. On his second mission,
when he married a free coloured woman,
he distributed thousands of guns to plantation workers. An obstacle to the growing
ambitions of Toussaint Louverture, he was
deported, accused by the black leader of
wanting to separate Saint Domingue from
France. The colony became independent
under black rule six years later.

As the prime cause of France's abolition
of slavery in February 1794, Sonthonax's
decree of general emancipation marks a
watershed in the history of antislavery, of
the Haitian Revolution and of the war for
the Caribbean. Hitherto the European
antislavery movement was primarily concerned with the slave trade and race
relations. For economic and prudential
reasons, slavery seemed too dangerous a
topic to tackle. In most of Saint Domingue
the institution was under pressure but
still intact until mid-1793. Just as the
simultaneous *levée en masse* kept France
republican, it was Sonthonax's mobilisation
of the blacks that kept most of the French
West Indies French through the 1790s,
though at the same time providing the
military experience that would enable the
Haitians to win their independence in 1803.
The French Republic's threat to American

slavery radically altered, even more than in Europe, the nature of warfare in the region with regard to tactics, propaganda and social consequences. There is now a full biography of Sonthonax – R. Stein, *Léger-Félicité Sonthonax: Lost Sentinel of the Republic* (Rutherford, 1985). His work as a colonial reformer is discussed in C.L.R. James, *The Black Jacobins* (New York, 1963); and D. Geggus, *Slavery, War and Revolution: the British occupation of Saint-Domingue* (Oxford, 1982). See also, J. Garran-Coulon, *Rapport sur les troubles de Saint-Domingue* (4 vols., Paris, 1795–97).

D. GEGGUS

SZENTMARJAY, József (1767–1795)
One of the directors of the Hungarian Jacobin conspiracy

Szentmarjay was a descendant of an ancient noble family. His father had worked as bailiff for the family of Count Barkóczi. After graduation from the Kassa (now Košice, Czechoslovakia) Academy of Law, Szentmarjay became the private secretary of Count Mihály Sztáray. There he became acquainted with the literature of the French Enlightenment and translated Rousseau's *Contrat social* into Hungarian. In 1790 he became the secretary of Baron László Orczy, one of the leaders of the reformist movement of noblemen in Pest (now Budapest). Szentmarjay then became a freemason and entered the 'Reading Circle' in Buda, where he made friends with József Hajnóczy (q.v.).

Szentmarjay was a devoted follower of the French Revolution. He translated articles from the *Moniteur*, a major source of information on the deliberations of the successive revolutionary governments, into Hungarian and circulated them among the university students. In spring 1794 Martinovics (q.v.) involved him in the Jacobin movement and appointed him one of the directors of the 'Society of Liberty and Equality'. The purpose of the Society was to emulate the French Revolution and bring about a bourgeois revolution in

Hungary. On 16 August 1794 he was arrested and transported to Vienna for questioning, then transferred to the Hungarian court, charged with high treason. He was sentenced to death on April 27 and beheaded on 20 May 1795.

Szentmarjay was therefore an active publicist of French revolutionary ideas within the Habsburg Empire and one of the organising forces behind the Hungarian Jacobin conspiracy. Although the bourgeois revolution was in many respects premature, the activities of Szentmarjay and his comrades anticipated the anti-imperial movements of the nineteenth century.

Further information on Szentmarjay's life and activities can be found in the following sources: Kálmán Benda (ed.), *A magyar jakobinusok iratai* (Documents of the Hungarian Jacobins), vols. 1–3 (Budapest, 1952–57), and Kálmán Benda, 'Die ungarischen Jakobiner', in Walter Markov (ed.), *Maximilien Robespierre, 1758–1794. Beiträge zu seinem 200. Geburstag* (1958; 2nd ed., Berlin, 1961), pp. 401–434.

KÁLMÁN BENDA

TALLIEN, Jean Lambert (1767–1820)
French revolutionary Jacobin and journalist, member of the Paris Commune and the National Convention

Tallien was born in Paris, the son of the butler of the Comte de Bercy. In 1789 he served as secretary, first to the deputy J. B. Brostaret and later to de Lameth. In December 1790, Tallien became a member of the Jacobin Club of Paris and in the same year he established the Société de Fraternelle in the Faubourg Saint-Antoine area to explain 'clearly and interestingly the principles of morality and of the constitution to both active and passive citizens'. His interests in club activism and the political education of the masses impelled him to establish the Société des Minimes in the east side of Paris. In August 1791 he also founded *L'ami des citoyens* which became the unofficial journal of the far left during the period between October 1791 and June 1793. His *L'ami des citoyens* was essentially a work of propaganda. Tallien and his associates sent sample copies of the newspaper to affiliates to counteract the effect of an aristocratic placard the *Chant du Coq*.

After the insurrection of 10 August 1792, Tallien became the secretary of the Paris Commune. Because of this position he was accused of being involved in the September massacres. Regarding his role Tallien wrote that 'in times of revolution and agitation it is necessary to draw a veil [over it] and let history take care to consecrate and appreciate this epoque of the revolution which is much more useful than one thinks'.

Tallien expected to be elected to the Convention for Paris, but his difference with Robespierre prevented him from gaining the seat. He was elected, however, for the Seine-et-Oise and soon became a notable opponent of the Girondins. He sided with the Montagnards in the party strife of the Convention and changed the name of his paper to the *Amis des Sans-culottes*. This cost him many subscribers from pro-Girondist clubs. He advocated denying Louis XVI a defence counsel and voted for his death. He served in the Committee of General Security on 15 October 1792 and again on 21 January 1793.

Tallien was very active in enlisting new members to the Jacobin party. While he and J.F.M. Goupilleau (of Fontenay) were on a recruitment mission in the departments of Indre-et-Loire and Loire-et-Cher, the Vendée rebellion broke out, and Tallien helped to mount a successful defence against the threat to the Indre-et-Loire. He imprisoned the priests who were supposedly stirring up trouble. All suspects and all the relatives of the émigrés were forced to report at the main town of their administrative districts. To quell further the uprising against the republic, he organised a network of *commissaires* with the power of instituting multiple arrests and disarming of suspects. Tallien even advocated obligatory loans from the rich and argued for strong punitive measures against hoarding of foods and necessary goods. Towards the end of July 1793 he returned to Paris.

The expulsion of the Girondins from the Convention (May–June 1793) brought revolt by the federalists to Bordeaux. Anti-Jacobin demonstrations by the Société Populaire de la Jeunesse Bordelaise had become quite intense. By August 1793 refractory priests, aristocrats, and émigrés congregated in Bordeaux, adding to the tension. The Convention sent Tallien to the departments of Gironde, Dordogne and Lot-et-Garonne to help repress the revolt. His duties were to capture the Girondist deputies and their supporters who had taken refuge in Bordeaux and in the surrounding areas. As emissaries of the Convention, Tallien and Ysabeau were forced to take refuge at La Reole, a Jacobin stronghold. Their presence encouraged the sans-culottes to overthrow the Girondin municipal government on 18 September.

Tallien, with the help of Ysabeau, now established a *commission militaire*, under the presidency of La Combe. This commission in a period of nine months tried over eight hundred rebels and put nearly three hundred of them to death. The commission claimed to have helped in the repression of a huge mercantile plot, which intended to starve the population by hoarding and refusing to continue business. The unravelling of this alleged conspiracy led to the arrest of approximately eighty businessmen. Tallien and his associates established a committee to review the appeals of the suspects, and which made the release of the businessmen conditional upon their payment of heavy fines. A vigilance committee complained about this to the local departmental Executive Council.

While he was in Bordeaux, Tallien became involved with Thérése Cabarrus, a wealthy ex-marquise and daughter of the Spanish court banker. She helped the rich to buy their passports from Tallien and Ysabeau. Soon Tallien's wealth, his style of living and his connection with Thérése made the local Jacobins suspicious of him and Ysabeau. Their secretary Peyren d'Herval had already denounced both of them in Paris. They responded by issuing innumerable pamphlets in their own defence, but the defamatory reports soon became so weighty that Tallien decided to go to Paris and make a statement in the Convention to clear himself. He was unsuccessful, however, in his defence before the Committee of Public Safety against charges of loose and luxurious living. On 12 Pluviôse, to silence their critics, Tallien and Ysabeau arrested members of the vigilance committee of Bordeaux. Accusing them of arbitrary actions, Tallien stated 'we proceed against schemers, false patriots and ultra-revolutionaries as courageously as we have proceeded against the enemies of liberty'. Through his letters to the National Club of Bordeaux he continued to plead his innocence.

On 3 Prairial (22 May 1794) the Committee of Public Safety arrested Thérése Cabarrus while she was in Paris. Tallien's relationship with her conformed to Robespierre's (q.v.) idea of a conspiracy of corrupt men connected with foreign courts through banking circles. In the Convention on 24 Prairial (12 June), Robespierre and Billaud-Varenne (q.v.) openly accused Tallien of lying and indirectly called him a conspirator. Billaud-Varenne stated, 'Tallien's impudence exceeds all bounds. He lies to the Assembly with incredible audacity.' The Jacobin Club immediately expelled Tallien. Imprisonment of Thérése and expulsion from the Jacobin Club heightened his fear for his own life. Fearing that they were on Robespierre's blacklist, Tallien and a handful of deputies conspired to overthrow him. On 9 Thermidor, interrupting Saint-Just's (q.v.) speech, Tallien exclaimed, 'I trembled for my country: I watched the formation of the new Cromwell's army, and I have armed myself with a dagger which shall pierce his breast if the Convention has not the courage to decree his accusation.' With these words he drew from his coat a dagger and waved it in the air. His intense emotional outburst apparently reversed Robespierre's fortune in the Convention.

On 13 Thermidor Tallien was appointed to the Committee of Public Safety. He now rapidly emerged as a leading spokesperson for the political right. In late 1794 and early 1795 he spearheaded much of the attacks on the Jacobins and their policy of the controlled economy. On 1er Brumaire Year III (22 October 1794), he re-established his newspaper, *L'ami des citoyens*, which became a mouthpiece of right-wing views, but severed his connection with it a few weeks later. On 6 Nivôse Year III (26 December 1794) he married Thérése. Her salon became a major centre of Thermidorian high society and of the political right. However, in early 1796 Thérése left him.

Tallien's reputation was tarnished by the émigré landing at Quiberon on 27 June 1795 and the subsequent massacre. He had been sent there to organise the defence of the west. He subsequently found himself out of favour with all sections of the political spectrum – royalists, conservative constitutionalists and former Montagnards. From 1798 to 1801 he served in Egypt, his return to Paris having been delayed by capture by the English. Thereafter in ill-health and financial difficulties he played a minor role. He died in 1820.

Tallien began his political career by identifying with the Parisian left. He established the Société de Fraternelle and Société des Minimes that served as centres for civic instruction. Through his newspaper, he popularised radical ideas and he identified himself with the goals of the sans-culottes when he renamed his newspaper *Ami des Sans-culottes*. Thus in the early stages of the revolution Tallien was undoubtedly a radical. But the requirements of national defence and the political struggle during the revolution put immense power in the hands of Montagnard deputies such as Tallien, who exploited the many new opportunities for amassing wealth. His apparent proclivity to such temptations made him the target of attacks by those for whom he had fought many revolutionary causes. A feeling of rejection by them and the vicious attacks upon him steered him to the political right.

There is relatively little critical assessment of Tallien in English. Michael L. Kennedy's 'The Jacobin Clubs and the Press: Phase Two,' *French Historical Stud-*

ies, vol XIII:4 (Fall, 1984), pp. 474–500 describes Tallien's activities during the early part of the revolution. A. Patrick, *The Men of the First French Republic* (Baltimore, 1972) provides brief information on Tallien's background and activities. J.M. Thomson's *The French Revolution* (New York, 1943) and J.B. Sirich's *The Revolutionary Committees in the Departments of France, 1793–1794* (Cambridge, Mass., 1943) deal with Tallien's activities in Bordeaux. Gerald A. Tate's *Tallien and Therezia de Cabarrus: A Romance of the French Revolution* (London, n.d.) describes the relationship between Tallien and Thérése. However, this is not a reliable work. A. Kuscinski's *Dictionnaire Des Conventionnels* (Paris, 1917), H. Lacape, *Notice sur Tallien* (Bordeaux, 1959), P. Leveel, 'La mission de Tallien, représentant du peuple en Indre-et-Loire, *Mem. de la. Soc. Archeolog. de Tour*, 54 (1958), E. Welvert, 'Tallien', *Revue Bleue* (1906, 5e serie), pp. 236–238, 256–269, and François Gendron's *La Jeunesse Dorée: Épisode de la Révolution Française* (Quebec, 1979) are good sources of information on Tallien's life and activities.

N. CHAUDHURI

TAUFFERER, Freiherr Siegfried von (1750–1796)
Austrian Jacobin

Siegfried von Taufferer was the second of nine children of Freiherr Anton von Taufferer, an imperial councillor and district governor of Upper Carniola. He grew up in Laibach, present-day Ljubljana in Yugoslavia, before going to Vienna to be educated at the prestigious Theresianum. In 1769 he embarked on a military career. At the same time he pursued his business interests in timber, and he devoted himself full-time to exporting timber after retiring from active military service. He was a freemason and a member of the Viennese masonic lodge 'Zur wahren Eintracht'. In 1787 he left the Imperial and Royal Army, and took over the stewardship of the estate of Count Theodor Batthány in Croatia.

Taufferer's early business enterprises were dogged by financial problems, and he was eventually forced to leave the Habsburg Empire. On his return in 1791 he was arrested and imprisoned for unpaid debts.

In Vienna he made the acquaintance of Martinovics (q.v.) and the Viennese Jacobins. He became a regular attender at the group's meetings at the Berghof, and had connections with many of the radical democrats of Vienna, although not with Andreas Riedel (q.v.). In April 1794 he left the city for Zagreb, and continued via Trieste, Ödenburg, Ljubljana and Udine to Venice, where he resumed his political activities. Taufferer had spent some time in the city in 1790 and had got to know Denen, a French legation secretary, and de las Casas, the Spanish ambassador. He now resumed his contact with Denen, who enlisted him for the French service, and he went on to Nice, where he became a captain on the French general staff and was sent to Genoa. Here he was employed as an interpreter and military adviser by the French embassy. Taufferer served actively in the French army in military conflicts with the Austrians, and suggested the formation of an international volunteer force recruited from Austrian, Piedmontese and other deserters.

While in Genoa Taufferer conceived a plan for revolution in Croatia, which he translated into French and had sent to Tilly, the French chargé d'affaires, who in turn presented it to the Committee of Public Safety in Paris. According to the Austrian authorities' official records, it was Taufferer's intention to procure money from the French government, and then go to Croatia, ostensibly on a business trip, in order to enlist support for a rebellion, first in Croatia and then in Carniola, northern Italy, the Dalmatian coast and the Banat. From here the revolution would spread to Hungary, Styria and Carinthia; finally supplies would be cut to the Imperial and Royal Army, and Vienna would be so effectively blockaded as to give rise to popular discontent there too, and create a revolutionary situation in the capital. His familiarity with Croatia and the neighbouring provinces, and the groundwork he claimed to have laid before his departure, were among the reasons he gave to the French for the particular ripeness of those provinces for revolutionary agitation.

The Austrian authorities judged the plan to be well thought out, indicating a knowledge of the area and considerable expertise in strategy and tactics. When they received intelligence of Taufferer's plan they informed the provincial governor of Carniola and attempts were made to find and arrest him. All such attempts were unsuccessful until Imperial troops took Taufferer and his men by surprise in Sestri in 1795. He was captured, interrogated and sent to Vienna to stand trial. He was found guilty and executed on 24 May 1796.

Although Taufferer was not closely involved in the Jacobin conspiracy in Vienna and Hungary of 1793–1794, he did attend meetings at the Berghof in the early 1790s. However, his importance lies in his plan, in collaboration with the French, for an armed insurrection posing a direct military threat to the monarchy in a part of the empire he knew well, and his raising of a revolutionary free corps to that end.

Further details of Taufferer's life and political activity may be found in the Ph.D. thesis of Dana Zwitter-Tehovnik, *Wirkungen der französischen Revolution in Krain* (Vienna University, 1975), published under the same title by the Historical Institute of Salzburg University (Vienna, Salzburg, 1975). His career is also discussed in Helmut Reinalter (ed.), *Jakobiner in Mitteleuropa* (Innsbruck, 1977).

TIM KIRK

THÉROIGNE DE MÉRICOURT, Anne Josèphe (1762–1817)
French republican and feminist

She was born Anne Josèphe Terwagne at Marcourt, Luxembourg, the daughter of a well-to-do peasant. Few activists of the French revolutionary period have had their biographies as embellished as has Théroigne; the actual details of her life are elusive and rather more prosaic than the popular image, but nonetheless remarkable.

Before 1789 Théroigne lived in comparative ease as a singer and courtesan in London, Paris and Rome but rapidly became involved in the enthusiasm of revolution on her return in May. Her first active involvement, in the women's insurrection of October 1789, gave her a certain notoriety; her democratic agitation and flamboyant attire also made her the butt of savage ridicule in the royalist press. Early in 1790 she established the short-lived Club des amis de la loi, presided over in her lodgings by Gilbert Romme (q.v.). While the Cordeliers Club welcomed a proposal she put to it in February, her corollary that she would be allowed an ongoing consultative voice was rejected.

In May 1790 she returned to Luxembourg to avoid arrest for her role in October 1789 but was arrested by Austrian authorities and imprisoned at Kufstein. Her imprisonment guaranteed her a certain popularity on her return to Paris in January 1792. However, her proposals to Tallien's (q.v.) Société fraternelle des Minimes in February and March that women had the right and duty to bear arms led to Jacobins such as Santerre (q.v.) and Collot (q.v.) rebuffing her and to a beating by her opponents.

Théroigne participated in the overthrow of the monarchy in August 1792 and was decorated by the insurgents. It appears that she killed the royalist journalist Suleau during the insurrection. During the next nine months she drew closer to the Girondins, notably Brissot (q.v.) and Pétion (q.v.), and, as the battle with Jacobins over the direction of the revolution spilled into the galleries and streets, became increasingly estranged from more radical women such as Léon (q.v.) and Lacombe (q.v.). Following her public manifesto to the sections of Paris and her defence of Brissot, she was attacked by a group of Jacobin women near the National Convention on 15 May 1793 and severely beaten. By mid-1794 Théroigne was under arrest and, on her release, her deteriorating mental condition forced her removal to an asylum. The last twenty years of her life were spent in confinement due to the general decline of her physical and mental health.

While Théroigne fatally distanced herself from the most militant women of the people, she is of unquestionable importance as one of the first organisers of popular societies in which women participated and for her insistence on women's civic rights, ridiculing 'absurd, immoral prejudices' and claiming women as men's equals in courage: 'it is time at last for women to leave behind their shameful inactivity, in which the ignorance, pride and injustice of men have kept them subservient for so long' (25 March 1792). In ideological and tactical terms she was closer to the militant women of the Jacobin movement, striving for women's participation in the struggle to safeguard the revolution, than she was to the individual feminists of the time. Ultimately, however, the combined weight of male ridicule and her own political choices were to result in a tragic collapse of her influence and health.

Further information on Théroigne's life can be found in: F. Hamel, *A Woman of the Revolution* (London, 1911); L. Lacour, *Trois femmes de la Révolution* (Paris, 1900); and R.B. Rose, *The making of the sans-culottes* (Manchester, 1983).

PETER McPHEE

THURIOT DE LA ROSIÈRE, Jacques Alexis (1753–1829)

French revolutionary jurist, member of the Legislative Assembly, president of the Convention, member of the Committee of Public Safety and dechristianiser

Thuriot was born at Sézanne (Marne), the son of a master carpenter. He was a relatively obscure advocate at Reims during the years leading up to the French Revolution. He plunged initially into revolutionary politics in 1789 as an elector of the municipality of Paris. The following year Thuriot's training and experience in the legal affairs of the late Ancien Régime procured for him a judgeship on the tribunal of the newly-created Sézanne district. However, scarcely more than a year after assuming these duties in the revolutionary magistracy, he was elected by his department (the Marne) to the Legislative Assembly, successor body to the National Constituent Assembly. As one of the most militant deputies in the Legislative Assembly, Thuriot argued for the application of severe measures against noble émigrés and clergy opposing the revolutionary church settlement, championed the cause of war against counter-revolutionary Europe, and justified the Parisian insurrection of 10 August 1792 that overthrew the monarchy.

Elected by his department soon thereafter to the National Convention, Thuriot de la Rosière became quite closely allied in that assemblage with Danton (q.v.) and the advanced faction known as the Mountain. He voted for Louis XVI's execution, denounced the Girondist politicians in the Convention and their prominent allies in the armies of the Republic, and enthusiastically embraced the campaign of dechristianisation that raged for a time in Paris and certain provincial departments. During this first hectic year of the Convention, Thuriot achieved the greatest political prominence he was ever to know: he served briefly as president of the Convention and (from April to September 1793) as a member of the Dantonist Committee of Public Safety. During the terror of 1793–4, Thuriot's association with Danton's clique apparently cost him much of his influence in public affairs; perhaps because of this, he helped to bring about Robespierre's (q.v.) fall in Thermidor (July 1794). Thuriot had a changeable political and judicial career under the Thermidorian Convention, Directory, and Napoleon. Marked by his regicide past, he fled from France at the accession of Louis XVIII in 1815. He lived in Liège (Belgium) until his death fourteen years later.

We do not know enough about Thuriot's pronouncements and activities after Thermidor to be able to affirm the long-term consistency of his views upon public issues. But in 1791–93 his radicalism was marked in two particular ways: he espoused the concept of 'careers open to talents', and he not only accepted Sieyès (q.v.) argument that the revolutionary state could reconstitute itself integrally and impose that constitution upon the hereditary monarch, he also endorsed the even more audacious notion that the state, if it saw fit, could dispense with the institution of monarchy altogether. In two further respects, Thuriot's radicalism carried him beyond even the Robespierre canons of 1793–94. First, he maintained that Christianity should be extirpated, and not merely regulated, by the secular state. Second, he advocated what a later age would know as an international 'civil war' of irreconcilable secular ideologies. He did this by extolling the necessity for a republican crusade, spearheaded by France, against a Europe still dominated by the institutions of monarchy, established religion, and antediluvian social hierarchy. Thuriot helped to father the militantly anticlerical republicanism of modern France, and like a number of his fellow-revolutionaries, he anticipated the ideological diplomacy and war of twentieth-century Europe.

In addition to the entry on Thuriot in J. Robinet, *Dictionnaire historique et biographique de la Révolution et de l'Empire 1789–1815* (Paris, 1899), there is a short article by G. de Froidcourt, 'Les conventionnels régicides réfugiés à Liège sous la Restauration: Thuriot de la Rosière et ses amis', *Bulletin de la Société royale de Vieux Liège*, 5 (1956).

B. STONE

TRENCK, Friedrich Wilhelm Freiherr von der (1726–1794)
German Jacobin writer and activist

Trenck came from an old East Prussian family; his father, Christoph Ehrenreich von der Trenck, was a major-general in the Prussian army. Trenck himself was born in Königsberg on 16 February 1726;

he too entered the Prussian army and became a standard-bearer in 1744 and served in the Second Silesian War. He was arrested in 1745 while trying to desert to the Austrian army where his cousin Franz was a Pandour colonel*. He fled from Glatz prison to Bohemia and lived in Austria and Russia until 1754. In 1754 he went to Danzig following the death of his mother in order to assert his East Prussian inheritance rights, and was arrested by the Prussian police. On the orders of Frederick he was taken to the fortress at Magdeburg where he made several failed escape attempts. He was amnestied after the end of the Seven Years' War and Maria Theresa appointed him a reserve major. He moved to Aachen in 1765 and married the daughter of a local patrician. There were to be eight children. In 1767 he turned to writing, and in 1772 he published a sharply anti-clerical weekly *Der Menschenfreund*. His didactic poem, written in alexandrines, *Der mazedonische Held in wahrer Gestalt*, compared the archetypal absolute monarch, Alexander the Great, with highway robbers.

In 1780 Trenck, who had in the meanwhile been a wine merchant in Aachen, moved with his family to Lower Austria, where he had bought up a number of small estates. After the death of Frederick II he published his *Selected Poems and Writings* in eight volumes and his autobiography in three volumes. In the latter he claimed to have been imprisoned on account of a love affair with Amalie, Frederick's sister, and to have been unjustly persecuted by the despotic king. His fairy-tale memoirs, which appealed to contemporary tastes, were translated into several languages and made him famous. After receiving a Prussian pension he left for Paris at the beginning of 1789, and witnessed the beginning of the revolution. He then travelled to Hungary, where he tried in vain to reclaim the confiscated estates of his cousin Franz, who had died in prison. His meetings with members of the aristocratic opposition in Hungary aroused the suspicion of the authorities; he was arrested, forbidden to take part in any political activity, and effectively deported from Austria.

In April 1792 Trenck left his family behind and moved to Altona, which belonged to Denmark and, since the reforms of Johann Friedrich Struensee, had enjoyed almost complete press freedom. Trenck's *Monatsschrift* and his *Proserpina*, two of the most radical Jacobin publications in the German language, appeared there between July 1792 and February 1793. However, since the journals were banned in almost all the German states, Trenck lost his livelihood. In March 1793 he sailed to France, where he tried in vain to establish himself, and quickly became involved in the power struggles between the Girondins and the Montagnards. As a former Austrian and Prussian officer he was not accepted as a member of the Jacobin Club. Two journals, *Journal de Trenck* and *Le raisonneur sur les affaires de l'Europe*, were complete failures. Denounced as an enemy spy and suspicious alien, the impoverished sixty-seven year old enemy of despotism was thrown into jail and spent the last ten months of his life in miserable conditions. He protested his innocence and support for the revolution in vain in no less than sixteen petitions to the Paris National Convention, its committees, and the Jacobin Club. He appeared before a tribunal on 7 Thermidor in the year II (25 July 1794) and was able to disprove the allegation that he was a Prussian spy; but on account of his confession that escape was the natural right of every prisoner, he was sentenced to death, and guillotined the same day.

Trenck's radicalism was therefore sincere and he sought to promote democratic ideals through his writings. As a political activist however he was hindered in his efforts to practise revolutionary politics by Prussian oppression on the one hand and French Jacobin suspicion of his aristocratic background on the other. His writing thus remains his chief contribution to the German radical tradition.

W. Grab's article 'Friedrich Freiherr von der Trenck – Hochstapler und Freiheitsmärtyrer', in W. Grab, *Ein Volk muß seine Freiheit selbst erobern. Zur Geschichte der deutschen Jakobiner* (Frankfurt, 1984), pp. 63–108, contains an extensive survey of sources and literature.

* Pandour: originally a South Slavonic irregular of the Austrian army noted for marauding and cruelty, later incorporated in the army.

W. GRAB

UNZER, Johann Christoph (1747–1809)
German Jacobin playwright and political publicist

Unzer was born in Wernigerode, the son of a doctor. He received a humanist education and became acquainted with the ideas of the Enlightenment under the influence of his teacher, Jakob Mauvillon, who taught at the Ilfeld monastery school. He graduated in medicine in 1771 at Göttingen University, and settled in Altona. From 1772 to 1780 he was editor of the Altona daily *Altonaischer Mercurius*, and from 1775 to 1789 he taught physics and natural history at the Altona *Christianeum*. However, the demands of his medical practice forced him to give up both jobs. His marriage to Dorothea Ackermann, a celebrated actress and the half-sister of F.L. Schröder, was unhappy. After the divorce Unzer sent his two sons to board with the deputy rector of the *Christianeum*, Masius Feldmann, who was a member of Schütz' (q.v.) Jewish-Christian masonic lodge 'Einigkeit und Toleranz'.

Unzer's tragedy *Diego und Leonore* which attacked the intolerance of the Roman Catholic clergy, had to be taken from the repertoire in 1778 at the request of the Imperial ambassador in Hamburg, Binder von Kriegelstein. His comedy, *Die neue Emma* dealt with the love of the daughter of Charlemagne for Eginhard. Together with F.L. Schröder, he adapted Wieland's translation of *King Lear* for the stage. He was friendly with Klopstock, G. H. Sieveking and J.H.A. Reimarus and took part in the 'festival of freedom' celebrating the achievements of the French Revolution on the first anniversary of the storming of the Bastille.

In the course of the following years Unzer became a radical democrat and welcomed the radicalisation of the French Revolution. He knew the Altona Jacobin G.F. Heiligenstedt (q.v.), who went to Berlin in the autumn of 1792 to take part in democratic agitation there, and continued to write to him after his imprisonment. The conservative Prussian ambassador in Hamburg, C.S. von Göchhausen, considered Unzer the 'chief of the Jacobins', and wanted to entice him into the embassy building, in order to have him abducted by recruiting officers.

Unzer remained in contact with French Republicans during the period of Jacobin rule and met the French emissaries Delamarre and Castera, who made trips to Copenhagen and Altona to make purchases on behalf of the French revolutionary army. When the French ambassador extraordinary Leonard Bourdon came to Hamburg and Altona there were secret meetings with French agents in Unzer's house. Unzer also took an active part in the work of the Altona National Theatre, which was run by J.F.E. Albrecht (q.v.) and F.W. von Schütz and their friends. He died in Göttingen in 1809.

As a playwright Unzer disseminated democratic ideals and was not fazed by the progressive radicalisation of the French Revolution. His political activity was only stymied after 1799 by the repressive régime of Kai von Reventlow as head of the Deutsche Kanzlei.

Unzer's political writings appeared in two volumes in Altona in 1811. Further details of his life are to be found in Berend Kordes, *Lexikon der jetzt lebenden schleswig-holsteinischen und eutinischen Schriftsteller* (Schleswig, 1797), p. 367, and the *Allgemeine Deutsche Biographie*, Vol. 39 (Leipzig, 1895), p. 334. See also W. Grab, *Demokratische Strömungen in Hamburg und Schleswig Holstein zur Zeit der ersten französischen Republik* (Hamburg, 1966), pp. 109–111, 226–28.

W. GRAB

USTERI, Paul (1768–1831)
Swiss statesman and publicist, a leader of the Helvetic Republic

Usteri was born in Zurich on 14 February 1768 into a prosperous academic family. He studied natural science and medicine at the Institute in Zurich and, more briefly, at Göttingen, from which he received his degree in 1788. He spent the next year travelling, then settled down to an impressively productive career as a scientist. From 1789 to 1798, in addition to practising medicine, he was a lecturer at the Institute in Zurich, and supervisor of the Botanical Gardens. He also published a number of works on botany and human biology, including the first journal of botanical science in German.

Usteri had been raised to take a lively interest in public life – his father had been a correspondent of Rousseau's – and as early as 1792 he was sufficiently intrigued by the unfolding events in France to remark that, if he were free to do so, he would gladly give up medicine to study history and politics. As it was, his contributions were considerable. A plan to publish a journal called *Bibliothek der freien Franken* was blocked by the Zurich censor, but in 1794 Usteri published anonymously several volumes entitled *Tagebuchs des Revolutionstribunals*. From 1795–98 he financed the publication of a series of francophile journals in Leipzig, where censorship was less severe: *Klio* (later *Neue Klio*) (1795–97, edited by Ludwig Huber (q.v.)); and *Beiträge zur französischen Revolution* (later *Humaniora*) (1795–96). All of these publications were republican and internationalist in their outlook, and featured articles by Konrad Oelsner (q.v.) and others from the Sieyès (q.v.) circle in Paris.

In April 1797 Usteri was chosen a member of the Zurich Greater Council, an honour that reflected his social standing rather than his politics, which were dogmatically republican, and not widely-shared in the city. On the basis of his close knowledge of events in Paris, he warned his fellow councillors that simmering discontent in the countryside against the canton's aristocratic system of rule amounted to an invitation to French intervention. But his argument that political prisoners should be released, and general reform undertaken, was not heeded. Following the French invasion of 1798 Usteri devoted himself to publicising the activities of the Cantonal Assembly in a periodical called *Schweizerischer Republikaner*, and in the pages of J.F. Cotta's (q.v.) *Allgemeine Zeitung*, to which he would contribute regularly for the next thirty years. In March he was himself chosen a member of the Assembly, and in April he was elected a senator of the soon-to-be-born Helvetic Republic. He subsequently became secretary, and, in September 1798, president of the Senate, in which post he devoted himself to the political education of his colleagues, most of whom were woefully inexperienced.

As a senator Usteri found himself out of sympathy with those, like Peter Ochs (q.v.) and Frederick La Harpe (q.v.), whose enthusiasm for the revolution led them to tolerate French domination of their own country. Usteri consistently opposed French hegemony in Switzerland, from the podium and in print, arguing that lasting reform could only be based on an uncoerced national consensus. He also tried to guard the fiscal health of the new state, opposing wholesale tax relief to the countryside on the grounds of equity and prudence. Above all, however, Usteri was a champion of civil liberties, most particularly freedom of the press, without which all political progress seemed to him impossible. In all these respects he stood with the moderate minority in the Senate, which did not, however, prevent him from serving on a variety of crucial commissions, including the one created in April 1798, to revise the constitution put forward by Ochs. Usteri was the principal author of the draft constitution that the commission returned to the Senate in March 1799. By then, however, La Harpe had established himself as a virtual dictator, ruling through the French-inspired Directory that he and Ochs had created. Usteri was among those who conspired to bring about La Harpe's fall,

which finally occurred in December.

The replacement of the Directory by a new Executive Committee did not improve Usteri's situation for long, however, since it too was hostile to democratic initiatives. In August he played a leading role in a second coup, in which the Executive Committee and the bi-cameral assembly (Senate and Greater Council) were dissolved, and replaced by a unified Legislative Assembly. Usteri was named to the presidency of this body in February 1801, and set his hand yet again to the drafting of a constitution. Since the appearance of Napoleon Bonaparte as First Consul of France, however, a movement to reverse the recent course of events had been building among conservative Swiss, who recognised that the French need for a quiescent ally between themselves and Austria might lead to a restoration of the old, historically stable federal structure. Usteri was a passionate opponent of these men, whom he attacked in print as 'Swiss Chouans'. The only effective answer to their campaign, however, was to bring an end to political unrest. This was not achieved, and in April 1801 Napoleon presented the Swiss with a draft constitution that included substantial concessions to the cantonalists.

In September 1801 the Legislative Assembly gave way to a new Federal Diet, which Usteri entered as a representative of the Canton of Zurich. A month later he was named president, in which capacity he rallied the anti-federalists in the chamber in an attempt to revise the new arrangements. The result was yet another coup, this time by the aristocratic cantonalist opposition that Usteri had effectively driven out of the Diet. Usteri was placed under house arrest until the original Napoleonic formula could be resurrected, and its opponents in the administration purged. For about a year thereafter Usteri was excluded from participation in the government of the federation. In July 1802, however, he became a member of the Zurich Cantonal Commission, and the following year travelled to Paris as a member of the committee that would finally accept Napoleon's Act of Mediation.

As a member of Zurich's ruling body, Usteri attempted to diffuse open opposition to the new system, on the grounds that further resistance to French policy was pointless. But he was nevertheless not trusted by the conservative majority in the city, and excluded from significant office. In 1806 his revision of the criminal code, aimed at reducing personal and political abuses by judges, was rejected out of hand. Throughout the Napoleonic period, however, he remained one of the most influential of Swiss political writers. Although his own *Republikaner* was suppressed in 1803, his connection to Cotta's *Allgemeine Zeitung* assured him a European audience, which he provided with a steady stream of critical articles on Swiss affairs, supported by confidential documents to which his office gave him access. His conduct was repeatedly a subject of debate before the Swiss Assembly, and of diplomatic protests against the *Allgemeine Zeitung*.

Except for his role as a journalist, Usteri played no part in Swiss public life during the Napoleonic period. With the collapse of the mediatised régime in 1813, however, he re-emerged, in alliance with his old opponent La Harpe, as a bitter opponent of the aristocracy. For the remainder of his life he was universally regarded as the most important spokesman for the liberal opposition in Switzerland, particularly through his reports in the *Aarauer Zeitung* (1814–21) and in the *Neue Zürcher Zeitung*, which he helped to establish as one of the leading newspapers of Europe. The alacrity with which he publicised official documents remained a recurring source of difficulty for him, and in June of 1828 led to a dramatic confrontation before the Zurich Cantonal Diet. Usteri defended himself in such stirring terms that further action against him was impossible. By the end of the following year most of the large Swiss cantons had abolished censorship altogether, a development for which he deserves substantial credit.

In 1830 Usteri was again drawn to the centre of political life. On 22 November 1830 Zurich was the scene of a major demonstration in favour of a democratic constitution. Usteri was chosen to head a reform commission, which presented the Greater Council with a new, more democratic charter on 15 February 1831. This was ratified by a popular referendum on 20 March; and on the 25th Usteri was chosen First Burgermeister of Zurich, and on the 28th President of the Greater Council. After thirty years in opposition he had achieved the highest office his community had to offer. The spirit in which he would have discharged his duties can be judged by his immediate appointment of the conservative leader David von Wys as his deputy, a gesture of reconciliation entirely in keeping with a career devoted to the principles of political enlightenment and open government. Two weeks later, at the age of sixty-three, he was dead, the victim of illness brought on by months of unremitting labour on behalf of the city in which he had spent his life.

Paul Usteri's political career was dominated by two general objectives: the political unification of Switzerland, and the establishment of civil liberties, particularly freedom of the press. For him all freedom was personal freedom, and he was distinctly intolerant of political expedients that abridged the rights of the individual, even in a nominally good cause. He assumed that the natural outcome of a sound constitution would be an aristocracy of talent and virtue, which would rule according to rational principles – the most important of which, for him, was centralisation of authority. He was, in this respect, a doctrinaire intellectual rather than a man of the people. But he did not fear the people unreasonably either. The rising of 1830 represented the emergence of political forces that he would not have called forth himself. But given a choice between the leadership of a popular party and a temporising alliance with reaction, he did not hesitate to choose the former.

Usteri has been the subject of a substantial biography by Gottfried Guggenbühl, *Bürgermeister Paul Usteri: Ein Sch-*

*weizerischer Staatsmann aus der Zeit der
französischen Vorherrschaft und des Früli-
beralismus* (2 vols., Aarau, 1924–31). The
prominence of his public role has assured
him of mention in any history of Switzerland in this period. For this the best guide
is the *Handbuch der Schweizer Geschichte*
(Zurich, 1977), vol. 2, pp. 785–918. One
should also consult the *Mémoires de Fréd-
éric-César La Harpe* in Jakob Vogel (ed.),
Schweizer-geschichtliche Studien (Bern,
1864); and Rudolf Luginbühl (ed.), *Aus
Philipp Albert Stapfer's Briefwechsel*
(Basel, 1891), which contains a number of
Usteri's letters.

DANIEL J. MORAN

VADIER, Marc Guillaume Alexis (1736–1828)

*French revolutionary Jacobin, member
of the Estates General, the Legislative
Assembly, the Convention, and
president of the Committee of General
Security*

Born in Pamiers (Ariège) in 1736, the son
of a tithe collector, Vadier was educated
at the Jesuit College, Pamiers, and then
at the Collège de l'Esquile, Toulouse. He
joined the Piedmont regiment in 1753, and
was promoted lieutenant in 1755. He
fought in the Battle of Rossbach, 1757,
and then resigned his commission. He
married in 1762, and was to have four
sons. He became the leading landowner in
his village of Montaut, near Pamiers, and
in 1770 purchased the office of *conseiller*
at the *présidial* court of Pamiers.

He was elected to the Estates-General
in 1789 as representative of the Third
Estate of the *sénéchaussée* of Pamiers. He
signed the Tennis Court Oath, and on 4
August 1789 supported the surrender of
the privileges of the Comté de Foix. He
defended the 'passive' citizens of Pamiers
against an attempt to partition a plot of
common land, known as La Boulbonne.
Vadier came into conflict here with his
local rivals, the Darmaing family, and in
this conflict he represented the interests of
Pamiers against those of the *chef-lieu*,
Foix.

During the period of the Legislative
Assembly, Vadier became president of the
district court of Mirepoix (Ariège). After
the flight to Varennes in 1791, he called,
in a rare public speech, for the suspension
of the king, but finding this view too
advanced for his audience, withdrew the
suggestion, and Marat (q.v.) accused him
of moral cowardice for so doing. In 1792
he denounced the royalist activities of the
Darmaing family, and was elected deputy
for the Ariège to the National Convention.
Vadier voted for the death of Louis XVI
without reprieve, and aligned himself with
Robespierre (q.v.) in opposing a national
referendum on the fate of the king. He
vigorously opposed the federalist revolt in
Toulouse. He was a member of the Jacobin
Club of Paris, the Convention's *Comité de
Secours Publics*, and in September 1793
he entered the Committee of General
Security. In Pluviôse Year II he was elected
its president, probably because he was the
oldest member, after the resignation of
Boucher St-Sauveur, and in the absence
of Ruhl (q.v.).

With the aid of his network of supporters
in the Ariège and Haute-Garonne, led by
his eldest son, known as Carpe-Vadier,
Vadier secured the arrest of the Darmaing
brothers, and other suspects from the
Ariège, including the so-called 'chapeaux
noirs' of Montaut. He wrote privately to
the Public Prosecutor, Fouquier-Tinville,
recommending the death sentence on several of these local enemies, and this he
obtained. Within the Committee of General Security, however, his chief responsibility was for political police in the Paris
area.

Vadier became a bitter and ironic antag-
onist of both Danton (q.v.), whom he
described as a stuffed turbot, and of
Robespierre, whose sententiousness he
detested. He had frequent consultations
with Fouquier-Tinville during the trial of
Danton, and even visited the jury while it
was deliberating, to argue successfully for
a conviction. He employed Taschereau to
spy on Robespierre, but he became a
double agent. Like other members of the
Committee of General Security, Vadier

was perhaps jealous of the increasing powers over political police exercised by the Committee of Public Safety. In addition, he resented Robespierre's pontifical role in the Cult of the Supreme Being, which Vadier may have interpreted as the beginning of a fatal policy of appeasement towards Catholicism. On 27 Prairial Year II, Vadier presented his report on the Catherine Théot affair. Théot, an eccentric visionary, had allegedly declared Robespierre the new messiah. Although Robespierre prevented the case from going before the Revolutionary Tribunal, Vadier used the affair to heap ridicule on the clerical counter-revolution, and also to undermine Robespierre's credibility. Some of the acrimony in Vadier's rhetoric may be explained by the bitterness caused by the deaths in the Year II of his wife, mother and two of his sons. Vadier promoted the Law of 21 Messidor Year II, which allowed the release of suspect artisans and agricultural workers at harvest time. When, however, he actively supported the overthrow of Robespierre on 9/10 Thermidor, he probably did not anticipate the relaxation of the terror.

He continued to mix in Jacobin circles, and to defend the Revolutionary Government in the Jacobin Club, and in the Convention, where he dramatically appeared with a pistol at his head, in response to Lecointre's accusations, which attempted to indict him and the leading survivors of the Revolutionary Government of tyranny and arbitrary rule. But in Ventôse Year III, Saladin's report on the ex-Montagnards accused Vadier of exerting illegal pressure on the Revolutionary Tribunal, and he went into hiding.

He was amnestied in Brumaire Year IV, but exiled from Paris in Floréal. He walked to Toulouse, where he was arrested in Prairial Year IV as an accomplice of the Babeuf (q.v.) conspiracy. Vadier typically denounced the conspiracy as a foreign plot, and used the Vendôme trial to make another strong public defence of the terror. He was acquitted, but detained by virtue of an unimplemented deportation order of the Year III. He was imprisoned in Cherbourg, where he met Buonarroti (q.v.), but was released in the Year VII.

He emerged from private life in the Hundred Days, to approve Napoleon's *Acte Additionnel*, and in 1815 he was arrested in Toulouse as a Bonapartist *fédéré*. The Bourbons exiled him as a regicide, and he settled in Brussels, where he renewed his acquaintance with Buonarroti, whose Robespierrist and Rousseauist sympathies Vadier challenged. He died in Brussels in 1828.

Described by his biographer as the 'Gascon Voltaire', for his acerbic tongue, Vadier was of an older generation than idealistic Rousseauists like Robespierre, who could not equal Vadier's boast of 'soixante ans de vertus'. Vadier used his enormous police powers to eliminate personal enemies, and he thus acquired a reputation as a bloodthirsty monster. Buonarroti described his political creed as simply a hatred of nobles and priests: if so, Vadier remained consistent in his political outlook throughout and beyond the revolutionary era.

There is further information on Vadier's life and political role in: M. Eude, 'Les Députés méridionaux membres des comités de gouvernement en 1793–1794', *Actes du 96e Congrès national des sociétés savantes. Toulouse, 1971, section d'histoire moderne et contemporaine* (Paris, 1976); M.A. Lyons, 'M.-G.-A. Vadier (1736–1828): The Formation of the Jacobin Mentality', *French Historical Studies*, X (1977), pp. 74–100; and A. Tournier, *Vadier, président du Comité de Sûreté Générale sous la Terreur* (Paris, n.d.).

MARTYN LYONS

VALCKENAER, Johan (1759–1821)
Dutch Jacobin, a leader of the Batavian Republic

Valckenaer was the son of a Leiden professor. Fluent in French and influenced by Voltaire and Rousseau, he became a law professor at the Frisian university of Franeker in 1781, just when the Patriot movement blossomed in reaction to the

Dutch defeat in the war with Britain. Although the Frisian movement initially united the provincial aristocracy and other elements, it quickly became divided and Valckenaer emerged as a leader of the democratic faction. His expulsion from his teaching post in 1787 made him a national Patriot hero and earned him an invitation to teach in the revolutionary stronghold of Utrecht, but the Prussian invasion of September 1787 forced him to flee the country.

From 1788 to 1795 Valckenaer lived in France, where he became embroiled in bitter disputes with some fellow émigrés. He supported the French Revolution, organised a local Jacobin club and joined the National Guard. In 1791 he supported an unrealistic proposal, modelled after the new French constitution, to turn the United Provinces into a constitutional monarchy, but he adapted to the increasing radicalism of the French Revolution and even accepted the necessity of the terror, although he only narrowly avoided arrest himself. As French armies neared the Netherlands after Thermidor, he published a pamphlet, *Le Noeud gordien débrouillé*, to persuade the French that they would gain by permitting the establishment of a genuinely democratic Dutch republic.

After the Batavian Revolution of 1795, Valckenaer returned home and became a leading advocate of a unitary constitution, based on popular sovereignty, that would eliminate all vestiges of traditional provincial autonomy. He also wanted a sweeping purge of former supporters of the Stadholder and the trial of the Orangist leaders and the Stadholder himself. Elected to the National Assembly of 1795–96, he was the unitarist minority's leading spokesman and edited an important weekly newspaper, the *Advocaat der Nationale Vrijheid*, but was unable to shake the more moderate federalists' majority. Accused, with little justification, of having sympathised with the Amsterdam cannoneers' rising of May 1796, and despairing of swaying the Assembly, Valckenaer became ambassador to Spain. From Madrid he welcomed the coup of 22 January 1798 which brought the unitarist radicals to power, but the French coup of 22 Floréal Year VI undermined their position and he returned to Spain in 1799 before quitting public life altogether in 1801.

Valckenaer remained loyal to his democratic and republican ideals in the Napoleonic period, but avoided compromising himself publicly. By 1813 concern for national independence led him to support an Orangist monarchy. He remained excluded from public life because of his revolutionary past until his death in 1821.

Valckenaer was among the most clear-headed and realistic of Dutch radicals. His experiences in the 1780s turned him against both the Stadholder and the Regent oligarchy, and from the French Revolution he learned the necessity of forceful measures to destroy old institutions. As Schama and others have noted, however, he remained aloof from popular movements and reluctant to incite violence; he wished to carry out even the most drastic measures legally. This attitude, characteristic of the Dutch radicals, explains his relatively limited achievements.

For Valckenaer's appeal to the French to establish a democratic Dutch republic, see his *Le noeud gordien débrouillé* (Paris, An III). There is an old study of Valckenaer: Jerome Alexandre Sillem, *Het Leven van Mr. Johan Valckenaer (1759–1821)* (Amsterdam, 1883); but for more recent appraisals, see Pieter Geyl, *La Révolution Batave 1783–98* (trans. J. Godard, Paris, 1971); and Simon Schama, *Patriots and Liberators* (New York, 1977).

J. POPKIN

VAN DER CAPELLEN TOT DEN POLL, Joan Derk (1741–1784)
Dutch Patriot

Van der Capellen was born into an aristocratic family at Tiel (in modern-day Gelderland). Educated at Utrecht University, he was more influenced by English writers in the Commonwealth tradition, such as Fletcher of Saltoun, than by the French Enlightenment. He entered the Estates of his province of Overijssel in 1772, overcoming strong resistance from the noble deputies, and used their meetings as a forum to state his views. His early opposition to British requests for Dutch aid against the American rebels in 1775 made him a national figure, and his translation of Richard Price's pro-American *Observations on Civil Liberty* in 1776 strongly influenced Dutch opinion, as well as bringing him to the attention of the American leaders. He helped organise Dutch support for the American cause, although the American official representative John Adams kept him at arm's length lest his radicalism scare away other supporters.

His quarrels with the nobles in Overijssel, who expelled him from the Estates in 1778, turned Van der Capellen against the traditional social structure there, but he rejected the usual alternative of supporting the Stadholder and became instead a spokesman for the province's common people, whose support he learned to mobilise effectively through petition campaigns and the press. The political turmoil following Dutch entry into the American war gave him the opportunity to expand his activities. In September 1781 he published an anonymous manifesto, *Aan het Volk van Nederland*, in which he accused the Stadholder of betraying the country and made a revolutionary appeal to the Dutch people as a whole to elect delegates who would supervise the traditional provincial institutions and defend liberty. Like the other Patriot leaders, however, he coupled radical initiatives like this with continued appeals to historic rights and institutions without any apparent sense of contradiction. Furthermore, his authorship of this inflammatory manifesto did not become known until long after his death.

Meanwhile, Van der Capellen continued to promote the Patriot cause both in Overijssel and on a national level. Official Dutch recognition of the United States in April 1782 marked a triumph for part of his programme, and he was readmitted to the Overijssel Estates on a wave of popular support the following autumn. He urged democratisation of the province's local institutions and town councils and supported the Vrijkorps movement for the formation of citizen militias in each town, while warning against letting them become middle-class instruments for the repression of the lower orders. Although the Dutch Patriot movement had traditionally looked to the wealthy province of Holland for leadership, Van der Capellen was honoured at a public banquet in Amsterdam in 1783, recognition of his national status. But he was becoming increasingly wary of the conservative 'Patriot Regents' who dominated the movement there, even though he had originally hoped that their instinctive hostility to the Stadholder could be used to further the democratic cause. By 1784 he had become convinced that true freedom required the rejection of the traditional Regent oligarchy as well as the Stadholder; he also saw the need for foreign protection if the Patriots were going to succeed and promoted a treaty with France. At the time of his sudden death in June 1784, he was just beginning to articulate the bases of a genuinely democratic polity.

Van der Capellen's death deprived the Patriot movement of its firmest democratic spokesman and most talented agitator. Although he had never reconciled the appeals to historical and to natural rights in his thinking, his practical experiences had made him the first clear advocate of national sovereignty in the Netherlands; had he lived longer, he might well have laid the foundations of an explicitly democratic programme.

There is a bicentenary edition of Van der Capellen's *Aan het Volk van Nederland* edited by W.F. Wertheim and A.H. Wertheim-Gijse Weenink (Weesp, 1981). The old standard biography – Murk de Jong Hendrikszoon, *Joan Derk van der Capellen* (Groningen and The Hague, 1921) – has now been supplemented by E. A. van Dijk *et al* (eds.), *De Wekker van de Nederlandse Natie. Joan Derk van der Capellen 1741–1784* (Zwolle, 1984). In addition, see Simon Schama, *Patriots and Liberators* (New York, 1977); Jan Willem Schulte Nordholt, *The Dutch Republic and Amer-*

ican Independence (trans. H. Rowen, Chapel Hill, N.C., 1982); Pieter Geyl, *La Révolution Batave 1783–98* (trans. J. Godard, Paris, 1971); and I. Leonard Leeb, *The ideological origins of the Batavian Revolution* (The Hague, 1973).

J. POPKIN

VARLET, Jean François (1764–?1831)
Parisian insurrectionary leader,
Jacobin, Enragé, a protagonist of direct democracy

Jean Varlet was born in Paris in 1764, the son of moderately wealthy bourgeois parents, and attended the Collège d'Harcourt, the college of La Harpe (q.v.) and Talleyrand, in the 1780s. At the outset of the revolution he had private means, and appears to have had no profession or vocation. Varlet began his career as a revolutionary activist in June 1789 as one of the group of agitators at the Palais Royal who organised the freeing of imprisoned army mutineers sympathetic to the popular cause. He became a member of the Jacobin Club, the Cordeliers Club, and of the most important Parisian popular society, the Société Fraternelle des deux Sexes. He was a copious pamphleteer and a notable street orator, making use of a decorated portable tribune and styling himself 'The Apostle of Liberty'.

In the summer of 1791 Varlet was imprisoned briefly for his part in the republican campaign of the Cordeliers and other popular societies that was extinguished by the massacre of the Champ de Mars. A year later he was one of the leaders of the anti-royalist popular demonstration of 20 June 1792 and of the renewed campaign for the dethronement of Louis XVI which led to the uprising of 10 August. He became intensely involved in the politics of the forty-eight 'Sections' into which Paris was divided, and particularly of the Droits-de-l'-Homme Section, on which he served at different times as secretary, president, and vice-president during 1793 and 1794.

In the spring of 1793 Varlet sought to organise a central committee of the Paris Sections as a power centre rivalling both the Commune (the Paris municipal government) and the Convention. He was implicated in the abortive uprising of 9–10 March 1793 which attempted to purge the Convention of moderates. Together with other 'Enragé' leaders, Jacques Roux (q.v.), Théophile Leclerc (q.v.), Pauline Léon (q.v.) and Claire Lacombe (q.v.), Varlet continued to agitate against the Convention, and was one of the leaders of the insurrection mounted by the Sections on 31 May–2 June which expelled the Girondin leaders and established Robespierrist domination over the Convention. As a result of the consolidation of Jacobin power that followed Varlet, whose challenge to the Convention's authority had been more far-reaching, was driven out of politics for a time. He re-emerged in September 1793 as a spokesman of the resistance of the Paris Sections to the efforts of the Convention and the Commune to re-establish a firm authority in Paris by curbing the Sections' independence and initiative.

Denounced by Robespierre (q.v.), Varlet was gaoled for two months, and after his release was careful not to cross the Jacobin régime again until after the overthrow of Robespierre in July 1794. At that time he joined Babeuf (q.v.) and other sans-culotte irreconcilables in a renewed campaign to restore the independence and power of the Section meetings which was part of a short-lived democratic opposition to the triumphant Thermidorians. This agitation was crushed in its turn and Varlet was arrested (for the fifth time) in September 1794. This time he was not released for more than a year.

Varlet's name appears as a potential supporter in lists drawn up by the Conspiracy of the Equals in 1796, but he does not seem to have associated himself again with Babeuf or played any active part in the Conspiracy. He was under police surveillance as a 'notorious anarchist' in June 1797, and was prominent in the last flicker of Jacobin activity in the summer of 1799.

In 1813 Varlet was living in poverty at

Meaux, and was said to be 'not at all dangerous'. In 1814 he published a Bonapartist pamphlet, and his Bonapartist sympathies were reaffirmed in a final pamphlet published at Nantes in 1831, where he played a minor part in local politics before disappearing from the record.

Varlet was not an original or profound thinker, but a militant agitator whose principles were expressed in constant action. In more than a dozen pamphlets and in public addresses he did however ground those principles in explicitly Rousseauistic arguments. This was particularly true of pamphlets published at the time of the elections to the Convention and soon after, in 1792 and 1793, in which Varlet sought to influence the shape of the new constitution with which the Convention was entrusted.

Varlet urged the deputies to imagine themselves as drawing up a 'social contract' for a 'community' of equal citizens. The social contract, moreover, ought especially to be directed towards the defence of the weak against the powerful. The poor were always in a majority, and their rights came before all else, particularly their right to limit 'acquisitive ambition' and to redress 'the enormous disproportion of wealth'. Like Jacques Roux, Varlet pressed for laws against usury, speculation, monopoly and food cornering, and, indeed, for the confiscation of property amassed by such means. In the summer of 1793 he advocated the 'extermination' of food and money speculators as part of his programme for the revolutionary agitation that prepared the uprising of 31 May.

Like Roux, and like other Jacobin radicals, however, Varlet stopped short at a fundamental critique of capitalist enterprise, instead distinguishing, in a traditional manner, between permissible, legitimate enterprise and reprehensible and illegitimate speculation. Nor did he elaborate any detailed plans for realising his objectives of suppressing poverty and redressing inequalities of wealth and income; he postulated no major reconstruction of society.

Varlet's central concern was rather with the institutionalising of direct, democratic control over government and administration. Starting from Rousseau's premise that sovereignty may be delegated but never represented, in a projected mandate or binding programme for the Convention, he recapitulated themes that had become familiar in the milieu of the Paris Districts, Sections, and popular societies since 1789. Peoples' mandatories, including those charged with executive government, must be chosen by the direct vote of primary assemblies, and subject to recall. All major acts of legislation must be submitted to the people for direct ratification. There should be an elected corps of censors to ensure the good conduct of the mandatories. The fundamental sanction completing this system of direct democracy was the popular right of insurrection against recalcitrant wielders of power. In practice Varlet was flexible in his choice of the basic institutions of popular vigilance: popular societies, section general assemblies, *ad hoc* revolutionary committees, were all pressed into service to maintain the insurrectionary pressure.

The Enragés, Varlet among them, have been depicted by some historians as the spokesmen of a developing proletarian class in conflict with the triumphant bourgeois revolution. Certaintly Varlet saw himself as the defender of the interests of the poor against the rich, and practical experience led him towards the recognition of a class conflict. In an address to the Cordeliers Club in June 1793 he divided society into three classes of 'shopkeepers' (*boutiquiers*), aristocrats and artisans, and urged the disarming of the first two classes, leaving the artisans in control. This programme did not, however, form part of any deeper or developed analysis.

In point of fact, Varlet's activities, rather than directly expressing the will of the masses, or of a nascent proletariat, tended to reflect the concerns of a militant minority or vanguard of sans-culotte revolutionaries. Within these limits his techniques proved particularly effective for organising a successful challenge to constitutional authority in the conditions of 1792–3 and for compelling the Jacobin Convention to take note of popular demands for controls on the economy in the interests of the poor. Only with the final defeat of the sans-culottes and the destruction of their institutions did such techniques become irrelevant to the course of the revolution, and Varlet with them. Similar agitational techniques were revived during the Paris uprisings of 1848 and 1871, but by this time Varlet was forgotten, except as a marginal note in the republican histories.

For Varlet's political opinions, see his *Projet d'un mandat spécial et impératif aux mandataires du peuple à la Convention nationale* (Paris, 1792), and *Declaration solennelle des droits de l'homme dans l'état social* (Paris, 1793). Further information on his life and activities can be found in R.B. Rose, *The Enragés: Socialists of the French Revolution?* (Sydney, 1968); M. Slavin, 'Jean Varlet as defender of direct democracy', *Journal of Modern History*, vol. 39, no. 4 (Dec. 1967), pp. 387–404; D. Guérin, *La lutte de classes sous la première république, bourgeois et 'bras nus' (1793–1797)* (Paris, 1946); and J.M. Zacker, *Dveshenye 'Beshenyih'* (Moscow, 1961).

R.B. ROSE

VERLOOY, Jan Baptist (1746–1797)
Belgian legal scholar, forefather of the Flemish movement, and democratic leader in the Brabant Revolution

The son of Jan Frans Verlooy, town clerk of Houtvenne, and Anna Wouters, Verlooy studied law at Louvain University. A brilliant student, he was apprenticed to the renowned and innovative legal scholar, Philippe Guillaume Malfait. Verlooy apparently remained an outsider to Brussels legal circles, concentrating on legal theory. He published the influential index of Brabant laws, *Codex Brabantica*, in 1787 and dedicated it to the Austrian minister, Joseph Crumpipen.

In 1789 Verlooy founded the secret revolutionary society, Pro Aris et Focis, in Brussels. If 3 million Belgians suffered under the despotic rule of the Austrian emperor, Joseph II, he explained, surely 300 thousand would be willing to fight for their independence. He suggested that each of the members of Pro Aris et Focis enlist six or seven friends each of whom would in turn enlist six or seven more members to support Van der Mersch's army as it approached their villages.

The Belgian victory over the Austrians allowed the provincial Estates to broaden their control over the provinces rather than giving the people sovereignty as Pro Aris et Focis had expected. Verlooy protested this usurpation of the people's sovereignty in his pamphlet, *Projet raisonné d'union des Provinces Belgiques* (1790). Driven from Brussels in the spring of 1790, he joined a number of other Belgian democrats in Lille as a member of Pro Patria, another secret revolutionary society.

When the French defeated the Austrians in November 1792, Verlooy assisted in the establishment of a French revolutionary government in Brussels. Elected as a Provisional Representative, he helped to organise the Société des Amis de liberté et d'égalité, the so-called Jacobins. He led the Brussels' vote for annexation to France just before the Austrians defeated the French in 1793. When the French returned in 1794, Verlooy served as mayor of Brussels. He died in 1797.

During the course of the Brabant Revolution, Verlooy was one of the most ardent opponents of the Estates. He protested that they no longer represented the diverse interests of the Belgian people in his pamphlets *Les auteurs secrets de la Révolution présente* and *Les intrigues du despotisme demasquées*. In his 1790 *Projet* he called on the bourgeoisie to write a new constitution that would guarantee them their natural rights. His exile in France radicalised him. In 1793 he wrote *Zyn geloof, vryheid, en eygendommen in gevaer?* praising the French revolutionary principles of equality, freedom of conscience, and property rights and calling on his countrymen to emulate their revolutionary neighbours.

Verlooy is probably better remembered in Belgium today as a Flemish nationalist. In his 1787 treatise, *Verhandeling op d'Onacht der moederlyke Tael in de Nederlanden*, he criticised the Flemish élite for adopting French. He urged them to return to Dutch, which he explained was the language of the common people and of freedom. One of his biographers cites the *Verhandeling* as a declaration of 'volksnationalisme'. Verlooy's arguments for a reform of the legal system, his espousal of Flemish nationalism, his struggle first against the Austrians and then the Estates, and his active support for the French occupation of Belgium all place him solidly in the late eighteenth-century 'democratic' revolutionary tradition.

A comprehensive study of all aspects of Verlooy's life is presented in Jan Van den Broeck, *J.B.C. Verlooy Vooruitstrevend jurist en politicus uit de 18de eeuw 1746/1797* (Antwerp, 1980). Other works that treat the various aspects of his life are: H. J. Elias, *Geschiedenis van de Vlaamse gedachte* (Antwerp, 1963); J. Nauwelaers, *Histoire des avocats au Souverain Conseil de Brabant* (Brussels, 1947); S. Tassier, *Les Démocrates belges de 1789* (Brussels, 1930); S. Tassier, *Histoire de la Belgique sous l'occupation française en 1792 et 1793* (Brussels, 1934); R. Devleeshouwer, *L'Arrondissement du Brabant sous l'occupation française, 1794–95* (Brussels, 1964); and J. Polasky, *Revolutionary Brussels, 1787–1793* (Brussels, 1985). A comprehensive bibliography of primary and secondary sources is provided at the end of Van den Broeck's book.

J. POLASKY

VINCENT, François Nicolas (1767–1794)
French revolutionary, Hébertist, and spokesman for the sans-culottes

Vincent was born in Paris in 1767. His father was a *concierge* of one of the Paris prisons. At the outset of the revolution, Vincent was clerk to a *procureur*. He joined the Cordeliers Club and soon acquired a reputation for his extreme views. From October 1792 he worked at the War Ministry under Pache (q.v.) but was dismissed by Bernouville who succeeded Pache in January 1793. However, Bouchotte recalled him and appointed him secretary general. Thereafter the Cordeliers took control of the Ministry of War through a series of Hébertist appointments.

Vincent was therefore at the core of the Hébertist faction that threatened the control of the revolution by the Committee of Public Safety in the winter of 1793–94. His short career was almost eclipsed in December 1793 when he was implicated in the 'foreign plot' revealed by the testimony of Fabre d'Eglantine (q.v.) and Chabot (q.v.) to the Committee of Public Safety. After brief incarceration Vincent was released on 2 February 1794 upon the intervention of Danton (q.v.) when it was revealed that the testimony was fabricated. He was arrested again on the night of March 13–14 as part of the Committee's coup against the Hébertists. Along with Hébert (q.v.) and fifteen others, Vincent was tried before the Revolutionary Tribunal for plotting against the Convention and was guillotined on 24 March 1794.

Vincent adhered to the vague quasi-petty bourgeois programme of the Hébertists. Features of the programme included sympathy to the needs of the sans-culottes; punishment of speculators and merchants who used the war crisis to reap large profits; militant republicanism; vigorous conduct of the war as a crusade against the conservative powers; rooting out traitors at home; and hostility towards Catholicism. In place of the latter, Vincent proposed a Cult of Reason centred on glorifying the revolution and the nation.

Based on the support of the sans-culottes, Vincent and other Hébertists controlled the more radical of the forty-eight Sections into which Paris was divided as well as the revolutionary Commune at the hôtel de ville. Demonstrations by masses of sans-culottes enabled the faction to extract notable concessions from the cowed deputies in the Convention. Among these were the regulatory Law of the

Maximum designed to control inflation of living costs and the Law of Ventôse providing for confiscation and resale of émigré property on terms that favoured acquisition by sans-culottes and peasants.

Such measures, however, were not fully endorsed by the more bourgeois Jacobins, and were half-heartedly implemented. After the fall of the Hébertists, and especially after the events of 9 Thermidor when the revolution swung to the right, these measures were repealed. The influence of Vincent and other Hébertists was therefore shortlived, but their programme was revived under other names during the revolutions of the nineteenth century.

There is no biography of Vincent, but see the sketch in J. Robinet et al, *Dictionnaire historique et biographique de la Révolution et de l'Empire 1789–1815* (Paris, 1899). See also, L. Jacob, *Hébert le Père Duchesne, chef des sans culottes* (Paris, 1960), and A. Soboul, *Les sans-culottes parisiens en l'an II* (Paris, 1961).

JOEL S. CLELAND

VOLLMER, Diederich Gottfried Leberecht (1768–1815)
German Jacobin and publicist of French revolutionary ideas

Vollmer was born in Thorn, but little is known about his early life until 1794, when he met G.F. Rebmann (q.v.) in Saxony. Rebmann wanted to publish Vollmer's translation of a speech by Robespierre (q.v.) and to found a Jacobin journal. Vollmer moved from Dresden with Rebmann to Dessau to open a bookshop. On 17 August 1794 he received a licence from the Danish authorities to set up the Royal Danish publishing house in Altona, where he could take advantage of the lenient Danish press laws to publish democratic writings that might encounter difficulties with censorship in other parts of Germany. Vollmer made the stepson of F.W. von Schütz (q.v.), Friedrich Bechtold, his partner in Altona.

After their deportation from Dessau, Vollmer and Rebmann moved to Erfurt, where Robespierre's speech and the first issues of the Jacobin journal, *Das neue graue Ungeheuer*, appeared. Vollmer also published other democratic works there. In December 1795 Vollmer and the printer Kramer were arrested on the charge of publishing a subversive journal, while Rebmann managed to get to Altona, where he sought refuge with Würzer (q.v.). In 1796 Vollmer also went to Altona, where his publishing house brought out more Jacobin publications than any other publishing house east of the Rhine. Among others they published *Die Geißel* (1797–1799), *Das neue graue Ungeheuer* and *Das neueste graue Ungeheuer* (1796–1800), *Die Schildwache* (1796–1797), *Die neue Schildwache* (1797–1798), *Briefe über Frankreich, die Niederlande und Teutschland* by G. Kerner (q.v.) (1797), and the 'documents' of the trial against the Silesian democrat Zerboni. Vollmer took an active part in the Altona National Theatre of J.F.E. Albrecht (q.v.), in which the north German Jacobins Unzer (q.v.), Schmieder (q.v.), Schütz, Evers and others were also involved, and published the *Theaterzeitung*, which Schütz edited from 1798 to 1800. He also participated financially in the theatre for a time, and lost a part of his investment capital when Danish troops occupied Hamburg.

Vollmer became a citizen of Hamburg on 15 March 1799 and received French citizenship the same year, when he ran a branch of his publishing house in French-occupied Mainz. The new Danish censorship law of 1 November 1799 prevented the publication of further democratic writing. Vollmer attempted to continue the sale of the company's publications in his Hamburg bookshop, until he was forbidden to do so by the Hamburg senate following the intervention of the imperial arch-chancellor Colloredo-Mansfeld (27 August 1800). In 1801 he dissolved his association with Bechtold, and in 1803 founded a new publishing house and bookshop in Hamburg which did not publish democratic works. This business was taken over by the publisher Johann Gottlieb Herold after Vollmer's death (30 April 1815), and continued under the name *Heroldsche*

Buchhandlung.

Vollmer was therefore an active member of Rebmann's radical circle in Altona and continued to support the French Revolution in its post-Jacobin phase. His importance lies in his attempt to popularise and spread democratic sentiments as a publisher of Jacobin books and pamphlets.

Further details of Vollmer's life may be found in Hans Schröder, *Lexikon der hamburgischen Schriftsteller bis zur Gegenwart* (Hamburg, 1851–1883). See also Paul T. Hoffmann, *Die Entwicklung des Altonaer Stadttheaters* (Altona, 1926) and W. Grab, *Demokratische Strömungen in Hamburg und Schleswig-Holstein zur Zeit der ersten französischen Republik* (Hamburg, 1966).

W. GRAB

VONCK, Jan François (1743–1792)
Belgian reformer and leader of the democrats in the Brabant Revolution

Jan François Vonck was born in Baerdegem to Jean Vonck and Elisabeth van Nuffel, prosperous peasants. He studied humanities at the Collège des Jesuites in Brussels and law at Louvain University. Graduating second in his class, he moved to Brussels in 1767 and was appointed *avocat fiscal* of Ste. Gudule and treasurer of the Abbaye de Forêt. He quickly earned a reputation as one of the best lawyers of the Conseil Souverain de Brabant. His short life was marked by feeble health.

In the spring of 1789, Vonck helped J.B.C. Verlooy (q.v.) to organise the secret revolutionary committee, Pro Aris et Focis. Initially, Vonck hoped to cooperate with Henri Van der Noot who had been leading the resistance in the Estates since 1787 against the Austrian emperor, Joseph II. Van der Noot rejected Vonck's suggestions for raising a Belgian army and continued to pursue diplomatic negotiations with the Triple Alliance for military support. The democratic lawyers, wholesale merchants, and professionals of Pro Aris et Focis recruited a general and armed, uniformed, and drilled Belgian volunteers.

In October 1789 Van der Noot and his supporters coalesced with Pro Aris et Focis to launch a military campaign. Much to the surprise of European observers, this so-called 'Army of the Moon' defeated the Austrians in December 1789. The declaration of Belgian independence, however, marked only the beginning of the democrats' battle for popular sovereignty. Throughout the spring of 1790, as the founder of a second revolutionary society, the Société Patriotique, Vonck challenged the re-establishment of the Estates and their assumption of sovereignty. Vonck wrote several major pamphlets and was a key supporter of the now mutinous Belgian army. Van der Noot's supporters chased Vonck out of Brussels in May 1790.

Across the border in Lille, Vonck organised Pro Patria. He remained more aloof than his fellow Brussels democrats from both the French who promised military assistance and the Austrians who offered reconciliation. When the Austrians defeated the straggling army of the Belgian Estates in the fall of 1790, Vonck did not return to Brussels with his fellow democrats. He refused to believe that a monarch or emperor, no matter how enlightened, would voluntarily allow the people to exercise their sovereignty. Vonck also rebuffed the overtures of the radical Belges et Liégeois in Paris who were campaigning for French aid in bringing the French Revolution to the Belgian provinces. He deplored their anti-clericalism which, he said, would have to be imposed by force on a believing nation. 'Que nous reste-t-il à faire,' he mused in a letter to a friend, 'Nous qui sommes placés entre les deux extrêmes.' (Vonck, Mss. 20737, Bibliothèque Royale, Brussels). Vonck, who had been plagued by ill health, died in December 1792 without returning to Belgium.

Throughout his life Vonck argued that the Belgians would have to build a new régime on the foundations of the old. In his first major pamphlet, *Vervolg van staetkundige onderrigtingen voor het Brabantse Volk*, he proposed doubling the Third Estate and including the secular clergy and lesser nobility in the first two

Estates. These reforms would provide representation for the useful and educated classes, he explained. He also urged that an executive, separate from the legislative powers, be established. In all of his later pamphlets, Vonck advised his fellow revolutionaries to build upon their medieval provincial constitutions, such as the Joyeuse Entrée with its principles of limited powers, rather than adopting French institutions. The Belgians were not ready for a National Assembly, he concluded. The advocate of moderate reform, Vonck was accepted as the spokesman and titular head of the Belgian democrats throughout the revolutionary period.

Most of Vonck's correspondence is preserved in the manuscript collection of the Albertine Library in Brussels and the Archives Générales du Royaume (Mss. 14891, 14892, 19648, and 20737.) An early biography is Paul Struye, *Jean François Vonck* (Brussels, 1927). Another older source is Théodore Juste, *Les Vonckistes* (Brussels, 1887). More general works on the Brabant Revolution include: Suzanne Tassier, *Les démocrates belges de 1789* (Brussels, 1930), and Janet Polasky, *Revolutionary Brussels, 1787–1793* (Brussels, 1985).

J. POLASKY

VOULLAND, Jean Henri (1751–1801)
French revolutionary, member of the Constituent Assembly and the National Convention, terrorist

Voulland was born a Protestant at Uzès (Gard). He became an *avocat*, practising in Toulouse and Nîmes, and subsequently a *subdélégué* to the Intendant of Languedoc. He represented the Third Estate of Nîmes and Beaucaire in the Estates-General. In the Constituent Assembly he appeared as the protégé of the Protestant pastor Rabaut St Etienne, who helped him to secure election to the Comité des Recherches. In October 1791 he was a member of the moderate Feuillant Club. Not until 1793 did Voulland disown these potentially embarrassing connections with the Prot-

estant (and federalist) community in the Gard department.

During the Legislative Assembly Voulland acted as judge on the Tribunal of Uzès, where he was elected to the National Convention. He voted for the death of Louis XVI and, in March 1793, was sent on a recruitment mission to the Gard and the Hérault, where his denunciations of refractory priests were particularly pronounced. On September 14, 1793 he was elected member of the Committee of General Security, where he was responsible for reports, and for the northern, eastern and south-eastern regions. He was an active member of the police committee, a frequent attender of its joint discussions with the Committee of Public Safety, and one who maintained close liaison with the Paris Revolutionary Tribunal. He also maintained close links with the Jacobins in his home department of the Gard, some of whom obtained posts, with Voulland's assistance, on the Revolutionary Tribunal in Paris. On October 20, 1793 he passed the decree which authorised the Committee of General Security to send arrested suspects directly before the Revolutionary Tribunal. Sénart, an agent of the C.S.G., described him as a cruel radical, with a violent temper, and an inclination to thump the table when contradicted. On 16 Frimaire Year II he was elected president of the Convention, and declared to one delegation that he was equally opposed to both atheism and fanaticism. In Prairial he was also president of the Jacobin Club.

Voulland played a leading role in rallying the Convention on 9/10 Thermidor against the Robespierrists and the rebel Commune of Paris. He secured the appointment of the future Director Barras as commander of the Convention's forces. Voulland was made responsible for the investigation of the so-called Robespierrist conspiracy, and for gathering the information which led to the execution of about 100 alleged accomplices of Robespierre (q.v.). He was later denounced by the Thermidorian Lecointre, and left the C.S.G. on 15 Fructidor Year II.

An order was issued for his arrest after

the rising of Prairial Year III, but Voulland escaped, and hid for over a year with a bookseller in the Palais-Royal. He was amnestied in the Year IV and, under the Directory, was employed in the secretariat of the Council of 500. He died in miserable circumstances in 1801. Lenôtre's assertion that Voulland experienced a religious conversion on his deathbed is a rumour, attributable to a royalist police report compiled in 1816.

Voulland was a very experienced administrator before the revolution began, which helps to account for his important contribution to the work of government committees during the revolution. For a few hours on the night of 9 Thermidor, he was a vital co-ordinator at the centre of the anti-Robespierrist operations. His career illustrates the strong links between radicalism and the Protestant religion in the sectarian areas of south-western France.

There is no biography of Voulland but information on his life can be found in Michel Eude, 'Les Députés méridionaux membres des comités du gouvernement en 1793–4', *Actes du 96e congrès national des sociétés savantes (Toulouse 1971), section d'histoire moderne et contemporaine* (Paris, 1976); and Martyn Lyons, 'The 9 Thermidor: motives and effects', *European Studies Review*, 5 (1975), pp. 123–46.

MARTYN LYONS

VREEDE, Pieter (1750–1837)
Leader of the Dutch Patriot movement

Pieter Vreede was born in Leiden, the son of a blanket and textile manufacturer. Employed by his father in the family firm, he became an early adherent of the Patriot movement. From 1778, he expressed his opposition to the stadholder, and specifically to the regent, the Duke of Brunswick. Using the pseudonyms Harmodius Friso and Frank de Vrij, Vreede attacked the stadholderate and a pamphlet entitled *De Oranjeboom* earned him the accolade of having the States offer a large reward for anyone who would identify him. Remaining undetected, he was able to continue his work, organising the Free Corps in his

home town and in 1785 writing with Wybo Fijnje (q.v.) the Patriot programme known as the *Leiden Draft*. Publishing the Draft under his own name made him far more widely known but in the following year he registered as a student at the University of Leiden and took little part in the Patriot revolt. Thus when the stadholder was restored in 1787, Vreede was left unmolested by the authorities.

For the next eight years, Vreede concerned himself with the family business, moving his main manufactory to Tilburg in Brabant, and a subsidiary from Emmerich in Prussia to Lier in the Austrian Netherlands. The move away from Holland undoubtedly helped to keep him safe from retribution after 1787 but he returned to the forefront of political life in 1795 after the French invasion by championing the cause of the 'Provincial Representatives of the People of Brabant' against the States-General in The Hague. The States had refused to accept the Brabanders as the equals of representatives from other provinces – a situation which arose from Brabant's inferior position under the old régime. Vreede mounted a virulent attack against the States-General whom he considered to be applying double standards. A delegation sent to the administrative capital, 's-Hertogenbosch only made matters worse and provoked the radical clubs and municipal councils still further. As the situation deteriorated, Vreede found himself losing control of the situation, and it was only the States' eleventh-hour acceptance of the Brabanders' claims which saved the day.

In 1796, Vreede was elected to the first National Assembly as representative for Bergen op Zoom and soon became allied with the more extreme elements among the unitarist democrats. Many members of the Assembly felt him to be a dangerous revolutionary and the Presidential chair consistently ignored his attempts to speak. For those, like Vreede, who saw the Assembly as the first step towards the establishment of a unitary republic, the proceedings of the body turned out to be a great disappointment. The conflict between the federalist and unitarist republicans continued unabated until a compromise was reached in December 1796. Nevertheless, this did not prevent Vreede and his political associates from bringing new reforms before the National Assembly. These included an attack on the status of the guilds, clearly an issue dear to the heart of Vreede, the entrepreneur; the emancipation of slaves in the colonies, and the introduction of religious freedom – a step which was bound to conflict with the pre-eminent position of the Reformed Church established by the synod of Dort in 1618.

At the same time that these specific measures were being discussed, the future structure of the Republic was also being debated. Vreede had experience of France under the Directory and was unwilling to see the Batavian Republic move in the same direction, towards what he termed 'constitutional anarchy'. His view remained that the only way in which democracy could be preserved was if the executive and even judiciary were subordinated to the representatives of the people. His championing of this form of democracy did little to enamour him to the more conservative factions within the National Assembly, nor to the French occupying power.

Although the Assembly agreed the final form of the constitution on 10 May 1797, it remained to be given popular assent through a plebiscite to be held on 8 August of that year. This gave the opponents of the definitive version time to organise their tactics. Opposition came from both federalists and the radical unitarists. Two days before the vote, Vreede and eleven like-minded colleagues published the *Address to the Batavian People*, known as the Manifesto of the 'Twelve Apostles'. In it, they asked all good patriots to vote against the constitution and put their trust in the election of a new national assembly. The effect of this document cannot be quantified, although it undoubtedly carried some weight, but the result of the plebiscite was an overwhelming rejection of the constitution – a rejection which left no further obvious means of progress.

The elections to a Second National Assembly, which resulted from the stalemate in the first, did reduce the numbers of patrician and moderate federalists, but this in turn only served to polarise still further the differences of opinion within the new body. Although Vreede occupied the presidential chair of the second assembly for a short time in late 1797, his ill-health forced him to return to Tilburg and he was not directly involved in the planning of the coup of January 1798. However, such was his renown that the French agent Delacroix refused to initiate the coup without first consulting with him. Thus Vreede left his sick-bed and returned to The Hague on 19 January in order to confer with Delacroix and his unitarist colleagues. Three days later, the coup brought to power a Directory of Five, of whom Vreede was the acknowledged leader. Although he could claim the credit for actually giving the Batavian Republic a new constitution during his brief period of ascendancy, Vreede was never so effective in government as he had been in opposition. His tendency to see every issue in black and white terms had been a positive advantage during his years as a polemicist and agitator, but faced with the day-to-day running of the Republic's government, he proved to have little grasp of administrative skills.

Vreede saw his basic task as being to ensure that the 'revolution' which had taken place was not undermined. To this end, he initiated a series of purging commissions which had a twofold purpose: firstly, to root out opponents of the Republic, and secondly, to restrict the number of people able to vote. In this way, the passage of the constitution was ensured, but only at the expense of alienating not only the localities, but also many of the Directory's erstwhile supporters. The commissions pursued their task with vigour, yet critics claimed that they disenfranchised many good republicans while leaving unrepentant Orangists unmolested.

Among the former supporters of the régime who were alienated in this way was

Herman Daendels (q.v.), and it was his intervention which effectively brought the Directory to an end. Although most of his colleagues were arrested, Vreede was able to escape from The Hague on 12 June 1798 and take sanctuary in Lier. After this second coup, the new government of the Republic showed no inclination to prosecute or victimise the former directors and when Vreede's wife died suddenly, he was allowed to return to Tilburg where he continued to run the family textile business. He appears to have played no further part in politics.

The reasons for Vreede's virulent stand against the stadholderate in the 1770s and 1780s are not altogether clear. Nor is his espousal of the cause of democracy and unitarism. Yet he became perhaps the most effective pamphleteer and polemicist of the early Patriot movement, using his undoubted natural talent against the evils of society as he saw it. Although he was able to remain in Brabant after 1787 and avoided the period in exile suffered by so many of his contemporaries, Vreede remained an acknowledged leader of the democrats – a position which was reinforced by his election to the two national assemblies of 1796 and 1797. Only when brought to power were his limitations exposed. The inability to negotiate or to deal with bureaucracy were major failings. More to the point, his attempt to steamroller the new constitution through a restricted electorate made him few friends. Thus the 'tribune of the Batavian democrats', whose oratory and polemical skill brought him to the leadership of the Republic, was unable to transform himself into a successful administrator – perhaps because he realised the contradiction of his own position. Was it possible for one who believed in the primacy of the people's representatives to find himself trying to manipulate or overrule the popular will?

The following sources provide information on Vreede's life and the political context in which he was active: S. Schama, *Patriots and Liberators* (New York, 1977); P.J. Blok and P.C. Molhuysen, *Nieuw Nederlandsch Biografisch Woordenboek*

(Leiden, 1911–1937); H.T. Colenbrander, *De Bataafsche Republiek* (Amsterdam, 1908); and P. Geyl, *De Patriottenbeweging 1780–1787* (Amsterdam, 1947).

BOB MOORE

WÄCHTER, Georg Philipp (1762–1837)
German writer and enthusiast of the French Revolution

Wächter was born in Uelzen, the son of a deacon. He studied theology in Göttingen, where he made the acquaintance of G.A. Bürger, who supported his plan to publish *Sagen der Vorzeit*. In 1786 Wächter returned to Hamburg, but became a teacher rather than a priest and worked on a number of journals, including the *Hamburgische Monatsschrift*, edited by H. C. Albrecht (q.v.). Seized by enthusiasm for the French Revolution he resolved, on the outbreak of the revolutionary wars, to take up arms on the side of the French. Together with his friend Philipp Wilhelm Diede he moved to the Rhineland, where the two volunteers were detained for some time by French émigrés for the loud singing of revolutionary songs.

Wächter joined the French army under General Dumouriez and became a captain in a cavalry regiment. He took part in the Battle of Jemappes in Belgium on 6 November 1792, where he suffered a slight head injury, and also fought at the Battle of Neerwinen (18 March 1793), when the revolutionary army was defeated. After this defeat Wächter returned to Hamburg, where he got a job as a schoolteacher. He published seven volumes of his *Sagen der Vorzeit*, several novels and short stories, and a play, *Wilhelm Tell*, which appeared in 1804, the same year as Schiller's version. He also published work on the history of Hamburg. The private school which he ran folded in 1827; he spent the last years of his life as an employee of the Hamburg municipal library, and undertook studies in history. He died in Hamburg in 1837.

The importance of Wächter's life and political activity lies in the fact that he is a good example of how the democratic ideas of the French Revolution were welcomed even by people who were not hitherto radical. Wächter joined the revolutionary army of his own free will, he was some kind of 'Interbrigadist', enthusiastic about the cosmopolitan ideas, and he was ready to sacrifice his life for the victory of the freedom army of the French – therefore he fought in two battles on the French side and was wounded for the revolutionary cause.

Further details of Wächter's life are to be found in the *Allgemeine deutsche Biographie*, vol. 40 (Leipzig, 1896), pp. 428–431, and in Hans Schröder (ed.) *Lexikon der hamburgischen Schriftsteller bis zur Gegenwart* (Hamburg, 1851–1883). His personal papers are in Hamburg University Library.

W. GRAB

WALCKIERS, Edouard Dominique Sébastien Joseph de (1758–1837)
Belgian reformer and wealthy financier of democratic organisations throughout the Brabant Revolution

Walckiers was born in Brussels in 1758. His father was *conseiller d'Etat et de robe* to the emperor of Austria, *grand bailli* of the city of Termonde, seigneur of Tronchiennes, Evere and Saint-Amand, and was made a vicomte by letters patent in 1786. His mother was a member of the Nettine banking family. Walckiers' participation in the anti-Austrian revolutions is surprising given his background. He served as *conseiller des finances* to Joseph II, as well as *grand bailli* of Termonde, and director of the Royal Treasury. He was connected through family relations to high finance in France and the Austrian Netherlands and enjoyed an exclusive commercial charter for trade with the Indies through the port of Ostende.

In 1787 Walckiers was chosen as captain of one of the units of armed volunteers in Brussels. He joined the secret revolutionary society, Pro Aris et Focis in 1789, funding their military preparations and bribing Austrian soldiers to desert. In 1790, angered by the re-establishment of the three Estates as sovereign power in the newly-independent Belgian provinces, he worked to enlist the support of the volunteers for the democratic opposition. He staged elaborate balls with the Duc d'Ursel and the Duc d'Arenberg, dined nightly with the officers of his company, and distributed pamphlets demanding that sovereignty be returned to the Belgian people. In February 1790 he urged the volunteers to refuse to swear an oath to the Estates, explaining that they should pledge their allegiance to the people instead. Influential among the middle bourgeoisie, he was hailed as the second Lafayette. In the end, however, the Estates prevailed and crowds of artisans hounded Walckiers, driving him into exile.

Walckiers took up residence at a chateau in Hem near Lille in 1790 with another banker, G. Herries. He lent financial support to the secret revolutionary committee of Belgian exiles, Pro Patria. He was an active member of its successor, the Société du Bien Public, formed in 1791. When the Austrians returned to the Belgian provinces, Walckiers worked unsuccessfully to effect a reconciliation between the Belgian democrats and the Austrians.

In December 1791, disappointed by the Austrians' refusal to cooperate, he organised the Belges et Liégeois Unis in Paris. The Liégeois, he wrote to his friend Vonck (q.v.), would help their more timid Belgian neighbours to throw off the despotism of both the Austrians and the privileged orders within Belgium. When the French took up the Belgian cause in 1792, Walckiers followed General Dumouriez back to the Belgian provinces. He helped to establish Jacobin societies in the provinces. He remained an avid support of the Jacobin Club in Brussels, rebuffing any suggestions that Belgium should not follow France's revolutionary example.

In his writings Walckiers called for the establishment of a new régime and the abolition of privilege. His pamphlet of 1791, *Bases de la Constitution à établir dans les Provinces Belgiques*, proclaimed the equality of all citizens before the law, calling for equal taxation and equal access to employment. He argued for reform of the Estates. He proposed doubling the representation of the Third Estate and holding a common meeting of the three Estates with a vote by head rather than order. In 1792 he is reported to have stood on street corners castigating his fellow citizens for their timidity in refusing to follow the French in eradicating religion.

Allied first with Dumouriez and then with the duc d'Orleans, Walckiers did not fare well in France. He was attacked by Marat (q.v.) in 1792. A number of arrest warrants were issued over the next several years. From Hamburg he helped to provision Paris in the middle of the 1790s, but he remained on the list of émigrés. Finally cleared, he returned to France and was given a minor post at the Administration des Biens Réunis. By this time he was apparently financially ruined. He died in Paris in 1837.

Walckiers' radicalism lay in his strong political and military leadership of, and financial commitment to, the forces of Belgian nationalism and liberalism against the representatives of dynastic monarchy during the Brabant Revolution. His writings also reveal a social component to his radicalism, a belief in equality of opportunity and greater political and economic rights for the less fortunate sections of Belgian society. His political career, however, went into eclipse in the mid-1790s.

Two rather different accounts of Walckiers' career are presented by J. Bouchary, 'Le banquier Ed. de Walckiers', *Annales historiques de la Révolution française* (March–April, 1938) and Suzanne Tassier, *Les démocrates belges de 1789* (Brussels, 1930) and *L'occupation française* (Brussels, 1934). See also, Janet Polasky, *Revolutionary Brussels, 1787–1793* (Brussels, 1985).

J. POLASKY

WEDEKIND, Georg Christian (1761–1831)
German revolutionary democrat

Wedekind was born in Göttingen in January 1761, the son of a pastor and teacher of philosophy. He studied medicine and was called to Mainz in 1785 to take up a position as doctor and teach at the university there. A man of very advanced ideas he belonged to the party of Stamm and Böhmer (q.v.), who welcomed Custine to Mainz following the first French offensive on the Rhine. He immediately became one of the leading revolutionary figures in Mainz and distinguished himself particularly in his speeches. The only important position he occupied was that of president of the Jacobin Club. While the rest of his family were arrested when the Prussians re-occupied the town, and held prisoner until 1794, he himself managed to escape (30 March 1793) with Hofmann (q.v.) to Strasbourg, where he worked as a doctor in a garrison-hospital. He suggested taking part in the republicanisation of the entire left bank and was appointed to the *Ecole Centrale* of the *département* of Mont-Tonerre. In 1796 he became editor of the *Rheinische Zeitung* at Strasbourg. In 1797 he returned to Mainz, where he organised the hospitals. From 1803–8 he was the new professor of medicine at Mainz, and established a high reputation. Unlike other Jacobins, he was not to remain in the service of France, and in 1808 he accepted the post of physician to the Grand Duke of Hesse-Darmstadt, who made him a baron in 1809. In 1816 he published a book on the nobility. He died in 1831 at Darmstadt.

In the first debates at the Jacobin Club he tried to demonstrate the practical application of Enlightenment ideas. This didactic concern characterised his speeches. He was conscious that he was not writing only for the nobility or the educated bourgeoisie, but so that he might be understood by everyone. Departing from the Enlightenment, he showed how its ideas could be radicalised in preparation for revolution. For him the rights of man were liberty, equality, property, security, and resistance to oppression, and he held that the laws of a revolutionary state should correspond to natural rights. The rights of a citizen were the same as those of the nation, and it was this right of the people which constituted popular sovereignty. It was in democracies that popular sovereignty was best realised. He outlined a new ideal based on the middle-class values of merit, work and virtue, always relating politics to morality and considering the right to property a sacred one. For him democracy was also a guarantee of peace. He demonstrated the advantages for Mainz in changing its system of government, proving first of all that all monarchies are bad, then explaining that in future the people would formulate their own laws. Mainz would become more prosperous when the city no longer had parasites to feed; its citizens would have fewer dues to pay if there were no more monasteries. To occupy an important office it was only necessary to be capable and virtuous. He also demonstrated the usefulness of freedom to commerce.

Wedekind did not follow the French model blindly, and often criticised the French Jacobin leaders, accusing the Parisian Jacobins of using the same means of oppression as princes in fettering the freedom of the press and governing in a very arbitrary manner. He contrasted them with the true Jacobins who wanted France and other countries to enjoy freedom and equality: the promulgation and implementation of legislation should express the will of the entire people. No part of the people should usurp an influence which would diminish that of another part of the nation, for then there would no longer be democracy, but concealed aristocracy. The tendency to think that the voice of the Jacobins was sovereign was an attack on popular sovereignty. It was for the Convention to govern, as the legally constituted authority. The greatest danger was the split between Jacobins and anti-Jacobins. The cause of humanity and truth might be sacrificed to the hatred between political parties, and it was essential to work to unite them. In

1795 he criticised the excesses of the Jacobins and supported the Directory and then Napoleon, though he subsequently became disillusioned with the policies of the latter.

Despite his criticism of the Parisian Jacobins, he lost none of his faith in the revolution. Unlike many Germans, he was particularly concerned that popular sovereignty should triumph, and that the wishes of the whole people should be expressed in legislation. He no more desired to suppress private property than the French revolutionaries. On the strength of both his words and his deeds, this Rhineland Jacobin can be counted among the true German revolutionaries.

Wedekind's political thought can be studied through a reading of his Mainz writings, especially G. C. Wedekind, *Drei Anreden an seine Mitbürger, gehalten am 27., 28. and 29. Oktober in der Gesellschaft der Freunde zu Mainz* (Mainz, 1792); *Über Aufklärung. Eine Anrede an seine lieben Mainzer, gehalten in der Gesellschaft der Volksfreunde zu Mainz am 28. Oktober im ersten Jahr der Freiheit und Gleichheit* (Mainz, 1792); *Über die Regierungsverfassungen. Eine Volksrede in der Gesellschaft der Freunde der Freiheit und Gleichheit gehalten zu Mainz am 5. November im ersten Jahr der Republik* (Mainz, 1792); *Über Freiheit und Gleicheit. Eine Anrede an seine Mitbürger gehalten in der Gesellschaft der Volksfreunde zu Mainz am 30. Oktober im ersten Jahr der Freiheit und Gleicheit* (Mainz, 1792); *Die Volksglückseligkeit* (Mainz, 1793); and *Die Rechte des Menschen und des Bürgers, wie sie die französische konstituierende Nationalversammlung 1791 proklamierte mit Erläuterungen* (Mainz, 1793). See also his *Bemerkungen und Fragen über das Jakobinerwesen von G. Wedekind* (Strasbourg, bei K. Fr. Pfeiffer im 3. Jahre der fränkischen Republik. [1794]). There is a short study of Wedekind by H. Mathy, 'Georg Wedekind, die politische Gedankenwelt eines Mainzer Medizinprofessors', in *Geschichtliche Landeskunde*, vol. 5 (Wiesbaden, 1968), pp. 177–205.

M. GILLI

WENNINGER, Joseph (1762–1833)
Austrian Jacobin

Joseph Wenninger was born on 25 January 1762 in Knittelfeld, Styria. His father, Peter Wenninger, was the owner of a small business involved in the transport of timber by water. He was educated at Judenburg, St Lamprecht and Graz before entering his father's business. In 1780 he married the widow of the owner of a similar timber business, which he inherited and ran for seventeen years (1780–1797). Wenninger was in many ways a respected local businessman and public worthy. He was mayor of Knittelfeld from 1786 to 1795 and was inspector of the school in Knittelfeld for thirty years. He survived his involvement with radicalism to become the local president of the Imperial and Royal Styrian Agricultural Society in 1819 and was awarded a civic honour in 1822.

The burghers of Styria were among the most organised and determined in their campaign for constitutional reform. In 1790 there had been demands for fairer representation on the provincial Diet, followed by the decision to send a petition to the emperor, Leopold II, and Wenninger, along with two others, was chosen to take the petition to court. The granting of the petition by the Commission on Grievances in Vienna caused a stir in a province where the attempts of the nobility to reimpose feudal labour services was meeting with determined opposition. The peasants themselves, following the example of the burghers, and availing themselves of the latters' contacts, went to Vienna with their own petition.

It was against this background of popular agitation and some sympathy on the part of the emperor that a circle of radicals around Wenninger and Georg Franz Dirnböck (q.v.) – referred to by a local aristocrat as 'the Jacobin Club' – met to discuss political ideas. As the political climate changed, and in particular as restrictions were placed on the freedom of press and association, such meetings, consisting largely of members of the local Diet, were forced to meet in private,

which in itself lent such gatherings a conspiratorial air.

Political discussion (more often than not centred on comparisons between the French and Austrian constitutions), the occasional singing of revolutionary songs, and the attempt to propagate ideas among the population, were – as in most parts of Austria – the most common activities of the radicals. The successful dissemination of democratic propaganda was more hopeful in Styria than in many places, since it was able to build on a history of co-operation between burghers and peasants, Diet members and electors from the period of reform under Joseph and Leopold. Organised by Wenninger and his colleague Franz Haas, the propaganda focused on popular demands for the commutation of tithes and an end to the war.

Wenninger and his circle cultivated their connections in Vienna and Wenninger himself travelled there in 1793. However, it was the participation of members of the so-called 'Styrian complicity', notably Dirnböck, Laurenz Schönberger and Ignaz Menz, in an oath-taking ceremony near Vienna which provided the authorities with the grounds for the arrest of the Styrian radicals, hitherto resisted by the liberal governor of the province, Count Welsperg, on the grounds of lack of evidence. Wenninger himself was charged with the dissemination of seditious literature and aiding and abetting a conspiracy. He was arrested, dismissed from his office as mayor of Knittelfeld and removed to Vienna, where he lost his mind during the investigation of the charges. At his trial he denied being a democrat, and supported by character references from locals who organised a petition, he was subsequently acquitted. He returned to Styria, where he continued to live as a respected member of the community. He died on 9 May 1833.

Wenninger was a practical politician drawn by the promise of reform under Joseph and Leopold to press the claims of the Styrian burghers for greater participation in local politics and government and to organise the citizens of the province against attempts by the local aristocracy to re-assert their feudal privileges over the peasantry. Undoubtedly a proponent of democratic ideas, he was the leader of a co-ordinated and pragmatic political campaign which was frustrated by the changing political climate which enabled the authorities to move against the radicals. The 'Styrian complicity' was more than the allegedly seditious 'oath in the Brühl', which precipitated the arrests of Wenninger and the other radicals, and was based on a history of singularly successful cooperation between burghers and peasants.

Further details of Wenninger's life and career are to be found in Elisabeth Führer, *Jakobiner in der Steiermark* (Phil. Diss., Vienna, 1965), which is a thorough account of the events surrounding the 'Styrian complicity'. See also Ernst Wangermann, *From Joseph II to the Jacobin Trials* (Oxford, 1959), and Helmut Reinalter (ed.), *Jakobiner in Mitteleuropa* (Innsbruck, 1977).

TIM KIRK

WÜRZER, Heinrich (1751–1835)
German Jacobin and publicist of revolutionary ideas

Würzer was born in Hamburg, the son of a confectioner. His father died when he was only five. His stepfather, a certain von Hagen, sent him to an orthodox Lutheran grammar school in order to educate him as a pastor. The fanatical intolerance of his teachers instilled in him a hatred and repugnance for dogmatic theology. He studied law and philosophy at Göttingen, and was then employed for five years as a tutor to the children of the Hanoverian ambassador in Vienna, Count von Wallmoden.

In 1779 he gained a doctorate at Göttingen, and began to lecture there. In 1782 he returned to Hamburg, where he worked as a private tutor and, in 1784, published the monthly journal *Deutsche Annalen*, which came out for six months. His essays were both cosmopolitan and patriotic in tone, and at the same time very respectful towards Frederick II of Prussia. He pressed

for improvements in the judicial system, made a plea for the extension of civil rights to the Jewish minority and appealed for the integration of the ideas of the French Enlightenment in Germany.

In 1788 Würzer moved to Berlin, where he met J.E. Biester, editor of the *Berliner Monatsschrift*, and attended the liberal salon of Henriette Herz. When he criticised the obscurantism of the powerful Prussian culture minister Wöllner, and demanded freedom of the press in his *Bemerkungen über das preußische Religionsedikt vom 9. Julius* (Leipzig, 1788) he was arrested and sentenced to six weeks' imprisonment. Following his release he published a weekly, *Etwas gegen die Langeweile an Feiertagen* (nine issues, 1789), and an equally short-lived journal, *Publikum und Theater*. In 1790 he married, set up a private school, and translated historical works from French. Because he refused to comply with Wöllner's legislative order and teach along the lines of the edict on religion, his school was closed.

For a time he considered emigrating to France with Pierre Villaume, but the September massacres of 1792 put him off. In 1793 he moved to Altona, where he published a *Revolutionskatechismus*, in which he tried to reconcile the differences in the political doctrines of Montesquieu and Rousseau, and argued that 'all citizens should be governed by a freely elected power, or at least by popular consent'. Although after the execution of the king, Würzer considered France a model for the political transformation of Germany, he distanced himself in the *Revolutionskatechismus* from the 'rough crowd'. During the 'Dictatorship of Freedom' of the Jacobins he became a supporter of Robespierre (q.v.), and in January and February 1794 he published the weekly *Historisches Journal*, which was the most radical mouthpiece of revolutionary democracy in Germany at the time. His collaborators were Elias Israel and H.S. Pappenheimer, both Jewish, and Charles Mercier, a Frenchman. Würzer criticised the expansionist policies of the absolutist powers and emphasised that France was a peace-loving nation, fighting for independence and freedom. The journal was prohibited after the fifth issue at the request of the Prussian, Austrian and British ambassadors in Hamburg.

Even after the fall of Robespierre, Würzer held to his democratic opinions; his *Neue Hyperboräische Briefe* (1795) justified the coercive measures of the Jacobin government, and attacked the rulers of Prussia and their Polish policy. In December 1795 Rebmann (q.v.) sought refuge with him following his flight from Erfurt. In 1796 Würzer published the weekly *Der politische Volksredner*, which emphasised the need for a revolution in Germany, and declared resistance to despotic authority to be the supreme human right. He held that those who had fallen during the French Revolution had died in order to erect a more just social order, while those who had died in dynastic wars had been sacrificed for princely interests. Both journals were published by the Verlagsgesellschaft von Altona.

Würzer took over the running of a school set up in 1793 by the Christian-Jewish masonic lodge 'Einigkeit und Toleranz'. His *Freimütige Gedanken über politische und religiöse Gegenstände* (Altona, 1797), which he dedicated to the Crown Prince, demonstrated his disillusionment with the policies of the Directory. The reactionary Danish censorship law of 1799 put an end to Würzer's political writing. He published a few articles in a cultural journal, *Hamburg und Altona* (1801–1806), and taught at the masonic school until its closure in 1808. In 1827 he moved to Berlin, where his two married daughters lived, and he died there at the age of eighty-four.

Würzer was undoubtedly profoundly influenced by the French Revolution and moved leftwards during the course of the 1790s to become a sympathiser of Jacobinism and a champion of the democratic revolution in Germany. As such his political ideals linked in with his commitment to religious and individual liberties, which he believed could only be guaranteed by democratic and republican government.

Reprints of the following pieces by Würzer are available: *Neue Hyperboräische Briefe* (Nendeln, Liechtenstein, 1976); *Der politische Volksredner* (Nendeln, Liechtenstein, 1976); and *Revolutionskatechismus* (Königstein/Taunus, 1977). Information on his life can be found in the following secondary sources: Berend Kordes, *Lexikon der jetzt lebenden schleswig-holsteinischen und eutinischen Schriftsteller* (Schleswig, 1797) p. 405f; D.L. Lübker and H. Schröder, *Lexikon der jetzt lebenden schleswig-holsteinischen, lauenburgischen und eutinischen Schriftsteller von 1796 bis 1828* (Altona and Schleswig, 1829–1831), p. 712; *Neuer Nekrolog der Deutschen,* Second Part (Weimar, 1837), p. 629ff.; W. Grab, *Demokratische Strömungen* (Hamburg, 1966), and W. Grab, *Leben und Werke norddeutscher Jakobiner* (Stuttgart, 1973), pp. 48–67. The latter contains excerpts from Würzer's works, pp. 152–248.

W. GRAB

ZIEGENHAGEN, Franz Heinrich (1753–1806)
German utopian socialist

Ziegenhagen was born in Strasbourg, the son of a doctor. He was raised in the spirit of pietism, and was taught at home by the famous educationlist J. Oberlin. He completed his commercial apprenticeship and became a cloth merchant. In 1775 he joined a masonic lodge in Regensburg during a business trip. He settled in Hamburg in 1780, and in 1788 bought an estate in nearby Billwärder, in order to set up the agricultural educational institute through which he hoped to contribute to the solution of social problems. In the 1790s he elaborated his utopian socialist philosophy, and put all his money into the establishment of model agricultural colonies. He appealed to princes, affluent citizens, universities, consistories and the French National Convention for financial support, but without success. He sold his estate in 1800, when his own financial resources were exhausted, tried in 1802 to start again in his native Alsace, and committed suicide there in 1806 after the final failure of his plans.

Ziegenhagen's social utopian ideas, which he elaborated in his book *Lehre vom richtigen Verhältnisse zu den Schöpfungswerken, und die durch öffentliche Einführung derselben allein zu bewirkende allgemeine Menschenbeglückung* (Hamburg, 1792) rest on the supposition that men should live 'according to nature', and thereby fulfil the will of God, in order to be happy, moral and good. In order to achieve this aim, and to do away with the debilitating and 'anti-creative' town life, he suggested the setting up of agricultural colonies, based on common property, shared work and planning, and a collective way of life. These colonies would be the germ of a future socialist society, which would provide everybody with freedom, social security and material abundance. Ziegenhagen composed a hymn to be sung in the assemblies of people devoted to his teachings, and asked Mozart to compose the music. Mozart's cantana, *Die ihr des unermeßlichen Weltalls Schöpfer ehrt*, is based on Ziegenhagen's text and was one of the composer's last pieces. The famous copper engraver, Daniel Chodowiecki, made several engravings showing how life would be in Ziegenhagen's colonies.

More extensive discussion of Ziegenhagen's ideas is to be found in J.J. Moschkovskaja, 'Zwei vergessene deutsche Utopisten des 18. Jahrhunderts', in *Zeitschrift für Geschichtswissenschaft* (1954), pp. 401–427, and in G. Steiner, *Franz Heinrich Ziegenhagen und seine Verhältnislehre* (East Berlin, 1962). Ziegenhagen's book was reprinted in 1980 by Topos-Verlag, Vaduz, Liechtenstein.

W. GRAB

ZSCHOKKE, Heinrich (1771–1848)
Swiss radical, publicist and literary figure

Although born in Magdeburg on 22 March 1771, the son of a clothier and member of the bourgeoisie of that city, Zschokke was closely associated not with his native Germany but rather with Switzerland, becoming a naturalised Swiss in 1803, living at Aarau for the greater part of his life and playing a prominent part in the politics and literary life of his adopted country. A leading literary figure, he managed to combine literature and politics in a remarkably busy and productive life. He commenced his literary career at an early age while a student of theology at Frankfurt-on-Oder, producing, in 1788, *Aballino*, a dramatic work which enjoyed great success throughout Germany. After being an actor he became a practising pastor in Magdeburg in 1792. He visited Switzerland for the first time in 1795, returning in 1796 after a side trip to Paris. In 1798 he became caught up in the political upheaval of that year and the establishment of the Helvetic Republic, acting as the representative of political refugees from the Grisons who sought aid from the infant republic. It was at this point that he began his long association with Aarau. He became an associate of Stapfer, the most effective minister of the republic in terms of lasting achievement and so helped in Stapfer's reforms of education. He became a government commissioner in 1799, first in Unterwald, then later in Tessin. After this he became prefect of Basle before temporarily withdrawing from politics to pursue a life of study at Biberstein. In 1803 he became a citizen of the canton of Argau and in 1807 settled permanently at Aarau, constructing his house at Blumenhalde in 1817–18. Here he continued his literary career, producing a constant flow of works on a wide and varied range of topics. He also found time to re-enter politics as a liberal and opponent of the restored régime. In 1829 he resigned from all of his public posts and helped in the replacement of the restoration constitution by a more democratic one. Afterwards he served as a deputy to the Diet in 1833, 1834 and 1837 as well as being a prominent figure in local politics until his death in 1848 at his home of Blumenhalde in Aarau.

Zschokke's writings were very diverse and give a clear picture of his political and philosophical views. The largest part in terms of bulk were devotional and theological works but he also wrote on politics, topography and history as well as producing many novels. Some of these were translated into English and other languages, enjoying a general popularity throughout Europe. The most popular was perhaps *The goldmaker's village*, a strongly didactic work first published in 1817. Didacticism was a pronounced feature of Zschokke's work and he clearly saw his writings as a personal contribution to the process of Enlightenment. As this comment suggests his views were broadly typical of the Aufkläurung. He believed profoundly in the doctrine of progress, seen as a move away from superstition and a social system based upon force towards one founded on reason and a culture of humanity. Although he conceived of this process as in some sense automatic, he also urged that it could be encouraged by reform and particularly education and individual endeavour. The general thrust of Zschokke's beliefs was strongly individualist – he saw the central features of progress as the liberation of individuals from the restraints of an unjust political and social hierarchy. He was also, as his many works show clearly, strongly committed to the notion of self-help and the dignity of work. One thing which distinguished him from many other Enlightenment thinkers was his profound, though idiosyncratic, religious faith.

There is no complete edition of his works – this is not surprising as his collected writings fill no fewer than forty volumes! Truly a life and career both creative and productive. There is no life of Zschokke in English and most of what has been written about him comes from the pens of literary scholars. The best place to start is perhaps with his autobiography, *Eine Selbitschau* (Aarau, 1842). Two important works are H. Schneiderreit, *H. Zschokke: seine weltanschaung* (1921) and E. Trosch, *J.K. Lavater, H. Zschokke und die Helvetische Revolution* (1926). Those unable to read German should consult the entry in *Dictionnaire historique et biographique de la Suisse* (Neuchâtel, 1924–29).

S. DAVIES

Index